Foundations of Biostatistics

M. Ataharul Islam · Abdullah Al-Shiha

Foundations of Biostatistics

 Springer

M. Ataharul Islam
ISRT
University of Dhaka
Dhaka
Bangladesh

Abdullah Al-Shiha
Department of Statistics and Operations
  Research
College of Science, King Saud University
Riyadh
Saudi Arabia

ISBN 978-981-13-4203-5   ISBN 978-981-10-8627-4   (eBook)
https://doi.org/10.1007/978-981-10-8627-4

This Springer imprint is published by the registered company Springer Nature Singapore Pte Ltd.
part of Springer Nature
The registered company address is: 152 Beach Road, #21-01/04 Gateway East, Singapore 189721,
Singapore

Preface

The importance of learning biostatistics has been growing very fast due to its increasing usage in addressing challenges in life sciences – in particular biomedical and biological sciences. There are challenges, both old and new, in nature, mostly attributable to interactive developments in the fields of life sciences, statistics, and computer science. The developments in statistics and biostatistics have been complementary to each other, biostatistics being focused to address the challenges in the field of biomedical sciences including its close links with epidemiology, health, biological science, and other life sciences. Despite the focus on biomedical-related problems, the need for addressing important issues of concern in the life science problems has been the source of some major developments in the theory of statistics. The current trend in the development of data science indicates that biostatistics will be in greater demand in the future.

The compelling motivation behind writing this book stemmed from our long experience of teaching the foundation course on biostatistics in different universities to students having varied background. The students seek a thorough knowledge with adequate background in both theory and applications, employing a more cohesive approach such that all the relevant foundation concepts can be linked as a building block. This book provides a careful presentation of topics in a sequence necessary to make the students and users of the book proficient in foundations of biostatistics. In other words, the understanding of any of the foundation materials is not left to the unfamiliar domain. In biostatistics, all these foundation materials are deeply interconnected and even a single source of unfamiliarity may cause difficulty in understanding and applying the techniques properly. In this textbook, immense emphasis is given on coverage of relevant topics with adequate details, to facilitate easy understanding of these topics by the students and users. We have used mostly elementary mathematics with minor exceptions in a few sections in order to provide a more comprehensive view of the foundations of biostatistics that are expected from a biostatistician in real-life situations.

There are 11 chapters in this book. Chapter 1 introduces basic concepts, and organizing and displaying data. One section includes the introduction to designing of sample surveys to make the students familiar with the steps necessary for collecting data. Chapter 2 provides a thorough background on basic summary statistics. The fundamental concepts and their applications are illustrated. In Chap. 3, basic probability concepts are discussed and illustrated with the help of suitable examples. The concepts are introduced in a self-explanatory manner. The applications to biomedical sciences are highlighted. The fundamental concepts of probability distributions are included in Chap. 4. All examples are self-explanatory and will help students and users to learn the basics without difficulty. Chapter 5 includes a brief introduction of continuous probability distributions, mainly normal and standard normal distributions. In this chapter, emphasis is given mostly to the appropriate understanding and knowledge about applications of these two distributions to the problems in biomedical science. The sampling distribution plays a vital role in inferential procedures of biostatistics. Without understanding the concepts of sampling distribution, students and users of biostatistics would not be able to face the challenges in comprehensive applications of biostatistical techniques. In Chap. 6, concepts of sampling distribution are illustrated with very simple examples. This chapter provides a useful link between descriptive statistics in Chap. 2 with inferential statistics in Chaps. 7 and 8. Chapters 7 and 8 provide inferential procedures, estimation, and tests of hypothesis, respectively. As a prelude to Chap. 6 along with Chaps. 7 and 8, Chaps. 3–5 provide very important background support in understanding the underlying concepts of biostatistics. All these chapters are presented in a very simple manner and the linkages are easily understandable by students and users. Chapters 9–11 cover the most extensively employed models and techniques that provide any biostatistician the necessary understanding and knowledge to explore the underlying association between risk or prognostic factors with outcome variables. Chapter 9 includes correlation and regression, and Chap. 10 introduces essential techniques of analysis of variance. The most useful techniques of survival analysis are introduced in Chap. 11 which includes a brief discussion about topics on study designs in biomedical science, measures of association such as odds ratio and relative risk, logistic regression and proportional hazards model. With clear understanding of the concepts illustrated in Chaps. 1–8, students and users will find the last three chapters very useful and meaningful to obtain a comprehensive background of foundations of biostatistics.

We want to express our gratitude to Halida Hanum Akhtar and Mahbub Elahi Chowdhury for the BIRPERHT data on pregnancy-related complications, the Health and Retirement Study (HRS), USA, M. Lichman, Machine Learning Repository (http://archive.ics.uci.edu/ml) of the Center for Machine Learning and Intelligent Systems, UCI, W. H. Wolberg, W. N. Street, and O. L. Mangasarian of the University of Wisconsin, Creators of the Breast Cancer Wisconsin Data Set, and NIPORT for BDHS 2014 and BMMS 2010 data. We would like to express our deep gratitude to the Royal Statistical Society for permission to reproduce the statistical tables included in the appendix, and our special thanks to Atinuke Phillips for her help. We also acknowledge that one table has been reproduced from

C. Dougherty's tables that have been computed to accompany the text 'Introduction to Econometrics' (second edition 2002, Oxford University Press, Oxford).

We are grateful to our colleagues and students at the King Saud University and the University of Dhaka. The idea of writing this book has stemmed from teaching and supervising research students at the King Saud University. We want to express our heartiest gratitude to the faculty members and the students of the Department of Statistics and Operations Research of the King Saud University and to the Institute of Statistical Research and Training (ISRT) of the University of Dhaka. Our special thanks to ISRT for providing every possible support for completing this book. We want to thank Shahariar Huda for his continued support to our work. We extend our deepest gratitude to Rafiqul I. Chowdhury for his immense help at different stages of writing this book. We want to express our gratitude to F. M. Arifur Rahman for his unconditional support to our work whenever we needed. We would like to thank Mahfuzur Rahman for his contribution in preparing the manuscript. Our special thanks to Amiya Atahar for her unconditional help during the final stage of writing this book. Further, we acknowledge gratefully the continued support from Tahmina Khatun, Jayati Atahar, and Shainur Ahsan. We acknowledge with deep gratitude that without help from Mahfuza Begum, this work would be difficult to complete. We extend our deep gratitude to Syed Shahadat Hossain, Azmeri Khan, Jahida Gulshan, Shafiqur Rahman, Israt Rayhan, Mushtaque Raza Chowdhury, Lutfor Rahman, Rosihan M. Ali, Adam Baharum, V. Ravichandran, and A. A. Kamil for their support. We are also indebted to M. Aminul Islam, P. K. Motiur Rahman, and Sekander Hayat Khan for their encouragement and support at every stage of writing this book.

Dhaka, Bangladesh   M. Ataharul Islam
Riyadh, Saudi Arabia   Abdullah Al-Shiha

Contents

About the Authors

M. Ataharul Islam is currently QMH Professor at ISRT, University of Dhaka, Bangladesh. He is a former professor of statistics at the University Sains Malaysia, King Saud University, University of Dhaka, and East West University, and was a visiting scholar at the University of Hawaii and University of Pennsylvania. He is the recipient of Pauline Stitt Award, WNAR Biometric Society Award for content and writing, University Grants Commission Award for book and research, and the Ibrahim Gold Medal for research. He has published more than 100 papers in international journals on various topics, particularly longitudinal and repeated measures data, including multistate and multistage hazards models, statistical models for repeated measures data, Markov models with covariate dependence, generalized linear models, and conditional and joint models for correlated outcomes.

Abdullah Al-Shiha is currently a professor of statistics at the Department of Statistics and Operations Research, King Saud University, Riyadh, Saudi Arabia. He has published in international journals on various topics, particularly experimental design. He has authored (and co-authored) books on this topic. In addition to his academic career, he has worked as a consultant and as a statistician with several governmental and private institutions, and has also received several research grants.

List of Figures

List of Tables

Chapter 1
Basic Concepts, Organizing, and Displaying Data

1.1 Introduction

Biostatistics has emerged as one of the most important disciplines in recent decades. A fast development in biostatistics has been experienced during the past decades due to interactive advancements in the fields of statistics, computer science, and life sciences. The process of development in biostatistics has been continuing to address new challenges due to new sources of data and growing demand for biostatisticians with sound background to face the needs. Biostatistics deals with designing studies, analyzing data, and developing new statistical techniques to address the problems in the fields of life sciences. It includes statistical analysis with special focus to the needs in the broad field of life sciences including public health, biomedical science, medicine, biological science, community medicine, etc. It may be noted that many of the remarkable developments in statistical science were stemmed from the needs in the biomedical sciences. A working definition of biostatistics states biostatistics as the discipline that deals with the collection, organization, summarization, and analysis of data in the fields of biological, health, and medical sciences including other life sciences. Sometimes, biostatistics is defined as a branch of statistics that deals with data relating to living organisms; however, due to rapid developments in the fields of statistics, computer science, and life sciences interactively, the role and scope of biostatistics have been widened to a large extent during the past decades. Despite the differences at an advanced level of applications of statistics and bio-statistics due to recent challenges, the fundamental components of both may be defined to encompass the procedures with similar guiding principles.

At the current stage of information boom in every sector, we need to attain an optimum decision utilizing the available data. The information used for making decision through a statistical process is called data. The decision about the underlying problem is to be made on the basis of a relatively small set of data that can be generalized for the whole population of interest. Here, the term population is used with specific meaning and a defined domain. For example, if an experimenter

© Springer Nature Singapore Pte Ltd. 2018
M. A. Islam and A. Al-Shiha, *Foundations of Biostatistics*,
https://doi.org/10.1007/978-981-10-8627-4_1

wants to know the prevalence of a disease among the children of age under 5 years in a small town, then the population is comprised of every child of under 5 years of age in that small town. In reality, it is difficult to conduct the study on the whole population due to cost, time, and skilled manpower needed to collect quality data. Under this circumstance, the population is represented statistically by a smaller set to help the experimenter to provide with the required information. At this stage, the experimenter faces two challenges: (i) to find the values that summarize the basic facts about the unknown characteristics of the population as sought in the study, and (ii) to make sure that the values obtained to characterize the sample can be shown to have adequate statistical support for generalizing the findings for the domain or more specifically the population from where the sample is drawn. These two criteria describe the essential foundations of both statistics and biostatistics.

The data obtained from experiments or surveys among the subjects can provide useful information concerning underlying reasons for such variations leading to important findings for the users, researchers, and policymakers. Using the techniques of biostatistics, we try to understand the underlying relationships and the extent of variation caused by the potential risk or prognostic factors. The identification of potential risk or prognostic factors associated with a disease, the efficacy of a treatment, the relationship between prognostic factors and survival status, etc. are some examples that can be analyzed by using biostatistical techniques.

Let us consider that an experimenter wants to know about the prevalence of diabetes in an urban community. There are two major types of diabetes mellitus, insulin-dependent diabetes mellitus (IDDM) or Type 1 diabetes and non-insulin-dependent diabetes mellitus (NIDDM) or Type 2 diabetes. The first type may occur among the young, but the other type usually occurs among relatively older population. To know the prevalence of the disease, we have to define the population living in the community as the study population. It would be difficult to conduct the study on the whole population because collection of blood glucose sample from each one of the population would take a very long time, would be very expensive, and a large number of skilled personnel with appropriate background for collecting blood samples need to be involved. In addition, the nonresponse rate would be very high resulting in bias in the estimate of prevalence rate. Thus, a sample survey would be a better choice in this situation considering the pressing constraints. For conducting the survey, the list of households in the community is essential, and then we may collect the data from the population. It is obvious that the result may deviate from the true population value due to use of a sample or a part of the population to find the prevalence of diabetes mellitus. The representation of the unknown population value by an estimate from the sample data is an important biostatistical concern to an experimenter.

A similar example is if we want to find whether certain factors cause a disease or not. It is difficult to establish a certain factor as a cause of that disease statistically alone, but we can have adequate statistical reasoning to provide insights to make conclusions that are of immense importance to understand the mechanism more logically. It may be noted here that biostatistics has been developing very extensively due to increasing demand for analyzing concerns regarding the health problems worldwide. Biostatistics covers a wide range of applications such as designing and conducting biomedical experiments and clinical trials, study of analyzing data from biological and biomedical studies along with the techniques to display the data meaningfully and developing appropriate computational algorithms, and also to develop statistical theories needed for analyzing and interpreting such data. It is very important to note that biostatisticians provide insights to analyze the problems that lead to advances in knowledge in the cross-cutting fields of biology, health policy, epidemiology, community medicine, occupational hazards, clinical medicine, public health policy, environmental health, health economics, genomics, and other disciplines. One major task of a biostatistician is to evaluate data as scientific evidence, so that the interpretations and conclusions from the data can be generalized for the populations from which the samples are drawn. A biostatistician must have (i) the expertise in the designing and conducting of experiments, (ii) the knowledge of relevant techniques of collecting data, (iii) an awareness of the advantages and limitations of employing certain techniques appropriate for a given situation and the analysis of data, and (iv) the understanding of employing the statistical techniques to the scientific contexts of a problem such that meaningful interpretations can be provided to address the objectives of a study. The results of a study should have the property of reproducibility in order to consider the validity of a study. The insights provided by a biostatistician essentially bridge the gap between statistical theories and applications to problems in biological and biomedical sciences.

The fundamental objective is to learn the basics about two major aspects of statistics: (i) descriptive statistics and (ii) inferential statistics. The descriptive statistics deals with organization, summarization, and description of data using simple statistical techniques, whereas the inferential statistics link the descriptive statistics measures from smaller data sets, called samples, with the larger body of data, called population from which the smaller data sets are drawn. In addition, the inferential techniques take into account analytical techniques in order to reveal the underlying relationships that might exist in the population on the basis of analysis from the sample data.

In this book, the elementary measures and techniques covering the following major issues will be addressed:

1. Descriptive statistics: This will address the organization, summarization, and analysis of data.
2. Inferential statistics: This will address the techniques to reach decision about characteristics of the population data by analyzing the sample data. The sample is essentially a small representative part of the population.

For understanding the underlying mechanism to address issues concerning inferential statistics, we need basic concepts of probability. Some important basic concepts of probability and probability distributions are included in this book for a thorough understanding of biostatistics.

1.2 Some Basic Concepts

Statistics
Statistics, as a subject, can be defined as the study of collection, organization, summarization, analysis of data, and the decision-making about the body of data called population on the basis of only a representative part of the data called sample. There are other usages of the term statistic in singular and statistics in plural senses. The term statistic is defined as a value representing a descriptive measure obtained from sample observations, and statistics is used in plural sense.

Population
The term population has a very specific meaning in statistics that may refer to human population or population of the largest possible set of values on which we need to conduct a study. For conducting a study on infants living in a certain rural community, all the infants in that community constitute the population of infants of that community at a particular time. In this case, the population is subject to change over time. If we shift the date of our reference time by 3 months, then the population of infants in the same community will be changed during the 3 months preceding the new date due to inclusion of additional newborn babies during the 3 months preceding the new date, exclusion of infant deaths during the 3 months preceding the new date, and exclusion of some infants who will be more than 1 year old during the 3-month period preceding the new study time because they cannot be considered as infants. A population of values is defined as the collection of all possible values at the specified time of study of a random variable for which we want to conduct the study. If a population is comprised of a fixed number of values, then the population is termed as a finite population and on the other hand if a population is defined to have an endless succession of values, then it is termed as an infinite population. Hence, a population is the collection of all the possible entities, elements, or individuals, on which we want to conduct a study at a specified time and want to draw conclusions regarding the objectives of that study. It may be noted that all the measurements of the characteristic of elements or individuals on which the study is conducted form the population of values of that characteristic or variable.

Example: Let us consider a study for estimating the prevalence of a disease among the children of age under 5 years in a community. Then, all the under 5 children in the community constitute the population for this study. If the objective of the study is to find the prevalence of a specific disease, then we need to define a variable for identifying each child under 5 in that community. The response may be coded as 1 for the presence of disease and 0 for the absence of disease at the time of study. The population of the variable prevalence of that disease is comprised of all the responses from each child of age under 5 year in that community.

Population Size (*N*)
The population size is the total number of subjects or elements in the population, usually denoted by N. In the previous example, the total number of children of age under 5 years in the community is the population size of the study area.

Sample
A sample is defined as the representative part of a population that needs to be studied in order to represent the characteristics of the population. The collection of sample data is one of the major tasks that use some well-defined steps to ensure the representativeness of the sample to represent the population from which the sample is drawn.

Example: In the hypothetical example of the population of children of age under 5 years in a community being conducted to study the prevalence of a disease, all the children of age under 5 years are included in the population for obtaining response regarding the status of that disease among the children. If only some of the children from the population are selected to represent all the children in the defined population, then it is called a sample.

Sample Size (*n*)
The number of individuals, subjects, or elements selected in the sample is called the sample size and is usually denoted by n.

Parameter
Parameter is defined to represent any descriptive characteristic or measure obtained from the population data. Parameter is a function of population values.

Example: Prevalence of heart disease in a population, average weight of patients suffering from diabetes in a defined population, average number of days suffered from seasonal flu by children of age under 5 years in a population, etc.

Statistic
Statistic is defined to represent any descriptive characteristic or measure obtained from sample data. In other words, statistic is a function of sample observations.

Example: Prevalence of heart disease computed from sample observations, average weight of patients suffering from diabetes obtained from sample observations, average number of days suffered from seasonal flu by children of age under 5 years computed from sample observations, etc.

Data
We have already used the term data in our previous discussion several times which indicates that data is one of the most extensively used terms in statistics. In the simplest possible way, we define data as the raw material of statistics. Data may be quantitative or qualitative in nature. The quantitative data may result from two sources: (i) measurements: temperature, weight, height, etc., and (ii) counts: number of patients, number of participants, number of accidents, etc. The qualitative data may emerge from attributes indicating categories of an element such as blood type, educational level, nationality, etc.

Sources of Data

The raw materials of statistics can be collected from various sources. Broadly, the sources of data are classified in terms of whether the data are being collected by either conducting a new study or experiment or from an existing source already collected by some other organization beforehand. In other words, data may be collected for the first time by conducting a study or experiment if the objectives of the study cannot be fulfilled on the basis of data from the existing sources. In some cases, there is no need to conduct a new study or experiment by collecting a new set of data because similar studies might have been conducted earlier but some of the analysis, required for fulfilling the objectives of a new study, might not be performed before. It may be noted here that most of the data collected by different agencies remain unanalyzed. Hence, we may classify the sources of data as the following types:

Primary Data: Primary data refer to the data being collected for the first time by either conducting a new study or experiment which has not been analyzed before. Primary data may be collected by using either observational studies for obtaining descriptive measures or analytical studies for analyzing the underlying relationships. We may conduct surveys or experimental studies to collect primary data depending on the objectives of the study. The data may be collected by employing questionnaires or schedules through observations, interviews, local sources, telephones, Internet, etc. Questionnaire refers to a series of questions arranged in a sequential order filled out by respondents and schedule is comprised of questions or statements filled out by the enumerators by asking questions or observing the necessary item in spaces provided.

Secondary Data: Secondary data refer to a set of data collected by others sometime in the past. Hence, secondary data does not represent the responses obtained at current time rather collected by someone else in the past for fulfilling specific objectives which might be different or not from that of the researchers or users. Sources of these data include data collected, compiled and published by government agencies, hospital records, vital registrations (collected and compiled by both government and non-government organizations), Internet sources, websites, internal records of different organizations, books, journal articles, etc.

Levels of Measurement

The data obtained either from the primary or secondary sources can be classified into four types of measurements or measurement scales. The four types or levels of measurement are nominal, ordinal, interval, and ratio scales. These measures are very important for analyzing data, and there are four criteria based on which these levels are classified. The four criteria for classifying the scales of measurements are identification, order, distance, and ratio. Identification indicates the lowest level of measuring scale which is used to identify the subject or object in a category and there are no meaningful order, difference between measures, and no meaningfully defined zero exists. The next higher level of measurement scale is order in the measure such as greater than, less than, or equal. It is possible to find a rank order of measurements. It is obvious that for measuring order by a scale both identification and order must be satisfied. This shows that a scale that measures order needs to satisfy identification criteria first implying that a measure for order satisfies two of the four properties, identification and order. Similarly, the next higher criterion is distance. To measure a distance, both identification and order criteria must be satisfied. It means that a distance measure, the interval scale, satisfies three criteria, identification, order, and distance. The highest level of criterion in measuring data is ratio that satisfies all the lower levels of criteria, identification, order, and distance and possesses an additional property of ratio. In this case, it is important to note that a meaningful ratio measure needs to satisfy the condition that zero exists in the scale such that it defines absolute zero for indicating the absence of any value. For any lower level measure, zero is not a precondition or necessity but for ratio measure the value of zero must exist with meaningful definition.

The levels of measurements are based on the four criteria discussed above. The levels or scales of measurements are discussed below:

1. **Nominal**: Nominal scale measure is used to identify by name or label of categories. The order, distance, and ratio of measurement are not meaningful, and thus can be used only for identification by names or labels of various categories. Nominal data measure qualitative characteristics of data expressed by various categories. Examples: gender (male or female), disease category (acute or chronic), place of residence (rural or urban), etc.

2. **Ordinal**: Ordinal data satisfy both identification and order criteria, but if we consider interval and ratio between measurements, then there is no meaningful interpretation in case of ordinal data. Examples: Educational level of respondent (no schooling, primary incomplete, primary complete, secondary incomplete, secondary complete, college, or higher), status of a disease (severe, moderate, normal), etc.

3. **Interval**: Interval data have better properties than the nominal and ordinal data. In addition to identification and order, interval data possess the additional property that the difference between interval scale measurements is meaningful. However, there is a limitation of the interval data due to the fact that there is no true starting point (zero) in case of interval scale data. Examples: temperature, IQ level, ranking an experience, score in a competition, etc. If we consider temperature data, then the zero temperature is arbitrary and does not mean the absence of any temperature implying that zero temperature is not absolute zero. Hence, any ratio between two values of temperature by Celsius or Fahrenheit scales is not meaningful.

4. **Ratio**: Ratio data are the highest level of measurements with optimum properties. Ratios between measurements are meaningful because there is a starting point (zero). Ratio scale satisfies all the four criteria including absolute zero implying that not only difference between two values but also ratio of two values is also meaningful. Examples: age, height, weight, etc.

Variable and Random Variable

The variable is defined as the measure of a characteristic on the elements. The element is the smallest unit on which the data are collected. The variable may take any value within a specified range for each element. However, this definition of variable does not express the underlying concept of a variable used in statistics adequately. It is noteworthy that the data in statistics are collected through a random experiment from a population. The sample collected from a population through a random experiment is called a random sample. There may be numerous possible random samples of size n from a population of size N. The selection of any value in a random sample that is drawn from the population depends on the chance or probability being assigned to draw each element of a sample. Hence, a random variable is subject to random variation such that it can take different values each with an associated probability. Examples: blood glucose level of respondents, disease status of individuals, gender, level of education, etc. The values of these random variables are not known until the selection of potential respondents and selection of a respondent from the defined population depend on associated probability.

Types of Random Variables

(1) Quantitative Random Variables

A quantitative random variable is a random variable that can be measured using scales of measurement. The value of a quantitative variable is measured numerically such as quantity that provides value in terms of measurements or counts. Examples: family size, weight, height, expenditure on medical care, number of patients, etc.

Types of Quantitative Random Variables

(a) Discrete Random Variables

A discrete random variable is defined as a random variable that takes only countable values from a random experiment. Examples: number of children ever born, number of accidents during specified time intervals, number of obese children in a family, etc.

(b) Continuous Random Variables

A continuous random variable is defined as a random variable that can take any value within a specified interval or intervals of values. More specifically, it can be said that a continuous random variable can take any value from one or more intervals resulting from a random experiment. Examples: height, blood sugar level, weight, waiting time in a hospital, etc.

(2) Qualitative Random Variables

The values of a qualitative random variable are obtained from a random experiment and take names, categories with or without meaningful ordering or attributes indicating to which category an element belongs. Examples: gender of respondent, type of hospital, level of education, opinion on the quality of medical care services, etc.

Types of Qualitative Random Variables

(a) Nominal Qualitative Variables

A nominal random variable is a qualitative variable that considers non-ranked and mutually exclusive categories of the variable. A nominal variable takes attributes such as names or categories that are used for identification only but cannot be ordered or ranked. Examples: sex, nationality, place of residence, blood type, etc.

(b) Ordinal Qualitative Variables

An ordinal variable is a qualitative variable that considers ranked and mutually exclusive categories of the variable. In other words, an ordinal variable takes the qualitative observations classified into various mutually exclusive categories that can be ranked. It is possible to order or rank the categories of an ordinal variable. Examples: severity of disease, level of satisfaction about the healthcare services provided in a community, level of education, etc.

The classification of variables is displayed in Fig. 1.1.

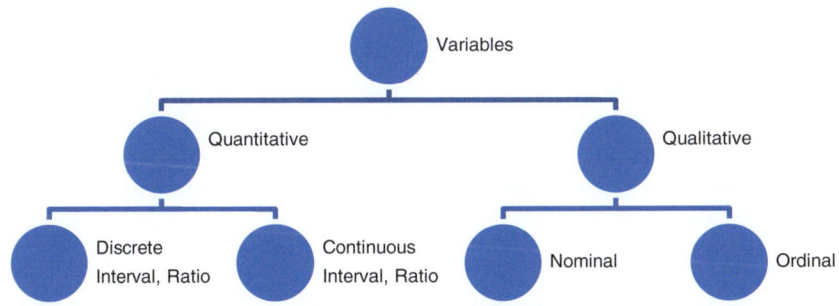

Fig. 1.1 Classification of variables by measurement scales

1.3 Organizing the Data

After collecting data, the major task is to organize data in such way that will help us to find information which are of interest to a study. Collection of data from a primary or secondary source is in a format that requires special techniques to arrange the data for answering the questions related to the objectives of a study or experiment. We need to organize the data from raw form in order to make suitable for such applications. In this section, some basic techniques for organization of data are discussed.

1.3.1 Frequency Distribution: Ungrouped

The data are collected on different variables from a well-defined population. Each variable can be organized and presented in a suitable form to highlight the main features of the data. One way to represent the sample data is to find the frequency distribution. In other words, the data are presented in a form where the characteristics of the original data are presented in a more meaningful way and the basic characteristics of the data are self-explanatory.

To organize the data using ungrouped frequency distribution for qualitative variables or discrete quantitative variables with a small number of distinct values are relatively easy computationally. The frequency of a distinct value from a sample represents the number of times the value is found in the sample. It means that if a value occurs 20 times then it is not necessary to write it 20 times rather we may use the frequency of that value 20, hence, it can be visualized in a more meaningful and useful way. The relative frequency is defined as the proportion of frequency for a value in the sample to the sample size. This can be multiplied by 100 to express it in percentage of the sample size. We can also find the frequency up to a certain value which is called the cumulative frequency.

In ungrouped form, data are displayed for each distinct value of the observations. In case of qualitative variable, the categories of a qualitative variable are summarized to display the number of times each category occurs. The number of times each category occurs is the frequency of that category and the table is called a frequency distribution table. Each observation is represented by only one category in a frequency distribution table such that the total frequency is equal to the sample size, n. An example below illustrates the construction of an ungrouped frequency distribution table.

Example 1.1
Let us consider hypothetical data on level of education of 16 women in a sample: 3, 5, 2, 4, 0, 1, 3, 5, 2, 3, 2, 3, 3, 2, 4, 1 where 0 = no education, 1 = primary incomplete, 2 = primary complete, 3 = secondary level education, 4 = college level education, and 5 = university level education.

Let variable = X = level of education (ordinal, qualitative), where the sample size = n = 16. The ordered array is 0, 1, 1, 2, 2, 2, 2, 3, 3, 3, 3, 3, 4, 4, 5, 5. The smallest value = 0 and the largest value = 5.

Frequency Bar Chart
A frequency bar chart displays the frequency distribution of a qualitative variable. The bar charts can take into account one or more classification factors. In a simple bar chart, we consider one classification factor. In a simple bar chart, a single bar for each category is drawn where the height of the bar represents the frequency of the category. For more than one classification factor, we may draw the bars for each category for the classification factors as clustered or stacked columns. In case of clustered bars, the bars for each category for all the classification factors are placed side by side. On the other hand, for the stacked bars, the segment of bars representing frequencies of each classification factor is stacked on top of one another. The following bar chart displays an example of a simple bar chart for the data on education level of 16 women as shown above (Fig. 1.2).

Dot Plot
An alternative to bar chart is dot plot. The most important advantage of dot plot is its simplicity. The dot plot displays a frequency distribution and grouped data points are represented by dots on a simple scale. Usually, dot plots display univariate quantitative data. It is used for relatively small or moderately large number of groups of data. Dot plots clearly show clusters and their gaps along with outliers, if any. To represent a frequency distribution, a dot plot simply provides number of

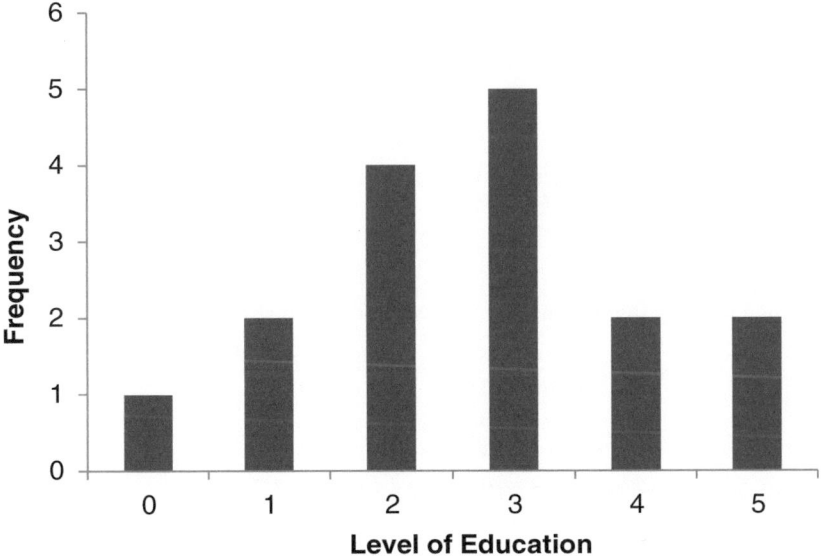

Fig. 1.2 Bar chart displaying frequency distribution of level of education

dots on the vertical axis against the values of the variable on the horizontal axis. Here, the bars are replaced by stacks of dots. From a dot plot, some descriptive measures such as mean, median, mode, and range can be obtained easily. It is also convenient to compare two or three frequency distributions using a dot plot.

An example of dot plot is displayed in Fig. 1.3. For constructing this diagram, the frequency distribution presented in Table 1.1 is used where the highest frequency occurs at level of education 3 for the women in the hypothetical sample.

Pie Chart

A pie chart is very commonly used to represent frequency distribution of qualitative variables using frequencies, percentage frequencies, or relative frequencies of categories of a qualitative variable. The pie or circle is divided into segments representing mutually exclusive categories of a qualitative variable, and the size of segment in a pie chart represents frequency, percentage frequency, or relative frequency of the corresponding category.

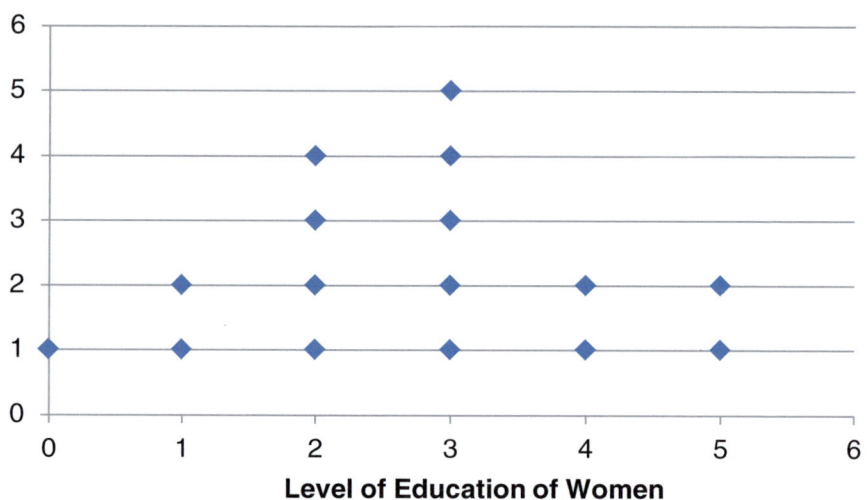

Fig. 1.3 Dot plot displaying level of education of women in a sample

Table 1.1 Frequency distribution of level of education of 16 women

Level of education	Frequency (f)	Relative frequency (f/n)	Percent frequency ((f/n)100)
0	1	0.0625	6.25
1	2	0.1250	12.50
2	4	0.2500	25.00
3	5	0.3125	31.25
4	2	0.1250	12.50
5	2	0.1250	12.50
Total	16	1.0000	100.00

A pie chart can be drawn using relative frequencies of a qualitative variable as follows:

(i)   A circle contains 360° which is equivalent to sample size n = total frequency or 1 in case of relative frequency.
(ii) Compute the relative frequency for each category.
(iii) Multiply relative frequency by 360° to find the share of angle size for the segment corresponding to the category. The total of all the angles corresponding to exhaustive and mutually exclusive categories is 360°.

Alternatively, percentage frequency can also be used to draw a pie chart following the guidelines stated below.

(i)   A circle contains 360° which is equivalent to sample size.
(ii) Compute the percentage frequencies for each category which add to 100% for all the categories combined.
(iii) Dividing percentage for each category by 100 provides relative frequency, and the size of the angle corresponding to a category is obtained by multiplying the relative frequency by 360°.

The following pie chart displays the level of education of women in a sample where the frequency distribution includes 1 in no school, 6 in primary, 5 in secondary, and remaining 4 in college categories. The total sample size is 16. The relative frequencies are 0.0625, 0.375, 0.3125, and 0.25, respectively, for no schooling, primary, secondary, and college levels, respectively. The angle sizes are obtained by multiplying the relative frequencies by 360° to draw the pie chart as displayed below. The sizes of angles for no schooling, primary schooling, secondary schooling, and college level education are 22.5°, 135°, 112.5°, 45°, and 45°, respectively. It can be checked that the total angle size in degrees for the pie chart is 22.5 + 135 + 112.5 + 45 + 45 = 360 (Fig. 1.4).

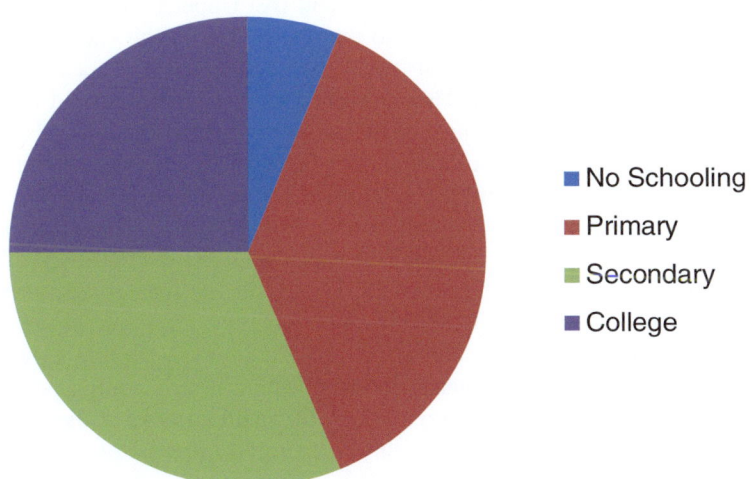

Fig. 1.4 Pie chart displaying level of education of women in a sample

1.3.2   Grouped Data: The Frequency Distribution

For ungrouped data, the frequency distribution is constructed for distinct values of categories or values of the variable. In case of continuous variables, the number of distinct values of the variable is too many and it is not meaningful or logical to construct the frequency distribution using all the distinct values of the variable observed in the sample. We know that the continuous random variable takes values from intervals, and in that case it would be logical to group the set of observations in intervals called class intervals. These class intervals are contiguous and nonoverlapping and selected suitably such that the sample observations can be placed in one and, only in one, of the class intervals. These groups are displayed in a frequency distribution table where the frequencies represent the number of observations recorded in a group. In grouped data, the choice of class intervals needs special attention. If the variable is quantitative and discrete such as size of household, then intervals such as 1–5, 6–10, 11–15, etc. are nonoverlapping. However, if we consider a continuous variable such as age of individuals admitted to a hospital, then the intervals 0–4, 5–9, 10–14, 15–19, etc. may raise the question what happens if someone reports age between the upper limit of an interval and lower limit of the next interval, for instance, if the reported age is 4 years 6 months. To avoid such ambiguity, if we may consider the intervals 0–5, 5–10, 10–15, etc., then there is clear overlapping between two consecutive age intervals because the upper limit of an interval is same as the lower limit of the next interval. To address this situation, we need to find the true class intervals which ensure continuity of the consecutive intervals and the values of the observations are considered to be nonoverlapping. A simple way to compute the true class interval is summarized here: (i) Find the gap between the consecutive class intervals, d = (lower limit of a class interval − upper limit of the preceding interval); (ii) Divide the gap, d, by 2, i.e., $d/2$; (iii) Lower limit of the true class interval can be obtained by subtracting $d/2$ from the lower limit of a class interval; and (iv) Upper limit of the true class interval can be obtained by adding $d/2$ to the upper limit of the class interval.

   In grouped data, the class intervals are to be constructed in a meaningful way depending on the nature of data. The number of class intervals should not be too small or too large. However, in most of the cases, the number of intervals depends on the purpose of the study. For example, if you conduct a survey to find the age composition of the patients admitted to a hospital, then the class intervals may be considered in five-yearly intervals such as 0–4, 5–9, 10–14, …, 90–94, where 90–94 is the last interval. Here, the last interval depends on the largest observed value. The five-yearly or ten-yearly age intervals are considered here to keep similarity with the age compositions available from other sources. However, if we need to construct intervals for data from laboratory tests, the intervals need to highlight the ranges usually employed for normal, mild complication, severe complication, etc. If these cut-off points are not taken into account, the main purpose of the table is not fulfilled and the table will not provide any meaningful information.

Let us consider that there are k intervals and the frequencies in those intervals are $f_1, \ldots, f_k$, then the sum of the frequencies is $\sum_{i=1}^{k} f_i = n$. Now, we can define the following terms necessary for constructing a table:

(i)   Frequency in the ith class interval: Number of observations in the ith class interval is $f_i, i = 1, 2, \ldots, k$.

(ii) Relative frequency in the ith class interval: Proportion of total observations in the ith class interval is f_i/n, where f_i is the frequency in the ith class interval and n is the sample size, $i = 1, 2, \ldots, k$.

(iii) Percentage relative frequency in the ith class interval: Percentage of total observations in the ith class interval is $(f_i/n) \times 100$, where f_i is the frequency in the ith class interval and n is the sample size.

(iv) Cumulative frequency: Number of observations less than or equal to the upper limit of a class interval is the cumulative frequency, usually denoted by F_i for the ith class interval. As all the observations are less than the upper limit of the last class interval, $F_k = n$. For instance, the cumulative frequency less than or equal to the upper limit of the first class interval is $F_1 = f_1$; similarly, the cumulative frequency less than or equal to the upper limit of the second class interval is $F_2 = f_1 + f_2$ (alternatively, $F_2 = F_1 + f_2$) which is the sum of frequencies in the first two classes, and the cumulative frequency less than or equal to the upper limit of the last class interval (or the kth class interval) is $F_k = f_1 + f_2 + \cdots + f_k = F_{k-1} + f_k$ which is the sum of frequencies in all the classes.

(v)   Relative cumulative frequency: Proportion of observations less than or equal to the upper limit of a class interval, which is F_i/n, is called the relative cumulative frequency corresponding to the upper limit of the ith class interval. As all the observations are less than the upper limit of the last class interval, the proportion of cumulative frequency in the last class is $(F_k/n) = (n/n) = 1$.

(vi) Percentage cumulative frequency: Percentage of observations less than or equal to the upper limit of the ith class interval which is $(F_i/n) \times 100$ is called the percentage cumulative frequency corresponding to the upper limit of the ith class interval. As all the observations are less than the upper limit of the last class interval, the corresponding percentage cumulative frequency is $(F_k/n) \times 100 = (n/n) \times 100 = 100$.

Example 1.2

The following data represent the weight of 24 women in kilograms taken from a randomly selected enumeration area of Bangladesh Demographic and Health Survey 2014.

Weight (in kilogram) of 24 women

46.4	53.2	52.8	42	50.8	43
51.9	59.2	55.1	38.9	49.7	43.1
42.2	52.7	49.8	50.7	44.8	49.2
47.7	42.9	52.9	54.1	45.4	49.9

In this example, let us denote the variable X = weight of women (in kg). The sample size is $n = 24$. The minimum weight observed in this sample is 38.9 kg. Similarly, the maximum weight is 59.2 kg. The range is the difference between the maximum and the minimum weights which is range = maximum weight − minimum weight = 59.2 kg − 38.9 kg = 20.3 kg. The possible class intervals include the lowest weight in the first and the largest weight in the last interval; we may use the following intervals of weight: 35.0–39.9, 40.0–44.9, 45.0–49.9, 50.0–54.9, and 55.0–59.9. There are 5 class intervals for grouping the weights (in kg) of 24 women in this example, where the smallest value, 38.9 kg, is included in the first interval, 35.0–39.9, and the largest value, 59.2 kg, is included in the last interval, 55.0–59.9.

Table 1.2 displays the construction of frequency distribution table for weights of women using tally marks. Then, dropping the column for tally marks from Table 1.2, we can display the grouped frequency distribution of the weights of 24 women as shown in Table 1.3.

Table 1.2 A frequency distribution table for weights of women for a selected enumeration area from BDHS 2014 ($n = 24$)

Class interval of weights of women (in kg)	Tally	Frequency (number of women)
35.0–39.9	|	1
40.0–44.9	𝍤|	6
45.0–49.9	𝍤||	7
50.0–54.9	𝍤|||	8
55.0–54.9	||	2

Table 1.3 A frequency distribution table for weights of women for a selected enumeration area from BDHS 2014 ($n = 24$)

Class interval of weights of women (in kg)	Frequency (number of women)
35.0–39.9	1
40.0–44.9	6
45.0–49.9	7
50.0–54.9	8
55.0–54.9	2

Mid-Points of Class Intervals
We can find the mid-point of a class interval as shown below:

$$\text{mid-point} = \frac{\text{lower limit} + \text{upper limit}}{2}.$$

It may be noted here that the mid-point of a class interval is considered as a repetitive or typical value for all observations in that interval.

True Class Intervals
In a frequency distribution table for a continuous variable, there cannot be any gap between two consecutive class intervals as displayed in Table 1.3. It is seen from Table 1.3 that the first class interval is 35.0–39.9 and the second class interval starts from 40.0 and ends at 44.9. Hence, there is a gap, $d = 40.0 - 39.9 = 0.1$, between the end point of the first interval and the starting point of the second interval. In other words, there is no continuity between these two points which violates the condition of continuity necessary for a continuous variable. To overcome this problem in constructing the frequency distribution of a continuous variable, let us compute the true class intervals or class boundaries as follows (Table 1.4):

d = gap between class intervals,
d = lower limit − upper limit of the preceding class interval,
true upper limit = upper limit + $d/2$, and
true lower limit = lower limit − $d/2$.

The computations mid-points of the first and last intervals are

mid-point of the first interval = $(34.95 + 39.95)/2 = 37.45$;
mid-point of the last interval = $(54.95 + 59.95)/2 = 57.45$.

It may be noted that (i) mid-point of a class interval can be used to represent all values of a class interval approximately, and (ii) there are no gaps between consecutive true class intervals. It may also be noted that the end point (true upper limit) of each true class interval equals to the starting point (true lower limit) of the next true class interval.

Cumulative Frequency Cumulative frequency of the first class interval = $F_1 = f_1$. Cumulative frequency of a class interval = frequency + cumulative frequency of the preceding class interval. Hence, it can be shown that

Table 1.4 Frequency distribution of weight of women (in kg) using true class intervals

Class interval	True class interval	Mid-point	Frequency
35.0–39.9	34.95–39.95	37.45	1
40.0–44.9	39.95–44.95	42.45	6
45.0–49.9	44.95–49.95	47.45	7
50.0–54.9	49.95–54.95	52.45	8
55.0–59.9	54.95–59.95	57.45	2

$$F_1 = f_1,$$
$$F_2 = F_1 + f_2,$$
$$F_3 = F_2 + f_3, \quad .$$
$$\vdots$$
$$F_k = F_{k-1} + f_k.$$

Relative Frequency and Percentage Frequency

Relative frequency = frequency/n,

Relative frequency of the ith class interval = $\frac{f_i}{\sum_{i=1}^{k} f_i} = \frac{f_i}{n}$.

Percentage frequency = Relative frequency $\times$ 100%.

Percentage frequency of the ith class interval = $\frac{f_i}{\sum_{i=1}^{k} f_i} \times 100\% = \frac{f_i}{n} \times 100\%$.

We can answer different types of questions from the information summarized in Table 1.5. Some examples are shown below using different columns of the table.

Frequency The most frequently responded weight of women belongs to the weight interval 50.0–54.9 kg and the number of women in this interval is 8.

Cumulative Frequency The number of women having weight less than 50 kg is 14.

Percentage Frequency The percentage of women with weights in the interval 50.0–54.9 kg is 33.4% which is one-third of the total number of women in the sample.

Cumulative Percentage Frequency The percentage of women with weight less than 55 kg is 58.4%.

Table 1.5 Frequency distribution, relative frequency distribution, cumulative relative frequency distribution, percentage frequency, and cumulative percentage frequency of weights (in kg) of women

Class interval	Frequency	Cumulative frequency	Relative frequency	Cumulative relative frequency	Percentage frequency	Cumulative percentage frequency
35.0–39.9	1	1	0.042	0.042	4.2	4.2
40.0–44.9	6	7	0.250	0.292	25.0	29.2
45.0–49.9	7	14	0.292	0.584	29.2	58.4
50.0–54.9	8	22	0.333	0.917	33.3	91.7
55.0–59.9	2	24	0.083	1.000	8.3	100.0

Table 1.6 Frequency distribution of weight of women (in kg) using true class intervals

Class interval	True class interval	Mid-point	Frequency	Cumulative frequency
35.0–39.9	34.95–39.95	37.45	1	1
40.0–44.9	39.95–44.95	42.45	6	7
45.0–49.9	44.95–49.95	47.45	7	14
50.0–54.9	49.95–54.95	52.45	8	22
55.0–59.9	54.95–59.95	57.45	2	24

1.4 Displaying Grouped Frequency Distributions

To display frequency, relative frequency, or percentage frequency distributions, we may consider one of the following graphs or plots:

(i)   The Histogram,
(ii) The Frequency Polygon,
(iii) Ogive, and
(iv) Stem-and-Leaf display.

For illustration of the graphs, the data on weights of 24 women presented in this section are summarized in Table 1.6. This table is a slightly extended version of Table 1.4.

Histogram
A histogram is constructed for continuous variable. In the X-axis, class boundaries or true class intervals and in the Y-axis, the frequencies or relative frequencies are used. The histogram displays the frequency distribution and that is why the underlying characteristics of a frequency distribution are well represented by a histogram. We can use the relative frequency to represent the frequency distribution. It is noteworthy that area of rectangle is proportional to the frequency in a histogram. If an interval is two times of other intervals, then the height for that interval in the Y-axis is height = (relative frequency/2), in other words, height = (relative frequency/width of the interval). The histogram is considered as very useful diagram for self-explanatory exposition of a data set. There are some disadvantages of histogram: (i) class boundaries are chosen arbitrarily and hence any change in the boundaries may change the appearance of a histogram quite substantially specially in case of small samples, (ii) the representation of a histogram by rectangular shapes assumes uniformity within each interval which may not be true in real-life frequency distributions and it depends largely on the width of an interval, and (iii) the comparison of two or more frequency distributions by histograms is not a convenient option.

Organizing and Displaying Data using Histogram: Using the data presented in Table 1.5, we can draw the following histogram (Fig. 1.5).

The Frequency Polygon
The frequency polygon is constructed for both continuous and discrete variables. We can use relative frequencies to draw a frequency polygon too. We can plot

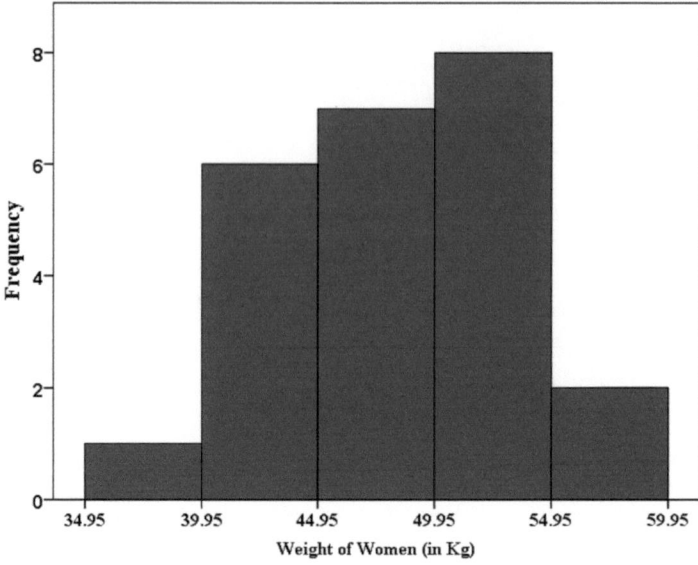

Fig. 1.5 Histogram of weight of women (in kg)

frequency corresponding to mid-point of each class. Mid-values of class intervals are plotted along the X-axis and frequencies are plotted at the Y-axis. The latter points are then joined by straight lines. The frequency polygon should be brought down at each end to the X-axis by joining it to the mid-values of the next outlying interval of zero frequency which is called the closed-ended frequency polygon and if the outlying interval of zero frequency is not considered then it is called the open-ended frequency polygon. The frequency polygon can be used for comparison by superimposing two or more polygons. Both histogram and frequency polygons are used to represent frequency distributions.

Example 1.3

Let us consider the following hypothetical frequency distribution of the age of 100 women (Table 1.7).

Table 1.7 Frequency distribution of age of 100 women

True class interval (age in years)	Frequency (No. of women)	Cumulative Frequency	Mid-points
14.5–19.5	8	8	17
19.5–24.5	16	24	22
24.5–29.5	32	56	27
29.5–34.5	28	84	32
34.5–39.5	12	96	37
39.5–44.5	4	100	42
Total	$n = 100$		

Width of the interval: W = true upper limit − true lower limit = $19.5 - 14.5 = 5.0$

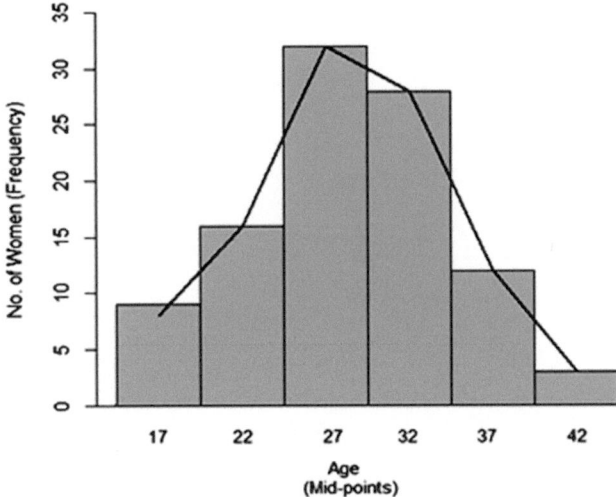

Fig. 1.6 Histogram and open-ended frequency polygon for displaying frequency distribution of age of 100 women

Frequency Polygon (Open)

The following frequency polygons represent the frequency of age of 100 women (Fig. 1.6).

Frequency Polygon (Closed)

See Figs. 1.7 and 1.8.

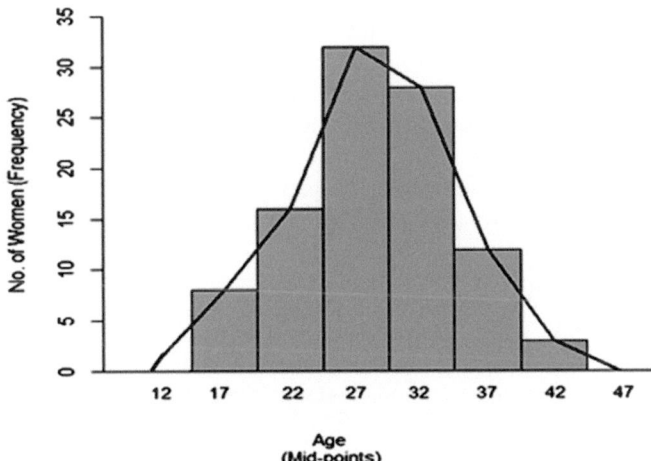

Fig. 1.7 Histogram and closed-ended frequency polygon for displaying frequency distribution of age of 100 women

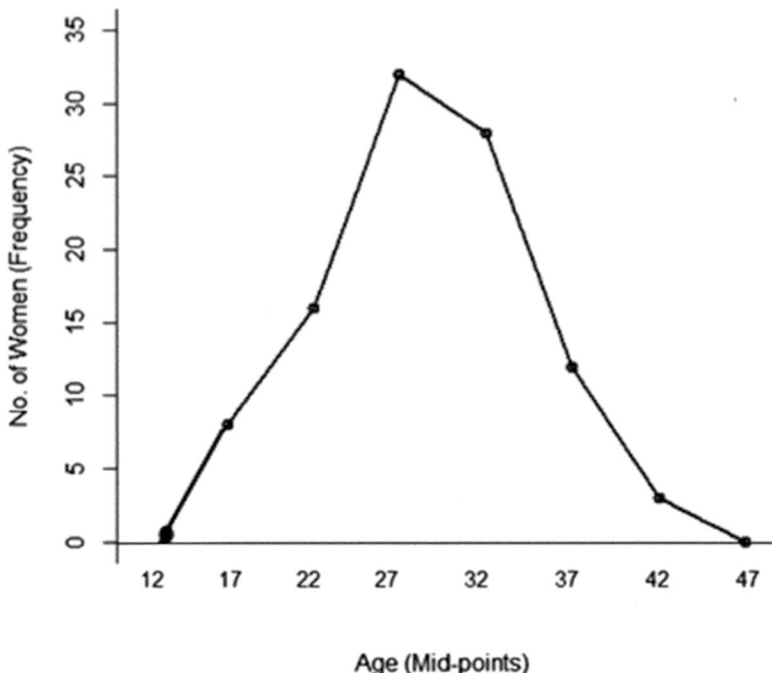

Fig. 1.8 A closed-ended frequency polygon for displaying frequency distribution of age of 100 women

Ogive
We can represent a cumulative frequency distribution by an ogive. An ogive can be constructed by considering the true class limits or boundaries in the horizontal axis and the cumulative frequencies in the vertical axis. Then, the cumulative frequencies are indicated corresponding to the upper limit of the class intervals. The cumulative frequency is zero at the lower limit of the first class interval and sample size, n, at the upper limit of the last class interval. After connecting all the points for cumulative frequencies using a line chart, we can draw an ogive. The ogive can be drawn by using relative cumulative frequencies or percentage cumulative frequencies in the vertical axis instead of cumulative frequencies as well (Fig. 1.9).

Stem-and-Leaf Display
The organization of data involves mainly ordering of the data and constructing a frequency distribution table. The ordering of data for a moderate or large data set does not provide a meaningful way to visualize characteristics inherent in the data. In tables, the original data are summarized and presented in a way that the original data are grouped, and it is not possible to examine the characteristics using

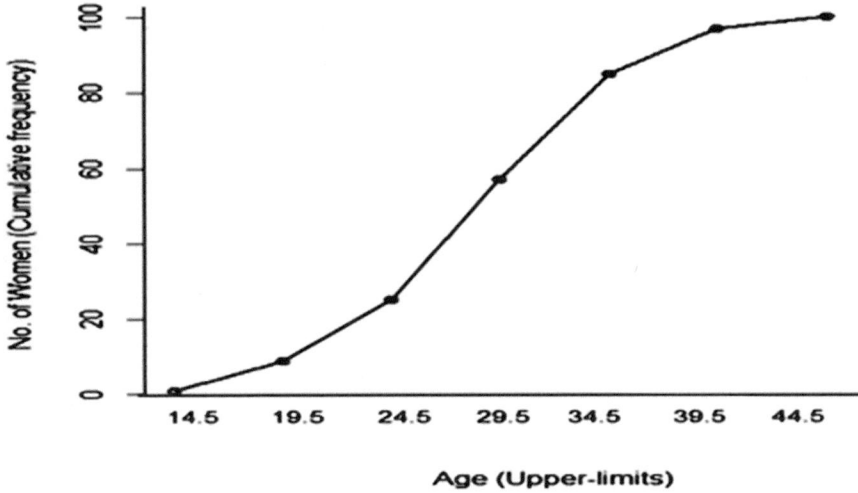

Fig. 1.9 An ogive displaying frequency distribution of age of 100 women

individual observations. In this context, the stem-and-leaf plot is an alternative approach where the original data are visible and the ordering of data is also done in the plot. In addition, this technique may be considered as a graphical representation as well. A simple way to explore data is stem-and-leaf display which is an exploratory data analysis technique. A stem-and-leaf display resembles a histogram which is useful for quantitative data sets. The purpose of a stem-and-leaf display is similar to a histogram. A stem-and-leaf display provides the following information: range of the data set, location of the highest concentration of measurements, reveals the presence or absence of symmetry in the data.

A major advantage of the stem-and-leaf plot is that it preserves the original data set. Another advantage is that the stem-and-leaf plot can be constructed during the tallying process, so an ordered array is not necessary to be performed separately. This is a very powerful but simple technique for exploring the data. Both the organization of data and some basic characteristics can be explored without much difficulty.

To construct a stem-and-leaf plot, we can follow the following steps:

(i)   Each measurement is partitioned into two parts: stem and leaf.
(ii) The stem part represents one or more of the initial digits, and the leaf part represents the remaining digits.
(iii) In a stem-and-leaf display, both stem and leaf parts are displayed.
(iv) In the display, the stem starts with the smallest value and ends with the largest value. The values are displayed in an ordered column. It may be noted that all the values within the range from the smallest to the largest values are included in the stem. If some values of the stem are not in the data, still the values are to be included in the stem of the display.

(v)   The leaves are placed on the right-hand side of the corresponding stems in the rows of the display. If there are more than one digit in the leaves, first digit is considered and remaining digits are ignored. If there are decimals in the observed sample data, then the decimals are omitted in the display.
(vi) We can draw a vertical line between the stems and leaves.

Example 1.4
Let us consider the following data on age of 25 women drawn randomly from an enumeration unit selected for a reproductive health study in Bangladesh in 2014 (BDHS, 2014):

39, 48, 40, 17, 23, 32, 31, 20, 38, 38, 27, 28, 45, 42, 36, 41, 22, 30, 33, 19, 36, 20, 36, 48, 22.

The stem-and-leaf display using the above data is

Stem	Leaf
1	79
2	3078202
3	9218860366
4	805218

After rearranging the leaf values in order of magnitude, we can show that

Stem	Leaf
1	79
2	0022378
3	0123666889
4	012588

From the above stem-and-leaf display, we can show that

smallest value = 17 years,
largest value = 48 years,
middle value = 33 years,
range = 48 years − 17 years = 31 years,
frequency of the women is the highest in the age group of 30s, and the most frequently occurred age is 36 years.

Some important features like the ones showed above are readily available from a stem-and-leaf plot.

1.5 Designing of Sample Surveys

We have mentioned in the previous sections that data are the raw materials for statistics. The drawing of a representative sample from the population is the most important part to make the statistical exercises meaningful. In this section, a brief description is highlighted for an understanding about the data collection procedures with introduction to the preliminary concepts necessary for the data collection procedures.

1.5.1 Introduction

It is known that the objective of statistics is to make inference about a population from information contained in a sample. Some of the concepts necessary to understand the data collection mechanism are described below.

Population: We have already defined population at the beginning of this chapter. In the context of sampling, let us define the population once again. The entire set of collection of elements about which we wish to make an inference can be defined as population. In sampling, we may call population as target population or universe too.

Element: An element is the smallest unit in a sampling on which data are collected. In other words, measurement on a variable is obtained from an element.

Sampling Unit: Sampling units are elements or group of elements that are defined clearly, can be identified without any ambiguity, and can be observed conveniently. If the sampling unit is an element, then we may call it sampling element.

Frame: An exhaustive and nonoverlapping list of all sampling units is called the sampling frame.

Sample: A sample is defined as the collection of sampling units or sampling elements selected for a study with specific objectives from the sampling frame.

1.5.2 Planning a Survey

Each item on the following checklist should be carefully considered in the planning of a survey.

(i) **Statement of objectives**: It is necessary to state the objectives of the survey at the planning stage. The stated objectives have to be very clear and precise. At every stage of survey design and its implementation, the stated objectives provide the guiding principles.

(ii) **Target population**: It is necessary to define the population to be sampled and it is called the target population due to its specified domain based on the objectives of the study as well as its exhaustive coverage of sampling units for selecting the sample. It is important to keep in mind that a sample must be selected from the target population such that each unit in the population can be assigned with a probability of being selected in the sample.

(iii) **Frame**: The sampling frame is comprised of the list of all sampling units from the entire population, nonoverlapping, and exhaustive. It is expected that there is close agreement between the target population and list of sampling units because sampling units are defined using the elements of the entire population.

(iv) **Sample design**: It is important to choose the design of the sample with special attention to number of sampling units/elements and method of selecting the sampling units/elements from the population in order to fulfill the stated objectives of a study.

(v) **Method of measurement**: At the planning stage, it is necessary to decide on the method of measurement. There are several methods of measurement employed in sampling including personal interviews, telephone interviews, mailed questionnaires, or direct observations.

(vi) **Measurement instrument**: To collect data from the elements of a survey, we need to specify the necessary measurements and the method of obtaining the relevant information using appropriate instruments to address the objectives of the study. This step requires a detailed plan necessary to set the questions for obtaining the data rigorously. The nonresponse and incorrect response can be minimized by a carefully designed instrument.

(vii) **Selection and training of fieldworkers**: With a very well-planned design, the success of a sample survey depends to a large extent on the selection, training of fieldworkers, and monitoring the collection of data at the field level. The fieldworkers are the most important persons responsible for collecting quality data at the field level. Hence, the implementation of the plans of a survey design heavily depends on the selection and training of fieldworkers on questionnaire and measurements for producing quality data.

(viii) **Pretest**: It is very useful to select a small sample and conduct pretesting prior to implement the survey design. The purpose of a pretest is to find whether there are deficiencies in the questionnaire or other data collecting measurement instrument, training of the fieldworkers, and monitoring of survey design activities. The pretest findings can provide useful feedbacks for making timely modifications prior to implementation at the field level.

(ix) **Organization of fieldwork**: To make a large-scale survey successful, the organization of fieldwork plays a vital role. The management of field activities at the field level involves careful monitoring activities of interviewers, coordinators, and data managers with possible backup support.

(x) **Organization of data management**: A carefully planned outline of han-
dling data at each stage of conducting a survey is an essential step. In
organizing data, different steps such as code plan, data entry, checking,
rechecking, editing, tabulation plan, analysis, etc. are to be planned very
carefully.

(xi) **Data analysis**: Data analysis is performed on the basis of the objectives of
the study.

1.5.3 Major Components of Designing a Sample Survey

The major components in designing sample surveys are

(i)   sample design,
(ii) survey measurements,
(iii) survey operations, and
(iv) statistical analysis and report writing.

Sample Design
The core component of designing a sample survey is sample design and depending
on the sample design of a sample survey, other components are planned. The
sample design includes the core tasks of sampling plan and inferential procedure.
The selection of sample from the population is designed in the sampling plan of a
sample survey. The sampling plan provides the methodology of selecting the
sampling units and illustrating the selection of elements to be included in the
sample from the sampling frame. The sampling plan provides the outline of relating
the sample to the target population. The inferential procedure provides specific plan
for estimation and tests based on the objectives stated for conducting a survey.

Survey Measurements
The survey measurements are very crucial that need careful expert opinion and
extensive literature review in the light of the underlying objectives of the study
before making measurements to be employed finally. A pretest can play a vital role
to obtain feedback on whether the measurements are relevant and observable. The
main concern regarding the survey measurements is about addressing the objectives
adequately by analyzing the data obtained from the survey. If there is problem with
core measurements necessary to obtain estimates relevant to the objectives of a
study, the purpose of conducting a sample survey is grossly undermined.

Survey Operations The collection of data is the most important task in a sample
survey because all the estimates needed to address the stated objectives are obtained
from the data that are collected from the field. At this stage, every operation needs
to be implemented very carefully because once the data are collected there will be
no way to repeat the whole process once again. The quality requirements are to be
ensured from the beginning and monitored and coordinated with extensive survey

operations strategy for ensuring quality of the data. The steps of survey operations include preparation of the process for data collection, training of the fieldwork team and management, data collection at the field level, review of field level operations for collecting data as an integral part, check for any inconsistency in the measurements and necessary remedial steps such as re-interview, repeated attempts to reduce the nonresponse, collection of the measurement instruments followed by data entry, consistency check, coding process, and storing of data for analysis.

Statistical Analysis and Report Writing
After the data have been collected at the field level, the processes of coding, editing, and processing for analysis are completed carefully. Once the data are processed, the next step is to use the data for conducting statistical analysis necessary in order to address the objectives of the sample survey and the findings are presented in a final report.

1.5.4 Sampling

In a very broad term, we can say that the primary objectives of conducting a sample survey are (i) to draw a random sample from the target population and (ii) to estimate the parameters of the target population from the sample.

Probability and Nonprobability Sampling
There are two broad classes of sampling: (i) probability sampling and (ii) nonprobability sampling. The definition of a random variable has been introduced in this chapter, and it is noted that a random variable has an associated probability such that each value of a random variable has a known and nonzero probability of being selected. In a probability sampling, there is an assigned probability for each element of being selected in the sample which is performed by applying the process of randomization. However, in case of a nonprobability sampling, the selection of elements does not use any randomization and there is no known probability of being selected. Only probability sampling can provide the estimated reliability of which can be evaluated. On the other hand, the reliability of an estimate based on nonprobability sampling cannot be evaluated and this weakness restricts a nonprobability sampling to generalize the estimates for any target population.

Probability Sampling A variety of probability sampling techniques have been developed to provide efficient practical sample designs:

  (i) Simple random sampling,
 (ii) Stratified sampling,
(iii) Systematic sampling,
 (iv) Cluster sampling,
  (v) Multistage sampling, etc.

Simple Random Sampling The simple random sampling is a simple but ideal sampling procedure but cannot be applied in many situations particularly in large surveys. A simple random sampling procedure is performed by drawing a sample of size n from a population of size N where each element in the population of size N has an equal probability or same chance of being included in the sample. In a simple random sampling, the chance of being selected for every possible sample of size n from a population of size N is same. Two types of simple random sampling are (i) simple random sampling with replacement and (ii) simple random sampling without replacement. We can use the random number tables for drawing a sample of size n from a population of size N. A random number table displays a set of integers that include all digits (0, 1, …, 9) with equal proportions approximately. It is noteworthy that there is no observable trend in the patterns of digits included in a generated random number table (see Appendix A.9).

Stratified Sampling It is important for sample survey to consider a strategy for a fixed cost to maximize the amount of information by implementing. It is not always possible to maximize the amount of information by using the simple random sampling for a fixed cost due to practical reasons and there is a need for alternative sampling procedures. One of the most popular alternatives is the stratified sampling which may increase the amount of information for a given cost.

In a simple random sampling procedure, the sample is drawn from a single population without separating the population elements into separate groups on the basis of any criteria. Sometimes, it would be cost-effective in terms of sample size if the population elements are classified into nonoverlapping groups termed as strata. Then, simple random sampling from each stratum provides the stratified sample. The reasons for choosing a stratified random sampling are as follows:

(i)   Stratification is performed usually if there is proven homogeneity within strata and there is heterogeneity between strata. In that case, the bound of error estimation is smaller for sample data from a stratified sampling compared to that of a simple random sample of same size.

(ii) Due to construction of strata by taking into account naturally formed groups such as rural and urban areas as strata, the cost per element is reduced to a large extent.

(iii) Sometimes, it is of great importance to obtain estimate for each stratum and a stratified random sampling provides the random sample for each stratum from which estimates for all the strata can be attained.

Systematic Sampling In a practical sense, both simple random sampling and stratified sampling may involve steps that may pose formidable difficulty for ensuring a feasible sample selection process in terms of time and cost. The systematic sampling procedure simplifies the sample selection process and it is used widely for practical reasons.

In a systematic sampling, the basic idea is very simple. Instead of sampling each unit at a time, an appropriate interval of units in the sampling frame is chosen and the starting point is selected randomly from the first interval of the list and every other element is selected at equal intervals from the list or frame. This systematic procedure of selecting the sample with randomization of the element in the first interval and selecting the remaining elements at equal intervals is known as the systematic sampling.

In a link systematic sampling, the first element is selected from the first k elements of the sampling frame and every kth element thereafter is selected from the complete list of elements. Often, the systematic sampling is used as an alternative to the simple random sampling for the reasons listed below:

(i) Selection of elements by simple or stratified random sampling is difficult and may be subject to error if the sampling frame is not updated or complete. In this case, the systematic sampling can provide a sample with less selection error at the field level.

(ii) Per unit cost may be reduced to a great extent for a systematic sampling as compared to simple random sampling.

Cluster Sampling If we consider cluster of elements or collection of elements instead of elements, then a cluster sampling can be employed to draw a sample. In a cluster sampling, the sampling units are cluster of elements and the clusters are selected using the simple random sampling. For a large sample survey, it is very costly to prepare the updated sampling frame of elements, and the cost is reduced substantially if a cluster of elements is considered as the sampling unit. The cost of obtaining measurements from elements increases if the selected elements are spread over at distant locations. On the other hand, the cost is reduced for a cluster sampling because the elements form a cluster at the same location. The cluster sampling can be used with minimum per unit cost under the following situations:

(i) The sampling frame of elements is either not available or may be very costly to obtain or update but the list of clusters can be obtained and updated easily.

(ii) The distance separating the elements cause increased cost per element in simple or stratified sampling but if the units are clusters then the cost of obtaining observations from each element reduces substantially.

There is noteworthy difference between construction of strata and clusters. The strata are constructed such that there is homogeneity within a stratum but heterogeneity between strata for the variable being measured from the elements. In constructing the cluster, on the other hand, we have to consider just the opposite, heterogeneity within the cluster, and homogeneity between clusters. If the heterogeneity within and homogeneity between clusters is satisfied, then the cluster sampling can produce estimates with very low cost per unit.

Multistage Sampling
It has been stated that cluster sampling is economical under certain circumstances but the cluster sampling may result in increased variance of the desired estimator for a large population with large size of clusters. This limitation restricts the use of cluster sampling to some extent. A possible remedy is to select only a small number of units from each cluster rather than collecting data from each element of the selected

clusters. In that case, we can increase the number of clusters in order to redistribute number of elements being selected per cluster to a larger number of clusters. In this case, two-stage sampling design is conducted. In the first stage, clusters are selected and at the second stage a specified number of elements are selected from each of the selected clusters. The first stage sampling units are called the primary sampling units (clusters) and the second stage units are called the secondary sampling units (elements). This sampling procedure is known as a two-stage sampling and can be further generalized to multistage sampling for three or higher stages.

Multistage sampling has been extensively used in practice in large-scale surveys. It is noteworthy that the multistage sampling is expected to be

(i) less efficient than single-stage sampling and more efficient than cluster sampling from the sampling variability point of view, and

(ii) more efficient than single-stage random sampling and less efficient than cluster sampling from the cost and operational point of view.

The main advantage of this sampling procedure is that, at the first stage, the frame of primary sampling units is required, which can be prepared easily. At the second stage, the frame of second stage units is required only for the selected PSUs, and so on.

The multistage sampling design is very flexible and allows different selection procedures at different stages depending on the requirement of the study. In many practical situations, the multistage sampling design may be considered as the only choice for selecting ultimate sampling units in the context of availability of suitable frame as well as cost per unit.

Design Effect (Deff)

With the more complex sampling plans such as multistage sampling, a useful quantity is the design effect (deff) of the plan. The design effect is described as the ratio of the variance of the estimate obtained by employing a more complex sampling technique such as the multistage sampling to the variance of the estimate that could be obtained from a simple random sampling of the same sample size. In general, the design effect is used for determining sample size and assessing the efficiency of a more complex sampling technique.

1.5.5 Methods of Data Collection

The major types of data collection methods are:

(i) personal interviews,
(ii) telephone interviews,
(iii) self-administered questionnaires, and
(iv) direct observation.

Personal Interviews

The personal interviews are conducted on the selected elements with questionnaires constructed beforehand and the responses are recorded. In most of the cases, the respondents agree to respond if contacted personally. The advantage of personal interview is obvious, ambiguity in a question can be explained, and reaction of a respondent can be noted on a question. There are some disadvantages too, particularly if the interviewers are not trained adequately or are biased toward certain potential responses, then that may influence the respondents and will result in bias in the sample data.

Telephone Interviews

Telephone interviews have become a very popular mode of conducting interviews, and the reasons for this popularity are (i) less expensive than personal interviews, (ii) less time is needed because interviewers do not have to travel to the respondents, and (ii) can be monitored whether the protocol is maintained or not. The problems with telephone interviews cannot be ignored. Some of the limitations are (i) there may be mismatch between sampling frame and list of telephone numbers, (ii) telephone directory may contain numbers do not belong to the potential respondents, (iii) there may be unlisted numbers, (iv) telephone interviews must be short so the number of questions need to be very few, and (v) the nonresponse rate can be much higher in telephone interviews.

Self-administered Questionnaires

Another very common mode is use of self-administered questionnaires. In this method, the questionnaires are either mailed or distributed using other means to selected individuals of the sample. Using this method, the cost of the survey can be minimized. The major limitation of the self-administered questionnaire method is a very low response rate.

Direct Observation

Sometimes, direct observation method is used to collect data if questionnaire method cannot provide necessary information effectively. If the objective of a study is to measure change in the behavior, occurrence of an event, physical condition, prevailing situation, etc., then a direct observation may provide necessary data that can reflect the objective of a study more appropriately and effectively. The direct observation method can use both the structured and unstructured observation methods; structured method may provide quantitative data and unstructured method results in qualitative data. The use of direct observation methods may be effective if the objective of the study is to provide estimates on indicators that do not involve responses from respondents directly but the observation method can sufficiently provide necessary data. This restricts the use of the direct observation method to studies with only very special needs of such data.

1.6 Summary

This chapter introduces biostatistics as a discipline that deals with designing studies, analyzing data, and developing new statistical techniques to address the problems in the fields of life sciences. This includes collection, organization, summarization, and analysis of data in the fields of biological, health, and medical sciences including other life sciences. One major objective of a biostatistician is to find the values that summarize the basic facts from the sample data and to make inference about the representativeness of the estimates using the sample data to make inference about the corresponding population characteristics. The basic concepts are discussed along with examples and sources of data, levels of measurement, and types of variables. Various methods of organizing and displaying data are discussed for both ungrouped and grouped data. The construction of table is discussed in details. This chapter includes methods of constructing frequency bar chart, dot plot, pie chart, histogram, frequency polygon, and ogive. In addition, the construction of stem-and-leaf display is discussed in details. All these are illustrated with examples. As the raw materials of statistics are data, a brief section on designing of sample surveys including planning of a survey and major components are introduced in order to provide some background about collection of data.

Exercises

1.1 Classify the following variables by the following types: (i) scale of measurement, (ii) quantitative or qualitative, (iii) if qualitative, nominal or ordinal, and (iv) if quantitative, discrete, or continuous:

    (i)   number of patients admitted to a hospital each day,
    (ii)   blood type of children,
    (iii) age of individuals in a study,
    (iv)   height of individuals in a study,
    (v)   weight of individuals in a study,
    (vi)   duration of stay in emergency care,
    (vii) level of education,
    (viii) years of schooling,
    (ix)   gender of respondent,
    (x)   survival status of patient suffered from heart disease,
    (xi)   place of delivery,
    (xii) current marital status,
    (xiii) number of children ever born,
    (xiv) pregnancy resulting in live birth or not,
    (xv)   duration of current pregnancy,
    (xvi) number of antenatal visits during pregnancy,

(xvii)   delivery by cesarean section or not,
(xviii) place of residence, and
(xix)   patient's level of satisfaction with service provided in a hospital.

1.2 Consider a study of 300 males aged 18 years or higher conducted in a city called *D*. The study indicates that there are 10% smokers. Answer the following questions:

   (i)   What is the sample?
   (ii) What is the population?
   (iii) What is the variable of interest?
   (iv) What is the scale of measurement used for the variable?

1.3 (i) What are the main purposes of constructing a table?
     (ii) What are the major steps in constructing a frequency distribution table?

1.4 Compare and contrast the following:

   (i)   sample and population,
   (ii) quantitative and qualitative variables,
   (iii) statistic and statistics,
   (iv) discrete and continuous variables, and
   (v)   class boundaries and class limits.

1.5 An experimenter recorded times (in minutes) to complete a procedure suggested to a sample of 50 patients with physical disability and the grouped frequency distribution is shown below.

Time (minutes)	20–29	30–39	40–49	50–59	60–69
Frequency	4	16	21	6	3

   (i) Find the true class limits.
   (ii) Find the relative and cumulative frequencies of the times to complete the suggested procedure.

1.6 (a) Compare and contrast between bar diagram and histogram.
     (b) Compare between histogram and frequency polygon.

1.7 How can you construct a stem-and-leaf display? What are the advantages of a stem-and-leaf display over histogram?

1.8 The following data show the number of hours 10 hospital patients had to stay in the emergency care after accident:
     17, 20, 22, 14, 14, 31, 14, 32, 25, 24.
     Construct a stem-and-leaf plot and comment on the characteristics of the data.

1.9 The following are the age of 30 patients (in years) seen in the emergency room of a hospital on Friday:
     30, 29, 18, 40, 36, 26,
     32, 39, 21, 42, 33, 20,

42, 20, 31, 37, 31, 22,
32, 41, 37, 42, 39, 46,
27, 38, 45, 46, 49, 27.

(a) Construct a frequency distribution table. Show the class intervals and true class intervals in the table.
(b) Obtain the relative frequency, percentage frequency, cumulative frequency, and cumulative relative frequency distributions.

1.10   Using the data in (1.9), construct

(i)   A histogram,
(ii) A frequency polygon,
(iii) An ogive,
(iv) A stem-and-leaf plot, and
(v)   Comment on the features of the data.

1.11   (a) What are the diagrams that we use most frequently in representing frequency distributions? Describe three important diagrams with their advantages and limitations.

(b) Describe the construction and use of the pie diagram and the line diagram.

1.12   The following data show weight (in kg) of 24 women in a study:
46.4, 53.2, 52.8, 42.0, 50.8, 43.0, 51.9, 59.2, 55.1, 38.9, 49.7, 49.9, 43.1, 42.2, 52.7, 49.8, 50.7, 44.8, 49.2, 47.7, 42.9, 52.9, 54.1, 45.4.
Prepare the following (show i–iv in a table):

(i)   A frequency distribution,
(ii) A relative frequency distribution,
(iii) A cumulative frequency distribution,
(iv) A cumulative relative frequency distribution,
(v)   A stem-and-leaf plot, and
(vi) Comment on the findings.

1.13   Use the data in question 1.12, to construct the following:

(i)   The histogram,
(ii) The frequency polygon, and
(iii) The ogive.

1.14   Heights (in cm) of 24 women in a study are shown below:
148.1, 158.1, 158.1, 151.4, 152.9, 159.1, 151.0, 158.2, 148.2, 147.3, 145.6, 155.1, 155.2, 149.7, 147.0, 152.2, 149.1, 145.2, 145.9, 149.7, 149.3, 152.3, 146.9, 148.2.

(a) Construct a frequency distribution table and show the following:

(i)   Class interval,
(ii) True class interval,

(iii) Frequency distribution,
(iv) Relative frequency distribution,
(v) Cumulative frequency distribution,
(vi) Relative cumulative frequency distribution,
(vii) Construct a stem-and-leaf plot, and
(viii) Comment on the main features of the data.

1.15 Use the data in Question 1.14 to construct the following:

(i) The histogram,
(ii) The frequency polygon, and
(iii) The ogive.

1.16 Fill in the following table on number of hours slept in a study on 100
individuals:

Class interval (number of hours)	True class interval	Frequency	Cumulative frequency	Relative frequency	Cumulative relative frequency
3.0–4.9		15			
5.0–6.9		40		B	C
7.0–8.9		30			
9.0–10.9		15	A	0.15	

Find the following values from the table above:

(a) The value of A is
(b) The value of B is
(c) The value of C is
(d) What percentage of observations is less than 9 h?
(e) The true class interval for the first class is
(f) The percentage of observations greater than 4.9 h is

1.17 Suppose we have conducted a study on 200 males with age more than
20 years living in a city. We want to estimate the average weight for the
males of age more than 20 years living in that city. It is found that the average
weight of the men is 76 kg.

(i) What is the variable in this study?
(ii) What is the sample size?
(iii) (a) What is the scale of the variable?
       (b) Is it qualitative or quantitative?
       (c) If quantitative, discrete or continuous?

1.18 Classify the following variables by (i) scale of measurement, (ii) quantitative or qualitative, and (iii) if quantitative, discrete, or continuous:

Variable	Scale of measurement	Qualitative/ quantitative	Attribute/discrete/ continuous
Blood group			
Time spent in exercise Daily			
Temperature of patients			
Quality of service			

Chapter 2
Basic Summary Statistics

2.1 Descriptive Statistics

In Chap. 1, we have displayed the techniques of organizing and displaying the data. In this chapter, we introduce the concept of summarization of data by means of descriptive measures. A descriptive measure computed from the values of a sample is called a statistic. A descriptive measure computed from the values of a population is called a parameter.

As we have mentioned earlier, for the variable of interest, there are N population values, and n sample of values. Let $X_1, X_2, \ldots, X_N$ be the population values (in general, they are unknown) of the variable of interest where the population size $= N$ and $x_1, x_2, \ldots, x_n$ be the sample values (these values are known) where the sample size $= n$.

A **parameter** is a measure, quantity, or numerical value obtained from the population values $X_1, X_2, \ldots, X_N$, and the value of a parameter is generally an unknown but constant value characterizing the population. As the value of a parameter is generally unknown but constant, we are interested in estimating a parameter to understand the characteristic of a population using the sample data.

A **statistic** is a measure, quantity, or numerical value obtained from the sample values $x_1, x_2, \ldots, x_n$ and values of statistics can be computed from the sample as functions of observations. Since parameters are unknown, statistics are used to approximate (estimate) parameters.

The necessity of descriptive statistics is quite self-explanatory. In Chap. 1, we have shown that the data can be organized and presented using figures and tables in order to display the important features and characteristics contained in data. However, tables and figures may not reveal the underlying characteristics very comprehensively. For instance, if we want to characterize the data with a single value, it would be very useful not only for communicating to everyone but also for making comparisons. Let us consider that we are interested in number of c-section births among the women during their reproductive period in different regions of a

© Springer Nature Singapore Pte Ltd. 2018
M. A. Islam and A. Al-Shiha, *Foundations of Biostatistics*,
https://doi.org/10.1007/978-981-10-8627-4_2

country. To collect information on this variable, we need to consider women who have completed their reproductive period. With tables and figures, we can display their frequency distributions. However, to compare tables and figures for different regions, it would be a very difficult task. In such situations, we need a single statistic which contains the salient feature of the data for a region. This single value can be a statistic such as arithmetic mean in this case. In case of a qualitative variable, it could be a proportion. With this single value, we can represent the whole data set in a meaningful way to represent the corresponding population character-istic and we may compare this value with similar other values at different times or for different groups or regions conveniently. A single value makes it very conve-nient to represent a whole data set of small, medium, or large size. This would be an ideal situation if we could have represented the important features of the data set using only a single value or a single measure but this may not be the case in reality. Sometimes, we may need more such measures to provide as much insight as possible.

The descriptive statistics are needed for representing the important features of data using only a few measures. These measures are known broadly as descriptive statistics. Four types of descriptive measures are commonly used for characterizing underlying features of data:

   (i) Measures of central tendency,
  (ii) Measures of dispersion,
 (iii) Measures of skewness, and
  (iv) Measures of kurtosis.

All these measures are used to characterize different features contained in a set of data. The first measure, central tendency or location, provides the central value around which all other values in the data set are located. In other words, the measure of central tendency provides the most important representative value of the data set. The dispersion quantifies or measures the variability in the data where variability between values of the data or difference between each value and the measure of central tendency may reflect how scattered the data are from a central value or what extent in variation among values of the data is there. The third measure is used to know whether there is symmetry from the central value or there exists asymmetry from the central value. The fourth measure indicates whether the data are more concentrated with high peak, low or normal peaks, or frequencies indicating extent of concentration of values.

2.2 Measures of Central Tendency

The values of a variable often tend to be concentrated around the center of the data. The center of the data can be determined by the measures of central tendency. A measure of central tendency is considered to be a typical (or a representative) value of the set of data as a whole. The measures of central tendency are sometimes referred as the measures of location too. The most commonly used measures of central tendency are the mean, the median, and the mode.

2.2.1   Mean

The Population Mean (μ)
If $X_1, X_2, \ldots, X_N$ are the population values, then the population mean is

$$\mu = \frac{X_1 + X_2 + \cdots + X_N}{N} = \frac{\sum_{i=1}^{N} X_i}{N}.$$

The population mean μ is a parameter. It is usually unknown, and we are interested to estimate its value.

The Sample Mean ($\bar{x}$)
If $x_1, x_2, \ldots, x_n$ are the sample values, then the sample mean is

$$\bar{x} = \frac{x_1 + x_2 + \cdots + x_n}{n} = \frac{\sum_{i=1}^{n} x_i}{n}.$$

It is noteworthy that the sample mean $\bar{x}$ is a statistic. It is known and we can calculate it from the sample. The sample mean $\bar{x}$ is used to approximate (estimate) the population mean, μ. A more precise way to compute the mean from a frequency distribution is

$$\bar{x} = \frac{f_1 x_1 + f_2 x_2 + \cdots + f_k x_k}{f_1 + f_2 + \cdots + f_k} = \frac{\sum_{i=1}^{k} f_i x_i}{n},$$

where f_i denotes the frequency of distinct sample observation $x_i, i = 1, \ldots, k$.

Example 2.1 Let us consider the data on number of children ever born reported by 20 women in a sample: 4, 2, 1, 0, 2, 3, 2, 1, 1, 2, 3, 4, 3, 2, 1, 2, 2, 1, 3, 2. Here $n = 20$. We want to find the average number of children ever born from this sample.
The sample mean is

$$\bar{x} = \frac{\sum_{i=1}^{n} x_i}{n} = \frac{4+2+1+0+2+3+2+1+1+2+3+4+3+2+1+2+2+1+3+2}{20}$$

$$= \frac{41}{20}$$

$$= 2.05.$$

Example 2.2 Employing the same data shown above, we can compute the arithmetic mean in a more precise way by using frequencies. We can construct a

Table 2.1 A frequency distribution table for number of children ever born of 20 women

i	Number of children ever born (x_i)	Number of women (f_i)
1	0	1
2	1	5
3	2	8
4	3	4
5	4	2
	Total	20

frequency distribution table from this data to summarize the data first. The frequency distribution table is displayed in Table 2.1.

Here, $n = \sum_{i=1}^{5} f_i = 20$ and $k = 5$. The value of k denotes the number of distinct values observed for the variable X in the sample. It means that number of times a value occurs becomes the frequency of that variable. The distinct values observed in this case are 0, 1, 2, 3, and 4 with frequencies 1, 5, 8, 4, and 2, respectively. The sample arithmetic can be computed from the above table easily as shown below:

$$\bar{x} = \frac{\sum_{i=1}^{k} f_i x_i}{\sum_{i=1}^{k} f_i} = \frac{\sum_{i=1}^{k} f_i x_i}{n}$$
$$= \frac{1 \times 0 + 5 \times 1 + 8 \times 2 + 4 \times 3 + 2 \times 4}{20}$$
$$= \frac{41}{20}$$
$$= 2.05.$$

Advantages and disadvantages of the arithmetic mean

Advantages of the arithmetic mean are

 (i)   Simplicity: The mean is easily understood and easy to compute.
 (ii) Uniqueness: There is one and only one mean for a given set of data.
 (iii) The mean takes into account all values of the data.

Disadvantage

 (i)   The main disadvantage of the arithmetic mean is that extreme values have an influence on the mean. Therefore, the mean may be distorted by extreme values (Table 2.2).
 (ii) The arithmetic mean cannot be used for qualitative data. The arithmetic mean can only be found for quantitative variables.

Example 2.3

Sample	Data						Mean
A	2	4	5	7	7	10	5.83
B	2	4	5	7	7	100	20.83

Table 2.2 Mean from two hypothetical sets of data

2.2.2 Median

The median of a finite set of numbers is that value which divides the ordered array into two equal parts. The numbers in the first part are less than or equal to the median, and the numbers in the second part are greater than or equal to the median.

Notice that 50% (or less) of the data are $\leq$ Median and 50% (or less) of the data are $\geq$ Median.

Calculating the Median

Let $x_1, x_2, \ldots, x_n$ be the sample values. The sample size (n) can be odd or even. The steps for computing the median are discussed below:

(i)   First, we order the sample to obtain the ordered array.

(ii) Suppose that the ordered array is

$$y_1, y_2, \ldots, y_n.$$

(iii) We compute the rank of the middle value(s):

$$\text{rank} = \frac{n+1}{2}.$$

(iv) If the sample size (n) is an odd number, there is only one value in the middle, and the rank will be an integer:

$$\text{rank} = \frac{n+1}{2} = m. \quad (m \text{ is integer}).$$

The median is the middle value of the ordered observations, which is

$$\text{Median} = y_m.$$

Ordered set (smallest to largest) $\rightarrow$	y_1	y_2	...	y_m **middle value**	...	y_n
Rank (or order) $\rightarrow$	1	2	...	**m**	...	n

(v)   If the sample size (n) is an even number, there are two values in the middle, and the rank will be an integer plus 0.5:

$$\text{rank} = \frac{n+1}{2} = m + 0.5.$$

Therefore, the ranks of the middle values are (m) and $(m + 1)$.

The median is the mean (average) of the two middle values of the ordered observations:

$$\text{Median} = \frac{y_m + y_{m+1}}{2}.$$

Ordered set	y_1	y_2	...	y_m	y_{m+1}	...	y_n
Rank (or order)	1	2		m	$m + 1$	...	n

Example 2.4 (Odd number) Find the median for the sample values: 10, 54, 21, 38, 53.

Solution

$n = 5$ (odd number)

There is only one value in the middle.

The rank of the middle value is

$$\text{rank} = \frac{n+1}{2} = \frac{5+1}{2} = 3. \ (m = 3)$$

Ordered set →	10	21	**38 (middle value)**	53	54
Rank (or order) →	1	2	**3 (m)**	4	5

The median = 38 (unit).

Example 2.5 (Even number) Find the median for the sample values: 10, 35, 41, 16, 20, 32.

Solution

$n = 6$ (even number)

There are two values in the middle. The rank is

$$\text{rank} = \frac{n+1}{2} = \frac{6+1}{2} = 3.5. \ (m = 3)$$

Ordered set →	10	16	**20 (middle value)**	**32 (middle value)**	35	41
Rank (or order) →	1	2	**3 (m)**	**4 (m + 1)**	5	6

The middle values are 20 and 32.

The median $= \frac{20+32}{2} = \frac{52}{2} = 26$ (unit).

It may be noted here that the unit of the median is the same as the unit of the data.

Advantages and disadvantages of the median

Advantages of the median are

(i)   Simplicity: The median is easily understood and easy to compute.
(ii) Uniqueness: There is only one median for a given set of data.
(iii) The median is not as drastically affected by extreme values as is the mean.

An example is illustrated in Table 2.3.

Disadvantages of median are as follows:

(i)   The median does not take into account all values of the sample after ordering the data in ascending order.
(ii) In general, the median can only be found for quantitative variables. However, in some cases, the median can be found for ordinal qualitative variables too.

2.2.3   Mode

The mode of a set of values is that value which occurs most frequently (i.e., with the highest frequency). If all values are different or have the same frequencies, there will be no mode. A set of data may have more than one mode (Table 2.4).

Example 2.6 It may be noted that the unit of the mode is same as the unit of the data.

Advantages and disadvantages of the mode

Advantages of the mode are

(i)   Simplicity: the mode is easily understood and easy to compute.
(ii) The mode is not as drastically affected by extreme values as is the mean (Table 2.5).
(iii) The mode may be found for both quantitative and qualitative variables.

Disadvantages of the mode are as follows:

(i)   The mode is not a good measure of location, because it depends on a few values of the data.
(ii) The mode does not take into account all values of the sample.
(iii) There might be no mode for a data set.
(iv) There might be more than one mode for a data set.

Example 2.7

Sample	Data						Median
A	9	4	5	9	2	10	7
B	9	4	5	9	2	100	7

Table 2.3 Median from two sets of data

Table 2.4 Mode from seven sets of data

Data set	Type	Mode(s)
26, 25, 25, 34	Quantitative	25
3, 7, 12, 6, 19	Quantitative	No mode
3, 3, 7, 7, 12, 12, 6, 6, 19, 19	Quantitative	No mode
3, 3, 12, 6, 8, 8	Quantitative	3 and 8
B C A B B B C B B	Qualitative	B
B C A B A B C A C	Qualitative	No mode
B C A B B C B C C	Qualitative	B and C

Table 2.5 Modes from two sets of data with and without extreme values

Sample	Data						Mode
A	7	4	5	7	2	10	7
B	7	4	5	7	2	100	7

2.2.4 Percentiles and Quartiles

The mean, median, and mode are the measures of central tendency. There are other measures, percentiles, and quartiles, which do not represent a measure of central tendency generally (with some exceptions such as median) but represent a measure of position. The measures of position indicate the location of a data set. The median is a special case of the family of parameters known as position parameters. These descriptive measures are called position parameters because they can be used to designate certain positions on the horizontal axis when the distribution of a variable is graphed. The position parameters include percentile and quartiles.

Percentile: Given a set of observations $x_1, x_2, \ldots, x_n$, the pth percentile, $P_p, p = 0, 1, 2, \ldots, 100$, is the value of X such that p percent or less of the observations are less than P_p and $(100 - p)$ percent or less of the observations are greater than P_p.

The 10th percentile is denoted by P_{10} where $P_{10} = \dfrac{10(n+1)}{100}$ th ordered value.

The 50th percentile is $P_{50} = \dfrac{50(n+1)}{100}$ th ordered value = median.

The median is a special case of percentile and it represents the 50th percentile.

Quartile: Given a set of observations $x_1, x_2, \ldots, x_n$, the rth quartile, $Q_r, r = 1, 2, 3$, is the value of X such that $(25 \times r)$ percent or less of the observations are less than Q_r and $[100 - (25 \times r)]$ percent or less of the observations are greater than Q_r.

For quartiles, we use the following formulas:

$$Q_1 = \frac{n+1}{4} \text{th ordered observation,}$$

$$Q_2 = \frac{2(n+1)}{4} \text{th ordered observation,}$$

$$Q_3 = \frac{3(n+1)}{4} \text{th ordered observation.}$$

The second quartile is $Q_2 = \frac{2(n+1)}{4} = \frac{n+1}{2} =$ median and this is equal to the 50th percentile.

2.3   Measures of Dispersion

The dispersion of a set of observations refers to the variation contained in the data. A measure of dispersion conveys information regarding the amount of variability present in a set of data. There are several measures of dispersion, some of which are range, variance, standard deviation, and coefficient of variation. In addition, some measures of dispersion based on percentiles and quartiles are also introduced in this section. The box-and-whisker plot is a very useful technique to summarize the data which is displayed in this section as well.

The variation or dispersion in a set of values refers to how spread out the values is from each other. The dispersion is small when the values are close together. There is no dispersion if the values are the same (Figs. 2.1, 2.2 and 2.3; Table 2.6).

Example 2.8 Let us consider the hypothetical data sets of size 5 with same measure of central tendency displayed in Table 2.6, say arithmetic mean in this case:

In this example, if we represent the samples by only measure of central tendency, or by arithmetic mean in this case, then all the samples have the same value. In other words, although we observe that the measure of central tendency remains

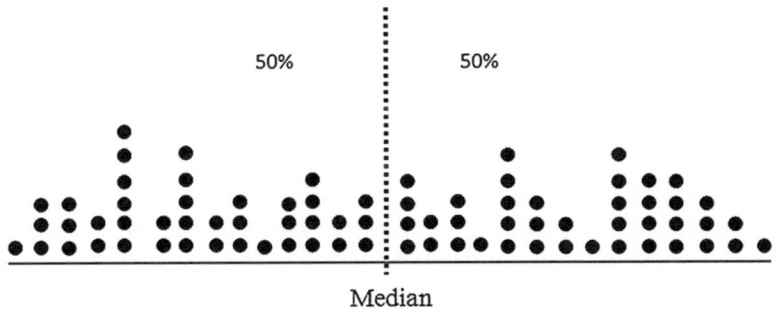

Fig. 2.1 Displaying median using a dot plot

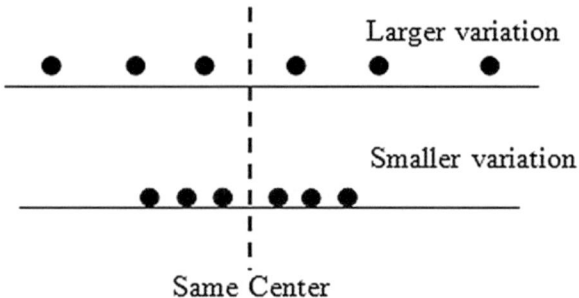

Fig. 2.2 Figure displaying smaller and larger variations using the same center

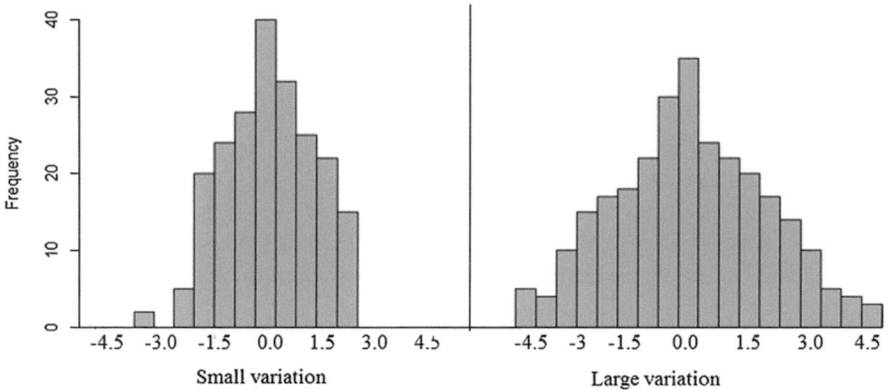

Fig. 2.3 Figure displaying small and large variations

Table 2.6 Four sets of data with same arithmetic mean	Data set 1	8, 9, 10, 11, 12	$\bar{x} = 10$
	Data set 2	6, 8, 10, 12, 14	$\bar{x} = 10$
	Data set 3	4, 7, 10, 13, 16	$\bar{x} = 10$
	Data set 4	2, 6, 10, 14, 18	$\bar{x} = 10$

same, the variation contained in each data set, or more specifically, the variation in values of a data set from its central value are not same at all. This indicates that the measure of central tendency alone fails to characterize different types of properties of data sets. We want to represent the data by a small number of measures, if possible by a single value, but sometimes a single value cannot represent the data adequately or sufficiently. The above example shows one such inadequacy. The measure of variation is an additional measure needed to characterize the data in addition to a measure of central tendency.

Some of the most important measures of dispersion are discussed below.

2.3.1   The Range

The range is the difference between the largest value (Max) and the smallest value (Min):

$$\text{Range } (R) = \text{Max} - \text{Min}.$$

Example 2.9 Find the range for the sample values: 26, 25, 35, 27, 29, 29.

Solution

$$\text{Max} = 35$$
$$\text{Min} = 25$$
$$\text{Range } (R) = \text{Max} - \text{Min} = 35 - 25 = 10.$$

The unit of the range is the same as the unit of the data. The usefulness of the range is limited. The range is a poor measure of the dispersion because it only takes into account two of the values, maximum and minimum; however, it plays a significant role in many applications to have a quick view of the dispersion in a data set.

2.3.2   The Variance

The variance is one of the most important measures of dispersion. The variance is a measure that uses the mean as a point of reference. More precisely, the variance provides an average measure of squared difference between each observation and arithmetic mean. The variance of the data is small when the observations are close to the mean, is large when the observations are spread out from the mean, and is zero (no variation) when all observations have the same value (concentrated at the mean). In other words, the variance shows, on an average, how close the values of a variable are to the arithmetic mean.

Deviations of sample values from the sample mean

Let $x_1, x_2, \ldots, x_n$ be the sample values, and $\bar{x}$ be the sample mean. The deviation of the value x_i from the sample mean $\bar{x}$ is

$$x_i - \bar{x}.$$

The squared deviation is

$$(x_i - \bar{x})^2.$$

The sum of squared deviations is

$$\sum_{i=1}^{n}(x_i - \bar{x})^2.$$

Figure 2.4 shows the deviations and squared deviations of the values from their mean.

The Population Variance, σ^2

Let $X_1, X_2, \ldots, X_N$ be the population values. The population variance, σ^2, is defined by

$$\sigma^2 = \frac{\sum_{i=1}^{N}(X_i - \mu)^2}{N}$$
$$= \frac{(X_1 - \mu)^2 + (X_2 - \mu)^2 + \cdots + (X_N - \mu)^2}{N} \quad (\text{unit})^2$$

where $\mu = \frac{\sum_{i=1}^{N}X_i}{N}$ is the population mean and N is the population size.

It may be noted here that σ^2 is a parameter because it is obtained from the population values, it is generally unknown. It is also always true that $\sigma^2 \geq 0$.

The Sample Variance, s^2

Let $x_1, x_2, \ldots, x_n$ be the sample values. The sample variance s^2 is defined by

$$s^2 = \frac{\sum_{i=1}^{n}(x_i - \bar{x})^2}{n}$$
$$= \frac{(x_1 - \bar{x})^2 + (x_2 - \bar{x})^2 + \cdots + (x_n - \bar{x})^2}{n},$$

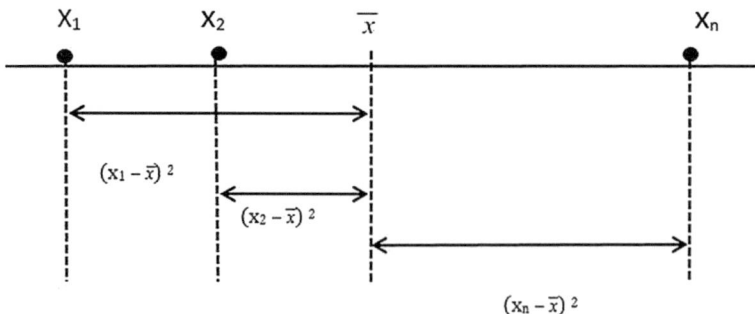

Fig. 2.4 Deviations and squared deviations of sample values from mean

where $\bar{x} = \frac{\sum_{i=1}^{n} x_i}{n}$ is the sample mean, and n is the sample size. It may be noted here that the estimate of the population variance can be obtained as

$$s^2 = \frac{\sum_{i=1}^{n} (x_i - \bar{x})^2}{n-1}$$
$$= \frac{(x_1 - \bar{x})^2 + (x_2 - \bar{x})^2 + \cdots + (x_n - \bar{x})^2}{n-1}.$$

For our estimate of the variance, we will use this formula to avoid ambiguity in the subsequent chapters. The underlying reason will be clear in the later chapters on estimation and test of hypothesis.

We can show that the numerator of the variance is

$$\sum_{i=1}^{n} (x_i - \bar{x})^2 = \sum_{i=1}^{n} x_i^2 - 2\bar{x} \sum_{i=1}^{n} x_i + \sum_{i=1}^{n} \bar{x}^2$$
$$= \sum_{i=1}^{n} x_i^2 - 2\bar{x}(n\bar{x}) + n\bar{x}^2$$
$$= \sum_{i=1}^{n} x_i^2 - n\bar{x}^2.$$

Hence, the sample variance is

$$s^2 = \frac{\sum_{i=1}^{n} x_i^2 - n\bar{x}^2}{n-1}.$$

Equivalently, we can also express the above for computational convenience as

$$s^2 = \frac{\sum_{i=1}^{n} x_i^2 - n\left(\sum_{i=1}^{n} x_i/n\right)^2}{n-1},$$

which is

$$s^2 = \frac{\sum_{i=1}^{n} x_i^2 - \left(\sum_{i=1}^{n} x_i\right)^2/n}{n-1}.$$

The estimate of the population variance as shown above will be used for inferential purposes in later sections. Hence, we have this expression of the sample variance subsequently to avoid any ambiguity.

We may note that

(i) s^2 is a statistic because it is obtained from the sample values and it is known.
(ii) s^2 is used to approximate (estimate) σ^2.
(iii) $s^2 \geq 0$, in other words, the sample variance is nonnegative.
(iv) $s^2 = 0$, this happens if all observations have the same value, indicating that there is no dispersion.

Using a frequency distribution, the sample variance with denominators n and $(n - 1)$ can be expressed as follows:

$$s^2 = \frac{\sum_{i=1}^{k} f_i (x_i - \bar{x})^2}{n},$$

and

$$s^2 = \frac{\sum_{i=1}^{k} f_i (x_i - \bar{x})^2}{n - 1}.$$

In both the cases, the arithmetic mean can be expressed as

$$\bar{x} = \frac{\sum_{i=1}^{k} f_i x_i}{\sum_{i=1}^{k} f_i} = \frac{\sum_{i=1}^{k} f_i x_i}{n}.$$

Example 2.10 We want to compute the sample variance of the following sample values: 10, 21, 33, 53, 54.

Solution
$n = 5$

$$\bar{x} = \frac{\sum_{i=1}^{n} x_i}{n} = \frac{\sum_{i=1}^{5} x_i}{5} = \frac{10 + 21 + 33 + 53 + 54}{5} = \frac{171}{5} = 34.2$$

$$s^2 = \frac{\sum_{i=1}^{n} (x_i - \bar{x})^2}{n - 1} = \frac{\sum_{i=1}^{5} (x_i - 34.2)^2}{5 - 1}.$$

$$s^2 = \frac{(10 - 34.2)^2 + (21 - 34.2)^2 + (33 - 34.2)^2 + (53 - 34.2)^2 + (54 - 34.2)^2}{4}$$

$$= \frac{1506.8}{4} = 376.7.$$

Another method for calculating sample variance:

x_i	$(x_i - \bar{x}) = (x_i - 34.2)$	$(x_i - \bar{x})^2 = (x_i - 34.2)^2$
10	−24.2	585.64
21	−13.2	174.24
33	−1.2	1.44
53	18.8	353.44
54	19.8	392.04
$\sum_{i=1}^{5} x_i = 171$	$\sum_{i=1}^{5} (x_i - \bar{x}) = 0$	$\sum (x_i - \bar{x})^2 = 1506.8$

$$\bar{x} = \frac{\sum_{i=1}^{5} x_i}{5} == \frac{171}{5} = 34.2 \quad \text{and} \quad s^2 = \frac{1506.8}{4} == 376.7.$$

Using the alternative methods, we can compute the sample variance for the same data as shown below:

$$s^2 = \frac{\sum_{i=1}^{n} x_i^2 - n\bar{x}^2}{n-1}$$

where

$$\sum_{i=1}^{5} x_i^2 = 10^2 + 21^2 + 33^2 + 53^2 + 54^2 = 100 + 441 + 1089 + 2809 + 2916 = 7355,$$

$$n\bar{x}^2 = 5 \times (34.2)^2 = 5 \times 1169.64 = 5848.20, \quad \text{and}$$

$$s^2 = \frac{\sum_{i=1}^{5} x_i^2 - n\bar{x}^2}{5-1} = \frac{7355 - 5848.20}{4} = \frac{1506.80}{4} = 376.70.$$

Similarly,

$$s^2 = \frac{\sum_{i=1}^{n} x_i^2 - \left(\sum_{i=1}^{n} x_i\right)^2/n}{n-1},$$

where

$$\sum_{i=1}^{5} x_i^2 = 10^2 + 21^2 + 33^2 + 53^2 + 54^2 = 100 + 441 + '1089 + 2809 + 2916 = 7355,$$

$$\left(\sum_{i=1}^{5} x_i\right)^2/5 = (171)^2/5 = \frac{29241}{5} = 5848.20, \quad \text{and}$$

$$s^2 = \frac{\sum_{i=1}^{5} x_i^2 - \left(\sum_{i=1}^{5} x_i\right)^2/5}{5-1} = \frac{7355 - 5848.20}{4} = \frac{1506.80}{4} = 376.70.$$

2.3.3 Standard Deviation

The variance represents squared units, and therefore is not appropriate measure of dispersion when we wish to express the concept of dispersion in terms of the original unit. The standard deviation is another measure of dispersion. The standard deviation is the positive square root of the variance and is expressed in the original unit of the data.

(i) Population standard deviation is $\sigma = \sqrt{\sigma^2}$.
(ii) Sample standard deviation is $s = \sqrt{s^2}$,

$$s = \sqrt{\frac{\sum_{i=1}^{n} (x_i - \bar{x})^2}{n - 1}}.$$

Example 2.11 For the previous example, the sample standard deviation is

$$s = \sqrt{s^2} = \sqrt{376.7} = 19.41.$$

2.3.4 Coefficient of Variation (C.V.)

Although the variance and the standard deviation are useful measures of variation of the values of a single variable for a single population, sometimes we need to compare the variation of two variables. In that case, we cannot use the variance or the standard deviation directly, because (i) the variables might have different units and (ii) the variables might have different means. For comparison, we need a measure of the relative variation that does not depend on either the units or on the values of means. This measure is called the coefficient of variation (C.V.).

The coefficient of variation is defined by

$$\text{C.V.} = \frac{s}{\bar{x}} \times 100\%.$$

It is clearly evident that the C.V. is free of unit and the standard deviation is divided by the corresponding arithmetic mean to make it comparable for different means.

To compare the variability of two sets of data (i.e., to determine which set is more variable), we need to calculate the following quantities:

Data set	Mean	Standard deviation	C.V.
1	$\bar{x}_1$	s_1	$\text{C.V.}_1 = \frac{s_1}{\bar{x}_1} 100\%$
2	$\bar{x}_2$	s_2	$\text{C.V.}_2 = \frac{s_2}{\bar{x}_2} 100\%$

The data set with the larger value of C.V. has larger variation which is expressed in percentage. The relative variability of the data set 1 is larger than the relative variability of the data set 2 if $\text{C.V.}_1 > \text{C.V.}_2$ and vice versa.

Example 2.12 Suppose we have two data sets from two samples:
Data set 1: Let us consider that from the data in sample 1, the mean and the standard deviation are $\bar{x}_1 = 66$ kg and $s_1 = 4.5$ kg, respectively. Hence, the coefficient of variation is

$$\text{C.V.}_1 = \frac{4.5}{66} \times 100\% = 6.8\%.$$

Data set 2: The mean and the standard deviation from the second sample are $\bar{x}_2 = 36$ kg and $s_2 = 4.5$ kg, respectively. The coefficient of variation for this data set is

$$\text{C.V.}_2 = \frac{4.5}{36} \times 100\% = 12.5\%.$$

Since C.V.$_2 >$ C.V.$_1$, the relative variability of the data set 2 is larger than the relative variability of the data set 1.

If we use the standard deviation to compare the variability of the two data sets, we will wrongly conclude that the two data sets have the same variability because the standard deviation of both sets is 4.5 kg.

2.3.5 Some Properties of $\bar{x}, s, s^2$

Let the sample values are $x_1, x_2, \ldots, x_n$ and let a and b are constants. Then, we can summarize the impact of the shift in origin and scale in the data on the variance and standard deviation as follows:

Case	Sample data	Sample mean	Sample standard deviation	Sample variance
1	$x_1, \ldots, x_n$	$\bar{x}$	s	s^2
2	$ax_1, \ldots, ax_n$	$a\bar{x}$	$\lvert a \rvert s$	$a^2 s^2$
3	$x_1 + b, \ldots, x_n + b$	$\bar{x} + b$	s	s^2
4	$ax_1 + b, \ldots, ax_n + b$	$a\bar{x} + b$	$\lvert a \rvert s$	$a^2 s^2$

Case 1 Case 1 represents the data without any change in the origin or scale. Hence, the mean, the standard deviation, and the variance represent the measures unaffected.

Example 2.13 Let us consider a hypothetical data set of size 5 as follows:

$$x_1 = 3, \quad x_2 = 1, \quad x_3 = 4, \quad x_4 = 2, \quad x_5 = 1.$$

Using these data, we obtain the following measures of central tendency and variation

$$\bar{x} = 2.2,$$
$$s = 1.3038,$$
$$s^2 = 1.7.$$

Case 2 In this case, we observe that the sample observations are multiplied by a scalar quantity, a. The difference between the data in Case 1 and Case 2 is that each observation in Case 1 is a times than the corresponding observation in Case 2. This may be termed as change in scale if divided or multiplied by a scalar quantity.

Example 2.14 Let us use the scalar quantity $a = 10$, and the data are now 30, 10, 40, 20, and 10 which are obtained multiplying by the scalar quantity 10. Due to change in scale by 10, the mean, standard deviation, and variance are obtained as follows:

$$\bar{x} = 2.2 \times 10 = 22,$$
$$s = 1.3038 \times 10 = 13.038,$$
$$s^2 = 1.7 \times 10^2 = 1.7 \times 100 = 170.$$

It is demonstrated here that mean, standard deviation, and variance all the measures are changed due to change in scale.

Case 3 In Case 3, the origin is shifted by an amount, b. Shift in origin means the values of sample data are shifted by an amount b which results in an increase or decrease of sample observations by b.

Example 2.15 Let us use the scalar quantity $b = 20$ and the data are now 23, 21, 24, 22, and 21 which are obtained by adding 20 to all the sample observations 3, 1, 4, 2, and 1, respectively. As we have shown, due to change in origin by 20, the mean, standard deviation, and variance are obtained as follows:

$$\bar{x} = 2.2 + 20 = 22.2,$$
$$s = 1.3038,$$
$$s^2 = 1.7.$$

It is shown that change in origin results in a change in the arithmetic mean but both standard deviation and variance remain unaffected.

Case 4 Case 4 demonstrates the impact of change in both origin and scale. Let us consider the scale value a and shift in origin by b. In other words, the observed values are multiplied by a and then b is added to the values after multiplying by a.

Example 2.16 Let us use the scalar quantity $a = 10$ and $b = 20$; then, the data are now 50, 30, 60, 40, and 30 which are obtained multiplying by the scalar quantity 10 and then by adding 20. Due to change in scale by 10 and shift in origin by 20, the mean, standard deviation, and variance are obtained as follows:

$$\bar{x} = 2.2 \times 10 + 20 = 42,$$
$$s = 1.3038 \times 10 = 13.038,$$
$$s^2 = 1.7 \times 10^2 = 1.7 \times 100 = 170.$$

It is demonstrated here that mean, standard deviation, and variance all these measures are changed due to change in scale and shift in origin. In this case, the arithmetic mean is affected by both change in scale and shift in origin but standard deviation and variance are affected due to change in scale only.

A more detailed example is shown below.

Example 2.17 Let us consider a sample of size 5 as follows: 5, 3, 2, 4, 1. Let $a = 3$ and $b = 5$. Then, the mean, variance, and standard deviations from the original data $x_1 = 5$, $x_2 = 3$, $x_3 = 2$, $x_4 = 4$, and $x_5 = 1$ are

$$\bar{x} = \frac{\sum_{i=1}^{5} x_i}{5} = \frac{5 + 3 + 2 + 4 + 1}{5} = \frac{15}{5} = 3,$$

$$s^2 = \frac{\sum_{i=1}^{5} x_i^2 - \left(\sum_{i=1}^{5} x_i\right)^2 / 5}{5 - 1} = \frac{5^2 + 3^2 + 2^2 + 4^2 + 1^2 - (15)^2 / 5}{4}$$

$$= \frac{55 - 45}{4} = \frac{10}{4} = 2.5,$$

$$s = \sqrt{2.5} = 1.5811.$$

Let us consider that the scale is changed by a, then the new data set is $ax_1, ax_2, \ldots, ax_n$. Here, $a = 3$ and $n = 5$; hence, the mean, the variance, and the standard deviation are

$$\text{mean} = a\bar{x} = 3 \times 3 = 9,$$

$$\text{variance} = a^2 s^2 = 9 \times 2.5 = 22.5 = 2.5, \text{ and}$$

$$\text{standard deviation} = |a|s = |3|\sqrt{2.5} = 3 \times 1.5811 = 4.7433.$$

This shows that change in the scale changes both the mean and the variance which implies change in the standard deviation as well.

If we shift the origin by 5 such that the new data set is $x_1 + b, x_2 + 5, \ldots, x_n + 5$, then the mean, variance, and standard deviation are

$$\text{mean} = \bar{x} + b = 3 + 5 = 8,$$

$$\text{variance} = s^2 = 2.5, \text{ and}$$

$$\text{standard deviation} = s = \sqrt{2.5} = 1.5811.$$

It is clearly observed that if the origin is shifted by any value, then the mean is shifted too but the variance and standard deviation remain unchanged. In other words, the mean is affected by a shift in the origin but variance and standard deviation are not affected.

Similarly, if we change both the scale and origin such that the new data set is $ax_1 + b, ax_2 + b, \ldots, ax_n + b$, then we obtain the following:

$$\text{mean} = a\bar{x} + b = 3 \times 3 + 5 = 9 + 5 = 14,$$
$$\text{variance} = a^2 s^2 = 9 \times 2.5 = 22.5 = 2, 5, \quad \text{and}$$
$$\text{standard deviation} = |a|s = |3|\sqrt{2.5} = 3 \times 1.5811 = 4.7433.$$

This shows that if we consider changes in both scale and origin, then the mean is affected by both but the variance and standard deviation need to be adjusted for only the quantity of the change in scale only. In other words, the measure of central tendency, mean, depends on both the scale and origin but the measures of dispersion, variance, and standard deviation are independent of change in the origin but depend on the change in the scale.

2.3.6 Interquartile Range

A disadvantage of the range is that it is computed using the two extreme values of the sample data, the smallest and the largest values. If the data contain extreme outlier values, then the range is affected by those outliers. To overcome this limitation of the range, an alternative measure called the interquartile range can be used. The interquartile range is computed by taking the difference between the third quartile and the first quartile. The interquartile range provides a more meaningful measure that represents the range of the middle 50% of the data. The interquartile range is defined as

$$\text{IQR} = Q_3 - Q_1,$$

where Q_3 is the third quartile and Q_1 is the first quartile. As the extreme values are not considered, the IQR is a more robust measure of variation in the data and is not affected by outliers. The semi-interquartile range is defined as

$$(Q_3 - Q_1)/2.$$

2.3.7 Box-and-Whisker Plot

We know that a measure of central tendency or location is a value around which other values are clustered. The variation or spread in the data from the central value is usually measured by a measure of dispersion. In addition, we want to know whether the data are symmetric or not. The box-and-whisker plot displays all these in a simple plot where the box contains features included in the middle 50% of the observations, and whiskers show the minimum and maximum values. For constructing a box-and-whisker plot, we need five points: three quartiles Q_1, Q_2, and Q_3, the minimum value and the maximum value. The box is constructed using Q_1, Q_2, and Q_3. The box-and-whisker plot represents the main features of the data very efficiently and precisely.

Steps of constructing a box-and-whisker plot are summarized below.

(i) The horizontal axis displays the variable of interest.
(ii) A box is drawn above the horizontal line. The first quartile is aligned with the left end of the box and the third quartile is aligned with the right end of the box.
(iii) The second quartile is aligned with a vertical line in the box.
(iv) A horizontal line from the left end of the box aligned to the smallest value of the sample data is a whisker to the left.
(v) A horizontal line from the right end of the box aligned to the largest value of the sample data is another whisker to the right.

Examination of box-and-whisker plot for a set of data reveals the following: (i) amount of spread, (ii) location of concentration, and (iii) symmetry of the data.

The box plots can be used for another very important data characteristic. In addition to the quartiles, the box plot can be used to identify the potential outliers in data. The first and third quartiles provide the basis for determining the fences for outliers or the observations which might be considered as outside of the box values. Rousseeuw et al. (1999) considered the upper fence as $Q_2 + 4(Q_3 - Q_2)$ and the lower fence as $Q_2 + 4(Q_1 - Q_2)$ where Q_2 is the median. For constructing the lower and upper fences of a box plot, we can use the following formulas:

$$\text{lower fence} = Q_1 - k(Q_3 - Q_1),$$
$$\text{upper fence} = Q_3 + k(Q_3 - Q_1).$$

Here, $(Q_3 - Q_1)$ is the interquartile range. Customarily, $k = 1.5$, and the lower and upper fences are

$$\text{lower fence} = Q_1 - 1.5(Q_3 - Q_1),$$
$$\text{upper fence} = Q_3 + 1.5(Q_3 - Q_1).$$

The outside observations or outliers can be plotted individually, beyond the fences, to have meaningful insights about the extreme data. The outliers are either the observations $<Q_1 - 1.5(Q_3 - Q_1)$ or the observations $>Q_3 + 1.5(Q_3 - Q_1)$. Hence, a modified box plot can also be constructed to display the individual observations outside the lower and upper fences.

Example Consider the following data set: 14.6, 24.3, 24.9, 27.0, 27.2, 27.4, 28.2, 28.8, 29.9, 30.7, 31.5, 31.6, 32.3, 32.8, 33.3, 33.6, 34.3, 36.9, 38.3, 44.0.

Here, $n = 20$.

$$Q_1 = \frac{n+1}{4} \text{th ordered observation} = \frac{20+1}{4} = 5.25\text{th ordered observation}$$

$$= \text{5th ordered observation} + (0.25)(27.4 - 27.2) = 27.2 + (0.25)(0.2) = 27.25$$

$$Q_2 = \frac{2(n+1)}{4} \text{th ordered observation} = \frac{20+1}{2} = 10.5\text{th ordered observation}$$

$$= \text{10th ordered observation} + (0.5)(31.5 - 30.7)$$

$$= 30.7 + (0.5)(31.5 - 30.7) = 31.1$$

$$Q_3 = \frac{3(n+1)}{4} \text{th ordered observation} = \frac{3(20+1)}{4} = 15.75\text{th ordered observation}$$

$$= \text{15th ordered observation} + (0.75)(33.6 - 33.3)$$

$$= 33.3 + (0.75)(33.6 - 33.3) = 33.525$$

IQR $= 33.525 - 27.25 = 6.275$

Range $= 44.0 - 14.6 = 29.4$

Ratio of IQR to Range (%) $= \dfrac{6.275}{29.4} \times 100 = 21\%$ of range.

Using the data shown in this example, we can construct the box-and-whisker plot or box plot. The traditional box plot is based on five points, Q_1, Q_2, and Q_3 for drawing the box and minimum and maximum values for the whiskers as shown in Fig. 2.5.

The second box plot shows the box plot where in addition to the box using Q_1, Q_2, and Q_3, the lower and upper fences are also shown. The lower and upper fences are

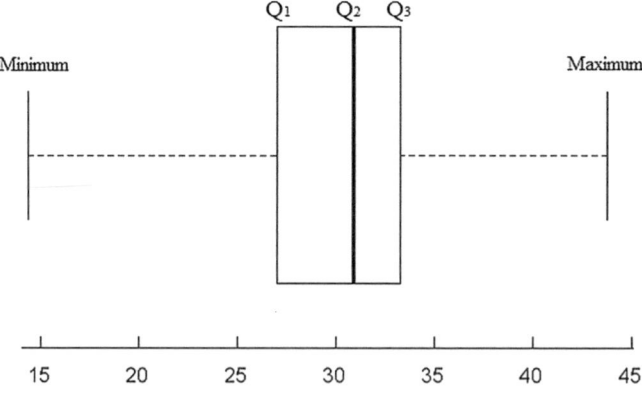

Fig. 2.5 Box-and-whisker plot

$$\text{lower fence} = Q_1 - 1.5(Q_3 - Q_1)$$
$$= 27.25 - 1.5 \times \text{IQR}$$
$$= 27.25 - 1.5 \times 6.275$$
$$= 17.8375$$

and

$$\text{upper fence} = Q_3 + k(Q_3 - Q_1)$$
$$= 33.525 + 1.5 \times \text{IQR}$$
$$= 33.525 + 1.5 \times 6.275$$
$$= 42.9375.$$

We can find the outliers from the observations either the observations $<Q_1 - 1.5(Q_3 - Q_1)$ or the observations $>Q_3 + 1.5(Q_3 - Q_1)$. It is observed that following this rule for detecting the outliers, there are two outliers in the sample data: one is less than the lower fence or outside the lower fence, 14.6, and the other value is greater than the upper fence or outside the upper fence, 44.0.

The results from sample data used for constructing Fig. 2.6 are sample size: 20, median: 31.1, minimum: 14.6, maximum: 44.0, first quartile: 27.25, third quartile: 33.525, interquartile range: 6.275, lower fence = 17.8375, upper fence = 42.9375, and outliers: 14.6, 44.0, as shown in Fig. 2.6.

2.4   Moments of a Distribution

The moments are used to summarize the characteristics of data. These are descriptive statistics if calculated from sample that can be used to explore characteristics of data such as central tendency, dispersion, skewness, and kurtosis. The measures of skewness and kurtosis are shape characteristics of the data which will be discussed in subsequent sections. We can define both the population and sample moments but for the sake of simplicity only sample moments are defined in this section. The moments can be classified as (i) the raw moments, (ii) the moments about any arbitrary value a, and (iii) the moments about mean or the central moments.

Let $x_1, x_2, \ldots, x_n$ be the n values assumed by the variable, X, then the quantity

$$m'_r = \frac{\sum_{i=1}^{n} x_i^r}{n}$$

is called the rth raw sample moment of the variable, X.

Fig. 2.6 Box-and-whisker plot displaying outliers from the sample data; sample size: 20, median: 31.1, minimum: 14.6, maximum: 44.0, first quartile: 27.25, third quartile: 33.525, interquartile range: 6.275, and outliers: 14.6, 44.0

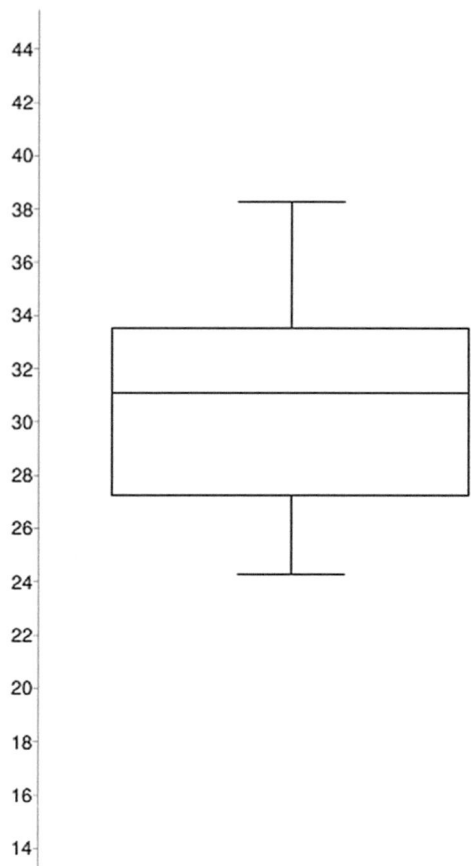

The rth sample moment about any value a, also denoted by m'_r, is defined as

$$m'_r = \frac{\sum_{i=1}^{n}(x_i - a)^r}{n}.$$

The rth central moment about mean or the rth moment about the mean is defined as

$$m_r = \frac{\sum_{i=1}^{n}(x_i - \bar{x})^r}{n}.$$

If $x_1, x_2, \ldots, x_k$ occur with frequencies $f_1, f_2, \ldots, f_k$, respectively, the above moments are

$$m'_r = \frac{\sum_{i=1}^{k} f_i x_i^r}{n},$$

$$m'_r = \frac{\sum_{i=1}^{k} f_i (x_i - a)^r}{n},$$

and

$$m_r = \frac{\sum_{i=1}^{k} f_i (x_i - \bar{x})^r}{n}.$$

Relation between Moments

The first raw moment is defined as

$$m'_1 = \frac{\sum_{i=1}^{k} f_i x_i}{n} = \bar{x}$$

which is the sample mean.

If $x_1, x_2, \ldots, x_k$ occur with frequencies $f_1, f_2, \ldots, f_k$, respectively, then

$$m'_1 = \frac{\sum_{i=1}^{k} f_i (x_i - a)}{n} = \frac{\sum_{i=1}^{k} f_i x_i - a \sum_{i=1}^{k} f_i}{n} = \bar{x} - a, \quad \text{and}$$

$$m_1 = \frac{\sum_{i=1}^{k} f_i (x_i - \bar{x})}{n} = \frac{\sum_{i=1}^{k} f_i x_i - \bar{x} \sum_{i=1}^{k} f_i}{n} = \bar{x} - \bar{x} = 0.$$

For the second moment,

$$m'_2 = \frac{\sum_{i=1}^{k} f_i (x_i - a)^2}{n}, \quad \text{and}$$

$$m_2 = \frac{\sum_{i=1}^{k} f_i (x_i - \bar{x})^2}{n} = \frac{\sum_{i=1}^{k} f_i \{(x_i - a) - (\bar{x} - a)\}^2}{n}$$

$$= \frac{\sum_{i=1}^{k} f_i \{(x_i - a)^2 - 2(x_i - a)(\bar{x} - a) + (\bar{x} - a)^2\}}{n}$$

$$= \frac{\sum_{i=1}^{k} f_i (x_i - a)^2}{n} - 2(\bar{x} - a)(\bar{x} - a) + (\bar{x} - a)^2$$

$$= \frac{\sum_{i=1}^{k} f_i (x_i - a)^2}{n} - (\bar{x} - a)^2$$

$$= m'_2 - m'^2_1.$$

By definition, this is the sample variance obtained from the data.

Similarly, it can also be shown that

$$m_3 = m_3' - 3m_2'm_1' + 2m_1'^3, and$$
$$m_4 = m_4' - 4m_3'm_1' + 6m_2'm_1'^2 - 3m_1'^4.$$

Example 2.19 Let us consider the following data from a sample: $x_1 = 2, x_2 = 1, x_3 = 4, x_4 = 0, x_5 = 2, n = 5$.

The sample raw moments are

$$m_1' = \frac{2+1+4+0+2}{5} = \frac{9}{5} = 1.8$$

$$m_2' = \frac{2^2 + 1^2 + 4^2 + 0^2 + 2^2}{5} = \frac{25}{5} = 5$$

$$m_3' = \frac{2^3 + 1^3 + 4^3 + 0^3 + 2^3}{5} = \frac{81}{5} = 16.2$$

$$m_4' = \frac{2^4 + 1^4 + 4^4 + 0^4 + 2^4}{5} = \frac{289}{5} = 57.8.$$

Using the relationships between raw and central moments, we can compute the central sample moments as follows:

$$m_2 = m_2' - m_1'^2 = 5 - (1.8)^2 = 1.76$$

$$m_3 = m_3' - 3m_2'm_1' + 2m_1'^3 = 16.2 - 3 \times 5 \times 1.8 + 2 \times (1.8)^3$$
$$= 0.864,$$

$$m_4 = m_4' - 4m_3'm_1' + 6m_2'm_1'^2 - 3m_1'^4 = 57.8 - 4 \times 16.2 \times 1.8 + 6 \times 5 \times (1.8)^2 - 3 \times (1.8)^4$$
$$= 6.8672.$$

2.5   Skewness

Skewness is the degree of asymmetry or departure of symmetry of a distribution. In a skew distribution, the mean tends to lie on the same side of the mode as the longer tail. In a symmetric distribution, the mean, the mode, and the median coincide. Some commonly used measures of skewness are discussed as shown in Fig. 2.7.

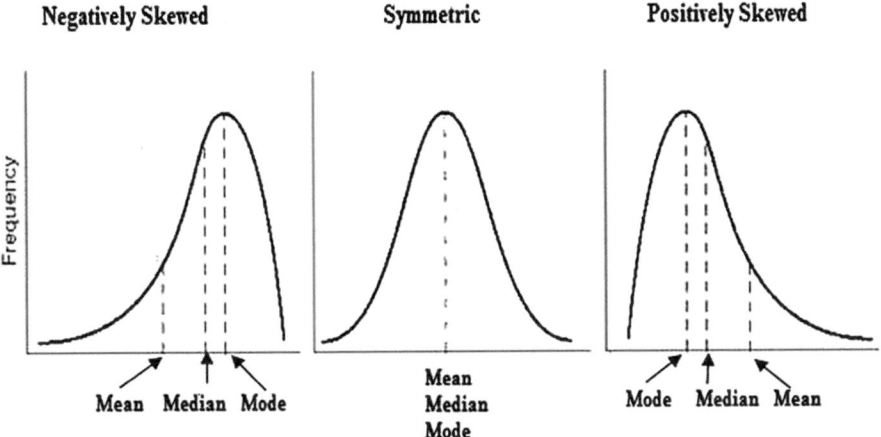

Fig. 2.7 Symmetric, negatively skewed, and positively skewed curves

Pearson's Measure

$$\text{skewness} = \frac{(\text{mean-mode})}{\text{standard deviation}}$$

$= 0$ for symmetry,

> 0 for positively skewed distribution,

< 0 for negatively skewed distribution.

Alternatively,

$$\text{skewness} = \frac{3(\text{mean-median})}{\text{standard deviation}}$$

$= 0$ for symmetry,

> 0 for positively skewed distribution,

< 0, for negatively skewed distribution.

Bowley's Measure

$$\text{skewness} = \frac{(Q_3 - Q_2) - (Q_2 - Q_1)}{(Q_3 - Q_1)}$$

$(Q_3 - Q_2) = (Q_2 - Q_1)$ for symmetry,

$(Q_3 - Q_2) > (Q_2 - Q_1)$ for positively skewed distribution,

$(Q_3 - Q_2) < (Q_2 - Q_1)$ for negatively skewed distribution.

Example 2.20 Consider the following data set: 14.6, 24.3, 24.9, 27.0, 27.2, 27.4, 28.2, 28.8, 29.9, 30.7, 31.5, 31.6, 32.3, 32.8, 33.3, 33.6, 34.3, 36.9, 38.3, 44.0.

Here, $n = 20$. $\bar{x} = 30.58$. There is no mode. The sample variance, $s^2 = 36.3417$ and the sample standard deviation, $s = 6.0284$.

$$Q_1 = \frac{n+1}{4}\text{th ordered observation} = \frac{20+1}{4} = 5.25\text{th ordered observation}$$

$$= 5\text{th ordered observation} + (0.25)(27.4 - 27.2) = 27.2 + (0.25)(0.2) = 27.25$$

$$\text{Median} = Q_2 = \frac{2(n+1)}{4}\text{th ordered observation} = \frac{20+1}{2} = 10.5\text{th ordered observation}$$

$$= 10\text{th ordered observation} + (0.5)(31.5 - 30.7)$$

$$= 30.7 + (0.5)(31.5 - 30.7) = 31.1$$

$$Q_3 = \frac{3(n+1)}{4}\text{th ordered observation} = \frac{3(20+1)}{4} = 15.75\text{th ordered observation}$$

$$= 15\text{th ordered observation} + (0.75)(33.6 - 33.3)$$

$$= 33.3 + (0.75)(33.6 - 33.3) = 33.525$$

$$IQR = Q_3 - Q_1 = 33.525 - 27.25 = 6.275.$$

As we cannot find any mode from the data shown in the example, it is not possible to compute the Pearson's measure of skewness using the following measure:

$$\text{skewness} = \frac{(\text{mean-mode})}{\text{standard deviation}}.$$

Hence, using the alternative measure, we can find the skewness:

$$\text{skewness} = \frac{3(\text{mean - median})}{\text{standard deviation}} = \frac{3(30.58 - 31.1)}{6.0284} = \frac{-1.56}{6.0284}$$

$$= -0.2588.$$

This shows that there is negative skewness in the distribution. Similarly, the Bowley's measure of skewness is

$$\text{skewness} = \frac{(Q_3 - Q_2) - (Q_2 - Q_1)}{(Q_3 - Q_1)} = \frac{(33.525 - 31.1) - (31.1 - 27.25)}{(33.525 - 27.25)}$$

$$= \frac{2.425 - 3.85}{6.275} = -0.2271.$$

This measure also confirms that there is negative skewness in the distribution.

Measure of Skewness Using Moments

For a symmetrical distribution, m_3 and any odd moment about mean is zero. Hence, a suitable measure of skewness is given by

$$b_1 = \frac{m_3^2}{m_2^3}, \quad \text{or}$$

$$\sqrt{b_1} = \frac{m_3}{m_2^{3/2}}.$$

This is the most important measure of skewness from theoretical point of view.

Example 2.21 Let us consider the following data from a sample: $x_1 = 2, x_2 = 1$, $x_3 = 4, x_4 = 0, x_5 = 2$, $n = 5$.

Then,

$$m_2 = 1.76,$$
$$m_3 = 0.864.$$

Hence, the measure of skewness employing moments is

$$b_1 = \frac{m_3^2}{m_2^3} = \frac{0.864^2}{1.76^3} = \frac{0.7465}{5.4518} = 0.1369$$

$$\sqrt{b_1} = \frac{m_3}{m_2^{3/2}} = 0.3700.$$

The above data indicates a positively skewed distribution.

The measure of skewness is -0.0817 for the weights of women in the data of 24 women shown in Chap. 1 which shows that weight of women data is negatively skewed.

2.6 Kurtosis

Kurtosis is the peakedness of a distribution, usually taken relative to a normal distribution. A distribution with a relatively high peak is called leptokurtic; a curve which is relatively flat topped is called platykurtic; a curve which is neither too peaked nor flat topped is called mesokurtic (Fig. 2.8).

The measure of kurtosis is

$$b_2 = \frac{m_4}{m_2^2} = \frac{n \sum_{i=1}^{n} (x_i - \bar{x})^4}{\left(\sum_{i=1}^{n} (x_i - \bar{x})^2 \right)^2}$$

and $b_2 - 3$

$= 0$, mesokurtic (not too high peak or not too flat topped)

<0, platykurtic (flat topped)

> 0, leptokurtic (high peak).

Example 2.22 Using the same data as displayed in the previous example, $x_1 = 2, x_2 = 1, x_3 = 4, x_4 = 0, x_5 = 2$, the second and fourth sample central moments are

Fig. 2.8 Figure displaying
leptokurtic, mesokurtic, and
platykurtic distributions

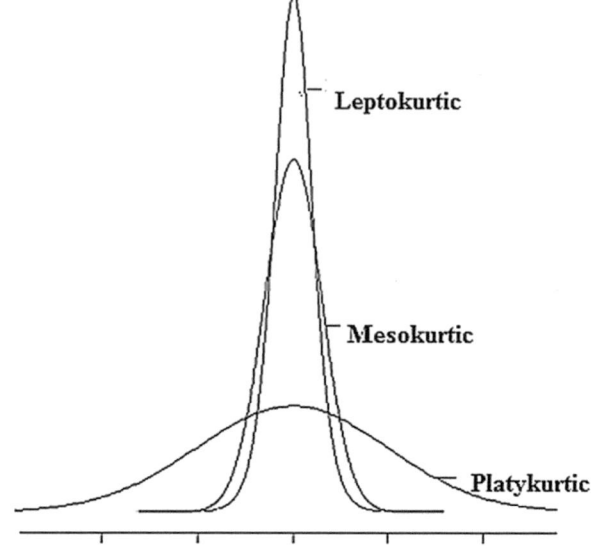

$$m_2 = 1.76,$$
$$m_4 = 6.8672.$$

$$b_2 = \frac{m_4}{m_2^2} = \frac{6.8672}{1.76^2} = 2.2169$$

and

$$b_2 - 3 = 2.2169 - 3 = -0.7831.$$

This indicates that the distribution is platykurtic or flat topped.

2.7   Summary

The basic descriptive statistics are introduced in this chapter. This chapter includes the basic measures of summary statistics, namely measures of central tendency, measures of dispersion, measures of skewness, and measures of kurtosis. These summary measures of descriptive statistics characterize the underlying features of data. The measures of central tendency include arithmetic mean, median, and mode with examples; advantages and disadvantages of the measures are highlighted. The measures of dispersion are discussed along with their properties. The measures of dispersion include range, variance, standard deviation, coefficient of variation, and interquartile range. In statistics and biostatistics, the first measure, central tendency or location, provides the central value around which all other values in the data set are located. In other words, the measure of central tendency provides the most important representative value of the data set. The dispersion quantifies or measures the variability in the data where variability between values of the data or difference between each value and the measure of central tendency may reflect how scattered the data are from a central value or what extent in variation among values of the data is there. The third measure is used to know whether there is symmetry from the central value or there exists asymmetry from the central value. The fourth measure indicates whether the data are more concentrated with high peak, low or normal peaks, or frequencies indicating extent of concentration of values.

Exercises

2.1 Are the following statements true? Write the correct answer giving appropriate justification:

(i) For any set of data $x_1, x_2, \ldots, x_n$ with mean $\bar{x}$ $\sum_{i=1}^{n} (x_i - \bar{x}) = 0$.

(ii) The standard deviation of a set of data does not depend on the units of measurement of the data.

(iii) The median of 0, -1, -2, -3, and 6 is 0.

(iv) If $n = 5$ and $\sum_{i=1}^{5} x_i = 10$, then $\sum_{i=1}^{5} x_i^2$ is not less than 20.

2.2 Consider the following sets of data:

E: 10, 15, 23, 30
F: 110, 115, 123, 130.

Is the data set F more dispersed than the data set E?

2.3 (a) The average and the standard deviation of weight of 24 women are $\bar{x} = 50$ kg and standard deviation $= 9.5$ kg. What are the average and standard deviation in pounds (1 kg $= 2.2046$ lb)?

(b) The average and the standard deviation of temperature of 50 patients in a sample are $\bar{x} = 37.8\,^{\circ}\text{C}$ and standard deviation $= 6.5\,^{\circ}\text{C}$. Let the conversion from *Celsius* to *Fahrenheit* scale can be obtained by using the relationship *Fahrenheit* $= 32 + 1.8\,^{\circ}\text{C}$. Find the average and standard deviation in Fahrenheit scale.

2.4 Are the following statements true? Justify your answer.
The median of a set of data is affected by extreme values.
If the range of data is zero, the standard deviation must also be zero.

2.5 (a) Define two measures of skewness and show how these measures indicate symmetry, positive skewness, and negative skewness.

(b) Show the following relationships: $(i)\, m_2 = m_2' - m_1'^2$, $(ii)\, m_3 = m_3' - 3m_2'm_1' + 2m_1'^3$. Also show that if $u_i = \frac{x_i - a}{c}$ then $m_r'(x) = c^r m_r'(u)$.

2.6   The following data show the number of hours 10 hospital patients had to stay at the emergency care after accident:
17, 20, 22, 14, 14, 31, 14, 32, 25, 24

(i) Compute the following:

(a) the mean, median, and mode,
(b) the sample variance,
(c) the interquartile range, and
(d) the coefficient of variation.

(ii) Construct the Box-and-Whisker plot.

2.7   (i) If for a sample we have $\Sigma X^2 = 12$, $\Sigma X = 4$, $n = 5$ then find the sample variance.
(ii) Consider the data given in the table below:

X	−1	0	1
Frequency	10	5	10

Find the following:

(i)   the mean,
(ii) the median,
(iii) the range,
(iv) the variance,
(v)   the standard deviation, and
(vi) the coefficient of variation.

2.8   Age (in years) of 50 patients in a study are summarized in the following table.

Age in years	Frequency f
10–19	12
20–29	23
30–39	15
	50

Find the following:

(i)   the mean,
(ii) the median,
(iii) the variance,
(iv) the standard deviation, and
(v)   the coefficient of variation.

2.9 (i) Define the raw and corrected moments. Show the relationship between the first two raw and corrected moments.

(ii) Construct the box-and-whisker plot using the following data: 10, 10, 14, 15, 15,15, 17, 19, 20, 25. Comment on the main features of these data.

(iii) Using the data in 8(b), find the skewness and comment on the finding.

2.10 (i) Use the following data on weight (in pounds) of 20 individuals in a sample: 100, 110, 114, 115, 115,115, 117, 119, 120, 135, 141, 143, 147, 150, 152, 157, 161, 162, 162, and 179 to compute the first four raw and corrected moments.

(ii) Compute the quartiles 1, 2, and 3.

(iii) Compute percentiles 23, 55, and 80.

(iv) Construct the box-and-whisker plot using the same data. Is there any outlier in the data? Comment on the main features of these data.

(v) Compute the measures of skewness and kurtosis using the moments.

2.11 Suppose we have two data sets with the following arithmetic means and standard deviations:

Data Set 1: $\bar{x}_1 = 60, s_1 = 30$
Data Set 2: $\bar{x}_2 = 40, s_2 = 30$

Compute the coefficient of variation and compare the variability in two data sets.

2.12 Consider the following data on age of 10 persons with allergy problems: 20, 25, 25, 30, 35, 30, 35, 40, 45, 40.

a. Find the following:

(i) Range
(ii) First quartile,
(iii) Second quartile,
(iv) Third quartile,
(v) Interquartile range,
(vi) Semi-interquartile range, and
(vii) Construct the box-and-whisker plot.

2.13 (i) If the sample variance of a variable, X, is 5, then what is the variance of $10X$?

(ii) If the sample variance of a variable, X, is 5, then what is the variance of $10X + 3$?

2.14 Show that $\sum_{i=1}^{n} (x_i - \bar{x})^2 = \sum_{i=1}^{n} x_i^2 - n\bar{x}^2$.

2.15 Consider the following data on the study hours of 10 students in a university: 3, 5, 4, 5, 6, 4, 5, 5, 7, 3.

(i) Find the range and interquartile range.
(ii) Construct the box-and-whisker plot.
(iii) Compute the Pearson's and Bowley's measures of skewness and comment.

2.16 (i) What are the measures of central tendency? How can you compute
         arithmetic mean, median, and mode?
      (ii) Suppose the following data represent the number of days in a hospital for
         12 patients suffering from diabetes-related complications:
         16, 10, 49, 15, 6, 15, 8, 19, 11. 22, 13, 17.

      (a) Compute: (i) arithmetic mean, (ii) median, and (iii) mode.
      (b) Which one is the best measure of central tendency in 15 (b)? Why?

2.17 (a) Using the data in 15 (b), construct the box-and-whisker plot and identify
         outliers, if any.
      (b) Compute the following using data in question 15 (b):

       (i) Range,
      (ii) Interquartile range, and
     (iii) Sample standard deviation.

2.18 If $x_1, x_2, \ldots, x_n$ are n observations from a sample with sample mean $\bar{x}$ and
      sample variance s^2, then find

       (i) Sample mean and variance for $x_1 + 5, x_2 + 5, \ldots, x_n + 5$ where b is a
            constant; and
      (ii) Sample mean and variance for $3x_1 + 5, 3x_2 + 5, \ldots, 3x_n + 5$.

2.19 Consider the following results from two samples of females:

	Sample 1	Sample 2
Age	25 years	20 years
Mean weight	130 lb	110 lb
Standard deviation	15 lb	10 lb

      Use a suitable measure of dispersion to compare the variability in the weight
      of the two 25- and 20-year-old females. What is your interpretation?

Reference

Rousseeuw, P. J., Ruts, I., & Tukey, J. W. (1999). The Bagplot: A Bivariate Boxplot. *The American Statistician, 53*(4), 382–387.

Chapter 3
Basic Probability Concepts

3.1 General Definitions and Concepts

As we have defined statistics, in broad terms, it deals with two major components, descriptive measures, and inference. Probability is the foundation for making inference about the population based on the sample as representative part of the population. In other words, probability is the link between population and sample in such a way that we can have an understanding about the degree of uncertainty in making decision about the population characteristics on the basis of sample characteristics with the help of underlying probabilities.

Probability
Probability is a measure used to measure the chance of the occurrence of some event. Probability measure ranges from 0 to 1, where 0 indicates impossibility and 1 indicates the certainty of the occurrence of an event.

Experiment
An experiment is a procedure (or process) that we perform whose outcomes are not predictable in advance.

Example: Experiment with coin tossing results in two outcomes, head or tail, but the outcome is not known until the coin is tossed or until the experiment is conducted. Here, the two outcomes, head and tail, are exhaustive, because one of these two outcomes must occur in each experiment and there are no other possible outcomes in this experiment.

Sample Space
The sample space of an experiment is the set of all possible outcomes of an experiment. Also, it is called the universal set and is denoted by Ω.

Example In the coin tossing experiment with a single coin, the possible outcomes are head (H) or tail (T). Hence, the sample space is $\Omega = \{H, T\}$.

© Springer Nature Singapore Pte Ltd. 2018
M. A. Islam and A. Al-Shiha, *Foundations of Biostatistics*,
https://doi.org/10.1007/978-981-10-8627-4_3

Event

Any subset of the sample space Ω is called an event. For example, in the coin tossing experiment, an event called success may occur if the outcome is a head (H). If a tail (T) appears, then it may be called failure. It may be noted that

(i) $\phi \subseteq \Omega$ is an event is an impossible event, and
(ii) $\Omega \subseteq \Omega$ is an event is a sure or certain event.

An example is shown here to illustrate the sample space and events.

Let us consider selecting a patient from a hospital room with six beds numbered from 1 to 6 and observing the patient of the selected bed. Here, the patients are identified by their respective bed numbers.

This experiment has six possible outcomes or elements.

The sample space is $\Omega = \{1, 2, 3, 4, 5, 6\}$.

Consider the following events and the elements corresponding to the events:

E_1 = getting an even number = $\{2, 4, 6\} \subseteq \Omega$,
E_2 = getting a number less than 4 = $\{1, 2, 3\} \subseteq \Omega$,
E_3 = getting 1 or 3 = $\{1, 3\} \subseteq \Omega$,
E_4 = getting an odd number = $\{1, 3, 5\} \subseteq \Omega$,
E_5 = getting a negative number = $\{\} = \phi \subseteq \Omega$, and
E_6 = getting a number less than 10 = $\{1, 2, 3, 4, 5, 6\} = \Omega \subseteq \Omega$.

Notation $n(\Omega)$ = number of outcomes (elements) in Ω and
$n(E)$ = number of outcomes (elements) in the event E.

Equally Likely Outcomes

The outcomes of an experiment are equally likely if the outcomes have the same chance of occurrence. In other words, an experiment resulting in equally likely outcomes is equally probable. It implies that if the sample space contains n equally likely outcomes, then it is likely that probability of each outcome is $1/n$. In case of the coin tossing example, the outcomes are (H, T) and the outcomes are equally likely for a fair coin. The probabilities of outcomes, Head or Tail, are equally likely with probability 1/2 for each outcome.

Mutually Exclusive Outcomes

In an experiment, if only one outcome is observed at a time excluding the occurrence of any other outcome, then it is called mutually exclusive.

Example: In the coin tossing experiment, if the outcome is observed to be head, the occurrence of tail is not possible at the same time and vice versa.

3.2 Probability of an Event

If the experiment has $n(\Omega)$ equally likely outcomes, then the probability of the event E is denoted by $P(E)$ and is defined by:

$$P(E) = \frac{n(E)}{n(\Omega)} = \frac{\text{number of outcomes in } E}{\text{number of outcomes in } \Omega}.$$

This is the classical definition of probability and under this definition the experiment should satisfy the condition of equally likely as an essential precondition which may not be true in many practical situations.

Example: If we conduct an experiment with a fair coin, then the outcomes H or T are equally likely but if we consider outcomes of defective and non-defective products from an experiment, the condition of equally likely outcomes may be violated because outcomes are not necessarily equally likely. In that case, we may use an alternative definition known as the relative frequency or empirical definition to measure the probability as stated below.

Let an event E occurs $n(E)$ times in a series of n trials, where n is the total number of trials or sample size, the trials are conducted under the same conditions in the experiment. Here, the ratio $\frac{n(E)}{n}$ is the relative frequency of the event E in n trials. If n tends to infinity, then we can define the probability of E as follows:

$$P(E) = \lim_{n \to \infty} \frac{n(E)}{n}.$$

Example 3.1 (Example of Classical Probability)

In the experiment for selecting patients identified by bed number of six patients as discussed in the previous example, suppose the bed number is selected at random. Determine the probabilities of the following events:

E_1 = the patient staying in a bed with even number,
E_2 = the patient staying in a bed with a number less than 4, and
E_3 = the patient staying in a bed with numbers 1 or 3.

Solution

$$\begin{aligned}
\Omega &= \{1, 2, 3, 4, 5, 6\} &&;& n(\Omega) &= 6 \\
E_1 &= \{2, 4, 6\} &&;& n(E_1) &= 3 \\
E_2 &= \{1, 2, 3\} &&;& n(E_2) &= 3 \\
E_3 &= \{1, 3\} &&;& n(E_3) &= 2
\end{aligned}$$

The outcomes are equally likely. Then, by definition the probabilities of the events, $E_1, E_2,$ and E_3 are

$$P(E_1) = \frac{3}{6}, \quad P(E_2) = \frac{3}{6}, \quad \text{and } P(E_3) = \frac{2}{6}.$$

Some Operations on Events

Let A and B be two events defined on the sample space Ω.

(i) **Union of Two events**: $(A \cup B)$

The event $A \cup B$ consists of all outcomes in A **or** in B **or** in both A and B. The event $A \cup B$ occurs if A occurs, **or** B occurs, **or** both A and B occur.

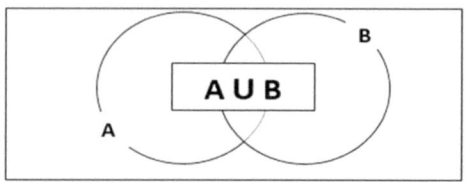

(ii) **Intersection of Two Events**: $(A \cap B)$

The event $A \cap B$ consists of all outcomes in both A **and** B. The event $A \cap B$ occurs if both A **and** B occur.

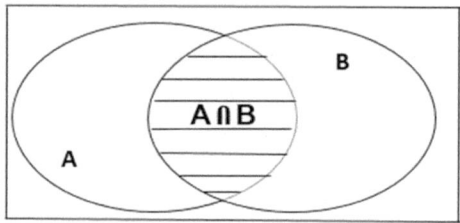

(iii) **Complement of an Event**: $(\overline{A})$ or (A^{C}) or (A')

The complement of the event A is denoted by $\overline{A}$. The event $\overline{A}$ consists of all outcomes of Ω that are not in A. The event $\overline{A}$ occurs if A does not.

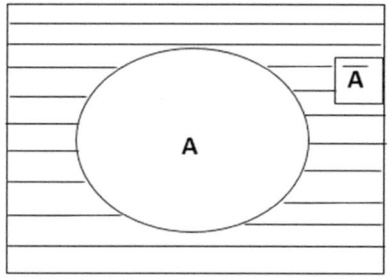

Example 3.2 (Classical Probability)

Experiment: Selecting a patient randomly from a hospital room having six beds numbered 1, 2, 3, 4, 5, and 6.

Define the following events:

$E_1 = \{2, 4, 6\}$ = selected an even number.
$E_2 = \{1, 2, 3\}$ = selecting a number <4.
$E_4 = \{1, 3, 5\}$ = selecting an odd number.

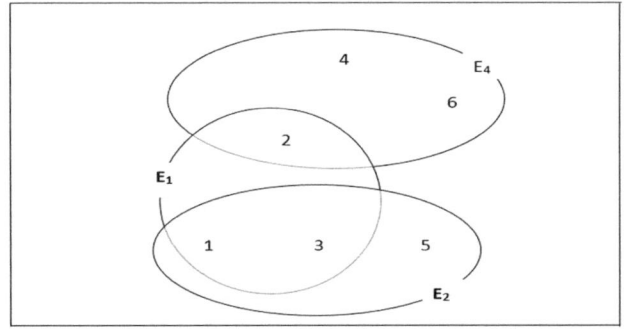

(1) $E_1 \cup E_2 = \{1, 2, 3, 4, 6\}$ = selecting an even number **or** a number less than 4.

$$P(E_1 \cup E_2) = \frac{n(E_1 \cup E_2)}{n(\Omega)} = \frac{5}{6}$$

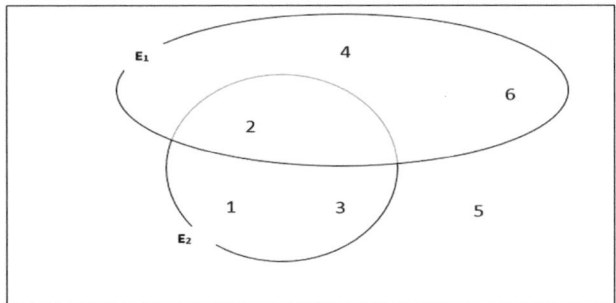

(2) $E_1 \cup E_4 = \{1, 2, 3, 4, 5, 6\} = \Omega$ = selecting an even number **or** an odd number.

$$P(E_1 \cup E_4) = \frac{n(E_1 \cup E_4)}{n(\Omega)} = \frac{6}{6} = 1.$$

It can be shown that $E_1 \cup E_4 = \Omega$ where E_1 and E_4 are called exhaustive events. The union of these events gives the whole sample space.

(3) $E_1 \cap E_2 = \{2\}$ = selecting an even number **and** a number less than 4.

$$P(E_1 \cap E_2) = \frac{n(E_1 \cap E_2)}{n(\Omega)} = \frac{1}{6}$$

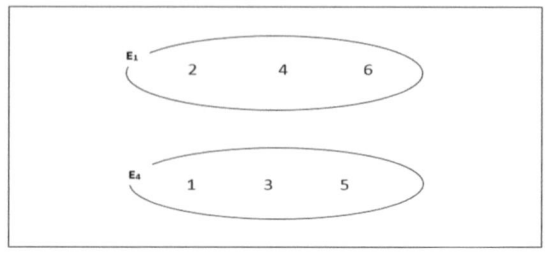

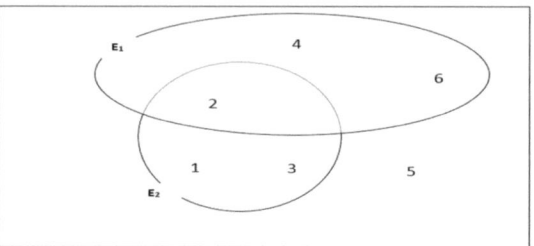

(4) $E_1 \cap E_4 = \phi$ = selecting an even number **and** an odd number.

$$P(E_1 \cap E_4) = \frac{n(E_1 \cap E_4)}{n(\Omega)} = \frac{n(\phi)}{6} = \frac{0}{6} = 0.$$

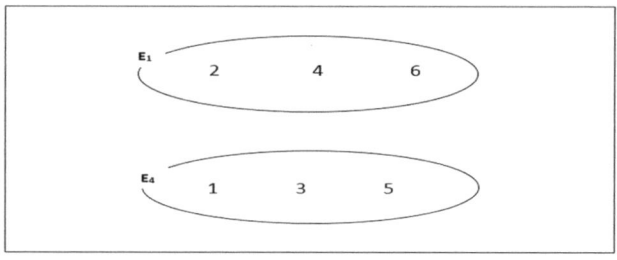

Note: $E_1 \cap E_4 = \phi$. In this case, E_1 and E_4 are called disjoint (or mutually exclusive) events. These kinds of events cannot occur simultaneously (together at the same time).

(5) The complement of E_1

$$\overline{E}_1 = \underline{\text{not}} \text{ selecting an even number} = \overline{\{2,4,6\}} = \{1,3,5\}$$
$$= \text{selecting an odd number.}$$
$$= E_4.$$

Mutually Exclusive (Disjoint) Events
The events A and B are disjoint (or mutually exclusive) if

$$A \cap B = \phi.$$

In this case, it is impossible that both events occur simultaneously (i.e., together in the same time). Hence,

(i) $P(A \cap B) = 0$
(ii) $P(A \cup B) = P(A) + P(B).$

If $A \cap B \neq \phi$, then A and B are not mutually exclusive (not disjoint).

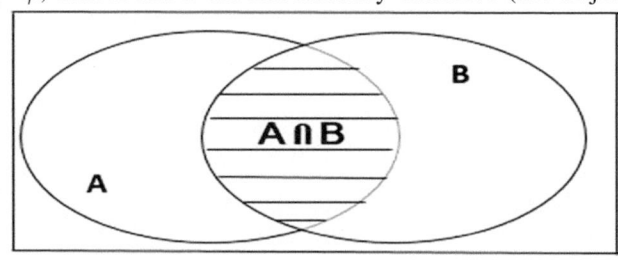

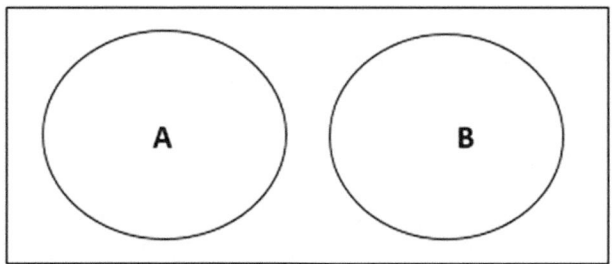

$A \cap B \neq \phi$	$A \cap B = \phi$
A and B are not mutually exclusive	A and B are mutually exclusive (disjoint)
It is possible that both events may occur at the same time.	It is impossible that both events occur at the same time.

Exhaustive Events
The events $A_1, A_2, \ldots, A_n$ are exhaustive events if

$$A_1 \cup A_2 \cup \ldots \cup A_n = \Omega.$$

For this case, $P(A_1 \cup A_2 \cup \ldots \cup A_n) = P(\Omega) = 1.$

Note

1. $A \cup \overline{A} = \Omega$ (A and $\overline{A}$ are exhaustive events),
2. $A \cap \overline{A} = \phi$ (A and $\overline{A}$ are mutually exclusive (disjoint) events),
3. $n(\overline{A}) = n(\Omega) - n(A)$, and
4. $P(\overline{A}) = 1 - P(A).$

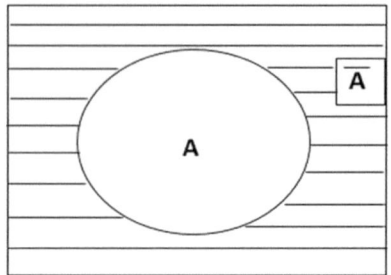

General Probability Rules

1. $0 \leq P(A) \leq 1$,
2. $P(\Omega) = 1$,
3. $P(\phi) = 0$, and
4. $P(\overline{A}) = 1 - P(A)$.

The Addition Rule

For any two events A and B:

$$P(A \cup B) = P(A) + P(B) - P(A \cap B)$$

and for any three events A, B, and C:

$$P(A \cup B \cup C) = P(A) + P(B) + P(C) - P(A \cap B) - P(A \cap C) \\ - P(B \cap C) + P(A \cap B \cap C).$$

$$P(A \cup B) = P(A) + P(B) - P(A \cap B)$$

Special Cases

1. For mutually exclusive (disjoint) events A and B,

$$P(A \cup B) = P(A) + P(B).$$

2. For mutually exclusive (disjoint) events $E_1, E_2, \ldots, E_n$,

$$P(E_1 \cup E_2 \cup \cdots \cup E_n) = P(E_1) + P(E_2) + \cdots + P(E_n).$$

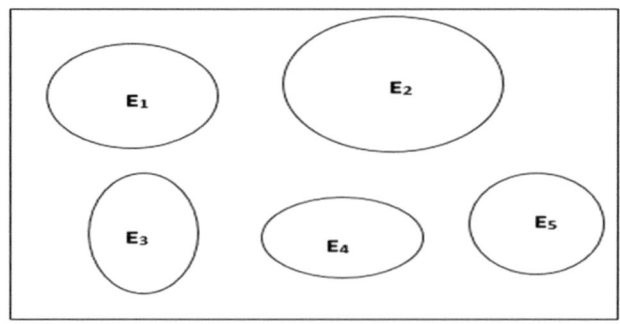

If the events $A_1, A_2, \ldots, A_n$ are exhaustive and mutually exclusive (disjoint) events, then

$$P(A_1 \cup A_2 \cup \cdots \cup A_n) = P(A_1) + P(A_2) + \cdots + P(A_n) = P(\Omega) = 1.$$

3.3 Marginal Probability

Given some variable that can be broken down into (m) categories designated by $A_1, A_2, \ldots, A_m$ and another jointly occurring variable that is broken down into (s) categories designated by $B_1, B_2, \ldots, B_s$ (Tables 3.1 and 3.2).

The marginal probability of A_i, $P(A_i)$, is equal to the sum of the joint probabilities of A_i with all categories of B. That is

$$P(A_i) = P(A_i \cap B_1) + P(A_i \cap B_2) + \cdots + P(A_i \cap B_s)$$
$$= \sum_{j=1}^{s} P(A_i \cap B_j).$$

For example,

$$P(A_2) = P(A_2 \cap B_1) + P(A_2 \cap B_2) + \cdots + P(A_2 \cap B_s)$$
$$= \sum_{j=1}^{s} P(A_2 \cap B_j).$$

We define the marginal probability of B_j, $P(B_j)$, in a similar way.

Example 3.3 (Relative Frequency or Empirical)

Let us consider a bivariate table for variables A and B. There are three categories for both the variables, $A_1, A_2,$ and A_3 for A and $B_1, B_2,$ and B_3 for B (Tables 3.3 and 3.4).

Table 3.1 Joint frequency distribution for m categories of A and s categories of B

	B_1	B_2	...	B_s	Total
A_1	$n(A_1 \cap B_1)$	$n(A_1 \cap B_2)$	...	$n(A_1 \cap B_s)$	$n(A_1)$
A_2	$n(A_2 \cap B_1)$	$n(A_2 \cap B_2)$	...	$n(A_2 \cap B_s)$	$n(A_2)$
.	.	.	.	.	.
.	.	.	.	.	.
.	.	.	.	.	.
A_m	$n(A_m \cap B_1)$	$n(A_m \cap B_2)$	...	$n(A_m \cap B_s)$	$n(A_m)$
Total	$n(B_1)$	$n(B_2)$	...	$n(B_s)$	n

Table 3.2 Joint probability distribution for m categories of A and s categories of B

	B_1	B_2	...	B_s	Marginal probability
A_1	$P(A_1 \cap B_1)$	$P(A_1 \cap B_2)$	...	$P(A_1 \cap B_s)$	$P(A_1)$
A_2	$P(A_2 \cap B_1)$	$P(A_2 \cap B_2)$	...	$P(A_2 \cap B_s)$	$P(A_2)$
.	.	.	.	.	.
.	.	.	.	.	.
.	.	.	.	.	.
A_m	$P(A_m \cap B_1)$	$P(A_m \cap B_2)$	...	$P(A_m \cap B_s)$	$P(A_m)$
Marginal probability	$P(B_1)$	$P(B_2)$	...	$P(B_s)$	1.00

Table 3.3 Number of elements in each cell

	B_1	B_2	B_3	Total
A_1	50	30	70	150
A_2	20	70	10	100
A_3	30	100	120	250
Total	100	200	200	500

Table 3.4 Probabilities of events

	B_1	B_2	B_3	Marginal probability
A_1	0.1	0.06	0.14	0.3
A_2	0.04	0.14	0.02	0.2
A_3	0.06	0.2	0.24	0.5
Marginal probability	0.2	0.4	0.4	1

For example,

$$P(A_2) = P(A_2 \cap B_1) + P(A_2 \cap B_2) + P(A_2 \cap B_3)$$
$$= 0.04 + 0.14 + 0.02$$
$$= 0.2.$$

3.4   Applications of Relative Frequency or Empirical Probability

Example 3.4 Let us consider a hypothetical data on four types of diseases of 200 patients from a hospital as shown below:

Disease type	A	B	C	D	Total
Number of patients	90	80	20	10	200

Experiment: Selecting a patient at random and observe his/her disease type. Total number of trials, sample size, in this case, is

$$n = 200.$$

Define the events

E_1 = the disease type of the selected patient is A,
E_2 = the disease type of the selected patient is B,
E_3 = the disease type of the selected patient is C, and
E_4 = the disease type of the selected patient is D.

Number of elements for each event is shown below:

$$n(E_1) = 90, \quad n(E_2) = 80,$$
$$n(E_3) = 20, \quad n(E_4) = 10.$$

Probabilities of the events are

$$P(E_1) = \frac{90}{200} = 0.45, \quad P(E_2) = \frac{80}{200} - 0.40,$$
$$P(E_3) = \frac{20}{200} = 0.1, \quad P(E_4) = \frac{10}{200} = 0.05.$$

Some Operations on the Events

1. $E_2 \cap E_4$ = the disease type of the selected patients is "*B*" **and** "*D*".
   $E_2 \cap E_4 = \phi$ (disjoint events/mutually exclusive events)

$$P(E_2 \cap E_4) = P(\phi) = 0.$$

2. $E_2 \cup E_4$ = the disease type of the selected patients is "*B*" **or** "*D*".

$$P(E_2 \cup E_4) = \begin{cases} \dfrac{n(E_2 \cup E_4)}{n(\Omega)} = \dfrac{80 + 10}{200} = \dfrac{90}{200} = 0.45 \\ \text{or} \\ P(E_2) + P(E_4) = \dfrac{80}{200} + \dfrac{10}{200} = \dfrac{90}{200} = 0.45, \end{cases}$$

   since $E_2 \cap E_4 = \phi$.

3. $\overline{E}_1$ = the disease type of the selected patients is not "*A*".

$$n(\overline{E}_1) = n - n(E_1) = 200 - 90 = 110$$
$$P(\overline{E}_1) = \frac{n(\overline{E}_1)}{n} = \frac{110}{200} = 0.55.$$

Another solution

$$P(E_1^C) = 1 - P(E_1) = 1 - 0.45 = 0.55.$$

It may be noted here that E_1, E_2, E_3, E_4 are mutually disjoint since $E_i \cap E_j = \phi$ $(i \neq j)$, and E_1, E_2, E_3, E_4 are exhaustive events since $E_1 \cup E_2 \cup E_3 \cup E_4 = \Omega$.

Example 3.5 (Relative Frequency or Empirical Probability)

The breast cancer databases (see Mangasarian et al. 1990) from the University of Wisconsin Hospitals include data on two variables, clump thickness categories 1–10 (A) and class referring to whether the case is malignant or benign (B). The study includes data on 699 instances. After combining clump thickness categories 1 and 2 as A_1, 3 and 4 as A_2, 5 and above as A_3, and denoting the benign category as B_1 and malignant category as B_2, Table 3.5 summarizes the cross-classified data for clump thickness and class.

Experiment: Selecting a case randomly.

The number of elements of the sample space is $n = 699$. Here, $n = 699$ is the sample size.

Some events and corresponding probabilities are shown below:

A_3 = the selected case has clump thickness of category 5 or higher

$$P(A_3) = \frac{n(A_3)}{n} = \frac{316}{699} = 0.4521.$$

B_2 = the selected case belongs to the malignant class

$$P(B_2) = \frac{n(B_2)}{n} = \frac{241}{699} = 0.3447.$$

$A_3 \cap B_2$ = the selected subject has clump thickness category 5 or above and the case is malignant,

$$P(A_3 \cap B_2) = \frac{n(A_3 \cap B_2)}{n} = \frac{210}{699} = 0.3004.$$

Table 3.5 Data on two variables, clump thickness, and class referring to whether the case is malignant or benign (B)

Clump thickness	Class		
	Benign (B_1)	Malignant (B_2)	Total
A_1	188	7	195
A_2	164	24	188
A_3	106	210	316
Total	458	241	699

$A_3 \cup B_2$ = the selected subject has clump thickness category 5 or above or the case is malignant, and

$$P(A_3 \cup B_2) = P(A_3) + P(B_2) - P(A_3 \cap B_2)$$
$$= \frac{316}{699} + \frac{241}{699} - \frac{210}{699}$$
$$= 0.4521 + 0.3448 - 0.3004$$
$$= 0.4965.$$

$\overline{A}_1$ = the selected subject does not belong to clump thickness categories 1 or 2
$$= A_1 \cup A_2 \cup A_3$$

$$P(\overline{A}_1) = 1 - P(A_1)$$
$$= 1 - \frac{n(A_1)}{n}$$
$$= 1 - \frac{195}{699} = 0.7210.$$

$A_2 \cup A_3$ = the selected subject belongs to clump thickness categories either A_2 or A_3

$$P(A_2 \cup A_3) = \frac{n(A_2 \cup A_3)}{n} = \frac{188 + 316}{699} = 0.7210$$
$$P(A_2 \cup A_3) = P(A_2) + P(A_3) = \frac{188}{699} + \frac{316}{699} = 0.7210,$$

since $A_2 \cap A_3 = \phi$.

Example 3.6 (Relative Frequency or Empirical Probability)
Let us consider a sample from a population of patients having health problems during a specified period. It was observed that 20% of the patients visited physicians but 41% of the patients had some medication. It was also observed that 15% of the patients visited physicians and used some prescribed medications.

In other words, among the patients having health problems,

20% of the patients visited physicians for consultation.
41% of the patients used some medications.
15% of the patients visited physicians and used some medications.

Experiment: Selecting a patient having health problems from this population.
Define the events

D = The selected patient visited physician.
M = The selected patient used medication.
$D \cap M$ = The selected patient visited physician and used some sort of medication.

Table 3.6 (a) An incomplete two-way table representing percentage of respondents by whether visited physician and whether used any medication. (b) A complete two-way table representing percentage of respondents by whether visited physician and whether used any medication

(a)

	M	$\overline{M}$	Total
D	15	?	20
$\overline{D}$	?	?	?
Total	41	?	100

(b)

	M	$\overline{M}$	Total
D	15	5	20
$\overline{D}$	26	54	80
Total	41	59	100

Percentages:

$$\%(D) = 20\% \quad \%(M) = 41\% \quad \%(D \cap M) = 15\%.$$

The complement events

$\overline{D}$ = The selected patient did not visit any physician.
$\overline{M}$ = The selected patient did not use any medication (Table 3.6).

The probabilities of the given events are

$$P(D) = \frac{\%(D)}{100\%} = \frac{20\%}{100\%} = 0.2$$

$$P(M) = \frac{\%(M)}{100\%} = \frac{41\%}{100\%} = 0.41$$

$$P(D \cap M) = \frac{\%(D \cap M)}{100\%} = \frac{15\%}{100\%} = 0.15.$$

Calculating probabilities of some events are illustrated below:

$D \cup M$ = the selected patient visited physician or used medication

$$P(D \cup M) = P(D) + (M) - P(D \cap M)$$
$$= 0.20 + 0.41 - 0.15 = 0.46.$$

$\overline{M}$ = The selected patient did not use medication

$$P(\overline{M}) = 1 - P(M) = 1 - 0.41 = 0.59,$$

$$P(\overline{M}) = \frac{59}{100} = 0.59.$$

$\overline{D}$ = The selected patient did not visit physician

$$P(\overline{D}) = 1 - P(D) = 1 - 0.20 = 0.80,$$
$$P(\overline{D}) = \frac{80}{100} = 0.80.$$

$\overline{D} \cap \overline{M}$ = the selected patient did not visit physician and did not use medication.
$$P(\overline{D} \cap \overline{M}) = \frac{54}{100} = 0.54.$$

$\overline{D} \cap M$ = the selected patient did not visit physician and used medication.
$$P(\overline{D} \cap M) = \frac{5}{100} = 0.05.$$

$D \cap \overline{M}$ = the selected patient visited physician and did not use medication.
$$P(D \cap \overline{M}) = \frac{5}{100} = 0.05.$$

$D \cup \overline{M}$ = the selected patient visited physician or did not use medication.
$$P(D \cup \overline{M}) = P(D) + (\overline{M}) - P(D \cap \overline{M})$$
$$= 0.20 + 0.59 - 0.26 = 0.53.$$

$\overline{D} \cup M$ = the selected patient did not visit physician or used medication.
$$P(\overline{D} \cup M) = P(\overline{D}) + (M) - P(\overline{D} \cap M)$$
$$= 0.80 + 0.41 - 0.26 = 0.95.$$

$\overline{D} \cup \overline{M}$ = the selected patient did not visit physician or did not use medication.
$$P(\overline{D} \cup \overline{M}) = P(\overline{D}) + (\overline{M}) - P(\overline{D} \cap \overline{M})$$
$$= 0.80 + 0.59 - 0.54 = 0.85.$$

3.5   Conditional Probability

The conditional probability of the event A when we know that the event B has already occurred is defined by

$$P(A|B) = \frac{P(A \cap B)}{P(B)}; \quad P(B) \neq 0.$$

$P(A|B)$ = The conditional probability of A given B.
The following figure shows the events graphically:

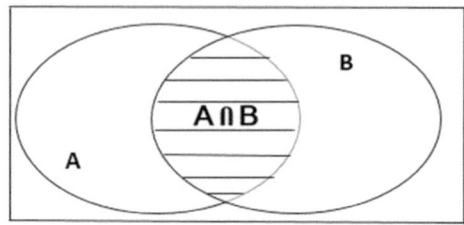

Notes:

1. $P(A|B) = \frac{P(A \cap B)}{P(B)} = \frac{n(A \cap B)/n(\Omega)}{n(B)/n(\Omega)} = \frac{n(A \cap B)}{n(B)}$
2. $P(B|A) = \frac{P(A \cap B)}{P(A)}$
3. For calculating $P(A|B)$, we may use any one of the following:

   i. $P(A|B) = \frac{P(A \cap B)}{P(B)}$
   ii. $P(A|B) = \frac{n(A \cap B)}{n(B)}$
   iii. Using the restricted table directly.

Multiplication Rules of Probability
For any two events A and B, we have

$$P(A \cap B) = P(B)P(A|B),$$
$$P(A \cap B) = P(A)P(B|A).$$

Example 3.7 Let us consider a hypothetical set of data on 600 adult males classified by their ages and smoking habits as summarized in Table 3.7.
   Consider the following event:
   $(B_1|A_2)$ = smokes daily given that age is between 30 and 39

Table 3.7 Two-way table displaying number of respondents by age and smoking habit of respondents smoking habit

		Daily (B_1)	Occasionally (B_2)	Not at all (B_3)	Total
Age	20–29 (A_1)	57	18	13	88
	30–39 (A_2)	200	55	90	345
	40–49 (A_3)	50	40	55	145
	50+ (A_4)	7	0	15	22
	Total	314	113	173	600

$$P(B_1) = \frac{n(B_1)}{n} = \frac{314}{600} = 0.523$$

$$P(B_1|A_2) = \frac{P(B_1 \cap A_2)}{P(A_2)}$$

$$= \frac{0.333}{0.575} = 0.579$$

$$\left\{ \begin{array}{c} P(B_1 \cap A_2) = \frac{n(B_1 \cap A_2)}{n} = \frac{200}{600} = 0.333 \\ P(A_2) = \frac{n(A_2)}{n} = \frac{345}{600} = 0.575 \end{array} \right\}$$

Another solution

$$P(B_1|A_2) = \frac{n(B_1 \cap A_2)}{n(A_2)} = \frac{200}{345} = 0.579.$$

Notice that

$$P(B_1) = 0.523$$
$$P(B_1|A_2) = 0.579$$
$$P(B_1|A_2) > P(B_1), \quad P(B_1) \neq P(B_1|A_2).$$

Example 3.8 (Multiplication Rule of Probability)

It was found from a study that 20% of the patients with some general health problems visited physicians and out of those who visited physicians 75% were prescribed some medications. If a person with health problem is selected randomly from the population, what is the probability that the person will use medicine? What is the percentage of patients who use medication?

Solution

Define the following events:

A = the event of visiting physician,

B = the event of using medication, and

$A \cap B$ = the event of visiting physician and using medication

= the event of experiencing both events.

Therefore, the probability of visiting physician and using medication is $P(A \cap B)$. From the given information, the probability of visiting physician is

$$P(A) = 0.2 \quad \left(\frac{20\%}{100\%} = 0.2 \right).$$

The probability of using medication given that the patient visited physician is

$$P(B|A) = 0.75 \quad \left(\frac{75\%}{100\%} = 0.75\right).$$

Now, we use the multiplication rule to find $P(A \cap B)$ as follows:

$$P(A \cap B) = P(A)P(B|A) = (0.2)(0.75) = 0.15.$$

We can conclude that 15% of the patients with general health problems visited physician and used medication.

Independent Events

There are three cases in a conditional probability for occurrence of A if B is given:

(i) $P(A|B) > P(A)$
     (given B increases the probability of occurrence of A),
(ii) $P(A|B) < P(A)$
     (given B decreases the probability of occurrence of A), and
(iii) $P(A|B) = P(A)$
     (given B has no effect on the probability of occurrence of A). In this case, A is independent of B.

Independent Events: Two events A and B are independent if one of the following conditions is satisfied:

(i) $P(A|B) = P(A)$,
(ii) $P(B|A) = P(B)$, and
(iii) $P(B \cap A) = P(A)P(B)$.

Note: The third condition is the multiplication rule of independent events.

Example 3.9 Suppose that A and B are two events such that

$$P(A) = 0.5, \quad P(B) = 0.6, \quad P(A \cap B) = 0.2.$$

These two events are not independent because

$$P(A)P(B) = 0.5 \times 0.6 = 0.3,$$
$$P(A \cap B) = 0.2,$$
$$P(A \cap B) \neq P(A)P(B).$$

Also,

$$P(A) = 0.5 \neq P(A|B) = \frac{P(A \cap B)}{P(B)} = \frac{0.2}{0.6} = 0.3333 \text{ and}$$

$$P(B) = 0.6 \neq P(B|A) = \frac{P(A \cap B)}{P(A)} = \frac{0.2}{0.5} = 0.4.$$

For this example, we may calculate probabilities of all events.

We can use a two-way table of the probabilities as follows:

	B	$\overline{B}$	Total
A	0.2	?	0.5
$\overline{A}$	?	?	?
Total	0.6	?	1.00

We complete Table 3.8:

$$P(\overline{A}) = 0.5$$
$$P(\overline{B}) = 0.4$$
$$P(A \cap \overline{B}) = 0.3$$
$$P(\overline{A} \cap B) = 0.4$$
$$P(\overline{A} \cap \overline{B}) = 0.1$$
$$P(A \cup B) = P(A) + P(B) - P(A \cap B) = 0.5 + 0.6 - 0.2 = 0.9$$
$$P(A \cup \overline{B}) = P(A) + P(\overline{B}) - P(A \cap \overline{B}) = 0.5 + 0.4 - 0.3 = 0.6.$$

The Addition Rule for Independent Events
If the events A and B are independent, then

$$P(A \cup B) = P(A) + P(B) - P(A \cap B)$$
$$= P(A) + P(B) - P(A)P(B).$$

Example 3.10 Suppose that 12 patients admitted with fever (F = high fever, $\overline{F}$ = low fever) in a hospital are selected randomly and asked their opinion about whether they were satisfied with the services in the hospital (S = satisfied, $\overline{S}$ = not satisfied). The table below summarizes the data.

	F (high fever)	$\overline{F}$ (low fever)	Total
S (satisfied)	2	1	3
$\overline{S}$ (not satisfied)	6	3	9
Total	8	4	12

The experiment is to randomly choose one of these patients. Consider the following events:

Table 3.8 A two-way table displaying probabilities

	B	$\overline{B}$	Total
A	0.2	0.3	0.5
$\overline{A}$	0.4	0.1	0.5
Total	0.6	0.4	1.00

S = satisfied with service and
F = high fever.

(a) Find the probabilities of the following events:

1. the chosen patient is satisfied with service in the hospital,
2. the chosen patient is suffering from high fever,
3. the chosen patient is satisfied with service and suffering from high fever, and
4. the chosen patient is satisfied with service and is not suffering from high fever.

(b) Find the probability of choosing a patient who is suffering from high fever given that the patient has high fever.
(c) Are the events S and F independent? Why?
(d) Are the events S and F disjoint? Why?

Solution

(a) The experiment has $n = 12$.
    P(patient is satisfied with service)

$$P(S) = \frac{n(S)}{n} = \frac{3}{12} = 0.25.$$

P(patient suffers from high fever)

$$P(F) = \frac{n(F)}{n} = \frac{8}{12} = 0.6667.$$

P(satisfied with service and suffers from high fever)

$$P(S \cap F) = \frac{n(S \cap F)}{n} = \frac{2}{12} = 0.16667.$$

P(satisfied with service and does not suffer from high fever)

$$P(S \cap \overline{F}) = \frac{n(S \cap \overline{F})}{n} = \frac{1}{12} = 0.0833.$$

(b) The probability of selecting a patient who suffers from high fever given that the patient is satisfied with service is

$$P(F|S) = \frac{P(S \cap F)}{P(S)} = \frac{2/12}{0.25} = 0.6667.$$

(c) The events S and F are independent because $P(F|S) = P(F)$.
(d) The events S and F are not disjoint because $S \cap F \neq \phi, n(S \cap F) = 2$.

3.6 Conditional Probability, Bayes' Theorem, and Applications

Bayes' theorem gives a posterior probability using the estimate used for a prior probability. This procedure is performed using the concept of the conditional probability. Let us consider that there are two states regarding the disease and two states stating the result of a test then the outcomes are

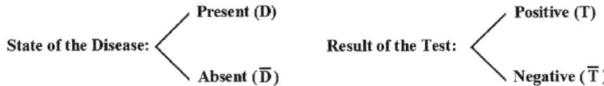

We define the following events:

D: the individual has the disease (presence of the disease),
$\overline{D}$: the individual does not have the disease (absence of the disease),
T: the individual has a positive screening test result, and
$\overline{T}$: the individual has a negative screening test result.

There are four possible situations as shown in the following table:

		Status of the disease	
		+ve (D: Present)	−ve ($\overline{D}$: Absent)
Result of the test	+ve (T)	Correct diagnosis	False positive result
	−ve ($\overline{T}$)	False-negative result	Correct diagnosis

We are interested in the true status of the disease for given test result which is a posterior probability. This is essentially a conditional probability, for instance, probability of being suffered from disease for the given fact that the screening test result shows positive. On the other hand, the estimate of the prevalence of the disease in the population may be considered as the prior probability which is a marginal probability and does not depend on any other condition. This helps us to understand or confirm how good the true status of the disease is for a given test result.

There are two false results that can happen in an experiment concerning disease status and test results.

1. **A false-positive** result: This is defined by a conditional probability

$$P(T|\overline{D}) = P(\text{positive result}|\text{absence of the disease})$$

and this result happens when a test shows a positive status if the true status is known to be negative.

2. **A false-negative** result: The false negative can be defined by the following conditional probability:

$$P(\overline{T}|D) = P(\text{negative result}|\text{presence of the disease}),$$

where the conditional probability states that a test shows a negative status; however, the true status is known to be positive.

Two Important Measures: The Sensitivity and Specificity of a Test

1. **The Sensitivity**: The conditional probability of a positive test given that the disease status is the presence of disease is

$$P(T|D) = P(\text{positive result of the test}|\text{presence of the disease}),$$

which is known as sensitivity of a test.
2. **The specificity**: The specificity is defined as

$$P(\overline{T}|\overline{D}) = P(\text{negative result of the test}|\text{absence of the disease}),$$

which is the probability of a negative test result given the absence of the disease.

To clarify these concepts, suppose we have a sample of (n) subjects who are cross-classified according to disease status and screening test result (Table 3.9).

For example, there are "a" subjects who have the disease and whose screening test result was positive.

From this table, we may compute the following conditional probabilities:

1. The probability of false-positive result

$$P(T|\overline{D}) = \frac{n(T \cap \overline{D})}{n(\overline{D})} = \frac{b}{b+d}.$$

2. The probability of false negative result

$$P(\overline{T}|D) = \frac{n(\overline{T} \cap D)}{n(D)} = \frac{c}{a+c}.$$

Table 3.9 Table displaying test result and true status of disease

Test result	Disease		
	Present (D)	Absent ($\overline{D}$)	Total
Positive (T)	a	b	$a + b = n$ (T)
Negative ($\overline{T}$)	c	d	$c + d = n$ ($\overline{T}$)
Total	$a + c = n$ (D)	$b + d = n$ ($\overline{D}$)	n

3. The sensitivity of the screening test

$$P(T|D) = \frac{n(T \cap D)}{n(D)} = \frac{a}{a+c}.$$

4. The specificity of the screening test

$$P(\overline{T}|\overline{D}) == \frac{n(\overline{T} \cap \overline{D})}{n(\overline{D})} = \frac{d}{b+d}.$$

The following conditional probabilities are used in biostatistics very extensively.

The predictive value positive: The predictive value positive is defined as the conditional probability

$$P(D|T) = P(\text{the subject has the disease}|\text{positive result}),$$

where the conditional probability states the chance of a subject has the disease given that the subject has a positive test result.

The predictive value negative: The predictive value negative is defined as the conditional probability

$$P(\overline{D}|\overline{T}) = P(\text{the subject does not have the disease}|\text{negative result}),$$

where the conditional probability states chance of a subject does not have the disease, given that the subject has a negative test result.

We calculate these conditional probabilities using the knowledge of the following:

1. The sensitivity of the test $= P(T|D)$,
2. The specificity of the test $= P(\overline{T}|\overline{D})$, and
3. The probability of the relevant disease in the general population, $P(D)$. It is usually obtained from another independent study or source.

We know that

$$P(D|T) = \frac{P(T \cap D)}{P(T)}.$$

Using the rules of probability, we have defined earlier, it can be shown that

$$P(T) = P(T \cap D) + P(T \cap \overline{D}),$$
$$P(T \cap D) = P(T|D)P(D),$$
$$P(T \cap \overline{D}) = P(T|\overline{D})P(\overline{D}),$$
$$P(T) = P(T|D)P(D) + P(T|\overline{D})P(\overline{D}).$$

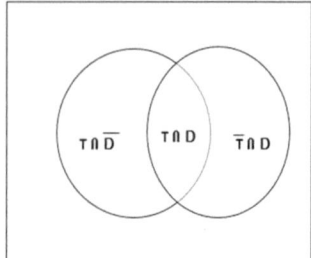

Therefore, we reach the following version of Bayes' theorem:

$$P(D|T) = \frac{P(T|D)P(D)}{P(T|D)P(D) + P(T|\overline{D})P(\overline{D})}.$$

It is noteworthy that

$P(T|D) = $ sensitivity,

$P(T|\overline{D}) = 1 - P(\overline{T}|\overline{D}) = 1-$specificity,
$P(D) = $ The probability of the relevant disease in the general population,

$$P(\overline{D}) = 1 - P(D).$$

To compute the predictive value negative of a test, we use the following statement of Bayes' theorem:

$$P(\overline{D}|\overline{T}) = \frac{P(\overline{T}|\overline{D})P(\overline{D})}{P(\overline{T}|\overline{D})P(\overline{D}) + P(\overline{T}|D)P(D)}.$$

It may be noted that $P(\overline{T}|\overline{D}) = $ specificity and $P(\overline{T}|D) = 1 - P(T|D) = 1 - $ sensitivity.

Example 3.11 Let us consider a study to examine the relationship between disease and a screening test result. Two samples were drawn from the population, one for the patients with symptoms of disease and another sample without symptoms of the disease. For both the samples, the screening tests were performed in order to confirm the disease status. The results are summarized in Table 3.10.

Based on another independent study, it is known that the percentage of patients with disease (the rate of prevalence of the disease) is 8 per 100.

Table 3.10 Table displaying test result and status of disease for the respondents with or without symptoms of a disease

	Disease status		
Test result	Present (D)	Absent ($\overline{D}$)	Total
Positive (T)	950	20	970
Negative ($\overline{T}$)	50	980	1030
Total	1000	1000	2000

Solution

Using these data, we estimate the following probabilities:

1. The sensitivity of the test

$$P(T|D) = \frac{n(T \cap D)}{n(D)} = \frac{950}{1000} = 0.95.$$

2. The specificity of the test:

$$P(\overline{T}|\overline{D}) = \frac{n(\overline{T} \cap \overline{D})}{n(\overline{D})} = \frac{980}{1000} = 0.98.$$

3. The probability of the disease in the general population, $P(D)$.

   The rate of disease in the relevant general population, $P(D)$, cannot be computed from the sample data given in the table. However, it is estimated from a different study that 8% of the population suffered from the disease. Therefore, $P(D)$ can be estimated as

$$P(D) = \frac{8\%}{100\%} = 0.08.$$

4. The predictive value positive of the test.

   We wish to estimate the probability that a subject who is positive on the test has the disease. We use the Bayes' theorem as follows:

$$P(D|T) = \frac{P(T|D)P(D)}{P(T|D)P(D) + P(T|\overline{D})P(\overline{D})}.$$

From the data displayed in table, we compute

$$P(T|D) = \frac{950}{1000} = 0.95, \text{ and}$$

$$P(T|\overline{D}) = \frac{n(T \cap \overline{D})}{n(\overline{D})} = \frac{20}{1000} = 0.02.$$

Substituting these results, we get

$$P(D|T) = \frac{(0.95)P(D)}{(0.95)P(D) + (0.02)P(\overline{D})}$$

$$= \frac{(0.95)(0.08)}{(0.95)(0.08) + (0.02)(1 - 0.08)} = 0.81.$$

As we see, in this case, the predictive value positive of the test is moderately high.

5. The predictive value negative of the test

We wish to estimate the probability that a subject who is negative on the test does not have the disease. Using the Bayes' formula, we obtain

$$P(\overline{D}|\overline{T}) = \frac{P(\overline{T}|\overline{D})P(\overline{D})}{P(\overline{T}|\overline{D})P(\overline{D}) + P(\overline{T}|D)P(D)}.$$

To compute $P(\overline{D}|\overline{T})$, we first compute the following probabilities:

$$P(\overline{T}|\overline{D}) = \frac{980}{1000} = 0.98,$$
$$P(\overline{D}) = 1 - P(D) = 1 - 0.08 = 0.92,$$
$$P(\overline{T}|D) = \frac{n(\overline{T} \cap D)}{n(D)} = \frac{50}{1000} = 0.05.$$

Substituting these values, we find

$$P(\overline{D}|\overline{T}) = \frac{P(\overline{T}|\overline{D})P(\overline{D})}{P(\overline{T}|\overline{D})P(\overline{D}) + P(\overline{T}|D)P(D)}$$
$$= \frac{(0.98)(0.92)}{(0.98)(0.92) + (0.05)(0.08)}$$
$$= 0.996.$$

As we see, the predictive value negative is very high.

3.7 Summary

The basic probability concepts are introduced in this chapter. It has been mentioned in Chap. 1 that probability plays a vital role to link the measures based on samples to the corresponding population values. The concept of random sampling provides the foundation for such links that depend on the concepts of probability. The definitions of probability along with experiment, sample space, event, equally likely, and mutually exclusive outcomes are highlighted. The important operations on events are discussed with examples. The concepts of marginal and conditional probabilities are discussed in a self-explanatory manner with several examples. The multiplication rules of probability and the concept of independent events are introduced in this chapter. The applications of conditional probability and Bayes' theorem in analyzing epidemiological data are shown. The measures of sensitivity and specificity of tests are illustrated with examples.

Exercises

3.1 Three patients are selected at random from a hospital. Consider that at each draw it is equally likely that the randomly drawn patient can be either male (*M*) or female (*F*).

    (i) Write the elements of the sample space.

    (ii) Write the elements corresponding to the event E = at least one of the selected patients is female.

    (iii) Define the event for the subset of sample space containing two male patients.

    (iv) Define the subset of sample space containing only male patients.

3.2 In Question 3.1, specify three patients by number of male patients out of three randomly selected patients.

    (i) Write the elements of the sample space.

    (ii) Define the subspace of the sample space corresponding to the event E_1 = two or more male patients.

    (iii) Define the subspace of the space corresponding to the event E_2 = less than two male patients.

    (iv) Define the subspace of the sample space corresponding to the event E_3 = three male patients.

3.3 Define the subspace of the sample space defined in Question 3.2 for the following events:

    (i) $E_1 \cup E_2$,

    (ii) $E_1 \cup E_3$,

    (iii) $E_2 \cap E_3$,

    (iv) $E_1 \cup E_2 \cup E_3$,

    (v) $(E_1 \cup E_2) \cap E_3$, and

    (vi) $(E_1 \cap E_3) \cup E_2$.

3.4 Define the subspace of the sample space defined in Question 3.2 for the following events:

    (i) $\bar{E}_1 \cup \bar{E}_2$,

    (ii) $\bar{E}_1 \cup \bar{E}_3$,

    (iii) $\bar{E}_1 \cap E_3$,

    (iv) $\bar{E}_2 \cap \bar{E}_3$,

    (v) $(\bar{E}_1 \cap \bar{E}_2) \cup E_3$, and

    (vi) $(\bar{E}_1 \cap \bar{E}_2) \cap E_3$.

3.5 For sample space of Exercise 3.2, find the following probabilities:

    (i) $P(E_1), P(E_2)$ and $P(E_3)$,

    (ii) $P(E_1 \cup E_2)$,

(iii) $P(E_1 \cup \overline{E}_3)$,
(iv) $P(E_1 \cap E_3)$,
(v) $P(\overline{E}_2 \cap \overline{E}_3)$,
(vi) $P(E_1 \cup E_2 \cup E_3)$,
(vii) $P[(\overline{E}_1 \cup E_2) \cap E_3]$, and
(viii) $P[(E_1 \cap E_3) \cup E_2]$.

3.6 The following table shows a hypothetical bivariate representation of 100,000 pregnant women by maternal age (A) and pregnancy-related deaths (B) in a community.

Maternal age in years (A)	Pregnancy-related deaths or survival (B)		Total
	Survived (B_1)	Died (B_2)	
<20 (A_1)	19,989	11	20,000
20–39 (A_2)	59,910	90	60,000
40–49 (A_3)	19,993	7	20,000
Total	99,892	108	100,000

Find the following probabilities:

(i) $P(A_1), P(A_2)$, and $P(A_3)$.
(ii) $P(B_1)$ and $P(B_2)$.
(iii) $P(B_2|A_1), P(B_2|A_2)$ and $P(B_2|A_3)$.
(iv) $P(B_1|A_1), P(B_1|A_2)$ and $P(B_1|A_3)$.
(v) Comment on your findings about pregnancy-related deaths and maternal age for the community.

3.7 In a study on incidence of common flu among the students of a university. Suppose the study was conducted on 200 male and female students during a semester. The data are summarized in the following table:

Gender of students (A)	Incidence of flu during semester (B)		Total
	Yes (Y)	No (N)	
Male (M)	15	85	100
Female (F)	20	80	100
Total	35	165	200

Suppose we pick a subject randomly from this group. Then, answer the following questions:

(i) Find $P(M \cap Y)$.
(ii) Find $P(\overline{M} \cap \overline{Y})$.

(iii) Find the probabilities $P(F)$ and $P(Y)$.
(iv) Find the probability $P(M \cup N)$.
(v) Find $P(Y|F)$ and $P(N|M)$.
(vi) Are the events Y and F independent?

3.8 Let us consider the following sample space and events:

$$\Omega = \{1, 2, 3, 4, 5, 6\}$$
$$E_1 = \{4, 5, 6\}$$
$$E_2 = \{1, 2, 3\}$$
$$E_3 = \{1, 2, 5, 6\}.$$

Find the following:

(i) $P(E_1), P(E_2), P(E_3)$.
(ii) $P(\overline{E_1}), P(\overline{E_3})$.
(iii) $P(E_1 \cap E_2), P(E_2 \cap E_3)$.
(iv) $P(\overline{E_1 \cap E_2})$.
(v) $P(E_1 \cup E_2), P(E_2 \cup E_3)$.

3.9 Suppose that the relationship between the performance of service in a hospital and whether the work is at day (D), night (N), or rotating shift (R) is of interest for a hospital administration. A hypothetical data set of 150 hospital workers is presented in the following table.

Shift	Performance of service		
	Poor (P)	Average (A)	Superior (S)
Day (D)	12	16	12
Night (N)	18	30	12
Rotating (R)	23	23	4

Calculate the probability that a worker selected at random

(i) Worked at night shift.
(ii) Performed of service is superior.
(iii) Performed average and served at day shift.
(iv) Performed poor given that the shift is rotating.
(v) Performed superior given that the shift is day.
(vi) Are the events poor performance and day shift independent?

3.10 The following data show the results obtained in a screening test for a disease on 10,000 persons based on a cross-sectional study.

Test result	True diagnosis	
	Disease	No disease
Positive	120	100
Negative	40	9740

Compute the following:

(i)   Probability that a randomly selected individual is having test result positive and true diagnosis diabetic.
(ii) Probability that a randomly selected individual is diabetic (true diagnosis).
(iii) Probability that an individual with negative test result (given) is truly diabetic.
(iv) Are the test results and true diagnosis independent?

3.11 Use the data given in Question 3.10 to answer the following:

(i)   sensitivity,
(ii) specificity,
(iii) false positive,
(iv) false negative,
(v)   predictive value positive, and
(vi) predictive value negative.

Reference

Mangasarian, O. L., Setiono, R., & Wolberg, W. H. (1990). Pattern recognition via linear programming: Theory and application to medical diagnosis. In T. F. Coleman & Y. Li (Eds.), *Large-scale numerical optimization* (pp. 22–30). Philadelphia: SIAM Publications.

Chapter 4
Probability Distributions: Discrete

4.1 Introduction

The concept of random variables plays a pivotal role in statistics. A variable is called a random variable if the value that the variable assumes in a given experiment is a chance or random outcome which cannot be known before the experiment is conducted. Some events can be defined using random variables.

There are two types of random variables: (i) discrete random variables, and (ii) continuous random variables. If observations on a quantitative random variable can assume only a countable number of values then the variable is defined as a discrete random variable. On the other hand, if observations on a quantitative random variable can assume any value from an interval, then the variable is defined as a continuous random variable.

We need to know the probability of observing a particular sample outcome in order to make any inference about the population from which the sample is drawn. This necessitates the knowledge about the probability of each outcome of the variable under consideration. It may be noted here that the relative frequencies provide the empirical foundation of the theoretical probability distribution of the underlying variable.

4.2 Probability Distributions for Discrete Random Variables

The probability distribution for a discrete random variable shows the probability associated with each value of the discrete random variable. The relative frequency based on the sample data approximates the probability distribution for a large sample size. The main properties of a discrete random variable are: (i) the probability of every value of a variable lies between 0 and 1; (ii) the sum of all

© Springer Nature Singapore Pte Ltd. 2018
M. A. Islam and A. Al-Shiha, *Foundations of Biostatistics*,
https://doi.org/10.1007/978-981-10-8627-4_4

probabilities of the variable is equal to 1; and (iii) the probabilities of a discrete random variable are additive.

The probability distribution of a discrete variable, X, can be shown for different number of outcome values of the variable. Some examples are shown below:

(i) $P(X = x), x = 0, 1;$
(ii) $P(X = x), x = 0, 1, \ldots, k;$
(iii) $P(X = x), x = 0, 1, \ldots, \infty.$

Case (i) may arise from an experiment where there are only two outcomes such as success or failure, defective or non-defective, disease or disease-free, yes or no, etc. This type of a discrete variable may result from an experiment with two outcomes where the outcomes may be qualitative in nature representing a nominal scale but in this case, we consider this variable as discrete variable with binary outcomes. Case (ii) variable is also discrete with $(k + 1)$ outcomes ranging from 0 to k. A typical example of this type of discrete variables is number of successes in an experiment which may be considered as a generalization of a binary variable in Case (i). In other words, sum of binary variables may result in this type of discrete variables. Case (iii) variables may take values ranging from 0 to infinity. In reality, we may observe large values instead of infinity indicating that there may be small or large values and the outcome values are not restricted to a specified upper limit. Some examples are number of accidents in a city during a specified time interval, number of experiments needed to get the first success, number of experiments required to obtain the rth success, etc.

It can be shown that for the abovementioned probability distributions, the probabilities add to 1:

(i) $P(X = 0) + P(X = 1) = \sum_{x=0}^{1} P(X = x) = 1;$

(ii) $P(X = 0) + P(X = 1) + \cdots + P(X = k) = \sum_{x=0}^{k} P(X = x) = 1;$

(iii) $P(X = 0) + P(X = 1) + \cdots = \sum_{x=0}^{\infty} P(X = x) = 1.$

First one represents a binary outcome with possible outcomes 0 or 1, second one shows that there are $k + 1$ possible distinct outcome values ranging from 0, 1 to k, and the third one shows that the number of possible distinct values of outcome is not specified, it may be very large. However, under all these circumstances, the probabilities add to one.

Example 4.1 The data on number of daily injury accidents for a period is used in this example (Leiter and Hamdan 1973). Let us define the following discrete random variable X = the number of daily injury accidents in a day.

The frequency distribution of number of injury accidents is displayed in Table 4.1.

Table 4.1 Frequency distribution of number of injury accidents in a day

$X = x$ (number of accidents)	Frequency of $X = x$ (number of days)
0	286
1	216
2	92
3	30
4	14
5	1
Total	639

Note that the possible values of the random variable X are
$X = 0, 1, 2, 3, 4, 5$.
Experiment: Selecting a day at random
Define the events

$(X = 0)$ = The event that on the selected day there was no accident,
$(X = 1)$ = The event that on the selected day there was one accident,
$(X = 2)$ = The event that on the selected day there were 2 accidents,
$(X = 3)$ = The event that on the selected day there were 3 accidents,
$(X = 4)$ = The event that on the selected day there were 4 accidents,
$(X = 5)$ = The event that on the selected day there were 5 accidents.

In general
$(X = x)$ = the event that on the selected day there were x accidents.
Using the relative frequency definition, we know that $n = 639$.
The number of elements of the event $(X = x)$ is $n(X = x)$ = frequency of x.

$$n(X = x) = \text{frequency of } x.$$

The probability of the event $(X = x)$ is (Table 4.2)

$$P(X = x) = \frac{n(X = x)}{n} = \frac{n(X = x)}{639}, \quad \text{for } x = 0, 1, 2, 3, 4, 5.$$

We can show that

$$P(X = x) = \frac{n(X = x)}{639} = \text{relative frequency} = \frac{\text{frequency}}{639}$$

The probability distribution of the discrete random variable X is given in Table 4.3.

Table 4.2 Relative frequency of number of accidents in a day

$X = x$	Frequency of $X = x$ $n(X = x)$	$P(X = x) = \frac{n(X=x)}{639}$ (relative frequency)
0	286	0.4476
1	216	0.3380
2	92	0.1440
3	30	0.0469
4	14	0.0219
5	1	0.0016
Total	639	1.0000

Table 4.3 Probability distribution of number of accidents in a day

$X = x$	$P(X = x) = f(x)$
0	0.4476
1	0.3380
2	0.1440
3	0.0469
4	0.0219
5	0.0016
Total	1.0000

The probability distribution of any discrete random variable X must satisfy the following three properties:

(i) $0 \le P(X = x) \le 1$,
(ii) $\sum_x P(X = x) = 1$, and
(iii) the probabilities are additive,
      for example, $P(X = 2 \text{ or } X = 3) = P(X = 2) + P(X = 3)$.

Some examples

(i) $P(X \ge 2) = P(X = 2) + P(X = 3) + P(X = 4) + P(X = 5) = 0.1440 +$
      $0.0469 + 0.0219 + 0.0016 = 0.2144.$
(ii) $P(X > 2) = P(X = 3) + P(X = 4) + P(X = 5) = 0.0469 + 0.0219 + 0.0016 = 0.0704.$
      [note : $P(X > 2) \ne P(X \ge 2)$]
(iii) $P(1 \le X < 3) = P(X = 1) + P(X = 2) = 0.3380 + 0.1440 = 0.4820.$

(iv) $P(X \le 2) = P(X = 0) + P(X = 1) + P(X = 2)$
      $= 0.4476 + 0,3380 + 0.1440 = 0.9296.$

This can be solved alternatively using the following relationship:

$$P(X \le 2) = 1 - P((\overline{X \le 2}))$$
$$= 1 - P(X > 2) = 1 - P(X = 3) - P(X = 4) - P(X = 5)$$
$$= 1 - 0.0469 - 0.0219 - 0.0016 = 1 - 0.0704 = 0.9296.$$

(v) $P(-1 \leq X < 2) = P(X = 0) + P(X = 1) = 0.4476 + 0.3380 = 0.7856.$
(vi) $P(-1.5 \leq X < 1.3) = P(X = 0) + P(X = 1) = 0.4476 + 0.3380 = 0.7856.$
(vii) $P(X = 3.5) = 0$
(viii) $P(X \leq 10) = P(X = 0) + P(X = 1) + P(X = 2) + P(X = 3) + P(X = 4) + P(X = 5) = P(\Omega) = 1$
(ix)   The probability that on the selected day there were at least 2 accidents

$$P(X \geq 2) = P(X = 2) + P(X = 3) + P(X = 4) + P(X = 5)$$
$$= 0.1440 + 0.0469 + 0.0219 + 0.0016 = 0.2144.$$

(x)   The probability that on the selected day there were at most 2 accidents

$$P(X \leq 2) = P(X = 0) + P(X = 1) + P(X = 2)$$
$$= 0.4476 + 0,3380 + 0.1440 = 0.9296.$$

(xi)   The probability that on the selected day there were more than 2 accidents

$$P(X > 2) = P(X = 3) + P(X = 4) + P(X = 5)$$
$$= 0.0469 + 0.0219 + 0.0016 = 0.0704.$$

(xii) The probability that on the selected day there were less than 2 accidents

$$P(X < 2) = P(X = 0) + P(X = 1) = 0.4476 + 0.3380 = 0.7856.$$

Graphical Presentation
The probability distribution of a discrete r. v. X can be graphically represented.

Example 4.2 The probability distribution of the random variable in the previous example is

$X = x$	$P(X = x) = f(x)$
0	0.4476
1	0.3380
2	0.1440
3	0.0469
4	0.0219
5	0.0016
Total	1.0000

The graphical presentation of this probability distribution is given in Fig. 4.1.

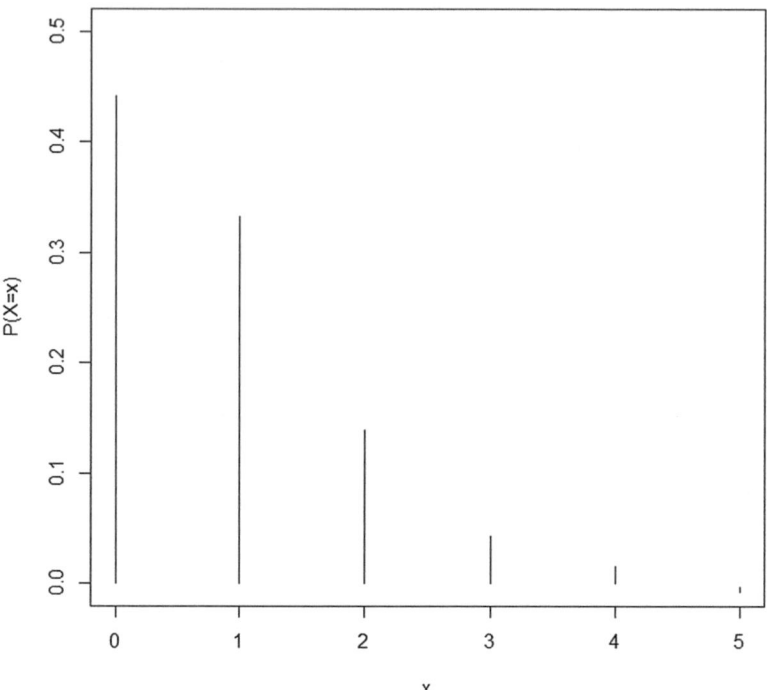

Fig. 4.1 Figure displaying probabilities of number of accidents

4.3 Expected Value and Variance of a Discrete Random Variable

The population mean and variance are introduced in Chap. 2. It is shown in Chap. 2 that if we use all the population values, then the population mean and variance can be defined. In this section, the population mean and variance are defined using corresponding probabilities of a variable. The population mean is defined as the expected value of a variable and it can be expressed as follows:

The population mean or expected value of a discrete random variable X is denoted by μ or μ_X and it is defined by

$$E(X) = \mu = \sum_x x P(X = x).$$

Similarly, the population variance of a discrete random variable X is denoted by σ^2 or σ_X^2 and it is defined by

$$\text{Var}(X) = E(X - \mu)^2 = \sigma^2 = \sum_x (x - \mu)^2 P(X = x).$$

An alternative expression for the variance of a variable, X, is

$$\text{Var}(X) = E(X - \mu)^2 = \sigma^2 = E(X^2) - [E(X)]^2,$$

where

$$E(X) = \mu \quad \text{and} \quad E(X^2) = \sum_x x^2 P(X = x).$$

Example 4.3 We wish to calculate the mean μ and the variance σ^2 of the discrete random variable X whose probability distribution is given by the following table:

x	$P(X = x)$
0	0.05
1	0.25
2	0.45
3	0.25

Solution

X	$P(X = x)$	$x\,P(X = x)$	$(x - \mu)$	$(x - \mu)^2$	$(x - \mu)^2$ $P(X = x)$
0	0.05	0	−1.9	3.61	0.1805
1	0.25	0.25	−0.9	0.81	0.2025
2	0.45	0.9	0.1	0.01	0.0045
3	0.25	0.75	1.1	1.21	0.3025
Total		$\mu = \sum x\,P(X = x) = 1.9$			$\sigma^2 = \sum (x - \mu)^2$ $P(X = x) = 0.69$

$$\mu = \sum_x x\,P(X = x) = (0)(0.05) + (1)(0.25) + (2)(0.45) + (3)(0.25) = 1.9$$

$$\sigma^2 = \sum_x (x - 1.9)^2\,P(X = x)$$
$$= (0 - 1.9)^2(0.05) + (1 - 1.9)^2(0.25) + (2 - 1.9)^2(0.45) + (3 - 1.9)^2(0.25)$$
$$= 0.69.$$

Alternatively, we can use the following table to find the variance of X:

X	$P(X=x)$	$x\,P(X=x)$	x^2	$x^2 P(X=x)$
0	0.05	0	0	0
1	0.25	0.25	1	0.25
2	0.45	0.9	4	1.80
3	0.25	0.75	9	2.25
Total		$\mu = \sum x\,P(X=x) = 1.9$		$\sum x^2 P(X=x)$ $= 4.30$

$$\text{Var}(X) = E(X-\mu)^2 = \sigma^2 = E(X^2) - [E(X)]^2 = 4.30 - 1.9^2 = 0.69.$$

Cumulative Distributions

The cumulative distribution function of a discrete random variable, X, is defined by

$$F(x) = P(X \le x) = \sum_{a \le x} P(X=a) \quad (\text{Sum over all values} \le x)$$

and this is denoted by $F(x)$.

Example 4.4 Calculate the cumulative distribution of the discrete random variable, X, with probability distribution given in the following table:

x	$P(X=x)$
0	0.05
1	0.25
2	0.45
3	0.25

Let us use the cumulative distribution to find

$$P(X \le 2), P(X<2), P(X \le 1.5), P(X<1.5), P(X>1), P(X \ge 1)$$

Solution

The cumulative distribution of X is

x	$P(X \le x)$	
0	0.05	$P(X \le 0) = P(X=0)$
1	0.30	$P(X \le 1) = P(X=0) + P(X=1)$
2	0.75	$P(X \le 2) = P(X=0) + P(X=1) + P(X=2)$
3	1.00	$P(X \le 3) = P(X=0) + \cdots + P(X=3)$

Using the cumulative distribution, the probabilities are

$$P(X \leq 2) = 0.75$$
$$P(X < 2) = P(X \leq 1) = 0.30$$
$$P(X \leq 1.5) = P(X \leq 1) = 0.30$$
$$P(X < 1.5) = P(X \leq 1) = 0.30$$
$$P(X > 1) = 1 - P\left(\overline{(X > 1)}\right) = 1 - P(X \leq 1) = 1 - 0.30 = 0.70$$
$$P(X \geq 1) = 1 - P\left(\overline{(X \geq 1)}\right) = 1 - P(X < 1) = 1 - P(X \leq 0)$$
$$= 1 - 0.05 = 0.95.$$

Example 4.5 Let us consider the following probability distribution for the variable X = number of children died to a mother in a village community from hypothetical relative frequencies.

x	Frequency	$P(X = x)$ Relative frequency
0	79	0.65
1	27	0.22
2	10	0.08
3	4	0.03
4	2	K
Total	122	1

(a) Find the value of K.
(b) Find the following probabilities:

    1. $P(X < 3)$
    2. $P(X \leq 3)$
    3. $P(X < 5)$
    4. $P(X < 1)$
    5. $P(X = 3.5)$

(c) Find the probability that a mother has lost at least two children.
(d) Find the probability that a mother has lost at most two children.
(e) Find the expected number of children died.
(f) Find the variance of X.

Solution

(a) $1 = \sum P(X = x) = 0.65 + 0.22 + 0.08 + 0.03 + K$

$1 = 0.98 + K$

$K = 1 - 0.98$

$K = 0.02$

The probability distribution of X is:

X	$P(X = x)$
0	0.65
1	0.22
2	0.08
3	0.03
4	0.02

(b) Finding the probabilities:

1. $P(X<3) = P(X = 0) + P(X = 1) + P(X = 2) = 0.65 + 0.22 + 0.08 = 0.95$
2. $P(X \leq 3) = P(X = 0) + P(X = 1) + P(X = 2) + P(X = 3) = 0.65 + 0.22 + 0.08 + 0.03 = 0.98$
3. $P(X<5) = P(X = 1) + P(X = 2) + P(X = 3) + P(X = 4) = P(\Omega) = 1$
4. $P(X<1) = P(X = 0) = 0.65$
5. $P(X = 3.5) = P(\phi) = 0$

(c) The probability that the mother has lost at least two children

$$P(X \geq 2) = P(X = 2) + P(X = 3) + P(X = 4) = 0.08 + 0.03 + 0.02 = 0.13$$

(d) The probability that the mother has lost at most two children

$$P(X \leq 2) = P(X = 0) + P(X = 1) + P(X = 2) = 0.65 + 0.22 + 0.08 = 0.95$$

(e) The expected number of children died

X	$P(X = x)$	$xP(X = x)$
0	0.65	0
1	0.22	0.22
2	0.08	0.16
3	0.03	0.09
4	0.02	0.08
Total	$\sum P(X = x) = 1$	$\mu = \sum x P(X = x) = 0.55$

The expected number of children died (mean of X) is

$$\mu = E(X) = 0 \times 0.65 + 1 \times 0.22 + 2 \times 0.08 + 3 \times 0.03 + 4 \times 0.02 = 0.55$$

(f) The variance of X: The following table displays the computation of population variance using relative frequency as probability.

X	$P(X=x)$	$(x-\mu)$	$(x-\mu)^2$	$(x-\mu)^2 P(X=x)$
0	0.65	−0.55	0.3025	0.1966
1	0.22	0.45	0.2025	0.0446
2	0.08	1.45	2.1025	0.1682
3	0.03	2.45	6.0025	0.1801
4	0.02	3.45	11.9025	0.2381
Total	1.00			$\sigma^2 = \sum (x-\mu)^2 P(X=x) = 0.8276$

The variance is $\sigma^2 = \sum (x - \mu)^2 P(X = x) = 0.8276$.

4.4   Combinations

Notation (n!):$n!$ is read "n factorial". It is defined by

$$n! = n(n-1)(n-2)\ldots(2)(1) \quad \text{for } n \geq 1$$

and for zero it is defined as

$$0! = 1.$$

Example: $5! = (5)(4)(3)(2)(1) = 120$
The number of different ways for selecting r objects from n distinct objects is denoted by $_nC_r$ or $\begin{pmatrix} n \\ r \end{pmatrix}$ and is given by

$$_nC_r = \frac{n!}{r!(n-r)!}; \quad \text{for } r = 0, 1, 2, \ldots, n$$

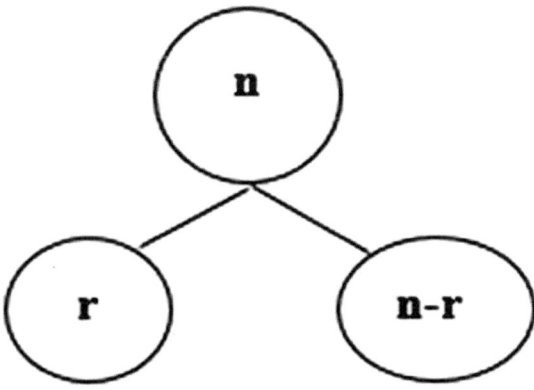

Notes:

1. $_nC_r$ is read as "n" choose "r".
2. $_nC_n = 1$, $_nC_0 = 1$,
3. $_nC_r = {}_nC_{n-r}$ (for example: $_{10}C_3 = {}_{10}C_7$
4. $_nC_r$ = number of unordered subsets of a set of (n) objects such that each subset contains (r) objects.

Example 4.6 For $n = 4$ and $r = 2$,

$$_4C_2 = \frac{4!}{2!(4-2)!} = \frac{4!}{2! \times 2!} = \frac{4 \times 3 \times 2 \times 1}{(2 \times 1) \times (2 \times 1)} = 6$$

$_4C_2 = 6$ = the number of different ways for selecting 2 objects from 4 distinct objects.

Example 4.7 Suppose that we have the set $\{a, b, c, d\}$ of ($n = 4$) objects.

We wish to choose a subset of two objects. The possible subsets of this set with two elements in each subset are

$$\{a,b\}, \{a,c\}, \{a,d\}, \{b,d\}, \{b,c\}, \{c,d\}$$

The number of these subsets is $_4C_2 = 6$.

4.5   Bernoulli Distribution

The Bernoulli distribution arises from a trial with two possible outcomes which are termed traditionally as success or failure. Each trial with two outcomes may be considered as a Bernoulli trial. The probabilities of success or failure are complementary to each other so that if the probability of success is denoted by p then the probability of failure is $1 - p$, where p satisfies $0 \leq p \leq 1$. One very familiar example is if we randomly draw an individual then the selected individual may or may not suffer from a disease at the time of survey with probability p of suffering from the disease and with probability $1 - p = q$ of not suffering from the disease. In that case, $p + q = 1$. A Bernoulli process consists of n repeated Bernoulli trials where trials are independent with a constant probability of success, p. The Bernoulli distribution plays a very important role in biostatistics and epidemiology.

The Bernoulli variable, X, is a binary variable with discrete probability mass function as shown below

$$f(x,p) = P(X = x) = \begin{cases} p^x(1-p)^{1-x} & \text{for } x = 0,1 \\ 0 & \text{otherwise.} \end{cases}$$

Here the parameter of the Bernoulli distribution is p which implies that if p is known then the probability distribution is completely specified.

The expected value and the variance of a Bernoulli variable X are

$$E(X) = \mu = p,$$
$$\text{Var}(X) = p(1 - p).$$

Example 4.8 In a study on reproductive health conducted in a rural area, question was asked to the women with their last pregnancy whether a pregnant woman had weight taken during the time of antenatal care visit. If the response was yes then the variable is defined as $X = 1$ for weight taken and $X = 0$ for weight not taken. Sample size is $n = 10$. The sample values of X are: 1, 1, 0, 1, 1, 1, 0, 1, 0, 1.

The frequency distribution table is displayed below

X	Frequency	Relative frequency
0	3	0.3
1	7	0.7
Total	10	1.0

Here $p = 0.7$ and $q = 1 - p = 0.3$ implying that weight was taken for 7 out of 10 women and weight was not taken for 3 out of 10 women. The expected value $E(X) = p = 0.7$ and the variance is $\text{Var}(X) = p(1 - p) = 0.7 \times 0.3 = 0.21$. It may be noted here that these relative frequencies are shown for a very small set of hypothetical data and with a large sample size, these relative frequencies will tend to corresponding true probabilities.

4.6   Binomial Distribution

Bernoulli Trial is an experiment with only two possible outcomes: S = success and F = failure (boy or girl, sick or well, dead or alive, etc.). Binomial distribution is a discrete distribution which is developed on the basis of a sequence of Bernoulli trials. Binomial distribution is used to model an experiment for which:

1. The experiment has a sequence of n Bernoulli trials.
2. The probability of success is $P(S) = p$, and the probability of failure is $P(F) = 1 - p = q$.
3. The probability of success $P(S) = p$ is constant for each trial.
4. The trials are independent, that is, the outcome of one trial has no effect on the outcome of any other trial.

In this type of experiment, we are interested in the discrete random variable representing the number of successes in the n trials.

Let X = number of successes in the n trials, then the possible values of X (number of success in n trails) are $x = 0, 1, 3, \ldots, n$.

The random variable, X, has a binomial distribution with parameters n and p, and we write $X \sim \text{Binomial}(n, p)$.

The probability distribution of X is given by

$$P(X = x) = \begin{cases} {}_nC_x p^x q^{n-x} & \text{for } x = 0, 1, 2, \ldots, n \\ 0 & \text{otherwise} \end{cases},$$

where ${}_nC_x = \frac{n!}{x!(n-x)!}$.

We can write the probability distribution of X as displayed in the following table:

X	$P(X = x)$
0	${}_nC_0\, p^0\, q^{n-0} = q^n$
1	${}_nC_1\, p^1\, q^{n-1}$
2	${}_nC_2\, p^2\, q^{n-2}$
$\vdots$	$\vdots$
n- 1	${}_nC_{n-1}\, p^{n-1}\, q^1$
n	${}_nC_n\, p^n\, q^0 = p^n$
Total	1

The Expected Value and the Variance of a Binomial Variable X

If $X \sim \text{Binomial}(n, p)$, then using expectations defined in the previous section, the expected value and the variance of a binomial variable X can be obtained.

The expected value or mean is $E(X) = \mu = np$ and the variance is $\text{Var}(X) = E(X - \mu)^2 = \sigma^2 = npq$.

Example 4.9 Suppose that the probability that an adult person is suffering from diabetes in a population is 0.10. Suppose that we randomly select a sample of 6 persons.

(1) Find the probability distribution of the random variable (X) representing the number of persons with diabetes in the sample.
(2) Find the expected number of persons with diabetes in the sample (mean of X).
(3) Find the variance of X.
(4) What is the probability that there will be exactly two persons with diabetes?
(5) What is the probability that there will be at most two persons with diabetes?
(6) What is the probability that there will be at least four persons with diabetes?

Solution

We are interested in the following random variable:

X = the number of persons with diabetes in the sample of six persons.

Notes:

(i)   Bernoulli trial: diagnosing whether a person has diabetes or not. There are two outcomes for each trial, diabetic (S) or nondiabetic (F).
(ii) Number of trials = 6 or $n = 6$.
(iii) Probability of success: $P(S) = p = 0.10$.
(iv) Probability of failure: $P(F) = q = 1 - p = 0.9$.
(v)   The trials are independent because of the fact that the result of each person does not affect the result of any other person since the selection was made at random.

The random variable, X, has a binomial distribution with parameters: $n = 6$ and $p = 0.10$, that is $X \sim$ Binomial (6, 0.10).
The possible values of X are $X = x$, where

$$x = 0, 1, 2, 3, 4, 5, 6.$$

(1) The probability distribution of X is

$$P(X = x) = \begin{cases} {}_6C_x(0.1)^x(0.9)^{6-x}; & x = 0, 1, 2, 3, 4, 5, 6 \\ 0; & \text{otherwise.} \end{cases}$$

The probabilities of all values of X are

$$P(X = 0) = {}_6C_0(0.1)^0(0.9)^6 = (1)(0.1)^0(0.9)^6 = 0.531441$$
$$P(X = 1) = {}_6C_1(0.1)^1(0.9)^5 = (6)(0.1)(0.9)^5 = 0.354294$$
$$P(X = 2) = {}_6C_2(0.1)^2(0.9)^4 = (15)(0.1)^2(0.9)^4 = 0.098415$$
$$P(X = 3) = {}_6C_3(0.1)^3(0.9)^3 = (20)(0.1)^3(0.9)^3 = 0.014580$$
$$P(X = 4) = {}_6C_4(0.1)^4(0.9)^2 = (15)(0.1)^4(0.9)^2 = 0.001215$$
$$P(X = 5) = {}_6C_5(0.1)^5(0.9)^1 = (6)(0.1)^5(0.9)^1 = 0.000054$$
$$P(X = 6) = {}_6C_6(0.1)^6(0.9)^0 = (1)(0.1)^6(1) = 0.000001$$

The probability distribution of X can be presented by the following table:

X	$P(X = x)$
0	0.531441
1	0.354294
2	0.098415
3	0.01458
4	0.001215
5	0.000054
6	0.000001

The probability distribution of X can be presented by the following graph (Fig. 4.2):

(2) The mean of the distribution (the expected number of men out of 6 with diabetes) is

$$\mu = np = (6)(0.1) = 0.6.$$

(3) The variance is

$$\sigma^2 = npq = (6)(0.1)(0.9) = 0.54.$$

(4) The probability that there will be exactly two men with diabetes is

$$P(X = 2) = 0.098415.$$

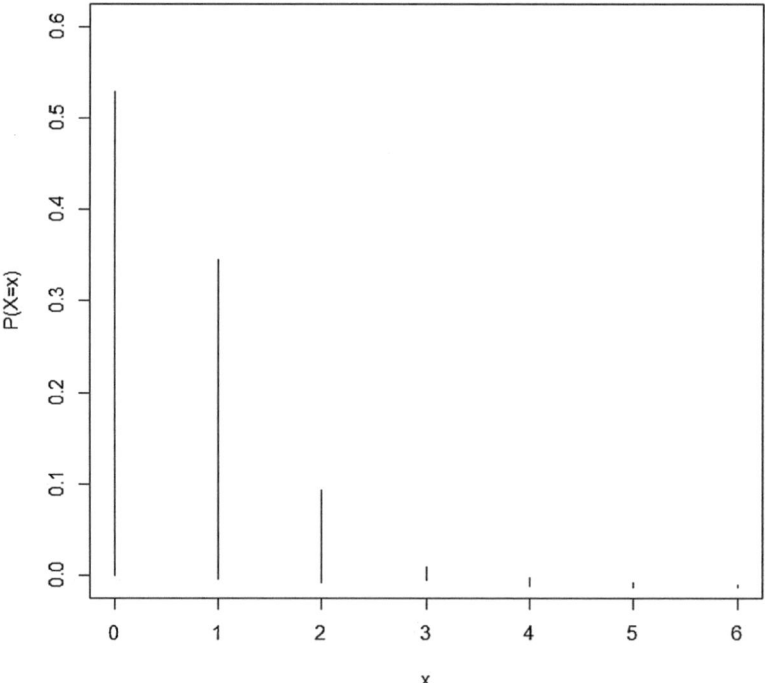

Fig. 4.2 Figure displaying binomial probabilities

(5) The probability that there will be at most two men with diabetes is

$$P(X \leq 2) = P(X = 0) + P(X = 1) + P(X = 2)$$
$$= 0.531441 + 0.354294 + 0.098415$$
$$= 0.98415.$$

(6) The probability that there will be at least four men with diabetes is

$$P(X \geq 4) = P(X = 4) + P(X = 5) + P(X = 6)$$
$$= 0.001215 + 0.000054 + 0.000001$$
$$= 0.00127.$$

Example 4.10 An experiment is conducted to select a sample of five patients admitted to the emergency care in a hospital randomly. Let the probability of selecting a patient with diabetes-related complications is 0.25. Here, the variable X denotes the number of patients admitted to the emergency care with diabetes-related complications. Then some of the typical questions relevant to the study can be outlined as follows:

(a) Find the probability distribution of X.
(b) Find the probability that at least two patients have diabetes-related complications.
(c) Find the probability that at most three patients have diabetes-related complications.
(d) Find the expected number of patients with diabetes-related complications.
(e) Find the variance of the number of patients with diabetes-related complications out of the five patients.

Solution
X = the number of patients out of five with diabetes-related complications
   The Bernoulli trial is the process of diagnosing the person with diabetes-related complications with
   p = probability of selecting a patient in emergency care with diabetes-related complications,
   $q = 1 - p$ = probability of selecting a patient in emergency care without diabetes-related complications.
   Here, $n = 5$ = number of patients selected randomly,

$$p = 0.25,$$

$$q = 1 - p = 0.75.$$

(a) X has a binomial distribution Binomial distribution with parameter $n = 5$ and $p = 0.25$ or $X \sim \text{Binomial}(5, 0.25)$.

The possible values of $X = x$ are $x = 0, 1, 2, 3, 4, 5$.
The probability distribution is

$$P(X = x) = \begin{cases} {}_nC_x p^x q^{n-x}; & \text{for } x = 0, 1, 2, \ldots, n \\ 0; & \text{otherwise} \end{cases}$$

$$P(X = x) = \begin{cases} {}_5C_x(0.25)^x(0.75)^{5-x}; & \text{for } x = 0, 1, 2, 3, 4, 5 \\ 0; & \text{otherwise} \end{cases}$$

X	$P(X = x)$
0	${}_5C_0 \times 0.25^0 \times 0.75^{5-0} = 0.23730$
1	${}_5C_1 \times 0.25^1 \times 0.75^{5-1} = 0.39551$
2	${}_5C_2 \times 0.25^2 \times 0.75^{5-2} = 0.26367$
3	${}_5C_3 \times 0.25^3 \times 0.75^{5-3} = 0.08789$
4	${}_5C_4 \times 0.25^4 \times 0.75^{5-4} = 0.01465$
5	${}_5C_5 \times 0.25^5 \times 0.75^{5-5} = 0.00098$
Total	$\sum P(X = x) = 1$

(b) The probability that at least two patients have diabetes-related complications is

$$\begin{aligned} P(X \geq 2) &= P(X = 2) + P(X = 3) + P(X = 4) + P(X = 5) \\ &= 0.26367 + 0.08789 + 0.01465 + 0.00098 \\ &= 0.36719. \end{aligned}$$

(c) The probability that at most three patients have diabetes-related complications is

$$\begin{aligned} P(X \leq 3) &= P(X = 0) + P(X = 1) + P(X = 2) + P(X = 3) \\ &= 0.23730 + 0.39551 + 0.26367 + 0.08789 \\ &= 0.98437. \end{aligned}$$

(d) The expected number of patients with diabetes-related complications out of the five patients is

$$\mu = np = 5 \times 0.25 = 1.25.$$

(e) The variance of the number of patients with diabetes-related complications is

$$\sigma^2 = npq = 5 \times 0.25 \times 0.75 = 0.93750.$$

4.7   The Poisson Distribution

The Poisson distribution is used to model a discrete random variable representing the number of occurrences or counts of some random events in an interval of time or space (or some volume of matter). The possible values of $X = x$ are $x = 0, 1, 2, 3, \ldots$

The discrete random variable, X, is said to have a Poisson distribution with parameter (average or mean) λ if the probability distribution of X is given by

$$P(X = x) = \begin{cases} \frac{e^{-\lambda}\lambda^x}{x!}; & \text{for } x = 0, 1, 2, 3, \ldots \\ 0; & \text{otherwise} \end{cases},$$

where $e = 2.71828$ (the natural number). We can write $X \sim$ Poisson (λ).

Mean and Variance of the Poisson Distribution

If $X \sim$ Poisson (λ), then it can be shown that the mean and variance are equal.

The expected value of X is $\mu = \lambda$, and the variance of X is $\sigma^2 = \lambda$.

Example 4.11 Some random quantities that can be modeled by Poisson distribution are

Note:

(i) λ is the expected value of the distribution.
(ii) If $X =$ the number of patients seen in the emergency unit in a day, and if $X \sim$ Poisson (λ), then

1. the expected value of patients seen every day in the emergency unit $= \lambda$,
2. the expected value of patients seen every month in the emergency unit $= 30\lambda$,
3. the expected value of patients seen every year in the emergency unit $= 365\lambda$, and
4. the expected value of patients seen every hour in the emergency unit $= \lambda/24$.

   (i)   number of patients in a waiting room in an hour,
   (ii) number of surgeries performed in a month,
   (iii) number of car accidents daily in a city,
   (iv) number of rats in each house in a particular city, etc.

Also, notice that

(i)   If $Y =$ the number of patients seen every month, then
      $Y \sim$ Poisson (λ^*), where $\lambda^* = 30\lambda$.
(ii) $W =$ the number of patients seen every year, then
      $W \sim$ Poisson (λ^*), where $\lambda^* = 365\lambda$,
(iii) $V =$ the number of patients seen every hour, then
      $V \sim$ Poisson (λ^*), where $\lambda^* = \frac{\lambda}{24}$.

Example 4.12 Suppose that the number of accidents per day in a city has a Poisson distribution with average 2 accidents.

(1) What is the probability that in a day

     (i) the number of accidents will be 5,
    (ii) the number of accidents will be less than 2.

(2) What is the probability that there will be six accidents in 2 days?
(3) What is the probability that there will be no accidents in an hour?

Solution

(1) X = number of accidents in a day

$$X \sim \text{Poisson}(2) \quad (\lambda = 2)$$

$$P(X = x) = \frac{e^{-2}2^x}{x!}; x = 0, 1, 2, \ldots$$

  (i) $P(X = 5) = \frac{e^{-2}2^5}{5!} = 0.036089$

 (ii) $P(X < 2) = P(X = 0) + P(X = 1) = \frac{e^{-2}2^0}{0!} + \frac{e^{-2}2^1}{1!} = 0.135335 + 0.270670 = 0.406005.$

(2) Y = number of accidents in 2 days

$$Y \sim \text{Poisson}(4) \quad (\lambda^* = 2\lambda = (2)(2) = 4)$$

$$P(Y = y) = \frac{e^{-4}4^y}{y!} : \quad y = 0, 1, 2\ldots$$

$$P(Y = 6) = \frac{e^{-4}4^6}{6!} = 0.1042.$$

(3) W = number of accidents in an hour

$$W \sim \text{Poisson}(0.083) \quad \left(\lambda^{**} = \frac{\lambda}{24} = \frac{2}{24} = 0.083\right)$$

$$P(W = w) = \frac{e^{-0.083}0.083^w}{w!} : \quad w = 0, 1, 2\ldots$$

$$P(W = 0) = \frac{e^{-0.083}(0.083)^0}{0!} = 0.9204.$$

Poisson Approximation for Binomial Distribution

Suppose that the random variable X has a binomial distribution with parameter n and p, that is $X \sim$ binomial (n, p). If the number of trial is large $(n \rightarrow \infty)$, and the probability of success is small $(p \rightarrow 0)$, and the quantity $\mu = np$ remains constant, then the binomial distribution, binomial (n, p), can approximated by Poisson distribution Poisson(μ), where $\mu = np$. That is, for large n and small p we have

Binomial $(n, p) \approx$ Poisson(μ)

$$\binom{n}{x} p^x (1 - p)^{n-x} \approx \frac{e^{-\mu} \mu^x}{x!}; \quad x = 0, 1, \ldots, n,$$

where $\mu = np$.

Example 4.13 Let us consider that X has a binomial distribution with parameters $n = 5000$ and $p = 0.002$. The probability that the number of success is less than or equal to 5 or $P(X \leq 5)$ can be obtained as follows.

Solution

(a) The probability of number of success less than or equal to 5 for $X \sim$ binomial (5000, 0.002):

$$P(X \leq 5) = \sum_{x=0}^{5} \binom{5000}{x} (0.002)^x (0.998)^{5000-x} = 0.0669$$

(b) We can use the Poisson approximation of binomial for this problem because $n = 5000$ is quite large and $p = 0.002$ is very small.

We can approximate the mean for Poisson distribution by the following relationship:

$$\mu = np = 5000 \times 0.002 = 10.$$

Using this as the parameter of the Poisson distribution as an approximation for binomial, we obtain the probability of less than or equal to 5 for with parameter $\mu = 10$, i.e., $X \sim$ Poisson(10).

$$P(X \leq 5) = \sum_{x=0}^{5} \frac{e^{-10} 10^x}{x!} = 0.0671.$$

We observe that the approximation is quite satisfactory.

4.8   Geometric Distribution

In an experiment, if we are interested in the random variable, X, representing the total number of trials required in order to obtain the success for the first time after $X - 1$ failures, then it follows a geometric distribution. The probability function of the random variable, X, is

$$f_X(x) = P(X = x) = \begin{cases} p(1 - p)^{x-1}; & x = 1, 2, 3, \ldots \\ 0; & \text{otherwise} \end{cases}$$

In this case, we can write $X \sim \text{Geometric}(p)$. The geometric distribution depends on only one parameter which is the probability of success (p). The variable X resembles in some sense incidence of disease.

Mean and Variance of the Geometric Distribution

The expected value and the variance of the geometric distribution are

$$\mu_X = E(X) = \frac{1}{p},$$

$$\sigma_X^2 = \text{Var}(X) = \frac{(1 - p)}{p^2}.$$

Example 4.14 Let us consider a hypothetical follow-up study on incidence of heart disease. The study is continued until the incidence of heart disease is diagnosed starting with no heart disease at the beginning of the study. Once an individual in the sample is diagnosed with heart disease, the number of follow-ups required is the variable X. We want to find the probability that the researcher needs to continue for four follow-ups to find an incidence case of heart disease. Let us assume that the probability of an incidence case is 0.3.

Solution

Let X be the random variable representing the number of follow-ups required to diagnose the incidence of heart disease. The random variable, X has a geometric distribution with parameter $p = 0.3$ that is

$$X \sim \text{Geometric}(p) = \text{Geometric}(0.30).$$

The probability function is

$$f_X(x) = P(X = x) = \begin{cases} 0.30 \times 0.7^{x-1}; & x = 1, 2, 3, \ldots \\ 0; & \text{otherwise.} \end{cases}$$

The probability that four follow-ups will be necessary to find an incidence case of heart disease at the fourth follow-up is

$$P(X = 4) = 0.3 \times (0.7)^3 = 0.1029.$$

4.9   Multinomial Distribution

The multinomial distribution is a generalization of the binomial distribution. As we have mentioned earlier, Bernoulli trial is an experiment that can have only two outcomes (either success or failure) and a binomial random variable is the number of times of obtaining the outcome of success when we independently perform the Bernoulli trial n times. Analogically, a multinomial trial is an experiment that can have k outcomes (say: $A_1, A_2, \ldots, A_k$). It is assumed that the probability of the ith outcome (A_i) is $p_i = P(A_i)$, where $(i = 1, 2, \ldots, k)$, and $\sum_{i=1}^{k} p_i = \sum_{i=1}^{k} P(A_i) = 1$.

Now, suppose that we independently repeat performing a multinomial trial n times with the probabilities $(p_1, p_2, \ldots, p_k)$ being constant in each trial, and let us define the random variable X_i to be the number of times we obtain the ith outcome (A_i). In this case, the random vector $(X_1, X_2, \ldots, X_k)$ follows a multinomial distribution with parameters $(n, p_1, p_2, \ldots, p_k)$, and the probability function of this multinomial distribution is:

$$P(X_1 = x_1, X_2 = x_2, \ldots, X_k = x_k) = \begin{cases} \frac{n!}{x_1! x_2! \ldots x_k!} p_1^{x_1} p_2^{x_2} \cdots p_k^{x_k}; & \text{when } \sum_{i=1}^{k} x_i = n \\ 0; & \text{otherwise.} \end{cases}$$

Some Notes

1. The event $(X_1 = x_1, X_2 = x_2, \ldots, X_k = x_k)$ means that the outcome (A_1) occurs (x_1) times, the outcome (A_2) occurs (x_2) times, $\ldots$, and the outcome (A_k) occurs (x_k) times when we independently repeat performing the multinomial trial (n) times.
2. $0 \leq p_i \leq 1$
3. $\sum_{i=1}^{k} p_i = \sum_{i=1}^{k} P(A_i) = 1$
4. $\sum_{i=1}^{k} x_i = n$
5. The value of one of the variables $(X_1, X_2, \ldots, X_k)$ can be determined by the values of the other variables, for example, $x_1 = n - \sum_{i=2}^{k} x_i$.
6. The random variable X_i follows a binomial distribution with parameters (n, p_i).
7. The mean of X_i is $n p_i$.
8. The variance of X_i is $n p_i (1 - p_i)$.

Example 4.15 Suppose that we have conducted a study on three different types of complications associated with a disease. The probability of suffering from complication type 1 is 0.1, complication type 2 is 0.3, and complication type 3 is 0.6. Let us select 6 patients randomly. Then, the following questions are asked.

(1) What is the probability of selecting 2, 1, and 3 patients with complication types 1, 2, and 3 respectively?
(2) What is the expected number of patients with complication type 2 in the sample?

Solution
The trial is the procedure of selecting six patients with complication types 1, 2, and 3. Let A_1 = complication type 1, A_2 = complication type 2, A_3 = complication type 3. The experiment is comprised of $n = 6$ trials. Then the probabilities of complication types are

$$p_1 = P(A_1) = P(\text{complication type 1}) = 0.1,$$
$$p_2 = P(A_2) = P(\text{complication type 2}) = 0.3, \text{and}$$
$$p_3 = P(A_3) = P(\text{complication type 3}) = 0.6.$$

Let us define X_1 = number of patients with complication type 1, X_2 = number of patients with complication type 2 and X_3 = number of patients with complication type 3. The random vector (X_1, X_2, X_3) follows a multinomial distribution with parameters $(n = 6, p_1 = 0.1, p_2 = 0.3, p_3 = 0.6)$.

(1) The event $(X_1 = 2, X_2 = 1, X_3 = 3)$ = the event of getting 2 with complication type 1, 1 with complication type 2 and 3 with complication type 3. The corresponding multinomial probability is

$$P(X_1 = 2, X_2 = 1, X_3 = 3) = \frac{6!}{2! \times 1! \times 3!} 0.1^2 \times 0.3^1 \times 0.6^3 = 0.039.$$

(2) The expected number of patients with type 2 complication in the sample = the expected value of $X_2 = np_2 = 6 \times 0.3 = 1.8$.

4.10   Hypergeometric Distribution

Let us consider a population with two types of elements (or 2 categories). Each element in the population can be classified as first type (success) or second type (failure). Let us define the following quantities: N = population size, K = number of elements of the first type in the population and $N - K$ = number of elements of the second type in the population. Suppose that we select a sample of n elements at random from this population, and define the random variable, X, to be the number of elements of first type (number of successes) in the sample. We are interested in finding the probability distribution of X.

To find the probability distribution of X, we should distinguish between two cases since there are two methods of selection, which are selection with replacement and selection without replacement.

(1) Case 1: If we select the elements of the sample at random and with replacement (i.e., each selected element is replaced back to the population before the next selection), then

$$X \sim \text{Binomial}(n, p)$$

where $p = \frac{K}{N}$.

(2) Second case: suppose that we select the elements of the sample at random and without replacement (i.e., each selected element is removed from the population before the next selection). When the selection is made without replacement, the random variable X has a hypergeometric distribution with parameters N, n, and K, and we write $X \sim h(N, n, K)$.

The probability distribution of X is given by

$$f(x) = P(X = x) = h(x; N, n, K) = \begin{cases} \dfrac{\binom{K}{x} \times \binom{N-K}{n-x}}{\binom{N}{n}} ; & x = 0, 1, 2, \ldots, n; \\ 0; & \text{otherwise.} \end{cases}$$

It should be noticed that the possible values of X must satisfy the following inequalities: $0 \leq x \leq K$ and $0 \leq n - x \leq N - K$ implying $0 \leq x \leq K$ and $n - N + K \leq x \leq n$ or $\max\{0, n - N + K\} \leq x \leq \min\{K, n\}$.

Mean and Variance

The expected value and the variance of the hypergeometric distribution $h(N, n, K)$ are

$$E(X) = \mu = n \times \frac{K}{N},$$

$$\text{Var}(X) = \sigma^2 = n \times \frac{K}{N} \times \left(1 - \frac{K}{N}\right) \times \frac{N-n}{N-1}.$$

Example 4.16 Consider a hypothetical study on admission to emergency care in a hospital with acute breathing problem. During the study period, 50 patients were admitted, 15 males and 35 females. A sample of five patients has been selected randomly without replacement.

(1) What is the probability that exactly one male patient is found in the sample?
(2) What is the expected number (mean) of males in the sample?
(3) What is the variance of number of males in the sample?

Solution
There are two types or categories male and female. Let X = number of males in the sample. We have $N = 50$, $K = 15$, and $n = 5$. Then X has a hypergeometric distribution with parameters $N = 50$, $n = 5$, and $K = 15$ which can be denoted by $X \sim h(N, n, K) = h(50, 5, 15)$ and the probability distribution of X is given by

$$f(x) = P(X = x) = h(x; 50, 5, 15) = \begin{cases} \dfrac{\dbinom{15}{x} \times \dbinom{35}{5-x}}{\dbinom{50}{5}}; & x = 0, 1, 2, \ldots, 15 \\ 0; & \text{otherwise} \end{cases}$$

but the values of X must satisfy: $0 \leq x \leq K$ and $n - N + K \leq x \leq n \Leftrightarrow 0 \leq x \leq 15$ and $-30 \leq x \leq 5$, hence, the probability distribution of X is given by

$$f(x) = P(X = x) = h(x; 50, 5, 15) = \begin{cases} \dfrac{\dbinom{15}{x} \times \dbinom{35}{5-x}}{\dbinom{50}{5}}; & x = 0, 1, 2, 3, 4, 5 \\ 0; & \text{otherwise.} \end{cases}$$

(1) The probability that exactly one male is found in the sample is

$$f(1) = P(X = 1) = h(1; 50, 5, 15) = \frac{\dbinom{15}{1} \times \dbinom{35}{5-1}}{\dbinom{50}{5}} = \frac{\dbinom{15}{1} \times \dbinom{35}{4}}{\dbinom{50}{5}}$$

$$= \frac{15 \times 52360}{2118760} = 0.3707$$

(2) The expected number of males is

$$E(X) = \frac{n \times k}{N} = \frac{5 \times 15}{50} = 1.50.$$

(3) The variance of the number of the females in the sample is

$$\mathrm{Var}(X) = \sigma^2 = n\frac{K}{N}\left(1 - \frac{K}{N}\right)\frac{N-n}{N-1}$$
$$= 5 \times \frac{15}{50} \times \left(1 - \frac{15}{50}\right) \times \frac{50-5}{50-1} = 0.9643.$$

The Relationship Between Hypergeometric and Binomial Distribution
The probability function of the binomial distribution is

$$b(x; n, p) = \binom{n}{x} p^x (1 - p)^{n-x}; \quad x = 0, 1, \ldots, n$$

and the probability function of the hypergeometric distribution is

$$h(x; N, n, K) = \frac{\binom{K}{x}\binom{N-K}{n-x}}{\binom{N}{n}}; \quad \max\{0, n-N+K\} \leq x \leq \min\{K, n\}.$$

If n is small compared to N and K, then the hypergeometric distribution $h(x; N, n, K)$ can be approximated by the binomial distribution $b(x; n, p)$, where $p = \frac{K}{N}$; i.e., for large N and K and small n, we have

$$h(x; N, n, K) \approx b\left(x; n, \frac{K}{N}\right)$$
$$\frac{\binom{K}{x}\binom{N-K}{n-x}}{\binom{N}{n}} \approx \binom{n}{x}\left(\frac{K}{N}\right)^x\left(1 - \frac{K}{N}\right)^{n-x}; \quad x = 0, 1, \ldots, n.$$

Note:

If n is very small compared to N and K, then there will be almost no difference between selection without replacement and selection with replacement $\left(\frac{K}{N} \approx \frac{K-1}{N-1} \approx \cdots \approx \frac{K-n+1}{N-n+1}\right).$

Example 4.17 Let us consider a random variable X follows a hypergeometric distribution with parameters $N = 10,000$, $n = 5$, and $K = 3000$, i.e.

$$X \sim h(N, n, K) = h(10,000, 5, 3000).$$

Find $P(X = 2)$ using the exact method and binomial approximation of hyper-geometric distribution.

Solution

(1) Exact method

The exact probability using hypergeometric distribution is

$$P(X = 2) = \frac{\binom{3000}{2}\binom{7000}{3}}{\binom{10,000}{5}} = 0.3088$$

(2) Approximate method

Since $n = 5$ is small relative to $N = 10000$ and $K = 3000$, we can approximate the hypergeometric probabilities using binomial probabilities as follows:

$$n = 5 (\text{number of trials})$$
$$p = K/N = 3000/10000 = 0.3 (\text{probability of success})$$

$$X \sim h(x; 10000, 5, 3000) \approx b(x; 5, 0.3)$$
$$P(X = 2; 5, 0.3) = \binom{5}{2}(0.3)^2(0.7)^3 = 0.3087$$

We notice that the approximation is very good.

4.11 Negative Binomial Distribution

The negative binomial distribution is based on an experiment consisting of a sequence of repeated independent Bernoulli trials. The experiment is continued until the rth success is obtained under the following conditions:

(i)   Each trial has only two outcomes (success and failure).
(ii) The trials are independent.
(iii) The probability of success $P(S) = p$ remains constant in each trial.
(iv) The number of success required is r, where r is a fixed given positive integer $(r = 1, 2, \ldots)$.
(v)   The experiment is immediately terminated once the rth success is obtained.

In the negative binomial experiment, we are interested in the random variable, X, representing the total number of trials required to obtain the first r successes for the first time. For example, let the experiment consists of independently continuing observing until r successes are observed and recording the number of trials required to obtain r successes.

In the negative binomial experiment, we should notice the following:

(i)   the number of successes is r (fixed number),
(ii) the number of trials is X (random variable),
(iii) the number of failures $= X - r$ (random),
(iv) the result of the last trial (the Xth trial) is success,
(v)   there are $r - 1$ successes and $X - r$ failures in the first $X - 1$ trails (the trials before the last one),
(vi) the number of trials required for obtaining the first r successes must not be less than r (i.e., $X \geq r$),
(vii) the set of possible values of X is $\{r, r + 1, r + 2, \dots\}$.

The probability function of the random variable, X, is

$$
f_X(x) = P(X = x) = \begin{cases} \binom{x-1}{r-1} p^r (1-p)^{x-r}; & x = r, r+1, r+2, \dots \\ 0; & \text{otherwise.} \end{cases}
$$

In this case, we write $X \sim NB(r, p)$. The negative binomial distribution depends on two parameters which are the number of successes (r) and the probability of success (p). The geometric distribution is a special case of the negative binomial distribution where $r = 1$. We should notice that $NB(1, p) = \text{Geometric}(p)$.

Mean and Variance
The mean (expected value) and the variance of the negative binomial distribution $NB(r, p)$ are

$$
\mu_X = E(X) = \frac{r}{p},
$$

$$
\sigma_X^2 = \text{Var}(X) = \frac{r(1-p)}{p^2}.
$$

Notes:

1. For the special case where $r = 1$, the negative binomial distribution $NB(1, p)$ is called the geometric distribution with parameter p, and in this case, the random variable $X \sim NB(1, p) = \text{Geometric}(p)$ represents the total number of trials required to obtain the first success.
2. In the case of negative binomial distribution, the number of trials is random and the number of successes is fixed. While in the case of binomial distribution, the number of trials is fixed and the number of successes is random.

Example 4.18 Let us consider a hypothetical study on utilization of health care services. For an elderly person, let the number of days required to make the rth visit to a community hospital is of interest. Let us also consider that the probability of a visit each time remains constant and it has been considered to be 0.4. The researcher wants to find the probability of number of days required to make the third visit since the start of the study. Suppose that the random variable X represents the total number of days required to visit the community clinic for the third time.

(1) Find the probability distribution of X.
(2) What is the expected number (mean) of days required for an elderly to visit the community clinic for the third time?
(3) What is the probability that 10 days will be needed to make the third visit to the community clinic?

Solution

(1) The random variable, X has a negative binomial distribution with parameters: $r = 3$ and $p = 0.4$, that is

$$X \sim NB(r, p) = NB(3, 0.4).$$

The probability function is

$$P(X = x) = \begin{cases} \binom{x-1}{2} \times 0.4^3 \times 0.6^{x-3}; & x = 3, 4, 5, \ldots \\ 0; & \text{otherwise.} \end{cases}$$

(2) The expected number (mean) of days required to make the third visit is

$$\mu_X = E(X) = \frac{r}{p} = \frac{3}{0.4} = 7.5.$$

(3) The probability that the researcher will have to wait for ten days to observe the third visit to the community clinic is

$$P(X = 10) = \binom{9}{2} 0.4^3 (0.6)^7 = 0.0645.$$

The negative binomial distribution provides answers to very useful questions regarding count data. The geometric distribution is a special case of the negative binomial distribution for $r = 1$. Sometimes, the negative binomial distribution is used as an alternative to the Poisson distribution if there is overdispersion in the data. As we know that in case of the Poisson distribution, there is equality of mean and variance which may not represent some count data in reality where the variance is greater than the mean resulting in overdispersion. The negative binomial distribution can be employed to analyze such data instead of the Poisson distribution.

4.12 Summary

The discrete probability distributions are introduced in this chapter. The general rules of discrete probability distributions are illustrated and the concepts of expected value and variance are shown. The rules are illustrated with a number of examples. This chapter includes brief introduction of the Bernoulli distribution, binomial distribution, Poisson distribution, geometric distribution, multinomial distribution, hypergeometric distribution, and negative binomial distribution. The important properties of these distributions are discussed and illustrated with examples. The applications of these useful distributions are given high priority in illustrations.

Exercises

4.1 Suppose that X be a discrete random variable with the following probability distribution:

X	$P(X = x)$
0	K
1	0.2
2	0.3
3	0.2
4	0.1

Find the following:

   (i)   the value of k;
  (ii)   the expected value of X;
 (iii)   the expected value of X^2;
 (iv)   the variance of X;
  (v)   the cumulative probability distribution of X;
 (vi) $P(X \leq 2)$;
(vii) $P(X > 2)$.

4.2 The following probability distribution represents probability of X = number of complications a person suffers at old age in a community.

X	0	1	2	3	4	5
$P(x)$	0.01	0.09	0.15	0.40	0.25	0.10

Find the probability that the number of complications is

    (a) 0;
    (b) more than 2;
    (c) more than or equal to 3;
    (d) $1 \leq X \leq 3$.

4.3   Suppose a diagnostic test conducted on five persons. The purpose is to determine probability of x, the number who suffer from a certain disease. Suppose that 20% of all the individuals suffer from the disease. Then find

    (a) $P(X = x)$;
    (b) the mean and standard deviation of X;
    (c) the probability of $X \leq 2$;
    (d) the probability of $X > 3$;
    (e) the probability of $X = 1$;
    (f) $P(2 < X \leq 4)$.

4.4   If the mean number of serious accidents per week in a city is six, find the probability of

    (a) $X = x$;
    (b) exactly seven accidents in a week;
    (c) six or more accidents in a week;
    (d) no accidents in a week;
    (e) fewer than three accidents in a week;
    (f) two accidents in a day;
    (g) no accident in four weeks;
    (h) variance of X.

4.5   Suppose that the percentage of pregnancy-related deaths during pregnancy is 25, 15% during delivery and 60% during postpartum period.

    (i)   What is the probability that out of seven pregnancy-related maternal deaths, two occurred during pregnancy, one during delivery, and remaining four during postpartum stage?
    (ii) What is the probability that all the maternal deaths occurred during postpartum period?
    (iii) What is the probability that none of the maternal deaths occurred during postpartum period?
    (iv) Find the expected number of pregnancy-related deaths during pregnancy, during delivery, and during postpartum stage.

4.6   Suppose that a study is conducted to obtain subjects with a rare disease with probability of success $p = 0.001$. Consider that the study is conducted on a large number of subjects where $n = 10,000$. Then find the probability of selecting less than or equal to 9 subjects with the rare disease.

4.7 A study is conducted to find the probability of diagnosing an individual with a complication associated with a certain disease. The subjects are observed every month since the diagnosis of the disease. If it is known that the probability of developing the complication is 0.2, then find the probability of developing the disease in 5 months. Write the probability function and find the mean and variance for number of months required for developing the complication among the subjects diagnosed with the disease.

4.8 Suppose that in a study on 20 patients, 14 patients are already registered and 6 patients need to register in a clinic. If 5 patients are selected randomly without replacement out of 20 patients for a quick survey regarding their disease status then what is the probability that 4 of the patients are not registered?

4.9 Suppose that in a study to diagnose a case with symptoms of infection among the patients after surgery is 0.2. What is the probability that the third infection case will be found after the seventh surgery?

Reference

Leiter, R. E., & Hamdan, M. A. (1973). Some bivariate models applicable to traffic accidents and fatalities. *International Statistical Review, 41*(1), 87–100.

Chapter 5
Probability Distributions: Continuous

5.1 Continuous Probability Distribution

Some important discrete distributions are introduced in Chap. 4. In many cases, we need to deal with a continuous variable which takes values from continuous scale in intervals rather than values of a variable which takes values from set of possible countable outcomes. Some examples of continuous variables are time from onset of a disease to an event such as recovery, height, weight, etc. In an interval, the values of the continuous variables are infinite or uncountable. In this chapter, an introduction of the continuous probability distributions is given with examples. The normal and standard normal distributions are discussed.

5.2 Continuous Probability Distributions

For any continuous random variable, X, there exists a function, $f(x)$, called the probability density function (pdf) of X, for which the following conditions apply:

(i) The total area under the curve of $f(x)$ equals to 1 (Fig. 5.1).
(ii) The probability that X lies between the points a and b equals to the area under the curve of $f(x)$ which is bounded by the point a and b.
(iii) In general, the probability of an interval event is given by the area under the curve of $f(x)$ corresponding to that interval.

If X is a continuous random variable then we can find probabilities as shown below (Figs. 5.2 and 5.3)

(i) $P(X = a) = 0$ for any a,
(ii) $P(X \leq a) = P(X < a) = F(a)$,
(iii) $P(X \geq b) = P(X > b) = 1 - F(b)$,
(iv) $P(a \leq X \leq b) = P(a \leq X < b) = P(a < X \leq b) = P(a < X < b)$,

© Springer Nature Singapore Pte Ltd. 2018
M. A. Islam and A. Al-Shiha, *Foundations of Biostatistics*,
https://doi.org/10.1007/978-981-10-8627-4_5

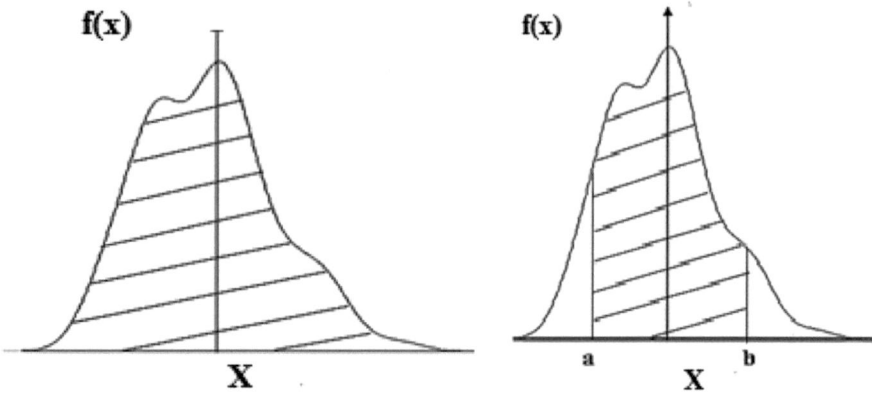

$$Total\ area = \int_{-\infty}^{\infty} f(x)\,dx = 1 \ and\ P(a \le X \le b) = \int_{a}^{b} f(x)\,dx = area$$

Fig. 5.1 Displaying areas under the probability density curves

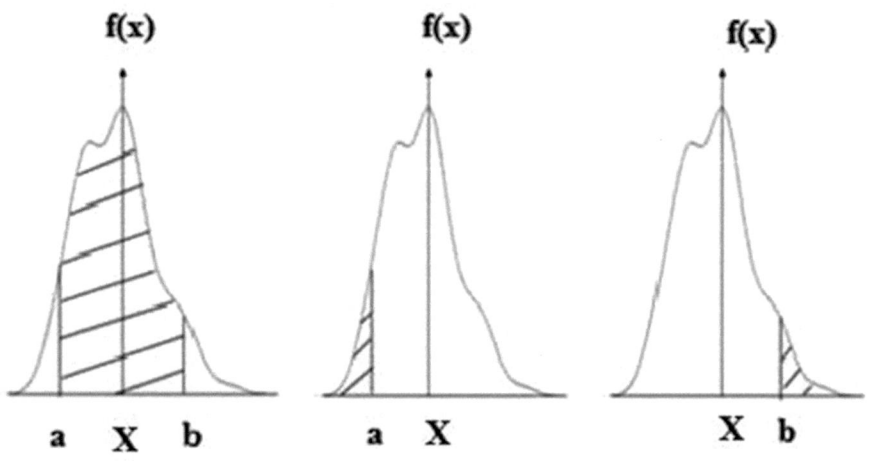

$$P(a \le X \le b) = \int_{a}^{b} f(x)\,dx = area \qquad P(X \le a) = \int_{-\infty}^{a} f(x)\,dx = area \qquad P(X \ge b) = \int_{b}^{\infty} f(x)\,dx = area$$

Fig. 5.2 Figures displaying areas

(v) $P(X \le x) = F(x),$

(vi) $P(X \ge a) = 1 - P(X < a) = 1 - P(X \le a) = 1 - F(a),$

(vii) $P(a \le X \le b) = P(X \le b) - P(X \le a) = F(b) - F(a)$ (Fig. 5.3).

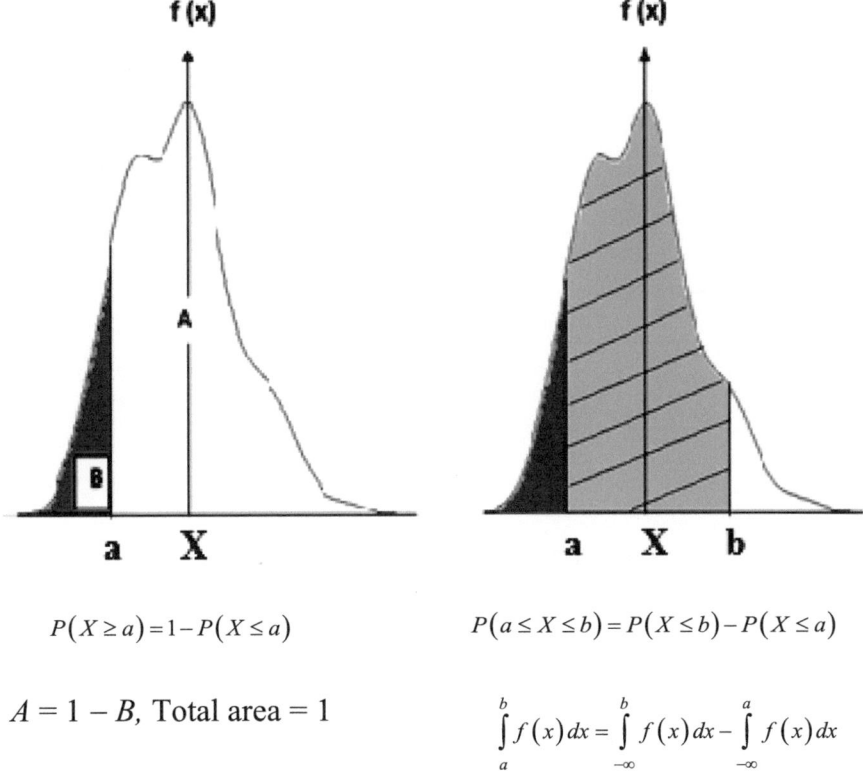

$$P(X \geq a) = 1 - P(X \leq a)$$

$$P(a \leq X \leq b) = P(X \leq b) - P(X \leq a)$$

$$A = 1 - B, \text{ Total area} = 1$$

$$\int_a^b f(x)\,dx = \int_{-\infty}^b f(x)\,dx - \int_{-\infty}^a f(x)\,dx$$

Fig. 5.3 Figures displaying probabilities greater than or equal to *a* and between *a* and *b*

5.3   The Normal Distribution

The normal distribution is one of the most important continuous probability density functions in statistics. It will be seen in the next chapters that the role of the normal density function is manyfold. Many measurable characteristics are normally or approximately normally distributed. The probability density function of the normal distribution is given by

$$f\left(x; \mu, \sigma^2\right) = \frac{1}{\sigma\sqrt{2\pi}} e^{-\frac{1}{2}\left(\frac{x-\mu}{\sigma}\right)^2}; \quad -\infty < x < \infty,$$

where (e = 2.71828) and (π = 3.14159).

The parameters of the distribution are the mean μ and the variance σ^2. The continuous random variable, *X*, which has a normal distribution possessing several important characteristics such as

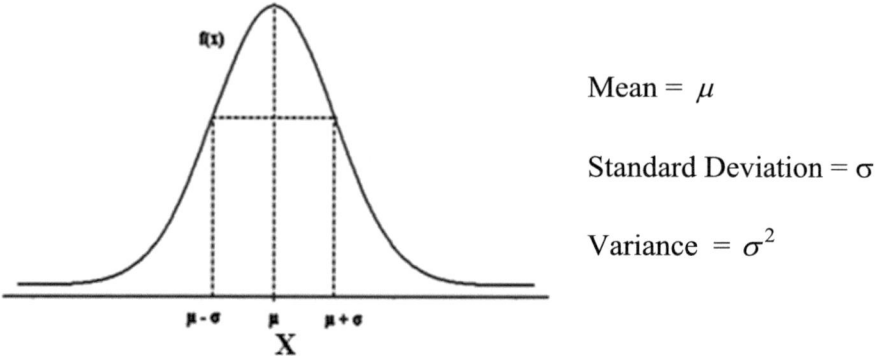

Mean = μ

Standard Deviation = σ

Variance = σ^2

Fig. 5.4 Figure displaying a normal distribution with mean μ and variance σ^2

(i) $-\infty < X < \infty,$

(ii) The area under the curve is 1 and it can be shown that

$$\int_{-\infty}^{\infty} f\left(x; \mu, \sigma^2\right) dx = \int_{-\infty}^{\infty} \frac{1}{\sigma\sqrt{2\pi}} e^{-\frac{1}{2}\left(\frac{x-\mu}{\sigma}\right)^2} dx = 1.$$

(iii) The density function of X, $f(x)$, is a bell-shaped curve (Fig. 5.4).

The highest point of the curve of $f(x)$ is at the mean μ. Hence, the mode = mean = μ.
The curve of $f(x)$ is symmetric about the mean μ.
In other words, mean = mode = median.
The normal distribution depends on two parameters

mean = μ and standard deviation = σ.

(vii) If the random variable, X, is normally distributed with mean μ and standard deviation σ (variance σ^2), we write $X \sim N\left(\mu, \sigma^2\right)$.

(viii) The location of the normal distribution depends on μ. The scale of the normal distribution depends on σ and if the values of these parameters are known then the normal distribution is fully specified (Fig. 5.5).

The location of the normal distribution depends on μ and its scale depends on σ as displayed in the figures here.

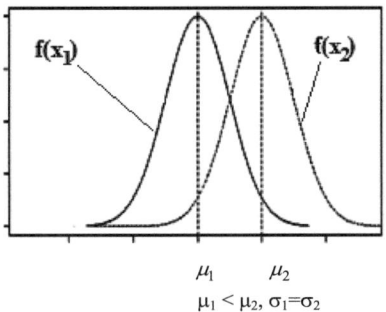

Suppose we have two normal distributions for variables X_1 and X_2 where $X_1 \sim N(\mu_1, \sigma_1^2)$ and $X_2 \sim N(\mu_2, \sigma_2^2)$.

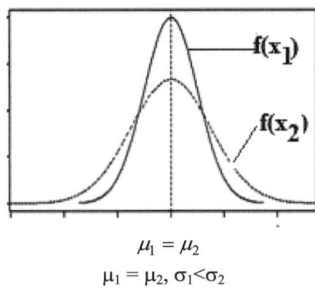

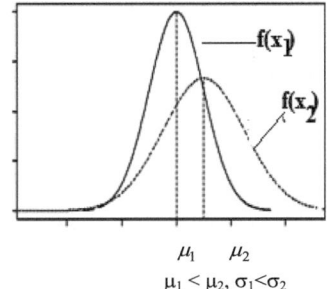

Fig. 5.5 Comparison of normal distributions with $X_1 \sim N(\mu_1, \sigma_1^2)$ and $X_2 \sim N(\mu_2, \sigma_2^2)$

5.4   The Standard Normal Distribution

The normal distribution with mean $\mu = 0$ and variance $\sigma^2 = 1$ is called the standard normal distribution and is denoted by Normal $(0,1)$ or $N(0,1)$. The standard normal random variable is denoted by Z, and we write

$$Z \sim N(0, 1).$$

It can be shown that if $X \sim$ Normal (μ, σ^2), then $Z = \frac{X-\mu}{\sigma} \sim$ Normal $(0,1)$. The mean and variance of the standard normal variate, Z, can be shown as follows:

$$E(Z) = E\left(\frac{X - \mu}{\sigma}\right) = \frac{E(X) - \mu}{\sigma} = \frac{E(X) - \mu}{\sigma} = \frac{\mu - \mu}{\sigma} = 0.$$

It may be noted here that μ and σ^2 are constants and we know that expected values on any constant remain same implying that $E(\mu) = \mu$ and $E\left(\frac{1}{\sigma}\right) = \frac{1}{\sigma}$. Similarly, variance of Z is

$$\text{Var}(Z) = \text{Var}\left(\frac{X - \mu}{\sigma}\right) = \frac{\text{Var}(X)}{\sigma^2} = \frac{\sigma^2}{\sigma^2} = 1.$$

In this case, as is shown in Chap. 2 that variance is independent of shift in origin (μ) but depends on the change in scale (σ) then $\text{Var}(aX) = a^2\text{Var}(X)$ where $a = \frac{1}{\sigma}$ and $\text{Var}(X) = \sigma^2$.

The probability density function (pdf) of $Z \sim N(0,1)$ is given by (Fig. 5.6)

$$f(z) = N(z; 0, 1) = \frac{1}{\sqrt{2\pi}} e^{-\frac{1}{2}z^2}$$

The standard normal distribution, $N(0,1)$, is very useful and plays a very important role in statistics because area under any normal curve can be calculated from the probabilities of the standard normal distribution due to the fact that both the mean and variance of the standard normal distribution are known hence the distribution is fully specified. The following figures indicate the area under specified range of the standard normal variate, Z (Fig. 5.7).

Calculating Probabilities of Normal (0,1)

We need to know various probability calculations using the standard normal distribution. The value for area under a specified value represents the corresponding probability. Suppose that $Z \sim N(0,1)$. For the standard normal distribution $Z \sim N(0, 1)$, there is a special table used to calculate probabilities of the form

$$P(Z \leq z).$$

(i) $P(Z \leq a)$ where $z = a$ can be found from the table for Z. The probability of less than or equal to $z = a$ is given. Sometimes probabilities greater than any value $z = a$ or probabilities in tail areas of a standard normal distribution are given too.

Fig. 5.6 Figure displaying a standard normal distribution

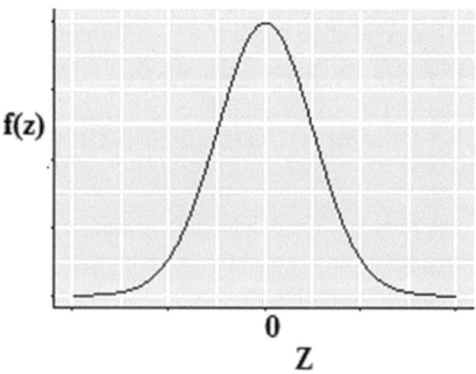

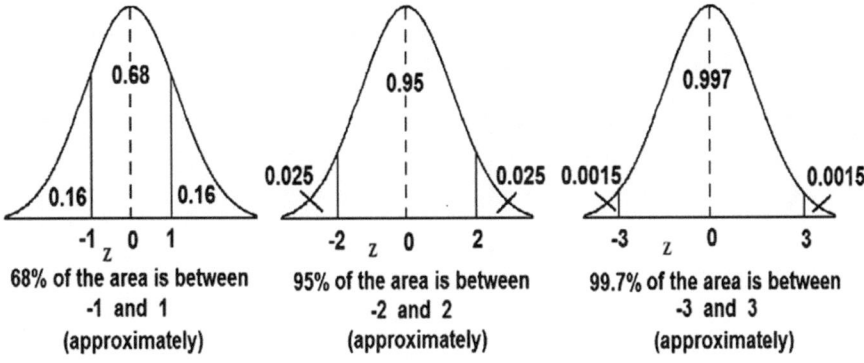

Fig. 5.7 Areas under standard normal distribution curve

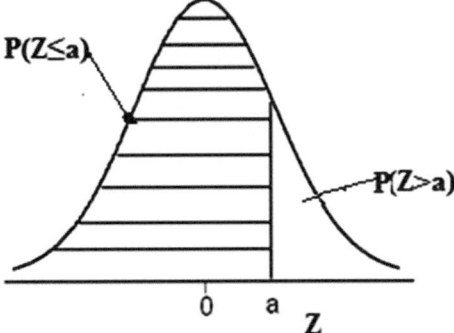

(ii) $P(Z > b) = 1 - P(Z \leq b)$ where $P(Z \leq b)$ can be obtained from the standard normal table for any specified value of $z = b$.

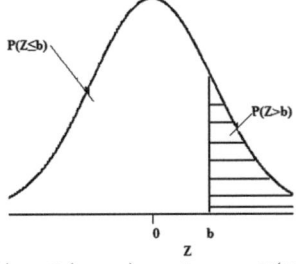

(iii) $P(a \leq Z \leq b) = P(Z \leq b) - P(z \leq a)$ where $P(Z \leq b)$ is   obtained   for $z = b$ and similarly $P(Z \leq a)$ for $z = a$ is also from the table.

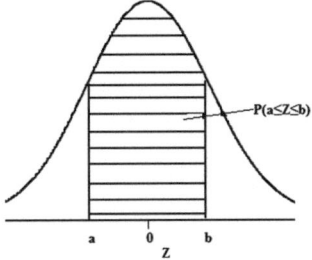

(iv) If $P(Z \leq a)$ where $a < 0$ then it can be obtained from the table where $P(Z \leq a)$ is shown for $a \geq 0$. In case of a positive value $P(Z \leq a)$ can be found directly from the table as:

z	0.00	0.01	0.02	...	0.09
0.01	0.5000	...	...		0.5359
...	...	...	...	...	....
3.6..	0.9998	...	...	...	0.9999

Example 5.1 If $z = 0.94$ then find the probability for $P(Z \geq 0.94)$. Using the relationship in (ii), we obtain

$$P(Z \geq 0.94) = 1 - P(Z \leq 0.94)$$
$$= 1 - 0.8264$$
$$= 0.1736$$

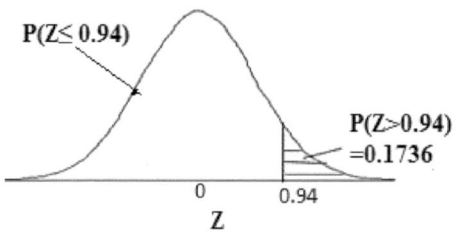

Z	0.00	...	0.04
:	:	:	⇓
:	...	...	⇓
0.9⇒	⇒	⇒	0.8264

Suppose that $Z \sim N(0,1)$ then using (i), we can calculate the probability of Z less than or equal to $z = 1.72$ as shown below

$$P(Z \leq 1.72) = 0.9573$$

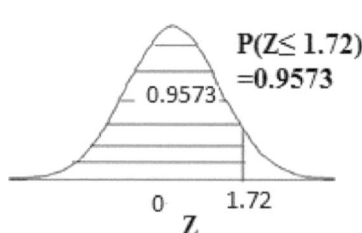

Z	0.00	0.01	0.02
:	⇓		
1.7⇒	0.9554		0.9573
:			

(3) If $Z \sim N(0, 1)$ then the area under $z = -1.65$ and $z = 1.48$ can be calculated using the standard normal table as follows

$$P(-1.65 \leq Z \leq 1.48) = P(Z \leq 1.48) -$$

$$P(Z \leq -1.65) = 0.9306 - 0.0548$$
$$= 0.8758$$

Z	0.00...	0.08
:	:	⇓
1.4	0.9192	0.9306
:	:	:

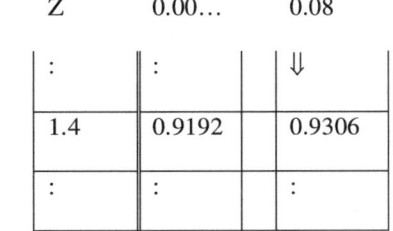

P(-1.65≤ Z≤ 1.48)
=0.8758

-1.65   0   1.48
          Z

(4) $P(Z \leq 0) = P(Z \geq 0) = 0.5$
(5) To find the value of Z, if area under that value is given, let us define $P(Z \leq z_a) = a$ where a is given and we want to find the value of z_a. As the normal curve is symmetric about zero, it can also be shown that $P(Z \leq z_{1-a}) = 1 - a$ implies that $z_a = -z_{1-a}$ because $P(Z \geq z_{1-a}) = 1 - P(Z \leq z_{1-a}) = 1 - (1 - a) = a$.

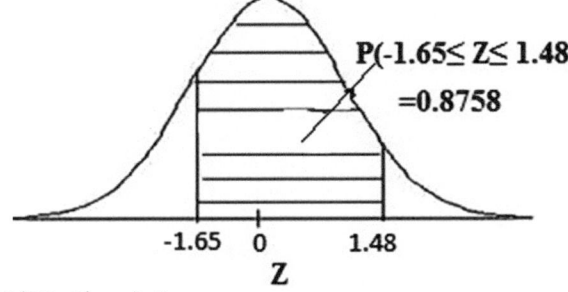

P(Z>z₁₋ₐ)=a

Z   z₁₋ₐ

From the above relationship, it is seen that $P(Z \geq z_{1-a}) = a$. From table, we can we can find this using the relationship

$$z_a = -z_{1-a}.$$

Some examples are displayed in the following figures:

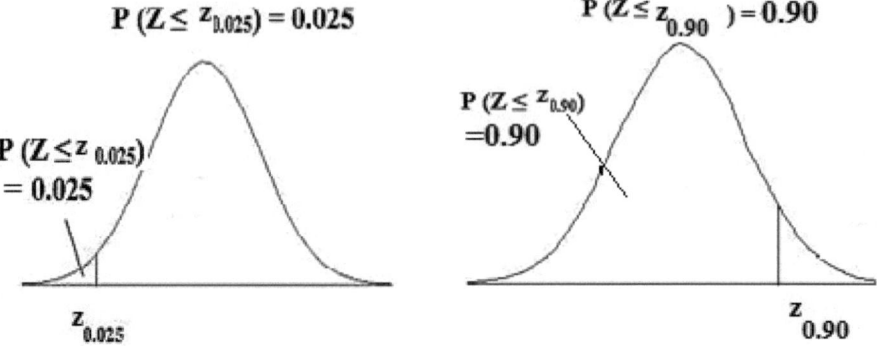

$P (Z \le z_{0.025}) = 0.025$

$P (Z \le z_{0.025}) = 0.025$

$z_{0.025}$

$P (Z \le z_{0.90}) = 0.90$

$P (Z \le z_{0.90}) = 0.90$

$z_{0.90}$

Example 5.2 Since the pdf of $Z \sim N(0, 1)$ is symmetric about 0, we have

$$z_{1-a} = -z_a, \text{ and}$$
$$z_a = -z_{1-a}.$$

For example, $Z_{0.48} = -Z_{1-0.48} = -Z_{0.52}$

$$Z_{0.73} = -Z_{1-0.73} = -Z_{0.27}.$$

Suppose that $Z \sim N(0, 1)$.
If $P(Z \le z_a) = 0.9306$
Then $z_a = 1.48$

$$z_{0.0694} = z_{1-0.9306} = -z_{0.9306} = -1.48$$

Z	...	0.08	...
:		⇑	
1.4	⇐	0.9306	
:			

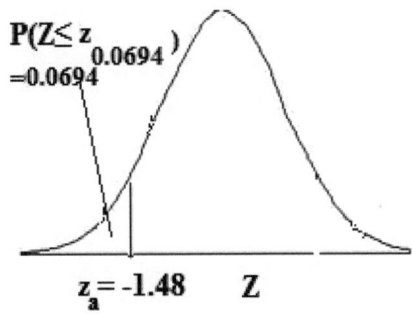

$P(Z \leq z_{0.0694})$
$= 0.0694$

$z_a = -1.48$ Z

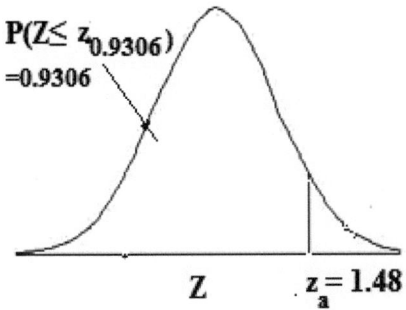

$P(Z \leq z_{0.9306})$
$= 0.9306$

Z $z_a = 1.48$

$$P(Z \leq z_a) = 0.9306, \ P(Z \leq Z_{0.9306}) = 0.9306,$$
$$z_a = z_{0.9306}, \ z_a = z_{0.9306} = 1.48,$$
$$P(Z \leq z_{1-a}) = P(Z \leq -z_a)$$
$$P(Z \leq z_{1-0.9306}) = P(Z \leq -z_{0.9306})$$
$$z_{0.0694} = z_{1-0.9306} = -z_{0.9306} = -1.48.$$

Example 5.3 Suppose that $Z \sim N(0, 1)$. Find the value of k such that

$$P(Z \leq k) = 0.0465.$$

Solution

$$k = -1.68, k = Z_{0.0465} = -1.68$$

Z	...	0.08	
:	:	⇑	
		⇑	
1.6	⇐⇐	0.9535	

Using the relationship $z_\alpha = -z_{1-\alpha}$ we find that

$$z_{0.0465} = z_{1-0.9535} = -z_{0.9535} = -1.68.$$

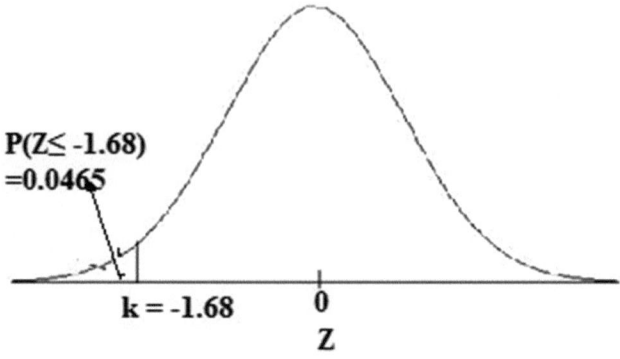

$P(Z \leq -1.68)$
$= 0.0465$

$k = -1.68$ 0
Z

Example 5.4 If $Z \sim N(0, 1)$, then some useful values are

$$z_{0.90} = 1.285,$$
$$z_{0.95} = 1.645,$$
$$z_{0.975} = 1.96, \text{ and}$$
$$z_{0.99} = 2.325.$$

Using the result $z_a = -z_{1-a}$, it can also be shown that

$$z_{0.10} = -z_{0.90} = -1.285,$$

$$z_{0.05} = -z_{0.95} = -1.645,$$

$$z_{0.025} = -z_{0.975} = -1.96, \text{ and}$$

$$z_{0.01} = -z_{0.99} = -2.325.$$

Calculating Probabilities of Normal (μ, σ^2)
Recall the result based on the relationship between X and Z
    $X \sim$ Normal (μ, σ^2) and $Z = \frac{X-\mu}{\sigma} \sim$ Normal $(0,1)$.
    Let us consider $X \leq a$ and if we subtract μ from X and divide by σ then we can rewrite equivalently

$$\frac{X - \mu}{\sigma} \leq \frac{a - \mu}{\sigma}$$

which is essentially

$$Z \leq \frac{a - \mu}{\sigma}.$$

Similarly, we can also show the following relationships:

1. $P(X \leq a) = P\left(Z \leq \frac{a-\mu}{\sigma}\right)$
2. $P(X \geq a) = 1 - P(X \leq a) = 1 - P\left(Z \leq \frac{a-\mu}{\sigma}\right)$
3. $P(a \leq X \leq b) = P(X \leq b) - P(X \leq a) = P\left(Z \leq \frac{b-\mu}{\sigma}\right) - P\left(Z \leq \frac{a-\mu}{\sigma}\right)$

Applications

Following examples show some applications of the normal distribution.

Example 5.5 Let us consider weight of women in reproductive age follows a normal distribution with mean 49 kg and variance 25 kg^2

(a) Find the probability that a randomly chosen woman in her reproductive age has weight less than 45 kg.
(b) What is the percentage of women having weight less than 45 kg?
(c) In a population of 20,000 women of reproductive age, how many would you expect to have weight less than 45 kg?

Solution Here the random variable, X = weight of women in reproductive age, population mean = 49 kg, population variance= σ^2 = 25 kg^2, population standard deviation = σ = 5 kg. Hence, $X \sim$ Normal (49,25).

(a) The probability that a randomly chosen woman in reproductive age has weight less than 45 kg is $P(X < 45)$.

$$
\begin{aligned}
P(X \leq 45) &= P\left(Z \leq \frac{45 - \mu}{\sigma}\right) \\
&= P\left(Z \leq \frac{45 - 49}{5}\right) \\
&= P(Z \leq -0.8) \\
&= 0.2119.
\end{aligned}
$$

(b) The percentage of women of reproductive age who have weight less than 45 kg is $P(X \leq 45) \times 100\% = 0.2119 \times 100\% = 21.19\%$
(c) In a population of 20,000 women of reproductive age, we would expect that the number of women with weight less than 45 kg is $P(X \leq 45) \times 20,000 = 0.2119 \times 20,000 = 4238$.

Example 5.6 Let us consider that the birth weight of girls in rural community of Bangladesh is 2.59 kg (μ) and the standard deviation is 0.43 kg (σ).

(a) Find the probability that a randomly chosen girl has a birth weight between 3.0 and 4.0 kg.
(b) What is the percentage of girls who have a birth weight between 3.0 and 4.0 kg?

(c) In a population of 100,000 girls, how many would you expect to have birth weight between 3.0 and 4.0 kg?

Solution The random variable is X = birth weight of a girl in rural community in Bangladesh, the population mean, $\mu = 2.59$ kg, the population standard deviation, $\sigma = 0.43$ kg, the population variance, $\sigma^2 = (0.43 \text{ kg})^2 = 0.1849 \text{ kg}^2$, and it is assumed that X is normally distributed then $X \sim N$ (2.59,0.1849).

(a) The probability that a randomly chosen girl has a birth weight between 3.0 and 4.0 kg is $P(3.0<X<4.0)$.

$$P(3.0<X<4.0) = P(X<4.0) - P(X\leq3.0)$$
$$= P\left(Z<\frac{4.0-\mu}{\sigma}\right) - P\left(Z\leq\frac{3.0-\mu}{\sigma}\right)$$
$$= P\left(Z<\frac{4.0-2.59}{0.43}\right) - P\left(Z\leq\frac{3.0-2.59}{0.43}\right)$$
$$= P(Z<3.27) - P(Z\leq0.95)$$
$$= 0.99946 - 0.82894 = 0.17052.$$

(b) The percentage of girls who have a birth weight between 3.0 and 4.0 kg is

$$P(3.0<X<4.0) \times 100\% = 0.17052 \times 100\% = 17.05\%$$

(c) In a population of 100,000 Bangladeshi girls community, we would expect that the number of babies with birth weight between 3.0 and 4.0 kg to be

$$P(3.0<X<4.0) \times 100,000 = 0.17052 \times 100,000 = 17,052 \text{ girls.}$$

5.5   Normal Approximation for Binomial Distribution

Suppose that the random variable, X, has a binomial distribution with parameters, n and p, that is $X \sim$ Binomial (n,p). If the number of trial is large $(n \to \infty)$, and the probability of success is close to half $(p \to 0.5)$, then the binomial distribution, binomial (n,p), can be approximated by Normal distribution $N(\mu, \sigma^2)$,where $\mu = np$ and $\sigma^2 = np(1-p)$. That is, for large n, we have

$$\text{Binomial}(n,p) \approx N(np, np(1-p)).$$

Then it can be shown that

$$\frac{X - np}{\sqrt{np(1-p)}} \approx N(0, 1).$$

As X is a discrete variable and it has limiting distribution that is $N(0,1)$, we need a continuity correction to obtain probability for an interval

$$P(X = x) = P(x - 0.5 < X < x + 0.5)$$
$$\approx P\left[\frac{x-0.5-np}{\sqrt{np(1-p)}} < Z < \frac{x+0.5-np}{\sqrt{np(1-p)}}\right].$$

Similarly, we can find the following probabilities using the limiting distribution:

$$P(X \le x) = P(X < x + 0.5) \approx P\left[Z < \frac{x + 0.5 - np}{\sqrt{np(1 - p)}}\right],$$

$$P(X \ge x) = P(X > x - 0.5) \approx P\left[Z > \frac{x - 0.5 - np}{\sqrt{np(1 - p)}}\right], \text{ and}$$

$$P(x_1 \le X \le x_2)$$
$$= P(x_1 - 0.5 < X < x_2 + 0.5) \approx P\left[\frac{x_1 - 0.5 - np}{\sqrt{np(1 - p)}} < Z < \frac{x_2 + 0.5 - np}{\sqrt{np(1 - p)}}\right].$$

The following figures illustrate the idea of the continuity correction for the case $P(X = x)$ and for the case $P(X \le x)$ (Fig. 5.8).

Fig. 5.8 Binomial probability using continuity correction for normal approximation

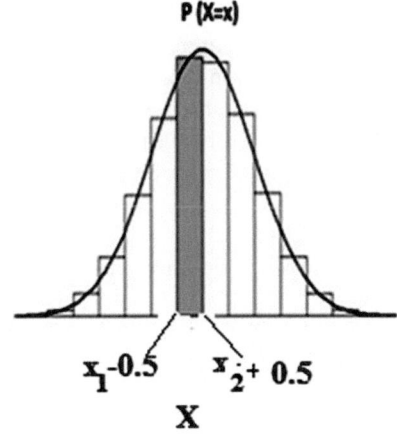

$P(X{=}x)$

$x_1{-}0.5$ $x_2{+}0.5$

X

Example 5.7 Suppose that the random variable X has a binomial distribution with parameters $n = 100$ and $p = 0.5$, i.e., $X \sim$ Binomial(100,0.5). Find $P(X \leq 45)$ using an exact method and an approximated method.

Solution

(a) Calculating the exact probability using the fact that $X \sim$ Binomial(100,0.5):

$$P(X \leq 45) = \sum_{x=0}^{45} \binom{100}{x} \times 0.5^x \times 0.5^{100-x} = 0.1841.$$

(b) Calculating the approximated probability using normal approximation

We notice that $n = 100$ (n is large) and $p = 0.5$. The mean and the variance of the distribution are, respectively,

$$\mu = np = 100 \times 0.5 = 50$$

$$\sigma^2 = np(1-p) = 100 \times 0.5 \times 0.5 = 25.$$

Therefore, we can approximate the distribution of X by the normal distribution with mean $\mu = 50$ and variance $\sigma^2 = 25$, as follows:

$$P(X \leq 45) = P(X < 45 + 0.5) = P(X < 45.5) \approx P\left(Z < \frac{45.5 - 50}{\sqrt{25}}\right) = 0.1841.$$

5.6   Summary

Two of the most essential continuous distributions, the normal probability distribution and the standard normal probability distribution, are discussed in this chapter with specific focus to the need of users who want to use these distributions in their applications. In this chapter, examples are displayed in a way that the users will be able to learn the applications of these distributions without ambiguity. The general rules of a continuous distribution are illustrated and the relationship between probability in an interval and cumulative probability are shown. The computational procedures of probabilities are illustrated with many examples and figures using the standard normal probability distributions.

Exercises

5.1 Find the following probabilities using the standard normal distribution:

   (i) $P(Z \leq 0)$,
   (ii) $P(Z = 1)$,
   (iii) $P(Z \leq 1)$,
   (iv) $P(Z \leq -1)$,

   (v) $P(Z \geq 1)$,
  (vi) $P(Z \geq -1)$,
 (vii) $P(Z \geq 1.75)$,
(viii) $P(Z \geq -1.75)$,
  (ix) $P(1.68 \leq Z \leq 2.75)$,
   (x) $P(-1 \leq Z \leq 1)$, and
  (xi) $P(-1 \leq Z \leq 2.45)$.

5.2   Find the values of the standard normal variate for the following probabilities:

   (i) $P(Z \leq z_a) = 0.975$,
  (ii) $P(Z \leq z_a) = 0.025$,
 (iii) $P(Z \leq z_{0.05}) =$,
  (iv) $P(Z \geq z_a) = 0.01$,
   (v) $P(Z \leq z_a) = 0.99$,
  (vi) $P(Z \geq z_a) = 0.35$, and
 (vii) $P(Z \geq z_a) = 0.65$.

5.3   Using the relationship $Z_a = -Z_{1-a}$, find the following values of the standard
       normal distribution variable:

   (i) $z_{0.2}$,
  (ii) $z_{0.7}$,
 (iii) $z_{0.01}$, and
  (iv) $z_{0.9}$.

5.4   For a normally distributed variable, X, where $X \sim N(25, 9)$, find the following
       probabilities:

   (i) $P(X \leq 25)$,
  (ii) $P(X \geq 10)$, and
 (iii) $P(15 \leq X \leq 40)$.

5.5   Suppose that the mean duration of suffering from a viral infection is dis-
       tributed normally with mean 10 days and standard deviation 5 days.

   (i)   Find the probability that a randomly selected subject will suffer for less
         than 7 days.
  (ii)   Find the probability that a randomly selected subject will suffer from the
         viral infection for more than 5 days.
 (iii)   Find the probability that the subject will suffer from the viral infection
         for 8 to 12 days.
  (iv)   Find the number of days above which 70% of the subjects will suffer
         from viral infection.

5.6 Suppose that the money spent for medical purpose in among the elderly in a community is $50 per month with a standard deviation $9.

   (i) Find the amount of money or less spent by an elderly person in a month such that the probability is 0.75.
   (ii) Find the probability that an elderly person will spend less than $30.
   (iii) Find the amount of money or more spent by an elderly subject with probability 0.9.

5.7 In a study, it is found that the proportion of underweight children under 5 years in a community is 0.41. Let the sample size $n = 200$ and the random variable X denotes the number of underweight children.

   (i) Find the probability that the number of underweight children is less than 40.
   (ii) Find the probability that the number of underweight children is greater than 90.
   (iii) Find the probability that the number of children lies between 50 and 80.

Chapter 6
Sampling Distribution

6.1 Sampling Distribution

The probability distribution of a statistic is called the sampling distribution of that statistic. The sampling distribution of the statistic is used to make statistical inference about the unknown parameter. There may be question regarding probability distribution of a statistic when the probability distribution of a variable is known. It involves the role of a random sample in statistics. Let us consider a variable, X, and the population of X is comprised of N elements denoted by $(X_1, \ldots, X_N)$ which means that whenever we draw a sample of size, n, the values in the sample must be selected from these elements in the population. Before a sample is drawn, we do not have any idea which values from the population are being selected although it is known that n values in the sample must be from N values in the population. In that case for each value of the sample, a random variable can be defined, which are denoted by $(X_1, \ldots, X_n)$. The realization of random sample can be represented as $X_1 = x_1, \ldots, X_n = x_n$ where $(x_1, \ldots, x_n)$. A random sample implies that each random variable in a random sample can take any of the N values from the population. In other words, n random variables in the random sample may take $N \times \ldots \times N = N^n$ possible samples with replacement. Here, the term with replacement indicates that if one value from the population is already selected can be considered for being selected again in subsequent draws in the same sample. That is the population values can be selected multiple times in a sample. To avoid this repetition in the same sample, we may use the other approach named as sampling without replacement. Sampling without replacement ensures that if one value is drawn already from the population in a sample, it will be dropped from the next selection. In that case, the number of possible samples is $N \times (N-1) \times \ldots \times (N-n+1)$ where there is no replacement in a single sample and considering the order of selection. However, due to change in the order of selection in the sample which occurs in $n!$ ways, there are $n!$ samples with same elements if the order is considered in samples. Hence, to select samples without repetition within the sample (without

© Springer Nature Singapore Pte Ltd. 2018
M. A. Islam and A. Al-Shiha, *Foundations of Biostatistics*,
https://doi.org/10.1007/978-981-10-8627-4_6

replacement) or between samples (disregarding order), we have $N \times (N-1) \times$

$\ldots \times (N - n + 1)/n! = \begin{pmatrix} N \\ n \end{pmatrix}$ samples without replacement disregarding the order

of selection in samples. This has a very useful interpretation with deep-rooted implications in statistics. Let us illustrate with a small population size in the following example.

Example 6.1 Let us consider a population with four elements represented by $X_1 = 1, X_2 = 3, X_3 = 2,$ and $X_4 = 4$. The population size is $N = 4$. We want to draw a sample of size $n = 2$. Let us define the random sample as (X_1, X_2). Then we can select the samples by either with replacement or without replacement.

With replacement: The number of samples with replacement is $2^4 = 16$. The samples are: (1, 1), (1, 3), (1, 2), (1, 4), (3, 1), (3, 3), (3, 2), (3, 4), (2, 1), (2, 3), (2, 2), (2, 4), (4, 1), (4, 3), (4, 2), (4, 4).

Without replacement: The number of samples without replacement in each sample is $4 \times 3 = 12$ and the samples are (1, 3), (1, 2), (1, 4), (3, 1), (3, 2), (3, 4), (2, 1), (2, 3), (2, 4), (4, 1), (4, 3), (4, 2). It is clearly seen from these possible samples that each sample is repeated $2! = 2 \times 1$ times if we disregard the order of selection such as (1, 3) and (3, 1). Hence, the number of samples without replacement within each sample (without replacement) and between samples (dis-

regarding order) is $\begin{pmatrix} 4 \\ 2 \end{pmatrix} = 6$. If we consider without replacement and disregard

order then the samples are: (1, 3), (1, 2), (1, 4), (3, 2), (3, 4), and (2, 4).

We have discussed about the random sample with or without replacement above. The important point here is that we select only one sample out of all the possible samples using with or without replacement. Let us consider a hypothetical situation where all the possible samples could be drawn of same sample size, n. In that situation, we could find the value of statistic for all the possible samples. As an example, let us consider about the statistic, sample mean. If there are N^n possible samples with replacement then the number of values of statistic, mean, will be N^n too. Similarly,

disregarding order the number of samples without replacement is $\begin{pmatrix} N \\ n \end{pmatrix}$. We can find

the frequency distribution and probability distribution of the mean based on these values. This probability distribution is known as the sampling distribution. In other words, probability distribution of a statistic is known as the sampling distribution.

6.2 Sampling Distribution of the Sample Mean

The sampling distribution of the sample mean is widely used in statistics. Suppose that we have a population with mean μ and variance σ^2 and let $X_1, X_2, \ldots, X_n$ be a random sample of size n selected randomly from this population. We know that the sample mean is

$$\bar{X} = \frac{\sum_{i=1}^{n} X_i}{n}.$$

Example 6.2 Let us consider a population of size $N = 5$ and a sample of size $n = 3$. The population elements are $X_1 = 30, X_2 = 25, X_3 = 40, X_4 = 27,$ and $X_5 = 35$. The random sample is (X_1, X_2, X_3). All the possible samples, disregarding order and obtained without replacement randomly, are shown below. The number of samples using without replacement and disregarding order is $\binom{5}{3} = 10$. The population mean is $\mu = \frac{\sum_{i}^{5} X_i}{5} = \frac{157}{5} = 31.40$.

The mean of the sample means is Table 6.1

$$\mu = \frac{\sum_{i}^{10} \bar{X}_i}{10} = \frac{314}{10} = 31.40.$$

The population mean of the variable X and the population mean of means from the random samples of size n are exactly the same. From the above example, we observe that in both the cases, the mean is 31.40. This can be summarized as

$$E(X) = \mu,$$
$$E(\bar{X}) = \mu.$$

This is an important property of the sampling distribution of mean.

It is observed that the value of the sample mean, $\bar{X}$, varies from one random sample to another. The value of $\bar{X}$ is random and it depends on the random sample. Hence, the sample mean $\bar{X}$ is a random variable. The probability distribution of $\bar{X}$ is called the sampling distribution of the sample mean, $\bar{X}$.

Table 6.1 Sample means of all possible samples of size 3 from a population of size 5

Sample	X_1	X_2	X_3	$\bar{X}$
1	30	25	40	31.67
2	30	25	27	27.33
3	30	25	35	30.00
4	30	40	27	32.33
5	30	40	35	35.00
6	30	27	35	30.67
7	25	40	27	30.67
8	25	27	35	29.00
9	25	40	35	33.33
10	40	27	35	34.00

For the sampling distribution of the sample mean, we need to know the form of the sampling distribution, the expected value of the mean of the sample mean, $\bar{X}$, and the variance of the sample mean, $\bar{X}$.

6.3 Some Important Characteristics of the Sampling Distribution of $\overline{X}$

Mean and Variance of $\overline{X}$

If $X_1, X_2, \ldots, X_n$ is a random sample of size n from any distribution with mean μ and variance σ^2, then:

1. The mean of $\overline{X}$ is

$$\mu_{\bar{X}} = \mu.$$

2. The variance of $\overline{X}$ is

$$\sigma_{\bar{X}}^2 = \frac{\sigma^2}{n}.$$

3. The standard deviation of $\overline{X}$ is called <u>the standard error</u> of $\overline{X}$ and is defined by

$$\sigma_{\bar{X}} = \sqrt{\sigma_{\bar{X}}^2} = \frac{\sigma}{\sqrt{n}}.$$

It may be noted here that the square root of the variance of a statistic is termed as standard error. In this case, the standard error of the sample mean is $\frac{\sigma}{\sqrt{n}}$.

6.4 Sampling from Normal Population

If $X_1, X_2, \ldots, X_n$ is a random sample of size n from a normal population with mean μ and variance σ^2 that is Normal (μ, σ^2), then the sample mean has a normal distribution with mean μ and variance σ^2/n that is

1. $\bar{X} \sim$ Normal $\left(\mu, \frac{\sigma^2}{n}\right)$.

The sampling distribution of the sample mean, $\bar{X}$, can be shown as

$$f(\bar{x}; \mu, \sigma^2/n) = \frac{1}{\sqrt{2\pi\sigma^2/n}} e^{-\frac{n}{2\sigma^2}(\bar{x}-\mu)^2}, \quad -\infty < \bar{x} < \infty.$$

This is also a normal distribution with the same expected value as the expected value of X but with a different variance. The expected value of $\bar{X}$ is

$$
\begin{aligned}
E(\bar{X}) &= E\left[\frac{X_1 + \ldots + X_n}{n}\right] \\
&= \frac{E(X_1) + \ldots + E(X_n)}{n} \\
&= \frac{\mu + \ldots + \mu}{n} \\
&= \mu.
\end{aligned}
$$

We know that the random samples can take values randomly from the population with probability density function $X \sim N(\mu, \sigma^2)$. Hence, $E(X_1) = \ldots = E(X_n) = \mu$. Similarly, the variance of the sample mean, if $X_1, \ldots, X_n$ are independent, is

$$
\begin{aligned}
\mathrm{Var}(\bar{X}) &= \mathrm{Var}\left[\frac{X_1 + \ldots + X_n}{n}\right] \\
&= \frac{\mathrm{Var}(X_1) + \ldots + \mathrm{Var}(X_n)}{n^2} \\
&= \frac{\sigma^2 + \ldots + \sigma^2}{n^2} \\
&= \frac{n\sigma^2}{n^2} \\
&= \frac{\sigma^2}{n}.
\end{aligned}
$$

For variance also, the random variable in a random sample satisfies the assumption that $X \sim N(\mu, \sigma^2)$ where population mean and population variance remain same for all the random variables in a random sample. Hence, it can be shown that $\mathrm{Var}(X_1) = \ldots = \mathrm{Var}(X_n) = \sigma^2$.

2. $Z = \frac{\bar{X} - \mu}{\sigma/\sqrt{n}} \sim$ Normal $(0, 1)$.

We use this result when sampling from normal distribution with known variance σ^2. As we have shown that if $X \sim N(\mu, \sigma^2)$ then $\bar{X} \sim N(\mu, \sigma^2/n)$ implying that the sampling distribution of the sample mean follows the normal distribution as well. Hence, the standardized normal variate can be obtained for the sample mean as a random variable which is

$$Z = \frac{\bar{X} - \mu}{\sigma/\sqrt{n}},$$

where $Z \sim N(0, 1)$.

6.4.1   Central Limit Theorem: Sampling from Non-normal Population

Let $X_1, X_2, \ldots, X_n$ be a random sample of size n from non-normal population with mean μ and variance σ^2. If the sample size n is large or if $n \rightarrow \infty$ then the sample mean has approximately a normal distribution with mean μ and variance σ^2/n that is

(i) $\bar{X} \approx \text{Normal}\left(\mu, \frac{\sigma^2}{n}\right)$,

(ii) $Z = \frac{\bar{X} - \mu}{\sigma/\sqrt{n}} \approx N(0, 1)$ Normal $(0, 1)$.

Note: "$\approx$" means "approximately distributed".

We can use this result when sampling from non-normal distribution with known variance σ^2 and with large sample size too.

6.4.2   If σ^2 is Unknown and Sample is Drawn from Normal Population

If $X_1, X_2, \ldots, X_n$ is a random sample of size n from a normal distribution with mean μ and unknown variance σ^2 that is Normal (μ, σ^2), then the statistic

$$T = \frac{\bar{X} - \mu}{S/\sqrt{n}}$$

has a t-distribution with $(n - 1)$ degrees of freedom, where S is the sample standard deviation given by

$$S = \sqrt{S^2} = \sqrt{\frac{\sum_{i=1}^{n}(X_i - \bar{X})^2}{n - 1}}.$$

We write

$$T = \frac{\bar{X} - \mu}{S/\sqrt{n}} \sim t(n-1),$$

where the sampling distribution of T is known as t-distribution with degrees of freedom $= df = v = n - 1$.

6.5 The T-Distribution

The Student's t-distribution is a distribution of a continuous random variable similar to Z defined earlier. The difference between t and Z lies in the fact that although both assume the random sample $X_1, X_2, \ldots, X_n$ is a random sample of size n from a normal distribution with mean μ and variance σ^2, i.e., $N(\mu, \sigma^2)$, σ^2 is assumed to be known for defining Z but it is not known for t and hence needs to be estimated. We defined Z as

$$Z = \frac{\bar{X} - \mu}{\sigma/\sqrt{n}} \sim N(0, 1)$$

which is theoretically correct if σ^2 is known. If σ^2 is unknown, we replace the population variance σ^2 with the sample variance

$$S^2 = \frac{\sum_{i=1}^{n} (X_i - \bar{X})^2}{n-1}$$

to define the following statistic known as T or Student's T

$$T = \frac{\bar{X} - \mu}{S/\sqrt{n}}.$$

Then we can define the statistic T more precisely as follows. If $(X_1, X_2, \ldots, X_n)$ is a random sample of size n from a normal distribution and the random variables are independent with mean μ and variance σ^2, i.e., $N(\mu, \sigma^2)$, then the statistic

$$T = \frac{\bar{X} - \mu}{S/\sqrt{n}}$$

has a t-distribution with $(n-1)$ degrees of freedom and we write $T \sim t_{(v)}$ or $T \sim t_{(n-1)}$. The t-distribution with v degrees of freedom is

$$f(t, v) = \frac{\overline{)(v+1)/2}}{\overline{)v/2}\sqrt{\pi v}} \left(1 + \frac{t^2}{v}\right)^{-\frac{(v+1)}{2}}, \quad -\infty < t < \infty.$$

The mean and variance of T are

$$E(T) = 0,$$
$$\mathrm{Var}(T) = \frac{v}{v-2}, v > 2.$$

The t-distribution is a continuous distribution, the value of random variable T ranges from $-\infty$ to $+\infty$ (that is, $-\infty < t < \infty$), the mean of T is 0, variance is $v/(v-2)$, and the shape of t-distribution is similar to the shape of the standard normal distribution. It may also be noted that t-distribution $\rightarrow$ standard normal distribution as $n \rightarrow \infty$.

The following figure displays the t-distribution curves for different degrees of freedom. It shows that as the degrees of freedom increases, the t-distribution curve tends to standard normal distribution (Figs. 6.1 and 6.2).

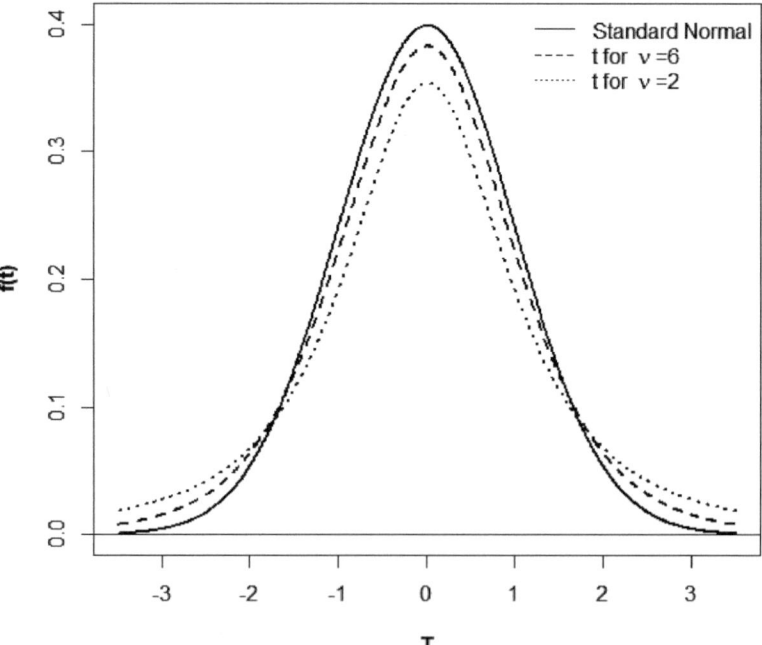

Fig. 6.1 Comparison between normal and t-distributions

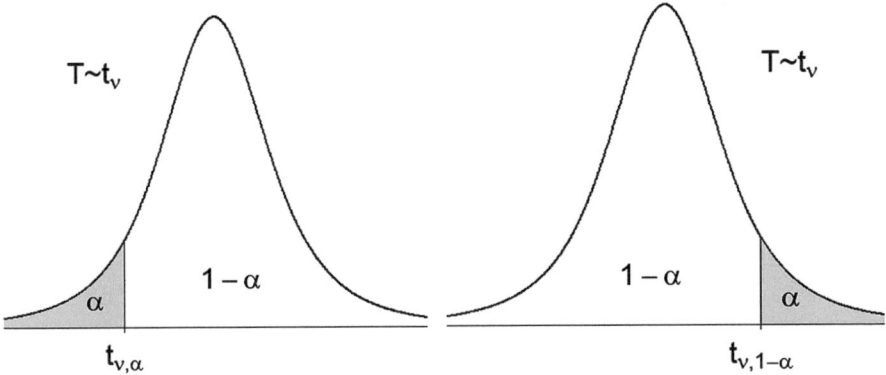

Fig. 6.2 Areas of *t*-distribution to the left and right tails

Area under the *t*-distribution curves is shown for $P(T < t_\alpha)$ and $P(T < t_{1-\alpha})$ in the figures displayed below. The mean of T is zero and the curve is symmetric that results in $t_\alpha = -t_{1-\alpha}$ or $t_{1-\alpha} = -t_\alpha$.

It may be noted here that

(i) t_α = the *t*-value under which we find an area equal to α = the *t*-value that covers an area of α to the left.
(ii) The value t_α satisfies: $P(T < t_\alpha) = \alpha$.
(iii) Since the curve of the pdf of $T \sim t(v)$ is symmetric about 0, we have

$$t_{1-\alpha} = -t_\alpha,$$

for example $t_{0.35} = -t_{1-0.35} = -t_{0.65}$, $t_{0.86} = -t_{1-0.86} = -t_{0.14}$.

(iv) In a table for *t*-distribution, the values of t_α are given for degrees of freedom. In other words, the value of t depends on degrees of freedom which implies that if the degree of freedom is specified then the area under a certain value of $T = t$ can be determined.

Example 6.3 Find the *t*-value with $v = 14$ that shows an area of

(a) 0.95 to the left,
(b) 0.95 to the right.

Solution
Here it is given that $v = 14$ which is and $T \sim t_{14}$ (Fig. 6.3).

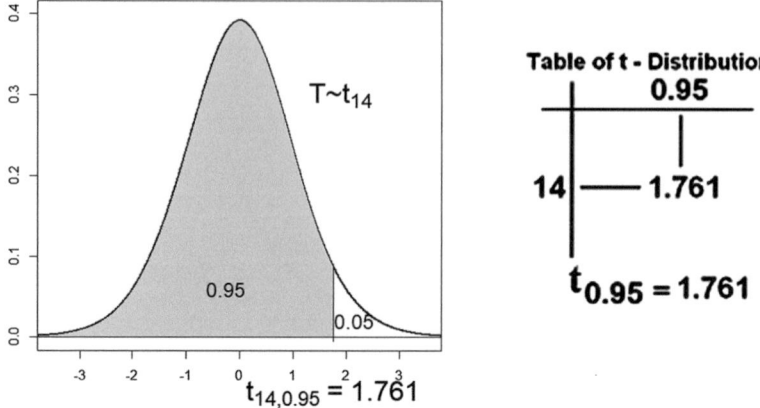

Fig. 6.3 Area of t to the left with 14 degrees of freedom

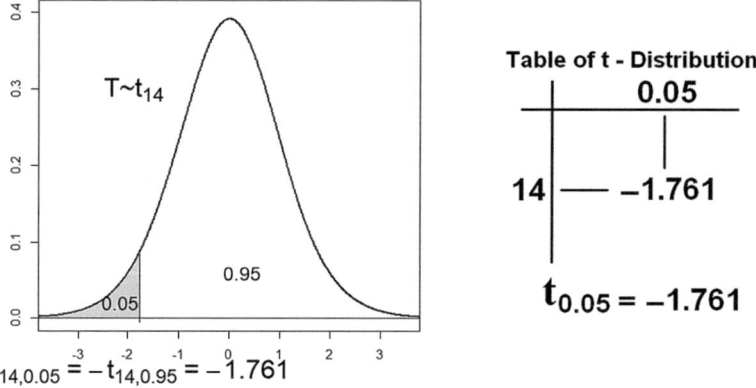

Fig. 6.4 Area of t to the right with 14 degrees of freedom

(a) The t-value that determines an area of 0.95 to the left is

$$t_{0.95} = 1.761.$$

(b) The t-value that leaves an area of 0.95 to the right is (Fig. 6.4)

$$t_{0.05} = -t_{1-0.05} = -t_{0.95} = -1.761$$

Note: Some t-tables contain values of α that are greater than or equal to 0.90. When we search for small values of α in these tables, we may use the fact that

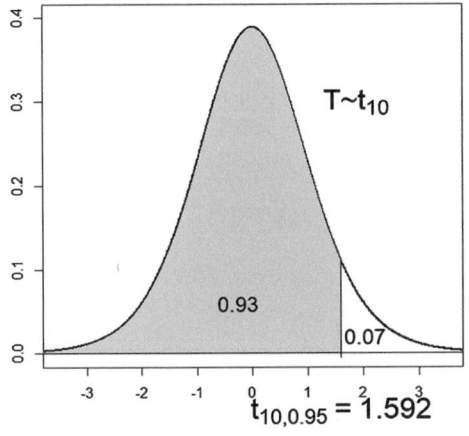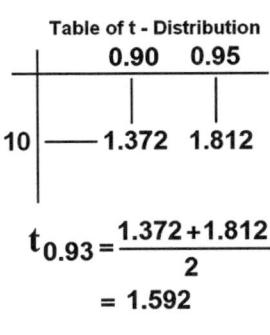

Fig. 6.5 $t_{0.93}$ for $v = 10$

$$t_{1-\alpha} = -t_\alpha$$

Example 6.4 For $v = 10$ degrees of freedom, find $t_{0.93}$ and $t_{0.07}$.

Solution

$t_{0.93}= (1.372 + 1.812)/2 = 1.592$ (from the table)
$t_{0.07} = -t_{1-0.07} = -t_{0.93} = -1.592$ (using the rule: $t_{1-\alpha} = -t_\alpha$) (Fig. 6.5)

Applications

Example 6.5 Let us consider that the temperature of patients with acute nephritis of renal pelvis origin may be greater than the individuals without having this disease rise and let the temperature of patients is normally distributed with the population mean 38.7 °C and the population standard deviation 1.82 Â °C. Find the probability that a random sample of 40 patients will have average temperature less than 38 °C.

Solution

X = the temperature of patient with acute nephritis of renal pelvis origin,
$\mu = 38.7$ °C,
$\sigma = 1.82$ °C,
$\sigma^2 = 3.31$ °C^2,
$X \sim N(38.7, 3.31)$,
Sample size, $n = 40$.

It has been shown earlier that the sampling distribution $\bar{X}$ is $\bar{X} \sim N(\mu, \sigma^2/n)$. The sample mean obtained from the sample of size 40 is $\bar{x} = 37$ and the population variance is assumed to be known as $\sigma^2 = 3.31 \; °C^2$. Hence, the standard error of the mean is $\sigma_{\bar{X}} = \sqrt{\frac{\sigma^2}{n}} = \sqrt{\frac{3.31}{40}} = \sqrt{0.08275} = 0.2877$.

Using the central limit theorem, $\bar{X}$ has a normal distribution with mean $\mu_{\bar{X}} = 38.7$ and variance $\sigma_{\bar{X}}^2 = 0.2877$ that is

$$\bar{X} \sim N\left(\mu, \frac{\sigma^2}{n}\right) = N(38.7, 0.2877)$$

$$Z = \frac{\bar{X} - \mu}{\sigma/\sqrt{n}} = \frac{\bar{X} - 38.7}{0.2877} \sim N(0, 1)$$

The probability that a random sample of 40 patients with acute nephritis of renal pelvis origin will have an average temperature of less than 38 °C is

$$\begin{aligned}
P(\bar{X} < 38) &= P\left(\frac{\bar{X} - \mu}{\sigma/\sqrt{n}} < \frac{38 - \mu}{1.82/\sqrt{40}}\right) \\
&= P\left(\frac{\bar{X} - 38.7}{1.82/\sqrt{40}} < \frac{38 - 38.7}{0.2877}\right) \\
&= P\left(Z < \frac{38 - 38.7}{0.2877}\right) \\
&= P(Z < -2.43) \\
&= 0.007549.
\end{aligned}$$

Example 6.6 If the mean and standard deviation of height of women in their reproductive age is 152 cm and standard deviation is 5 cm then find the probability that a random sample of size 50 women will yield a mean height between 150 and 154 cm.

Solution

X = the height of a woman in her reproductive period,
$\mu = 152$ cm,
$\sigma = 5$ cm,
$\sigma^2 = 25 \; cm^2$,
$X \sim N(152, 25)$,
Sample size, $n = 50$.

It has been shown earlier that the sampling distribution $\bar{X}$ is $\bar{X} \sim N(\mu, \sigma^2/n)$. The standard error of the mean is $\sigma_{\bar{X}} = \sqrt{\frac{\sigma^2}{n}} = \sqrt{\frac{25}{50}} = \sqrt{0.50} = 0.7071$.

Using the central limit theorem, $\bar{X}$ has a normal distribution with mean $\mu_{\bar{X}} = 152$ cm and variance $\sigma_{\bar{X}}^2 = 0.50 \; cm^2$ that is

$$\bar{X} \sim N\left(\mu, \frac{\sigma^2}{n}\right) = N(152, 0.50)$$

and it can be shown that

$$Z = \frac{\bar{X} - \mu}{\sigma/\sqrt{n}} = \frac{\bar{X} - 152}{0.7071} \sim N(0, 1).$$

The probability that the random sample of 50 women will yield average height in-between 150 and 154 cm is

$$P(150 < \bar{X} < 154) = P\left(\frac{150 - \mu}{5/\sqrt{50}} < \frac{\bar{X} - \mu}{\sigma/\sqrt{n}} < \frac{154 - \mu}{5/\sqrt{50}}\right)$$

$$= P\left(\frac{150 - 152}{5/\sqrt{50}} < Z < \frac{154 - 152}{5/\sqrt{50}}\right)$$

$$= P(-1.4142 < Z < 1.4142)$$

$$= P(Z < 1.4142) - P(Z < -1.4142)$$

$$= 0.9213 - 0.0787 = 0.8426$$

Example 6.7 *t*-distribution for single sample

Let us consider that in a rural population, the mean weight of women in their reproductive ages is 52 kg. The population variance is not known. Using the data from a sample of size $n = 24$ from a normally distributed population, the sample variance is $s^2 = 90.0217$. Find the probability that a randomly selected woman of childbearing age has weight less than 49 kg. Also, find the probability that a randomly selected woman of childbearing age has weight in between 49 and 53 kg.

Solution

X = the weight of women in their childbearing age in a rural community,
$\mu = 52$ kg

$$S = \sqrt{90.0217} = 9.4880 \, \text{kg},$$

$$X \sim N(\mu, \sigma^2),$$

sample size, $n = 24$.

It is shown earlier that if σ^2 is unknown, then we use the sample variance and replace the population variance σ^2 with

$$S^2 = \frac{\sum_{i=1}^{n} (X_i - \bar{X})^2}{n - 1}.$$

The Student's T is defined as

$$T = \frac{\bar{X} - \mu}{S/\sqrt{n}},$$

where $T \sim t_{(v)}$ or $T \sim t_{(n-1)}$. The standard error of the mean for unknown variance is $\sqrt{\frac{S^2}{n}} = \sqrt{\frac{90.0217}{24}} = \sqrt{3.7509} = 1.9367$.

Now using the above results, we obtain

$$T = \frac{\bar{X} - \mu}{S/\sqrt{n}} = \frac{\bar{X} - 52}{1.9367}$$

which is $t_{(23)}$.

The probability that a random sample of weights of 24 women in their child-bearing period is less than 49 kg is

$$P(\bar{X} < 49) = P\left(\frac{\bar{X} - \mu}{S/\sqrt{n}} < \frac{49 - \mu}{9,4880/\sqrt{24}}\right)$$

$$= P\left(\frac{\bar{X} - \mu}{S/\sqrt{n}} < \frac{49 - 52}{1.9367}\right)$$

$$= P\left(T < \frac{49 - 52}{1.9367}\right) = P(T < -1.5490) = 0.0675.$$

Now if we want to find the probability that a randomly selected woman will have weight in between 49 and 53 kg then

$$P(49 < \bar{X} < 53) = P\left(\frac{49 - \mu}{9,4880/\sqrt{24}} < \frac{\bar{X} - \mu}{S/\sqrt{n}} < \frac{53 - \mu}{9,4880/\sqrt{24}}\right)$$

$$= P\left(\frac{49 - 52}{1.9367} < \frac{\bar{X} - \mu}{S/\sqrt{n}} < \frac{53 - 52}{1.9367}\right)$$

$$= P\left(\frac{49 - 52}{1.9367} < T < \frac{53 - 52}{1.9367}\right)$$

$$= P(-1.5490 < T < 0.5163).$$

From the t-table, this probability can be obtained from the following:

$$P(-1.5490 < T < 0.5163) = P(T < 0.5163) - P(T < -1.5490)$$
$$= 0.6947 - 0.0675 = 0.6272.$$

6.6   Distribution of the Difference Between Two Sample Means $(\bar{X}_1 - \bar{X}_2)$

The difference between two sample means where random samples are considered for two different populations is of interest in many applications. Let the two random samples from populations 1 and 2 are denoted by $(X_{11}, \ldots, X_{1n_1})$ for the first sample with sample size n_1 and $(X_{21}, \ldots, X_{2n_2})$ for the second sample with sample size n_2. Here the first population is characterized with mean μ_1 and variance σ_1^2 and the second population with mean μ_2 and variance σ_2^2. We are interested in comparing μ_1 and μ_2, or equivalently, making inferences about the difference between the means $(\mu_1 - \mu_2)$. In this case, to make any inference about the difference between two means, we need the sampling distribution of the difference between two means. Let us assume that we independently select a random sample of size n_1 from the first population and another random sample of size n_2 from the second population. Let $\bar{X}_1$ and S_1^2 be the sample mean and the sample variance of the first sample and $\bar{X}_2$ and S_2^2 be the sample mean and the sample variance of the second sample. Then the sampling distribution of $\bar{X}_1 - \bar{X}_2$ is used to make inferences about $\mu_1 - \mu_2$.

The Sampling Distribution of $\bar{X}_1 - \bar{X}_2$

The mean, the variance, and the standard error of $\bar{X}_1 - \bar{X}_2$ are:
Mean of $\bar{X}_1 - \bar{X}_2$

$$\mu_{\bar{X}_1 - \bar{X}_2} = \mu_1 - \mu_2$$

Variance of $\bar{X}_1 - \bar{X}_2$

$$\sigma_{\bar{X}_1 - \bar{X}_2}^2 = \frac{\sigma_1^2}{n_1} + \frac{\sigma_2^2}{n_2},$$

Standard error of $\bar{X}_1 - \bar{X}_2$

$$\sigma_{\bar{X}_1 - \bar{X}_2} = \sqrt{\sigma_{\bar{X}_1 - \bar{X}_2}^2} = \sqrt{\frac{\sigma_1^2}{n_1} + \frac{\sigma_2^2}{n_2}}.$$

If the two random samples are selected from normal distributions (or non-normal distributions with large sample sizes) with known variances σ_1^2 and, σ_2^2 then the difference between the sample means $(\bar{X}_1 - \bar{X}_2)$ has a normal distribution with mean $(\mu_1 - \mu_2)$ and variance $(\sigma_1^2/n_1) + (\sigma_2^2/n_2)$ that is

$$\bar{X}_1 - \bar{X}_2 \sim N\left(\mu_1 - \mu_2, \frac{\sigma_1^2}{n_1} + \frac{\sigma_2^2}{n_2}\right)$$

and

$$Z = \frac{(\bar{X}_1 - \bar{X}_2) - (\mu_1 - \mu_2)}{\sqrt{\frac{\sigma_1^2}{n_1} + \frac{\sigma_2^2}{n_2}}} \sim N(0, 1).$$

In the above mentioned sampling distribution for the difference between two means, the population variances are assumed to be known. If that assumption does not hold true then we need to replace the population variance by the sample variance as shown before in case of single sample. Let us consider that the difference between the sample means is

$$\bar{X}_1 - \bar{X}_2 \sim N\left(\mu_1 - \mu_2, \frac{\sigma_1^2}{n_1} + \frac{\sigma_2^2}{n_2}\right)$$

as before and the sample variances for samples 1 and 2 are

$$S_1^2 = \frac{\sum_{i=1}^{n_1}(X_{1i} - \bar{X}_1)^2}{n_1 - 1}, \text{ and}$$

$$S_2^2 = \frac{\sum_{i=1}^{n_2}(X_{2i} - \bar{X}_2)^2}{n_2 - 1}.$$

Then we can define the statistic T as follows:

$$T = \frac{(\bar{X}_1 - \bar{X}_2) - (\mu_1 - \mu_2)}{\sqrt{\frac{S_1^2}{n_1} + \frac{S_2^2}{n_2}}} \sim t_{(n_1 + n_2 - 2)}$$

which is distributed as t with $(n_1 + n_2 - 2)$ degrees of freedom. Here, degrees of freedom are reduced by 2 from the total sample size, one from each sample, due to the following reasons: (i) Initially, we assumed that the random variables in the random samples from populations 1 and 2 have probability distributions $X_{1i} \sim N(\mu_1, \sigma_1^2)$ and $X_{2i} \sim N(\mu_2, \sigma_2^2)$ respectively; (ii) If σ_1^2 and σ_2^2 are unknown then while defining S_1^2 and S_2^2 for the random samples 1 and 2 respectively to replace the corresponding population variances, we need to assume that population means remain fixed that means the random samples have expected values equal to the population means that are given by the sample means from the two random samples. This restricts the random sample such that $(n_1 - 1)$ and $(n_2 - 1)$ values of random samples 1 and 2 can be drawn randomly from populations 1 and 2, respectively, without restrictions but to satisfy the condition that the random samples have the means equal to the population means, one of the values from each random sample has to be constrained to make the random sample mean equal to the corresponding population. (iii) Hence, one degree of freedom is lost from each sample resulting in a total degrees of freedom $= (n_1 - 1) + (n_2 - 1) = (n_1 + n_2 - 2)$.

Application

Example 6.8 Let us consider birth weights of two groups of babies with means and standard deviations of 3.3 and 0.6 kg for the first group and 3.1 and 0.5 kg for the second group. Find the probability of difference between means of birth weights from random samples of two groups of babies is greater than 0.3 kg. Let the sample size for the first group is 100 and the second group is 125. Also, find the probability of a difference between mean weights of two groups of babies between 0.1 and 0.3 kg.

Solution
For the first group:

$$\mu_1 = 3.3 \text{ kg}, \ \sigma_1 = 0.6 \text{ kg}, \ \sigma_1^2 = 0.36 \text{ kg}^2, \ n_1 = 100.$$

For the second group:

$$\mu_2 = 3.1 \text{ kg}, \ \sigma_2 = 0.5 \text{ kg}, \ \sigma_2^2 = 0.25 \text{ kg}^2, \ n_2 = 125.$$

The mean, the variance, and the standard error of $\bar{X}_1 - \bar{X}_2$ are shown below. Mean of $\bar{X}_1 - \bar{X}_2$ is

$$\mu_{\bar{X}_1 - \bar{X}_2} = \mu_1 - \mu_2 = 3.3 - 3.1 = 0.2.$$

The variance of $\bar{X}_1 - \bar{X}_2$ is

$$\sigma_{\bar{X}_1 - \bar{X}_2}^2 = \frac{\sigma_1^2}{n_1} + \frac{\sigma_2^2}{n_2} = \frac{0.36}{100} + \frac{0.25}{125} = 0.0056.$$

The standard error of $\bar{X}_1 - \bar{X}_2$ is

$$\sigma_{\bar{X}_1 - \bar{X}_2} = \sqrt{\sigma_{\bar{X}_1 - \bar{X}_2}^2} = \sqrt{0.0056} = 0.0748.$$

The sampling distribution of $\bar{X}_1 - \bar{X}_2$ is

$$\bar{X}_1 - \bar{X}_2 \sim N(0.2, 0.0056).$$

It can be shown that

$$Z = \frac{(\bar{X}_1 - \bar{X}_2) - 0.2}{\sqrt{0.0056}} \sim N(0, 1).$$

We can now find the probability of the difference between means of birth weights greater than 0.3 kg from the following steps:

$$P(\bar{X}_1 - \bar{X}_2 > 0.3) = P\left(\frac{(\bar{X}_1 - \bar{X}_2) - (\mu_1 - \mu_2)}{\sqrt{\frac{\sigma_1^2}{n_1} + \frac{\sigma_2^2}{n_2}}} > \frac{0.3 - (\mu_1 - \mu_2)}{\sqrt{\frac{\sigma_1^2}{n_1} + \frac{\sigma_2^2}{n_2}}} \right)$$

$$P\left(Z > \frac{0.3 - 0.2}{\sqrt{0.0056}}\right) = P\left(Z > \frac{0.3 - 0.2}{0.0748}\right) = P(Z > 1.3368)$$
$$= 1 - P(Z \leq 1.3368) = 1 - 0.9082 = 0.0918.$$

Similarly, the probability of a difference in between 0.1 and 0.3 kg can be obtained from

$$P(0.1 < \bar{X}_1 - \bar{X}_2 < 0.3) = P\left(\frac{0.1 - (\mu_1 - \mu_2)}{\sqrt{\frac{\sigma_1^2}{n_1} + \frac{\sigma_2^2}{n_2}}} < \frac{(\bar{X}_1 - \bar{X}_2) - (\mu_1 - \mu_2)}{\sqrt{\frac{\sigma_1^2}{n_1} + \frac{\sigma_2^2}{n_2}}} < \frac{0.3 - (\mu_1 - \mu_2)}{\sqrt{\frac{\sigma_1^2}{n_1} + \frac{\sigma_2^2}{n_2}}}\right)$$

Hence

$$P\left(\frac{0.1 - 0.2}{\sqrt{0.0056}} < Z < \frac{0.3 - 0.2}{\sqrt{0.0056}}\right) = P\left(\frac{0.1 - 0.2}{0.0748} < Z < \frac{0.3 - 0.2}{0.0748}\right)$$
$$= P(1.3368 < Z < 1.3368) = P(Z < 1.3368)$$
$$- P(Z < 1.3368)$$
$$= 0.9082 - 0.0918 = 0.8164.$$

Application

Example 6.9 Let us consider weights of women in their reproductive age from two populations. Suppose that the mean for populations 1 and 2 are 50 kg and 49 kg respectively. The population variances are unknown and samples are drawn randomly of size 12 and 10, respectively, from populations 1 and 2. The sample variances are 30 kg^2 for sample 1 and 25 kg^2 for sample 2. Then find the probability of a difference between the sample means is greater than 3 kg. Also, find the probability of a difference between the average weights in-between 1 and 2 kg.

For the first set:

$\mu_1 = 50\,\text{kg}$, $S_1 = 5.48\,\text{kg}$, $S_1^2 = 30\,\text{kg}^2$, $n_1 = 12$.

For the second set:

$\mu_2 = 49\,\text{kg}$, $S_2 = 5\,\text{kg}$, $S_2^2 = 25\,\text{kg}^2$, $n_2 = 10$.

The mean, the variance, and the standard error of $\bar{X}_1 - \bar{X}_2$ are:
Mean of $\bar{X}_1 - \bar{X}_2$ is

$$\mu_{\bar{X}_1 - \bar{X}_2} = \mu_1 - \mu_2 = 50 - 49 = 1.$$

The sample variance of $\bar{X}_1 - \bar{X}_2$ is

$$S^2_{\bar{X}_1 - \bar{X}_2} = \frac{S^2_1}{n_1} + \frac{S^2_2}{n_2} = \frac{30}{12} + \frac{25}{10} = 5.$$

The standard error of $\bar{X}_1 - \bar{X}_2$ is

$$S_{\bar{X}_1 - \bar{X}_2} = \sqrt{S^2_{\bar{X}_1 - \bar{X}_2}} = \sqrt{5} = 2.2361.$$

We can define the statistic T by

$$T = \frac{(\bar{X}_1 - \bar{X}_2) - (\mu_1 - \mu_2)}{\sqrt{\frac{S^2_1}{n_1} + \frac{S^2_2}{n_2}}} \sim t_{(n_1 + n_2 - 2)}.$$

To find the probability of the difference between means of weights less than 3 kg

$$P(\bar{X}_1 - \bar{X}_2 < 3) = P\left(\frac{(\bar{X}_1 - \bar{X}_2) - (\mu_1 - \mu_2)}{\sqrt{\frac{S^2_1}{n_1} + \frac{S^2_2}{n_2}}} > \frac{3 - (\mu_1 - \mu_2)}{\sqrt{\frac{S^2_1}{n_1} + \frac{S^2_2}{n_2}}}\right)$$

$$P\left(T > \frac{3-1}{\sqrt{5}}\right) = P\left(T > \frac{2}{2.2361}\right) = P(T > 0.4472)$$

$$= 1 - P(T \le 0.4472) = 1 - 0.6702 = 0.3298.$$

Here, the degrees of freedom of t is 20.

Similarly, the probability of a difference in between 0.1 and 0.3 kg can be obtained from

$$P(0.1 < \bar{X}_1 - \bar{X}_2 < 0.3) = P\left(\frac{0.1 - (\mu_1 - \mu_2)}{\sqrt{\frac{\sigma^2_1}{n_1} + \frac{\sigma^2_2}{n_2}}} < \frac{(\bar{X}_1 - \bar{X}_2) - (\mu_1 - \mu_2)}{\sqrt{\frac{\sigma^2_1}{n_1} + \frac{\sigma^2_2}{n_2}}} < \frac{0.3 - (\mu_1 - \mu_2)}{\sqrt{\frac{\sigma^2_1}{n_1} + \frac{\sigma^2_2}{n_2}}}\right).$$

Hence

$$P\left(\frac{0.1 - 0.2}{\sqrt{0.0056}} < Z < \frac{0.3 - 0.2}{\sqrt{0.0056}}\right) = P\left(\frac{0.1 - 0.2}{0.0748} < Z < \frac{0.3 - 0.2}{0.0748}\right)$$

$$= P(1.3368 < Z < 1.3368) = P(Z < 1.3368)$$

$$- P(Z < 1.3368)$$

$$= 0.9082 - 0.0918 = 0.8164.$$

6.7 Distribution of the Sample Proportion ($\hat{p}$)

Let us define a random variable X = number of elements or subjects with a specified characteristic A. Let n = total number of elements in the sample. The probability that a randomly selected subject or element has characteristic A is denoted as p which is essentially the proportion of elements or subjects with characteristic A in the population. We know from the Bernoulli distribution that each subject or element in a Bernoulli trial has a probability, p. Let us define $X_i = 1$, if the ith Bernoulli trial results in selecting an element or subject with characteristic A, $X_i = 0$, otherwise. If a sequence of n Bernoulli trials is performed independently then the number of successes is X and it can be expressed as a binomial variable. The random sample of size n is $(X_1, \ldots, X_n)$. Here $X = \sum_{i=1}^{n} X_i$ = the number of elements or subjects selected with characteristic A. Then the proportion is defined for a random sample of size n as

$$\hat{p} = \frac{X}{n}$$

which is a statistic.

We have to use the sampling distribution of p to make inferences about the parameter, p. The mean of the sample proportion ($\hat{p}$) is the population proportion (p) that is

$$\mu_{\hat{p}} = p.$$

It is known that $E(X_i) = p$ and $E(X) = E\left(\sum_{i=1}^{n} X_i\right) = \sum_{i=1}^{n} E(X_i) = np$. The variance of the sample proportion p can be defined as

$$\mathrm{Var}(\hat{p}) = \sigma_{\hat{p}}^2 = \mathrm{Var}\left(\frac{X}{n}\right) = \frac{\mathrm{Var}(X)}{n^2},$$

where

$$\mathrm{Var}(X) = \mathrm{Var}\left(\sum_{i=1}^{n} X_i\right) = \sum_{i=1}^{n} \mathrm{Var}(X_i) = np(1-p) = npq.$$

Hence, the variance of the sample proportion is

$$\sigma_{\hat{p}}^2 = \frac{np(1-p)}{n^2} = \frac{pq}{n}.$$

The standard error of the sample proportion, $\hat{p}$, is

$$\sigma_{\hat{p}} = \sqrt{\frac{p(1-p)}{n}} = \sqrt{\frac{pq}{n}}.$$

For large sample size ($n \geq 30$, $np > 5$, $nq > 5$), the sample proportion $(\hat{p})$ has approximately a normal distribution with mean $\mu_{\hat{p}} = p$ and a variance $\sigma_{\hat{p}}^2 = pq/n$ that is

$$\hat{p} \sim N\left(p, \frac{pq}{n}\right),$$

$$Z = \frac{\hat{p} - p}{\sqrt{\frac{pq}{n}}} \sim N(0, 1).$$

Example 6.10 Let us suppose that the proportion of under 5 children with underweight for their height is 17%. If a sample of 50 under 5 children is selected at random, find the probability that

1. the proportion of children in the sample will be underweight for their height is greater than 0.3, and
2. the proportion of children in the sample will be underweight for their height is between 0.1 and 0.2.

Solution
The sample size is $n = 50$ which is greater than 30 and we may use the Central Limit Theorem to obtain the sampling distribution characteristics of proportion. The percentage of underweight children for their height is 17% which means that the proportion of underweight children for their height is $p = 0.17$.
   Hence, the mean, variance, and standard error of $\hat{p}$ are

$$\mu_{\hat{p}} = p = 0.17,$$
$$\sigma_{\hat{p}}^2 = \frac{p(1-p)}{n} = \frac{0.17 \times 0.83}{50} = \frac{0.1411}{50} = 0.0028,$$
$$\sigma_{\hat{p}} = 0.0531.$$

The asymptotic distribution of the sample proportion using the Central Limit Theorem is standardized normal distribution as shown below

$$Z = \frac{\hat{p} - p}{\sqrt{\frac{p(1-p)}{n}}} \approx N(0, 1).$$

Then the probability that the sample proportion of underweight children for height greater than 0.3 is

$$P(\hat{p} > 0.3) = P\left(\frac{\hat{p} - p}{\sqrt{\frac{p(1-p)}{n}}} > \frac{0.3 - p}{\sqrt{\frac{p(1-p)}{n}}} \right)$$

$$= 1 - P\left(\frac{\hat{p} - p}{\sqrt{\frac{p(1-p)}{n}}} \le \frac{0.3 - p}{\sqrt{\frac{p(1-p)}{n}}} \right)$$

$$= 1 - P\left(Z \le \frac{0.3 - p}{\sqrt{\frac{p(1-p)}{n}}} \right) = 1 - P\left(Z \le \frac{0.3 - 0.17}{0.0531} \right)$$

$$= 1 - P(Z \le 2.4482) = 1 - 0.9928 = 0.0072.$$

Similarly, the probability that the sample proportion of underweight children for height lies between 0.1 and 0.2 is

$$P(0.1 < \hat{p} < 0.2) = P\left(\frac{0.1 - p}{\sqrt{\frac{p(1-p)}{n}}} < \frac{\hat{p} - p}{\sqrt{\frac{p(1-p)}{n}}} < \frac{0.2 - p}{\sqrt{\frac{p(1-p)}{n}}} \right)$$

$$= P\left(Z < \frac{0.2 - p}{\sqrt{\frac{p(1-p)}{n}}} \right) - P\left(Z \le \frac{0.1 - p}{\sqrt{\frac{p(1-p)}{n}}} \right)$$

$$= P\left(Z < \frac{0.2 - 0.17}{0.0531} \right) - P\left(Z \le \frac{0.1 - 0.17}{0.0531} \right)$$

$$= P(Z < 0.5650) - P(Z \le -1.3183)$$

$$= 0.7140 - 0.0937 = 0.6203.$$

6.8   Distribution of the Difference Between Two Sample Proportions, $(\hat{p}_1 - \hat{p}_2)$

Let us consider random samples of size n_1 and n_2, respectively, from two different populations. The random samples are defined as $(X_{11}, \ldots, X_{1n_1})$ for population 1 and $(X_{21}, \ldots, X_{2n_2})$ for population 2. The variables in the random samples in both the cases are assumed to be Bernoulli trials for selecting elements or subjects randomly with characteristic A, then let us define

$X_1 = \sum_{i=1}^{n_1} X_{1i}$ = number of elements or subjects with characteristic A in the first random sample,

$X_2 = \sum_{i=1}^{n_2} X_{2i}$ = number of elements or subjects with characteristic A in the second random sample,

p_1 = proportion of elements of type (A) in the first population,
p_2 = proportion of elements of type (A) in the second population.

We are interested in comparing p_1 and p_2, or equivalently, making inferences about $p_1 - p_2$. Let us assume that we <u>independently</u> select the random samples of size n_1 from the first population and another random sample of size n_2 from the second population, then

$\hat{p}_1 = \frac{X_1}{n_1}$ = sample proportion of elements or subjects with characteristic A in random sample 1,

$\hat{p}_2 = \frac{X_2}{n_2}$ = sample proportion of elements or subjects with characteristic A in random sample 2, and

$\hat{p}_1 - \hat{p}_2$ = difference between sample proportions.

The Sampling Distribution of $\hat{p}_1 - \hat{p}_2$
The mean of the difference between sample proportions $(\hat{p}_1 - \hat{p}_2)$ is

$$\mu_{\hat{p}_1 - \hat{p}_2} = p_1 - p_2.$$

We can show that

$$E(X_{1i}) = p_1 \text{ and } E(X_1) = E\left(\sum_{i=1}^{n_1} X_{1i}\right) = \sum_{i=1}^{n_2} E(X_{1i}) = n_1 p_1,$$

and

$$E(X_{2i}) = p_2 \text{ and } E(X_2) = E\left(\sum_{i=1}^{n_2} X_{2i}\right) = \sum_{i=1}^{n_2} E(X_{2i}) = n_2 p_2.$$

Hence

$$\mu_{\hat{p}_1 - \hat{p}_2} = E(\hat{p}_1 - \hat{p}_2) = E\left(\frac{X_1}{n_1} - \frac{X_2}{n_2}\right) = \frac{E(X_1)}{n_1} - \frac{E(X_2)}{n_2} = p_1 - p_2.$$

The variance of the difference between two sample proportions where random samples are drawn independently is

$$\text{Var}(\hat{p}_1 - \hat{p}_2) = \sigma^2_{\hat{p}_1 - \hat{p}_2} = \text{Var}\left(\frac{X_1}{n_1} - \frac{X_2}{n_2}\right) = \frac{\text{Var}(X_1)}{n_1^2} + \frac{\text{Var}(X_2)}{n_2^2},$$

where

$$\mathrm{Var}(X_1) = \mathrm{Var}\left(\sum_{i=1}^{n_1} X_{1i}\right) = \sum_{i=1}^{n_1} \mathrm{Var}(X_{1i}) = n_1 p_1 (1 - p_1) = n_1 p_1 q_1$$

and

$$\mathrm{Var}(X_2) = \mathrm{Var}\left(\sum_{i=1}^{n_2} X_{2i}\right) = \sum_{i=1}^{n_2} \mathrm{Var}(X_{2i}) = n_2 p_2 (1 - p_2) = n_2 p_2 q_2,$$

The variance of the difference between two sample proportions is

$$\sigma^2_{\hat{p}_1 - \hat{p}_2} = \frac{n_1 p_1 (1 - p_1)}{n_1^2} + \frac{n_2 p_2 (1 - p_2)}{n_2^2} = \frac{p_1 q_1}{n_1} + \frac{p_2 q_2}{n_2}.$$

The standard error of the sample proportion, $\hat{p}_1 - \hat{p}_2$, is

$$\sigma_{\hat{p}_1 - \hat{p}_2} = \sqrt{\frac{p_1 q_1}{n_1} + \frac{p_2 q_2}{n_2}}.$$

For large samples sizes, the Central Limit Theorem can be used to show that the difference between two sample means is asymptotically normal and the standardized normal statistic can be defined as

$$Z = \frac{(\hat{p}_1 - \hat{p}_2) - (p_1 - p_2)}{\sqrt{\frac{p_1 q_1}{n_1} + \frac{p_2 q_2}{n_2}}} \sim N(0, 1).$$

Example 6.11 Suppose that stunting among under 5 children in rural and urban areas in a region are 45 and 36% respectively. We have randomly and independently selected a sample of 120 rural and 100 urban children of under 5 years. What is the probability that the difference between the sample proportions, $\hat{p}_1 - \hat{p}_2$, is between 0.10 and 0.20?

Solution
The proportions in the populations are defined as

p_1 = population proportion of under 5 children with stunting in rural area,
p_2 = population proportion of under 5 children with stunting in urban area.

The estimates are
$\hat{p}_1$ = sample proportion of under 5 children with stunting in rural area,
$\hat{p}_2$= sample proportion of under 5 children with stunting in urban area.

The population proportions given are $p_1 = 0.45$ for rural area and $p_2 = 0.36$ for urban area and sample size for rural and urban areas are $n_1 = 120$ and $n_2 = 100$, respectively. The difference between sample proportions is

$$\mu_{\hat{p}_1 - \hat{p}_2} = p_1 - p_2 = 0.45 - 0.36 = 0.09$$

The variance and standard error of the difference between two sample estimates can also be obtained as shown below

$$\begin{aligned} \sigma^2_{\hat{p}_1 - \hat{p}_2} &= \frac{p_1 \times q_1}{n_1} + \frac{p_2 \times q_2}{n_2} \\ &= \frac{0.45 \times 0.55}{120} + \frac{0.36 \times 0.64}{100} \\ &= 0.0021 + 0.0023 \\ &= 0.0044. \end{aligned}$$

The standard error of the difference between two sample proportions is

$$\begin{aligned} \sigma_{\hat{p}_1 - \hat{p}_2} &= \sqrt{\frac{p_1 \times q_1}{n_1} + \frac{p_2 \times q_2}{n_2}} \\ &= \sqrt{0.0044} \\ &= 0.0663. \end{aligned}$$

To find the probability of the difference between the sample proportions, $\hat{p}_1 - \hat{p}_2$, between 0.10 and 0.20, we follow the steps shown below:

$$\begin{aligned} P(0.10 < \hat{p}_1 - \hat{p}_2 < 0.20) &= P\left(\frac{0.10 - (p_1 - p_2)}{\sqrt{\frac{p_1 q_1}{n_1} + \frac{p_2 q_2}{n_2}}} < \frac{\hat{p}_1 - \hat{p}_2 - (p_1 - p_2)}{\sqrt{\frac{p_1 q_1}{n_1} + \frac{p_2 q_2}{n_2}}} < \frac{0.20 - (p_1 - p_2)}{\sqrt{\frac{p_1 q_1}{n_1} + \frac{p_2 q_2}{n_2}}} \right) \\ &= P\left(\frac{0.10 - (p_1 - p_2)}{\sqrt{\frac{p_1 q_1}{n_1} + \frac{p_2 q_2}{n_2}}} < Z < \frac{0.20 - (p_1 - p_2)}{\sqrt{\frac{p_1 q_1}{n_1} + \frac{p_2 q_2}{n_2}}} \right) \\ &= P\left(\frac{0.10 - 0.10}{0.0663} < Z < \frac{0.20 - 0.10}{0.0633} \right) \\ &= P(0 < Z < 1.5798) \\ &= P(Z < 1.5798) - P(Z \le 0) \\ &= 0.9429 - 0.5 = 0.4429. \end{aligned}$$

6.9 Chi-Square Distribution (χ^2—Distribution)

We learned about the standardized normal distribution in Chap. 5. Let us consider a random sample of size n, $(X_1, \ldots, X_n)$, from a normal population with mean μ and variance σ^2 expressed as $X \sim N(\mu, \sigma^2)$ then the standardized normal variable is defined by

$$Z = \frac{X - \mu}{\sigma} \sim N(0, 1).$$

The random sample is drawn independently from the identical normal distribution $X \sim N(\mu, \sigma^2)$. This implies that X_i, $i = 1, \ldots, n$ is drawn independently from the population such that $X_i \sim N(\mu, \sigma^2)$ that is each variable in the random sample has an identical distribution. Then a chi-square is defined as the sum of squared standardized normal variables for known μ and σ^2 as shown below

$$\chi^2 = \sum_{i=1}^{n} Z_i^2,$$

where this is called chi-square statistic with n degrees of freedom and is denoted by χ_n^2.

It is not practical to use chi-square in situations when the population mean and the variance are not known. Another problem with the chi-square statistic described above is that the normality assumption may not hold in many instances. Let us discuss these situations. If the mean and the variance of the normal population from where the random sample is drawn are not known then we can define the following components of a chi-square

$$
\begin{aligned}
\chi_n^2 &= \sum_{i=1}^{n} \left(\frac{X_i - \mu}{\sigma} \right)^2 \\
&= \sum_{i=1}^{n} \left[\frac{(X_i - \bar{X})^2 + (\bar{X} - \mu)^2}{\sigma^2} \right] \\
&= \sum_{i=1}^{n} \frac{(X_i - \bar{X})^2}{\sigma^2} + \frac{n(\bar{X} - \mu)^2}{\sigma^2} \\
&= \sum_{i=1}^{n} \frac{(X_i - \bar{X})^2}{\sigma^2} + \frac{(\bar{X} - \mu)^2}{\sigma^2/n}
\end{aligned}
$$

As we have shown earlier that $\bar{X} \sim N(\mu, \sigma^2/n)$ and $\frac{\bar{X} - \mu}{\sigma/\sqrt{n}} \sim N(0, 1)$ then it follows that

$$\frac{(\bar{X} - \mu)^2}{\sigma^2/n} = Z^2 \sim \chi_1^2.$$

The other component is

$$\sum_{i=1}^{n} \frac{(X_i - \bar{X})^2}{\sigma^2} = \frac{(n-1)S^2}{\sigma^2} \sim \chi_{n-1}^2,$$

where $S^2 = \frac{\sum_{i=1}^{n}(X_i-\bar{X})^2}{n-1}$ and one degree of freedom is lost in the component of chi-square due to replacing μ by $\bar{X}$ or, in other words, the sample mean is estimated to replace the population mean that constrains the computation of chi-square by one degree of freedom.

A continuous random variable X is defined to have a chi-square distribution if the probability density function is

$$f(x) = \frac{1}{)(r/2)2^{r/2}} x^{r/2-1} e^{-x/2}, 0 < x < \infty.$$

This is a chi-square distribution with r degrees of freedom. The expected value is r and the variance is $2r$.

In most of the applications, we are interested in obtaining the critical value of the χ^2-distribution which is that value of the random variable X that leaves an area equal α to the right, this value is denoted by $\chi_\alpha^2(n)$. More precisely, the critical value $\chi_\alpha^2(n)$ is that value satisfying the following condition

$$P(X > \chi_\alpha^2(n)) = \alpha.$$

Figure 6.6 illustrates this value.

Special tables are available in literature where we can find the critical values, $\chi_\alpha^2(n)$, for several values of α and n. The following figure illustrates how to use these tables to find the value after determining the value of α and the value of the degrees of freedoms $n = df$:

Fig. 6.6 Figure displaying the shape of a chi-square distribution

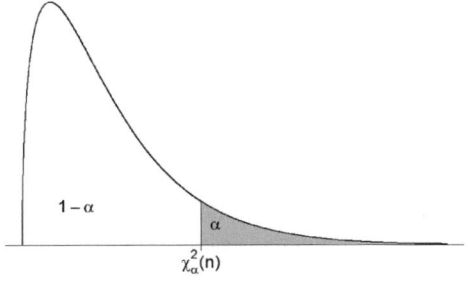

$1-\alpha$

α

$\chi_\alpha^2(n)$

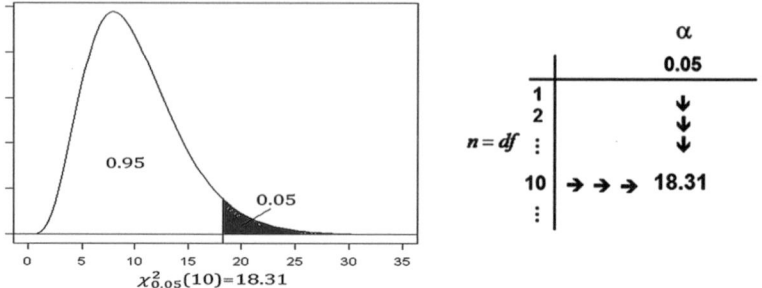

Fig. 6.7 Area of chi-square with 10 degrees of freedom

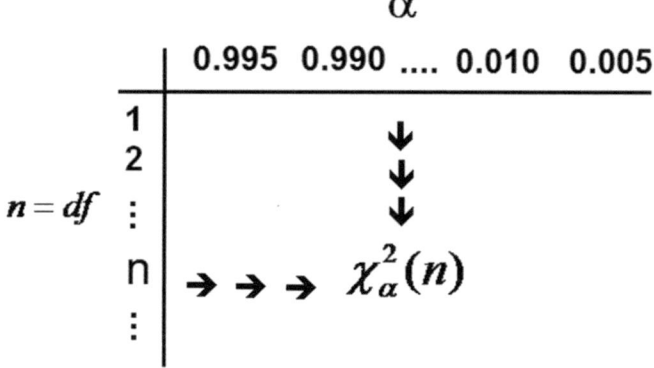

Example 6.12 (1) Suppose that the random variable X has a χ^2 distribution with parameter $r = 10$, i.e., $X \sim \chi^2(10)$. Find the value of the random variable X that leaves an area equal $\alpha = 0.05$ to the right of it.

Solution

The value of the random variable X that leaves an area equal $\alpha = 0.05$ to the right of it is $\chi^2_{0.05}(10) = 18.31$. Figure 6.7 illustrates this value.

6.10 *F*-Distribution

The *F*-distribution is an important continuous distribution used in many statistical applications. To introduce this distribution, suppose that we have two independent chi-square random variables X and Y with degrees of freedoms n and m, respectively, i.e., $X \sim \chi^2(n)$ and $Y \sim \chi^2(m)$. The random variable F which is defined by the following ratio:

$$F = \frac{X/n}{Y/m}$$

has an *F*-distribution with parameters *n* and *m*, and we write $F \sim F(n, m)$. The *F*-distribution is characterized by two parameters *n* and *m* and we can find the probabilities of *F* on the basis of these degrees of freedom. In general, the *F*-distribution is used extensively to compare sample variances and it has a wide range of applications to compare two or more samples.

The sampling distribution of *F* is the probability density function of the ratio $F = \frac{X/n}{Y/m}$ where $X \sim \chi^2(n)$ and. $Y \sim \chi^2(m)$, *n* and *m* are degrees of freedom, respectively. The sampling distribution of *F* is given by the density function

$$g(f) = \frac{\overline{)\,(n+m)/2}(n/m)^{n/2}}{\overline{)\,n/2})m/2} \frac{f^{n/2-1}}{(1+nf/m)^{(n+m)/2}}, \quad 0 < f < \infty.$$

In most of the applications, we are interested in obtaining the critical value of *F* which is that value of the random variable *F* that leaves an area equal α to the right, this value is denoted by $F_\alpha(n, m)$. More precisely, the critical value $F_\alpha(n, m)$ is that value satisfying the following condition:

$$P(F > F_\alpha(n, m)) = \alpha.$$

Figure 6.8 illustrates this value.

A special table is available in literature where we can find the critical value $F_\alpha(n, m)$ for several values of *n*, *m*, and α. The following figure illustrates how to use these tables to find the critical value $F_\alpha(n, m)$ after determining the value of α and the values of the degrees of freedoms *n* and *m*:

Fig. 6.8 Figure displaying the shape of an *F*-distribution

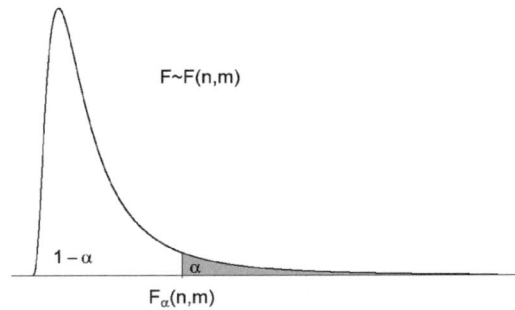

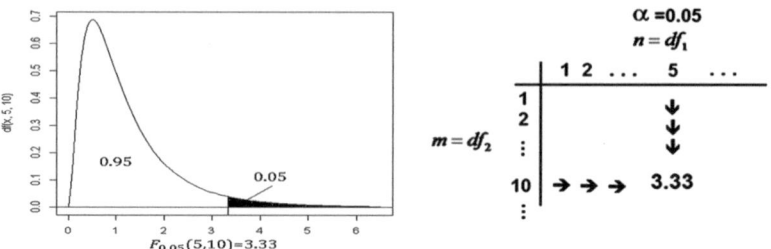

Fig. 6.9 Figure displaying F-distribution with (5, 10) degrees of freedom

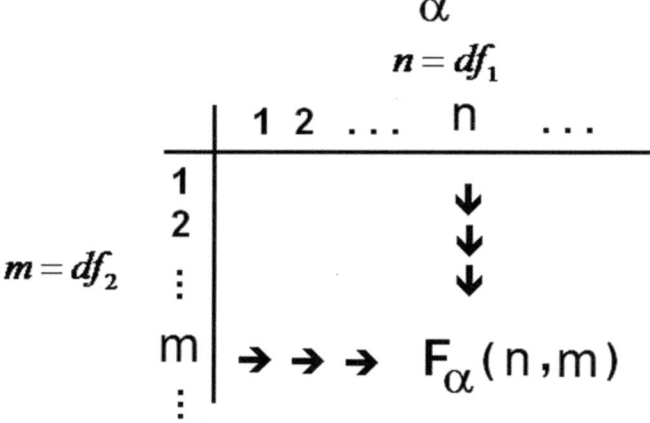

Example 6.13 Suppose that the random variable F has an F-distribution with parameters $n = 5$ and $m = 10$, i.e., $F \sim F(5, 10)$. Find the value of the random variable F that leaves an area equal $\alpha = 0.05$ to the right of it.

Solution
The value of the random variable F that leaves an area equal $\alpha = 0.05$ to the right of it is $F_{0.05}(5, 10) = 3.33$. Figure 6.9 illustrates this value.

6.11 Summary

In this chapter, the concepts of sampling distribution are introduced. The meaning of a sampling distribution is illustrated with examples in order to provide the users with fundamental concepts in a step-by-step procedure. The sampling distributions of mean for both small and large samples are discussed. The underlying assumptions about the distributions from which the samples are drawn and about the population variance are also highlighted. Similarly, the sampling distributions of difference between two means along with the underlying assumptions about the populations are shown with examples. The sampling distributions of sample proportion and difference between two proportions are discussed with examples. The sampling distributions included in this chapter are normal, t, chi-square, and F-distributions.

Exercises

6.1 Suppose that a population is comprised of 10 elements. The elements of the population are $X_1 = 10, X_2 = 7, X_3 = 15, \ X_4 = 16, X_5 = 5, X_6 = 11, X_7 = 14, \ X_8 = 8, X_9 = 15, X_{10} = 11$.
In other words, the population size is $N = 10$. A sample of size $n = 2$ is to be drawn randomly.

    (i) How many samples can be drawn with replacement?
    (ii) How many samples can be drawn without replacement?
    (iii) Find the sample means of all possible samples that can be drawn without replacement.
    (iv) Find the population mean, μ.
    (v) Find the population variance, σ^2.
    (vi) Find the expected value of the sample mean, $\bar{X}, \mu_{\bar{X}}$.
    (vii) Find the variance of the sample mean, $\bar{X}, \sigma_{\bar{X}}^2$.
    (viii) Using the above results, are the following statements true?

        (a) $\mu_{\bar{X}} = \mu$;
        (b) $\sigma_{\bar{X}}^2 = \frac{\sigma^2}{n}$.

6.2 Suppose X is distributed as normal with population mean 10 and population variance 4. For a random sample of size 9, what is the sampling distribution of the sample mean, $\bar{X}$? Also, define the standard normal variate using the given information.

6.3 Let us consider a non-normal population with mean 150 and variance 25. How can you find the sampling distribution of the sample mean for a random sample of size $n = 100$? What are the underlying preconditions for the asymptotic sampling distribution?

6.4 Find the following values for $v = 14$:

    (a) (i) $t_{0.05}$,
        (ii) $t_{0.95}$,
        (iii) $t_{0.01}$,
        (iv) $t_{0.025}$, and
        (v) $t_{0.001}$.

6.5 Find the following probabilities:

    (i) $P(-1.476 < T < 1.476)$ for $v = 5$,
    (ii) $P(-1.7959 < T < 1.7959)$ for $v = 11$,

(iii) $P(-2.1009 < T < 2.1009)$ for $v = 18$,
(iv) $P(T < -2.500)$ for $v = 23$, and
(v) $P(T > 2.500)$ for $v = 23$.

6.7   Suppose that the variable X be a normal distribution with population mean 15 and standard deviation 3.5. A study is conducted with sample size $n = 70$.

(i)   What is the sampling distribution of the sample mean $\bar{X}$?
(ii)   Find the probability $P(\bar{X} < 17)$.
(iii)   Find the probability $P(\bar{X} > 12)$.
(iv)   Find the probability $P(12 < \bar{X} < 17)$.

6.8   Let X be distributed with population mean 40 and variance 16 where the population is not normal. If a random sample of size 100 is drawn from the population then find:

(i)   the sampling distribution of the sample mean $\bar{X}$,
(ii)   the probability $P(\bar{X} < 25)$,
(iii)   the probability $P(\bar{X} > 45)$,
(iv)   the probability $P(30 < \bar{X} < 50)$.

6.9   Let the variable X be normal with population mean 125 but the population variance is unknown. A random sample of size 16 is drawn from the population and the sample variance is obtained where the sample variance s^2 is 81. Then find:

(i)   the sampling distribution of the sample mean $\bar{X}$,
(ii)   the probability $P(\bar{X} < 100)$,
(iii)   the probability $P(\bar{X} > 150)$,
(iv)   the probability $P(90 < \bar{X} < 150)$.

6.10   The population mean, and variance of a characteristic, X, of two groups of individuals are $\mu_1 = 25, \sigma_1^2 = 9$ for group 1 and $\mu_2 = 31, \sigma_2^2 = 12$ for group 2. In a study on the difference between two population means, the sample sizes for groups 1 and 2 are 100 and 150, respectively.

(i)   Show the sampling distribution of the difference between two population means.
(ii)   Find the probability $P(\bar{X}_1 - \bar{X}_2 > 10)$.
(iii)   Find the probability $P(\bar{X}_1 - \bar{X}_2 < 5)$.
(iv)   Find the probability $P(2 < \bar{X}_1 - \bar{X}_2 < 7)$.

6.11   Suppose that the population mean and variance of a variable, X, for group A are
$\mu_1 = 10$ and $\sigma_1^2 = 5$ and for group B are $\mu_2 = 12$ and $\sigma_2^2 = 7$. A study is conducted to find the difference between two population means. The sample sizes for groups A and B are 11 and 14, respectively.

(i)   What is the sampling distribution of $\bar{X}_1 - \bar{X}_2$?

(ii)   Find the probability $P(\bar{X}_1 - \bar{X}_2 > 4)$.

(iii)   Find the probability $P(\bar{X}_1 - \bar{X}_2 < 1)$.

(iv)   Find the probability $P(1 < \bar{X}_1 - \bar{X}_2 < 4)$.

6.12   In a population, the proportion of infants suffering from high fever during the month of December in a community is believed to be 0.2. A random sample of 100 infants is drawn randomly from the population.

(i)   What is the sampling distribution of sample proportion for large sample size?

(ii)   Find the probability that more than 30% of the infants suffered from high fever.

(iii)   What is the probability that less than 10% of the infants suffered from high fever.

(iv)   What is the probability that the proportion of infants suffered from high fever lies between 0.1 and 0.3?

6.13   Two independent samples are drawn from male and female populations with proportion of a complication associated with a chronic disease. The proportion of complication among the male population is 0.25 and among the female population is 0.20. The sample size for male is 150 and for female is 175.

(i)   What is the sampling distribution of the difference between sample proportions for male and female?

(ii)   Find the probability that the difference between male and female proportions is less than 1%.

(iii)   Find the probability that the probability of a difference between male and female proportions having complications greater than 10%.

(iv)   What is the probability that the difference between proportions of male and female suffering from complications lies between 0.03 and 0.07?

Chapter 7
Estimation

7.1 Introduction

Statistical inference refers to the methods by which we arrive at a conclusion about a population on the basis of the information contained in a sample drawn from that population. The sample is drawn from a population randomly and hence a random sample of size n considers a method of selecting a sample with predetermined probability. We have discussed about the sampling distribution of statistics in Chap. 6 and it is shown that a sampling distribution provides the underlying probability distribution of the statistics by which we try to generalize for population. As the sampling distribution is based on all the possible samples from a population of size N, the expected value, variance, and other population characteristics can be obtained theoretically from the statistics of a random sample. Statistical inference is comprised of two broad components: (i) estimation and (ii) test of hypothesis. Estimation refers to the methods of finding the value of statistic from a sample corresponding to its population value such that it satisfies some good properties to represent a parameter. On the other hand, once we obtain a value to estimate the corresponding population value or parameter, it is needed to know whether the sample value used as an estimate is close to the true value. This issue is of great importance in statistics and there are various techniques to make comment or to make decision about generalizing the estimates obtained by estimating parameters for the population as a whole. As the estimates are obtained from randomly drawn samples, it is likely that the values we consider to be population characteristics may differ from the true value. It means that although drawn from the population, a sample estimate may not be exactly equal to the corresponding parameter. Hence, as a statistician or biostatistician, it is necessary to provide procedures to make decision about the population values such that with the help of underlying sampling distribution, we may come up with decision about the population value where underlying probability distribution of statistic or sampling distribution plays an important role.

© Springer Nature Singapore Pte Ltd. 2018
M. A. Islam and A. Al-Shiha, *Foundations of Biostatistics*,
https://doi.org/10.1007/978-981-10-8627-4_7

Let us consider two examples here to highlight the role of estimation and test in biostatistics. In the first example, let us consider a study to find the mean duration of breastfeeding in a population. A random sample $(X_1, \ldots, X_n)$ is considered with $X \sim f(x; \mu, \sigma^2)$ and the sample observations are $X_1 = x_1, \ldots, X_n = x_n$. The sample mean of the duration is found to be $\bar{x}$. Let the sampling distribution of $\bar{X}$ be known or assumed and we also know that $E(\bar{X}) = \mu$ where μ is the population mean of the population from which the random sample is drawn. Then the statistical procedure to establish $\bar{x}$ as an estimate of μ is called a method of estimation. Once we obtain an estimate for μ, the next step is to confirm whether the population mean is a specified value, say $\mu = \mu_0$. Based on the sample mean and also using the sampling distribution of the sample mean, we may not reject or reject the hypothesis that the mean duration of breastfeeding in the population is $\mu = \mu_0$. This is a typical problem of test of hypothesis. In other words, a test of hypothesis is used to generalize the findings from the sample estimates for the population from where the sample is drawn randomly. In a study on old age population, the proportions of males and females suffering from high blood pressure are estimated. The sample values or statistics are $\hat{p}_1$ and $\hat{p}_2$ and the corresponding parameters are p_1 and p_2, respectively. In this case, $\hat{p}_1$ and $\hat{p}_2$ may be used to estimate the population values or parameters p_1 and p_2. The estimates are computed from sample values as $\hat{p}_1 = \frac{X_1}{n_1}$ and $\hat{p}_2 = \frac{X_2}{n_2}$ where X_1 and X_2 are number of males and females with high blood pressure, and n_1 and n_2 are number of males and females in the survey. The sample values or statistics of proportions with high blood pressure among males and females are used to represent the population values. As the sample is drawn randomly, we can show that expected values of the sample proportions are equal to the parameters. The way the sample values are chosen to estimate the parameters is a technique of estimation. Once we have the estimates, let us test for the hypothesis that proportion of males and females suffering from high blood pressure are the same in the population. If not same, then either males or females may suffer from high blood pressure at a higher proportion. Using the sampling distribution of difference between sample proportions, we can come up with a decision regarding non-rejection or rejection of the hypothesis. The means to test the difference or equality of sample proportions is performed by using a method of test of hypothesis. We try to arrive at a correct decision about the population characteristic on the basis of a sample value known as estimate and a test of hypothesis.

7.2   Estimation

Let us assume that some characteristics of the elements in a population be represented by a random variable X with probability density $f(x; \theta)$ where the form of the probability density function is assumed known except that it contains an unknown parameter, θ. If θ were known, the density function would be completely specified, and there would be no need to make inferences about it. We assume that the values

$(x_1, \ldots, x_n)$ of a random sample $(X_1, \ldots, X_n)$ from $f(x; \theta)$ can be observed. It is desired to estimate the value of the unknown parameter, θ.

This estimation can be made in two ways:

i. Point estimation: If some statistic, say $\bar{X}$, represents or estimates the unknown parameter, μ, then $\bar{X}$ is called a point estimator. A point estimate is a single value such as $\bar{X} = \bar{x}$ used to estimate the corresponding population parameter. Hence, a point estimator is a statistic that represents the function of random variables of a random sample to represent or estimate an unknown parameter and any single value of the statistic or more specifically estimator in this case used to estimate the parameter is a point estimate.

ii. Interval estimation: Let us define two statistics, L and U, where $L < U$ such that (L, U) constitutes an interval for which the probability can be determined that it contains the unknown parameter. An interval estimate consists of two numerical values defining a range of values that most likely includes the parameter being estimated with a specified degree of confidence.

There are two problems that we need to address in point estimation:

(i) to desire some means of obtaining a statistic to use as an estimator,
(ii) to select criteria and techniques to define and find best estimator among many possible estimators.

7.2.1 Methods of Finding Point Estimators

Let $X_1, \ldots, X_n$ be a random sample from a population density or mass function, $f_X(x, \theta)$, which is denoted as $f(x, \theta)$ in this book for simplicity, where the form of the density is known but the parameter is unknown. We need to find statistics, functions of observations to be used as estimator of the parameter.

Estimator and Estimate

Any statistic is a function of observable random variables that is itself a random variable. The value of statistic that is used to estimate the parameter, say θ, is called the estimator of the parameter θ. Any specific value of the estimator from a sample is called as estimate. Example: $\bar{X} = \frac{\sum_{i=1}^{n} X_i}{n}$ is an estimator of mean μ and $\bar{x} = \frac{\sum_{i=1}^{n} x_i}{n}$ is an estimate where $X_1 = x_1, \ldots, X_n = x_n$ are the realizations of the variable by the sample observations. It may be noted here that the estimator, $\bar{X}$, is a random variable because it is a function of observable random variables $X_1, \ldots, X_n$ and the estimate, $\bar{x}$, is a specific value of the function from the sample observations.

Sometimes, it is an easy task to find estimators, for example, estimating a parameter with its sample analogue is usually reasonable. In particular, the sample mean is a good estimate for the population mean. In more complicated models, we need to use a more methodical way. The most extensively used techniques of

estimating parameters are: (i) method of moments, (ii) method of maximum likelihood, and (iii) method of least squares. We will illustrate the first two methods
very briefly in this section and the third method will be discussed in Chap. 9.

Method of Moments

The method of moments is the oldest technique for estimating parameters of a
probability distribution. This method is simple to use and almost always yields
some sort of estimate. However, method of moments sometimes provides estimator
that needs improvement. If other methods are intractable, method of moments can
be a good starting point.

Let $(X_1, \ldots, X_n)$ be a sample from a population with probability density function
(pdf) or probability mass function (pmf), $f_X(x, \theta)$, then the method of moments
estimators is found by equating the first k sample moments to the corresponding
k population moments if there are k parameters to be estimated, and solving the
resulting system of simultaneous equations, we obtain the estimates. In other words,
if there is a single parameter, then we have to use the first sample moment and
equating with the first population moment. Similarly, if there are two parameters,
we can use the first two sample and population moments.

If there are k parameters, then we need first k raw sample and population
moments as defined below:

$$
\begin{array}{ll}
\text{Sample Moments} & \text{Population Moments} \\
m_1' = \dfrac{\sum_{i=1}^{n} x_i}{n} & \mu_1' = E(X) \\
m_2' = \dfrac{\sum_{i=1}^{n} x_i^2}{n} & \mu_2' = E(X^2) \\
\vdots & \vdots \\
m_k' = \dfrac{\sum_{i=1}^{n} x_i^k}{n} & \mu_k' = E(X^k)
\end{array}
$$

Then the estimates are obtained for the k parameters by solving the following
simultaneous equations:

$$
\begin{aligned}
\tilde{\mu}_1' &= m_1', \\
\tilde{\mu}_2' &= m_2', \\
&\vdots \\
\tilde{\mu}_k' &= m_k'.
\end{aligned}
$$

Example 7.1 Let $(X_1, \ldots, X_n)$ be a random sample from a Poisson distribution with
parameter λ, then

$$
\mu_1' = E(X) = \lambda
$$

and

$$m_1' = \frac{\sum_{i=1}^n x_i}{n} = \bar{x}.$$

Hence, the method of moments estimate for λ is

$$\tilde{\lambda} = \bar{x}.$$

Method of Maximum Likelihood

The concept of a joint distribution arises if we draw a random sample of size n from a multivariate population. If a sample of size n is drawn from a population simultaneously, we need to define the underlying joint probability for $X_1 = x_1, \ldots, X_n = x_n$. The joint probability density or mass function is

$$f(x_1, \ldots, x_n; \theta)$$

where this joint distribution expresses the probability distribution for the random sample values $X_1 = x_1, \ldots, X_n = x_n$. Here θ is unknown. The joint distribution involves not only parameters of a univariate distribution but also parameters for association or correlation between random sample variables $X_1, \ldots, X_n$. However, if the random variables $X_1, \ldots, X_n$ are independent then there is a simple relationship between joint distribution and univariate distributions as shown below

$$f(x_1, \ldots, x_n; \theta) = f(x_1; \theta) \ldots f(x_n; \theta).$$

It means that the joint distribution is the multiplication of marginal probabilities under independence of the random variables.

It is stated in case of a random sample that the joint probability of $X_1 = x_1, \ldots, X_n = x_n$ is of concern in a joint distribution and once the parameter is known, then the probabilities of observed values for n random variables can be obtained. Now if we consider that for a random sample the values of variables are known, i.e., the sample observations $x_1, \ldots, x_n$ are given, then what the likely estimate of θ would be for which the probability of θ is maximum. This idea leads to the concept of the likelihood function.

The concept of the theory of likelihood is not only the most popular but also the most useful technique with very important properties for deriving estimates of parameters of any probability distribution. If $X_1, \ldots, X_n$ are independently and identically distributed random variables with pdf or pmf $f(x, \theta)$ then the likelihood function is defined by

$$L(\theta | x_1, \ldots, x_n) = \prod_{i=1}^n f(x_i | \theta).$$

The left-hand side defines the probability of the likely values of parameter for given observed values $x_1, \ldots, x_n$ of a random sample and the right-hand side is the joint probability of $X_1 = x_1, \ldots, X_n = x_n$ for a given θ. The left-hand side is equal to the right-hand side only when the random variables $X_1, \ldots, X_n$ independently and identically distributed. It may be noted here that for each sample point x, let there be a parameter value at which $L(\theta|x)$ is expected to attain its maximum as a function of θ, if x is held fixed. A maximum likelihood estimator (MLE) of the parameter θ based on a sample $X_1, \ldots, X_n$ is $\hat{\theta}(X)$ or simply $\hat{\theta}$.

If the likelihood function is differentiable in θ, then the MLE is obtained by solving the following equation:

$$\frac{\delta}{\delta\theta} L(\theta|x_1, \ldots, x_n) = 0.$$

The likelihood function for k parameters, $\theta_1, \ldots, \theta_k$ is

$$L(\theta_1, \ldots, \theta_k|x_1, \ldots, x_n) = \prod_{i=1}^{n} f(x_i|\theta_1, \ldots, \theta_k)$$

and the maximum likelihood equations are

$$\frac{\delta}{\delta\theta_1} L(\theta_1, \ldots, \theta_k|x_1, \ldots, x_n) = 0,$$

$$\vdots$$

$$\frac{\delta}{\delta\theta_k} L(\theta_1, \ldots, \theta_k|x_1, \ldots, x_n) = 0.$$

The maximum likelihood estimates are obtained by solving the maximum likelihood equations and the estimates are denoted by $\hat{\theta}_1, \ldots, \hat{\theta}_k$.

To confirm maximization, we need to find the second derivatives of the likelihood functions and negative value of the second derivatives indicate that the estimates provide maximum likelihood. The second derivatives are

$$\frac{\delta^2}{\delta\theta_1^2} L(\theta_1, \ldots, \theta_k|x_1, \ldots, x_n) < 0,$$

$$\vdots$$

$$\frac{\delta^2}{\delta\theta_k^2} L(\theta_1, \ldots, \theta_k|x_1, \cdots, x_n) < 0.$$

It is noteworthy that instead of the likelihood functions, we can use the log-likelihood functions for making the equations more convenient to obtain the same solutions. The log-likelihood function for k parameters, $\theta_1, \ldots, \theta_k$ is

$$\ln L(\theta_1, \ldots, \theta_k|x_1, \ldots, x_n) = \sum_{i=1}^{n} \ln f(x_i|\theta_1, \ldots, \theta_k)$$

and the maximum log-likelihood equations are

$$\frac{\delta}{\delta\theta_1} \ln L(\theta_1, \ldots, \theta_k | x_1, \ldots, x_n) = 0,$$

$$\vdots$$

$$\frac{\delta}{\delta\theta_k} \ln L(\theta_1, \ldots, \theta_k | x_1, \ldots, x_n) = 0.$$

and the second derivatives are

$$\frac{\delta^2}{\delta\theta_1^2} \ln L(\theta_1, \ldots, \theta_k | x_1, \ldots, x_n) < 0,$$

$$\vdots$$

$$\frac{\delta^2}{\delta\theta_k^2} \ln L(\theta_1, \ldots, \theta_k | x_1, \ldots, x_n) < 0.$$

Some important properties of the maximum likelihood estimators are summarized here: (i) Invariance Property: If $\hat{\theta}$ is a maximum likelihood estimator of θ, then $g(\hat{\theta})$ is the maximum likelihood estimator of $g(\theta)$ where $g(\theta)$ is a function of θ; (ii) Asymptotically Unbiased: The maximum likelihood estimator, $\hat{\theta}$, is asymptotically unbiased such that $E(\hat{\theta}) \to \theta$ as $n \to \infty$ but not necessarily exactly unbiased; (iii) Consistency: Under certain regularity conditions, the maximum likelihood estimator $\hat{\theta}$ is a consistent estimator of θ; and (iv) Normality: Under regularity conditions, the maximum likelihood estimator $\hat{\theta}$ is asymptotically normally distributed with mean θ.

Example 7.2 Let $X_1, \ldots, X_n$ be *iid* Bernoulli (p).
     The likelihood function is

$$L(p | x_1, \ldots, x_n) = \prod_{i=1}^{n} p^{x_i} (1 - p)^{1 - x_i}$$

$$= p^y (1 - p)^{n - y}, y = \sum x_i$$

$$\ln L(p | | x_1, \ldots, x_n) = y \ln p + (n - y) \ln(1 - p)$$

$$\frac{\delta \ln L(p)}{\delta p} = \frac{y}{p} - \frac{n - y}{(1 - p)} = 0$$

$$\text{or } \hat{p} = \frac{y}{n}.$$

7.2.2 Interval Estimation

We have discussed about point estimation in the previous section. From point estimation, it has been observed that a single value represents the parameter in point estimation. The use of point estimation for generalizing the result from sample to population is relatively simple and convenient but it may not provide some important information regarding the extent of error associated with the point estimate. In other words, if a point estimate is accompanied by a measure of the extent of error associated with a point estimate then the reliability of an estimate becomes more meaningful and the extent of confidence about the estimation can also be assigned to such estimation.

An interval estimate of θ is an interval (L, U) containing the true value of θ with a probability of $1 - \alpha$ where $1 - \alpha$ is called the confidence coefficient (level), L = lower limit of the confidence interval, and U = upper limit of the confidence interval. Hence, we can express the $100(1 - \alpha)\%$ two-sided confidence interval as $P(L \leq \theta \leq U) = 1 - \alpha$. Similarly, we can define the one-sided lower confidence interval as $P(L \leq \theta) = 1 - \alpha$ where L is the one-sided lower confidence limit for θ and $P(\theta \leq U) = 1 - \alpha$ where U is the one-sided upper confidence limit for θ. It is important to remember that L and U are random variables, not θ, hence the interpretation of confidence interval needs a very careful attention. As θ remains constant which is a parameter, we can only interpret in terms of whether the parameter θ is included in the interval or not. Furthermore, the interval constructed from a single sample cannot provide the probability statement but it has to be interpreted in reference to the construction of similar intervals for each sample repeated a very large number of times with same sample size from the same population. In other words, the sampling distribution of the pivotal quantity provides the necessary background for both construction and interpretation of confidence interval.

The most extensively used method of finding confidence interval is the Pivotal Quantity Method. In addition, sometimes other statistical methods are also employed. Another method, known as the confidence sets, is also used for constructing confidence intervals. The most commonly used technique, the Pivotal Quantity Method, is highlighted in this chapter.

Pivotal Quantity Method: Let us consider a random sample $X_1, \ldots, X_n$ of size n from the population density $X \sim f(x, \theta)$ and let $Q = q(X_1, \ldots, X_n; \theta)$ where Q is a function of random variables $X_1, \ldots, X_n$ and parameter θ such that the sampling distribution of Q does not depend on θ then Q is defined as a pivotal quantity. Based on the pivotal quantity, we obtain the confidence intervals using the sampling distribution of pivotal quantity. Let us define the following probability with lower and upper limits or bounds for the pivotal quantity, $Q = q(X_1, \ldots, X_n; \theta)$:

$$P[q_1(X_1, \ldots, X_n; \theta) < Q < q_2(X_1, \ldots, X_n; \theta)] < 1 - \alpha$$

then after some algebraic manipulation, we arrive at the confidence interval for the parameter with confidence coefficient $1 - \alpha$ as

$$P[L(X_1, \ldots, X_n; \theta) < \theta < U(X_1, \ldots, X_n; \theta)] < 1 - \alpha,$$

where L and U are lower and upper bounds, limits or lower and upper end points of the confidence interval. The lower and upper limits are computed from a sample $X_1 = x_1, \ldots, X_n = x_n$

$$L = l(x_1, \ldots, x_n) \text{ and } U = u(x_1, \ldots, x_n).$$

Some examples of pivotal quantities are shown below:

(i) $Z = \frac{\bar{X} - \mu}{\sigma/\sqrt{n}}$ where $Z \sim N(0, 1)$ does not depend on μ,

(ii) $T = \frac{\bar{X} - \mu}{S/\sqrt{n}}$ where $T \sim t_{n-1}$ does not depend on μ,

(iii) $\chi^2 = \sum_{i=1}^{n} \frac{(X_i - \bar{X})^2}{\sigma^2} = \frac{(n-1)S^2}{\sigma^2} \sim \chi^2_{n-1}$ does not depend on σ^2, and (Fig. 7.1).

(iv) $F = \frac{X/(n-1)}{Y/(m-1)} \sim F(n-1, m-1)$ where $X \sim \chi^2(n-1), Y \sim \chi^2(m-1)$,

$$\chi^2(n-1) = \sum_{i=1}^{n} \frac{(X_i - \bar{X})^2}{\sigma_X^2} = \frac{(n-1)S_X^2}{\sigma_X^2} \sim \chi^2_{n-1} \text{ and}$$

$$\chi^2(m-1) = \sum_{i=1}^{m} \frac{(Y_i - \bar{Y})^2}{\sigma_Y^2} = \frac{(m-1)S_Y^2}{\sigma_Y^2} \sim \chi^2_{m-1}$$

,

and it is seen that F does not depend on the parameters σ_X^2 and σ_Y^2.

All these statistics satisfy the conditions required for pivotal quantity, hence, can be employed to construct confidence intervals (Fig. 7.2).

7.2.3 Estimation of Population Mean (μ)

In this section, we are interested in estimating the parameters of population such as the mean of a certain population (μ). Let us define the population and sample characteristics as displayed below.

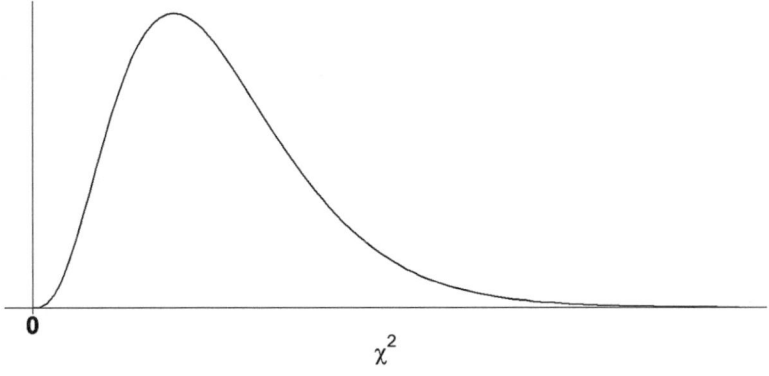

Fig. 7.1 Chi-square distribution

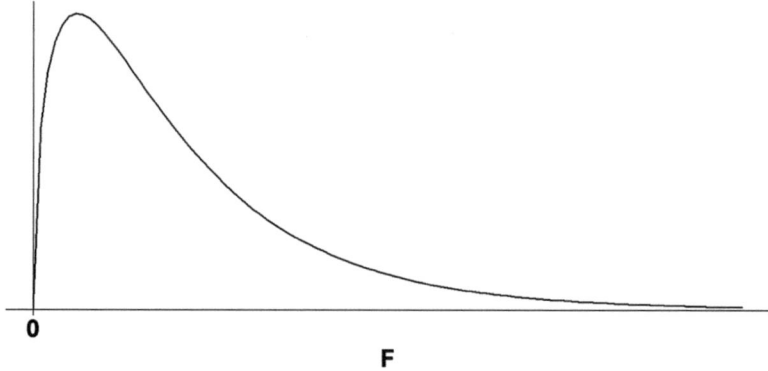

Fig. 7.2 F-distribution

Population	Sample
Population size $= N$	Sample size $= n$
Population values: $X_1, \ldots, X_N$	Sample values: $X_1, \ldots, X_n$
Population mean: $\mu = \frac{\sum_{i=1}^{N} X_i}{N}$	Sample mean: $\bar{X} = \frac{\sum_{i=1}^{n} X_i}{n}$
Population variance: $\sigma^2 = \frac{\sum_{i=1}^{N}(X_i-\mu)^2}{N}$	Sample variance: $S^2 = \frac{\sum_{i=1}^{n}(X_i-\bar{X})^2}{n-1}$

(i) **Point Estimation of μ**

A point estimate of the mean is a single number used to estimate (or approximate) the true value of μ. Let us consider a random sample of size n, $X_1, \ldots, X_n$ with $X \sim N(\mu, \sigma^2)$. Then the sample mean of the random sample is $\bar{X} = \frac{1}{n}\sum_{i=1}^{n} X_i$ and the sample mean computed from observations $X_1 = x_1, \ldots, X_n = x_n$ is $\bar{x} = \frac{1}{n}\sum_{i=1}^{n} x_i$. It should be noted here that $\bar{X}$ is a variable and $\bar{x}$ is a value of the variable $\bar{X}$ from observations of the random sample. We obtain the estimator of the sample mean using the maximum likelihood method as shown below.

The likelihood function is

$$L(\mu, \sigma^2; x_1, \ldots, x_n) = \prod_{i=1}^{n} f(x_i; \mu, \sigma^2)$$

$$= \frac{1}{(2\pi\sigma^2)^{n/2}} \prod_{i=1}^{n} e^{-\frac{1}{2\sigma^2}(x_i-\mu)^2}$$

$$= \frac{1}{(2\pi\sigma^2)^{n/2}} e^{-\frac{1}{2\sigma^2}\sum_{i=1}^{n}(x_i-\mu)^2}$$

and the log-likelihood function can be shown as

$$\ln L\left(\mu, \sigma^2; x_1, \ldots, x_n\right) = -\frac{n}{2}\ln\left(2\pi\sigma^2\right) - \frac{1}{2\sigma^2}\sum_{i=1}^{n}(x_i - \mu)^2.$$

The maximum likelihood estimate of the population mean, μ, is found by solving the equation

$$\frac{\partial \ln L}{\partial \mu} = -\frac{2}{2\sigma^2}\sum_{i=1}^{n}(x_i - \mu)(-1) = \frac{1}{\sigma^2}\sum_{i=1}^{n}(x_i - \mu) = 0$$

and the maximum likelihood estimate is

$$\hat{\mu} = \frac{\sum_{i=1}^{n}x_i}{n}.$$

The estimator of the population for the random sample is denoted as $\hat{\mu} = \bar{X} = \frac{\sum_{i=1}^{n}X_i}{n}$ which is a random variable.

(ii) Confidence Interval (Interval Estimate) of μ

An interval estimate of μ is an interval (L, U) containing the true value of μ with a probability of $1 - \alpha$ where $1 - \alpha =$ is called the confidence coefficient, $L =$ lower limit of the confidence interval, and $U =$ upper limit of the confidence interval. The $100(1 - \alpha)\%$ confidence interval is $P(L \leq \mu \leq U) = 1 - \alpha$ where L and U are variables and different samples will produce different values of end points of confidence interval L and U. From any sample data, we can find $L = l$ and $U = u$.

A. Let us consider the case when σ is known.

If $X_1, \ldots, X_n$ is a random sample of size n from a normal distribution with mean μ and known variance σ^2, then let us define the pivotal quantity

$$Z = \frac{\bar{X} - \mu}{\sigma/\sqrt{n}}.$$

This statistic is independent of parameters μ and σ and Z is a variable with probability distribution $N(0, 1)$. The probability of $1 - \alpha$ can be obtained from the following interval:

$$P(z_{\alpha/2} < Z < z_{1-\alpha/2}) = 1 - \alpha.$$

Here $1 - \alpha$ is the confidence coefficient. We know that Z is a function of sample observations and population mean and it can be shown in the interval

$$P\left(z_{\alpha/2} < Z = \frac{\bar{X} - \mu}{\sigma/\sqrt{n}} < z_{1-\alpha/2}\right) = 1 - \alpha$$
$$= P\left(z_{\alpha/2} \times \sigma/\sqrt{n} < \bar{X} - \mu < z_{1-\alpha/2} \times \sigma/\sqrt{n}\right) = 1 - \alpha$$
$$= P\left(-\bar{X} + z_{\alpha/2} \times \sigma/\sqrt{n} < -\mu < -\bar{X} + z_{1-\alpha/2} \times \sigma/\sqrt{n}\right) = 1 - \alpha$$
$$= P\left(\bar{X} - z_{1-\alpha/2} \times \sigma/\sqrt{n} < \mu < \bar{X} - z_{\alpha/2} \times \sigma/\sqrt{n}\right) = 1 - \alpha.$$

The above interval is the $(1 - \alpha)100\%$ confidence interval for population mean μ where σ is assumed to be known. We know that $Z_{\alpha/2} = -Z_{1-\alpha/2}$, hence, the interval can be expressed as

$$P(\bar{X} - z_{1-\alpha/2} \times \sigma/\sqrt{n} < \mu < \bar{X} + z_{1-\alpha/2} \times \sigma/\sqrt{n}) = 1 - \alpha.$$

The lower and upper limits or end points of this confidence interval are

$$L = \bar{X} - z_{1-\alpha/2} \times \sigma/\sqrt{n} \text{ and}$$
$$U = \bar{X} + z_{1-\alpha/2} \times \sigma/\sqrt{n}.$$

From observed data of a sample, the end points are

$$l = \bar{x} - z_{1-\alpha/2} \times \sigma/\sqrt{n} \text{ and}$$
$$u = \bar{x} + z_{1-\alpha/2} \times \sigma/\sqrt{n}.$$

The lower and upper limits or bounds for $(1 - \alpha)100\%$ confidence interval can be expressed in the following ways too:

$$\bar{x} \pm z_{1-\alpha/2} \times \sigma/\sqrt{n}, \text{ or}$$
$$\left(\bar{x} - z_{1-\alpha/2} \times \sigma/\sqrt{n}, \bar{x} + z_{1-\alpha/2} \times \sigma/\sqrt{n}\right).$$

The confidence interval with a probability of $(1 - \alpha)$ can be interpreted as the probability $(1 - \alpha)$ of containing μ in the interval. In other words, the probability of containing μ interval does not imply the probability of μ being included in a particular interval because the probability statement is not about any specific interval rather about large number of such intervals either containing μ or not. If μ is contained $(1 - \alpha)100\%$ of the times in confidence intervals constructed from a large number of repeated samples, then it refers to $(1 - \alpha)100\%$ confidence interval.

B. **If $X_1, \ldots, X_n$ is a random sample of size n from a non-normal distribution with mean μ and known variance σ^2, and if the sample size n is large**

If $X_1, \ldots, X_n$ is a random sample of size n from a non-normal distribution with mean μ and known variance σ^2 and the sample size is large then the pivotal quantity is

$$Z = \frac{\bar{X} - \mu}{\sigma/\sqrt{n}},$$

which is independent of parameters μ and σ, and Z is asymptotically $N(0,1)$.

The $(1 - \alpha)100\%$ confidence interval for population mean μ, if σ is assumed to be known and sample size is large, is similar as

$$P(\bar{X} - z_{1-\alpha/2} \times \sigma/\sqrt{n} < \mu < \bar{X} + z_{1-\alpha/2} \times \sigma/\sqrt{n}) = 1 - \alpha.$$

The lower and upper limits of this confidence interval are

$$L = \bar{X} - z_{1-\alpha/2} \times \sigma/\sqrt{n}, \text{and}$$
$$U = \bar{X} + z_{1-\alpha/2} \times \sigma/\sqrt{n}.$$

The lower and upper bounds for sample data are

$$l = \bar{x} - z_{1-\alpha/2} \times \sigma/\sqrt{n} \text{ and}$$
$$u = \bar{x} + z_{1-\alpha/2} \times \sigma/\sqrt{n}.$$

The lower and upper limits or bounds for $(1 - \alpha)100\%$ confidence interval for the population parameter μ if and population variance σ^2 for large sample non-normal population can be expressed in the following ways too:

$$\bar{x} \pm z_{1-\alpha/2} \times \sigma/\sqrt{n}, \text{or}$$
$$\left(\bar{x} - z_{1-\alpha/2} \times \sigma/\sqrt{n}, \bar{x} + z_{1-\alpha/2} \times \sigma/\sqrt{n}\right).$$

We may summarize the findings from both A and B as noted below.

(i)   We are $(1 - \alpha)100\%$ confident that the true value of μ belongs to the interval, $(\bar{X} - z_{1-\frac{\alpha}{2}}\frac{\sigma}{\sqrt{n}}, \bar{X} + z_{1-\frac{\alpha}{2}}\frac{\sigma}{\sqrt{n}})$;

(ii) Upper limit of the confidence interval $= \bar{X} + z_{1-\frac{\alpha}{2}}\frac{\sigma}{\sqrt{n}}$;

(iii) Lower limit of the confidence interval $= \bar{X} - z_{1-\frac{\alpha}{2}}\frac{\sigma}{\sqrt{n}}$;

(iv) $z_{1-\frac{\alpha}{2}} = $ reliability coefficient;

(v) $z_{1-\frac{\alpha}{2}} \times \frac{\sigma}{\sqrt{n}} = $ margin of error $= $ precision of the estimate;

(vi) In general, the interval estimate (confidence interval) may be expressed as follows:

$$\bar{X} \pm z_{1-\frac{\alpha}{2}}\sigma_{\bar{X}},$$

which means
estimator ± (reliability coefficient) × (standard error) or
estimator ± margin of error.

Confidence Interval for μ: σ is Unknown

We have already introduced and discussed the t-distribution. In this section, we discuss some applications of t-statistic to obtain confidence intervals.

A. Confidence Interval for μ for the Case when σ is Unknown and the Population is Normal

If $X_1, \ldots, X_n$ is a random sample of size n from a normal distribution with mean μ and unknown variance σ^2, then the pivotal quantity may be defined as

$$T = \frac{\bar{X} - \mu}{S/\sqrt{n}}$$

where $S^2 = \frac{\sum_{i=1}^{n}(X_i - \bar{X})^2}{n-1}$, $T \sim t_{n-1}$ and the $1 - \alpha$ probability can be obtained from

$$P(t_{(n-1),\alpha/2} < T < T_{(n-1),1-\alpha/2}) = 1 - \alpha.$$

Here $1 - \alpha$ is the confidence coefficient. It is known that T is a function of sample observations and population mean and the interval can be expressed as

$$P\left(t_{(n-1),\alpha/2} < T = \frac{\bar{X} - \mu}{S/\sqrt{n}} < t_{(n-1),1-\alpha/2}\right) = 1 - \alpha$$
$$= P(t_{(n-1),\alpha/2} \times S/\sqrt{n} < \bar{X} - \mu < t_{(n-1),1-\alpha/2} \times S/\sqrt{n}) = 1 - \alpha$$
$$= P(-\bar{X} + t_{(n-1),\alpha/2} \times S/\sqrt{n} < -\mu < -\bar{X} + t_{(n-1),1-\alpha/2} \times S/\sqrt{n}) = 1 - \alpha$$
$$= P(\bar{X} - t_{(n-1),1-\alpha/2} \times S/\sqrt{n} < \mu < \bar{X} - t_{(n-1),\alpha/2} \times S/\sqrt{n}) = 1 - \alpha.$$

The above interval is the $(1 - \alpha)100\%$ confidence interval for population mean μ where σ is unknown. It has been shown earlier that for a t-distribution $t_{(n-1),\alpha/2} = -t_{(n-1),1-\alpha/2}$, hence, the interval can be expressed as

$$P(\bar{X} - t_{(n-1),1-\alpha/2} \times S/\sqrt{n} < \mu < \bar{X} + t_{(n-1),1-\alpha/2} \times S/\sqrt{n}) = 1 - \alpha.$$

The lower and upper limits of this confidence interval are

$$L = \bar{X} - t_{(n-1),1-\alpha/2} \times S/\sqrt{n} \text{ and}$$
$$U = \bar{X} + t_{(n-1),1-\alpha/2} \times S/\sqrt{n}.$$

The lower and upper limits for $(1 - \alpha)100\%$ confidence interval from sample data for σ unknown can be expressed in following ways too:

$$\bar{x} \pm t_{(n-1),1-\alpha/2} \times s/\sqrt{n}, \text{ or}$$

$$\left(\bar{x} - t_{(n-1),1-\alpha/2} \times s/\sqrt{n}, \bar{x} + t_{(n-1),1-\alpha/2} \times s/\sqrt{n}\right),$$

where $\bar{x} = \frac{\sum_{i=1}^{n} x_i}{n}$ and $s^2 = \frac{\sum_{i=1}^{n}(x_i-\bar{x})^2}{n-1}$.

Notes:

1. We are $(1-\alpha)100\%$ confident that the true value of μ is contained in the interval

$$\left(\bar{X} - t_{(n-1),1-\frac{\alpha}{2}}\frac{S}{\sqrt{n}}, \bar{X} + t_{(n-1),1-\frac{\alpha}{2}}\frac{S}{\sqrt{n}}\right).$$

2. $\hat{\sigma}_{\bar{X}} = \frac{S}{\sqrt{n}}$ (estimate of the standard error of $\bar{x}$)
3. $t_{(n-1),1-\frac{\alpha}{2}}$ = reliability coefficient
4. In this case, we replace σ by s and z by t.
5. In general, the interval estimate (confidence interval) may be expressed as follows:

$$\bar{X} \pm t_{(n-1),1-\frac{\alpha}{2}}\hat{\sigma}_{\bar{X}}$$

which is
estimator $\pm$ (reliability coefficient) $\times$ (estimate of the standard error)
Notes: Finding Reliability Coefficient

(1) We find the reliability coefficient $Z_{1-\frac{\alpha}{2}}$ from the Z-table as follows (Fig. 7.3):
(2) We find the reliability coefficient $t_{(n-1),1-\frac{\alpha}{2}}$ from the t-table as follows: (df =
    = n − 1) (Fig. 7.4)

Example 7.3 Suppose that $Z \sim N(0,1)$. Find $Z_{1-\frac{\alpha}{2}}$ for the following cases:

(1) $\alpha = 0.1$ (2) $\alpha = 0.05$ (3) $\alpha = 0.01$

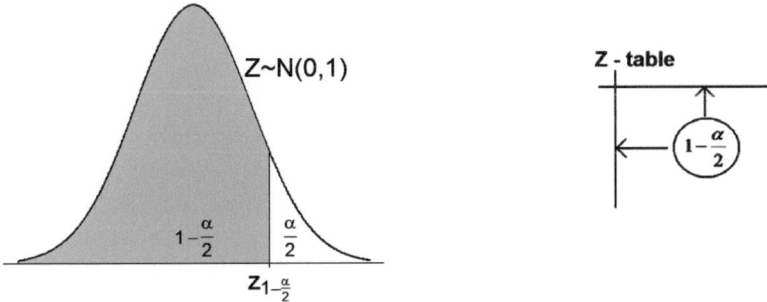

Fig. 7.3 Finding reliability coefficient using Z-table

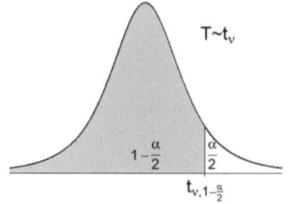
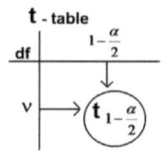

Fig. 7.4 Finding reliability coefficient using t-table

Solution

(1) For $\alpha = 0.1$:

$1 - \frac{\alpha}{2} = 1 - \frac{0.1}{2} = 0.95$ From **Z-table**

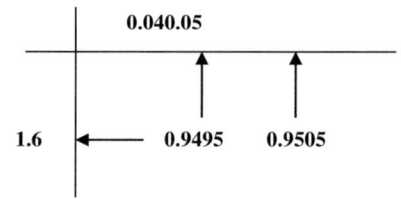

$\Rightarrow Z_{1-\frac{\alpha}{2}} = Z_{0.95} = 1.645$

(2) For $\alpha = 0.05$:

$1 - \frac{\alpha}{2} = 1 - \frac{0.05}{2} = 0.975$ From **Z-table**

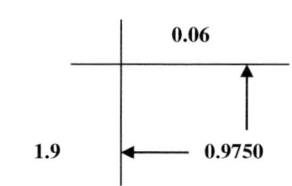

$\Rightarrow Z_{1-\frac{\alpha}{2}} = Z_{0.975} = 1.96.$

(3) For $\alpha = 0.01$:

$1 - \frac{\alpha}{2} = 1 - \frac{0.01}{2} = 0.995$ From **Z-table**

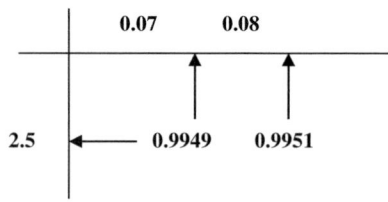

$\Rightarrow Z_{1-\frac{\alpha}{2}} = Z_{0.995} = 2.575$

Example 7.4 Suppose that $t \sim t(30)$. Find $t_{1-\frac{\alpha}{2}}$ for $\alpha = 0.05$.

Solution
Here,

$$df = \nu = 30 \text{ From } \textbf{t-table}$$
$$1 - \frac{\alpha}{2} = 1 - \frac{0.05}{2} = 0.975$$

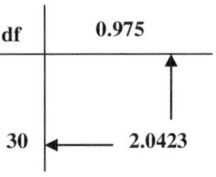

$$\Rightarrow t_{1-\frac{\alpha}{2}} = t_{0.975} = 2.0423$$

Example 7.5 (**The case where σ^2 is known**)

Confidence Interval for μ if σ^2 is Assumed to be Known
Let us consider that in a study, a random sample of 123 patients admitted to a hospital with old age complications has the mean age, 55 years. If it is assumed that the sample is drawn from a normal population with unknown mean, μ, and known population variance, $\sigma^2 = 82$, then we want to find the 90% confidence interval for the population mean.

Solution
Here, the variable X represents the age of patients with old age complications. The parameter of interest is $\mu = $ the population mean age of patients admitted to the hospital with old age complications. The population variance is assumed to be known and $\sigma^2 = 82$. We can write $X \sim N(\mu, 82)$. We can find the maximum likelihood estimate of the population mean, $\hat{\mu} = \bar{x} = 55$. The sample size is $n = 123$.

Point Estimation
For constructing the confidence interval, we need to find a point estimate for μ first. The sample mean is the maximum likelihood estimate for a normal distribution, hence,

$\bar{x} = 55$ is a point estimate for μ, and
$$\hat{\mu} = 55.$$

Interval Estimation
We need to find 90% C. I. for μ where $90\% = (1 - \alpha)100\%$.
   The confidence coefficient is

$$1 - \alpha = 0.9$$

and $\alpha = 0.1$. For a two-sided confidence interval, $\frac{\alpha}{2} = 0.05$ and $1 - \frac{\alpha}{2} = 0.95$. The reliability coefficient is: $Z_{1-\frac{\alpha}{2}} = Z_{0.95} = 1.645$

The 90% confidence interval for μ is

$$\left(\bar{x} - Z_{1-\frac{\alpha}{2}}\frac{\sigma}{\sqrt{n}}, \bar{x} + Z_{1-\frac{\alpha}{2}}\frac{\sigma}{\sqrt{n}}\right).$$

For the given data, we obtain

$$\left(55 - (1.645)\frac{9.055}{\sqrt{123}}, 55 + (1.645)\frac{9.055}{\sqrt{123}}\right)$$

and the confidence interval for the population mean age of elderly patients with old age complications is

$$(53.6569, 56.3431).$$

We may interpret this confidence interval in following way: if the samples of the same size were drawn repeatedly a very large number of times from the same population then in 90% of the times the true value of the population mean would be included in the intervals. For this example even if the distribution were not normal, we might have used the same interval because the sample size is large enough for the application of the central limit theorem.

Example 7.6 **Confidence Interval for μ if σ^2 is Unknown**
Let us consider a hypothetical study on the height of women in their adulthood. A sample of 24 women is drawn from a normal distribution with population mean μ and variance σ^2. The sample mean and variance of height of the selected women are 151 cm and 18.65 cm^2 respectively. Using given data, we want to construct a 99% confidence interval for the mean height of the adult women in the population from which the sample was drawn randomly.

Solution
Let us summarize the information provided in this example.
    The random variable X represents the height of women in their adulthood.
    The population mean μ is unknown. The population variance is σ^2. The variable X is distributed as $X \sim N(\mu, \sigma^2)$.
    The sample size is 24. The sample mean and standard deviations are $\bar{x} = 151$ and $s = 4.32$.

(a) **Point Estimation**

We need to find a point estimate for μ.
It may be noted that $\bar{x} = 151$ is a point estimate for μ.
We obtain $\hat{\mu} = 151$ cm.

(b) **Interval Estimation**

We need to find 99% C. I. for μ, where $99\% = (1-\alpha)100\%$ and as $1 - \alpha = 0.99$, it can be shown that $\alpha = 0.01$. For a two-sided interval, we define $\frac{\alpha}{2} = 0.005$ and $1 - \frac{\alpha}{2} = 0.995$. The sample size is $n = 24$.

The reliability coefficient is $t_{v,1-\frac{\alpha}{2}} = t_{23,0.995} = 2.807$

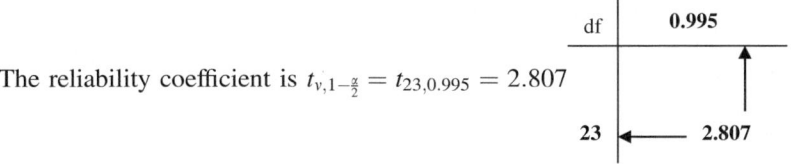

From **t-table**
99% confidence interval for μ is:
The confidence interval for the population mean when the population variance is unknown can be constructed from the following:

$$\bar{x} \pm t_{1-\alpha/2} \times s/\sqrt{n}$$

where for 99% confidence interval, the lower and upper limits are

$$l = \bar{x} - t_{1-\alpha/2} \times s/\sqrt{n}$$
$$= 151 - 2.807 \times 4.32/\sqrt{24}$$
$$= 151 - 2.4753$$
$$= 148.5247,$$

and

$$u = \bar{x} + t_{1-\alpha/2} \times s/\sqrt{n}$$
$$= 151 + 2.807 \times 4.32/\sqrt{24}$$
$$= 151 + 2.4753$$
$$= 153.4753.$$

This can be expressed more precisely as $(148.5247, 153.4753)$.

If the random samples of size 24 were drawn very large number of times from the same population then out of all intervals constructed for each sample, 99% of the times the population mean would be contained in the intervals. It may be noted here that for large sample size, the test statistic T would tend to standard normal variate, Z, asymptotically.

7.2.4   Estimation of the Difference Between Two Population Means ($\mu_1 - \mu_2$)

Suppose that we have two populations such that the first population is characterized with mean μ_1 and variance σ_1^2 and the second population with mean μ_2 and variance σ_2^2. We are interested in comparing μ_1 and μ_2, or equivalently, making inferences about the difference between the means ($\mu_1 - \mu_2$). We select independently a random sample of size n_1 from the first population and another random sample of size n_2 from the second population. Let $\bar{X}_1$ and S_1^2 be the sample mean and the sample variance of the first sample and $\bar{X}_2$ and S_2^2 be the sample mean and the sample variance of the second sample. The sampling distribution of $\bar{X}_1 - \bar{X}_2$ is used to make inferences about $\mu_1 - \mu_2$.

The sampling distribution of the difference between two sample means has been discussed and the following results are summarized about the sampling distribution of the difference between two sample means:

1. Mean of $\bar{X}_1 - \bar{X}_2$ is $\mu_{\bar{X}_1 - \bar{X}_2} = \mu_1 - \mu_2$
2. Variance of $\bar{X}_1 - \bar{X}_2$ is $\sigma_{\bar{X}_1 - \bar{X}_2}^2 = \frac{\sigma_1^2}{n_1} + \frac{\sigma_2^2}{n_2}$
3. Standard error of $\bar{X}_1 - \bar{X}_2$ is $\sigma_{\bar{X}_1 - \bar{X}_2} = \sqrt{\frac{\sigma_1^2}{n_1} + \frac{\sigma_2^2}{n_2}}$
4. If the two random samples were selected from normal distributions (or non-normal distributions with large sample sizes) with known variances σ_1^2 and σ_2^2, then the difference between the sample means $(\bar{X}_1 - \bar{X}_2)$ has a normal distribution with mean $(\mu_1 - \mu_2)$ and variance $((\sigma_1^2/n_1) + (\sigma_2^2/n_2))$, that is

$$\bar{X}_1 - \bar{X}_2 \sim N\left(\mu_1 - \mu_2, \frac{\sigma_1^2}{n_1} + \frac{\sigma_2^2}{n_2}\right)$$

and we can show that

$$Z = \frac{(\bar{X}_1 - \bar{X}_2) - (\mu_1 - \mu_2)}{\sqrt{\frac{\sigma_1^2}{n_1} + \frac{\sigma_2^2}{n_2}}} \sim N(0, 1).$$

(i) **Point Estimation of $\mu_1 - \mu_2$**

It can be shown that $\bar{X}_1 - \bar{X}_2$ is a point estimator for $\mu_1 - \mu_2$.

(ii) **Interval Estimation (Confidence Interval) of $\mu_1 - \mu_2$**

We will consider two cases.

A. **First Case: σ_1^2 and σ_2^2 are known**

If σ_1^2 and σ_2^2 are known, we use the following pivotal quantity to find an interval estimate for $\mu_1 - \mu_2$.

$$Z = \frac{(\bar{X}_1 - \bar{X}_2) - (\mu_1 - \mu_2)}{\sqrt{\frac{\sigma_1^2}{n_1} + \frac{\sigma_2^2}{n_2}}}$$

A $(1 - \alpha)100\%$ confidence interval for $\mu_1 - \mu_2$ is obtained from the following probability statement:

$$P(z_{\alpha/2} < Z < z_{1-\alpha/2}) = 1 - \alpha.$$

and it can be shown that

$$P\left(z_{\alpha/2} < Z = \frac{(\bar{X}_1 - \bar{X}_2) - (\mu_1 - \mu_2)}{\sqrt{\frac{\sigma_1^2}{n_1} + \frac{\sigma_2^2}{n_2}}} < z_{1-\alpha/2}\right) = 1 - \alpha$$

$$= P\left(z_{\alpha/2} \times \sqrt{\frac{\sigma_1^2}{n_1} + \frac{\sigma_2^2}{n_2}} < (\bar{X}_1 - \bar{X}_2) - (\mu_1 - \mu_2) < z_{1-\alpha/2} \times \sqrt{\frac{\sigma_1^2}{n_1} + \frac{\sigma_2^2}{n_2}}\right) = 1 - \alpha$$

$$= P\left(\begin{array}{c} -(\bar{X}_1 - \bar{X}_2) + z_{\alpha/2} \times \sqrt{\frac{\sigma_1^2}{n_1} + \frac{\sigma_2^2}{n_2}} < -(\mu_1 - \mu_2) < -(\bar{X}_1 - \bar{X}_2) \\ + z_{1-\alpha/2} \times \sqrt{\frac{\sigma_1^2}{n_1} + \frac{\sigma_2^2}{n_2}} \end{array}\right) = 1 - \alpha$$

$$= P\left[\begin{array}{c} (\bar{X}_1 - \bar{X}_2) - z_{1-\alpha/2} \times \sqrt{\frac{\sigma_1^2}{n_1} + \frac{\sigma_2^2}{n_2}} < (\mu_1 - \mu_2) < (\bar{X}_1 - \bar{X}_2) \\ - z_{\alpha/2} \times \sqrt{\frac{\sigma_1^2}{n_1} + \frac{\sigma_2^2}{n_2}} \end{array}\right] = 1 - \alpha.$$

The above interval for the difference between two population means is the $(1 - \alpha)$ 100% confidence interval if population variances are assumed to be known. Using the known relationship $z_{\alpha/2} = -z_{1-\alpha/2}$, the interval can be expressed as

$$P\left[(\bar{X}_1 - \bar{X}_2) - z_{1-\alpha/2} \times \sqrt{\frac{\sigma_1^2}{n_1} + \frac{\sigma_2^2}{n_2}} < (\mu_1 - \mu_2) < (\bar{X}_1 - \bar{X}_2) + z_{1-\alpha/2} \times \sqrt{\frac{\sigma_1^2}{n_1} + \frac{\sigma_2^2}{n_2}}\right]$$

$$= 1 - \alpha$$

The lower and upper limits of this confidence interval are

$$L = (\bar{X}_1 - \bar{X}_2) - z_{1-\alpha/2} \times \sqrt{\frac{\sigma_1^2}{n_1} + \frac{\sigma_2^2}{n_2}} \text{ and}$$

$$U = (\bar{X}_1 - \bar{X}_2) + z_{1-\alpha/2} \times \sqrt{\frac{\sigma_1^2}{n_1} + \frac{\sigma_2^2}{n_2}}$$

and the values from sample data are

$$l = (\bar{x}_1 - \bar{x}_2) - z_{1-\alpha/2} \times \sqrt{\frac{\sigma_1^2}{n_1} + \frac{\sigma_2^2}{n_2}} \text{ and}$$

$$u = (\bar{x}_1 - \bar{x}_2) + z_{1-\alpha/2} \times \sqrt{\frac{\sigma_1^2}{n_1} + \frac{\sigma_2^2}{n_2}}$$

Alternative ways to represent the lower and upper limits for $(1 - \alpha)$ 100% confidence interval of the difference between two population means are

$$(\bar{x}_1 - \bar{x}_2) \pm z_{1-\alpha/2} \times \sqrt{\frac{\sigma_1^2}{n_1} + \frac{\sigma_2^2}{n_2}}, \text{ or}$$

$$\left((\bar{x}_1 - \bar{x}_2) - z_{1-\alpha/2} \times \sqrt{\frac{\sigma_1^2}{n_1} + \frac{\sigma_2^2}{n_2}}, (\bar{x}_1 - \bar{x}_2) + z_{1-\alpha/2} \times \sqrt{\frac{\sigma_1^2}{n_1} + \frac{\sigma_2^2}{n_2}} \right).$$

B. Second Case: Unknown equal variances: $(\sigma_1^2 = \sigma_2^2 = \sigma^2$ is unknown)

Let us consider two random samples $X_{11}, \ldots, X_{1n_1}$ and $X_{21}, \ldots, X_{2n_2}$ with probability density functions $X_1 \sim N(\mu_1, \sigma_1^2)$ and $X_2 \sim N(\mu_2, \sigma_2^2)$, respectively, for samples 1 and 2.

The point estimate of the difference between two population means is $\bar{X}_1 - \bar{X}_2$.

If σ_1^2 and σ_2^2 are equal but unknown $(\sigma_1^2 = \sigma_2^2 = \sigma^2)$, then the pooled estimate of the common variance σ^2 is

$$S_p^2 = \frac{(n_1 - 1)S_1^2 + (n_2 - 1)S_2^2}{n_1 + n_2 - 2},$$

where $S_1^2 = \frac{\sum_{i=1}^{n_1}(X_{1i} - \bar{X}_1)^2}{n_1 - 1}$ and $S_2^2 = \frac{\sum_{i=1}^{n_1}(X_{2i} - \bar{X}_2)^2}{n_2 - 1}$ are the variance of the first and second samples, respectively.

If σ_1^2 and σ_2^2 are assumed to be equal but unknown then the pivotal quantity to find an interval estimate for $\mu_1 - \mu_2$ is

$$T = \frac{(\bar{X}_1 - \bar{X}_2) - (\mu_1 - \mu_2)}{\sqrt{S_p^2 \left(\frac{1}{n_1} + \frac{1}{n_2}\right)}},$$

where $T \sim t_{n_1 + n_2 - 2}$.

A $(1 - \alpha)100\%$ confidence interval for $\mu_1 - \mu_2$ can be obtained by using the pivotal quantity as shown below

$$P(t_{(n_1 + n_2 - 2), \alpha/2} < T < t_{(n_1 + n_2 - 2), 1 - \alpha/2}) = 1 - \alpha.$$

and it can also be shown that

$$P\left(t_{(n_1 + n_2 - 2), \alpha/2} < T = \frac{(\bar{X}_1 - \bar{X}_2) - (\mu_1 - \mu_2)}{\sqrt{S_p^2 \left(\frac{1}{n_1} + \frac{1}{n_2}\right)}} < t_{(n_1 + n_2 - 2), 1 - \alpha/2}\right) = 1 - \alpha$$

$$= P\left(t_{(n_1 + n_2 - 2), \alpha/2} \times \sqrt{S_p^2 \left(\frac{1}{n_1} + \frac{1}{n_2}\right)} < (\bar{X}_1 - \bar{X}_2) - (\mu_1 - \mu_2)\right.$$

$$\left. < t_{(n_1 + n_2 - 2), 1 - \alpha/2} \times \sqrt{S_p^2 \left(\frac{1}{n_1} + \frac{1}{n_2}\right)}\right) = 1 - \alpha$$

$$= P\left(-(\bar{X}_1 - \bar{X}_2) + t_{(n_1 + n_2 - 2), \alpha/2} \times \sqrt{S_p^2 \left(\frac{1}{n_1} + \frac{1}{n_2}\right)} < -(\mu_1 - \mu_2)\right.$$

$$\left. < -(\bar{X}_1 - \bar{X}_2) + t_{(n_1 + n_2 - 2), 1 - \alpha/2} \times \sqrt{S_p^2 \left(\frac{1}{n_1} + \frac{1}{n_2}\right)}\right) = 1 - \alpha$$

$$= P\left[\begin{array}{c} (\bar{X}_1 - \bar{X}_2) - t_{(n_1 + n_2 - 2), 1 - \alpha/2} \times \sqrt{S_p^2 \left(\frac{1}{n_1} + \frac{1}{n_2}\right)} < (\mu_1 - \mu_2) \\ < (\bar{X}_1 - \bar{X}_2) - t_{(n_1 + n_2 - 2), \alpha/2} \times \sqrt{S_p^2 \left(\frac{1}{n_1} + \frac{1}{n_2}\right)} \end{array}\right] = 1 - \alpha.$$

The above interval for the difference between two population means is the $(1 - \alpha)$ 100% confidence interval if population variances are assumed to be unknown and equal. Using the known relationship $t_{(n_1 + n_2 - 2), \alpha/2} = -t_{(n_1 + n_2 - 2), 1 - \alpha/2}$, the interval can be expressed as

$$P\left[\begin{array}{c} (\bar{X}_1 - \bar{X}_2) - t_{(n_1 + n_2 - 2), 1 - \alpha/2} \times \sqrt{S_p^2 \left(\frac{1}{n_1} + \frac{1}{n_2}\right)} \\ < (\mu_1 - \mu_2) < (\bar{X}_1 - \bar{X}_2) - t_{(n_1 + n_2 - 2), \alpha/2} \times \sqrt{S_p^2 \left(\frac{1}{n_1} + \frac{1}{n_2}\right)} \end{array}\right] = 1 - \alpha.$$

The lower and upper limits of this confidence interval are

$$L = (\bar{X}_1 - \bar{X}_2) - t_{(n_1 + n_2 - 2), 1 - \alpha/2} \times \sqrt{S_p^2 \left(\frac{1}{n_1} + \frac{1}{n_2} \right)}, \text{and}$$

$$U = (\bar{X}_1 - \bar{X}_2) + t_{(n_1 + n_2 - 2), 1 - \alpha/2} \times \sqrt{S_p^2 \left(\frac{1}{n_1} + \frac{1}{n_2} \right)}.$$

The lower and upper bounds from sample data can be shown as

$$l = (\bar{x}_1 - \bar{x}_2) - t_{(n_1 + n_2 - 2), 1 - \alpha/2} \times \sqrt{s_p^2 \left(\frac{1}{n_1} + \frac{1}{n_2} \right)}, \text{and}$$

$$u = (\bar{x}_1 - \bar{x}_2) + t_{(n_1 + n_2 - 2), 1 - \alpha/2} \times \sqrt{s_p^2 \left(\frac{1}{n_1} + \frac{1}{n_2} \right)},$$

where $s_p^2 = \frac{(n_1 - 1)s_1^2 + (n_2 - 1)s_2^2}{n_1 + n_2 - 2}$, $s_1^2 = \frac{\sum_{i=1}^{n_1}(x_{1i} - \bar{x}_1)^2}{n_1 - 1}$ and $s_2^2 = \frac{\sum_{i=1}^{n_1}(x_{2i} - \bar{x}_2)^2}{n_2 - 1}$.

The $(1 - \alpha)100\%$ lower and upper limits of confidence interval, using sample data for difference between two population means if the population variances are unknown but assumed to be equal, are shown alternatively as follows:

$$(\bar{x}_1 - \bar{x}_2) \pm t_{(n_1 + n_2 - 2), 1 - \alpha/2} \times \sqrt{s_p^2 \left(\frac{1}{n_1} + \frac{1}{n_2} \right)}, \text{or}$$

$$\left((\bar{x}_1 - \bar{x}_2) - t_{(n_1 + n_2 - 2), 1 - \alpha/2} \times \sqrt{s_p^2 \left(\frac{1}{n_1} + \frac{1}{n_2} \right)}, (\bar{x}_1 - \bar{x}_2) \right.$$
$$\left. + t_{(n_1 + n_2 - 2), 1 - \alpha/2} \times \sqrt{s_p^2 \left(\frac{1}{n_1} + \frac{1}{n_2} \right)} \right).$$

Example 7.7 (**Case 1: σ_1^2 and σ_2^2 are known**)

Let us consider an experiment for comparing duration of stay of patients in intensive care unit of a hospital with complication types A and B. Two random samples are drawn for types A and B with sample sizes 100 and 70, respectively. Both the random samples are drawn from normally distributed populations with mean and variance μ_A and σ_A^2 for type A and μ_B and σ_B^2 for type B. The mean duration of stay with complication type A is 40 h and with complication type B is 50 h. If the population variances for mean duration of stay with complication types A and B are known to be 15 and 20, respectively, then the interval estimation of the difference in the population means of duration of stay with complication types A and B is to be determined. The experimenter wants to find the 95% confidence interval for $\mu_A - \mu_B$.

Solution

Let us summarize the information provided in this example in the following table.

Surgery	Type (A)	Type (B)
Sample size	$n_A = 100$	$n_B = 70$
Sample mean	$\bar{x}_A = 40$	$\bar{x}_B = 50$
Population variance	$\sigma_A^2 = 15$	$\sigma_B^2 = 20$

A point estimate for $\mu_A - \mu_B$ is

$$(\bar{x}_A - \bar{x}_B) = 40 - 50 = -10.$$

To find a 95% confidence interval for $\mu_A - \mu_B$, we can define

$$95\% = (1 - \alpha)100\%$$

which implies that $0.95 = (1 - \alpha)$, $\alpha = 0.05$ and $\alpha/2 = 0.025$.
The reliability coefficient is $z_{1-\alpha/2} = z_{0.975} = 1.96$.
A 95% C.I. for $\mu_A - \mu_B$ is defined as

$$(\bar{x}_A - \bar{x}_B) \pm Z_{1-\frac{\alpha}{2}} \sqrt{\frac{\sigma_A^2}{n_A} + \frac{\sigma_B^2}{n_B}}.$$

The lower and upper limits can be computed as follows:

$$-10 \pm Z_{0.975} \sqrt{\frac{15}{100} + \frac{20}{70}}$$

which provides

$$l = -10 - 0.8540 = -10.8540$$

and

$$u = -10 + 0.8540 = -9.1460.$$

The above 95% confidence interval of the difference between two means can also be shown as

$$-10.8540 < \mu_A - \mu_B < -9.1460.$$

This confidence interval can be interpreted as: if the samples were drawn from populations A and B with sizes n_A and n_B, respectively, very large number of times then the true difference in the population means would be included in the intervals in 95% of times. There is a link between confidence interval and hypothesis testing because in both the cases we use the statistic known as pivotal quantity in constructing the confidence interval and test statistic in case of testing a null hypothesis. For instance, since the confidence interval does not include zero, we may conclude that the sample data do not provide evidence in favor of equality of two population means and it may be said that the population means are not equal ($\mu_A - \mu_B \neq 0$ or equivalently, $\mu_A \neq \mu_B$). This will be discussed in more details in Chap. 8.

Example 7.8 **(Case II: $\sigma_1^2 = \sigma_2^2$ unknown)**

In the previous example, population variances for populations A and B are assumed to be known. In reality, the population variances are generally not known. Now let us consider a study where samples are drawn from normal populations on the variables $X_1 =$ time taken for remission of body temperature from high fever to normalcy with medication type A and $X_2 =$ time taken for remission of body temperature from high fever to normalcy with medication type B which are assumed to be distributed as follows

$$X_A \sim N(\mu_A, \sigma_A^2) \text{ and } X_B \sim N(\mu_B, \sigma_B^2).$$

The parameters are unknown. The sample data from populations A and B on time taken for remission of body temperature from high fever (in hours) are displayed below

Type A: 55, 70, 35, 48, 71, 40
Type B: 30, 35, 52, 64, 25, 45

The experimenter wants to find the 95% confidence interval of the difference between mean times of remission of body temperature from high to normal using medication types A and B. Let us assume that the population variances are equal, i.e., $\sigma_A^2 = \sigma_B^2 = \sigma^2$.

Solution

First we calculate the mean and the variances of the two samples, and we get

Surgery	Type (A)	Type (B)
Sample size	$n_A = 6$	$n_B = 6$
Sample mean	$\bar{x}_A = 53.17$	$\bar{x}_B = 41.83$
Sample variance	$S_A^2 = 226.97$	$S_B^2 = 214.97$

(1) A point estimate for $\mu_A - \mu_B$ is

$$\bar{x}_A - \bar{x}_B = 53.17 - 41.83 = 11.34.$$

(2) To find the 95% confidence interval for $\mu_A - \mu_B$, we need to state the following:

$$(1 - \alpha) = 0.95, \alpha = 0.05 \text{ and } \alpha/2 = 0.025.$$

It is assumed that the population variances are equal, hence, the pooled variance can be employed to compute the pivotal quantity, statistic t. In that case, the degree of freedom for T, is $v = n_A + n_B - 2 = 10$. The reliability coefficient is

$$t_{10,1-\alpha/2} = t_{10,0.975} = 2.228.$$

The pooled estimate of the common variance is

$$
\begin{aligned}
s_p^2 &= \frac{(n_A - 1)s_A^2 + (n_B - 1)s_B^2}{n_A + n_B - 2} \\
&= \frac{(6 - 1) \times 226.97 + (6 - 1) \times 214.97}{6 + 6 - 2} \\
&= 220.97.
\end{aligned}
$$

The 95% confidence interval for $\mu_A - \mu_B$ is

$$(\bar{x}_A - \bar{x}_B) \pm t_{1-\frac{\alpha}{2}}\sqrt{\frac{s_p^2}{n_A} + \frac{s_p^2}{n_B}}$$

The lower and upper limits of the confidence interval using the sample data from populations A and B are

$$
\begin{aligned}
l &= (\bar{x}_A - \bar{x}_B) - t_{1-\frac{\alpha}{2}}\sqrt{\frac{s_p^2}{n_A} + \frac{s_p^2}{n_B}} \\
&= (53.17 - 41.83) - 2.228 \times \sqrt{\frac{220.97}{6} + \frac{220.97}{6}} \\
&= 11.34 - 19.12 \\
&= -7.78
\end{aligned}
$$

and

$$
\begin{aligned}
u &= (\bar{x}_A - \bar{x}_B) + t_{1-\frac{\alpha}{2}}\sqrt{\frac{s_p^2}{n_A} + \frac{s_p^2}{n_B}} \\
&= (53.17 - 41.83) + 2.228 \times \sqrt{\frac{220.97}{6} + \frac{220.97}{6}} \\
&= 11.34 + 19.12 \\
&= 30.46.
\end{aligned}
$$

This can be shown as

$$-7.78 < \mu_A - \mu_B < 30.46.$$

95% of the times, the confidence interval for difference between the true population means would include the true difference between the population means out of all the intervals calculated for each of the samples of same size drawn repeatedly very large number of times. Since the confidence interval includes zero, we conclude that the two population means may be equal ($\mu_A - \mu_B = 0$, equivalently, $\mu_A = \mu_B$). Therefore, we may conclude that the mean time required for remission of body temperature is the same for the two types.

7.2.5 Estimation of a Population Proportion (P)

If we recall from Chap. 6, the random variable X = number of elements or subjects with a specified characteristic A, N = total number of elements in the population and n = total number of elements in the sample. The probability of a randomly selected subject or element has characteristic A is denoted by p which is essentially the proportion of elements or subjects with characteristic A in the population. We defined $X_i = 1$, if the ith Bernoulli trial results in selecting an element or subject with characteristic A, $X_i = 0$, if the selected element does not have characteristic A. After conducting the trial on n elements of the sample independently, we have $X = \sum_{i=1}^{n} X_i$ = the number of elements or subjects selected with characteristic A.

The joint distribution of n Bernoulli variables $(X_1, \ldots, X_n)$, if X_i s are independently and identically distributed, is

$$f(x_1, \ldots, x_n; p) = \prod_{i=1}^{n} f(x_i, p) = \prod_{i=1}^{n} p^{x_i}(1-p)^{(1-x_i)} = p^x(1-p)^{n-x}$$

and the distribution of $X = x$, where X is the sum of n Bernoulli variables, is

$$f(x; n, p) = \binom{n}{x} p^x(1-p)^{n-x}$$

where the number of mutually exclusive events is $\binom{n}{x}$. This probability function is similar to the likelihood function of the Bernoulli distribution for $X_1, \ldots, X_n$ but the difference between the Bernoulli and binomial trials is that in Bernoulli trial, we are interested in the sequence of outcomes for elements in a Bernoulli trial but in total number of successes, X, out of n in a binomial distribution where n is fixed. Then the likelihood function of p for known value of n is

$$L(p;x) = f(x;n,p) = \binom{n}{x} p^x (1-p)^{n-x}.$$

The log-likelihood function is

$$\ln L(p;x) = \ln \binom{n}{x} + x \ln p + (n-x) \ln(1-p).$$

Differentiating with respect to p, we obtain the likelihood equation

$$\frac{\partial}{\partial p} \ln L(p;x) = \frac{x}{p} - \frac{n-x}{1-p} = 0.$$

Solving this equation for p, we obtain the maximum likelihood estimate $\hat{p} = \frac{x}{n}$. This is the point estimate of p. The maximum likelihood estimator is the statistic $\hat{P} = \frac{X}{n}$.

In Chap. 6, we have shown that $E(\hat{P}) = p$ and $\mathrm{Var}(\hat{P}) = \frac{p(1-p)}{n}$ and it is also shown for large sample size using the Central Limit Theorem

$$\hat{P} \approx N\left(p, \frac{p(1-p)}{n}\right).$$

The pivotal quantity can be defined for population proportion or probability p as

$$Z = \frac{\hat{P} - p}{\sqrt{\frac{p(1-p)}{n}}}$$

Then the probability of $1 - \alpha$ can be shown approximately to be in the interval

$$P\left(z_{\alpha/2} < Z = \frac{\hat{P} - p}{\sqrt{\frac{p(1-p)}{n}}} < z_{1-\alpha/2}\right) = 1 - \alpha.$$

The confidence interval for p with confidence coefficient $1 - \alpha$ can be expressed as

$$P\left(z_{\alpha/2} \times \sqrt{\frac{p(1-p)}{n}} < \hat{P} - p < z_{1-\alpha/2} \times \sqrt{\frac{p(1-p)}{n}}\right) = 1 - \alpha$$

$$= P\left(-\hat{P} + z_{\alpha/2} \times \sqrt{\frac{p(1-p)}{n}} < -p < -\hat{P} + z_{1-\alpha/2} \times \sqrt{\frac{p(1-p)}{n}}\right) = 1 - \alpha$$

$$= P\left(\bar{X} - z_{1-\alpha/2} \times \sqrt{\frac{p(1-p)}{n}} < p < \bar{X} - z_{\alpha/2} \times \sqrt{\frac{p(1-p)}{n}}\right) = 1 - \alpha.$$

The above interval is the $(1 - \alpha)$ 100% confidence interval for population proportion p for large sample size. Using the relationship $Z_{\alpha/2} = -Z_{1-\alpha/2}$ for standard normal distribution, the confidence interval can be expressed as

$$P\left(\hat{P} - z_{1-\alpha/2} \times \sqrt{\frac{p(1-p)}{n}} < p < \hat{P} + z_{1-\alpha/2} \times \sqrt{\frac{p(1-p)}{n}}\right) = 1 - \alpha.$$

The lower and upper limits or end points of this confidence interval are

$$L = \hat{P} - z_{1-\alpha/2} \times \sqrt{\frac{p(1-p)}{n}} \text{ and}$$

$$U = \hat{P} + z_{1-\alpha/2} \times \sqrt{\frac{p(1-p)}{n}}.$$

Using the sample data, the lower and upper limits of the confidence interval are

$$l = \hat{p} - z_{1-\alpha/2} \times \sqrt{\frac{\hat{p}(1-\hat{p})}{n}} \text{ and}$$

$$u = \hat{p} + z_{1-\alpha/2} \times \sqrt{\frac{p(1-p)}{n}}.$$

Alternative Methods

The method of constructing confidence interval of a proportion discussed above is based on the asymptotic normality of the sample proportion. This is the most popular way to present confidence interval for proportion or binomial parameter p. However, several studies such as studies by Agresti and Coull (1998) and Brown et al. (2001) showed that this method, known as the Wald confidence interval for p, first proposed by Laplace (1812) and may be considered as one of the oldest confidence intervals proposed for a parameter, may provide very erratic behavior of the coverage probability even for a large n, where the value of large n may be quite arbitrary and vague in case of sample proportion. The Wald confidence interval for p based on asymptotic normality may produce small coverage probability. It is also known that the coverage probability is poor for p near 0 or 1. In many cases even with the assumption that $n \times \min(p, 1 - p)$ should be at least 5 (some prefer 10) may produce poor coverage for p near 0 or 1. Brown et al. (2001) showed that even when this condition is satisfied, there is no guarantee that the coverage probability is close to confidence level. As an alternative, Clopper and Pearson (1934) exact method is suggested for p where a hypothesized value for p, say p_0, is used to compute lower and upper end points as shown below

$$\sum_{x=k}^{n} \binom{n}{x} p_0^x (1-p_0)^{n-x} = \frac{\alpha}{2}, \text{ and}$$

$$\sum_{x=0}^{k} \binom{n}{x} p_0^x (1-p_0)^{n-x} = \frac{\alpha}{2}.$$

In this exact method, the lower and upper bounds are 0 and 1 for $x = 0$ and $x = n$, respectively. This exact method provides interval estimator with guaranteed coverage of at least $1 - \alpha$ for every possible value of p (Agresti and Coull 1998). It may be noted here that this method depends on a test value for $p = p_0$. The choice of $p = p_0$ will play a major role in obtaining the coverage probability or confidence coefficient by using the exact method. Brown et al. (2001) pointed out that for any fixed p, the coverage probability may be much higher than $1 - \alpha$ unless n is quite large and that is why it may not be considered as a good choice for practical use because it may lead to inaccurate confidence interval. The cumulative probabilities for selected values of n and p are shown in Appendix.

Two methods of constructing confidence intervals that may perform better as recommended by Brown et al. (2001) are summarized below.

(i) The Wilson Interval

This confidence interval for p was introduced by Wilson (1927). In this method, the end points are based on solutions of the equations

$$\frac{\hat{p} - p_0}{\sqrt{p_0(1-p_0)}} = \pm z_{\alpha/2},$$

where $p = p_0$ is called the null value or null hypothesis value of p. The form of the confidence interval for p is

$$\left(\hat{p} + \frac{z_{\alpha/2}^2}{2n} \pm z_{\alpha/2} \sqrt{\left[\hat{p}(1-\hat{p}) + z_{\alpha/2}^2/4n \right]/n} \right) / (1 + z_{\alpha/2}^2/n).$$

This interval is also known as the score confidence interval. Here, the standard error of the estimator of p is based on the null hypothesis value of p rather than maximum likelihood estimators as used in case of the Wald confidence interval. It is shown by Agresti and Coull that score confidence interval tends to perform much better than the Wald or exact intervals for obtaining coverage probability close to the confidence level.

(ii) The Agresti–Coull Interval

The Wald interval would be the best choice for the students to use and remember for its simplicity. The score confidence may be little difficult although it has attractive properties and it performs much better. Agreti and Coull suggested an alternative similar to the Wald interval in terms of its form but performs better than the Wald interval and they named it as the "add two successes and two failures" adjusted Wald interval. In this method, instead of $\hat{p} = \frac{X}{n}$, it is suggested that $\tilde{p} = \frac{\tilde{X}}{\tilde{n}}$, where $\tilde{X} = X + z_{\alpha/2}^2/2$ and $\tilde{n} = n + z_{\alpha/2}^2$. For 95% confidence interval for p, $\alpha = 0.05$ so that $z_{\alpha/2} = 1.96 \approx 2$ and $z_{\alpha/2}^2 = 1.96^2 \approx 4$, the Agresti–Coull point estimator is

$$\tilde{p} = \frac{\tilde{X}}{\tilde{n}} = \frac{X + 2}{n + 4}.$$

The Agresti–Coull confidence interval with confidence level $1 - \alpha$ is

$$\tilde{p} \pm z_{\alpha/2} \frac{\tilde{p}(1 - \tilde{p})}{\sqrt{\tilde{n}}},$$

where the lower and upper end points are

$$l = \tilde{p} - z_{\alpha/2} \frac{\tilde{p}(1 - \tilde{p})}{\sqrt{\tilde{n}}}, \text{ and}$$

$$u = \tilde{p} + z_{\alpha/2} \frac{\tilde{p}(1 - \tilde{p})}{\sqrt{\tilde{n}}}.$$

Both the Wilson interval and Agresti–Coull interval are centered on the same value, $\tilde{p}$, and Agresti–Coull intervals are never shorter than the Wilson intervals (Brown et al. 2001).

Example 7.9 In a study on the diagnosis of acute inflammations of urinary bladder and acute nephritises, a sample of 120 is considered (Czerniak and Zarzycki 2003). Out of 120 in the sample, 50 are found to have acute nephritis of renal pelvis origin. Then we want to find the point estimate and the 95% confidence interval for the true proportion of acute nephritis of renal pelvis origin.

Solution
The variable is X = number of subjects having acute nephritis of renal pelvis origin. The sample size is $n = 120$. The number of subjects with acute nephritis of renal pelvis origin is 50. The sample proportion is

$$\hat{p} = \frac{x}{n} = \frac{50}{120} = 0.4167.$$

A point estimate for p is $\hat{p} = 0.4167$.
For constructing the 95% confidence interval for proportion, p, let us define
The confidence coefficient = $1 - \alpha = 0.95, \alpha = 0.05, \alpha/2 = 0.025$.
The reliability coefficient = $z_{1-\alpha/2} = z_{0.975} = 1.96$.
The 95% confidence interval for proportion of acute nephritis of renal pelvis region is

$$P\left(\hat{P} - z_{1-\alpha/2} \times \sqrt{\frac{p(1-p)}{n}} < p < \hat{P} + z_{1-\alpha/2} \times \sqrt{\frac{p(1-p)}{n}}\right) = 1 - \alpha.$$

The lower and upper limits of the confidence interval using the sample data are

$$l = \hat{p} - z_{1-\alpha/2} \times \sqrt{\frac{\hat{p}(1-\hat{p})}{n}}$$

$$= 0.4167 - 1.96 \times \sqrt{\frac{0.4167 \times 0.5833}{120}}$$

$$= 0.4167 - 0.0882$$

$$= 0.3285$$

and

$$u = \hat{p} + z_{1-\alpha/2} \times \sqrt{\frac{\hat{p}(1-\hat{p})}{n}}$$

$$= 0.4167 + 1.96 \times \sqrt{\frac{0.4167 \times 0.5833}{120}}$$

$$= 0.4167 + 0.0882$$

$$= 0.5049.$$

As it is shown that the above method may fail to provide a reasonably good confidence interval for proportion, two alternative methods are also used here for a comparison.

The Wilson Interval

The Wilson confidence interval considers

$$\frac{\hat{p} - p_0}{\sqrt{p_0(1-p_0)}} = \pm z_{\alpha/2}$$

where $p = p_0$ is called the null value or null hypothesis value of p. It may be noted here that $z_{\alpha/2} = -(1 - z_{\alpha/2})$. Let $p = 0.50$, hence

$$\frac{\hat{p} - p_0}{\sqrt{p_0(1-p_0)}} = \frac{0.4167 - 0.5}{\sqrt{0.5 \times 0.5}} = -0.1666.$$

The form of the confidence interval for p is

$$\left(\hat{p} + \frac{z_{\alpha/2}^2}{2n} \pm z_{\alpha/2}\sqrt{\left[\hat{p}(1-\hat{p}) + z_{\alpha/2}^2/4n\right]/n}\right) / (1 + z_{\alpha/2}^2/n).$$

The lower and upper limits are

$$l = \left(\hat{p} + \frac{z_{\alpha/2}^2}{2n} + z_{\alpha/2}\sqrt{\left[\hat{p}(1-\hat{p}) + z_{\alpha/2}^2/4n\right]/n} \right) / (1 + z_{\alpha/2}^2/n)$$

$$= \left(\frac{0.4167 + \dfrac{(-0.1666)^2}{2 \times 120} + (-0.1666\times}{\sqrt{\left[0.4167 \times 0.5833 + (-0.1666)^2/(4 \times 120)\right]/120}} \right) /[1 + (-0.1666)^2/120]$$

$$= 0.4092$$

$$u = \left(\hat{p} + \frac{z_{\alpha/2}^2}{2n} - z_{\alpha/2}\sqrt{\left[\hat{p}(1-\hat{p}) + z_{\alpha/2}^2/4n\right]/n} \right) / (1 + z_{\alpha/2}^2/n)$$

$$= \left(\frac{0.4167 + \dfrac{(-0.1666)^2}{2 \times 120} - (-0.1666\times}{\sqrt{\left[0.4167 \times 0.5833 + (-0.1666)^2/(4 \times 120)\right]/120}} \right) /[1 + (-0.1666)^2/120]$$

$$= 0.4242.$$

The Agresti–Coull Interval

Agresti and Coull suggested an alternative similar to the Wald interval shown as the first example that performs better than the Wald interval and it is called as "add two successes and two failures" adjusted Wald interval.

In this method, instead of $\hat{p} = \frac{X}{n}$, we use the estimator $\tilde{p} = \frac{\tilde{X}}{\tilde{n}}$,

where $\tilde{X} = X + z_{1-\alpha/2}^2/2$ and $\tilde{n} = n + z_{1-\alpha/2}^2$. For 95% confidence interval for p, $\alpha = 0.05$ so that $z_{1-\alpha/2} = 1.96 \approx 2$ and $z_{1-\alpha/2}^2 = 1.96^2 \approx 4$, the Agresti–Coull point estimator is

$$\tilde{p} = \frac{\tilde{X}}{\tilde{n}} = \frac{X+2}{n+4} = \frac{50+2}{120+4} = 0.4194.$$

The Agresti–Coull confidence interval with confidence level 0.95 is

$$\tilde{p} \pm z_{0.95} \times \frac{\tilde{p}(1-\tilde{p})}{\sqrt{\tilde{n}}},$$

where the lower and upper end points are

$$l = \tilde{p} - z_{1-\alpha/2} \times \frac{\tilde{p}(1-\tilde{p})}{\sqrt{\tilde{n}}}$$

$$= 0.4194 - 2 \times \frac{0.4194 \times 0.5806}{\sqrt{124}}$$

$$= 0.4194 - 0.0437$$

$$= 0.3757,$$

and

$$u = \tilde{p} + z_{1-\alpha/2} \times \frac{\tilde{p}(1-\tilde{p})}{\sqrt{\tilde{n}}}$$

$$= 0.4194 + 2 \times \frac{0.4194 \times 0.5806}{\sqrt{124}}$$

$$= 0.4194 + 0.0437$$

$$= 0.4631.$$

Both the Wilson interval and Agresti–Coull interval are centered on the same value, $\tilde{p}$, but it is seen that the Agresti–Coull interval is larger than the Wilson interval.

7.2.6 *Estimation of the Difference Between Two Population Proportions* $(p_1 - p_2)$

Let us define two independent random samples $(X_{11}, \ldots, X_{1n_1})$ and $(X_{21}, \ldots, X_{2n_2})$ with sample size n_1 and n_2, respectively. The random sample 1 is drawn from $X_{1i} \sim \text{Bernoulli}(p_1)$ and the second sample from $X_{2i} \sim \text{Bernoulli}(p_2)$. Here $X_{1i} = 1$, if the ith Bernoulli trial (or simply ith element of the random sample 1) results in selecting an element with a specified characteristic A in sample 1; $X_{1i} = 0$, otherwise and $X_{2i} = 1$, if the ith Bernoulli trial (or simply ith element of the random sample 2) results in selecting an element with a specified characteristic A in sample 2; $X_{2i} = 0$, otherwise. Then let us define $X_1 = \sum_{i=1}^{n_1} X_{1i}$ and $X_2 = \sum_{i=1}^{n_1} X_{2i}$ representing number of elements with characteristic A in samples 1 and 2, respectively. The probability distributions of $X_1 = \sum_{i=1}^{n_1} X_{1i}$ and $X_2 = \sum_{i=1}^{n_1} X_{2i}$ are then $X_1 \sim \text{Binomial}(p_1)$ for random sample and the second sample from $X_2 \sim \text{Binomial}(p_2)$.

The point estimator of the difference between two parameters is
$\hat{p}_1 - \hat{p}_2 = \frac{X_1}{n_1} - \frac{X_2}{n_2}$.

The expected value and variance of these statistics are

$$
\begin{aligned}
E(\hat{p}_1 - \hat{p}_2) &= E\left[\frac{X_1}{n_1} - \frac{X_2}{n_2}\right] \\
&= \frac{E(X_1)}{n_1} - \frac{E(X_2)}{n_2} \\
&= \frac{n_1 p_1}{n_1} - \frac{n_2 p_2}{n_2} \\
&= p_1 - p_2.
\end{aligned}
$$

The variance is

$$
\begin{aligned}
\mathrm{Var}(\hat{p}_1 - \hat{p}_2) &= \mathrm{Var}\left[\frac{X_1}{n_1} - \frac{X_2}{n_2}\right] \\
&= \frac{\mathrm{Var}(X_1)}{n_1^2} + \frac{\mathrm{Var}(X_2)}{n_2^2} \\
&= \frac{n_1 p_1 (1 - p_1)}{n_1^2} + \frac{n_2 p_2 (1 - p_2)}{n_2^2} \\
&= \frac{p_1 (1 - p_1)}{n_1} + \frac{p_2 (1 - p_2)}{n_2}.
\end{aligned}
$$

If both n_1 and n_2 are large then the pivotal quantity is

$$
Z = \frac{(\hat{p}_1 - \hat{p}_2) - (p_1 - p_2)}{\sqrt{\frac{\hat{p}_1(1-\hat{p}_1)}{n_1} + \frac{\hat{p}_2(1-\hat{p}_2)}{n_2}}} \approx N(0, 1).
$$

Then the confidence level $1 - \alpha$ can be shown approximately as

$$
P\left(z_{\alpha/2} < Z = \frac{(\hat{p}_1 - \hat{p}_2) - (p_1 - p_2)}{\sqrt{\frac{p_1(1-p_1)}{n_1} + \frac{p_2(1-p_2)}{n_2}}} < z_{1-\alpha/2}\right) = 1 - \alpha.
$$

The confidence interval for $p_1 - p_2$ with confidence coefficient $1 - \alpha$ can be expressed as

$$
P\left(\begin{array}{c} z_{\alpha/2} \times \sqrt{\dfrac{p_1(1-p_1)}{n_1} + \dfrac{p_2(1-p_2)}{n_2}} < (\hat{p}_1 - \hat{p}_2) - (p_1 - p_2) \\[4mm] < z_{1-\alpha/2} \times \sqrt{\dfrac{p_1(1-p_1)}{n_1} + \dfrac{p_2(1-p_2)}{n_2}} \end{array}\right) = 1 - \alpha
$$

$$
= P\left(\begin{array}{c} -(\hat{p}_1 - \hat{p}_2) + z_{\alpha/2} \times \sqrt{\dfrac{p_1(1-p_1)}{n_1} + \dfrac{p_2(1-p_2)}{n_2}} < -(p_1 - p_2) \\[4mm] < -(\hat{p}_1 - \hat{p}_2) + z_{1-\alpha/2} \times \sqrt{\dfrac{p_1(1-p_1)}{n_1} + \dfrac{p_2(1-p_2)}{n_2}} \end{array}\right) = 1 - \alpha
$$

$$
= P\left(\begin{array}{c} (\hat{p}_1 - \hat{p}_2) - z_{1-\alpha/2} \times \sqrt{\dfrac{p_1(1-p_1)}{n_1} + \dfrac{p_2(1-p_2)}{n_2}} < (p_1 - p_2) \\[4mm] < (\hat{p}_1 - \hat{p}_2) - z_{\alpha/2} \times \sqrt{\dfrac{p_1(1-p_1)}{n_1} + \dfrac{p_2(1-p_2)}{n_2}} \end{array}\right) = 1 - \alpha.
$$

Using the relationship $Z_{\alpha/2} = -Z_{1-\alpha/2}$ and replacing p_1 and p_2 by maximum likelihood estimators in the lower and upper end points, the confidence interval can be expressed as

$$
P\left(\begin{array}{c} (\hat{p}_1 - \hat{p}_2) - z_{1-\alpha/2} \times \sqrt{\dfrac{\hat{p}_1(1-\hat{p}_1)}{n_1} + \dfrac{\hat{p}_2(1-\hat{p}_2)}{n_2}} < (p_1 - p_2) < (\hat{p}_1 - \hat{p}_2) \\[4mm] + z_{1-\alpha/2} \times \sqrt{\dfrac{\hat{p}_1(1-\hat{p}_1)}{n_1} + \dfrac{\hat{p}_2(1-\hat{p}_2)}{n_2}} \end{array}\right)
$$
$$
= 1 - \alpha.
$$

The lower and upper limits or end points of this confidence interval, using the estimates of the proportions, are

$$
l = (\hat{p}_1 - \hat{p}_2) - z_{1-\alpha/2} \times \sqrt{\frac{\hat{p}_1(1-\hat{p}_1)}{n_1} + \frac{\hat{p}_2(1-\hat{p}_2)}{n_2}} \text{ and}
$$

$$
u = (\hat{p}_1 - \hat{p}_2) + z_{1-\alpha/2} \times \sqrt{\frac{\hat{p}_1(1-\hat{p}_1)}{n_1} + \frac{\hat{p}_2(1-\hat{p}_2)}{n_2}}.
$$

Example 7.10 A researcher was interested in comparing the proportion of people suffering from breathing problem in two cities, A and B. A random sample of 2500 people is taken from city A, and another independent random sample of 2000 people is taken from city B. It is found that 110 people in city A and 74 people in city B have been found with breathing problem. The researcher is interested in finding the 90% confidence interval of the difference between the two proportions.

Solution

Let us define the parameters and estimators for the populations A and B:

p_1 population proportion of people having breathing problem in city A,
p_2 population proportion of people having breathing problem in city B,
x_1 number of people with breathing problem in the sample from city A,
x_2 number of people with breathing problem in the sample from city B,
n_1 sample size for city A,
n_2 sample size for city B,
$\hat{p}_1$ sample proportion of the sample from city A, and
$\hat{p}_2$ sample proportion of the sample from city B.

The point estimates of proportions with breathing problems in cities A and B are shown below:

$$\hat{p}_1 = \frac{x_1}{n_1} = \frac{110}{2500} = 0.044,$$

$$\hat{p}_2 = \frac{x_2}{n_2} = \frac{74}{2000.} = 0.037$$

Point Estimation for $p_1 - p_2$:

The point estimate for the difference between the two proportions, $p_1 - p_2$, is

$$\hat{p}_1 - \hat{p}_2 = 0.044 - 0.037 = 0.007.$$

The lower and upper limits or end points of this confidence interval, using the estimates of the proportions, are

$$l = (\hat{p}_1 - \hat{p}_2) - z_{1-\alpha/2} \times \sqrt{\frac{\hat{p}_1(1-\hat{p}_1)}{n_1} + \frac{\hat{p}_2(1-\hat{p}_2)}{n_2}}$$

$$= 0.007 - 1.645 \times \sqrt{\frac{0.044 \times 0.956}{2500} + \frac{0.037 \times 0.963}{2000}}$$

$$= 0.007 - 0.0097$$

$$= -0.0027$$

and

$$u = (\hat{p}_1 - \hat{p}_2) + z_{1-\alpha/2} \times \sqrt{\frac{\hat{p}_1(1 - \hat{p}_1)}{n_1} + \frac{\hat{p}_2(1 - \hat{p}_2)}{n_2}}$$

$$= 0.007 + 1.645 \times \sqrt{\frac{0.044 \times 0.956}{2500} + \frac{0.037 \times 0.963}{2000}}$$

$$= 0.007 + 0.0097$$

$$= 0.0167.$$

The 95% confidence interval for the difference between two proportions for cities A and B is $(-0.0027, 0.0167)$. This includes 0 that indicates the no difference between the proportions.

7.3 Summary

In this chapter, the concepts and applications of estimation are discussed. The methods of point estimation namely the method of maximum likelihood and the method of moments are introduced in this chapter. The interval estimation is also highlighted in this chapter and the construction of confidence intervals are discussed at length. The construction of confidence interval for single population mean, difference between two population means, single population proportion, and difference between two population proportions are shown with examples under different underlying assumptions about population as well as about small or large sample sizes. The pivotal quantities under the assumption of known or unknown variances are also highlighted. In addition to the traditional Wald method, alternative methods of interval estimation of the population proportion namely the exact method, the Wilson method and the Agresti–Coull method are also illustrated with examples.

Exercises

7.1 Define the following briefly with example:

    (i) Parameter,
    (ii) Statistic,
    (iii) Estimator,
    (iv) Estimate.

7.2 Find the estimator of the parameter of the Bernoulli distribution using the method of moments.

7.3 Write the probability mass function of the geometric distribution and find the estimator of the parameter using method of moments.

7.4 Using the method of moments, find the estimator of the parameters of a normal distribution.

7.5

(i) What is the difference between joint density function and likelihood function?

(ii) Write the likelihood function for a Poisson distribution.

(iii) Find the likelihood estimators of the parameters of a Poisson distribution.

7.6 Use the method of moments to estimate the parameter of the following distribution:

$$f(y, \theta) = \frac{1}{\theta} e^{-\frac{y}{\theta}}.$$

7.7

(i) Find the $100(1 - \alpha)\%$ confidence interval for the population mean μ if the variance σ^2 is known.

(ii) Consider that the time necessary for conducting a surgery is distributed as normal with population mean μ and variance σ^2, where variance is known. A study is conducted to find the estimate of the population mean. The sample size is $n = 40$ and the estimated mean time is $\bar{x} = 25$ minutes. The population variance is known to be 15 min^2. Find the 99% confidence interval of the population mean time of performing the surgery. Interpret your result.

7.8

(i) Find the $100(1 - \alpha)\%$ confidence interval for the population mean μ if the variance σ^2 is known. A sample of size n is drawn from a non-normal population with the population mean μ and known variance σ^2.

(ii) A study is conducted on children under 5 years regarding duration of breathing problem (in days) due to environmental problems in a city. The size of the sample is 75. The probability distribution of the variable, duration of breathing problem, is not normal. The population mean is μ and the variance is known $\sigma^2 = 3$ days^2. The estimated mean time is $\bar{x} = 5$ days. Find the 95% confidence interval of the population mean duration of breathing problem among children of under 5 years. Interpret your result.

7.9

(i) Find the $100(1 - \alpha)\%$ confidence interval for the population mean μ if the variance σ^2 is unknown.

(ii) In a study on blood glucose level among adult population, it is found that the mean glucose level and standard deviation are 80 mg/dL and 27 mg/dL, respectively. The sample size is 21. Find the 95% confidence interval of the population mean glucose level among adult population. Interpret your result.

7.10

(i) Find the $100(1 - \alpha)\%$ confidence interval for difference between two population means if σ_1^2 and σ_2^2 are unknown and assumed to be equal.

(ii) An experiment was conducted to compare time duration of stay in a hospital with two types of complications (A) and (B) and 9 patients with complication type A and 16 patients with complication type B were selected randomly. The average time lengths were 12 days for A and 7 days for B and sample variances were 8 days^2 for A and 5 days^2 for B. Assuming equality of variances in the populations, find the 99% confidence interval for the difference in population means of A and B.

7.11

(i) Find the 90% confidence interval for population proportion, p, if $\hat{p} = 0.4$ and $n = 100$ using the asymptotic normality assumption.

(ii) Use the alternative methods: (a) exact method, (b) Wilson interval and (c) Agresti–Coull interval for constructing confidence interval.

(iii) Compare all these confidence intervals and comment on the suitability of confidence intervals for the given data.

7.12 Among the adult males and females, a study is conducted to estimate the proportion of diabetics. The sample sizes are 250 for males and 200 for females. It is found from the estimates from the samples that the proportion of diabetics among males is 10% and among females is 7%. Find the 95% confidence interval of the difference between population proportions for males and females.

7.13

(i) What is interval estimation? Define the $100\ (1 - \alpha)\%$ confidence interval and illustrate with a pivotal quantity.

(ii) Find the $100(1 - \alpha)\%$ confidence interval for the difference between two population means for two correlated variables.

7.14

(i) Briefly describe the method of estimating parameters by the method of maximum likelihood.

(ii) Let $X_1, \ldots, X_n$ be a random sample from the following population: $f(x, \mu, 5) = \frac{1}{\sqrt{10\pi}} e^{-\frac{1}{10}(x-\mu)^2}$, and find the maximum likelihood estimators of the parameters. If $\hat{\mu}$ is the ML estimator of μ then find the ML estimator of μ^2.

7.15 Consider the following probability mass functions:

$$f(x, \text{n}, \text{p}) = \binom{n}{x} p^x q^{n-x}, x = 0, 1, \ldots, \text{n};$$

Find the estimator of p using the method of moments and the method of maximum likelihood.

7.16 Find the $100(1 - \alpha)\%$ confidence interval for the difference between two means, $\mu_1 - \mu_2$, if σ_1^2 and σ_2^2 are unknown and assumed to be unequal and sample sizes are small; also indicate what would be the confidence interval if the sample sizes are large.

7.17 Consider the following probability mass function:

$$f(x, \theta) = \frac{e^{-\theta}\theta^x}{x!}, x = 0, 1, \ldots$$

   (i) Find the estimator of the parameter of the above pmf for a random sample $X_1, \ldots, X_n$ using the method of moments.
   (ii) Find the estimator of the parameter of the above pmf for a random sample $X_1, \ldots, X_n$ using the method of maximum likelihood.
   (iii) What is the invariance property of a maximum likelihood estimator?

7.18 Find the $100(1 - \alpha)\%$ confidence interval for the following:

   (i) difference between two population means if σ_1^2 and σ_2^2 are unknown and assumed to be equal, and
   (ii) difference between two population means if σ_1^2 and σ_2^2 are unknown and assumed to be unequal.

7.19

   (i) Suppose $X_1, \ldots, X_n$ are an iid sample from a population with pdf or pmf $f(x|\theta_1, \ldots, \theta_k)$ then find the joint density or mass function and then define the likelihood function. How can you estimate the parameters using the likelihood function?
   (ii) Find the likelihood estimates of the parameters of the following distributions:
   $(a) f(x, \lambda) = \lambda e^{-x\lambda}$, and $(b) f(x, \mu, 1) = \frac{1}{\sqrt{2\pi}} e^{-\frac{1}{2}(x-\mu)^2}$.

7.20

   (a) Let $X_1, \ldots, X_n$ be an iid random sample from a population with pdf or pmf $f(x|\theta_1, \ldots, \theta_k)$. Briefly show the estimating equations for estimating parameters $\theta_1, \ldots, \theta_k$ using method of moments.

(b) Use the method of moments to estimate the parameters of the following distributions:

$(i)\, f(x, \theta) = \frac{1}{\theta} e^{-x/\theta}$, and (ii) $f(x, \mu, \sigma^2) = \frac{1}{\sqrt{2\pi\sigma^2}} e^{-\frac{1}{2\sigma^2}(x-\mu)^2}$.

7.21

(a) Suppose $X_1, \ldots, X_n$ are an iid sample from a population with pdf or pmf $f(x|\theta_1, \ldots, \theta_k)$ then find the joint density or mass function and then define the likelihood function. How can you estimate the parameters using the likelihood function?

(b) Find the likelihood estimates of the parameters of the following distributions:

$(i)\, f(x, \lambda) = \lambda e^{-x\lambda}$, and (ii) $f(x, p) = p^x (1-p)^{1-x}, x = 0, 1$.

References

Agresti, A., & Coull, B. A. (1998). Approximate is better than "exact" for interval estimation of binomial proportions. *The American Statistician, 52*(2), 119–226.

Brown, L. D., Cai, T. T., & DasGupta, A. (2001). Interval estimation for a binomial proportion. *Statistical Science, 16*(2), 101–133.

Clopper, C. J., & Pearson, E. S. (1934). The use of confidence or fiducial limits illustrated in the case of the binomial. *Biometrika, 26*, 404–413.

Czerniak, J., & Zarzycki, H. (2003). Application of rough sets in the presumptive diagnosis of urinary system diseases, Artificial Intelligence and Security in Computing Systems. *ACCS 2002 9th International Conference Proceedings* (pp. 41–51). Kluwer Academic Publishers.

Laplace, P. S. (1812). *The'orie analytique des probabilities*. Paris: Courcier.

Wilson, E. B. (1927). Probable inference, the law of succession, and statistical inference. *Journal of the American Statistical Association, 22*, 209–212.

Chapter 8
Hypothesis Testing

8.1 Why Do We Need Hypothesis Testing?

The hypothesis testing deals with answering research questions about the unknown parameters of the population or, in other words, confirming or denying some conjectures or statements about the unknown parameters. In the chapter on estimation (Chap. 7), we have shown point and interval estimation of unknown parameters from random samples. The estimation procedures ensure that the random samples provide us good estimates to represent the corresponding population values called parameters, which are unknown. Once we obtain the estimate, the next important phase is to confirm whether the estimate represents the population value adequately. This question arises because there are various estimates that can be obtained from random samples depending on a specified sample size. The possible variations in the estimates are discussed in sampling distribution presented in Chap. 6. As there are various estimates that can be obtained from random samples of fixed size, each one competing to represent the population value or parameter, it may be a difficult task to confirm whether the estimate from the sample can be considered as the value representing the parameter of a population from which the sample is drawn. Although we consider usually a single sample from the population using random sampling, the concept of underlying sampling distribution provides us insights regarding the possible distribution and its characteristics that help us in understanding the nature of variability in the sampling distribution of the statistic used to estimate the parameter. The process that involves making a decision about the parameter on the basis of a random sample is called the test of hypothesis, where hypothesis is a statement about the parameter and test involves a method that helps to make a decision about the statement about the parameter.

© Springer Nature Singapore Pte Ltd. 2018
M. A. Islam and A. Al-Shiha, *Foundations of Biostatistics*,
https://doi.org/10.1007/978-981-10-8627-4_8

8.2 Null and Alternative Hypotheses

Let us consider a population with some unknown parameter θ. We are interested in testing (confirming or denying) some hypotheses about θ. A hypothesis is a statement about one or more populations. A research hypothesis is the statement about a population parameter that motivates the research. We may define a statistical hypothesis as a statement about the population, which can be evaluated by an appropriate statistical technique. For example, if θ is an unknown parameter of the population, we might be interested in testing the statement stating that $\theta \geq \theta_0$ against $\theta < \theta_0$ (for some specific value θ_0) or $\theta = \theta_0$ against $\theta \neq \theta_0$.

We usually test the null hypothesis (H_0) against the alternative (or the research) hypothesis (H_1 or H_A) by choosing one of the following situations:

(i) $H_0: \theta = \theta_0$ against $H_1: \theta \neq \theta_0$,
(ii) $H_0: \theta \geq \theta_0$ against $H_1: \theta < \theta_0$,
(iii) $H_0: \theta \leq \theta_0$ against $H_1: \theta > \theta_0$.

There are two types of statements about the unknown parameter we need to consider in testing of hypothesis, one is null hypothesis and another is alternative hypothesis, as shown in the examples above. The hypothesis that is being tested provides a statement about the unknown parameter or population denoted by H_0. We may accept or reject the null hypothesis on the basis of evidence from the sample data as well from the underlying sampling distribution of the statistic being used to estimate the unknown parameter. Rejection of a null hypothesis leads to another hypothesis known as alternative hypothesis. While acceptance of a null hypothesis implies that there is not much evidence to reject the statement in the null hypothesis, an alternative hypothesis implies that if we cannot accept the null hypothesis or more specifically if we do not have enough evidence in favor of the null hypothesis or to support the null hypothesis, we may accept the alternative statement called the alternative hypothesis denoted usually by H_1. A simple example of a null hypothesis is $H_0: \theta = \theta_0$ and the corresponding alternative hypothesis is $H_1: \theta \neq \theta_0$. These hypotheses imply that if we do not have sufficient evidence to reject the null hypothesis $H_0: \theta = \theta_0$, it may lead to non-rejection of the null hypothesis statement. By non-rejection of this null hypothesis, we are not saying that this value is exactly equal to the population value but it may be interpreted that there is not much evidence to reject this hypothesis. It may also be noted that, from random samples, we may obtain estimates close to θ_0 and for each of those values the null hypothesis may not be rejected, which may lead to non-rejection of the null hypothesis.

8.3 Meaning of Non-rejection or Rejection of Null Hypothesis

Let us consider a study on a disease and we are interested in finding the proportion of individuals suffering from the disease in the population. The proportion of individuals suffering from the disease in the population is denoted by p. The value of p is unknown. A random sample is considered and the observed values of the random sample provide an estimated p, say $\hat{p} = 0.17$. We want to test for the null hypothesis statement $H_0: p = 0.15$ against the alternative hypothesis $H_1: p \neq 0.15$. If we fail to reject the null hypothesis based on the fact that the estimated value from the sample, 0.17, is not exactly equal to the hypothesized population value of 0.15, still we do not have sufficient evidence to reject this null hypothesis. This might happen with some other estimates from different random sample values as well due to the sampling distribution variation in the possible samples with same sample size having drawn from the same population with parameter, p. Hence, the non-rejection or rejection of null hypothesis should be interpreted very carefully with a proper understanding of the underlying concepts correctly. It needs to be remembered that failure to reject H_0 does not imply that the null hypothesis is true rather it indicates that there is no sufficient evidence to reject H_0 or no sufficient evidence to support the alternative hypothesis, H_1. Another point to be remembered in hypothesis testing is that the formulation of hypothesis needs very careful consideration and understanding about the underlying probability of the random sample variables as well as about the sampling distribution of the statistic being used to estimate the unknown parameter for arriving at an acceptable decision statistically.

One-sided and Two-sided Tests
Both the null and alternative hypotheses have to be stated before the test is performed. Depending on the objectives of the study, the formulation of the hypothesis can be either one tailed or two tailed referring to one-sided or two-sided tests. A statistical test in which the alternative hypothesis states the value of the parameter either above the value specified by H_0 or below the value specified by H_0 is called a one-sided test or one-tailed test.

Examples

(i)
$H_0: \theta = \theta_0,$
$H_1: \theta > \theta_0;$

(ii)
$H_0: \theta = \theta_0,$
$H_1: \theta < \theta_0.$

On the other hand, if the alternative hypothesis states in a test that the value of the parameter can be taken from either side of the stated null hypothesis value it leads to a two-sided or two-tailed test.

Example

$$H_0: \theta = \theta_0,$$
$$H_1: \theta \neq \theta_0.$$

8.4   Test Statistic

For testing hypothesis, we need a statistic which provides the sampling distribution for defining the probability of accepting or rejecting the stated null hypothesis which is called the test statistic. The test statistic is a statistic defined as a function of random sample variables and parameters and the test statistic may also be considered as a random variable. The sampling distribution of the test statistic is independent of the parameters for which the test of hypothesis is performed. Two of the most familiar and widely used test statistics corresponding to their hypotheses are shown below.

(i) Test for $H_0: \mu = \mu_0, H_1: \mu \neq \mu_0$ assuming that the random sample is drawn from $X \sim N(\mu, \sigma^2)$, where σ^2 is known. The sampling distribution of $\bar{X} = \sum_{i=1}^{n} X_i/n$ is $\bar{X} \sim N(\mu, \sigma^2/n)$. Then, the test statistic can be obtained from the standard normal variable

$$Z = \frac{\bar{X} - \mu}{\sigma/\sqrt{n}} \sim N(0, 1)$$

by replacing μ with μ_0 under the null hypothesis. Hence, the test statistic is (Fig. 8.1)

$$Z = \frac{\bar{X} - \mu_0}{\sigma/\sqrt{n}}.$$

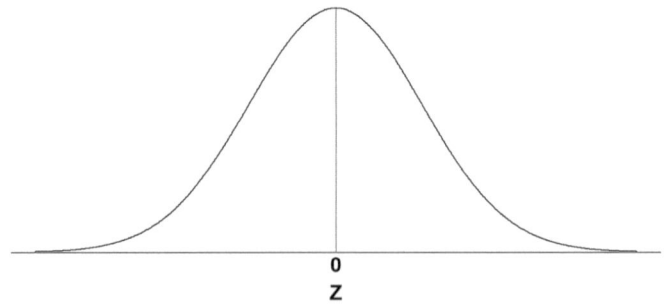

Fig. 8.1 Standard normal distribution

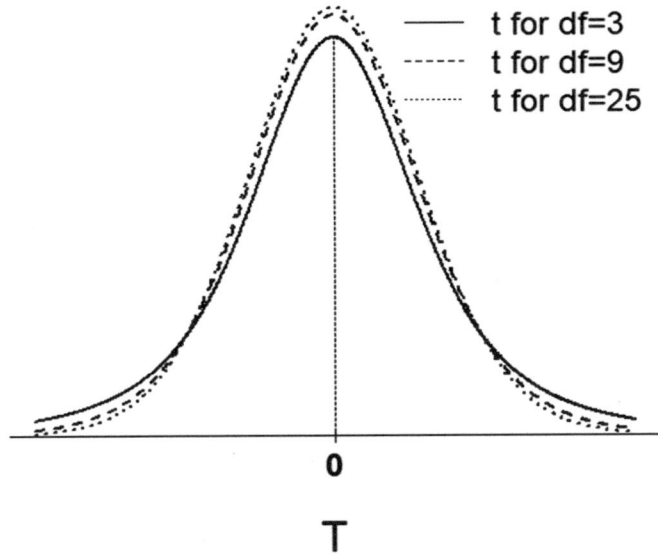

Fig. 8.2 t-distributions with degrees of freedom 3, 9, and 25

(ii)   Test for $H_0: \mu = \mu_0, H_1: \mu \neq \mu_0$ assuming that the random sample is drawn
from $X \sim N(\mu, \sigma^2)$, where σ^2 is unknown. The sampling distribution of $\bar{X} = \sum_{i=1}^{n} X_i/n$ is $\bar{X} \sim N(\mu, \sigma^2/n)$. Then, the test statistic can be obtained from the
standard normal variable

$$T = \frac{\bar{X} - \mu}{S/\sqrt{n}} \sim t_{n-1}$$

by replacing μ with μ_0 under the null hypothesis (Fig. 8.2). Hence, the test statistic is

$$T = \frac{\bar{X} - \mu_0}{S/\sqrt{n}}.$$

8.5   Types of Errors

In performing a test of hypothesis, the decision-making process is not free from
making errors. There are two types of errors arising from accepting or rejecting the
null hypothesis. If we reject a null hypothesis when it is true, it is called the Type I
error. The probability of Type I error is denoted by α. The probability of Type I
error is called the size of the test or level of significance too. The second type of
error is due to failing to reject the null hypothesis, when it is false. The probability
of Type II error is denoted by β. The correct decisions are: (i) reject the null

hypothesis if the null hypothesis is false, and (ii) failing to reject the null hypothesis if the null hypothesis is true. In performing a test, our goal is to keep both the Type I and II errors minimum or in many instances a fixed. These decisions can be shown in a 2×2 table as shown below.

| | | Condition of null hypothesis H_0 | |
		H_0 is true	H_0 is false
Possible action (decision)	Fail to reject H_0	Correct decision	Type II error
	Reject H_0	Type I error	Correct decision

We can define this decision procedure more precisely using the conditional probabilities as summarized below.

(i) P (Type I error) $= P$ (reject $H_0|H_0$ is true) $= \alpha$

This probability statement shows the chance of rejecting a null hypothesis when in reality the null hypothesis is true. This probability is fixed at the pre-experiment stage and the rejection region is determined by the Type I error rate. In order to control the overall erroneous rejections, the Type I error rate is fixed at a low level before the experiment is conducted.

(ii) P (Type II error) $= P$(fail to reject $H_0|H_0$ is false) $= \beta$

In the above probability statement, the chance of failing to reject a null hypothesis when it might be false is stated. This probability should be kept as low as possible.

(iii) P (fail to reject $H_0|H_0$ is true) $= 1 - \alpha$

The above probability statement shows the chance of failure to reject a null hypothesis, when it is true that results in a correct decision of non-rejection of the null hypothesis if given that the null hypothesis is true. If the probability of Type I error is fixed then the complementary event of not making an error by non-rejection of the null hypothesis is also fixed at the pre-experiment stage.

(iv) P (reject $H_0|H_0$ is false) $= 1 - \beta$

The probability of rejecting a null hypothesis when it is truly false is stated in (iv). This is the probability of making a right decision by rejecting the null hypothesis when it might be false. This probability is called the power of the test.

The probabilities of correct decisions, subject to the condition that the underlying null and alternative hypotheses values are known, are shown in (iii) for non-rejection of a null hypothesis if it is true, and in (iv) for rejection of a null hypothesis if it is false. It has to be remembered here that underlying population value is not known generally in most of the cases, but we may consider a hypothetical value based on which the test is performed. So when we say that the null hypothesis is given to be true or false it provides only a hypothetical statement about the population value, there might be other competing null hypothesis values that could be tested with equal importance in many cases. Hence, the test is conducted under a hypothetical situation about the underlying population and in a relative sense, the probability statements leading to specific decisions about the population value reflect only one of the many hypothetical situations. We try to use a test for which the probability of correct decisions (iii) and (iv) are maximized. If we decrease the probability of one type of error it may increase the probability of other types of error for a fixed sample size. However, both the probabilities of Type I and Type II errors will decrease with an increase in sample size. Usually we consider a fixed probability of Type I error, α. The probability of non-rejection of the null hypothesis if it is true is used in constructing a confidence interval as confidence level or confidence coefficient. Similarly, the probability of rejecting a null hypothesis when it is false is called the power of a test and by increasing the power of a test we try to minimize the Type II error.

8.6   Non-rejection and Critical Regions

The non-rejection and critical regions are defined on the basis of the null and alternative hypotheses as well as the test statistic. It is shown that the test statistic is also a variable and there is sampling distribution from which we can find the probabilities of greater than or smaller than some specified values of the test statistic. The specification of these values are based on two criteria: (i) the alternative hypothesis, one-sided or two-sided, and (ii) specification of Type I error, α. If the test is one-sided, then based on the alternative hypothesis, we may define the critical region either to the left or to the right side of the sampling distribution of the test statistic. On the other hand, if the test is two-sided then the critical region is defined to both the left- and right-hand sides of the sampling distribution of the test statistic. The critical region may be defined as the region of a sample space with the property that if the observed value of a test statistic for testing a null hypothesis against an alternative falls in that region then the null hypothesis is rejected. Depending on the alternative hypothesis, the critical region is defined on one or both sides of the sampling distribution of a test statistic. The non-rejection region may be defined as the region with the property that if the observed value of a test statistic for testing a null hypothesis against an alternative falls in that region then the null hypothesis is not rejected. It implies that the non-rejection region is the region under the sampling distribution complementary to the critical region. The value of the test statistic that separates the critical region and non-rejection region is called a critical value for a one-sided test and there are two critical values for a two-sided test. The level of significance, α, determines the size of a test and the critical region depends on the choice of α. Usually, the choices of α are 0.05, 0.01 or in some cases 0.001.

8.7 *p*-Value

Let us consider a test statistic, Z, to test the null hypothesis $H_0: \mu = \mu_0$ against the alternative hypothesis $H_1: \mu > \mu_0$ for a random sample of size n.

Instead of a fixed size of a test, sometimes many users prefer to use a *p*-value to report the result of a test. Currently, there is a debate in the statistical community regarding the conclusions based on statistical significance by using the *p*-value which is commonly misused and misinterpreted (Wasserstein and Lazar 2016). Although it is used by the applied statisticians widely, statisticians may disagree in some situations on its appropriate use and on its interpretation as a measure of evidence (Goodman 1992; Hung et al. 1997). In their ASA's statement on *p*-values, context, process, and purpose, Wasserstein and Lazar (2016) defined informally that a *p*-value is the probability under a specified statistical model that a statistical summary of the data would be equal to or more extreme than its observed value. The *p*-value is a random variable derived from the test statistic and used for testing a null hypothesis in analyzing a set of data. According to Hung et al. (1997), "the *p*-value is derived from the perspective of a test of hypothesis in which a test statistic is calculated from results of a given set of data and, under the assumption that the null hypothesis is true, the distribution of the test statistic is used to obtain the tail probability of observing that result or a more extreme result." The probability of Type I error, α, is a pre-experiment error rate that determines the rejection region and the purpose of the fixed Type I error is to control the overall frequency of making erroneous rejections of the null hypothesis.

Some principles of *p*-values stated in the ASA's statement on *p*-values are quoted from Wasserstein and Lazar (2016)

   (i)   "*P*-values can indicate how incompatible the data are with a specified statistical model.

  (ii)   *P*-values do not measure the probability that the studied hypothesis is true, or the probability that the data were produced by random chance alone.

 (iii)   Scientific conclusions and business or policy decisions should not be based only on whether a *p*-value passes a specific threshold.

 (iv)   A proper inference requires full reporting and transparency.

  (v)   A *p*-value, or statistical significance, does not measure the size of an effect or the importance of a result.

 (vi)   By itself, a *p*-value does not provide a good measure of evidence regarding a model or hypothesis."

In case of a test statistic employed to test a null hypothesis against an alternative hypothesis, *p*-value is the probability of the test statistic under null hypothesis would be equal to or more extreme than its observed value. Let us consider an example to illustrate the computation of *p*-values.

Example 1: For testing a null hypothesis $H_0: \mu = \mu_0$ against an alternative hypothesis $H_1: \mu \neq \mu_0$ assuming that the random sample $(X_1, \ldots, X_n)$ is from a population $X \sim N(\mu, \sigma^2)$. The test statistic is

$$Z = \frac{\bar{X} - \mu_0}{\sigma/\sqrt{n}}$$

and the sampling distribution of Z is $Z \sim N(0, 1)$. Then, the observed values of random samples are $X_1 = x_1, \ldots, X_n = x_n$ and the sample mean is

$$\bar{x} = \frac{\sum_{i=1}^{n} x_i}{n}.$$

Now, we can obtain the value of the test statistic for the given sample and under the null hypothesis as

$$z = \frac{\bar{x} - \mu_0}{\sigma/\sqrt{n}}.$$

Then, we can define the *p*-value as the probability under a specified statistical hypothesis that the test statistic value from the data would be equal to or more extreme than its observed value stated by

$$p\text{-value} = P(Z > |z|) + P(Z < -|z|).$$

Here, the absolute value of z is used to define the tail areas for observed value or more extreme values to both the tail areas in case of either a negative or a positive value of the test statistic. In case of a two-sided alternative, more extreme values of the test statistic can be obtained from the left or right tail areas of the sampling distribution. For a positive value of z, it can be shown directly as

$$p\text{-value} = P(Z > z) + P(Z < -z)$$

because the standard normal distribution is symmetric and the tail areas are greater than z and less than $-z$. Similarly, for a negative value of z, the *p*-value for the two-sided test is (Fig. 8.3)

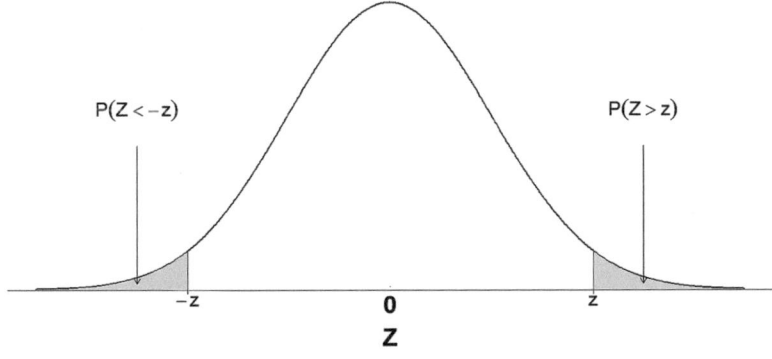

Fig. 8.3 Figure displaying standard normal distribution with two-sided critical regions

$$p\text{-value} = P(Z<z) + P(Z > -z).$$

For a one-sided test for a null hypothesis $H_0\!: \mu = \mu_0$ versus an alternative hypothesis $H_1\!: \mu > \mu_0$, the p-value is

$$p\text{-value} = P(Z > z).$$

Alternatively, this can be defined as

$$p\text{-value} = 1 - P(Z<z) = 1 - F(z)$$

where $F(z)$ is the distribution function value (cumulative probability) of the standard normal at $Z = z$ (Fig. 8.4).

If the tail area is to the left side of a one-sided test for a null hypothesis $H_0\!: \mu = \mu_0$ versus an alternative hypothesis $H_1\!: \mu < \mu_0$, the p-value is

$p\text{-value} = P(Z<z)$. This can be defined alternatively as
$$p\text{-value} = P(Z<z) = F(z)$$

where $F(z)$ is the distribution function value (cumulative probability) of the standard normal at $Z = z$ (Fig. 8.5).

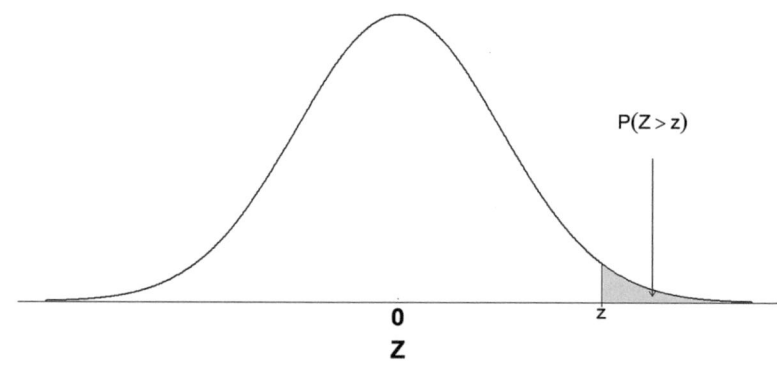

Fig. 8.4 Figure displaying standard normal distribution with critical region to the right tail

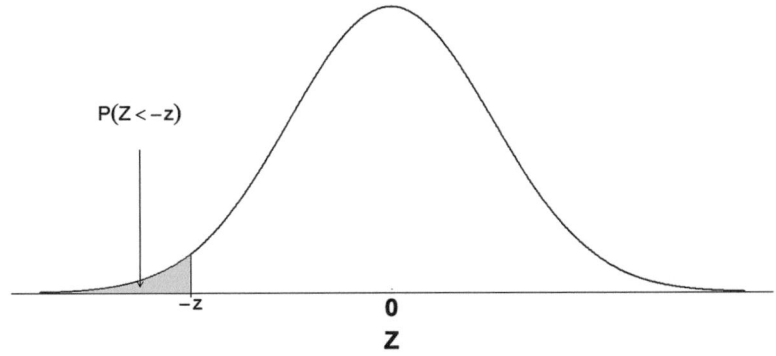

$P(Z < -z)$

$-z$

0

z

Fig. 8.5 Figure displaying standard normal distribution with critical region to the right tail

8.8   The Procedure of Testing H_0 (Against H_A)

The test procedure for not rejecting H_0 or rejecting H_0 involves the following steps:

Steps 1. Specify the statements for null and alternative hypotheses and the size of the test or level of significance, α.

Steps 2. Carefully note the following: (i) probability distribution of the random variable from which the sample is drawn, (ii) if $X \sim N(\mu, \sigma^2)$ and the test is about the population mean then whether the variance is known or unknown, and (iii) sample size, n, and whether the sample size is small or large. This step will vary depending on whether we consider a test for mean, proportion or variance from single or multiple populations, and size of sample.

Steps 3. Find: (i) the point estimator of the parameter being tested, (ii) the sampling distribution of the point estimator, (ii) the test statistic and (iii) the sampling distribution of the test statistic.

Steps 4. Calculate the value of the test statistic from the data and find the critical value to define the rejection region and non-rejection or acceptance region.

Steps 5. Make decision and interpret result based on whether the calculated value of the test statistic falls in the critical region or non-rejection region. Alternatively, the p-value is computed by determining the probability of observed or more extreme values from the sampling distribution of the test statistic.

8.9 Hypothesis Testing: A Single Population Mean (μ)

1. σ^2 is known

Suppose that $X_1, \ldots, X_n$ is a random sample of size n from a distribution (or population) with mean μ and variance σ^2. Then, the steps of performing the test of hypothesis regarding a single population mean are shown below.

Step 1: Let the null and alternative hypotheses are $H_0: \mu = \mu_0$ versus $H_1: \mu \neq \mu_0$. The level of significance is α, say $\alpha = 0.05$.

Step 2: Two different cases are considered.

Case 1: Let the probability distribution of X is $X \sim N(\mu, \sigma^2)$ for the random sample $X_1, \ldots, X_n$ and let us assume that σ^2 is known. Here the sample size is n, small or large.

Case 2: Alternatively, the random sample is drawn from a non-normal population with mean μ and variance σ^2 and sample size is large.

Step 3: The point estimator of μ is $\bar{X} = \frac{\sum_{i=1}^{n} X_i}{n}$. The sampling distributions for two different cases specified in step 2 are

Case 1: $\bar{X} \sim N(\mu, \sigma^2/n)$, the standard error of $\bar{X}$ is $\sigma/\sqrt{n}$.

Case 2: For a large sample size, it can be shown asymptotically that $\bar{X} \approx N(\mu, \sigma^2/n)$, the standard error of $\bar{X}$ is $\sigma/\sqrt{n}$ approximately.

The statistic for both cases 1 and 2 is

$$Z = \frac{\bar{X} - \mu}{\sigma/\sqrt{n}}$$

where the sampling distribution of Z is $Z \sim N(0, 1)$ for case 1 and if the sample size is large then approximately $Z \approx N(0, 1)$ for case 2.

Step 4: The observed value of the test statistic from the sample data $X_1 = x_1, \ldots, X_n = x_n$ is

$$z = \frac{\bar{x} - \mu_0}{\sigma/\sqrt{n}}.$$

The critical values for a two-sided alternative are $z_{\alpha/2}$ and $z_{1-\alpha/2}$ (Fig. 8.6).

Step 5: If $z < z_{\alpha/2}$ or $z > z_{1-\alpha/2}$ then the test statistic value from the sample data falls in the rejection region and the decision is in favor of rejecting the null hypothesis. On the other hand, if $z > z_{\alpha/2}$ and $z < z_{1-\alpha/2}$ then the test statistic falls in the non-rejection region. In this case, the decision is in favor of non-rejection of null hypothesis as evident from the sample data (Fig. 8.7).

2. σ^2 is unknown

Let us consider that $X_1, \ldots, X_n$ be a random sample of size n from a normal distribution (or population) with mean μ and variance σ^2 where σ^2 is not known.

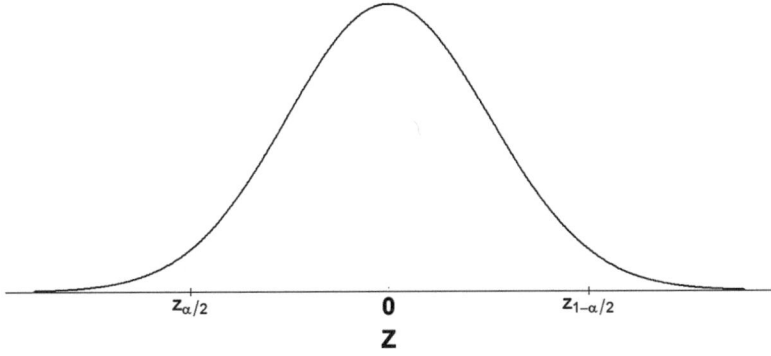

Fig. 8.6 Figure displaying standard normal distribution with critical values for two-sided alternative

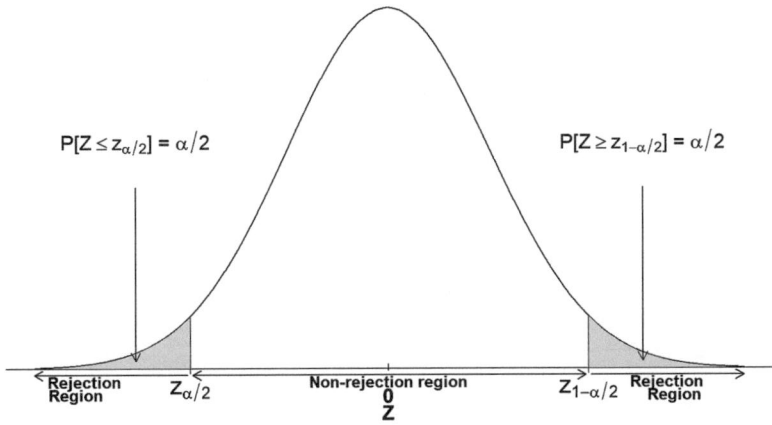

Fig. 8.7 Figure displaying standard normal distribution with non-rejection and rejection regions

The steps of performing the test of hypothesis regarding a single population mean are shown below.

Step 1: The null and alternative hypotheses are $H_0: \mu = \mu_0$ versus $H_1: \mu \neq \mu_0$. The level of significance is α, say $\alpha = 0.05$.

Step 2: Two different cases are considered.

Case 1: Let us assume that the probability distribution of X is $X \sim N(\mu, \sigma^2)$ for the random sample $X_1, \ldots, X_n$ and let σ^2 be unknown. The sample size n is small.

Case 2: Alternatively, the random sample is drawn from a normal population with mean μ and variance σ^2 and sample size is large.

Step 3: The point estimator of μ is $\bar{X} = \frac{\sum_{i=1}^{n} X_i}{n}$. The sampling distributions for two different cases specified in step 2 are

Case 1: $\bar{X} \sim N(\mu, \sigma^2/n)$, the standard error of $\bar{X}$ is $\sigma/\sqrt{n}$.

Case 2: For a large sample size, it can be shown asymptotically that $\bar{X} \approx N(\mu, \sigma^2/n)$, the standard error of $\bar{X}$ is $\sigma/\sqrt{n}$ approximately.

The test statistic for case 1 is

$$T = \frac{\bar{X} - \mu_0}{S/\sqrt{n}}$$

where σ is replaced by its estimator S and the sampling distribution of T is $T \sim t_{n-1}$ for case 1 and if the sample size is large then T is approximately standard normal and can be expressed as $Z \approx N(0,1)$ for case 2.

Step 4: The observed value of the test statistics for cases 1 and 2 from the sample data $X_1 = x_1, \ldots, X_n = x_n$ are

Case 1: $t = \frac{\bar{x} - \mu_0}{s/\sqrt{n}}$

The critical values for a two-sided alternative are $t_{(n-1),\alpha/2}$ and $t_{(n-1),1-\alpha/2}$.

Case 2: $z = \frac{\bar{x} - \mu_0}{s/\sqrt{n}}$

The critical values for a two-sided alternative are $z_{\alpha/2}$ and $z_{1-\alpha/2}$.

Step 5: The decision for cases 1 and 2 can be made as follows:

Case 1: It is mentioned that case 1 represents a random sample drawn from normal population, where the population variance is unknown. Then to perform the test for the population mean, we have considered a t-test statistic with $(n-1)$ degrees of freedom. If $t < t_{(n-1),\alpha/2}$ or $t > t_{(n-1),1-\alpha/2}$, then the test statistic value from the sample data falls in the rejection region and the decision is in favor of rejecting the null hypothesis. However, if $t_{(n-1),\alpha/2} < t < t_{(n-1),1-\alpha/2}$ then the test statistic falls in the non-rejection region. In this case, the decision based on the sample data is in favor of non-rejection of the null hypothesis (Fig. 8.8).

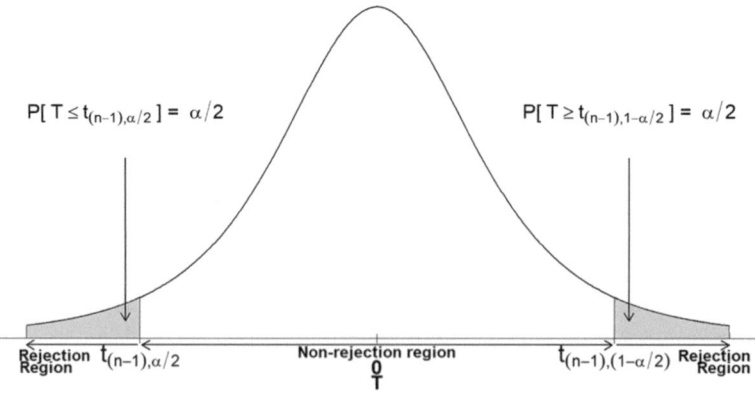

Fig. 8.8 Figure displaying t-distribution with non-rejection and rejection regions

Case 2: In this case also the random sample is assumed to be drawn from a normal population with variance unknown. Then, the test statistic tends to follow a standard normal distribution for a large sample size. If the value of the test statistic is $z < z_{\alpha/2}$ or $z > z_{1-\alpha/2}$, then the sample data favor rejection of the null hypothesis because the test statistic value from sample data falls in the critical or rejection region. If $z_{\alpha/2} < z < z_{1-\alpha/2}$ then the test statistic falls in the non-rejection region and the decision is in favor of non-rejection of null hypothesis.

Example 8.1 Test for μ, σ^2 is known.

The example we have employed to illustrate the confidence interval for population mean for known population variance is used here. In that example, we have considered a random sample of 123 patients admitted to a hospital with old age complications. The sample mean age is 55 years. The population variance is assumed to be $\sigma^2 = 82$. Let us assume that the population is normal with mean μ and variance $\sigma^2 = 82$. Then a test is performed to know whether the population mean is $\mu = 50$.

In this example, $X_1, \ldots, X_n$ is a random sample of size n from a distribution (or population) with mean μ and variance σ^2.

Step 1: The null and alternative hypotheses are

$$H_0: \mu = 50 \text{ versus } H_1: \mu \neq 50.$$

The level of significance is $\alpha = 0.05$.

Step 2: The probability distribution of X is $X \sim N(\mu, \sigma^2)$ for the random sample $X_1, \ldots, X_n$ and let us assume that σ^2 is known.

Step 3: The point estimator of μ is $\bar{X} = \frac{\sum_{i=1}^{n} X_i}{n}$ and its sampling distribution is $\bar{X} \sim N(\mu, \sigma^2/n)$, the standard error of $\bar{X}$ is $\sigma/\sqrt{n}$.

The statistic is

$$Z = \frac{\bar{X} - \mu}{\sigma/\sqrt{n}}$$

where the sampling distribution of Z is $Z \sim N(0, 1)$.

Step 4: The observed value of the test statistic from the sample data is

$$z = \frac{\bar{x} - \mu_0}{\sigma/\sqrt{n}} = \frac{55 - 50}{9.06/\sqrt{123}} = \frac{5}{0.8169} = 6.1207.$$

The critical values for a two-sided alternative are $z_{0.025} = -196$ and $z_{0.975} = 1.96$ (Fig. 8.9).

Step 5: The calculated value of the test statistic is 6.1207 which is greater than the critical value, i.e., $z > z_{0.975}$ where $z = 6.1207$ and $z_{0.975} = 1.96$. It shows that the test statistic value from the sample data falls in the rejection region and the decision is in favor of rejecting the null hypothesis.

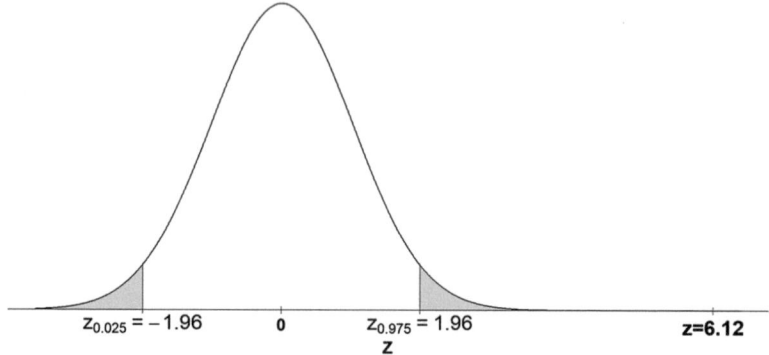

$z_{0.025} = -1.96$ 0 $z_{0.975} = 1.96$ $z = 6.12$

z

Fig. 8.9 Figure displaying critical regions for test about population mean, when variance is known

Example 8.2 Test for μ, σ^2 is unknown.

Using the data on height of women in their adulthood presented in Chap. 7, an example for test on population mean (when σ^2 is unknown) is shown here. A hypothetical sample of 24 women considered here is assumed to be drawn from a normal distribution with population mean μ and variance σ^2. The sample mean and variance of height of the selected women are 151 cm and 18.65 cm^2 respectively. Then, let us test for the null hypothesis whether population mean is 153 cm or not.

Solution

The random sample $X_1, \ldots, X_n$ is assumed to be drawn from a normal distribution with mean μ and variance σ^2 where σ^2 is not known.

Step 1: The null and alternative hypotheses are

$H_0: \mu = 153$ versus $H_1: \mu \neq 153$. The level of significance is $\alpha = 0.05$.

Step 2: The probability distribution of X is $X \sim N(\mu, \sigma^2)$ for the random sample $X_1, \ldots, X_n$ and let σ^2 be unknown. The sample size n is small.

Step 3: The point estimator of μ is $\bar{X} = \frac{\sum_{i=1}^{n} X_i}{n}$ and $\bar{X} \sim N(\mu, \sigma^2/n)$, the standard error of $\bar{X}$ is $\sigma/\sqrt{n}$.

The test statistic is

$$T = \frac{\bar{X} - \mu_0}{S/\sqrt{n}}$$

and the sampling distribution of T is $T \sim t_{n-1}$,

Step 4: The observed value of the test statistics is

$$t = \frac{\bar{x} - \mu_0}{s/\sqrt{n}} = \frac{151 - 153}{4.32/\sqrt{24}} = \frac{-2}{0.8818} = -2.2681$$

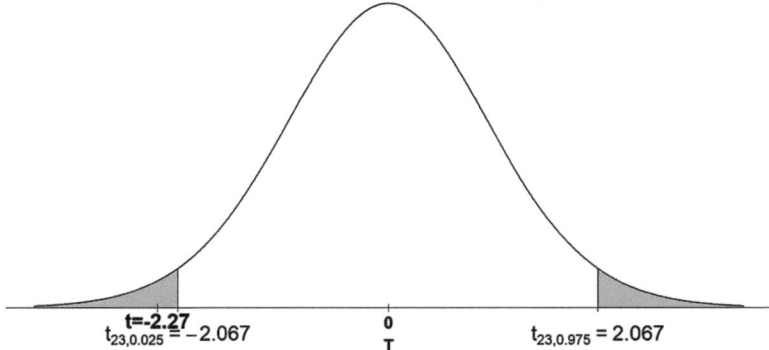

Fig. 8.10 Figure displaying critical regions for test about population mean when variance is unknown

where $n = 24$ and $s = +\sqrt{s^2} = +\sqrt{18.65} = 4.32$.

The critical values for a two-sided alternative are $t_{23,0.025} = -2.067$ and $t_{23,0.975} = 2.067$ (Fig. 8.10).

Step 5: The calculated value of the test statistic, t, appears to be less than the critical value at the lower tail, i.e., $t < t_{(n-1),\alpha/2}$, hence the test statistic value from the sample data falls in the rejection region and the decision is in favor of rejecting the null hypothesis.

8.10   Hypothesis Testing: The Difference Between Two Population Means: Independent Populations

Suppose that we have two independent populations where the first population is characterized with parameters mean $= \mu_1$ and variance $= \sigma_1^2$ and the second population with mean $= \mu_2$ and variance $= \sigma_2^2$. The random samples from the first and second populations are $(X_{11}, \ldots, X_{1n_1})$ and $(X_{21}, \ldots, X_{2n_2})$ respectively. Let us denote the probability distributions for the variables for the first and second random samples as $X_1 \sim D(\mu_1, \sigma_1^2)$ and $X_2 \sim D(\mu_2, \sigma_2^2)$, respectively, where D represents underlying population distribution. Here, we are interested in comparing μ_1 and μ_2, or equivalently, making inferences about the difference between the means $(\mu_1 - \mu_2)$. Let us select a random sample of size n_1 from the first population and another random sample of size n_2 from the second population independently and let $\bar{X}_1$ and S_1^2 be the sample mean and the sample variance of the first random sample and $\bar{X}_2$ and S_2^2 be the sample mean and the sample variance of the second random sample. The sampling distribution of $\bar{X}_1 - \bar{X}_2$ is used to make inferences about $(\mu_1 - \mu_2)$.

The steps discussed in the previous section can be used to illustrate the testing of hypothesis of difference between two population means. The steps are highlighted below.

1. σ_1^2 and σ_2^2 are known

Suppose that the random samples from the first population is $(X_{11}, \ldots, X_{1n_1})$ with sample size n_1 and the random sample from the second population is $(X_{21}, \ldots, X_{2n_2})$ with sample size n_2.

Step 1: The null and alternative hypotheses are $H_0: \mu_1 - \mu_2 = 0$ versus $H_1: \mu_1 - \mu_2 \neq 0$. The level of significance is α, say $\alpha = 0.05$.

Step 2: Two different cases are considered.

Case 1: Let the probability distribution of X_1 is $X_1 \sim N(\mu_1, \sigma_1^2)$ for the random sample $X_{11}, \ldots, X_{1n_1}$ and X_2 is $X_2 \sim N(\mu_2, \sigma_2^2)$ for the random sample $X_{21}, \ldots, X_{2n_2}$ let us assume that σ_1^2 and σ_2^2 are known.

Case 2: Alternatively, let the probability distribution of X_1 is non-normal for the random sample $X_{11}, \ldots, X_{1n_1}$ with mean μ_1 and variance σ_1^2 and X_2 is non-normal for the random sample $X_{21}, \ldots, X_{2n_2}$ with mean μ_2 and variance σ_2^2 for the random sample $X_{21}, \ldots, X_{2n_2}$. Let us assume that σ_1^2 and σ_2^2 are known and sample sizes for both the samples are large.

Step 3: The point estimator of μ_1 is $\bar{X}_1 = \frac{\sum_{i=1}^{n_1} X_{1i}}{n_1}$ and μ_2 is $\bar{X}_2 = \frac{\sum_{i=1}^{n_2} X_{2i}}{n_2}$. The sampling distributions of $\bar{X}_1 - \bar{X}_2$ for two different cases specified in step 2 are summarized below.

Case 1: $\bar{X}_1 - \bar{X}_2 \sim N(\mu_1 - \mu_2, \sigma_1^2/n_1 + \sigma_2^2/n_2)$ and the standard error of

$\bar{X}_1 - \bar{X}_2$ is $\sigma_1/\sqrt{n_1} + \sigma_2/\sqrt{n_2}$.

Case 2: For large sample, it can be shown asymptotically that

$\bar{X}_1 - \bar{X}_2 \approx N(\mu_1 - \mu_2, \sigma_1^2/n_1 + \sigma_2^2/n_2)$ and the standard error of $\bar{X}_1 - \bar{X}_2$ is approximately $\sigma_1/\sqrt{n_1} + \sigma_2/\sqrt{n_2}$.

The statistic for both cases 1 and 2 is

$$Z = \frac{\bar{X}_1 - \bar{X}_2 - (\mu_1 - \mu_2)}{\sqrt{\sigma_1^2/n_1 + \sigma_2^2/n_2}}$$

where the sampling distribution of Z is $Z \sim N(0, 1)$ for case 1 and if the sample sizes are large then approximately $Z \approx N(0, 1)$ for case 2.

Step 4: The observed value of the test statistic from the sample data $X_{11} = x_{11}, \ldots, X_{1n_1} = x_{1n_1}$ for sample 1 and $X_{21} = x_{21}, \ldots, X_{2n_2} = x_{2n_2}$ for sample 2 is

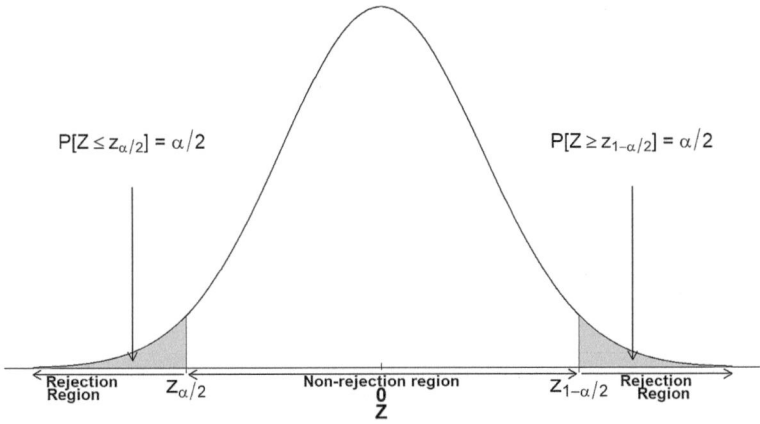

Fig. 8.11 Figure displaying critical regions for test about equality of population means when population variances are known

$$z = \frac{\bar{x}_1 - \bar{x}_2}{\sqrt{\sigma_1^2/n_1 + \sigma_2^2/n_2}}.$$

The critical values for a two-sided alternative are $z_{\alpha/2}$ and $z_{1-\alpha/2}$ (Fig. 8.11).

Step 5: The rejection region is defined by $z < z_{\alpha/2}$ or $z > z_{1-\alpha/2}$. If the test statistic's value from the sample data falls in the rejection region, the decision is in favor of rejecting the null hypothesis. On the other hand, if $z_{\alpha/2} < z < z_{1-\alpha/2}$ then the value of the test statistic falls in the non-rejection region and the decision is in favor of non-rejection of null hypothesis as evident from the sample data.

2. σ_1^2 and σ_2^2 are unknown

Let us consider the random sample from the first population is $(X_{11}, \ldots, X_{1n_1})$ with sample size n_1 and from the second population is $(X_{21}, \ldots, X_{2n_2})$ with sample size n_2. The variance of both the populations 1 and 2 are unknown.

Step 1: The null and alternative hypotheses are $H_0 : \mu_1 - \mu_2 = 0$ versus $H_1 : \mu_1 - \mu_2 \neq 0$. The level of significance is α, say $\alpha = 0.05$.

Step 2: Two different cases are considered.

Case 1: Let $X_1 \sim N(\mu_1, \sigma_1^2)$ and $X_2 \sim N(\mu_2, \sigma_2^2)$ and σ_1^2 and σ_2^2 are unknown.

Case 2: Let the probability distribution of X_1 is non-normal for the random sample $X_{11}, \ldots, X_{1n_1}$ with mean μ_1 and variance σ_1^2 and X_2 is non-normal for the random sample $X_{21}, \ldots, X_{2n_2}$ with mean μ_2 and variance σ_2^2 for the random sample $X_{21}, \ldots, X_{2n_2}$. In this case also, σ_1^2 and σ_2^2 are unknown and sample size for both the samples are large.

Step 3: The point estimators of population means: the estimator of μ_1 is $\bar{X}_1 = \frac{\sum_{i=1}^{n_1} X_{1i}}{n_1}$ and the estimator of μ_2 is $\bar{X}_2 = \frac{\sum_{i=1}^{n_2} X_{2i}}{n_2}$. The sampling distribution of $\bar{X}_1 - \bar{X}_2$ for 1 and 2 are summarized below.

Case 1: $\bar{X}_1 - \bar{X}_2 \sim N(\mu_1 - \mu_2, \sigma_1^2/n_1 + \sigma_2^2/n_2)$.

Case 2: For large sample, it can be shown asymptotically that

$$\bar{X}_1 - \bar{X}_2 \approx N(\mu_1 - \mu_2, \sigma_1^2/n_1 + \sigma_2^2/n_2).$$

The test statistic for case 1 is

$$T = \frac{\bar{X}_1 - \bar{X}_2}{\sqrt{S_1^2/n_1 + S_2^2/n_2}}$$

where the sampling distribution of T is $T \sim t_\nu$ for case 1.

The denominator of T shown above, which is the standard error of the estimators of two population means, may be estimated under different assumptions about the population variances. We address two different situations here.

Case 1(i) The population variances of two independent populations are unknown but assumed to be equal which imply $\sigma_1^2 = \sigma_2^2 = \sigma^2$. The sample variances are defined as

$$S_1^2 = \frac{\sum_{i=1}^{n_1} (X_{1i} - \bar{X}_1)^2}{n_1 - 1} \quad \text{and} \quad S_2^2 = \frac{\sum_{i=1}^{n_2} (X_{2i} - \bar{X}_2)^2}{n_2 - 1}.$$

For equality of population variances a pooled estimator of population variance is preferred as shown below

$$S_p^2 = \frac{\sum_{i=1}^{n_1} (X_{1i} - \bar{X}_1)^2 + \sum_{i=1}^{n_2} (X_{2i} - \bar{X}_2)^2}{n_1 + n_2 - 2} = \frac{(n_1 - 1)S_1^2 + (n_2 - 1)S_2^2}{n_1 + n_2 - 2}.$$

Under this assumption of equality of variances, the test statistic is redefined as

$$T = \frac{\bar{X}_1 - \bar{X}_2}{S_p \sqrt{(1/n_1) + (1/n_2)}}.$$

Here, T is $T \sim t_\nu$ and the degrees of freedom $\nu = n_1 + n_2 - 2$.

Case 1(ii) If the population variances are assumed to be unequal and unknown then we have to deal with $\sigma_1^2 \neq \sigma_2^2$ and the pooled estimator of the variance can not be used. In this case, the test statistic is

$$T = \frac{\bar{X}_1 - \bar{X}_2}{\sqrt{S_1^2/n_1 + S_2^2/n_2}}$$

where the sampling distribution of T is $T \sim t_\nu$ as shown earlier and the degrees of freedom is obtained by using the following approximation popularly known as the Satterthwaite approximation introduced in 1946 (Satterthwaite 1946)

$$\nu = \frac{\left(s_1^2/n_1 + s_2^2/n_2\right)^2}{\left[\left(s_1^2/n_1\right)^2/(n_1 - 1)\right] + \left[\left(s_2^2/n_2\right)^2/(n_2 - 1)\right]}.$$

Usually, this approximation is not an integer and we can approximate the degrees of freedom by rounding the result to the nearest integer.

The test statistic for case 2 is

$$Z = \frac{\bar{X}_1 - \bar{X}_2}{\sqrt{S_1^2/n_1 + S_2^2/n_2}}$$

where the sampling distribution of Z is asymptotically $Z \approx N(0, 1)$ if sample sizes are large for case 2.

Step 4: The values of the test statistics for cases 1 and 2 are shown below.

The value of the test statistic from sample data for case 1(i) is

$$t = \frac{\bar{x}_1 - \bar{x}_2}{s_p \sqrt{(1/n_1) + (1/n_2)}}$$

and the critical values for the two-tailed test at the left and right tail areas are $t_{n_1 + n_2 - 2, \alpha}$ and $t_{n_1 + n_2 - 2, 1 - \alpha}$.

Similarly, the test statistic from sample data for case 1(ii) is

$$t = \frac{\bar{x}_1 - \bar{x}_2}{\sqrt{s_1^2/n_1 + s_2^2/n_2}}.$$

The critical values are $t_{\nu, \alpha}$ and $t_{\nu, 1 - \alpha}$, where the degrees of freedom, ν, is

$$\nu = \frac{\left(s_1^2/n_1 + s_2^2/n_2\right)^2}{\left[\left(s_1^2/n_1\right)^2/(n_1 - 1)\right] + \left[\left(s_2^2/n_2\right)^2/(n_2 - 1)\right]}.$$

For case 2, the value of the test statistic for large sample size is

$$z = \frac{\bar{x}_1 - \bar{x}_2}{\sqrt{\sigma_1^2/n_1 + \sigma_2^2/n_2}}.$$

The critical values for a two-sided alternative are $z_{\alpha/2}$ and $z_{1-\alpha/2}$. Here, the sampling distribution of Z is asymptotically $Z \approx N(0, 1)$ if sample sizes are large.

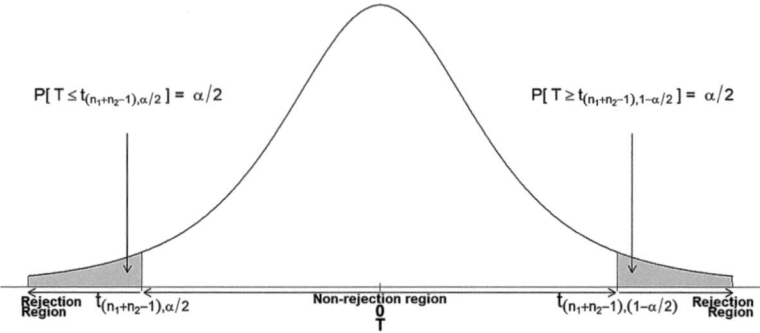

Fig. 8.12 Figure displaying critical regions for test about equality of population means when population variances are unknown

Step 5: The decision is based on test statistic value from sample data as displayed in Step 4.

Case 1: The rejection region is defined by $t < t_{n_1+n_2-2,\alpha/2}$ or $t > t_{n_1+n_2-2,1-\alpha/2}$. The decision is in favor of rejecting the null hypothesis if the test statistic value, t, falls in the rejection region. On the other hand, if $t_{\alpha/2} < t < t_{1-\alpha/2}$ then the value of the test statistic falls in the non-rejection region, and the decision is in favor of non-rejection of null hypothesis as we observe from the sample data (Fig. 8.12).

Case 2: The rejection region is defined by $z < z_{\alpha/2}$ or $z > z_{1-\alpha/2}$. If the test statistic value from the sample data, z, falls in the rejection region, the decision is in favor of rejecting the null hypothesis. On the other hand, if $z_{\alpha/2} < z < z_{1-\alpha/2}$ then the value of the test statistic falls in the non-rejection region and the decision is in favor of non-rejection of null hypothesis (Fig. 8.13).

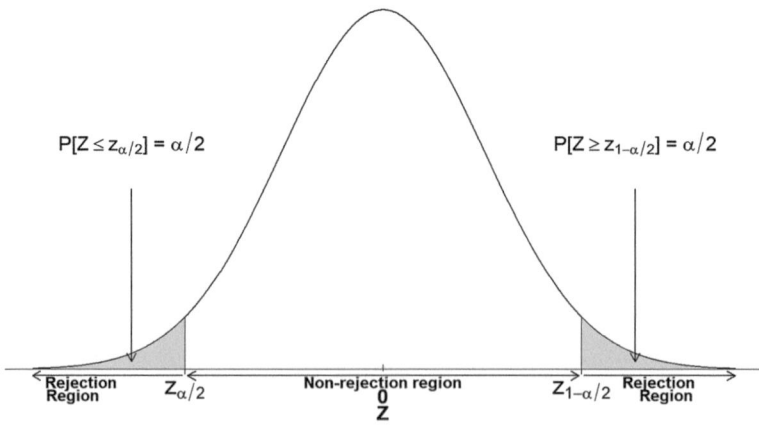

Fig. 8.13 Figure displaying critical regions for test about equality of population means when population variances are unknown but sample sizes are large

Example 8.3 Test for Equality of μ_1 and μ_2 if σ_1^2 and σ_2^2 are known.

In a study on birth weights measured within 72 h of birth (BBS, 2005), mean birth weights of rural and urban areas are estimated to be 2622 g ($n_1 = 2774$) and 2698 g ($n_2 = 311$) respectively. Let us assume that the standard deviations of birth weights in rural area (439 g) and urban area (389 g) represent their population values. For known σ_1^2 and σ_2^2, we want to test for the equality of mean birth weights in rural and urban areas at 1% level of significance.

Solution

Let us consider two random samples $(X_{11}, \ldots, X_{1n_1})$ with sample size n_1 from $N(\mu_1, \sigma_1^2)$ and $(X_{21}, \ldots, X_{2n_2})$ with sample size n_2 from $N(\mu_2, \sigma_2^2)$.

Step 1: The null and alternative hypotheses are

$H_0: \mu_1 - \mu_2 = 0$ versus $H_1: \mu_1 - \mu_2 \neq 0$. The level of significance is $\alpha = 0.01$.

Step 2: The probability distribution of X_1 is approximately $X_1 \sim N(\mu_1, \sigma_1^2)$ for the rural area and X_2 is approximately $X_2 \sim N(\mu_2, \sigma_2^2)$ for the urban area, let us assume that σ_1^2 and σ_2^2 are known.

Step 3: The point estimators of μ_1 and μ_2 are

$$\bar{X}_1 = \frac{\sum_{i=1}^{n_1} X_{1i}}{n_1} \text{ and } \bar{X}_2 = \frac{\sum_{i=1}^{n_2} X_{2i}}{n_2}.$$

The sampling distribution of $\bar{X}_1 - \bar{X}_2$ is

$$\bar{X}_1 - \bar{X}_2 \sim N(\mu_1 - \mu_2, \sigma_1^2/n_1 + \sigma_2^2/n_2).$$

The test statistic is

$$Z = \frac{\bar{X}_1 - \bar{X}_2}{\sqrt{\sigma_1^2/n_1 + \sigma_2^2/n_2}}$$

where the sampling distribution of Z is approximately $Z \sim N(0, 1)$.

Step 4: The observed value of the test statistic is

$$
\begin{aligned}
z &= \frac{\bar{x}_1 - \bar{x}_2}{\sqrt{\sigma_1^2/n_1 + \sigma_2^2/n_2}} \\
&= \frac{2622 - 2698}{\sqrt{192721/2774 + 151321/311}} \\
&= \frac{-76}{23.5804} \\
&= -3,2230.
\end{aligned}
$$

The critical values for a two-sided alternative are $z_{0.005} = -2.575$ and $z_{0.995} = 2.575$ (Fig. 8.14).

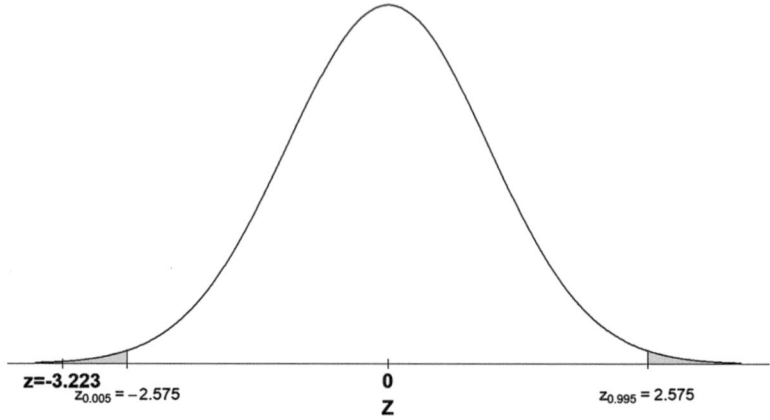

Fig. 8.14 Figure displaying critical regions for test about equality of population means when population variances are known

Step 5: The rejection region is defined by $z < z_{0.005}$ or $z > z_{0.995}$ and as the value of the test statistic from the sample data falls in the rejection region, the decision is in favor of rejecting the null hypothesis of equality of the birth weights in rural and urban areas.

Example 8.4 Test for Equality of μ_1 and μ_2 if σ_1^2 and σ_2^2 are unknown.

Case 1 σ_1^2 and σ_2^2 are unknown but Assumed to be Equal.

In a study on heights, two samples of height of women are drawn randomly from normal populations with means μ_1 and μ_2 and variances σ_1^2 and σ_2^2 respectively. The size of sample 1 is 28 and sample 2 is 24. The sample 1 mean and variance are 151.88 cm and 26.53 cm^2 and sample 2 mean and variance are 150.99 cm and 18.65 cm^2. It is of interest to test the equality of two population means if population variances are unknown.

Solution

The sample from the first population is $(X_{11}, \ldots, X_{1n_1})$ with sample size n_1 and from the second population is $(X_{21}, \ldots, X_{2n_2})$ with sample size n_2. The variance of both the populations 1 and 2 are unknown.

Step 1: The null and alternative hypotheses are
$H_0: \mu_1 - \mu_2 = 0$ versus $H_1: \mu_1 - \mu_2 \neq 0$.
The level of significance is $\alpha = 0.05$.

Step 2: Let $X_1 \sim N(\mu_1, \sigma_1^2)$ and $X_2 \sim N(\mu_2, \sigma_2^2)$ and σ_1^2 and σ_2^2 are unknown.

Step 3: The point estimator μ_1 is $\bar{X}_1 = \frac{\sum_{i=1}^{n_1} X_{1i}}{n_1}$ and μ_2 is $\bar{X}_2 = \frac{\sum_{i=1}^{n_2} X_{2i}}{n_2}$. The sampling distribution of $\bar{X}_1 - \bar{X}_2$ is

$$\bar{X}_1 - \bar{X}_2 \sim N(\mu_1 - \mu_2, \sigma_1^2/n_1 + \sigma_2^2/n_2).$$

The test statistic is

$$T = \frac{\bar{X}_1 - \bar{X}_2}{\sqrt{S_1^2/n_1 + S_2^2/n_2}}$$

where the sampling distribution of T is $T \sim t_\nu$.

If the population variances of two independent populations are unknown but assumed to be equal which imply $\sigma_1^2 = \sigma_2^2 = \sigma^2$. The estimator of the pooled variance under the assumption of equality of population variances is

$$S_p^2 = \frac{\sum_{i=1}^{n_1}(X_{1i} - \bar{X}_1)^2 + \sum_{i=1}^{n_2}(X_{2i} - \bar{X}_2)^2}{n_1 + n_2 - 2} = \frac{(n_1 - 1)S_1^2 + (n_2 - 1)S_2^2}{n_1 + n_2 - 2}.$$

The test statistic is redefined as

$$T = \frac{\bar{X}_1 - \bar{X}_2}{S_p\sqrt{(1/n_1) + (1/n_2)}}.$$

Here, T is $T \sim t_\nu$ and the degrees of freedom $\nu = n_1 + n_2 - 2$.

Step 4: The values of the test statistic is

$$t = \frac{\bar{x}_1 - \bar{x}_2}{s_p\sqrt{(1/n_1) + (1/n_2)}},$$

where

$$\hat{\mu}_1 - \hat{\mu}_2 = \bar{x}_1 - \bar{x}_2 = 151.88 - 150.99 = 0.89,$$

$$s_p^2 = \frac{(n_1 - 1)s_1^2 + (n_2 - 1)s_2^2}{n_1 + n_2 - 2}$$

$$= \frac{27 \times 26.53 + 23 \times 18.65}{50}$$

$$= 23.45,$$

and $s_p = 4.84$.

The value of t is

$$t = \frac{\bar{x}_1 - \bar{x}_2}{s_p\sqrt{(1/n_1) + (1/n_2)}}$$

$$= \frac{0.89}{4.84\sqrt{(1/28) + (1/24)}}$$

$$= 0.6610.$$

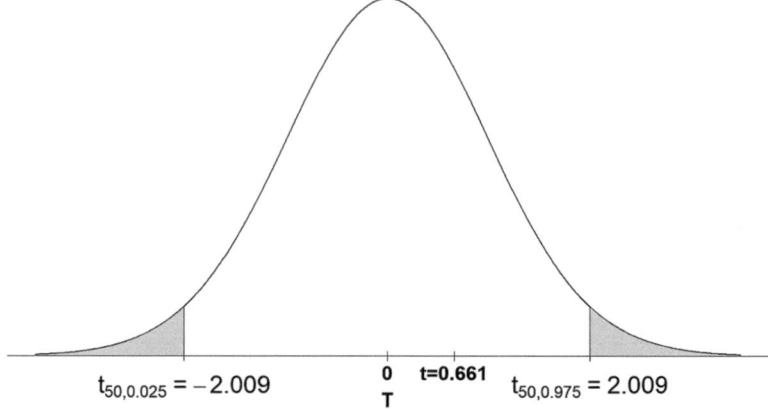

$t_{50,0.025} = -2.009$ **0**   **t=0.661** $t_{50,0.975} = 2.009$
                      T

Fig. 8.15 Figure displaying critical regions for test about equality of population means when population variances are unknown

The critical values for the two-tailed test at the left and right tail areas are $t_{50,0.025} = -2.009$ and $t_{50,0.975} = 2.009$ (Fig. 8.15).

Step 5: The non-rejection region is defined by $t_{\alpha/2} < t < t_{1-\alpha/2}$. The decision is in favor of not rejecting the null hypothesis because the test statistic value, t, falls in the non-rejection region. We may conclude that we may not reject the null hypothesis of equality of mean heights of women from two different populations.

Example 8.5 Test for Equality of μ_1 and μ_2 if σ_1^2 and σ_2^2 are unknown and assumed to be unequal.

Case II σ_1^2 and σ_2^2 are unknown and assumed to be unequal.

Let us consider that a study was conducted to collect data on weight of women in two areas, denoted by area 1 and area 2. Using the data on weight from both the samples we have found the mean weights of women in areas 1 and 2 are 48.68 and 49.34 kg, respectively. The sample variances are 25.50 kg^2 for area 1 and 90.02 kg^2 in area 2. We have to test for the equality of two population means of women in areas 1 and 2 at 5% level of significance.

Solution
Step 1: The null and alternative hypotheses are

$$H_0: \mu_1 - \mu_2 = 0 \text{ versus } H_1: \mu_1 - \mu_2 \neq 0.$$

The level of significance is $\alpha = 0.05$.

Step 2: Let $X_1 \sim N(\mu_1, \sigma_1^2)$ and $X_2 \sim N(\mu_2, \sigma_2^2)$, where σ_1^2 and σ_2^2 are unknown and assumed to be unequal.

Step 3: The point estimators of population means the estimator of μ_1 is $\bar{X}_1 = \frac{\sum_{i=1}^{n_1} X_{1i}}{n_1}$ and the estimator of μ_2 is $\bar{X}_2 = \frac{\sum_{i=1}^{n_2} X_{2i}}{n_2}$. The sampling distribution of $\bar{X}_1 - \bar{X}_2$ is $\bar{X}_1 - \bar{X}_2 \sim N(\mu_1 - \mu_2, \sigma_1^2/n_1 + \sigma_2^2/n_2)$.

The test statistic is

$$T = \frac{\bar{X}_1 - \bar{X}_2}{\sqrt{S_1^2/n_1 + S_2^2/n_2}}$$

where the sampling distribution of T is $T \sim t_\nu$.

The Satterthwaite approximation of degrees of freedom is

$$
\begin{aligned}
\nu &= \frac{\left(s_1^2/n_1 + s_2^2/n_2\right)^2}{\left[\left(s_1^2/n_1\right)^2/(n_1 - 1)\right] + \left[\left(s_2^2/n_2\right)^2/(n_2 - 1)\right]} \\
&= \frac{(25.51/24 + 76.91/28)^2}{\left[(25.51/24)^2/23\right] + \left[(76.91/28)^2/27\right]} \\
&= \frac{(25.51/24 + 76.91/28)^2}{\left[(25.51/24)^2/23\right] + \left[(76.91/28)^2/27\right]} \\
&\approx 44.
\end{aligned}
$$

Step 4: The test statistic from sample data is

$$
\begin{aligned}
t &= \frac{\bar{x}_1 - \bar{x}_2}{\sqrt{s_1^2/n_1 + s_2^2/n_2}} \\
&= \frac{-0.72}{\sqrt{25.51/24 + 76.91/28}} \\
&= -0.3692
\end{aligned}
$$

where the degrees of freedom is approximately 44. The critical values for the two-tailed test are $t_{44,0.025} = -2.0154$ and $t_{44,0.975} = 2.0154$ (Fig. 8.16).

Step 5: The decision is in favor of not rejecting the null hypothesis because the test statistic value, $t = 0.3692$, falls in the non-rejection region, $t_{\alpha/2} < t < t_{1-\alpha/2}$. This decision implies that the null hypothesis of equality of weights of women in areas 1 and 2 may not be rejected.

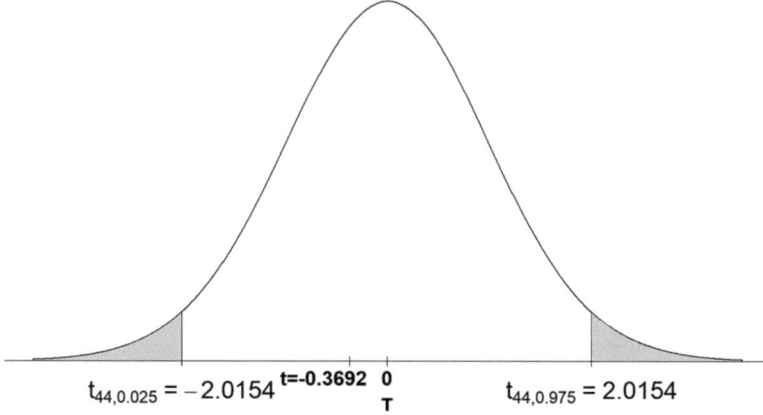

$t_{44,0.025} = -2.0154$ $t=-0.3692$ 0 $t_{44,0.975} = 2.0154$
$\qquad\qquad\qquad\qquad\qquad\qquad$ T

Fig. 8.16 Figure displaying critical regions for test about equality of population means when population variances are unknown and unequal

8.11 Paired Comparisons

In this section, we are interested in comparing the means of two correlated variables from normal populations. In other words, we wish to make statistical inference for the difference between the means of two correlated normal populations. Paired t-test is used for testing the equality of the means of two related normal populations. Examples of related populations are: (i) height of the father and height of his son, (ii) weight of subjects before and after a diet program, (iii) pulse rate of patient before and after a medical treatment, (iv) hemoglobin level of the patient before and after the medical treatment, etc. It is clear from the examples that data are observed in pairs. In a paired comparison, we perform a test to arrive at a decision whether there is any difference between the population means. In the before and after receiving a treatment experiments, if the difference in the means is not statistically significant then it indicates that there is not much evidence in favor of rejecting the null hypothesis of no difference in the correlated variables representing outcomes before and after the experiment is conducted.

Let us consider n pairs of a random sample $(X_1, Y_1), \ldots, (X_n, Y_n)$ and the observations in the sample are $(x_1, y_1), \ldots, (x_n, y_n)$. We assume that the data are continuous and differences in the matched pairs follow a normal probability distribution. It is noteworthy that the assumption of normality is required for the difference in the pairs of variables, $D = X - Y$, not for the original variables, X and Y. The observed difference in pairs is denoted by $d = x - y$.

Let us consider that the differences in pairs, $D_i = X_i - Y_i, i = 1, \ldots, n$, follow a normal probability density with mean μ_D and variance σ_D^2. The estimator for the population mean of the differences is denoted by

$$\bar{D} = \frac{\sum_{i=1}^{n} D_i}{n}$$

and the corresponding sample mean from the observed data is

$$\bar{d} = \frac{\sum_{i=1}^{n} d_i}{n}.$$

Similarly, the sample variance of the differences for the random pairs is $S_d^2 = \frac{\sum_{i=1}^{n}(D_i - \bar{D})^2}{n-1}$ and the corresponding sample variance from the observed data is $s_d^2 = \frac{\sum_{i=1}^{n}(d_i - \bar{d})^2}{n-1}$.

The steps of performing the test of hypothesis regarding the mean difference in the pairs of variables are discussed below.

Step 1: The null and alternative hypotheses are $H_0: \mu_D = \mu_X - \mu_Y = 0$ versus $H_1: \mu_D \neq 0$. The level of significance is α, say $\alpha = 0.05$.

Step 2: Let us assume that the probability distribution of D is $D \sim N(\mu_D, \sigma_D^2)$ for the random sample of pairs $(X_1, Y_1), \ldots, (X_n, Y_n)$ and let σ_D^2 be unknown. The random sample is comprised of n pairs.

Step 3: The point estimator of μ_D is

$$\bar{D} = \frac{\sum_{i=1}^{n} D_i}{n}.$$

The sampling distribution of $\bar{D}$ is summarized below.

(i) $E(\bar{D}) = E(\bar{X} - \bar{Y}) = \mu_X - \mu_Y = \mu_D$,

(ii) $\bar{D} \sim N(\mu_D, \sigma_D^2/n)$, the standard error of $\bar{D}$ is $\sigma_D/\sqrt{n}$.

The test statistic for testing the difference in the means of the paired variables is

$$T = \frac{\bar{D} - \mu_D}{S_d/\sqrt{n}}$$

where σ_D is replaced by its estimator S_d and the sampling distribution of T is $T \sim t_{n-1}$.

Step 4: The observed value of the test statistic from the sample data $(x_1, y_1), \ldots, (x_n, y_n)$ is

$$t = \frac{\bar{d}}{s_d/\sqrt{n}}$$

The critical values for a two-sided alternative are $t_{(n-1),\alpha/2}$ and $t_{(n-1),1-\alpha/2}$ (Fig. 8.17).

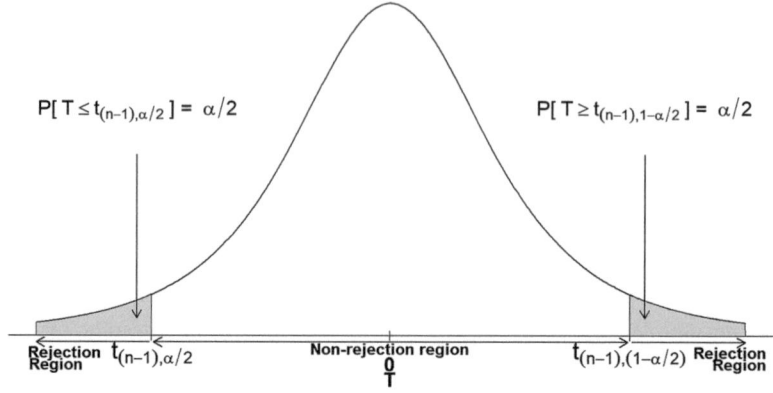

$P[T \le t_{(n-1),\alpha/2}] = \alpha/2$ $P[T \ge t_{(n-1),1-\alpha/2}] = \alpha/2$

Rejection Region $t_{(n-1),\alpha/2}$ Non-rejection region 0 T $t_{(n-1),(1-\alpha/2)}$ Rejection Region

Fig. 8.17 Figure displaying critical regions for test about equality of population means using paired t-test

Step 5: If $t < t_{(n-1),\alpha/2}$ or $t > t_{(n-1),1-\alpha/2}$ then the test statistic value from the sample data falls in the rejection region and the decision is in favor of rejecting the null hypothesis. However, if $t_{(n-1),\alpha/2} < t < t_{(n-1),1-\alpha/2}$ then the test statistic falls in the non-rejection region. In this case, the decision based on the sample data is in favor of non-rejection of the null hypothesis.

Example 8.6 Paired t-test.

Let us consider the following paired hypothetical data on 10 individuals displaying their weights in kg before (X) and after (Y) a diet program was introduced in order to find any possible change in weight of subjects of age 15–49 years attributable to the diet program.

Individual	1	2	3	4	5	6	7	8	9	10
x	53	51	43	59	55	39	50	42	53	51
y	50	50	45	53	52	42	51	40	50	52

The research question is whether the diet program could make any difference in the weight of subjects. Consider $\alpha = 0.05$.

Solution

The steps of a paired t-test are discussed below.

Step 1: The null and alternative hypotheses are

$$H_0: \mu_D = \mu_X - \mu_Y = 0 \text{ versus } H_1: \mu_D \neq 0.$$

The level of significance is $\alpha = 0.05$.

Step 2: It is assumed that the probability distribution of D is $D \sim N(\mu_D, \sigma_D^2)$, where $D = X - Y$ for pairs $(X_1, Y_1), \ldots, (X_n, Y_n)$, and let σ_D^2 be unknown.

Step 3: The point estimator of μ_D is

$$\bar{D} = \frac{\sum_{i=1}^{n} D_i}{n}.$$

The expected value and variance of $\bar{D}$ are
$E(\bar{D}) = E(\bar{X} - \bar{Y}) = \mu_X - \mu_Y$, $\text{Var}(\bar{D}) = \sigma_D^2/n$ and
$\bar{D} \sim N(\mu_D, \sigma_D^2/n)$, the standard error of $\bar{D}$ is $\sigma_D/\sqrt{n}$.
The test statistic is

$$T = \frac{\bar{D} - \mu_D}{S_d/\sqrt{n}}$$

where $T \sim t_{n-1}$.

Step 4: The observed value of the test statistic from the sample data
$(x_1, y_1), \ldots, (x_n, y_n)$ is

$$t = \frac{\bar{d}}{s_d/\sqrt{n}}$$

Using the paired data, we compute the values of d as shown in the following
table

Individual	1	2	3	4	5	6	7	8	9	10
x	53	51	43	59	55	39	50	42	53	51
y	50	50	45	53	52	42	51	40	50	52
d	3	1	−2	6	3	−3	−1	2	3	−1

Here, $n = 10$ and we can estimate the mean of the differences in x and y as

$$\bar{d} = \frac{\sum_{i=1}^{10} d_i}{10} = \frac{11}{10} = 1.1$$

and

$$s_d^2 = \frac{\sum_{i=1}^{10} (d_i - \bar{d})^2}{10 - 1}$$
$$= \frac{\sum_{i=1}^{10} d_i^2 - 10 \times \bar{d}^2}{9}$$
$$= \frac{83 - 10 \times 1.21}{9}$$
$$= 7.88.$$

The standard deviation is $s_d = 2.81$.

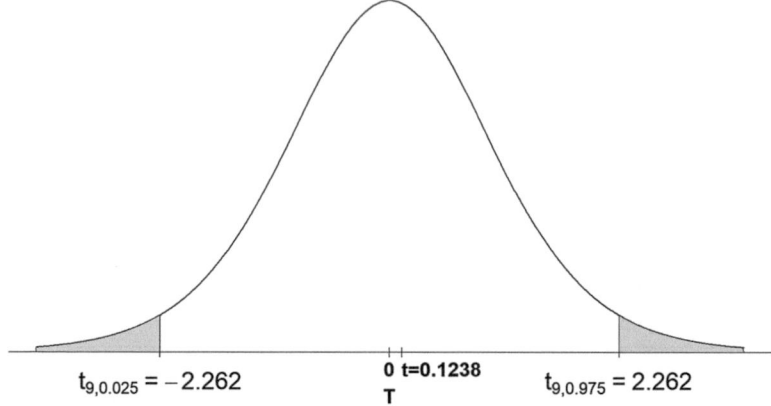

Fig. 8.18 Figure displaying critical regions for paired *t*-test using the sample data

Hence, we can obtain the value of *t* for sample of paired data as

$$
\begin{aligned}
t &= \frac{\bar{d}}{s_d/\sqrt{n}} \\
&= \frac{1.1}{2.81/\sqrt{10}} \\
&= 0.1238.
\end{aligned}
$$

The critical values for a two-sided alternative are $t_{9,0.025} = -2.262$ and $t_{9,0.975} = 2.262$ (Fig. 8.18).

Step 5: The value of *t* from sample data is 0.1238, which lies in the non-rejection region $t_{(n-1),\alpha/2} < t < t_{(n-1),1-\alpha/2}$, i.e., $-2.262 < t < 2.262$. Hence, it shows that the decision, based on the sample data, may be in favor of non-rejection of the null hypothesis that there is no difference in the weight of individuals attributable to the diet program.

8.12 Hypothesis Testing: A Single Population Proportion (*P*)

The sampling distribution of estimator of population proportion, *p*, is discussed in Chap. 6. The point and interval estimators are presented in Chap. 7. For a sequence of *n* Bernoulli trials, performed independently, the number of successes is denoted by *X* and it can be expressed as a binomial variable. The random sample of size *n* from Bernoulli population with population proportion, *p*, is $(X_1, \ldots, X_n)$. Here, $X = \sum_{i=1}^{n} X_i$ = the number of elements or subjects selected with characteristic A. Then estimator of the proportion is defined for a random sample of size *n* as

$$\hat{p} = \frac{X}{n}$$

which is a statistic.

The steps for testing the null hypothesis on the population proportion are summarized below. Suppose that $X_1, \ldots, X_n$ is a random sample of size n from a sequence of Bernoulli trials with probability of success, p.

Step 1: Let the null and alternative hypotheses are $H_0: p = p_0$ versus $H_1: p \neq p_0$. The level of significance is α, say $\alpha = 0.05$.

Step 2: Let the probability distribution of X is $X \sim \text{Binomial}(n, p)$ and let us assume that n is known and large.

Step 3: The point estimator of p is

$$\hat{p} = \frac{X}{n}.$$

We have shown in Chap. 6 that the mean and variance of the number of successes, X are

$$E(X) = E\left(\sum_{i=1}^{n} X_i\right) = \sum_{i=1}^{n} E(X_i) = np, \text{ and}$$

$$\text{Var}(X) = \text{Var}\left(\sum_{i=1}^{n} X_i\right) = \sum_{i=1}^{n} \text{Var}(X_i) = np(1-p) = npq.$$

For a large sample size, we can use the normal approximation of binomial variable, X, with parameters $\mu = np_0$ and $\sigma^2 = np_0(1 - p_0)$ under the null hypothesis. The test statistic is

$$Z = \frac{X - np_0}{\sqrt{np_0(1 - p_0)}}$$

where the sampling distribution of Z is approximately $Z \approx N(0, 1)$.

For small sample size, we can either use exact binomial probabilities under null hypothesis or a Poisson approximation to find the tail probabilities if the value of p under null hypothesis is close to 0 or 1.

Step 4: Using the normal approximation, the value of the test statistic from the sample data is

$$z = \frac{x - np_0}{\sqrt{np_0(1 - p_0)}}.$$

The critical values for a two-sided alternative are $z_{\alpha/2}$ and $z_{1-\alpha/2}$ (Fig. 8.19).

Step 5: If the test statistic value is either $z < z_{\alpha/2}$ or $z > z_{1-\alpha/2}$ then the sample data falls in the rejection region and the decision is in favor of rejecting the null

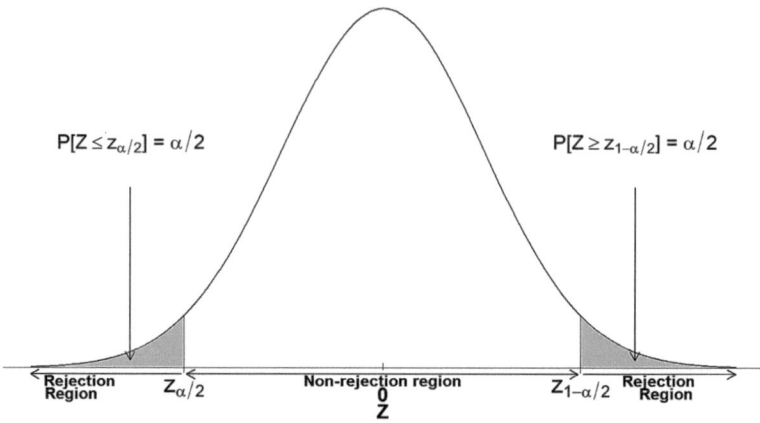

$P[Z \le z_{\alpha/2}] = \alpha/2$ $P[Z \ge z_{1-\alpha/2}] = \alpha/2$

Rejection $z_{\alpha/2}$ Non-rejection region $z_{1-\alpha/2}$ Rejection
Region   0   Region
                                                    Z

Fig. 8.19 Figure displaying critical regions for test about population proportion assuming normality approximation

hypothesis. On the other hand, if $z_{\alpha/2} < z < z_{1-\alpha/2}$ then the test statistic value is in the non-rejection region and the decision is in favor of non-rejection of null hypothesis for the given sample data.

Example 8.7 In a study on the diagnosis of acute inflammations of the urinary bladder and acute nephritises, a sample of 120 subjects is considered (Czerniak and Zarzycki 2003). The inflammation of urinary bladder is found among 59 out of 120 subjects. The hypothesis needs to be tested is whether the true population proportion is 50% of the total subjects in the population. The level of significance is $\alpha = 0.05$.

Solution
The steps in testing the whether the specified value is the true population proportion are illustrated here.
  Step 1: $H_0 : p = 0.5$ versus $H_1 : p \ne 0.5$.
  The level of significance is $\alpha = 0.05$.
  Step 2: $X \sim \text{Binomial}(n, p)$, n is known and large.
  Step 3: The point estimator of p is
$\hat{p} = \frac{X}{n}$. The expected value and variance of the estimator are

$$E(X) = np, \tag{and}$$

$$\text{Var}(X) = np(1 - p).$$

  The test statistic is approximately normal under null hypothesis with parameters $\mu = np_0$ and $\sigma^2 = np_0(1 - p_0)$ which is

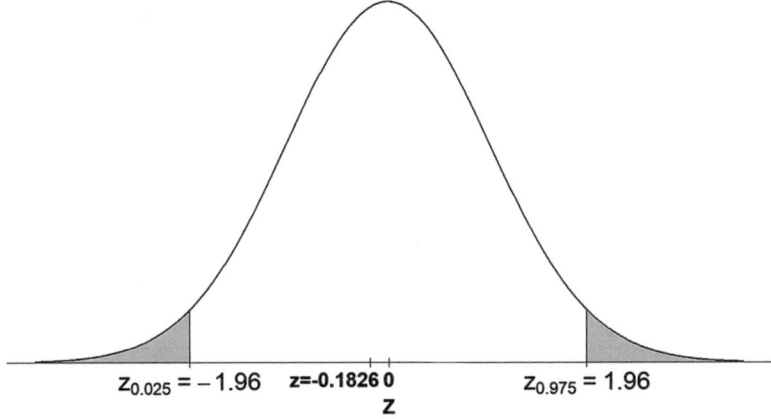

Fig. 8.20 Figure displaying critical regions for test about population proportion using sample data assuming normality approximation

$$Z = \frac{X - np_0}{\sqrt{np_0(1 - p_0)}}$$

where the sampling distribution of Z is approximately $Z \approx N(0, 1)$.

Step 4: Using the normal approximation, the value of the test statistic from the sample data is

$$z = \frac{x - np_0}{\sqrt{np_0(1 - p_0)}}$$
$$= \frac{59 - 120 \times 0.5}{\sqrt{120 \times 0.5 \times 0.5}}$$
$$= -0.1826.$$

The critical values for a two-sided alternative are $z_{0.025} = -1.96$ and $z_{0.975} = 1.96$.

Step 5: The test statistic value from the sample data is -0.1826, which falls in the non-rejection region $-1.96 < z < 1.96$ and the decision is in favor of non-rejection of null hypothesis that the true population proportion is 0.5 (Fig. 8.20).

8.13   Hypothesis Testing: The Difference Between Two Population Proportions ($P_1 - P_2$)

In this section, we are interested in testing some hypotheses about the difference between two population proportions ($p_1 - p_2$). Suppose that we have two populations with p_1 = population proportion of the first population, p_2 = population proportion of the second population. We want to compare p_1 and p_2, or equivalently, to make inferences about $p_1 - p_2$. If we select a random sample of size n_1 from the first Bernoulli population with parameter p_1 and another random sample of size n_2 from the second Bernoulli population with parameter p_2 then let X_1 = number of elements of type A in the first sample and X_2 = number of elements of type A in the second sample. Then, we can define $\hat{p}_1 = \frac{X_1}{n_1}$ = the sample proportion of the first sample and $\hat{p}_2 = \frac{X_2}{n_2}$ = the sample proportion of the second sample. The sampling distribution of $\hat{p}_1 - \hat{p}_2$ is used to make inferences about $p_1 - p_2$.

For large n_1 and n_2, we can show asymptotically

$$Z = \frac{(\hat{p}_1 - \hat{p}_2) - (p_1 - p_2)}{\sqrt{\frac{p_1 q_1}{n_1} + \frac{p_2 q_2}{n_2}}} \sim N(0, 1)$$

where $q_1 = 1 - p_1$ and $q_2 = 1 - p_2$.

The steps for testing the null hypothesis on the equality of population proportions are shown below.

Step 1: The null and alternative hypotheses are $H_0 : p_1 = p_2$ versus $H_1 : p_1 \neq p_2$. The level of significance is α, say $\alpha = 0.05$.

Step 2: Let the probability distribution of X_1 and X_2 are $X_1 \sim \text{Binomial}(n_1, p_1)$ and $X_2 \sim \text{Binomial}(n_2, p_2)$ respectively.

Step 3: The point estimator of p_1 and p_2 are

$$\hat{p}_1 = \frac{X_1}{n_1}$$

and

$$\hat{p}_2 = \frac{X_2}{n_2}.$$

The mean and variance of the difference between two population proportions, assuming independence of X_1 and X_2, are

$$E(\hat{p}_1 - \hat{p}_2) = p_1 - p_2, \text{ and}$$
$$\text{Var}(\hat{p}_1 - \hat{p}_2) = \frac{p_1(1 - p_1)}{n_1} + \frac{p_2(1 - p_2)}{n_2}.$$

For large sample sizes n_1 and n_2, we can use the following test statistic as an approximation of difference between two binomial proportions with parameters $\mu_{\hat{p}_1 - \hat{p}_2} = p_1 - p_2$ and $\sigma^2_{\hat{p}_1 - \hat{p}_2} = \frac{p_1(1-p_1)}{n_1} + \frac{p_2(1-p_2)}{n_2}$.

The test statistic is

$$Z = \frac{\hat{p}_1 - \hat{p}_2 - (p_1 - p_2)}{\sqrt{\frac{p_1(1-p_1)}{n_1} + \frac{p_2(1-p_2)}{n_2}}}$$

and under the null hypothesis of equality of these proportions, the test statistic becomes

$$Z = \frac{\hat{p}_1 - \hat{p}_2}{\sqrt{\frac{p_1(1-p_1)}{n_1} + \frac{p_2(1-p_2)}{n_2}}}$$

where the sampling distribution of Z is approximately $Z \approx N(0, 1)$.

Step 4: Using the normal approximation, the value of the test statistic from the sample data is

$$z = \frac{\hat{p}_1 - \hat{p}_2}{\sqrt{\frac{\hat{p}_1(1-\hat{p}_1)}{n_1} + \frac{\hat{p}_2(1-\hat{p}_2)}{n_2}}}.$$

However, under the null hypothesis $p_1 = p_2$, hence, a pooled estimator of p can be computed

$$\hat{p} = \frac{x_1 + x_2}{n_1 + n_2}.$$

Then, z can be redefined as

$$z = \frac{\hat{p}_1 - \hat{p}_2}{\sqrt{\hat{p}(1 - \hat{p})\left[\frac{1}{n_1} + \frac{1}{n_2}\right]}}.$$

We can find the critical values for a two-sided alternative, $z_{\alpha/2}$ and $z_{1-\alpha/2}$ (Fig. 8.21).

Step 5: If the test statistic value is either $z < z_{\alpha/2}$ or $z > z_{1-\alpha/2}$ then the sample data favor rejection of the null hypothesis that there is equality of population proportions. On the other hand, if $z_{\alpha/2} < z < z_{1-\alpha/2}$ then the test statistic value is in the non-rejection region and the decision is in favor of non-rejection of null hypothesis for the sample data.

Example 8.8 In Chap. 7, we have shown an example of constructing confidence interval of difference between two proportions. The same hypothetical data are

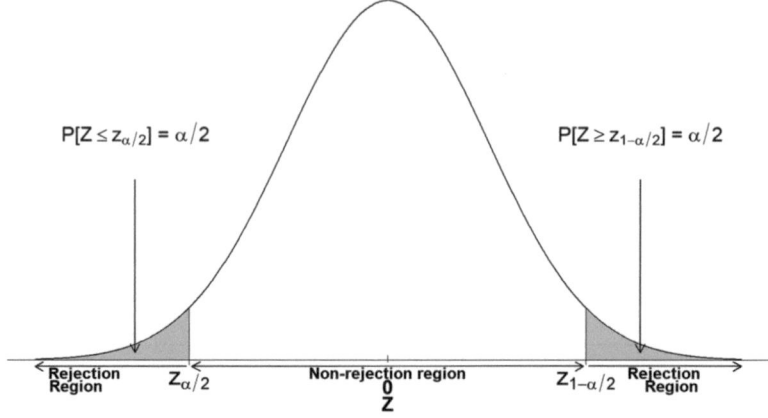

$P[Z \le z_{\alpha/2}] = \alpha/2$ $P[Z \ge z_{1-\alpha/2}] = \alpha/2$

Rejection Region $z_{\alpha/2}$ Non-rejection region $z_{1-\alpha/2}$ Rejection Region

0

Z

Fig. 8.21 Figure displaying critical regions for test about equality of population proportions assuming normality approximation

employed in this chapter to illustrate the procedure for testing the hypothesis of equality of two population proportions. Let us consider that a researcher has conducted a study to compare the proportion of people suffering from breathing problem in two cities, A and B. In a random sample of 2500 people from city A, 110 are suffering from breathing problem and in another independent random sample of 2000 people, 74 people from city B are found to have breathing problem. The researcher wants to test for equality of proportions of people suffering from breathing problem in cities A and B. The level of significance is 0.05.

Solution
The steps for conducting the test hypothesis for the example are illustrated below.
   Step 1: $H_0: p_1 = p_2$ versus $H_1: p_1 \ne p_2$.
   The level of significance is α, say $\alpha = 0.05$.
   Step 2: The independent probability distributions for number of people suffering from breathing problem in cities A and B, respectively, are
   $X_1 \sim \text{Binomial}(n_1, p_1)$ for city A and $X_2 \sim \text{Binomial}(n_2, p_2)$ for city B.
   Step 3: The point estimator of p_1 and p_2 are

$$\hat{p}_1 = \frac{X_1}{n_1}$$

and

$$\hat{p}_2 = \frac{X_2}{n_2}.$$

Assuming independence of X_1 and X_2, the mean and variance of the difference between two population proportions are

$$E(\hat{p}_1 - \hat{p}_2) = p_1 - p_2, \quad \text{and} \quad \text{Var}(\hat{p}_1 - \hat{p}_2) = \frac{p_1(1 - p_1)}{n_1} + \frac{p_2(1 - p_2)}{n_2}.$$

For large sample size, the test statistic under null hypothesis is

$$Z = \frac{\hat{p}_1 - \hat{p}_2}{\sqrt{\frac{p_1(1-p_1)}{n_1} + \frac{p_1(1-p_1)}{n_1}}}$$

where the sampling distribution of Z can be shown approximately as $Z \approx N(0, 1)$.

Step 4: The estimates of p_1 and p_2 as well as the pooled estimator of p can be computed

$$\hat{p}_1 = \frac{x_1}{n_1} = \frac{110}{2500} = 0.044,$$

$$\hat{p}_2 = \frac{x_2}{n_2} = \frac{74}{2000} = 0.037,$$

and

$$\begin{aligned} \hat{p} &= \frac{x_1 + x_2}{n_1 + n_2}. \\ &= \frac{110 + 74}{2500 + 2000} \\ &= 0.041. \end{aligned}$$

Then z can be obtained as

$$\begin{aligned} z &= \frac{\hat{p}_1 - \hat{p}_2}{\sqrt{\hat{p}(1 - \hat{p}) \left[\frac{1}{n_1} + \frac{1}{n_2}\right]}} \\ &= \frac{0.044 - 0.037}{\sqrt{0.041 \times 0.959 \left[\frac{1}{2500} + \frac{1}{2000}\right]}} \\ &= 1.1771. \end{aligned}$$

We can find the critical values for a two-sided alternative, $z_{0.025} = -1.96$ and $z_{0.975} = 1.96$ (Fig. 8.22).

Step 5: The test statistic value falls in the non-rejection region, $-196 < z < 1.96$, so the decision is made in favor of non-rejection of the null hypothesis that the proportion of population with breathing problem is the same in cities A and B.

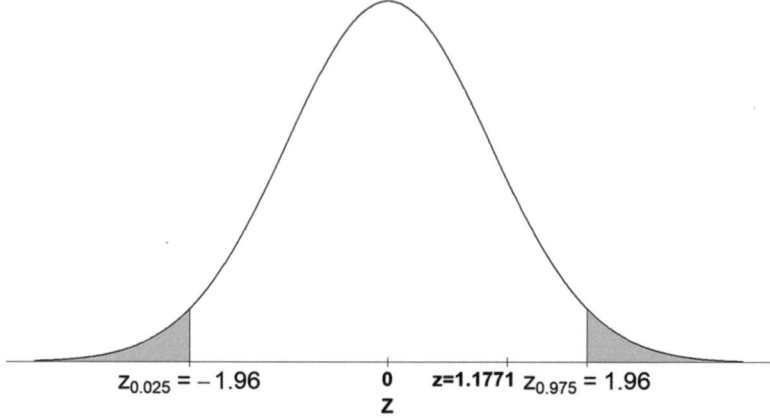

$$Z_{0.025} = -1.96 \qquad 0 \qquad z=1.1771 \quad Z_{0.975} = 1.96$$
$$Z$$

Fig. 8.22 Figure displaying critical regions for test about equality of population proportions using sample data assuming normality approximation

8.14 Summary

The concepts and techniques of hypothesis testing are introduced in this chapter. The definition and concept of null and alternative hypotheses, rejection and non-rejection of null hypothesis, one-sided and two-sided tests, test statistic, types of error, critical region, and p-value are discussed with examples. The step-by-step procedures of testing a null hypothesis against an alternative are shown in this chapter. The hypothesis testing procedures are illustrated with examples for single mean and single proportion and difference between two means and two proportions under various situations arising from assumptions about population (normal or non-normal), sample size (small or large), population variance (known or unknown), and sample sizes equal or unequal in case of two samples. In addition, if the equality of population means is tested for correlated data then the paired t-test is shown with an example. This chapter includes many examples to illustrate the procedures in easy steps.

Exercises

8.1 Explain the following briefly with example:

  (i)   Null and alternative hypotheses,
  (ii) Non-rejection and rejection of null hypothesis,
  (iii) One-sided and two-sided tests,
  (iv) Test statistic,
  (v)   Type I and Type II errors,
  (vi) Level of significance,
  (vii) Critical region, and
  (viii) P-value.

8.2 Let us consider the age (in years) of 40 respondents from a study on women in their reproductive ages. The data are listed below.

28, 44, 20, 28, 19, 40, 21, 29, 32, 21, 18, 27, 23, 34, 38, 33, 23, 21, 28, 19,
36, 31, 25, 18, 28, 39, 42, 41, 21, 36, 25, 25, 43, 22, 41, 34, 25, 37, 34, 21.

    (i)   It is of interest to researcher whether the population mean age is 28 years or not. What are the null hypothesis and alternative hypothesis?

    (ii) Perform the test of hypothesis at level of significance = 0.01 stating the underlying assumptions.

    (iii) What is your conclusion?

8.3 Let us consider a study on cholesterol level (in mg/dL) in a community. The sample size is 135. The sample mean and standard deviation are 175 and 30 mg/dL respectively. Can we say that the population mean of cholesterol level is 165 mg/dL? Perform the test for a one-sided test (greater than the null hypothesis value) with $\alpha = 0.05$.

8.4 Let us consider a study of sample size 15 on systolic blood pressure (mm Hg). The sample mean and standard deviation are 120 and 20 mm Hg respectively. Test for the null hypothesis that the population mean of the systolic blood pressure is 125 mm Hg, $H_0: \mu = 125$ mm Hg. The alternative hypothesis is $H_1: \mu > 125$ mm Hg. Consider the level of significance value for this test be $\alpha = 0.01$. What is your conclusion?

8.5 In a study on cholesterol level of men and women, it is of interest to know whether the cholesterol level of men (m) and women (w) are the same. The mean cholesterol level for men and women, say, are 177 mg/dL for men and 173 mg/dL for women. The standard deviation of cholesterol level for men is 32 mg/dL and for women is 28 mg/dL. The number of men and women in the study are 70 and 65 respectively. Test for the following null and alternative hypotheses assuming that the population variances for men and women are unknown but equal:

$$H_0: \mu_m = \mu_w$$
$$H_1: \mu_m \neq \mu_w.$$
$$\text{Let } \alpha = 0.05$$

Does your conclusion change if you assume unknown but unequal variances instead of unknown but equal variances for men and women?
Summarize your comments.

8.6 In a study on blood glucose level among adult men (m) and women (w), it is found that the mean glucose level and standard deviation for men are 85 and 29 mg/dL and for women are 75 and 25 mg/dL respectively. The number of men and women are 12 and 9 respectively. Perform the test on the following null and alternative hypotheses for $\alpha = 0.05$:

$$H_0: \mu_m = \mu_w.$$
$$H_1: \mu_m > \mu_w.$$

Comment on your test results.

8.7   An experiment was conducted to compare time duration of stay in a hospital with two types of complications (A) and (B) and 9 patients with complication type A and 16 patients with complication type B were selected randomly. The average time lengths were 12 days for A and 7 days for B and sample variances were 8 days^2 for A and 5 days^2 for B. Assuming equality of variances in the populations, test for the equality of population means at 1% level of significance.

8.8   Let the proportion of obese children estimated from a sample of size 100 is 0.15. Test for the following null and alternative hypotheses at 5% level of significance and comment on your findings:

$$H_0: p = 0.20.$$
$$H_1: p \neq 0.20.$$

8.9   Among the adult males and females, a study is conducted to estimate the proportion of diabetics. The sample sizes are 250 for males and 200 for females. It is found from the estimates from the samples that the proportion of diabetics among males is 10% and among females is 7%. Test for the equality of proportions of diabetics among males and females in the population at 5% level of significance. Consider the one-sided alternative that the proportion of diabetics is higher among the males.

8.10 Following results are given from two independent random samples: $\hat{p}_1 = 0.3, n_1 = 49$, and $\hat{p}_2 = 0.5, n_2 = 81$. Test for the equality of two population proportions and then comment on the test result.

8.11 Following results are given from two independent random samples: $\bar{x}_1 = 20, s_1^2 = 16, n_1 = 10$, and $\bar{x}_2 = 25, s_2^2 = 16, n_2 = 12$. State the null and alternative hypotheses for testing the equality of two population means and comment on the result, if σ_1^2 and σ_2^2 are unknown and assumed to be equal.

8.12 The following hypothetical data show the systolic blood pressure (SBP) of 10 subjects before and after exercise:

SBP before exercise (mm Hg)	SBP after exercise (mm Hg)
115	125
120	132
100	114
125	130
121	130
117	132
106	119

(continued)

(continued)

SBP before exercise (mm Hg)	SBP after exercise (mm Hg)
118	131
110	121
117	128

Perform the test for the null hypothesis that there is no difference in the mean of systolic blood pressure due to exercise. What would be a reasonable alternative hypothesis? Justify your choice of the alternative hypothesis. Comment on your test result. The level of significance is 0.05.

References

Czerniak, J., & Zarzycki, H. (2003). Application of rough sets in the presumptive diagnosis of urinary system diseases, Artificial Intelligence and Security in Computing Systems. *ACCS 2002 9th International Conference Proceedings* (pp. 41–51). Kluwer Academic Publishers.

Goodman, S. N. (1992). A comment on replication. P-values and evidence. *Statistics in Medicine, 11*(7), 875–879.

Hung, H. M., O'Neill, R. T., Bauer, P., & Kohne, K. (1997). The behavior of the P-value when the alternative hypothesis is true. *Biometrics, 53*(1), 11–22.

Satterthwaite, F. E. (1946). An approximate distribution of variance components. *Biometrics Bulletin, 2*(6), 110–114.

Wasserstein, R. L., & Lazar, N. A. (2016). The ASA's statement on p-values: Context, process, and purpose. *The American Statistician, 70*(2), 129–133. https://doi.org/10.1080/00031305.2016.1154108.

Chapter 9
Correlation and Regression

9.1 Introduction

In many applications, we may want to study the underlying nature of relationships among the variables. Furthermore, we may also want to utilize these relationships for predicting or estimating the values of some variables (outcome variables) on the basis of the given values of other variables (explanatory variables). By exploring the underlying relationships, we can find whether there is any association between variables as well as whether there is dependence of outcome variables on explanatory variables that can provide necessary inputs required for useful decisions. Some examples of these relationships are (i) relationship between height and weight, (ii) relationship between weight and cholesterol level, (iii) relationship between income and expenditure on health care, etc. In these studies, we are interested in answering several important questions, some of which are

(i) Is there a relationship between the variables? What is the nature of this relationship? What is the strength of this relationship?
(ii) If there is a relationship between the variables, how can we formulate it mathematically? How can we interpret it? What are the policy implications? What is the significance of such finding in explaining the underlying truth in population?

Suppose that we are interested in studying the relationship between the height of the person and his weight in a certain population of a community. In this case, we select a random sample of size n from this population, and then we measure the height (X) and the weight (Y) of each individual in the sample. The random sample of pairs of variables is

$$(X_1, Y_1), (X_2, Y_2), \ldots, (X_n, Y_n).$$

The observations of the sample will be a set of pairs $(x_1, y_1), (x_2, y_2), \ldots, (x_n, y_n)$

© Springer Nature Singapore Pte Ltd. 2018
M. A. Islam and A. Al-Shiha, *Foundations of Biostatistics*,
https://doi.org/10.1007/978-981-10-8627-4_9

where x_i and y_i are, respectively, the height and the weight of the ith individual in the sample ($i = 1, 2, ..., n$). In this example, we want to explore the nature and strength of the relationship between the variable X (height) and the variable Y (weight).

The first step in exploring the relationship between Y and X is to construct the scatter diagram.

Scatter Diagram

If we graph the pairs of values of the variables X and Y in a diagram where values of one variable are represented by X-axis, while the values of the other variable are represented by Y-axis then plotting the pairs of values simultaneously using dots is called a scatter diagram. It may be noted here that in a scatter diagram, one dot represents two values, one for the variable X and the other for the variable Y. The following figure illustrates a typical shape of scatter diagram:

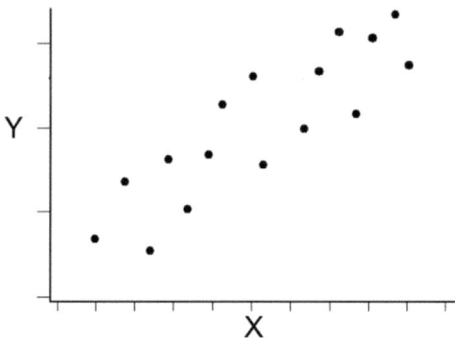

9.2   Correlation Analysis

The correlation analysis deals with studying the existence, nature, and strength of the linear relationship between the variables. In particular, if the variables X and Y are quantitative (interval or ratio scale), we are interested in studying the strength of the linear relationship between these variables. Another assumption for the measure of correlation based on quantitative data is that the pairs of observations for the variables X and Y are drawn from a bivariate normal distribution. Another measure of correlation is discussed in this chapter for the pairs of data that can be ranked.

There are several measures of correlation called coefficients of correlation. These measures are used to measure the strength of the linear relationship between the variables X and Y. On the basis of the values of these measures, we may determine the direction and the strength of the linear relationship between the variables. We may observe the following situations:

(i)   The coefficient of correlation is positive if the large values of Y are associated with large values of X which implies that the values of Y tend to be large with large values of X, and vice versa.

(ii) The coefficient of correlation is negative if the large values of Y are associated with small values of X implying that the values of Y tend to be large with small values of X, and vice versa.

(iii) The coefficient of correlation is zero if the values of Y are not linearly affected by the values of X.

It may also be noted here that the existence of correlation indicating a linear association between variables does not necessarily imply that there is a cause and effect relationship between the variables.

The following figures illustrate some typical cases.

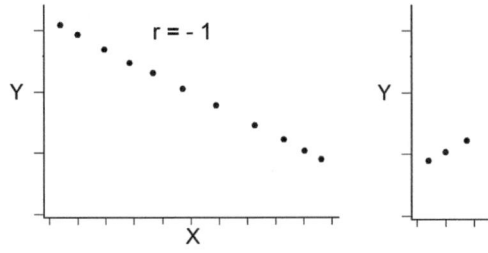
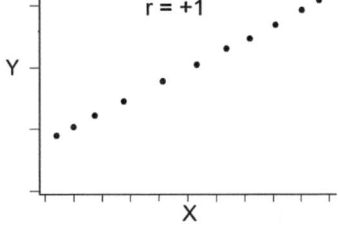

(a) Complete (perfect) negative linear   (b) Complete (perfect) positive linear

correlation   correlation

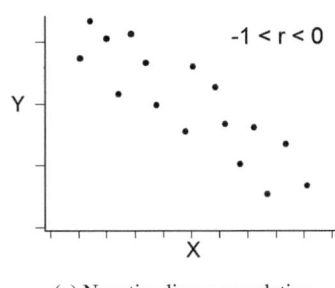

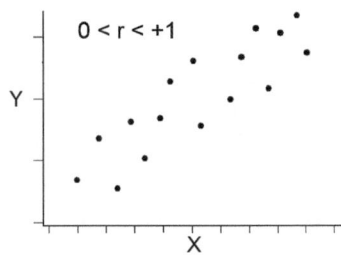

(c) Negative linear correlation   (d) Positive linear correlation

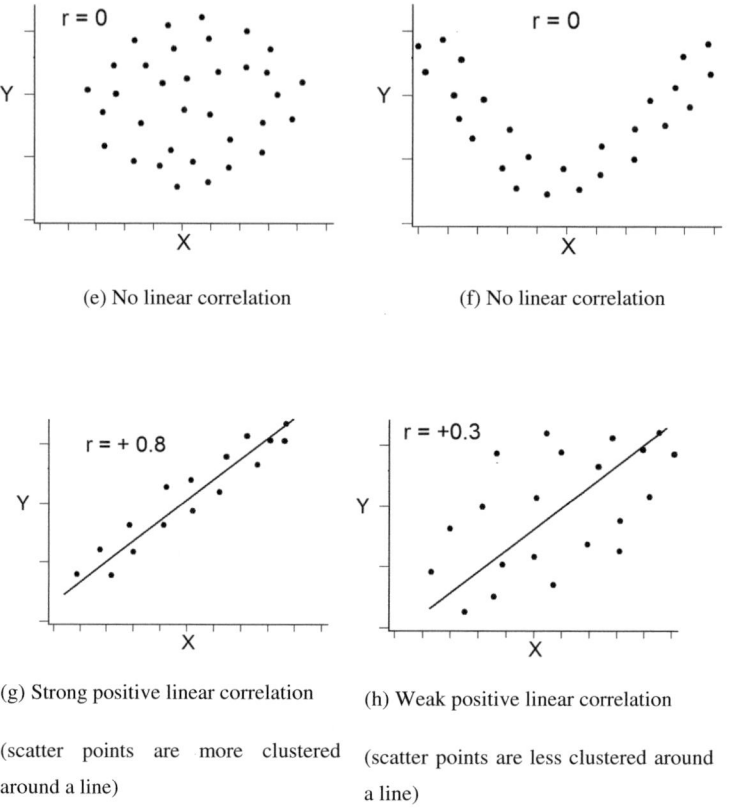

(e) No linear correlation   (f) No linear correlation

(g) Strong positive linear correlation   (h) Weak positive linear correlation

(scatter points are more clustered around a line)   (scatter points are less clustered around a line)

There are several measures used to measure the correlation or association between variables. Two of these measures commonly employed are

(i) Pearson's correlation coefficient: This measure is used in the case where both variables are quantitative.
(ii) Spearman's Rank Correlation coefficient: This measure is used in the case where the variables can be expressed as ranks.

9.2.1 Pearson's Correlation Coefficient

The Pearson's correlation coefficient provides a measure of the strength of linear relationship between two variables, say X and Y. As we have mentioned earlier, this measure can be used when both variables are ratio or interval scaled.

Definition

The population correlation coefficient for N pairs of population values $(X_1, Y_1), (X_2, Y_2), \ldots, (X_N, Y_N)$ is defined by

$$
\begin{aligned}
\rho &= \frac{\sum_{i=1}^{N} (X_i - \mu_X)(Y_i - \mu_Y)}{\sqrt{\sum_{i=1}^{N} (X_i - \mu_X)^2 / N} \sqrt{\sum_{i=1}^{N} (Y_i - \mu_Y)^2 / N}} \\
&= \frac{E[(X - \mu_X)(Y - \mu_Y)]}{\sqrt{E(X - \mu_X)^2} \sqrt{E(Y - \mu_Y)^2}} \\
&= \frac{\sigma_{XY}}{\sqrt{\sigma_X^2} \sqrt{\sigma_Y^2}}
\end{aligned}
,
$$

where $\mu_X = \sum_{i=1}^{N} X_i / N$, $\mu_Y = \sum_{i=1}^{N} Y_i / N$, $\sigma_{XY} = \sum_{i=1}^{N} (X_i - \mu_X)(Y_i - \mu_Y) / N$, $\sigma_X^2 = \sum_{i=1}^{N} (X_i - \mu_X)^2$ and $\sigma_Y^2 = \sum_{i=1}^{N} (Y_i - \mu_Y)^2$.

As we cannot measure the population correlation coefficient generally due to lack of observing the pairs of values from the population, we estimate it by the sample correlation coefficient.

The sample correlation coefficient for n given pairs of observations $(x_1, y_1), \ldots, (x_n, y_n)$ is denoted by r and is defined by

$$
\begin{aligned}
r &= \frac{\sum_{i=1}^{n} (x_i - x)(y_i - \bar{y}) / n}{\sqrt{\sum_{i=1}^{n} (x_i - x)^2 / n} \sqrt{\sum_{i=1}^{n} (y_i - \bar{y})^2 / n}} \\
&= \frac{\sum_{i=1}^{n} (x_i - x)(y_i - \bar{y})}{\sqrt{\sum_{i=1}^{n} (x_i - x)^2} \sqrt{\sum_{i=1}^{n} (y_i - \bar{y})^2}} \\
&= \frac{S_{xy}}{\sqrt{S_{xx}} \sqrt{S_{yy}}} ,
\end{aligned}
$$

where $S_{xy} = \sum_{i=1}^{n} (x_i - \bar{x})(y_i - \bar{y})$, $S_{xx} = \sum_{i=1}^{n} (x_i - \bar{x})^2$, and $S_{yy} = \sum_{i=1}^{n} (y_i - \bar{y})^2$.

The computational formula for calculating r is shown below

$$
r = \frac{\sum_{i=1}^{n} x_i y_i - n \bar{x} \bar{y}}{\sqrt{\sum_{i=1}^{n} x_i^2 - n(\bar{x})^2} \sqrt{\sum_{i=1}^{n} y_i^2 - n(\bar{y})^2}}
$$

which can be expressed in the following form too:

$$
r = \frac{n \sum_{i=1}^{n} x_i y_i - \sum_{i=1}^{n} x_i \sum_{i=1}^{n} y_i}{\sqrt{n \sum_{i=1}^{n} x_i^2 - \left(\sum_{i=1}^{n} x_i\right)^2} \sqrt{n \sum_{i=1}^{n} y_i^2 - \left(\sum_{i=1}^{n} y_i\right)^2}} .
$$

9.2.2 Two Important Properties of the Correlation Coefficient

Two important properties of the Pearson's correlation coefficient are discussed here.

1. The correlation coefficient between two variables is independent of origin and scale of measurement.

Proof Let us consider the original variables X and Y and the pairs of n observation drawn from (X, Y) are $(x_1, y_1), \ldots, (x_n, y_n)$. Then, let us consider four constant values a, b, c, and d, and let us define two variables W and Z such that $W = aX + b$ and $Z = cY + d$, then it can be shown that the correlation coefficient between X and Y, r_{xy}, is equal to the correlation coefficient between W and Z, r_{wz}. The n pairs of observations from (W, Z) are $(w_1, z_1), \ldots, (w_n, z_n)$.

The arithmetic means, sum of product and sum of squares of the variables W and Z are

$$\bar{w} = \frac{\sum_{i=1}^n w_i}{n} = \frac{\sum_{i=1}^n (ax_i + b)}{n} = a\bar{x} + b,$$

$$\bar{z} = \frac{\sum_{i=1}^n z_i}{n} = \frac{\sum_{i=1}^n (cy_i + d)}{n} = c\bar{y} + d,$$

$$S_{wz} = \sum_{i=1}^n (w_i - \bar{w})(z_i - \bar{z})$$

$$= \sum_{i=1}^n (ax_i + b - a\bar{x} - b)(cy_i + d - c\bar{y} - d)$$

$$= ac \sum_{i=1}^n (x_i - \bar{x})(y_i - \bar{y}) = acS_{xy},$$

$$S_{ww} = \sum_{i=1}^n (w_i - \bar{w})^2$$

$$= \sum_{i=1}^n (ax_i + b - a\bar{x} - b)^2$$

$$= a^2 \sum_{i=1}^n (x_i - \bar{x})^2 = a^2 S_{xx},$$

$$S_{zz} = \sum_{i=1}^n (z_i - \bar{z})^2 = \sum_{i=1}^n (cy_i + d - c\bar{y} - d)^2$$

$$= c^2 \sum_{i=1}^n (y_i - \bar{y})^2 = c^2 S_{yy}.$$

The correlation coefficient between W and Z is

$$r_{wz} = \frac{\sum_{i=1}^{n}(w_i - \bar{w})(z_i - \bar{z})}{\sqrt{\sum_{i=1}^{n}(w_i - \bar{w})^2}\sqrt{\sum_{i=1}^{n}(z_i - \bar{z})^2}}$$

$$= \frac{S_{wz}}{\sqrt{S_{ww}}\sqrt{S_{zz}}} = \frac{acS_{xy}}{\sqrt{a^2 S_{xx}}\sqrt{c^2 S_{yy}}}$$

$$= \frac{S_{xy}}{\sqrt{S_{xx}}\sqrt{S_{yy}}} = r_{xy}.$$

The above result proves that the correlation coefficient between two variables is independent of origin and scale of measurement.

2. The value of the correlation coefficient lies between -1 and $+1$.

Proof As we know that the correlation coefficient is independent of origin and scale, let us assume that $\bar{x} = \bar{y} = 0$. Let us consider the following nonnegative expression:

$$Q = \sum_{i=1}^{n}(ax_i - y)^2,$$

where a is any constant value.
   Then, we can show that

$$Q = \sum_{i=1}^{n}(ax_i - y)^2 = \sum_{i=1}^{n}(a^2 x_i^2 - 2ax_i y_i + y_i^2) \geq 0$$

which is

$$\left(a^2 \sum_{i=1}^{n} x_i^2 - 2a \sum_{i=1}^{n} x_i y_i + \sum_{i=1}^{n} y_i^2 \geq 0\right)$$

As the above inequalities hold for any value of a, let us put $a = \frac{\sum_{i=1}^{n} x_i y_i}{\sum_{i=1}^{n} x_i^2}$, then, the above inequality can be expressed as

$$\left(\frac{\sum_{i=1}^{n} x_i y_i}{\sum_{i=1}^{n} x_i^2}\right)^2 \sum_{i=1}^{n} x_i^2 - 2\left(\frac{\sum_{i=1}^{n} x_i y_i}{\sum_{i=1}^{n} x_i^2}\right) \sum_{i=1}^{n} x_i y_i + \sum_{i=1}^{n} y_i^2 \geq 0$$

and

$$\frac{\left(\sum_{i=1}^{n} x_i y_i\right)^2}{\sum_{i=1}^{n} x_i^2} - \frac{2\left(\sum_{i=1}^{n} x_i y_i\right)^2}{\sum_{i=1}^{n} x_i^2} + \sum_{i=1}^{n} y_i^2 \geq 0.$$

Multiplying both sides by $\sum_{i=1}^{n} x_i^2$, we have

$$-\left(\sum_{i=1}^{n} x_i y_i\right)^2 + \left(\sum_{i=1}^{n} x_i^2\right)\left(\sum_{i=1}^{n} y_i^2\right) \geq 0$$

which can be expressed as

$$\left(\sum_{i=1}^{n} x_i^2\right)\left(\sum_{i=1}^{n} y_i^2\right) \geq \left(\sum_{i=1}^{n} x_i y_i\right)^2$$

and dividing both sides by $\left(\sum_{i=1}^{n} x_i^2\right)\left(\sum_{i=1}^{n} y_i^2\right)$

$$1 \geq \frac{\left(\sum_{i=1}^{n} x_i y_i\right)^2}{\left(\sum_{i=1}^{n} x_i^2\right)\left(\sum_{i=1}^{n} y_i^2\right)} = r^2.$$

It means that

$$r^2 \leq 1$$

which proves $-1 \leq r \leq 1$.

Some important points to be remembered about the correlation coefficient are listed below.

1. The value of r lies between -1 and $+1$, inclusive, that is $-1 \leq r \leq +1$.
2. If the correlation (linear association) is positive and strong, then the value of r is close to $+1$.
3. If the correlation (linear association) is negative and strong, then the value of r is close to -1.
4. If the correlation (linear association) is weak, then the value of r is close to 0.
5. If there is no correlation (no linear association) between the variables, i.e., if there is no linear relationship between the variables, then the value of r equals 0. However, this does not mean that there is no other form of nonlinear relationship between the variables.
6. A positive correlation with value ($r = +a$) and a negative correlation with value ($r = -a$) (where $0 < a \leq 1$) have the same strength and opposite directions.
7. The existence of correlation (linear association) between variables, even if it is strong, does not imply that there is a cause and effect relationship between them. For instance, a strong positive correlation between income and saving does not mean that more income causes more saving.

Example 9.1

Let us consider weight (kg) and height (cm) of 12 children under 5 years of age. Assume that the sample of children was drawn randomly. It is of interest to find the strength of linear relationship between height (X) and weight (Y) of children under 5 years of age.

i	x_i	y_i	i	x_i	y_i
1	72.1	7.4	7	92.5	11.5
2	93.5	11.3	8	93.5	12.2
3	78.9	9.8	9	97.7	12.3
4	85.2	12.1	10	79.9	10.5
5	89.1	11.6	11	83.2	9.3
6	100.3	13.2	12	68.8	6.6

(1) Draw the scatter diagram. What indications does the scatter diagram reveal?
(2) Calculate Pearson's correlation coefficient (r).

The scatter plot below displays the pairs of sample data for height and weight of the children. In this diagram, each point in a scatter plot represents pairs of values where X-axis represents height and Y-axis represents weight. It shows that there is a linear relationship between height and weight because as the height increases, the weight also increases linearly. Hence, there is a positive correlation between the variables height and weight of children (Fig. 9.1).

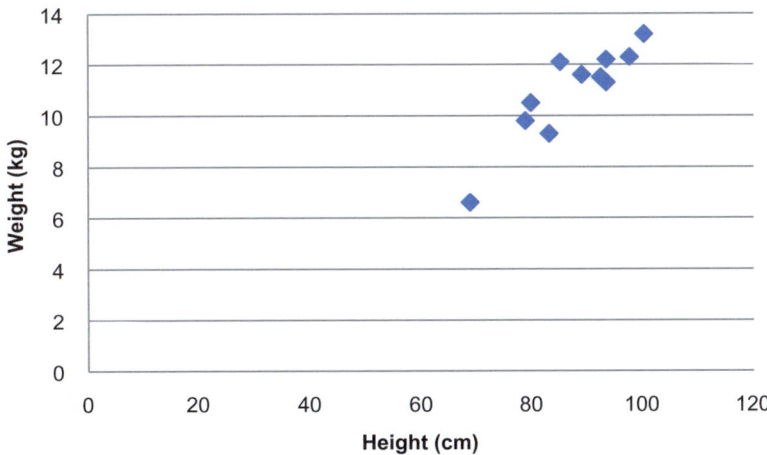

Fig. 9.1 Scatter plot of height and weight of 12 children of age under 5 years

(2) The computation of Pearson's correlation coefficient is illustrated below for the height and weight data of 12 children. We have shown that the Pearson's correlation coefficient can be computed using the following formula

$$r = \frac{\sum_{i=1}^{n} x_i y_i - n\bar{x}\bar{y}}{\sqrt{\sum_{i=1}^{n} x_i^2 - n(\bar{x})^2}\sqrt{\sum_{i=1}^{n} y_i^2 - n(\bar{y})^2}}.$$

Table 9.1 can be used to facilitate the computation of the correlation coefficient from the sample data.

$$\bar{x} = \frac{\sum_{i=1}^{12} x_i}{12} = \frac{1034.7}{12} = 86.225$$

$$\bar{y} = \frac{\sum_{i=1}^{12} y_i}{12} = \frac{127.8}{12} = 10.65$$

The correlation coefficient then can be estimated as

$$\begin{aligned} r &= \frac{\sum_{i=1}^{n} x_i y_i - n\bar{x}\bar{y}}{\sqrt{\sum_{i=1}^{n} x_i^2 - n(\bar{x})^2}\sqrt{\sum_{i=1}^{n} y_i^2 - n(\bar{y})^2}} \\ &= \frac{11224.7 - 12 \times 86.225 \times 10.65}{\sqrt{90307.29 - 12 \times (86.225)^2}\sqrt{1406.38 - 12 \times (10.65)^2}} \\ &= 0.92. \end{aligned}$$

Table 9.1 Table for computation of Pearson's correlation coefficient on height and weight of 12 children under 5 years of age

x Height (cm)	y Weight (kg)	xy	x^2	y^2
72.1	7.4	533.54	5198.41	54.76
93.5	11.3	1056.55	8742.25	127.69
78.9	9.8	773.22	6225.21	96.04
85.2	12.1	1030.92	7259.04	146.41
89.1	11.6	1033.56	7938.81	134.56
100.3	13.2	1323.96	10060.09	174.24
92.5	11.5	1063.75	8556.25	132.25
93.5	12.2	1140.70	8742.25	148.84
97.7	12.3	1201.71	9545.29	151.29
79.9	10.5	838.95	6384.01	110.25
83.2	9.3	773.76	6922.24	86.49
68.8	6.6	454.08	4733.44	43.56
$\sum x_i = 1034.7$	$\sum y_i = 127.8$	$\sum x_i y_i = 11224.7$	$\sum x_i^2 = 90307.29$	$\sum y_i^2 = 1406.38$

The measure of correlation coefficient shows that: (i) there is a positive linear relationship between height and weight of children under 5 years of age, and (ii) the linear relationship between height and weight of children appears to be quite strong.

9.2.3   Inferences About the Correlation Coefficient

In the previous section, we have seen that the first step in studying the relationship between two quantitative phenomena are construction of the scatter diagram and calculating the value of the correlation coefficient using Pearson's correlation coefficient, r. Indeed, the calculated value of r is used as a point estimate for the true value of the coefficient of linear correlation between X and Y, denoted by ρ.

The second step is to test the significance of the true value of (ρ) and constructing confidence intervals about it.

(i)   Testing hypotheses about the coefficient of linear correlation (ρ)

Suppose that $(X_1, Y_1), (X_2, Y_2)\ldots, (X_n, Y_n)$ is a random sample of size n taken from a bivariate normal distribution with linear correlation coefficient ρ.

We are interested in knowing whether there is a correlation between the variables X and Y ($\rho \neq 0$) or not ($\rho = 0$). Also, we are interested in knowing the nature of the linear correlation in case it exists; whether it is positive ($\rho > 0$) or negative ($\rho < 0$). In other words, we aew interested in testing hypotheses according to one of the following cases:

(a) $\begin{cases} H_0: \rho = 0 \\ H_1: \rho \neq 0 \end{cases}$	(b) $\begin{cases} H_0: \rho \leq 0 \\ H_1: \rho > 0 \end{cases}$	(c) $\begin{cases} H_0: \rho \geq 0 \\ H_1: \rho < 0 \end{cases}$

The test statistic for testing these hypotheses for r from the pairs of random sample data $(X_1, Y_1), \ldots, (X_n, Y_n)$ is

$$T = \frac{r\sqrt{n-2}}{\sqrt{1-r^2}}$$

where r is the estimator of the Pearson's coefficient of correlation. Under $H_0: \rho = 0$, the test statistic T has a t-distribution with degrees of freedom $= v = n - 2$.

The test statistic value of T from observed sample data $(x_1, y_1), \ldots, (x_n, y_n)$ is

$$t = \frac{r\sqrt{n-2}}{\sqrt{1-r^2}}$$

where r is computed from the sample data. The decision of rejecting or not rejecting $H_0: \rho = 0$ will be as follows according to the three cases mentioned above:

(a) For the first case: We reject H_0: $\rho = 0$ against H_1: $\rho \neq 0$ at the level of significance α if $t > t_{(n-2),1-\alpha/2}$ or if $t < -t_{(n-2),1-\alpha/2}$. That is we reject H_0: $\rho = 0$
if $|t| > t_{(n-2),\alpha/2}$.

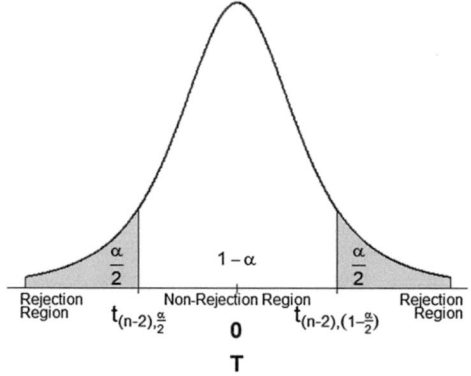

(b) For the second case: We reject H_0: $\rho \leq 0$ against H_1: $\rho > 0$ at the level of
significance α if $t > t_{(n-2),1-\alpha}$.

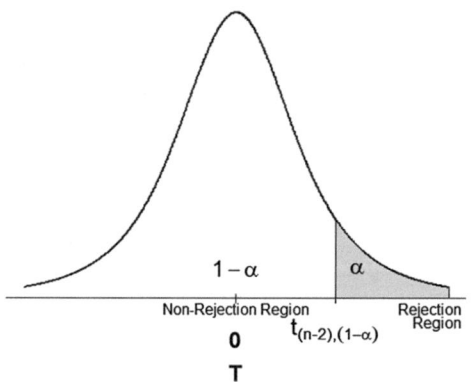

(c) For the third case: We reject H_0: $\rho \geq 0$ against H_1: $\rho < 0$ at the level of significance α if $t < -t_{(n-2),1-\alpha}$.

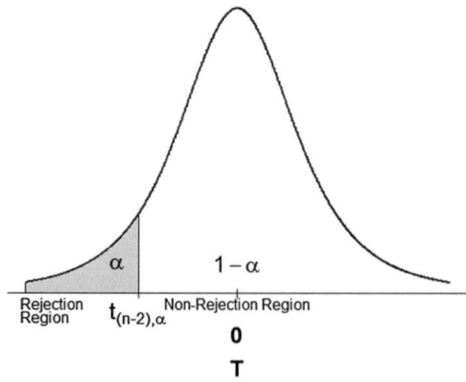

A more general approach of testing the null hypothesis H_0: $\rho = \rho_0$ against one- or two-sided alternatives is based on Fisher's transformation of r which tends to normal distribution with an increase in the sample size. The Fisher's transformation of r is

$$Z = \frac{1}{2}\ln\left(\frac{1+r}{1-r}\right)$$

and $\text{Var}(Z) = \frac{1}{n-3}$.

Here, Z is approximately normally distributed with an expected value $\frac{1}{2}\ln\left(\frac{1+\rho}{1-\rho}\right)$ and variance $\frac{1}{n-3}$.

The test statistic value of Z for the sample data is

$$z = \frac{\frac{1}{2}\ln\left[\frac{1+r}{1-r}\right] - \frac{1}{2}\ln\left[\frac{1+\rho_0}{1-\rho_0}\right]}{\sqrt{\frac{1}{n-3}}}.$$

Confidence intervals for the coefficient of correlation (ρ) is obtained from the Fisher's transformation shown above and the confidence interval for ρ are computed from the following:

$$z \pm z_{1-\alpha/2}\sqrt{\frac{1}{n-3}}$$

where let us denote

$$z_L = z - z_{1-\alpha/2}\sqrt{\frac{1}{n-3}},$$

and

$$z_U = z + z_{1-\alpha/2}\sqrt{\frac{1}{n-3}}.$$

Using inverse Fisher's transformation, we can find

$$z = \frac{1}{2}\ln\left(\frac{1+r}{1-r}\right)$$

which can be expressed as

$$\ln\left(\frac{1+r}{1-r}\right) = 2z$$
$$\Rightarrow \frac{1+r}{1-r} = e^{2z}$$
$$\Rightarrow 1+r = (1-r)e^{2z}$$
$$\Rightarrow r(e^{2z}+1) = e^{2z} - 1$$
$$\Rightarrow r = \frac{e^{2z}-1}{e^{2z}+1}.$$

The lower and upper limits of the confidence interval

$$r_L = \frac{e^{2z_L}-1}{e^{2z_L}+1},$$

and

$$r_U = \frac{e^{2z_U}-1}{e^{2z_U}+1}.$$

A $(1-\alpha)100\%$ confidence interval for ρ is:

$$\frac{e^{2z_L}-1}{e^{2z_L}+1} < \rho < \frac{e^{2z_U}-1}{e^{2z_U}+1}.$$

Example 9.2
Using the data displayed in Example 9.1, answer the following questions.

(1) Find a point estimate for the correlation coefficient between X and Y.
(2) Find a 95% confidence interval for the correlation coefficient between X and Y.
(3) Do the data provide us with a sufficient evidence to conclude that there is a linear relationship between X and Y? Suppose $\alpha = 0.05$.

Solution
In the previous example, we found that the value of the Pearson's correlation coefficient is $r = 0.92$.

(1) A point estimate for the correlation coefficient between X and Y is

$$r = +0.92$$

(2) In ordered to calculate a 95% confidence interval for the correlation coefficient between X and Y, we calculate the following quantities:

$$z = \frac{1}{2}\ln\left(\frac{1+r}{1-r}\right) = \frac{1}{2}\ln\left(\frac{1+0.92}{1-0.92}\right) = 1.589$$

$$z_L = z - \frac{z_{1-\alpha/2}}{\sqrt{n-3}} = 1.589 - \frac{z_{0.975}}{\sqrt{9}} = 1.589 - \frac{1.96}{\sqrt{9}} = 0.9357,$$

$$z_U = z + \frac{z_{1-\alpha/2}}{\sqrt{n-3}} = 1.589 + \frac{z_{0.975}}{\sqrt{9}} = 1.589 + \frac{1.96}{\sqrt{9}} = 2.2423.$$

Now, a 95% confidence interval for ρ is

$$\frac{\exp(2z_L) - 1}{\exp(2z_L) + 1} < \rho < \frac{\exp(2z_U) - 1}{\exp(2z_U) + 1}$$

$$\frac{\exp(2 \times 0.9357) - 1}{\exp(2 \times 0.9357) + 1} < \rho < \frac{\exp(2 \times 2.2423) - 1}{\exp(2 \times 2.2423) + 1}$$

and the 95% confidence interval for the population correlation coefficient can be expressed as

$$0.7332 < \rho < 0.9777.$$

Therefore, we can say that if the paired random samples of same size would be repeated a very large number of times from the same population and the confidence interval is constructed for each sample then 95% of the times the confidence intervals may include the true population correlation coefficient.

(3) We need to test the following hypotheses:
H_0: $\rho = 0$ implies that there is no linear relationship between X and Y
H_1: $\rho \neq 0$ implies that there is a linear relationship between X and Y

Let us assume that X and Y have a joint bivariate normal distribution, then we can use the t-test as shown below.
The value of the test statistics is

$$t = \frac{r\sqrt{n-2}}{\sqrt{1-r^2}} = \frac{0.92 \times \sqrt{12-2}}{\sqrt{1-0.92^2}} = 7.4232$$

From the t-table, and using $df = v = 12 - 2 = 10$, we find the critical values for the lower and upper tails

$$t_{(n-2),0.025} = t_{10,0.025} = -2.228 \text{ and } t_{(n-2),0.975} = t_{10,0.975} = 2.228.$$

Since $|t| > t_{(n-2),1-\alpha/2}$, we reject H_0: $\rho = 0$ at $\alpha = 0.05$, and we conclude that there is evidence from the sample data of a linear relationship between X and Y.

An alternative test can also be used based on Fisher's transformation. The assumption in that case is that either the joint distribution of X and Y is a bivariate normal distribution or the sample size is sufficiently large, then under the null hypothesis

$$z = \frac{\frac{1}{2} \ln \left[\frac{1+r}{1-r} \right]}{\sqrt{\frac{1}{n-3}}}$$

and the test statistic follows approximately a standard normal distribution.

9.3   Spearman's Rank Correlation Coefficient

As we mentioned earlier, Pearson's correlation coefficient can be used only when both variables are quantitative. In addition to the Pearson's correlation coefficient for ratio or interval scale data, the Spearman's correlation coefficient is introduced in this section for the ordinal qualitative scale data. The assumption of the bivariate normality is not required as an underlying assumption for the Spearman's correlation coefficient.

It may be noted here that the Spearman's correlation coefficient is a statistical measure of the strength of a monotonic relationship between paired data from variables X and Y. Here the monotonic relationship shows that if the value of one variable increases than the value of other variable may also increase or if the value of one variable increases then the value of other variable decreases. There is similarity in the interpretation of the Pearson's and the Spearman's correlation, e.g., the value closer to +1 or −1 indicates the stronger monotonic relationship in case of the Spearman's correlation.

In the case where variables can be expressed as ordinal qualitative (a qualitative variable whose values can be ordered or ranked), we can use the Spearman's rank correlation coefficient. If both the variables are quantitative but it is possible to transform the variables in rank orders then also we can use the Spearman's rank correlation. This can also be employed in some situations when the original data have nonlinear monotonic relationships but after transforming into rank orders the relationship tends to be linear.

Suppose that $(X_1, Y_1), (X_2, Y_2), \ldots, (X_n, Y_n)$ is a random sample of size, n, of paired variables. Let us define the following variables:

$$V_i = \text{Rank of } X_i = r(X_i)$$

$$W_i = \text{Rank of } Y_i = r(Y_i)$$

where $i = 1, 2, \ldots, n$. In the case where same values (ties) exist, each one of these values will receive the mean value of their ranks.

Definition

Spearman's rank correlation coefficient of the variables X and Y is denoted by r_S and can be expressed similar to the Pearson's correlation coefficient of the variables V and W. More specifically, Spearman's rank correlation coefficient of the variables X and Y is defined by

$$r_S = \frac{\sum_{i=1}^{n} (V_i - \overline{V})(W_i - \overline{W})}{\sqrt{\sum_{i=1}^{n} (V_i - \overline{V})^2} \sqrt{\sum_{i=1}^{n} (W_i - \overline{W})^2}}$$

$$= \frac{\sum_{i=1}^{n} V_i W_i - n\overline{V}\,\overline{W}}{\sqrt{\sum_{i=1}^{n} V_i^2 - n(\overline{V})^2} \sqrt{\sum_{i=1}^{n} W_i^2 - n(\overline{W})^2}}$$

$$= \frac{n \sum_{i=1}^{n} V_i W_i - \sum_{i=1}^{n} V_i \sum_{i=1}^{n} W_i}{\sqrt{n \sum_{i=1}^{n} V_i^2 - \left(\sum_{i=1}^{n} V_i\right)^2} \sqrt{n \sum_{i=1}^{n} W_i^2 - \left(\sum_{i=1}^{n} W_i\right)^2}}$$

where $V_i = r(x_i)$, $W_i = r(y_i)$, $\overline{V} = \frac{\sum_{i=1}^{n} V_i}{n}$, $\overline{W} = \frac{\sum_{i=1}^{n} W_i}{n}$,

If there are no ties, or if the number of ties is small, we may use the following simpler formula to calculate the Spearman's rank correlation (r_S)

$$r_S = 1 - \frac{6 \sum_{i=1}^{n} D_i^2}{n(n^2 - 1)}$$

where $D_i = r(X_i) - r(Y_i)$.

Example 9.3

Let us consider the following hypothetical data on two different methods of measuring the severity of a disease, say both are measured on a scale of 100. The first method is denoted as A and the second method as B. The number of subjects drawn randomly is 10. The hypothetical scores are shown below.

i	1	2	3	4	5	6	7	8	9	10
x_i	54	35	72	67	38	81	66	48	69	15
y_i	50	45	65	73	44	80	66	52	77	20

Let us find the Spearman's rank correlation coefficient, r_S, between the variables X and Y.

Solution

For computing the rank correlation, let us illustrate the procedures based on a method similar to the Pearson's method as shown below

$$\frac{\sum_{i=1}^{n} v_i w_i - n\bar{v}\bar{w}}{\sqrt{\sum_{i=1}^{n} v_i^2 - n(\bar{v})^2}\sqrt{\sum_{i=1}^{n} w_i^2 - n(\bar{w})^2}}$$

and the Spearman's method

$$r_S = 1 - \frac{6\sum_{i=1}^{n} d_i^2}{n(n^2 - 1)}.$$

Table 9.2 provides the computations necessary for the first method. From Table 9.2, we obtain

$$\bar{v} = \frac{\sum_{i=1}^{10} v_i}{10} = \frac{55}{10} = 5.5,$$

$$\bar{w} = \frac{\sum_{i=1}^{10} w_i}{10} = \frac{55}{10} = 5.5,$$

and

$$\begin{aligned}
r &= \frac{\sum_{i=1}^{n} v_i w_i - n\bar{v}\bar{w}}{\sqrt{\sum_{i=1}^{n} v_i^2 - n(\bar{v})^2}\sqrt{\sum_{i=1}^{n} w_i^2 - n(\bar{w})^2}} \\
&= \frac{377 - 10 \times 5.5 \times 5.5}{\sqrt{385 - 10 \times 5.5^2}\sqrt{385 - 10 \times 5.5^2}} \\
&= 0.90.
\end{aligned}$$

It shows that there is a positive association in the ranking of A and B indicating that both the scores ranked the severity of the disease quite similarly with little deviation (Table 9.3).

Table 9.2 Table for computation of rank correlation using Pearson's method

x	y	v	w	vw	v^2	w^2
54	50	5	4	20	25	16
35	45	2	3	6	4	9
72	65	9	6	54	81	36
67	73	7	8	56	49	64
38	44	3	2	6	9	4
81	80	10	10	100	100	100
66	66	6	7	42	36	49
48	52	4	5	20	16	25
69	77	8	9	72	64	81
15	20	1	1	1	1	1
		$\sum v_i = 55$	$\sum w_i = 55$	$\sum v_i w_i = 377$	$\sum v_i^2 = 385$	$\sum w_i^2 = 385$

Table 9.3 Table for computation of rank correlation using the Spearman's method

x	y	v	w	d	d^2
54	50	5	4	1	1
35	45	2	3	-1	1
72	65	9	6	3	9
67	73	7	8	-1	1
38	44	3	2	1	1
81	80	10	10	0	0
66	66	6	7	-1	1
48	52	4	5	-1	1
69	77	8	9	-1	1
15	20	1	1	0	0
		$\sum v_i = 55$	$\sum w_i = 55$	$\sum d_i = 0$	$\sum d_i^2 = 16$

Using the Spearman's method, we obtain

$$r_S = 1 - \frac{6 \sum_{i=1}^n d_i^2}{n(n^2 - 1)}$$
$$= 1 - \frac{6 \times 16}{10(100 - 1)}$$
$$= 0.90.$$

This value is same as the one obtained by using the Pearson's method. It may deviate in some cases due to ties in the ranks. We notice that there is a strong positive association between X and Y in the sense that an increase in the score by one method is associated with increase in the score of the other method of measuring the severity of the disease.

9.4 Regression Analysis

In this section, the basic concepts of regression analysis are introduced. We introduce the simple linear regression model first. The usual purpose of regression analysis is to explain and predict the change in the magnitude of an outcome variable in terms of change in magnitude of an explanatory variable in case of a simple regression model. The variable to be explained is called the dependent variable, outcome variable, or response variable, usually denoted by Y, and the remaining variable for which change in outcome variable is studied is known as the independent, predictor, or explanatory variable, usually denoted by X. For instance, Y may denote the weight of an individual and X may represent associated height or daily calorie intake. Generally, one does not predict the exact value of the occurrence. We are usually satisfied if the predictions are, on the average, reasonably close.

The statistician usually wants to find the equation of the curve of best fit to express the relationship of the variables.

The regression analysis deals with studying the form of the relationship between the variables in order to find a mathematical equation relating the outcome variables with explanatory variables. Once the mathematical form of the relationship is determined, we can utilize it to predict the value of the response (dependent) variable (Y) by knowing the value of the predictor (independent) variable (X). In other words, the objective of regression analysis is to estimate the mean of response variable (Y) by using the value of the predictor variable (X). For instance, we might be interested in predicting the blood pressure level of a person by using his weight, or predicting the height of an adult male by using the height of his father.

9.4.1   Simple Linear Regression Model

The first step in regression analysis is to estimate the model or the form of the relationship relating the response variable (Y) with the predictor or explanatory variable (X). One of the most useful relationships which has a lot of applications is the linear relationship between response and predictor variables. The following figure presents some examples for linear and nonlinear relationships.

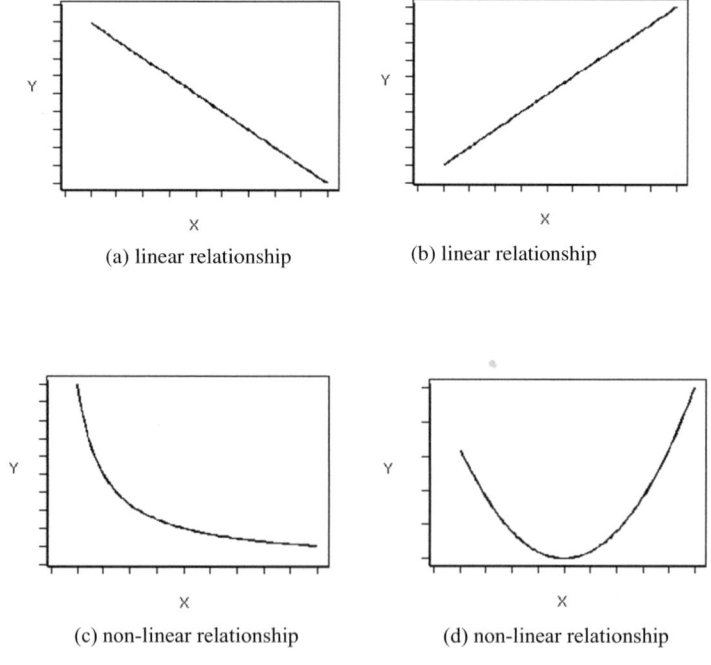

| (a) linear relationship | (b) linear relationship |
| (c) non-linear relationship | (d) non-linear relationship |

If the relationship between Y and X is linear, then it can be represented by a line called the regression line. In this case, it is possible to fit a line on the scatter diagram that describes this relationship. To introduce the simple linear regression model, suppose that the random sample of paired variables are

$$(X_1, Y_1), (X_2, Y_2), \ldots, (X_n, Y_n).$$

We may state that the expectation of Y given X, $E(Y|X)$, is a linear regression model or a regression function of Y upon X if it can be expressed as

$$E(Y|X) = \beta_0 + \beta_1 X.$$

This model is called a simple regression model because it takes into account a single independent variable X to explain the dependent variable, Y. There are two regression parameters in this model which are unknown constants, β_0 is an intercept and β_1 is a slope known as the regression coefficient of the independent variable, X. Let us consider the relationship between the independent and dependent variables for a random sample, $(X_i, Y_i), i = 1, \ldots, n$. The linear regression model for each pair of independent and dependent variables for the ith subject can be shown in the following form

$$E(Y_i|X_i) = \beta_0 + \beta_1 X_i, \quad i = 1, \ldots, n.$$

Now, we can rewrite the model for each value of the outcome variable for a corresponding given value of X_i as follows

$$Y_i = \beta_0 + \beta_1 X_i + \varepsilon_i, \quad i = 1, \ldots, n$$

where the ε_i are the experimental errors and are distributed such that $E(\varepsilon_i) = 0$ and $\text{Var}(\varepsilon_i) = \sigma^2, i = 1, \ldots, n$.

The above model includes an additional term because this is not a model for the population mean based on given value of the independent variable, rather this model may contain error due to its deviation from the population mean which is shown in the following expression of the model

$$Y_i = E(Y_i|X_i) + \varepsilon_i,$$

where $E(Y_i|X_i) = \beta_0 + \beta_1 X_i, i = 1, \ldots, n$. A comparison between the model for the population mean for given values of independent variable and the relationship between independent and dependent variables needs to be understood clearly in order to interpret the results without any ambiguity.

The following assumptions are necessary for estimating the parameters of the regression model:

(i)   The expected value of the error variable is zero, i.e., $E(\varepsilon_i) = 0$ for all i;

(ii) The variance of the error variable is $\mathrm{Var}(\varepsilon_i) = \sigma^2$ for all i;

(iii) The error variables are independent, i.e., ε_i and ε_j are independent for any i and j $(i \neq j)$, and

(iv) The independent variables and the error variables are independent, i.e., X_j and ε_i are independent for all i and j.

Under these assumptions, it can be shown that the least squares estimators of β_0 and β_1 are minimum variance unbiased estimators (Best Linear Unbiased Estimators). The least squares estimation procedure will be introduced in the next section.

A fifth assumption, the assumption that the residuals ε_j are normally distributed, though not needed for the least squares estimation but is needed to make confidence interval statements and to apply tests of significance:

(v)   Normality: In conjunction with assumptions (i)–(iv), this assumption implies that $\varepsilon_i \sim N(0, \sigma^2)$.

9.4.2   *Estimation of β_0 and β_1*

The parameters of the regression model, β_0 and β_1, are unknown population values. We have to estimate these parameters using the sample data. We have discussed about estimation procedures in Chap. 7 and two methods of estimating parameters are highlighted there, one is the method of moments and the other one is the method of maximum likelihood. For estimating the parameters of a regression model, we generally use a third method known as the method of least squares. The method of least squares is preferred for estimating parameters of a linear regression model because of its good properties for the linear regression models, some of which will be highlighted in this chapter. The most important criterion for employing the least squares method for estimating the parameters of a linear regression model is the fact that the error in fitting a linear regression model to the sample data is kept minimum that provides the model fit a desirable acceptance to the users who prefer applications to data with strong measurable properties.

The error term in the regression model is the deviation between the observed value of the dependent variable and the expected value of the dependent variable for given value of the independent variable which is

$$\varepsilon = Y - (\beta_0 + \beta_1 X).$$

Here, ε represents the distance between the observed values of Y to the line represented by $E(Y|X) = \beta_0 + \beta_1 X$ which shows the error in representing the observed values of Y by the regression line. We want to minimize $\sum_{i=1}^{n} \varepsilon_i^2$ such that the estimates of the parameters confirm the minimum errors. For convenience, we define

$$Q = \sum_{i=1}^{n} \varepsilon_i^2 = \sum_{i=1}^{n} (Y_i - \beta_0 - \beta_1 X_i)^2$$

where n denotes the number of observations in the sample. To minimize Q, we take the partial derivative of Q with respect to each of the two parameters that we are estimating and set the resulting expressions equal to zero. Thus,

$$\frac{\partial Q}{\partial \beta_0} = 2 \sum_{i=1}^{n} (Y_i - \beta_0 - \beta_1 X_i)(-1) = 0$$

and

$$\frac{\partial Q}{\partial \beta_1} = 2 \sum_{i=1}^{n} (Y_i - \beta_0 - \beta_1 X_i)(-X_i) = 0$$

Dropping 2 and -1 from the estimating equations, the solutions for β_0 and β_1 are obtained by solving the equations which are generally called normal equations

$$\sum_{i=1}^{n} (Y_i - \beta_0 - \beta_1 X_i) = 0$$

$$\sum_{i=1}^{n} \left(X_i Y_i - \beta_0 X_i - \beta_1 X_i^2 \right) = 0$$

Solving the first normal equation and replacing β_0 by $\hat{\beta}_0$ and β_1 by $\hat{\beta}_1$, we obtain

$$n\hat{\beta}_0 = \sum_{i=1}^{n} Y_i - \hat{\beta}_1 \sum_{i=1}^{n} X_i$$

and the estimator of β_0

$$\hat{\beta}_0 = \overline{Y} - \hat{\beta}_1 \overline{X}.$$

Similarly, the equation for β_1 can be solved by expressing the equation in the following form and replacing β_0 by $\hat{\beta}_0$ and β_1 by $\hat{\beta}_1$, we obtain

$$\hat{\beta}_1 \sum_{i=1}^{n} X_i^2 = -\hat{\beta}_0 \sum_{i=1}^{n} X_i + \sum_{i=1}^{n} X_i Y_i$$

and using $\hat{\beta}_0 = \overline{Y} - \hat{\beta}_1 \overline{X}$ and replacing $\hat{\beta}_0$ by $\overline{Y} - \hat{\beta}_1 \overline{X}$, it is seen that

$$\hat{\beta}_1 \sum_{i=1}^{n} X_i^2 = -(\overline{Y} - \hat{\beta}_1 \overline{X}) \sum_{i=1}^{n} X_i + \sum_{i=1}^{n} X_i Y_i$$

and we rewrite the equation

$$\hat{\beta}_1 \sum_{i=1}^{n} X_i^2 - n\hat{\beta}_1 \overline{X}^2 = \sum_{i=1}^{n} X_i Y_i - n\overline{X}\,\overline{Y}$$

and solving for β_1, we obtain the estimator

$$\hat{\beta}_1 = \frac{\sum_{i=1}^{n} X_i Y_i - n\overline{X}\,\overline{Y}}{\sum_{i=1}^{n} X_i^2 - n\hat{\beta}_1 \overline{X}^2} = \frac{\sum_{i=1}^{n} (X_i - \overline{X})(Y_i - \overline{Y})}{\sum_{i=1}^{n} (X_i - \overline{X})^2} = \frac{S_{XY}}{S_{XX}}.$$

The estimated model is

$$\hat{Y}_i = \hat{\beta}_0 + \hat{\beta}_1 X_i$$

and the model for observed Y is

$$Y_i = \hat{\beta}_0 + \hat{\beta}_1 X_i + e_i$$

where the estimated residuals are

$$e_i = Y_i - (\hat{\beta}_0 + \hat{\beta}_1 X_i), \quad i = 1, \ldots, n.$$

The residual sum of squares is defined by

$$\text{Residual SS} = \text{RSS} = \sum_{i=1}^{n} \left(Y_i - \hat{Y}_i\right)^2 = \sum_{i=1}^{n} \left(Y_i - \hat{\beta}_0 - \hat{\beta} X_i\right)^2$$

and the regression sum of squares (Reg SS) is

$$\sum_{i=1}^{n} \left(\hat{Y}_i - \overline{Y}\right)^2 = \sum_{i=1}^{n} \left(\hat{\beta}_0 + \hat{\beta}_1 X_i - \hat{\beta}_0 - \hat{\beta}_1 \overline{X}\right)^2$$

$$= \hat{\beta}_1^2 \sum_{i=1}^{n} (X_i - \overline{X})^2$$

$$= \left(\frac{S_{XY}}{S_{XX}}\right)^2 S_{XX}$$

$$= \frac{S_{XY}^2}{S_{XX}}$$

where $\overline{Y} = \hat{\beta}_0 + \hat{\beta}_1 \overline{X}$.

The total sum of squares is

$$\text{Total SS} = \sum_{i=1}^{n} \left(Y_i - \overline{Y}\right)^2$$

which can be rewritten and expanded in the following form

$$\sum_{i=1}^{n} \left(Y_i - \overline{Y}\right)^2 = \sum_{i=1}^{n} \left(Y_i - \widehat{Y}_i + \widehat{Y}_i - \overline{Y}\right)^2$$

$$= \sum_{i=1}^{n} \left(Y_i - \widehat{Y}_i\right)^2 + \sum_{i=1}^{n} \left(\widehat{Y}_i - \overline{Y}\right)^2 + 2 \sum_{i=1}^{n} \left(Y_i - \widehat{Y}_i\right)\left(\widehat{Y}_i - \overline{Y}\right).$$

In the product term, $Y_i - \widehat{Y}_i = e_i$ and $\widehat{Y}_i - \overline{Y} = \hat{\beta}_1(X_i - \overline{X})$. It can be shown that the product term is zero. Hence, the total sum of squares of the dependent variable, Y, can be partitioned into two components

$$\text{Total SS} = S_{YY} = \sum_{i=1}^{n} \left(Y_i - \overline{Y}\right)^2 = \sum_{i=1}^{n} \left(Y_i - \widehat{Y}_i\right)^2 + \sum_{i=1}^{n} \left(\widehat{Y}_i - \overline{Y}\right)^2,$$

which can be rewritten as

$$S_{YY} = \text{RSS} + \frac{S_{XY}^2}{S_{XX}}$$

and the residual sum of squares can be obtained from

$$\text{RSS} = S_{YY} - \frac{S_{XY}^2}{S_{XX}} = S_{YY}\left(1 - \frac{S_{XY}^2}{S_{XX}S_{YY}}\right) = S_{YY}\left(1 - r_{XY}^2\right)$$

where the measure of Pearson's correlation coefficient from the sample data is $r_{XY} = \frac{S_{XY}}{S_{XX}S_{YY}}$ that shows the strength of linear relationship between variables X and Y. It has been shown here that

$$\text{Total SS} = \text{Residual SS} + \text{Regression SS}$$

which provides the important logical background for testing of hypotheses including the measure of goodness of fit of a regression model.

9.4.3   Interpretations of the Parameters of the Regression Line

The parameters of the population regression model, $Y = \beta_o + \beta_1 X + \varepsilon$, are β_0 and β_1. The first parameter, β_0, is the intercept of the line; it is the value of Y when $X = 0$. The second parameter, β_1, is the slope of the regression line; it is the amount of change in the value of Y, on average, when the value of X is increased by one unit. In particular, the value of β_1 determines the nature of the linear relationship between X and Y. If there is no linear relationship between X and Y, then $\beta_1 = 0$; if there is a positive linear relationship, then $\beta_1 > 0$; if there is a negative linear relationship, then $\beta_1 < 0$. The estimated regression model is $\widehat{Y} = \hat{\beta}_0 + \hat{\beta}_1 X$ and the observed value of the dependent variable can be shown as $Y = \hat{\beta}_0 + \hat{\beta}_1 X + e = \widehat{Y} + e$, where e is the estimated error from the sample data.

The estimates of β_0 and β_1 that minimize the differences between the observed values of the dependent variable and the regression line are called the least squares estimates. The vertical differences between the scatter points and the regression line are illustrated in the following figure

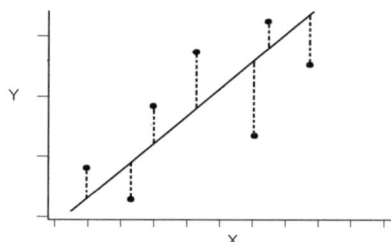

9.4.4   Properties of the Least Squares Estimators and the Fitted Regression Model

The least squares estimators $\hat{\beta}_0$ and $\hat{\beta}_1$ have several important properties. Some of the properties are discussed here. Let us consider the least squares estimators

$$\hat{\beta}_0 = \overline{Y} - \hat{\beta}_1 \overline{X},$$

and

$$\hat{\beta}_1 = \frac{\sum_{i=1}^{n} \left(X_i - \overline{X}\right)\left(Y_i - \overline{Y}\right)}{\sum_{i=1}^{n} \left(X_i - \overline{X}\right)^2}.$$

The above estimators are linear combinations of the observations, Y_i. For example

$$\hat{\beta}_1 = \frac{\sum_{i=1}^n (X_i - \overline{X})(Y_i - \overline{Y})}{\sum_{i=1}^n (X_i - \overline{X})^2}$$

$$= \frac{\sum_{i=1}^n (X_i - \overline{X})Y_i}{\sum_{i=1}^n (X_i - \overline{X})^2}$$

$$= \sum_{i=1}^n C_i Y_i$$

where $\dfrac{(X_i - \overline{X})}{\sum_{i=1}^n (X_i - \overline{X})^2} = C_i$ and $\sum_{i=1}^n (X_i - \overline{X})\overline{X} = 0$.

(i) The least squares estimators $\hat{\beta}_0$ and $\hat{\beta}_1$ are unbiased estimators of model parameters β_0 and β_1. To show this for $\hat{\beta}_1$, let us consider

$$E\left(\hat{\beta}_1\right) = E\left(\sum_{i=1}^n C_i Y_i\right)$$

$$= \sum_{i=1}^n C_i E(Y_i)$$

$$= \sum_{i=1}^n C_i(\beta_0 + \beta_1 X_i)$$

$$= \beta_0 \sum_{i=1}^n C_i + \beta_1 \sum_{i=1}^n C_i X_i.$$

It can be shown from the linear function that $\sum_{i=1}^n C_i = 0$ and $\sum_{i=1}^n C_i X_i = 1$, and using these results we prove the following property of the least squares estimator

$$E\left(\hat{\beta}_1\right) = \beta_0 \times 0 + \beta_1 \times 1 = \beta_1$$

which proves that $\hat{\beta}_1$ is an unbiased estimator of β_1.

(ii) The estimator $\hat{\beta}_0$ is an unbiased estimator of β_0 .

We know that $\hat{\beta}_0 = \overline{Y} - \hat{\beta}_1 \overline{X}$.
The expected value of $\hat{\beta}_0$ is

$$E(\hat{\beta}_0) = E(\overline{Y}) - \overline{X}E(\hat{\beta}_1)$$
$$= \beta_0 + \beta_1 \overline{X} - \beta_1 \overline{X}$$
$$= \beta_0$$

confirming that $\hat{\beta}_0$ is an unbiased estimator of β_0.

(iii) The variance of $\hat{\beta}_1$ can be obtained as

$$\text{Var}\left(\hat{\beta}_1\right) = \text{Var}\left(\sum_{i=1}^n C_i Y_i\right)$$

$$= \sum_{i=1}^n C_i^2 \text{Var}(Y_i)$$

$$= \sigma^2 \sum_{i=1}^n C_i^2$$

where $\sum_{i=1}^n C_i^2 = \dfrac{\sum_{i=1}^n \left(X_i - \overline{X}\right)^2}{\left(\sum_{i=1}^n \left(X_i - \overline{X}\right)^2\right)^2} = \dfrac{1}{\sum_{i=1}^n \left(X_i - \overline{X}\right)^2}$. Hence,

$$\text{Var}\left(\hat{\beta}_1\right) = \dfrac{\sigma^2}{\sum_{i=1}^n \left(X_i - \overline{X}\right)^2}.$$

(iv) The variance of $\hat{\beta}_0$ is

$$\text{Var}\left(\hat{\beta}_0\right) = \text{Var}\left(\overline{Y} - \hat{\beta}_1 \overline{X}\right)$$

$$= \text{Var}\left(\overline{Y}\right) + \overline{X}^2 \text{Var}\left(\hat{\beta}_1\right) - 2\overline{X}\,\text{Cov}\left(Y, \hat{\beta}_1\right)$$

$$= \sigma^2\left(\dfrac{1}{n} + \dfrac{\overline{X}^2}{\sum_{i=1}^n \left(X_i - \overline{X}\right)^2}\right)$$

where $\text{Cov}\left(Y, \hat{\beta}_1\right) = 0$.

(v) The covariance between $\hat{\beta}_0$ and $\hat{\beta}_1$ is

$$\text{Cov}\left(\hat{\beta}_0, \hat{\beta}_1\right) = -\overline{X}\,\dfrac{\sigma^2}{\sum_{i=1}^n \left(X_i - \overline{X}\right)^2}.$$

(vi) The mean square residual is an unbiased estimator of σ^2. It can be shown that

$$E\left(\dfrac{\sum_{i=1}^n e_i^2}{(n-2)}\right) = \sigma^2 \text{ and } \hat{\sigma}^2 = \dfrac{\sum_{i=1}^n e_i^2}{(n-2)} = \text{residual mean square} = MS_{\text{Res}}.$$

From the above equation, it can be shown that the expected value of the error mean square is the variance

$$E\left(\frac{\sum_{i=1}^{n} e_i^2}{n-2}\right) = \sigma^2$$

which implies that the error mean square is an unbiased estimator of the variance.

Example 9.4

The data set we have used for computing the Pearson's correlation coefficient is employed, here, for showing the estimation and tests for the simple regression model introduced in this section. We have considered weight (kg) and height (cm) of 12 children under 5 years of age drawn randomly. The estimation and tests for simple regression model for variables height (X) and weight (Y) of children under 5 years of age are shown here.

Table 9.4 shows the computations necessary for estimating parameters of the regression model

$$Y_i = \beta_0 + \beta_1 X_i + \varepsilon_i, \quad i = 1, \ldots, 12.$$

The least squares estimators of β_0 and β_1 are

$$\hat{\beta}_0 = \overline{Y} - \hat{\beta}_1 \overline{X},$$

Table 9.4 Height (x) and weight (y) of 12 children under 5 years of age and calculations necessary for estimating the parameters of a simple regression model

x Height (cm)	y Weight (kg)	xy	x^2	y^2
72.1	7.4	533.54	5198.41	54.76
93.5	11.3	1056.55	8742.25	127.69
78.9	9.8	773.22	6225.21	96.04
85.2	12.1	1030.92	7259.04	146.41
89.1	11.6	1033.56	7938.81	134.56
100.3	13.2	1323.96	10060.09	174.24
92.5	11.5	1063.75	8556.25	132.25
93.5	12.2	1140.70	8742.25	148.84
97.7	12.3	1201.71	9545.29	151.29
79.9	10.5	838.95	6384.01	110.25
83.2	9.3	773.76	6922.24	86.49
68.8	6.6	454.08	4733.44	43.56
$\sum x = 1034.7$	$\sum y = 127.8$	$\sum xy = 11224.7$	$\sum x^2 = 90307.29$	$\sum y^2 = 1406.38$

and

$$\hat{\beta}_1 = \frac{\sum_{i=1}^{n} X_i Y_i - n\overline{X}\,\overline{Y}}{\sum_{i=1}^{n} X_i^2 - n\hat{\beta}_1 \overline{X}^2} = \frac{\sum_{i=1}^{n} (X_i - \overline{X})(Y_i - \overline{Y})}{\sum_{i=1}^{n} (X_i - \overline{X})^2} = \frac{S_{XY}}{S_{XX}}.$$

The estimated model is

$$\widehat{Y}_i = \hat{\beta}_0 + \hat{\beta}_1 X_i$$

and the model for observed Y is

$$Y_i = \hat{\beta}_0 + \hat{\beta}_1 X_i + e_i.$$

We need the estimated means, sum of products, and sum of squares as shown below

$$\overline{x} = \frac{\sum_{i=1}^{12} x_i}{12} = \frac{1034.7}{12} = 86.225$$

$$\overline{y} = \frac{\sum_{i=1}^{12} y_i}{12} = \frac{127.8}{12} = 10.65,$$

$$S_{xy} = \sum_{i=1}^{n} (x_i - \overline{x})(y_i - \overline{y})$$

$$= \sum_{i=1}^{n} x_i y_i - n\overline{x}\overline{y}$$

$$= 11224.7 - 12 \times 86.225 \times 10.65$$

$$= 205.14,$$

and

$$S_{xx} = \sum_{i=1}^{12} (x_i - \overline{x})^2$$

$$= \sum_{i=1}^{12} x_i^2 - n\overline{x}^2$$

$$= 90307.29 - 12 \times (86.225)^2$$

$$= 1090.28.$$

The estimates of regression parameters are

$$\hat{\beta}_1 = \frac{\sum_{i=1}^{n} x_i y_i - n\bar{x}\bar{y}}{\sum_{i=1}^{n} x_i^2 - n\bar{x}^2}$$

$$= \frac{205.14}{1090.28}$$

$$= 0.1882$$

$$\hat{\beta}_0 = \bar{y} - \hat{\beta}_1 \bar{x}$$

$$= 10.65 - 0.1882 \times 86.225$$

$$= -5.5775.$$

The fitted model is

$$\widehat{Y}_i = \hat{\beta}_0 + \hat{\beta}_1 X_i$$

$$= -5.5775 + 0.1882 X_i$$

and the model for observed Y is

$$Y_i = \hat{\beta}_0 + \hat{\beta}_1 X_i + e_i$$

$$= -5.5775 + 0.1882 X_i + e_i.$$

The estimated error can be obtained as

$$e_i = Y_i - (-5.5775 + 0.1882 X_i).$$

We know that the unbiased estimator of the population variance σ^2 is the mean square error s^2 from the sample data. The mean square error computed from the sample data is shown in below (Table 9.5)

$$s^2 = \frac{\sum_{i=1}^{n} (y_i - \hat{y}_i)^2}{n-2} = \frac{6.7104}{10} = 0.67104.$$

9.4.5   Hypothesis Testing on the Slope and Intercept

We are often interested in testing hypotheses and constructing confidence intervals about the model parameters. These procedures require that we make the additional assumption that the model errors ε_i are normally distributed. Thus, we add to complete the assumptions by stating that the errors are normally and independently distributed with mean 0 and variance σ^2, abbreviated $NID(0, \sigma^2)$.

Table 9.5 Height (x) and weight (y) of 12 children under 5 years of age and calculations necessary for estimating the variance

x Height (cm)	y Weight (kg)	$\hat{y}$	e_i	e_i^2
72.1	7.4	7.99172	−0.59172	0.350133
93.5	11.3	12.0192	−0.7192	0.517249
78.9	9.8	9.27148	0.52852	0.279333
85.2	12.1	10.45714	1.64286	2.698989
89.1	11.6	11.19112	0.40888	0.167183
100.3	13.2	13.29896	-0.09896	0.009793
92.5	11.5	11.831	−0.331	0.109561
93.5	12.2	12.0192	0.1808	0.032689
97.7	12.3	12.80964	−0.50964	0.259733
79.9	10.5	9.45968	1.04032	1.082266
83.2	9.3	10.08074	−0.78074	0.609555
68.8	6.6	7.37066	−0.77066	0.593917
$\sum x = 1034.7$	$\sum y = 127.8$	127.8005		6.7104

Tests for the Parameters

Suppose that we wish to test the hypothesis that the slope equals a constant, say β_{10}. The appropriate hypotheses are

$$H_0: \beta_1 = \beta_{10}$$

$$H_1: \beta_1 \neq \beta_{10}$$

where a two-sided alternative is specified. Since the errors ε_i are $NID(0, \sigma^2)$, the observations Y_i are $NID(\beta_0 + \beta_1 X_i, \sigma^2)$. Now $\hat{\beta}_1$ is a linear combination of the observations, so $\hat{\beta}_1$ is normally distributed with mean β_1 and variance σ^2/S_{XX} using the mean and variance of $\hat{\beta}_1$ as shown earlier. Therefore, the statistic

$$Z = \frac{\hat{\beta}_1 - \beta_{10}}{\sqrt{\sigma^2/S_{XX}}}$$

is distributed $N(0, 1)$ if the null hypothesis is true. If σ^2 were known, we could use Z to test the null hypothesis. Generally, σ^2 is unknown. We have already seen that MS_{Res} is an unbiased estimator of σ^2. It can be shown that $(n-2)MS_{Res}/\sigma^2$ follows a χ_{n-2}^2 distribution and that MS_{Res} and $\hat{\beta}_1$ are independent. By the definition of a t statistic,

$$T = \frac{\hat{\beta}_1 - \beta_{10}}{\sqrt{MS_{Res}/S_{XX}}}$$

follows a t_{n-2} distribution if the null hypothesis is true. The degree of freedom associated with t is the degree of freedom associated with MS_{Res}. The null hypothesis is rejected if

$$|t| > t_{(n-2),1-\alpha/2}.$$

The denominator of this test statistic, t, is often called the estimated standard error or simply, the standard error of the slope. That is,

$$se(\hat{\beta}_1) = \sqrt{\frac{MS_{Res}}{S_{XX}}}.$$

Therefore, we often see T written as

$$T = \frac{\hat{\beta}_1 - \beta_{10}}{se(\hat{\beta}_1)}.$$

A similar procedure can be used to test hypothesis about the intercept. To test

$$H_0: \beta_0 = \beta_{00}$$

$$H_1: \beta_0 \neq \beta_{00}$$

we would use the following test statistic:

$$T = \frac{\hat{\beta}_0 - \beta_{00}}{\sqrt{MS_{Res}\left(\frac{1}{n} + \frac{\overline{X}^2}{S_{XX}}\right)}} = \frac{\hat{\beta}_0 - \beta_{00}}{se(\hat{\beta}_0)}$$

where $se(\hat{\beta}_0) = \sqrt{MS_{Res}(1/n + \overline{X}^2/S_{XX})}$ is the standard error of the intercept. We may reject the null hypothesis if

$$|t| > t_{(n-2),1-\alpha/2}.$$

9.4.6 Testing Significance of Regression

A very important special case of the hypothesis is

$$H_0: \beta_1 = 0$$

$$H_1: \beta_1 \neq 0$$

These hypotheses relate to the significance of regression. Failing to reject $H_0: \beta_1 = 0$ implies that there is no linear relationship between X and Y. This may imply either of the following:

 (i) X is of little value in explaining the variation in Y and that the best estimator of Y for any X is $\widehat{Y} = \overline{Y}$;
 (ii) The true relationship between X and Y is not linear. Therefore, failing to reject $H_0: \beta_1 = 0$ is equivalent to saying that there is no linear relationship between X and Y.

Alternatively if $H_0: \beta_1 = 0$ is rejected, this implies that X is of value in explaining the variability in Y. However, rejecting $H_0: \beta_1 = 0$ could mean either of the following:

 (i) that the straight-line model is adequate;
 (ii) better results could be obtained with the addition of higher order polynomial terms in X.

The test procedure for $H_0: \beta_1 = 0$ is as follows:

$$T = \frac{\widehat{\beta}_1}{se(\widehat{\beta}_1)}.$$

The hypothesis of significance of regression would be neglected if

$$|t| > t_{(n-2),1-\alpha/2}.$$

9.4.7 Analysis of Variance

We may also use an analysis of variance approach to test the significance of a regression. The analysis of variance is based on a partitioning of total variability in the response variable Y. To obtain this partitioning, let us begin with

$$Y_i - \overline{Y} = (\widehat{Y}_i - \overline{Y}) + (Y_i - \widehat{Y}_i).$$

Squaring both sides of the above equation and summing over all n observations produces

$$\sum_{i=1}^{n}(Y_i - \overline{Y})^2 = \sum_{i=1}^{n}(\widehat{Y}_i - \overline{Y})^2 + \sum_{i=1}^{n}(Y_i - \widehat{Y}_i)^2 + 2\sum_{i=1}^{n}(\widehat{Y}_i - \overline{Y})(Y_i - \widehat{Y}_i).$$

The product term can be rewritten as

$$2\sum_{i=1}^{n}(\widehat{Y}_i - \overline{Y})(Y_i - \widehat{Y}_i) = 2\sum_{i=1}^{n}\widehat{Y}_i(Y_i - \widehat{Y}_i) - 2\overline{Y}\sum_{i=1}^{n}(Y_i - \widehat{Y}_i)$$

$$= 2\sum_{i=1}^{n}\widehat{Y}_i e_i - 2\overline{Y}\sum_{i=1}^{n}e_i = 0$$

where $\sum_{i=1}^{n} e_i = 0$ and $\sum_{i=1}^{n}\widehat{Y}_i e_i = 0$.
Therefore,

$$\sum_{i=1}^{n}(Y_i - \overline{Y})^2 = \sum_{i=1}^{n}(\widehat{Y}_i - \overline{Y})^2 + \sum_{i=1}^{n}(Y_i - \widehat{Y}_i)^2.$$

This equation is the fundamental analysis of variance identity for a regression model. Symbolically, we usually write

$$SS_{\text{Total}} = SS_{\text{Reg}} + SS_{\text{Res}}.$$

The total sum of squares, SS_{Total}, has $df_T = n - 1$ degrees of freedom due to reduction of one degree of freedom resulting from the constraint $\sum_{i=1}^{n}(Y_i - \overline{Y})$ on the deviations $Y_i - \overline{Y}$. There are two components in the analysis of variance, regression, and residual. It has been shown that SS_{Reg} is completely determined by one parameter, namely, $\hat{\beta}_1$, and $SS_{\text{Reg}} = \hat{\beta}_1 S_{XY}$, hence $df_{\text{Reg}} = 1$ degree of freedom. The component of residual sum of squares is obtained from the deviations $Y_i - \widehat{Y}_i$, where $\widehat{Y}_i$ depends on estimates $\hat{\beta}_0$ and $\hat{\beta}_1$. The number of parameters estimated for computing SS_{Res} causes reduction in the degrees of freedom and $df_{\text{Res}} = n - 2$. Hence, it is shown that

$$df_{\text{Total}} = df_{\text{Reg}} + df_{\text{Res}}$$
$$(n - 1) = 1 + (n - 2).$$

We can use the usual analysis of variance F test to test the hypothesis $H_0: \beta_1 = 0$. By definition

Table 9.6 The analysis of variance table for a simple regression model

Source of variation	Sum of square	df	Mean squares	F
Regression	$SS_{\text{Reg}} = \hat{\beta}_1 S_{XY} - n\bar{Y}^2$	1	$SS_{\text{Reg}}/1$	$F = MS_{\text{Reg}}/MS_{\text{Res}}$
Residual	$SS_{\text{Res}} = SS_{\text{Total}} - \hat{\beta}_1 S_{Xy}$	$n-2$	$SS_{\text{Res}}/(n-2)$	

$$F = \frac{SS_{\text{Reg}}/df_{\text{Reg}}}{SS_{\text{Res}}/df_{\text{Res}}} = \frac{SS_{\text{Reg}}/1}{SS_{\text{Res}}/(n-2)} = \frac{MS_{\text{Reg}}}{MS_{\text{Res}}}$$

follows the $F_{1,(n-2)}$ distribution. Therefore, to test the hypothesis $H_0: \beta_1 = 0$, test statistic is computed and the null hypothesis is rejected if

$$F > F_{\alpha,1,(n-2)}.$$

The test procedure is summarized in Table 9.6
The t statistic as defined earlier is

$$T = \frac{\hat{\beta}_1}{se(\hat{\beta}_1)} = \frac{\hat{\beta}_1}{\sqrt{MS_{\text{Res}}/SS_X}}$$

could be used for testing for significance of regression. However, squaring both sides, we obtain

$$T^2 = \frac{\hat{\beta}_1^2 SS_X}{MS_{\text{Res}}} = \frac{\hat{\beta}_1 S_{XY}}{MS_{\text{Res}}} = \frac{MS_{\text{Reg}}}{MS_{\text{Res}}}.$$

Thus, T^2 is identical to F of the analysis of variance approach for the special case where the square of a T variable with $(n-2)$ degrees of freedom is equivalent to an F variable with 1 and $(n-2)$ degrees of freedom. For testing the null hypothesis $H_0: \beta_1 = 0$ in a simple regression problem, the t-test has advantages because one-sided alternatives such as $H_1: \beta_1 < 0$ or $H_1: \beta_1 > 0$ can also be performed using the t-test.

9.4.8 Interval Estimation in Simple Linear Regression

Under the assumption that $\varepsilon_i \sim NID(0, \sigma^2)$, it can be shown that

(i) $\hat{\beta}_0$ has a normal distribution with mean β_0 and variance

$$\text{Var}(\hat{\beta}_0) = \sigma^2 \left(\frac{1}{n} + \frac{\overline{X}^2}{S_{XX}} \right).$$

(ii) $\hat{\beta}_1$ has a normal distribution with mean β_1 and variance $\text{Var}(\hat{\beta}_1) = \sigma^2/S_{XX}$.

(iii) $\text{Cov}(\hat{\beta}_0, \hat{\beta}_1) = \sigma^2(-\overline{X}/S_{XX})$.

(iv)   Residual SS, $RSS = S_{YY} - (S_{XY}^2/S_{XX})$, then RSS/σ^2 has a χ^2 distribution with $(n-2)$ df and $\hat{\sigma}^2 = RSS/(n-2)$ is an unbiased estimator for σ^2.

(v)   If we substitute $\hat{\sigma}^2$ for σ^2 in $V(\hat{\beta}_0)$ and $V(\hat{\beta}_1)$ given in (i) and (ii), we obtain the estimated variances

$$\hat{V}\text{ar}(\hat{\beta}_0) = \hat{\sigma}^2 \left(\frac{1}{n} + \frac{\overline{X}^2}{S_{XX}} \right),$$

and

$$\hat{V}\text{ar}(\hat{\beta}_1) = \frac{\hat{\sigma}^2}{S_{XX}}$$

where $\hat{\sigma}^2 = \frac{\sum_{i=1}^{n} e_i^2}{(n-2)}$ is the mean square residual denoted by $s^2 = \frac{\sum_{i=1}^{n} \left(Y_i - \hat{Y}_i \right)^2}{(n-2)}$, which is an unbiased estimator of σ^2.

Test statistics for the regression parameters are

$$T = \frac{\hat{\beta}_0 - \beta_0}{se(\hat{\beta}_0)} \sim t_{n-2}$$

$$T = \frac{\hat{\beta}_1 - \beta_1}{se(\hat{\beta}_1)} \sim t_{n-2}.$$

Therefore, a $100(1-\alpha)\%$ confidence interval on the slope β_1 is given by

$$\hat{\beta}_1 - t_{(n-2),1-\alpha/2}se(\hat{\beta}_1) \leq \beta_1 \leq \hat{\beta}_1 + t_{(n-2),1-\alpha/2}se(\hat{\beta}_1).$$

Similarly, a $100(1-\alpha)\%$ confidence interval on the intercept β_0 is given by

$$\hat{\beta}_0 - t_{(n-2),1-\alpha/2}se(\hat{\beta}_0) \leq \beta_0 \leq \hat{\beta}_0 + t_{(n-2),1-\alpha/2}se(\hat{\beta}_0).$$

The interpretation of confidence interval for parameters β_1 and β_0: If we repeat taking samples of size n from the same population very large number of times and if we construct confidence interval for each parameter from each sample then the proportion of those intervals that will include the true population value (β_1 in the first confidence interval and β_0 in the second interval) is $1 - \alpha$.

If the errors are normally and independently distributed then the sampling distribution of

$$\frac{(n-2)MS_{\text{Res}}}{\sigma^2} \sim \chi^2_{n-2}.$$

Thus,

$P[\chi^2_{(n-2),\alpha/2} \leq \frac{(n-2)MS_{\text{Res}}}{\sigma^2} \leq \chi^2_{(n-2),1-\alpha/2}] = 1 - \alpha$. and consequently a $100(1 -$ $\alpha)\%$ confidence interval on σ^2 is

$$P\left[\frac{(n-2)MS_{\text{Res}}}{\chi^2_{(n-2),1-\alpha/2}} \leq \sigma^2 \leq \frac{(n-2)MS_{\text{Res}}}{\chi^2_{(n-2),\alpha/2}}\right] = 1 - \alpha.$$

9.4.9   Interval Estimation of Mean Response

In many situations of applications of regression models, the estimation of mean response is of major concern. This problem involves estimation of the mean response, $E(Y)$, for a given value of the independent variable, X. For example, let X_0 be the given value of X for which we wish to estimate the mean response, say $E(Y|X_0)$. Let us assume that X_0 is any value within the range of the sample data on the independent variable, X. The expected value, $E(Y|X_0)$, is

$$\widehat{E}(Y|X_0) = \hat{\beta}_0 + \hat{\beta}_1 X_0.$$

To obtain a $100(1 - \alpha)\%$ confidence interval of $E(Y|X_0)$, we need to find the sampling distribution of $\widehat{E}(Y|X_0)$. It can be shown that

$$E(Y|X_0) = \beta_0 + \beta_1 X_0$$

and the variance of $\widehat{E}(Y|X_0)$ is

$$\begin{aligned}
\text{Var}[\widehat{E}(Y|X_0)] &= \text{Var}[\overline{Y} + \hat{\beta}_1(X_0 - \overline{X})] \\
&= \frac{\sigma^2}{n} + \frac{\sigma^2(X_0 - \overline{X})^2}{SS_X} \\
&= \sigma^2\left[\frac{1}{n} + \frac{(X_0 - \overline{X})^2}{SS_X}\right].
\end{aligned}$$

Then, it follows that

$$\widehat{E}(Y|X_0) = \hat{\beta}_0 + \hat{\beta}_1 X_0 \sim N\left(\beta_0 + \beta_1 X_0, \sigma^2\left[\frac{1}{n} + \frac{(X_0 - \overline{X})^2}{SS_X}\right]\right).$$

It can be shown that $\text{cov}(\overline{Y}, \hat{\beta}_1) = 0$. Thus, the sampling distribution of

$$T = \frac{\widehat{E}(Y/X_0) - E(Y/X_0)}{\sqrt{MS_{\text{Res}}\left(\frac{1}{n} + \frac{(X_0 - \overline{X})^2}{SS_X}\right)}}$$

is t with $n - 2$ degrees of freedom. Consequently, a $100(1 - \alpha)\%$ confidence interval on the mean response at the point $X = X_0$ is

$$\widehat{E}(Y/X_0) - t_{(n-2),1-\alpha/2}\sqrt{MS_{\text{Res}}\left(\frac{1}{n} + \frac{(X_0 - \overline{X})^2}{SS_X}\right)} \leq E(Y/X_0)$$

$$\leq \widehat{E}(Y/X_0) + t_{(n-2),1-\alpha/2}\sqrt{MS_{\text{Res}}\left(\frac{1}{n} + \frac{(X_0 - \overline{X})^2}{SS_X}\right)}.$$

Interval Estimation of Prediction

Let the regression equation be

$$\widehat{Y} = \hat{\beta}_0 + \hat{\beta}_1 X$$

is used for predicting Y for given values of X.

Let X_F be a future value of X. Then, we predict the corresponding value of Y by

$$\widehat{Y}_F = \hat{\beta}_0 + \hat{\beta}_1 X_F.$$

The true value of Y_F is

$$Y_F = \beta_0 + \beta_1 X_F + \varepsilon_F.$$

Hence, the prediction error is

$$\widehat{Y}_F - Y_F = (\hat{\beta}_0 - \beta_0) + (\hat{\beta}_1 - \beta_1)X_F - \varepsilon_F$$

and

$$E(\widehat{Y}_F - Y_F) = E(\hat{\beta}_0 - \beta_0) + E(\hat{\beta}_1 - \beta_1)X_F - E(\varepsilon_F) = 0.$$

Then, the variance is

$$\begin{aligned}
\mathrm{Var}(\widehat{Y}_F - Y_F) &= \mathrm{Var}(\hat{\beta}_0 - \beta_0) + X_F^2 \mathrm{Var}(\hat{\beta}_1 - \beta_1) \\
&\quad + 2X_F \mathrm{Cov}(\hat{\beta}_0 - \beta_0, \hat{\beta}_1 - \beta_1) + \mathrm{Var}(\varepsilon_F) \\
&= \sigma^2 \left(\frac{1}{n} + \frac{\overline{X}^2}{S_{XX}} \right) + \sigma^2 \cdot \frac{X_F^2}{S_{XX}} - 2X_F \sigma^2 \cdot \frac{\overline{X}}{S_{XX}} + \sigma^2 \\
&= \sigma^2 \left[1 + \frac{1}{n} + \frac{(X_F - \overline{X})^2}{S_{XX}} \right].
\end{aligned}$$

The estimated variance is

$$\widehat{\mathrm{Var}}(\widehat{Y}_F - Y_F) = MS_{\mathrm{Res}} \left[1 + \frac{1}{n} + \frac{(X_F - \overline{X})^2}{S_{XX}} \right].$$

Consequently, a $100(1 - \alpha)\%$ prediction interval on a future observation at the point $X = X_F$ is

$$\widehat{Y}_F - t_{(n-2),1-\alpha/2} \sqrt{MS_{\mathrm{Res}} \left(1 + \frac{1}{n} + \frac{(X_F - \overline{X})^2}{SS_X} \right)} \leq Y_F$$

$$\leq \widehat{Y}_F + t_{(n-2),1-\alpha/2} \sqrt{MS_{\mathrm{Res}} \left(1 + \frac{1}{n} + \frac{(X_F - \overline{X})^2}{SS_X} \right)}$$

The prediction interval widens with an increase in the distance between X_F and $\overline{X}$ and is minimum at $X = X_F$.

9.4.10 Coefficient of Determination of the Regression Model

The coefficient of determination is a quantitative measure used to evaluate the appropriateness and the adequacy of fitting the assumed regression model to the sample data in terms of the performance of the model in explaining the variation in Y.

The coefficient of determination is denoted by R^2. It measures the proportion of variation in the values of Y that can be explained by the regression model. The total variation in the values of Y is measured by the quantity $\sum_{i=1}^{n} (Y_i - \overline{Y})^2$.

The coefficient of determination is defined by

$$R^2 = \frac{\sum_{i=1}^{n} (\hat{Y}_i - \bar{Y})^2}{\sum_{i=1}^{n} (Y_i - \bar{Y})^2} = \frac{SS_{\text{Reg}}}{SS_{\text{Total}}}$$

where

$$\hat{Y}_i = \hat{\beta}_0 + \hat{\beta}_1 X_i, \quad i = 1, 2, \ldots, n.$$

Alternatively,

$$R^2 = 1 - \frac{\sum_{i=1}^{n} (Y_i - \hat{Y}_i)^2}{\sum_{i=1}^{n} (Y_i - \bar{Y})^2} = 1 - \frac{SS_{\text{Res}}}{SS_{\text{Total}}}.$$

The coefficient of determination, R^2, can be shown as the squared correlation between Y and $\hat{Y}$ and it measures the proportion of total variation about the mean $\bar{Y}$ explained by the regression model. If we multiply the coefficient of multiple determination by 100 then it interprets percentage of total variation about the mean explained by the regression model. The coefficient of determination ranges between 0 and 1, a value near zero indicates that the regression model either fails or performs poorly to explain the total variation and a value near 1 indicates that the regression model explains the total variation either with near perfection or performs very well. A large value of R^2 shows that the regression model performs strongly in explaining the variation of the response variable by the explanatory variable included in the model.

Some important characteristics of R^2 are summarized below.

1. The value of R^2 is between zero and one, both inclusive, i.e., $0 \le R^2 \le 1$.
2. The larger the value of R^2 the better the regression model explains the variation of Y.
3. Large values of R^2 indicate that the regression model fits the observation very well. Small values of R^2 indicate that the regression model does not fit the observation well.
4. If $R^2 = 1$, then the regression model explains all variations of Y, which means that all observations lie on the regression line, i.e., there is a perfect correlation between Y and X.
5. If $R^2 = 0$, then the regression model cannot explain the variation of Y at all, which means there is no linear relationship between Y and X.
6. We can show that

$$R^2 = 1 - \frac{\sum_{i=1}^{n} (Y_i - \hat{Y}_i)^2}{\sum_{i=1}^{n} (Y_i - \bar{Y})^2}$$

which implies that if the residual sum of squares decreases then R^2 increases and if the residual sum of squares increases then R^2 decreases. This provides the fundamental measure of the fit of a regression model to the sample data.

Example 9.5

For the data in the previous example, let us illustrate the interval estimation of parameters and tests for the model and parameters. The following results are summarized from the previous example:

$$\bar{x} = 86.225, \quad \bar{y} = 10.65, \quad S_{xy} = 205.14, \quad S_{xx} = 1090.28.$$

We can also compute the total sum of squares of the dependent variable Y from the sample data as

$$S_{yy} = \sum_{i=1}^{n} (y_i - \bar{y})^2$$

$$= \sum_{i=1}^{n} y_i^2 - n\bar{y}^2$$

$$= 45.309.$$

The estimates of regression parameters are $\hat{\beta}_0 = -5.5775$ and $\hat{\beta}_1 = 0.1882$. The fitted model is

$$\widehat{Y}_i = -5.5775 + 0.1882X_i$$

and the model for observed Y is

$$Y_i = \hat{\beta}_0 + \hat{\beta}_1 X_i + e_i$$
$$= -5.5775 + 0.1882X_i + e_i.$$

The estimated error can be obtained as

$$e_i = Y_i - (-5.5775 + 0.1882X_i).$$

Table 9.7 provides necessary calculations for estimating the variance.

We know that the unbiased estimator of the population variance σ^2 is the mean square error s^2 from the sample data. The mean square error computed from the sample data is shown below

$$s^2 = \frac{\sum_{i=1}^{n} (y_i - \hat{y}_i)^2}{n-2} = \frac{6.7104}{10} = 0.67104.$$

The error sum of squares is 6.7104.

Table 9.7 Height (*X*) and Weight (*Y*) of 12 children under 5 years of age and calculations necessary for estimating the variance

x Height (cm)	y Weight (kg)	$\hat{y}$	e_i	e_i^2
72.1	7.4	7.99172	−0.59172	0.350133
93.5	11.3	12.0192	−0.7192	0.517249
78.9	9.8	9.27148	0.52852	0.279333
85.2	12.1	10.45714	1.64286	2.698989
89.1	11.6	11.19112	0.40888	0.167183
100.3	13.2	13.29896	−0.09896	0.009793
92.5	11.5	11.831	−0.331	0.109561
93.5	12.2	12.0192	0.1808	0.032689
97.7	12.3	12.80964	-0.50964	0.259733
79.9	10.5	9.45968	1.04032	1.082266
83.2	9.3	10.08074	−0.78074	0.609555
68.8	6.6	7.37066	−0.77066	0.593917
$\sum x = 1034.7$	$\sum y = 127.8$	$\sum \hat{y}_i = 127.08$		6.7104

Subtracting the error sum of squares from the total sum of squares of *Y*, we obtain the regression sum of squares for the model which is

the regression sum of squares = $\sum_{i=1}^{n} (\hat{y}_i - \bar{y})^2$
= s_{yy} − error sum of squares
= 45.309 − 6.710 = 38.599.

A 95% confidence interval for β_1 using the sample data is obtained by computing

$$\hat{\beta}_1 \pm t_{(n-2),1-\alpha/2}\sqrt{\frac{s^2}{s_{XX}}}$$

which is

$$0.1882 \pm t_{10,0.975}\sqrt{\frac{0.67104}{1090.28}}$$
$$= 0.1882 \pm 2.228 \times 0.0248$$
$$= 0.1882 \pm 0.0553.$$

The 95% confidence interval for β_1 is (0.1329, 0.2453) and notice that the interval does not include the null value.

(ii) Calculating the coefficient of determination (R^2)

(a) First method: using the formula $R^2 = \sum_{i=1}^{n} (\hat{Y}_i - \bar{Y})^2 / \sum_{i=1}^{n} (Y_i - \bar{Y})^2$:

$$R^2 = \frac{\sum_{i=1}^{n} (\widehat{Y}_i - \overline{Y})^2}{\sum_{i=1}^{n} (Y_i - \overline{Y})^2} = \frac{38.599}{45.309} = 0.8519.$$

The positive square root of the coefficient of determination is

$$R = 0.9229.$$

Since the value of coefficient of determination is $R^2 = 0.8519$, we conclude that 85% of the total variation in the values of Y can be explained by the regression model.

(b) Second method: using the formula $R^2 = r^2$:

In a previous example, we have found that the Pearson's coefficient of correlation is $r = +0.9229$. Therefore, the coefficient of determination is

$$R^2 = r^2 = (+0.9229)^2 = 0.8519.$$

9.4.11 Tests for the Parameters

The tests for the regression parameters are illustrated using the sample data. The null and alternative hypotheses for β_1 are

$$H_0: \beta_1 = 0$$

$$H_1: \beta_1 \neq 0$$

where a two-sided alternative is specified. Here the error ε_i is $NID(0, \sigma^2)$, the random variables Y_i is $NID(\beta_0 + \beta_1 X_i, \sigma^2)$. The test statistic is

$$Z = \frac{\widehat{\beta}_1 - 0}{\sqrt{\sigma^2 / S_{XX}}}$$

if σ^2 is known. However, as σ^2 is unknown and we know that $MS_{Res} = s^2$ is an unbiased estimator of σ^2, the test statistic for unknown variance is

$$T = \frac{\widehat{\beta}_1 - \beta_{10}}{\sqrt{MS_{Res} / S_{XX}}}$$

which follows a t_{n-2} distribution if the null hypothesis is true. The degree of freedom associated with t is the degree of freedom associated with MS_{Res}. We may reject the null hypothesis if

$$|t| > t_{(n-2),1-\alpha/2}.$$

Therefore, the value of t statistic from the sample data is

$$t = \frac{\hat{\beta}_1 - 0}{se(\hat{\beta}_1)}$$

$$= \frac{\hat{\beta}_1}{\sqrt{s^2/S_{xx}}}$$

$$= \frac{0.1882}{\sqrt{0.6710/1090.28}}$$

$$= 7.5862$$

and the critical values are $t_{10,0.025} = -2.228$ and $t_{10,0.975} = 2.228$. The test statistic value falls in the critical region so the null hypothesis of no relationship between height and weight of children under 5 years of age may be rejected.

Similarly, to test hypothesis about the intercept

$$H_0: \beta_0 = 0$$

$$H_1: \beta_0 \neq 0$$

we can use the test statistic

$$T = \frac{\hat{\beta}_0 - 0}{\sqrt{MS_{Res}\left(\frac{1}{n} + \frac{\bar{x}^2}{S_{XX}}\right)}} = \frac{\hat{\beta}_0}{s\hat{e}(\hat{\beta}_0)}$$

where $s\hat{e}(\hat{\beta}_0) = \sqrt{MS_{Res}(1/n + \bar{X}^2/S_{XX})}$ is the standard error of the intercept. We may reject the null hypothesis if

$$|t| > t_{(n-2),1-\alpha/2}.$$

We can compute the value of the test statistic using the sample data

$$t = \frac{\hat{\beta}_0}{\sqrt{MS_{Res}\left(\frac{1}{n} + \frac{\bar{x}^2}{S_{xx}}\right)}}$$

$$= \frac{-5.5775}{\sqrt{0.6710\left(\frac{1}{12} + \frac{(86.225)^2}{1090.28}\right)}}$$

$$= -2.5917$$

and we have shown that the critical values are $t_{10,0.025} = -2.228$ and $t_{10,0.975} = 2.228$. This test also shows that the null hypothesis may be rejected because the test statistic value from the sample data falls in the critical at 5% level of significance.

9.4.12   Testing Significance of Regression

The test for model, in case of the simple regression is similar to testing the t-test performed for the regression parameter, β_1. The null and alternative hypotheses are

$$H_0: \beta_1 = 0$$

$$H_1: \beta_1 \neq 0.$$

These hypotheses relate to the significance of regression. Failing to reject $H_0: \beta_1 = 0$ implies that there is no linear relationship between X and Y.

The test procedure for $H_0: \beta_1 = 0$ is shown for the sample data already. This is a special case for simple regression model only. To generalize the procedure for multiple regression model, we need to use the analysis of variance procedure which is illustrated below.

Analysis of Variance

The analysis of variance procedure is based on the components of variance from the fact that

Total SS = Regression SS + Error SS., which is expressed previously as

$$SS_{\text{Total}} = SS_{\text{Reg}} + SS_{\text{Res}}.$$

The test procedure is summarized in Table 9.8.

The test statistic for testing $H_0: \beta_1 = 0$ is

$$F = \frac{MS_{\text{Reg}}}{MS_{\text{Res}}} = \frac{38.599}{0.671} = 57.525$$

follows the $F_{1,10}$ distribution. The critical region is defined by

$$F > F_{0.05,1,10}$$

where $F_{0.05,1,10} = 4.96$. The test statistic value from the sample data is 57.525 that falls in the critical region, hence, we may reject the null hypothesis that there is no linear relationship between height and weight. It may be shown that $F_{0.05,1,10} = t^2_{0.025,10} = (2.228)^2 = 4.96$.

Table 9.8 The analysis of variance table for a simple regression model on height and weight of children under 5 years of age

Source of variation	Sum of square	df	Mean squares	F
Regression	38.599	1	38.599	57.525
Residual	6.710	10	0.671	
Total	45.309			

9.5 Multiple Linear Regression

A regression model that involves more than one regressor variable is called a multiple regression model. The simple regression model is introduced in previous sections and we extend the simple regression for several independent variables in this section, so that the regression model for an outcome variable can be expressed as a linear function of several explanatory variables. In many instances the outcome or response variable cannot be explained adequately by a single independent variable rather there may multiple factors that may cause change in the outcome variable. A multiple regression model that might describe this relationship is

$$E(Y|X_1, X_2, X_3) = \beta_0 + \beta_1 X_1 + \beta_2 X_2 + \beta_3 X_3$$

which can also be expressed in the following form for the random sample of variables Y, X_1, X_2 and X_3

$$Y = \beta_0 + \beta_1 X_1 + \beta_2 X_2 + \beta_3 X_3 + \varepsilon$$

where Y denotes the response variable, X_1, X_2 and X_3 denote the explanatory or independent variables 1, 2, and 3. This is the multiple linear regression model with three regressor variables. The term linear is used because the above equation is a linear function of the unknown parameters β_0, β_1 and β_2.

In general, the response Y may be related to k regressor or predictor variables. The model

$$Y = \beta_0 + \beta_1 X_1 + \cdots + \beta_k X_k + \varepsilon$$

is called a multiple linear regression model with k regressors. The parameters $\beta_j, j = 0, 1, 2, \ldots, k$ are called the regression coefficients. It is interesting to note as we have seen in case of a single regression model that the parameter β_j measures the expected change in the outcome Y per unit change in X_j keeping the remaining regressor variables $X_{j'} (j' \neq j)$ constant. Sometimes, we call these regression coefficients as partial coefficients.

A multiple linear regression model may be considered as an empirical function too, which is employed to approximate the true underlying relationships. Although the true functional relationship between $X_1, X_2, \ldots, X_k$ and Y is unknown the linear regression model can provide an adequate representation of the underlying linear relationship.

Models that are more complex in structure may often still be analyzed by multiple linear regression techniques. For example, consider the cubic polynomial model

$$Y = \beta_0 + \beta_1 X + \beta_2 X^2 + \beta_3 X^3 + \varepsilon.$$

If we let $X_1 = X, X_2 = X^2$, and $X_3 = X^3$, then the equation can be rewritten as

$$Y = \beta_0 + \beta_1 X_1 + \beta_2 X_2 + \beta_3 X_3 + \varepsilon$$

which is a multiple linear regression model with three regressor variables.

Models that include interaction effects may also be analyzed by multiple linear regression methods. For example, suppose that the model is

$$Y = \beta_0 + \beta_1 X_1 + \beta_2 X_2 + \beta_{12} X_1 X_2 + \varepsilon.$$

If we let $X_3 = X_1 X_2$ and $\beta_3 = \beta_{12}$, then the equation can be rewritten as

$$Y = \beta_0 + \beta_1 X_1 + \beta_2 X_2 + \beta_3 X_3 + \varepsilon$$

which is a linear regression model.

9.5.1   Estimation of the Model Parameters

The method of least squares can be used to estimate the regression coefficients . Suppose that $n > k$ observations are available, and let Y_i denote the ith observed response and X_{ij} denote the ith observation or level of regressor X_j. Let us assume that the error term ε in the model has $E(\varepsilon) = 0$ and $\text{Var}(\varepsilon) = \sigma^2$ and that the errors are uncorrelated.

Further, we assume that the regressor variables $X_1, X_2, \ldots, X_k$ are fixed variables. In representing a regression model, we consider the model as a conditional model as follows:

$$E(Y|X_1, \ldots, X_k) = \beta_0 + \beta_1 X_1 + \ldots + \beta_k X_k$$

where the model assumes that the values of $X_1, X_2, \ldots, X_k$ are supposed to be given. This model provides a relationship for average outcome for given values of the explanatory variables. In other words, the population model for showing the relationship between outcome and explanatory variables assume an average relationship between average outcome and fixed values of explanatory variables. The tests of hypotheses and construction of confidence intervals will require to assume that the conditional distribution of Y-given $X_1, X_2, \ldots, X_k$ be normal with mean

$\beta_0 + \beta_1 X_1 + \cdots + \beta_k X_k$ and variance σ^2.

We may write the regression model for the ith individual as

$$Y_i = \beta_0 + \beta_1 X_{i1} + \cdots + \beta_k X_{ik} + \varepsilon_i, \quad i = 1, \ldots, n$$

$$= \beta_0 + \sum_{j=1}^{k} \beta_j X_{ij} + \varepsilon_i, \quad i = 1, 2, \ldots \ldots, n.$$

The least squares function is

$$Q(\beta_0, \beta_1, \ldots, \beta_k) = \sum_{i=1}^{n} \varepsilon_i^2$$

$$= \sum_{i=1}^{n} \left(Y_i - \beta_0 - \sum_{j=1}^{k} \beta_j X_{ij} \right)^2$$

The function Q must be minimized with respect to $\beta_0, \beta_1, \ldots, \beta_k$. The least squares estimators of $\beta_0, \beta_1, \ldots, \beta_k$ must satisfy

$$\left. \frac{\partial Q}{\partial \beta_0} \right|_{\hat{\beta}_0, \hat{\beta}_1, \ldots, \hat{\beta}_k} = -2 \sum_{i=1}^{n} \left(Y_i - \hat{\beta}_0 - \sum_{j=1}^{k} \hat{\beta}_j X_{ij} \right) = 0$$

and

$$\left. \frac{\partial Q}{\partial \beta_j} \right|_{\hat{\beta}_0, \hat{\beta}_1, \ldots, \hat{\beta}_k} = -2 \sum_{i=1}^{n} \left(Y_i - \hat{\beta}_0 - \sum_{j=1}^{k} \hat{\beta}_j X_{ij} \right) X_{ij} = 0, \quad j = 1, 2, \ldots, k.$$

Simplifying the above equations, we obtain the least squares normal equations

$$n\hat{\beta}_0 + \hat{\beta}_1 \sum_{i=1}^{n} X_{i1} + \hat{\beta}_2 \sum_{i=1}^{n} X_{i2} + \cdots + \hat{\beta}_k \sum_{i=1}^{n} X_{ik} = \sum_{i=1}^{n} Y_i,$$

$$\hat{\beta}_0 \sum_{i=1}^{n} X_{i1} + \hat{\beta}_1 \sum_{i=1}^{n} X_{i1}^2 + \hat{\beta}_2 \sum_{i=1}^{n} X_{i1} X_{i2} + \cdots + \hat{\beta}_k \sum_{i=1}^{n} X_{i1} X_{ik} = \sum_{i=1}^{n} X_{i1} Y_i,$$

.

.

.

$$\hat{\beta}_0 \sum_{i=1}^{n} X_{ik} + \hat{\beta}_1 \sum_{i=1}^{n} X_{ik} X_{i1} + \hat{\beta}_2 \sum_{i=1}^{n} X_{ik} X_{i2} + \cdots + \hat{\beta}_k \sum_{i=1}^{n} X_{ik}^2 = \sum_{i=1}^{n} X_{ik} Y_i.$$

Note that there are $p = k + 1$ normal equations, one for each of the unknown regression coefficients. The solution to the normal equations will be the least squares estimators $\hat{\beta}_0, \hat{\beta}_1, \ldots, \hat{\beta}_k$.

In matrix notation, the model is

$$Y = X\beta + \varepsilon$$

where

$$Y = \begin{bmatrix} Y_1 \\ Y_2 \\ \cdot \\ \cdot \\ \cdot \\ Y_n \end{bmatrix},$$

$$X = \begin{bmatrix} 1 & X_{11} & X_{12} & \cdots & X_{1k} \\ 1 & X_{21} & X_{22} & \cdots & X_{2k} \\ \vdots & & & & \\ 1 & X_{n1} & X_{n2} & \cdots & X_{nk} \end{bmatrix},$$

$$\beta = \begin{bmatrix} \beta_0 \\ \beta_1 \\ \cdot \\ \cdot \\ \cdot \\ \beta_k \end{bmatrix}, \quad \varepsilon = \begin{bmatrix} \varepsilon_1 \\ \varepsilon_2 \\ \cdot \\ \cdot \\ \cdot \\ \varepsilon_n \end{bmatrix}.$$

In general, Y is an $n \times 1$ vector of the observations, X is an $n \times p$ matrix of the levels of the regressor variables, β is a $p \times 1$ vector of the regression coefficients, and ε is an $n \times 1$ vector of random errors.

We wish to find the vector of least squares estimators, $\hat{\beta}$, that minimizes

$$Q(\beta) = \sum_{i=1}^{n} \varepsilon_i^2 = \varepsilon'\varepsilon = (Y - X\beta)'(Y - X\beta).$$

Note that $Q(\beta)$ may be expressed as

$$Q(\beta) = Y'Y - \beta'X'Y - Y'X\beta + \beta'X'X\beta$$
$$= Y'Y - 2\beta'X'Y + \beta'X'X\beta$$

since $\beta'X'Y = Y'X\beta$ because these are scalars.

The least squares estimators must satisfy the following equations:

$$\left.\frac{\partial S}{\partial \beta}\right|_{\hat{\beta}} = -2X'Y + 2X'X\beta = 0$$

which simplifies to

$$X'X\beta = X'Y.$$

These equations are called the least squares normal equations. They are matrix analogue of the scalar presentations shown for simple regression model.

The matrix form of the normal equations are

$$
\begin{bmatrix}
n & \sum_{i=1}^{n} X_{i1} & \sum_{i=1}^{n} X_{i2} & \cdots & \sum_{i=1}^{n} X_{ik} \\
\sum_{i=1}^{n} X_{i1} & \sum_{i=1}^{n} X_{i1}^2 & \sum_{i=1}^{n} X_{i1}X_{i2} & \cdots & \sum_{i=1}^{n} X_{i1}X_{ik} \\
\vdots & & & & \\
\sum_{i=1}^{n} X_{ik} & \sum_{i=1}^{n} X_{ik}X_{i1} & \sum_{i=1}^{n} X_{ik}X_{i2} & \cdots & \sum_{i=1}^{n} X_{ik}^2
\end{bmatrix}
\begin{bmatrix}
\hat{\beta}_0 \\
\hat{\beta}_1 \\
\vdots \\
\hat{\beta}_k
\end{bmatrix}
=
\begin{bmatrix}
\sum_{i=1}^{n} Y_i \\
\sum_{i=1}^{n} X_{i1}Y_i \\
\vdots \\
\sum_{i=1}^{n} X_{ik}Y_i
\end{bmatrix}
$$

To solve the normal equations, let us multiply both sides by the inverse of $X'X$. Thus, the least squares estimator of β are

$$\hat{\beta} = (X'X)^{-1}(X'Y)$$

provided that the inverse matrix $(X'X)^{-1}$ exists. The $(X'X)^{-1}$ matrix will always exist if the regressors are linearly independent, that is, if no column of the X matrix is a linear combination of the other columns.

The fitted regression model corresponding to the levels of the regressor variables

$$X_i' = [1, X_{i1}, \ldots, X_{ik}]$$

is

$$\widehat{Y}_i = X_i\hat{\beta} = \hat{\beta}_0 + \sum_{j=1}^{k} \hat{\beta}_j X_{ij}.$$

By definition,

$$e_i = Y_i - \widehat{Y}_i.$$

Then, the n residuals may be conveniently written in matrix notation as

$$e = \begin{bmatrix} e_1 \\ e_2 \\ \vdots \\ e_n \end{bmatrix} = \begin{bmatrix} Y_1 - \widehat{Y}_1 \\ Y_2 - \widehat{Y}_2 \\ \vdots \\ Y_n - \widehat{Y}_n \end{bmatrix}.$$

9.5.2   Properties the Least Squares Estimators

The statistical properties of the least squares estimator $\widehat{\beta}$ may be easily demonstrated.

Unbiasedness

$$\begin{aligned} E(\widehat{\beta}) &= E[(X'X)^{-1}X'Y] \\ &= E[(X'X)^{-1}X'(X\beta + \varepsilon)] \\ &= E[(X'X)^{-1}X'X\beta + (X'X)^{-1}X'\varepsilon] = \beta \end{aligned}$$

since $E(\varepsilon) = 0$ and $(X'X)^{-1}X'X = I$. Thus $\widehat{\beta}$ is an unbiased estimator of β.

Variance–Covariance

The covariance matrix of $\widehat{\beta}$ is expressed by

$$\begin{aligned} \mathrm{Cov}(\widehat{\beta}) &= E[\widehat{\beta} - E(\widehat{\beta})][\widehat{\beta} - E(\widehat{\beta})]' \\ &= (X'X)^{-1}\sigma^2. \end{aligned}$$

Example 9.6

Using the matrix $(X'X)^{-1}$, we obtain variances and covariances for the simple linear regression as follows:

$$\text{cov}\left(\widehat{\beta}\right) = \text{cov}\begin{pmatrix} \widehat{\beta}_0 \\ \widehat{\beta}_1 \end{pmatrix} = \begin{pmatrix} \text{var}\left(\widehat{\beta}_0\right) & \text{cov}\left(\widehat{\beta}_0, \widehat{\beta}_1\right) \\ \text{cov}\left(\widehat{\beta}_0, \widehat{\beta}_1\right) & \text{var}\left(\widehat{\beta}_1\right) \end{pmatrix}$$

$$= \sigma^2 (X'X)^{-1}$$

$$= \frac{\sigma^2}{n\sum_{i=1}^n X_i^2 - \left(\sum_{i=1}^n X_i\right)^2} \begin{pmatrix} \sum_{i=1}^n X_i^2 & -\sum_{i=1}^n X_i \\ -\sum_{i=1}^n X_i & n \end{pmatrix}$$

$$= \frac{\sigma^2}{n\sum_{i=1}^n (X_i - \overline{X})^2} \begin{pmatrix} \sum_{i=1}^n X_i^2/n & -\overline{X} \\ -\overline{X} & 1 \end{pmatrix}.$$

Hence,

$$\text{var}\left(\widehat{\beta}_0\right) = \frac{\sigma^2 \sum_{i=1}^n X_i^2/n}{\sum_{i=1}^n (X_i - \overline{X})^2},$$

$$\text{var}\left(\widehat{\beta}_1\right) = \frac{\sigma^2}{\sum_{i=1}^n (X_i - \overline{X})^2},$$

$$\text{cov}\left(\widehat{\beta}_0, \widehat{\beta}_1\right) = \frac{-\sigma^2 \overline{X}}{\sum_{i=1}^n (X_i - \overline{X})^2}.$$

The least squares estimator $\widehat{\beta}$ is the best linear unbiased estimator of β. If we further assume that the errors ε_i are normally distributed, then $\widehat{\beta}$ is also the maximum likelihood estimator of β. The maximum likelihood estimator is minimum variance unbiased estimator of β.

As in simple linear regression, we may show that residual mean square is an unbiased estimator of σ^2.

Let us define the sum of squares of residual as

$$SS_{\text{Res}} = \sum_{i=1}^n (Y_i - \widehat{Y}_i)^2$$

$$= \sum_{i=1}^n e_i^2 = e'e.$$

Then it can be shown that

$$E(SS_{\text{Res}}) = (n - p)\sigma^2.$$

So

$$E(MS_{\text{Res}}) = E\left(\frac{SS_{\text{Res}}}{n-p}\right) = \sigma^2.$$

The unbiased estimator of the variance is

$$\hat{\sigma}^2 = MS_{\text{Res}} = \frac{SS_{\text{Res}}}{(n-p)}.$$

9.5.3 The Coefficient of Multiple Determination

The coefficient of multiple determination is introduced in the coefficient of determination and is defined by

$$R^2 = \frac{\sum_{i=1}^{n}(\hat{Y}_i - \bar{Y})^2}{\sum_{i=1}^{n}(Y_i - \bar{Y})^2} = \frac{SS_{\text{Reg}}}{SS_{\text{Total}}}$$

where $\hat{Y}_i = \hat{\beta}_0 + \hat{\beta}_1 X_{i1} + \cdots + \hat{\beta}_k X_{ik}, i = 1, 2, \ldots, n$.

As we have seen earlier for a simple regression model, alternatively, R^2 can be expressed as

$$R^2 = 1 - \frac{\sum_{i=1}^{n}(Y_i - \hat{Y}_i)^2}{\sum_{i=1}^{n}(Y_i - \bar{Y})^2} = 1 - \frac{SS_{\text{Res}}}{SS_{\text{Total}}}.$$

The R^2 measures the proportion of total variation about the mean $\bar{Y}$ explained by the fitted regression model $\hat{Y}_i = \hat{\beta}_0 + \hat{\beta}_1 X_{i1} + \cdots + \hat{\beta}_k X_{ik}, i = 1, 2, \ldots, n$. The regression sum of squares is $\hat{\beta}'X'Y$ due to coefficients β_0 and β_1 and if we consider the sum of squares for regression model given β_0, the regression sum of squares can be shown as $\hat{\beta}'X'Y - n\bar{Y}^2$ and the corrected total sum of squares is $Y'Y - n\bar{Y}^2$. Using these notations, the coefficient of multiple determination is

$$R^2 = \frac{\hat{\beta}'X'Y - n\bar{Y}^2}{Y'Y - n\bar{Y}^2}.$$

Some Properties of
R^2 and R

1. The range of R^2 is $0 \le R^2 \le 1$.
2. $R = r_{Y\hat{Y}}$; that is, the multiple correlation is equal to the simple correlation between observed Y and $\hat{Y}$.

3. By including an additional variable to the regression model the value of R^2 can be increased.
4. If the explanatory variables are mutually orthogonal, then R^2 can be partitioned into k components.
5. R^2 is invariant to linear transformations on X and scale change on Y.

9.5.4 Tests for Significance of Regression

The test for significance of regression is a test to determine if there is a linear relationship between the response Y and any of the regressors $X_1, X_2, \ldots, X_k$. This procedure is often thought of as an overall or global test of model adequacy. The appropriate hypotheses are

$$H_0: \beta_1 = \beta_2 = \cdots = \beta_k = 0$$

$$H_1: \beta_j \neq 0 \text{ for at least one } j.$$

Rejection of the null hypothesis implies that at least one of the regressors $X_1, X_2, \ldots, X_k$ contributes significantly to the model.

The test procedure is a generalization of the analysis of variance used in simple linear regression. The total SS is partitioned into two components:

$$SS_T = SS_{\text{Reg}} + SS_{\text{Res}}.$$

If the null hypothesis is true then

$$\frac{SS_{\text{Reg}}}{\sigma^2} \approx \chi_k^2$$

and

$$\frac{SS_{\text{Res}}}{\sigma^2} \approx \chi_{n-k-1}^2.$$

Hence,

$$F = \frac{SS_{\text{Reg}}/k}{SS_{\text{Res}}/(n-k-1)} = \frac{MS_{\text{Reg}}}{MS_{\text{Res}}} \approx F_{k,n-k-1}.$$

The partitioning of total variation is shown in the analysis of variance table for total variation about mean or the corrected total sum of squares (Table 9.9)

$$SS_T = SS_{\text{Reg}} + SS_{\text{Res}}$$

Table 9.9 Analysis of variance table for the regression model

Source of variation	Sum of squares	df	Mean squares	F
Regression	$SS_{\text{Reg}} = \hat{\beta}'S_{XY} - n\bar{Y}^2$	k	SS_{Reg}/k	$MS_{\text{Reg}}/MS_{\text{Res}}$
Residual	$SS_{\text{Res}} = SS_T - \hat{\beta}'S_{Xy}$	$n - k - 1$	$SS_{\text{Res}}/(n - k - 1)$	
Total	$SS_T = Y'Y - n\bar{Y}^2$	$n - 1$		

where

$$SS_{\text{Total}} = Y'Y - \frac{\left(\sum Y_i\right)^2}{n},$$

$$SS_{\text{Reg}} = \hat{\beta}'X'Y - \frac{\left(\sum Y_i\right)^2}{n},$$

and

$$SS_{\text{Res}} = Y'Y - \hat{\beta}'X'Y.$$

9.5.5   Tests on Regression Coefficients

Once we reject the null hypothesis H_0: $\beta_1 = \beta_2 = \cdots = \beta_k = 0$ then it is logical to perform tests on every regression coefficient in the regression model to identify the explanatory variables having statistically significant relationship with the response variable. It is important to keep in mind that with inclusion of an additional variable the regression sum of squares always increases and residual sum of squares decreases. However, a good model needs to satisfy an important criterion of modeling the data which is: if with a minimum number of variables in a model that provides the explanatory power equal to or close to the models with additional variables that indicates that the additional variables would not increase the explanatory power of the model significantly rather will result in increase in the variance of the fitted value and also the residual mean square. Hence, it is needed to test for the significance of each regression coefficient in the model to identify the variables which contribute significantly and which do not.

The hypotheses for testing the significance of any individual regression coefficient are

$$H_0: \beta_j = 0 \quad \text{and} \quad H_1: \beta_j \neq 0.$$

The test statistic for this hypothesis is

$$T = \frac{\hat{\beta}_j - \beta_j}{se(\hat{\beta}_j)} \approx t_{n-k-1}$$

which can be expressed under the null hypothesis as

$$T = \frac{\hat{\beta}_j}{\sqrt{\hat{\sigma}^2 C_{jj}}} = \frac{\hat{\beta}_j}{se(\hat{\beta}_j)}$$

where C_{jj} is the diagonal element of $(X'X)^{-1}$ corresponding to $\hat{\beta}_j$. The null hypothesis H_0: $\beta_j = 0$ is rejected if $|t| > t_{(n-k-1),1-\alpha/2}$. Therefore, a $100(1 - \alpha)\%$ confidence interval on regression coefficient β_j is given by

$$\hat{\beta}_j - t_{\alpha/2,n-2}se(\hat{\beta}_j) \leq \beta_j \leq \hat{\beta}_j + t_{\alpha/2,n-2}se(\hat{\beta}_j).$$

9.5.6 Confidence Interval for Mean Response

We may construct a confidence interval on the mean response at a particular point, such as $X_{01}, X_{02}, \ldots, X_{0k}$ where the values of variables are within the range of the values in the sample data. Let us define the vector X_0 as

$$X_0 = \begin{bmatrix} 1 \\ X_{01} \\ X_{02} \\ \vdots \\ X_{0k} \end{bmatrix}$$

The fitted value at this point is

$$\hat{Y}_0 = \hat{X}_0 \hat{\beta}.$$

This is an unbiased estimator of $E(Y/X_0)$, since $E(\hat{Y}_0) = X_0'\beta = E(Y|X_0)$, and the variance of $\hat{Y}_0$ is

$$\mathrm{Var}(\hat{Y}_0) = \sigma^2 X_0'(X'X)^{-1}X_0.$$

Therefore, a $100(1 - \alpha)$ percent confidence interval on the mean response at the point $X_{01}, X_{02}, \ldots, X_{0k}$ is

$$\hat{Y}_0 - t_{\alpha/2,n-p}\sqrt{\hat{\sigma}^2 X_0'(X'X)^{-1}X_0} \leq E(Y/X_0) \leq \hat{Y}_0 + t_{\alpha/2,n-p}\sqrt{\hat{\sigma}^2 X_0'(X'X)^{-1}X_0}$$

9.5.7   Prediction of New Observations

The regression model can be used to predict future observations on Y corresponding to particular values of the regressor variables, for example, $X_{F1}, X_{F2}, \ldots\ldots, X_{Fk}$. If $X_F' = [1, X_{F1}, X_{F2}, \ldots\ldots, X_{Fk}]$, then a point estimate of the future observation Y_F at the point $X_{F1}, X_{F2}, \ldots\ldots, X_{Fk}$ is

$$\widehat{Y}_F = X_F' \hat{\beta}.$$

A $100(1 - \alpha)$ percent confidence interval for this future observation at the point $X_{F1}, X_{F2}, \ldots, X_{Fk}$ is

$$\widehat{Y}_F - t_{(n-k-1),1-\alpha/2} \sqrt{\hat{\sigma}^2 (1 + X_F'(X'X)^{-1} X_F)} \leq Y_F)$$
$$\leq \widehat{Y}_F + t_{(n-k-1),1-\alpha/2} \sqrt{\hat{\sigma}^2 (1 + X_F'(X'X)^{-1} X_F)}$$

Example 9.7

The data set used for this application is 5% random sample from the first wave of the Health and Retirement Study (HRS 2010). The outcome variable is weight (in kg) of the respondents and the independent variables are height (in cm), gender (male = 1, female = 0), sum of conditions (0, ..., 5) ever had. The selected sample size is 301.

In this example, a multiple linear regression model is fitted. The study was conducted on elderly people. The outcome variable is weight (Y) and the explanatory variables are height (X_1), gender (X_2, 1 for male and 0 for female), and number of health conditions ever had (X_3). The regression model is

$$E(Y|X_1, X_2, X_3) = \beta_0 + \beta_1 X_1 + \beta_2 X_2 + \beta_3 X_3.$$

This model can be expressed in the following form too

$$Y = \beta_0 + \beta_1 X_1 + \beta_2 X_2 + \beta_3 X_3 + \varepsilon.$$

The least squares estimates of the parameters are

$$\hat{\beta}_0 = -50.127, \hat{\beta}_1 = 0.751, \hat{\beta}_2 = -4.309 \text{ and } \hat{\beta}_3 = 1.123.$$

To test for the regression model, the null hypothesis is

$$H_0: \beta_1 = \beta_2 = \beta_3 = 0$$

and the alternative hypothesis can be stated as at least one of the regression coefficients is not zero. The analysis of variance table shows that the null hypothesis can be rejected and there is evidence that one or more of the explanatory variables are significantly associated with weight of elderly people. The value of the test statistic, F, from the sample data is 49.357 (p-value < 0.001). The value of R^2 is 0.333 which implies that 33% of the total variation in the outcome variable can be explained by the regression model considered in this example. Alternatively, it can be said that two-thirds of the variation remains unexplained although the model appears to be a statistically significant one. The search for the best possible model needs to be in the list of priorities to delineate possible strategies by a researcher.

As the overall model appears to be significant, we need to find the variables that are significantly associated with weight of elderly people. The null and alternative hypotheses for testing the significance of three regression coefficients are (Table 9.10)

$$H_{01}: \beta_1 = 0, \quad H_{11}: \beta_1 \neq 0,$$
$$H_{02}: \beta_2 = 0, \quad H_{12}: \beta_2 \neq 0,$$
$$H_{03}: \beta_3 = 0, \quad H_{13}: \beta_3 \neq 0.$$

From the analysis of variance table, we observe that height is significantly and positively associated (p-value < 0.001) with weight. Gender appears to have a negative association with weight, males demonstrate lower weight compared to

Table 9.10 Estimation and tests on the fit of multiple regression model for weight of elderly people

A. Coefficient of multiple determination

R	R square	Adjusted R square	Std. error of the estimate	Durbin–Watson
0.577	0.333	0.326	13.351	2.131

B. ANOVA table

Model	Sum of squares	df	Mean square	F	Sig.
Regression	26393.106	3	8797.702	49.357	0.000
Residual	52938.618	297	178.245		
Total	79331.724	300			

C. Parameter estimates of multiple regression model

Model	$\hat{\beta}$		t-value	p-value	95.0% confidence interval for $\hat{\beta}$	
	B	Std. error			Lower bound	Upper bound
Intercept	−50.127	20.551	−2.439	0.015	−90.571	−9.683
Height	0.751	0.116	6.486	0.000	0.523	0.979
Gender	−4.309	2.312	−1.864	0.063	−8.858	0.240
Number of conditions ever had	1.123	0.730	1.540	0.125	−0.313	2.559

females at older age (p-value = 0.063) but null hypothesis that there is no association between number of conditions ever had and weight may not be rejected. The 95% confidence intervals are also included in the table.

9.6 Summary

The concepts of correlation and regression are introduced in this chapter. The measures of correlation are discussed for both Pearson's product moment and Spearman's rank correlation and the important properties of correlation coefficient are discussed with examples. The estimation and test procedures for population correlation coefficient are illustrated. Both the simple and multiple regression models are also introduced with necessary theoretical background with examples. The method of least squares is demonstrated for estimating regression parameters. The variances are obtained and unbiased estimator of the variance are shown. The properties of estimators of regression parameters are also highlighted. The coefficient of multiple determination, the F tests for a regression model and Wald tests for testing the significance of regression parameters are illustrated. The analysis of variance and the components of variance are shown too. The extra sum of squares principle is also introduced in this chapter. The procedures of constructing the confidence intervals of the regression parameters are included in this chapter. This is a self-explanatory chapter on the concepts and techniques of correlation and regression with many illustrations.

Exercises

9.1 (i) Define the coefficient of correlation with an example.

(ii) Consider the following data on weight of women in kg (Y) and height in cm (X).

The sample size is 20.

(iii) Find the correlation between X and Y and interpret your result.

(iv) Test for the null and alternative hypotheses: $H_0: \rho = 0.5, H_1: \rho \neq 0.5$.

(v) Construct the 95% confidence interval of the population correlation coefficient.

X	Y
148.1	46.4
158.1	53.2
158.1	52.8
151.4	42.0
152.9	50.8
159.1	43.0
151.0	51.9
158.2	59.2

(continued)

(continued)

X	Y
148.2	55.1
147.3	38.9
145.6	49.7
155.1	49.9
155.2	43.1
149.7	42.2
147.0	52.7
152.2	49.8
149.1	50.7
145.2	44.8
145.9	49.2
149.7	47.7

9.2 (i) Define a simple regression model. What are the assumptions?

(ii) Obtain the least squares estimators of the parameters of the simple regression model.

(iii) Obtain the least squares estimates of the parameters of a simple regression model using data in 9.1(ii). Consider Y as the dependent and X as the independent variable. Interpret your results.

9.3 (i) Define the Pearson's coefficient of correlation and show that it does not depend on the change in origin and scale.

(ii) Find the Pearson's coefficient from the following data and comment on the relationship between X and Y:

X	Y
1	3
2	4
3	6
2	5
1	2

9.4 (i) Write the population and estimated simple regression model. What are the underlying assumptions?

(ii) Find the least squares estimates of the parameters of a simple regression model.

(iii) Fit the regression model using data in 3 (ii) and interpret the nature of relationship between X and Y.

9.5 (i) Define correlation coefficient and demonstrate how can you interpret +ve and −ve correlations.

(ii) Show that the correlation coefficient lies between −1 and +1.

(iii) Show that coefficient of correlation between two variables is independent of origin and scale of measurement.

9.6 (i) Define the simple regression model indicating the underlying assumptions.

(ii) Show that the Total SS = Regression SS + Residual SS.

(iii) Obtain the least squares estimates of the parameters of the simple regression model.

9.7 (i) Write the population and estimated regression models. What are the assumptions of a regression model?

(ii) Obtain the least squares estimators of the parameters of a simple regression model, $Y = \beta_0 + \beta_1 X + \varepsilon$.

(iii) Find the variance of $\hat{\beta}_0$ and $\hat{\beta}_1$.

9.8 (i) Define the correlation coefficient and graphically show: (i) no correlation, (ii) positive correlation, and (iii) negative correlation.

(ii) Show that $-1 \leq r \leq 1$.

(iii) Compute the correlation coefficient using the following data and interpret your result:

X	Y
5	2
4	4
3	5
5	1
1	2
4	3
7	7
5	3
8	6
7	5
9	7
6	3
3	2
8	5
9	8
4	3

9.9 (a) Consider a regression model $Y = \beta_0 + \beta_1 X + \varepsilon$. What are the assumptions of a regression model? Show that $\mathrm{Var}(\hat{\beta}_1) = \sigma^2 / \sum_{i=1}^{n} (X_i - \overline{X})^2$.
(b) Show that the coefficient of regression is independent of origin, but in general, depends on the scale of measurement.
(c) Using the data in 8 (iii) find the following:

    (i) $\hat{\beta}_0$ and $\hat{\beta}_1$;
    (ii) Estimated regression model;
    (iii) Residual sum of squares, total sum of squares, regression sum of squares;
    (iv) Estimate the variance of $\hat{\beta}_0$ and $\hat{\beta}_1$;
    (vi) R^2 and it is interpretation.
    (v) Construct the analysis of variance table.
    (vi) Perform the tests on regression parameters stating the null and alternative hypotheses.
    (vii) Construct the 95% confidence interval for β_0 and β_1.
    (viii) Comment on the fit of the regression model.

9.10 (i) Define the Spearman's rank correlation.
(ii) How can you measure the rank correlation coefficient for a group of n individuals with two characteristics A and B?
(iii) Following data shows the ranks given by two judges in an essay competition for students in a college participated by 10 students:

Student	Judge 1	Judge 2
1	3	2
2	1	1
3	2	3
4	5	5
5	4	4
6	6	6
7	9	7
8	10	9
9	7	8
10	8	10

Find the Spearman's rank correlation and interpret your result.

9.11 (a) Define the simple regression model indicating the underlying assumptions. Show that the Total SS = Regression SS + Residual SS.
(b) Obtain the least squares estimates of the parameters of the simple regression model.
(c) Show that $E\left(\dfrac{\sum_{i=1}^{n} e_i^2}{n-2}\right) = \sigma^2$ for a simple regression model.

9.12   Show that $\hat{\beta}_0$ and $\hat{\beta}_1$ are unbiased estimators of β_0 and β_1 in a simple regression model. Also, find the variances of $\hat{\beta}_0$ and $\hat{\beta}_1$.

9.13   Let there be n pairs of observations $(x_1, y_1), \ldots, (x_n, y_n)$

    (i)   Write the population regression model;

    (ii)   What are the assumptions for a regression model?

    (iii)   Show equations for estimating the parameters of a regression model using the least squares method.

9.14   Using the following data, estimate the parameter of a regression model and interpret your estimates.

X:	2	1	3	2	5
Y:	4	3	5	3	6

9.15   Let there be 5 pairs of observations given below:

X	Y	X^2	Y^2	XY
0	2			
1	3			
1	2			
2	4			
3	5			
$\sum_{i=1}^{5} X_i =$	$\sum_{i=1}^{5} Y_i =$	$\sum_{i=1}^{5} X_i^2 =$	$\sum_{i=1}^{5} Y_i^2 =$	$\sum_{i=1}^{5} X_i Y_i =$

(a)   Compute the following from the above table:

$$\overline{X} =$$

$$\overline{Y} =$$

$$\sum_{i=1}^{5} (X_i - \overline{X})^2 =$$

$$\sum_{i=1}^{5}(Y_i-\overline{Y})^2 =$$

$$\sum_{i=1}^{5}(X_i-\overline{X})(Y_i-\overline{Y}) =$$

(b) Calculate the Pearson's correlation coefficient;
(c) Interpret the correlation coefficient obtained in (a);
(d) Is the correlation coefficient independent of

    (i) change in origin?:
    (ii) change in scale?:

(e) Write the population regression model considering Y as the outcome variable and X as the explanatory variable;
(f) Write the estimated regression model;
(g) Find the regression sum of squares and residual sum of squares.
(h) Construct the analysis of variance table.
(i) Perform tests on the parameters of the regression model.
(j) Comment on your findings.

9.16 (a) For a regression model, $Y = X\beta + \varepsilon$, where X is $(n \times (k+1))$ and β is $(k+1) \times 1$ vector of parameters, then find the estimators of β.

(b) Show that $\text{Cov}(\hat{\beta}) = (X'X)^{-1}\sigma^2$ for the above model.

9.17 Let us consider a model with k regressors, $Y = X\beta + \varepsilon$, where Y is $n \times 1$, X is $n \times p$, β is $p \times 1$, and $p = k + 1$. If we partition $\beta = [array*20l\beta_1 - \beta_2]$, where β_1 is $(p-r) \times 1$ and β_2 is $r \times 1$, then illustrate the test procedure for $H_0: \beta_2 = 0$.

9.18 Briefly discuss the role of R^2, adjusted R^2, and residual mean square in selecting the best regression model.

9.19 Let us consider the following data on height (in cm), age (in months) and weight (in kg) of 25 children as shown below:

Age (X_1)	Height (X_2)	Weight (Y)
10	72.1	7.4
55	93.5	11.3
15	78.9	9.8
20	85.2	12.1
31	89.1	11.6

(continued)

(continued)

Age (X_1)	Height (X_2)	Weight (Y)
56	100.3	13.2
43	92.5	11.5
40	93.5	12.2
46	97.7	12,3
28	79.9	10.5
33	83.2	9.3
16	68.8	6.6
42	111.0	17.3
46	89.6	13.7
32	93.7	13.7
23	82.2	10.2
51	95.0	12.5
50	104.6	14.5
27	87.1	11.0
28	80.9	10.6
19	79.0	9.0
15	76.2	7.1
54	98.3	11.8
58	101.5	13.0
7	71.9	8.2

Answer the following questions using the output given below:

(a) Fit the linear regression model: $Y = X\beta + \varepsilon$.
(b) Find the R^2 and interpret.
(c) Test for the overall regression hypothesis: $H_0: \beta_1 = \beta_2 = 0$.
(d) Test for $H_0: \beta_j = 0, j = 1, 2$.
(e) Construct the 99% confidence intervals of the parameters of regression model.

9.20 Consider a regression model: $Y = X\beta + \varepsilon$ where Y is $n \times 1$ vector of observations, X is $n \times p$ matrix of regressor variables, β is a $p \times 1$ vector of
regression coefficients and ε is an $n \times 1$ vector of random errors.

(i)   What are the assumptions need to be stated for this model?
(ii) Obtain the least squares estimators of β.
(iii) Show that $E(\hat{\beta}) = \beta$.
(iv) Show that $Cov(\hat{\beta}) = (X'X)^{-1}\sigma^2$.
(v)   Briefly show that $E(s^2) = \sigma^2$.

9.21   Show the analysis of variance table for the model in Question 9.19 and write the steps for testing the following hypotheses specifying the alternative hypotheses, test statistics and comments based on the values of test statistics:

   (i) $H_0: \beta_1 = \cdots = \beta_k = 0$,
        and
   (ii) $H_0: \beta_j = 0, j = 1, 2, \ldots, k$.

9.22   Consider a regression model: $Y = X\beta + \varepsilon$, where Y is $n \times 1$ vector of observations, X is $n \times p$ matrix, β is a $p \times 1$ vector of regression coefficients and ε is an $n \times 1$ vector of random errors.

   (a)   Write the expression for residual sum of squares.
   (b)   Write the expression for mean square residual.
   (c)   Construct the ANOVA table for $n = 40$ and $k = 3$:
   (d)   From the ANOVA table in (c), show the test for $H_0: \beta_1 = \beta_2 = \beta_3 = 0$.
   (e)   How can you comment from (d)?
   (f)   Construct the 95% confidence interval for $\beta_j, j = 1, 2, 3$.
   (g)   What is the extra sum of squares principle? Comment on the null hypothesis $H_0: \beta_3 = 0$ using the extra sum of squares principle.

Reference

HRS (Health And Retirement Study) (2014). *Public use dataset*. Produced and distributed by the University of Michigan with funding from the National Institute on Aging (grant number NIAU01AG09740). Ann Arbor, MI.

Chapter 10
Analysis of Variance

10.1 Introduction

The technique of analysis of variance (ANOVA) is used to compare several means of several populations. It can be considered as a generalization of the t-test that is used for comparing two means from two populations.

For example, suppose that a researcher conducted a study to compare the effects of four different types of medical training programs $(T_1, T_2, T_3,$ and $T_4)$ on the attainment of students. In order to compare these training programs, the researcher selected 24 medical students in the same level of study and who obtained the same grade in a placement test. Then, the researcher randomly divided these students into four groups each with six students. After that, the researcher randomly applied each training program on one of the four groups of students. In the end of the program, the researcher obtained the marks of the students (out of 15) which are summarized in the following table:

		Observations (marks)					
Treatments	Program (T_1)	11.6	7.3	11.4	11.0	8.6	9.2
	Program (T_2)	6.2	8.1	9.8	5.1	7.0	8.6
	Program (T_3)	11.9	8.1	12.6	14.2	10.7	11.4
	Program (T_4)	10.5	15.0	11.8	13.7	14.7	12.8

One of the goals that the researcher wants to accomplish is to know whether real (or significant) differences exist between the means of the students' marks for the different programs. In other words, the researcher wants to know whether the type of training program has an effect on the educational attainment measured by the marks of the students. In this example, and based on the ANOVA methodology, the type of the training program is called the treatment factor (or independent variable), and the mark is called the response (or dependent variable) which is that quantity measured on the experimental units. The different training programs

© Springer Nature Singapore Pte Ltd. 2018
M. A. Islam and A. Al-Shiha, *Foundations of Biostatistics*,
https://doi.org/10.1007/978-981-10-8627-4_10

$(T_1, T_2, T_3,$ and $T_4)$ are called the treatments or the levels of the factor, whereas a student who receives one of the treatments and on which we measure the response is called an experimental unit. The design of this kind of experiment is called the completely randomized design.

The existence of real differences between the means of marks for the different training program indicates that the type of the training program has an effect on the educational attainment of the students.

10.2 Completely Randomized Design: One-Way Classification

The completely randomized design (CRD) is one of the simplest and useful designs. In this design, we have one factor of interest that might have an effect on the response of interest. The response variable is denoted by Y. Suppose that the treatment factor has a levels (or a treatments). Each level of the factor corresponds to a population. We select independent random samples of size n from the a populations; a sample from each population. Each population represents a level of the factor; that is, each population represents a treatment.

The goal is to answer the following questions: Are all population means equal? Are some of them different? In other words, we need to answer the following question: Does the factor significantly affect the response?

Statistically speaking, we need to test the following null and alternative hypotheses:

$$H_0: \mu_1 = \mu_2 = \cdots = \mu_a$$
$$H_1: \mu_i \neq \mu_j \text{ for some } i \text{ and } j,$$

where μ_i is the mean of the ith population $(i = 1, 2, \ldots, a)$.

Rejecting $H_0: \mu_1 = \mu_2 = \cdots = \mu_a$ indicates that there exist significant differences between the populations' means, which means that there is a significant effect of the factor on the response. In this case, we wish to know which means are different and to estimate the difference between the means.

10.2.1 Analysis of Variance Technique

The analysis of variance technique is based on partitioning the total variation in the observations of the response variable into several components; each component measures some source of variation.

Suppose that we have a treatments, and there are n observations for each treatment, and let y_{ij} be the jth observation of the ith treatment, where $(i = 1, 2, \ldots, a)$ and $(j = 1, 2, \ldots, n)$. The total variation in the observations of the response variable (Y) can be measured by the quantity $\sum_{i=1}^{a} \sum_{j=1}^{n} (y_{ij} - \bar{y}_{..})^2$, where $\bar{y}_{..}$ is the grand average of all observations. The observations can be arranged in the following layout:

	Treatments				Grand
	1	2	...	a	
Observations	y_{11}	y_{21}	...	y_{a1}	–
	y_{12}	y_{22}	...	y_{a2}	–
	$\vdots$	$\vdots$	$\vdots$	$\vdots$	–
	y_{1n}	y_{2n}	...	y_{an}	–
Total	$y_{1.}$	$y_{2.}$	...	$y_{a.}$	$y_{..}$
Mean	$\bar{y}_{1.}$	$\bar{y}_{2.}$	...	$\bar{y}_{a.}$	$\bar{y}_{..}$

We define the total number of observations by

$$N = an.$$

We define the total and the average of the observations of the ith treatment, respectively, by

$$y_{i.} = \sum_{j=1}^{n} y_{ij}$$

$$\bar{y}_{i.} = \frac{y_{i.}}{n} = \frac{\sum_{j=1}^{n} y_{ij}}{n}.$$

We also define the grand total and the grand average of all observations, respectively, by

$$y_{..} = \sum_{i=1}^{a} \sum_{j=1}^{n} y_{ij} = \sum_{i=1}^{a} y_{i.}$$

$$\bar{y}_{..} = \frac{y_{..}}{an} = \frac{\sum_{i=1}^{a} \sum_{j=1}^{n} y_{ij}}{N} = \frac{\sum_{i=1}^{a} y_{i.}}{N}.$$

The ultimate goals of the ANOVA are as follows:

(1) Testing the equality of the treatments' means $(H_0: \mu_1 = \mu_2 = \cdots = \mu_a)$.
(2) Estimating the differences between the treatments' means $(\mu_i - \mu_j)$, and determining which the different means are.

10.2.2   Decomposition of the Total Sum of Squares

As we mentioned earlier, the total variation in the observations as a whole can be measured by the corrected total sum of squares which is defined by

$$\text{SSTOT} = \sum_{i=1}^{a} \sum_{j=1}^{n} (y_{ij} - \bar{y}_{..})^2.$$

The degrees of freedom associated with this sum of squares is

$$\text{df}_{\text{TOT}} = an - 1 = N - 1.$$

If we divide the corrected total sum of squares by its degrees of freedom, we obtain the ordinary sample variance of all observations, that is,

$$S^2 = \frac{\text{SSTOT}}{\text{df}_{\text{TOT}}} = \frac{\text{SSTOT}}{N - 1} = \frac{\sum_{i=1}^{a} \sum_{j=1}^{n} (y_{ij} - \bar{y}_{..})^2}{N - 1}.$$

This quantity is a measure of the total variation in all observations.

There are two sources of the total variation which are as follows:

(1) The first kind of variation is due to the differences between the treatments.
(2) The second kind of variation is due to the random error.

According to these two sources of variation, we can partition the total sum of squares $\text{SSTOT} = \sum_{i=1}^{a} \sum_{j=1}^{n} (y_{ij} - \bar{y}_{..})^2$ into two components which are as follows:

(1) The treatment sum of squares (SSTRT):

This quantity measures the differences between the treatment means and defined by

$$\text{SSTRT} = n \sum_{i=1}^{a} (\bar{y}_{i.} - \bar{y}_{..})^2.$$

The degrees of freedom associated with this sum of squares are

$$\text{df}_{\text{TRT}} = a - 1.$$

Notice that the treatment sum of squares, $\text{SSTRT} = n \sum_{i=1}^{a} (\bar{y}_{i.} - \bar{y}_{..})^2$, measures the sum of squares of the differences between the treatment averages $(\bar{y}_{i.})$ and the grand average of the observations $(\bar{y}_{..})$. A large value of SSTRT indicates the existence of differences between the treatment' means, consequently, we reject the hypothesis of the equality of the treatments' means $(H_0: \mu_1 = \mu_2 = \cdots = \mu_a)$ for large values of SSTRT.

(2) The error sum of squares (SSE):

This quantity measures the differences between the observations within treatments and is defined by

$$\text{SSE} = \sum_{i=1}^{a} \sum_{j=1}^{n} (y_{ij} - \bar{y}_{i \cdot})^2$$

The degrees of freedom associated with this sum of squares are

$$\text{df}_E = N - a.$$

Notice that the error sum of squares, $\text{SSE} = \sum_{i=1}^{a} \sum_{j=1}^{n} (y_{ij} - \bar{y}_{i \cdot})^2$, measures the sum of squares of the differences between the observations (y_{ij}) and their average $(\bar{y}_{i \cdot})$ within treatments.

Algebraically, it can be shown that the total sum of squares, $\text{SSTOT} = \sum_{i=1}^{a} \sum_{j=1}^{n} (y_{ij} - \bar{y}_{\cdot \cdot})^2$, is the sum of two components; the first component is (SSTRT) and the second component is (SSE). That is,

$$\text{SSTOT} = \text{SSTRT} + \text{SSE}$$

and equivalently, we may write

$$\sum_{i=1}^{a} \sum_{j=1}^{n} (y_{ij} - \bar{y}_{\cdot \cdot})^2 = n \sum_{i=1}^{a} (\bar{y}_{i \cdot} - \bar{y}_{\cdot \cdot})^2 + \sum_{i=1}^{a} \sum_{j=1}^{n} (y_{ij} - \bar{y}_{i \cdot})^2.$$

Similarly, we can partition the degrees of freedom associated with the total sum of squares $(\text{df}_{TOT} = N - 1)$ into two components as follows:

$$\text{df}_{TOT} = \text{df}_{TRT} + \text{df}_E$$

and equivalently, we may write

$$N - 1 = (a - 1) + (N - a).$$

10.2.3   Pooled Estimate of the Variance

Suppose that the observations of the ith treatment are

$$y_{i1}, y_{i2}, \ldots, y_{in}.$$

The sample variance of the observations of the ith treatment is

$$S_i^2 = \frac{\sum_{j=1}^{n} (y_{ij} - \bar{y}_{i.})^2}{n-1}.$$

This variance is associated with $(n-1)$ degrees of freedoms. The pooled estimate of the variance using the sample variances of all treatments is

$$
\begin{aligned}
S_p^2 &= \frac{(n-1)S_1^2 + (n-1)S_2^2 + \cdots + (n-1)S_a^2}{(n-1) + (n-1) + \cdots + (n-1)} \\
&= \frac{\sum_{i=1}^{a} (n-1)S_i^2}{\sum_{i=1}^{a} (n-1)} \\
&= \frac{\sum_{i=1}^{a} \sum_{j=1}^{n} (y_{ij} - \bar{y}_{i.})^2}{\sum_{i=1}^{a} (n-1)} \\
&= \frac{\text{SSE}}{N-a}.
\end{aligned}
$$

This quantity is called the mean square error (MSE).

Mean Squares

When we divide the sum of squares (SS) by its degrees of freedom (df), we obtain what is called mean square (MS), i.e.,

$$\text{MS} = \frac{\text{SS}}{\text{df}}.$$

We will define the following means of squares:

(1) The treatment mean square (MSTRT):
   This mean square is defined as follows:

$$\text{MSTRT} = \frac{\text{SSTRT}}{\text{df}_{\text{TRT}}} = \frac{\text{SSTRT}}{a-1}.$$

(2) The error mean square (MSE):
   This mean square is defined as follows:

$$\text{MSE} = \frac{\text{SSE}}{\text{df}_{\text{E}}} = \frac{\text{SSE}}{N-a}.$$

As we mentioned earlier, the error mean square (MSE) is nothing but the pooled estimate of the variance, i.e., $\text{MSE} = S_p^2$.

10.2.4 *Testing the Equality of Treatments' Means*

We summarize the procedure of testing the equality of treatments' means $(H_0: \mu_1 = \mu_2 = \cdots = \mu_a)$ by the following steps:

(1) Determining the hypotheses:
As we mentioned earlier, ANOVA is concerned with testing the following null hypothesis:

$$H_0: \mu_1 = \mu_2 = \cdots = \mu_a \text{ (no difference between means)}$$

against the following alternative hypothesis:

$$H_1: \mu_i \neq \mu_j \text{ for some } i \text{ and } j \text{ (there are some differences).}$$

(2) Determining the level of significance (α):
We select one of the common values of the significance level (α) which are 0.1, 0.05, 0.025, or 0.01.
(3) Determining the test statistic:
The test statistic used to test the equality of treatments' means is

$$F_0 = \frac{\text{MSTRT}}{\text{MSE}}.$$

Under H_0 (i.e., when H_0 is correct), the test statistic $F_0 = \frac{\text{MSTRT}}{\text{MSE}}$ has an F-distribution with the following degrees of freedoms:

$$df_1 = df_{TRT} = a - 1$$
$$df_2 = df_E = N - a$$

that is $F_0 \sim F(a - 1, N - a)$.
(4) Determining the rejection region (RR) of H_0:
The rejection region consists of the values of F_0 which are greater than the critical value $F_\alpha(a - 1, N - a)$. The following figure shows the rejection region (RR) and non-rejection region of H_0:

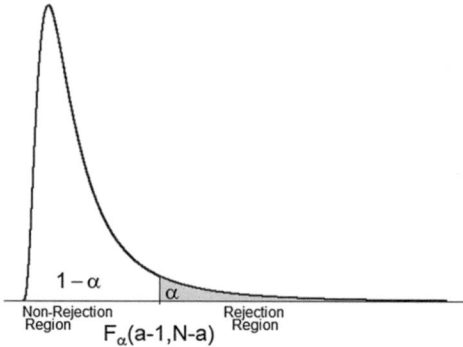

(5) Determining the decision rule:

We reject $H_0: \mu_1 = \mu_2 = \cdots = \mu_a$ at the significant level α if

$$F_0 > F_\alpha(a - 1, N - a).$$

ANOVA Table

The information needed to perform the ANOVA procedure is usually summarized in so-called ANOVA table as follows:

Source of variation	Sum of squares	Degrees of freedom	Mean squares	F-ratio (F_0)
Treatments (between treatments)	$SSTRT = n \sum_{i=1}^{a} (\bar{y}_{i\cdot} - \bar{y}_{\cdot\cdot})^2$	$a - 1$	$MSTRT = \frac{SSTRT}{a-1}$	$F_0 = \frac{MSTRT}{MSE}$
Error (within treatments)	$SSE = \sum_{i=1}^{a} \sum_{j=1}^{n} (y_{ij} - \bar{y}_{i\cdot})^2$ $= SSTOT - SST$	$N - a$	$MSE = \frac{SSE}{N-a}$	
Total	$SSTOT = \sum_{i=1}^{a} \sum_{j=1}^{n} (y_{ij} - \bar{y}_{\cdot\cdot})^2$	$N - 1$		

Computational Formulas

In order to simplify calculating the sum of squares used in ANOVA table, we may use the following equivalent formulas:

$$SSTOT = \sum_{i=1}^{a} \sum_{j=1}^{n} y_{ij}^2 - \frac{y_{\cdot\cdot}^2}{N}$$

$$SSTRT = \frac{1}{n} \sum_{i=1}^{a} y_{i\cdot}^2 - \frac{y_{\cdot\cdot}^2}{N}$$

$$SSE = SSTOT - SSTRT \text{ (by subtraction)}.$$

The quantity $\frac{y_{..}^2}{N}$ is called the correction factor.

Example 10.1 A researcher wanted to compare the efficiency of four different types of medical training programs $(T_1, T_2, T_3,$ and $T_4)$. In order to compare the efficiency of these training programs, the researcher selected 24 medical students in the same level and who obtained the same grade in a placement test. Then, the researcher randomly divided these students into four groups each with six students. After that, the researcher randomly applied each program on one of the four groups of students. In the end of program, the researcher obtained the marks of the students (out of 15), which are summarized in the following table:

		Observations (marks)					
Treatments	Program (T_1)	11.6	7.3	11.4	11.0	8.6	9.2
	Program (T_2)	6.2	8.1	9.8	5.1	7.0	8.6
	Program (T_3)	11.9	8.1	12.6	14.2	10.7	11.4
	Program (T_4)	10.5	15.0	11.8	13.7	14.7	12.8

Do these data provide us with a sufficient evidence to conclude that there are significant differences among the training programs? In other words, does the type of training program significantly affect the student attainment? Use $\alpha = 0.05$.

Solution

We want to test $(H_0: \mu_1 = \mu_2 = \mu_3 = \mu_4)$ against $(H_1: \mu_i \neq \mu_j$ for some i and $j)$ at $\alpha = 0.05$.

There are four treatments (programs): $a = 4$.
There are six observations in each sample: $n = 6$.
The total number of observation is $N = an = 24$.
The following table summarizes the totals and the averages:

	Treatments (programs)				Grand
	T_1	T_2	T_3	T_4	
Observations y_{ij}	11.6	6.2	11.9	10.5	–
	7.3	8.1	8.1	15.0	–
	11.4	9.8	12.6	11.8	–
	11.0	5.1	14.2	13.7	–
	8.6	7.0	10.7	14.7	–
	9.2	8.6	11.4	12.8	–
Total $(y_{i.})$	59.1	44.8	68.9	78.5	$y_{..} = 251.3$
Average $(\bar{y}_{i.})$	9.850	7.467	11.483	13.083	$\bar{y}_{..} = 10.471$

In order to calculate the sums of squares, we first calculate the following quantities:

$$\frac{y_{..}^2}{N} = \frac{(251.3)^2}{24} = 2631.3204$$

$$\sum_{i=1}^{a}\sum_{j=1}^{n} y_{ij}^2 = (11.6)^2 + \cdots + (12.8)^2 = 2800.65$$

$$\sum_{i=1}^{a} y_{i.}^2 = (59.1)^2 + (44.8)^2 + (68.9)^2 + (78.5)^2 = 16409.31.$$

Calculate the sums of squares (SS) using the calculating formulas:

$$\text{SSTOT} = \sum_{i=1}^{a}\sum_{j=1}^{n} y_{ij}^2 - \frac{y_{..}^2}{N} = 2800.65 - 2631.3204 = 169.3296$$

$$\text{SSTRT} = \frac{1}{n}\sum_{i=1}^{a} y_{i.}^2 - \frac{y_{..}^2}{N} = \frac{1}{6}(16409.31) - 2631.3204 = 103.5646$$

$$\text{SSE} = \text{SSTOT} - \text{SSTRT} = 169.3296 - 103.5646 = 65.765.$$

Calculate the degrees of freedoms (df):

$$\text{df}_{\text{TRT}} = a - 1 = 4 - 1 = 3$$
$$\text{df}_{\text{E}} = N - a = 24 - 4 = 20$$
$$\text{df}_{\text{TOT}} = N - 1 = 24 - 1 = 23.$$

Calculate the means of squares (MS):

$$\text{MSTRT} = \frac{\text{SSTRT}}{a - 1} = \frac{103.5646}{4 - 1} = 34.5215$$
$$\text{MSE} = \frac{\text{SSE}}{N - a} = \frac{65.765}{24 - 4} = 3.2883.$$

We notice that the value of the treatment mean squares (MSTRT) is more than ten times as the value of the error mean squares (MSE), and this indicates that the treatment means are likely to be different.

Calculate the value of the test statistics (F_0):

$$F_0 = \frac{\text{MSTRT}}{\text{MSE}} = \frac{34.5215}{3.2883} = 10.498.$$

Finding the critical Value $(F_\alpha(a-1, N-a))$:

$$F_{0.05}(3,\ 20) = 3.10.$$

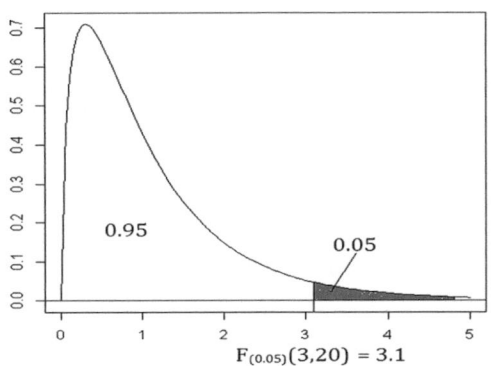
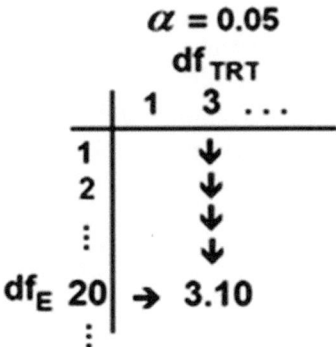

ANOVA Table
We summarize the above calculations in the following ANOVA table:

Source of variation	Sum of squares	Degrees of freedom	Mean squares	F-ratio (F_0)
Treatments (between treatments)	103.5646	3	34.5215	10.498
Error (within treatments)	65.765	20	3.2883	
Total	169.3296	23		

Decision
Since $F_0 > F_{0.05}(3,\ 20)$, we reject $H_0: \mu_1 = \mu_2 = \mu_3$ at the significance level $\alpha = 0.05$, and we conclude that the treatments' means are significantly different, which mean that the type of the training program has an effect on the student attainment.

10.2.5 Estimation of the Differences Between the Treatment Means $(\mu_1 - \mu_2)$

A point estimate and a $(1 - \alpha)100\%$ confidence interval of the mean of the ith treatment (μ_i) are, respectively, as follows:

$$\hat{\mu}_i = \bar{y}_{i\cdot}$$

$$\bar{y}_{i\cdot} - t_{\alpha/2}(N - a)\sqrt{\frac{\text{MSE}}{n}} < \mu_i < \bar{y}_{i\cdot} + t_{\alpha/2}(N - a)\sqrt{\frac{\text{MSE}}{n}},$$

where $i = 1, 2, \ldots, a$, and $t_{\alpha/2, N-a}$ is the critical value of t-distribution, with degrees of freedom df $= N-a$, that leaves an equal $\alpha/2$ to the left.

A point estimate and a $(1 - \alpha)100\%$ confidence interval of the difference between the mean of the ith treatment and the mean of the jth treatment $(\mu_i - \mu_j)$ are, respectively, as follows:

$$\hat{\mu}_i - \hat{\mu}_j = \bar{y}_{i\cdot} - \bar{y}_{j\cdot}$$

$$(\bar{y}_{i\cdot} - \bar{y}_{i\cdot}) - t_{\alpha/2}(N - a)\sqrt{\frac{2\times\text{MSE}}{n}} < \mu_i - \mu_j < (\bar{y}_{i\cdot} - \bar{y}_{i\cdot}) + t_{\alpha/2}(N - a)\sqrt{\frac{2\times\text{MSE}}{n}},$$

where $i, j = 1, 2, \ldots, a$.

Separation of Means and Pairwise Comparisons

As we mentioned earlier, if the hypothesis of the equality of the treatment means $(H_0: \mu_1 = \mu_2 = \cdots = \mu_a)$ is rejected, we conclude that there are some differences between the treatment means. In this case, we wish to know which means are different, and we wish to estimate the differences between the different means. We usually make comparisons between the means in order to find where the differences are. These comparisons are done by testing some hypotheses about the differences between all possible pairs of means of the form $(\mu_i - \mu_j)$. The number of all possible pairs of means is $\binom{a}{2} = a(a - 1)/2$.

Fisher's Least Significant Difference Method

We will compare all possible pairs of means (pairwise comparison) using the Fisher's Least Significant Difference Method:

In this procedure, we are interested in testing all hypotheses of the following form:

$$H_o^{ij}: \mu_i - \mu_j = 0$$
$$H_1^{ij}: \mu_i - \mu_j \neq 0$$

for all values $i, j = 1, 2, \ldots, a$ where $i \neq j$. The test statistic used in this method is

$$t_o = \frac{\bar{y}_{i\cdot} - \bar{y}_{j\cdot}}{\sqrt{\frac{2\times\text{MSE}}{n}}}.$$

We reject $H_o^{ij}: \mu_i = \mu_j$ if

$$|t_o| = \left|\frac{\bar{y}_{i\cdot} - \bar{y}_{j\cdot}}{\sqrt{\frac{2\times\text{MSE}}{n}}}\right| > t_{\frac{\alpha}{2}}(N - a)$$

which implies that

$$\left|\bar{y}_{i\cdot} - \bar{y}_{j\cdot}\right| > t_{\frac{\alpha}{2}}(N - a) \times \sqrt{\frac{2 \times \text{MSE}}{n}}.$$

The quantity on the right-hand side of the last inequality is called the least significant difference (LSD), i.e.,

$$\text{LSD} = t_{\frac{\alpha}{2}}(N - a) \times \sqrt{\frac{2 \times \text{MSE}}{n}}.$$

Therefore, we reject $H_o^{ij}: \mu_i = \mu_j$ if

$$\left|\bar{y}_{i\cdot} - \bar{y}_{j\cdot}\right| > \text{LSD}.$$

Example 10.2 Consider the data in the previous example.

(1) Compare all possible pairs of means using $\alpha = 0.05$.
(2) Construct 95% confidence intervals for the differences between all pairs of means $\left(\mu_i - \mu_j\right)$.

Solution

(1) There are $\binom{a}{2} = \binom{4}{2} = 6$ possible pairs of means. The least significant difference (LSD) is

$$\text{LSD} = t_{\frac{\alpha}{2}}(N - a) \times \sqrt{\frac{2 \times \text{MSE}}{n}}$$

$$= t_{0.025}(20) \times \sqrt{\frac{2 \times 3.2883}{6}}$$

$$= 2.086 \times 1.0469$$

$$= 2.1839.$$

For any pair of means (μ_i, μ_j), if $|\bar{y}_{i\cdot} - \bar{y}_{j\cdot}| > 2.1839$, we conclude that the means μ_i and μ_j are significantly different (i.e., we reject $H_o^{ij}: \mu_i = \mu_j$).

We summarize the calculations in the following table:

Pair of means (μ_i, μ_j)	Absolute difference of the corresponding averages $\|\bar{y}_{i\cdot} - \bar{y}_{j\cdot}\|$	Conclusion
(μ_1, μ_2)	$\|\bar{y}_{1\cdot} - \bar{y}_{2\cdot}\| = \|9.85 - 7.467\| = 2.383$	$\|\bar{y}_{1\cdot} - \bar{y}_{2\cdot}\| > \text{LSD}$ (Significant)
(μ_1, μ_3)	$\|\bar{y}_{1\cdot} - \bar{y}_{3\cdot}\| = \|9.85 - 11.483\| = 1.633$	$\|\bar{y}_{1\cdot} - \bar{y}_{3\cdot}\| < \text{LSD}$
(μ_1, μ_4)	$\|\bar{y}_{1\cdot} - \bar{y}_{4\cdot}\| = \|9.85 - 13.083\| = 3.233$	$\|\bar{y}_{1\cdot} - \bar{y}_{4\cdot}\| > \text{LSD}$ (Significant)
(μ_2, μ_3)	$\|\bar{y}_{2\cdot} - \bar{y}_{3\cdot}\| = \|7467 - 11.483\| = 4.016$	$\|\bar{y}_{2\cdot} - \bar{y}_{3\cdot}\| > \text{LSD}$ (Significant)
(μ_2, μ_4)	$\|\bar{y}_{2\cdot} - \bar{y}_{4\cdot}\| = \|7.467 - 13.083\| = 5.616$	$\|\bar{y}_{2\cdot} - \bar{y}_{4\cdot}\| > \text{LSD}$ (Significant)
(μ_3, μ_4)	$\|\bar{y}_{3\cdot} - \bar{y}_{4\cdot}\| = \|11.483 - 13.083\| = 1.6$	$\|\bar{y}_{3\cdot} - \bar{y}_{4\cdot}\| < \text{LSD}$

From this table, we notice that the mean of the second treatments (μ_2) is significantly different from all other means.

(2) A 95% confidence interval for the difference $(\mu_i - \mu_j)$ is

$$(\bar{y}_{i\cdot} - \bar{y}_{i\cdot}) \pm t_{\alpha/2}(N - a) \times \sqrt{\frac{2\text{MSE}}{n}}$$

$$(\bar{y}_{i\cdot} - \bar{y}_{i\cdot}) \pm t_{0.025}(20) \times \sqrt{\frac{2 \times 3.2883}{6}}$$

$$(\bar{y}_{i\cdot} - \bar{y}_{i\cdot}) \pm 2.086 \times 1.0469$$

$$(\bar{y}_{i\cdot} - \bar{y}_{i\cdot}) \pm 2.1839.$$

We summarize the calculations in the following table:

Difference: $\mu_i - \mu_j$	Point estimate: $\bar{y}_{i\cdot} - \bar{y}_{i\cdot}$	$(1 - \alpha)100\%$ C.I. for $(\mu_i - \mu_j)$: $(\bar{y}_{i\cdot} - \bar{y}_{i\cdot}) \pm 2.1839$
$\mu_1 - \mu_2$	2.383	$0.199 < \mu_1 - \mu_2 < 4.567$
$\mu_1 - \mu_3$	-1.633	$-3.817 < \mu_1 - \mu_3 < 0.551$
$\mu_1 - \mu_4$	-3.233	$-5.417 < \mu_1 - \mu_4 < -1.049$
$\mu_2 - \mu_3$	-4.016	$-6.200 < \mu_2 - \mu_3 < -1.832$
$\mu_2 - \mu_4$	-5.616	$-7.800 < \mu_2 - \mu_4 < -3.432$
$\mu_3 - \mu_4$	-1.600	$-3.784 < \mu_3 - \mu_4 < 0.584$

We noticed that all 95% confidence intervals involving the observations of the response variable into three componentsmean of the second treatment (μ_2) do not contain zero. Therefore, we conclude that μ_2 is different of all other means.

10.3   Randomized Completely Block Design

The randomized completely block design (RCBD) is one of the most important designs, and it is used in many applications. It can be considered as a generalization of the paired t-test that used in comparing the means of two related populations.

It is used when the researcher wants to eliminate the effect of some controlled extraneous source of variation (called nuisance factor) from the comparisons of the treatment means.

As we have seen, the completely randomized design is useful when the experimental units are homogenous. However, in many situations, it might be difficult to find homogenous experimental units due to many practical reasons. In his case, we may use the randomized completely block design in order to increase the precision of the comparisons of the treatment means.

To show the usefulness of RCBD, suppose that in the previous example demonstrated in the last section, where the researcher wanted to compare the efficiency of four medical training programs, the students in the first and second groups (who received T_1 and T_2) were females, and the students in the third and fourth groups (who received T_3 and T_4) were males. In this case, two factors are involved in the design; the first factor is the type of program, whereas the second factor is the gender. The result of the ANOVA procedure of the CRD in the example showed that there are significant differences between treatment means. Since there are two factors involved, it is not clear in this situation which factor causes the differences. Indeed, the factor of interest is the type of program, whereas the gender is a nuisance factor whose effect must be eliminated. The CRD fails to remove the effect of the gender on the treatment comparisons, since it affects the response (student attainment) besides the factor of interest which is the type of program.

Another candidate nuisance factor in the previous example might be the study's level of the student. Suppose that students in the first group who received treatment T_1 were students at the bachelors' level (B_1), the students in the second group who received treatment T_2 were at the masters' level (B_2), the students in the third group who received treatment T_3 were doctoral students (B_3), and the students in the fourth group who received treatment T_4 were postdoctoral students (B_4), In this case, two factors are involved in the design; the first factor is the type of program, whereas the second factor is the level of study. The result of ANOVA procedure of the CRD in the example showed that there are significant differences between treatment means. Since there are two factors involved, it is not clear in this situation which factor causes the differences. Indeed, the factor of interest is the type of program, whereas the level of study is a nuisance factor whose effect must be eliminated. The CRD fails to remove the effect of the level of study on the treatment comparisons, since it affects the response (student attainment) besides the factor of interest which is the type of program.

10.3.1 The Model and the Estimates of Parameters

An alternative design used when we want to remove the effect of a controlled nuisance factor is the RCBD.

The RCBD is characterized by the following features:

1. We partition the experimental units into several blocks.
2. The number of blocks must be equal to the number of different levels of the nuisance factor. The nuisance factor is that factor we wish to eliminate its effect from the treatment comparisons.
3. Each block should contain homogenous experimental units.
4. The number of experimental units in each block must be equal to the number of treatments (number of different levels of the factor of interest).
5. After forming the blocks, each treatment is randomly applied once and only once in each block.
6. Each treatment must appear in each block only one time.

The following figure illustrates the layout of the RCBD for the case in which we have a treatments $(T_1, T_2, \ldots, T_a)$, and b blocks $(B_1, B_2, \ldots, B_b)$:

Blocks

B_1	B_2	B_3	$\cdots\cdots$	B_b
T_2	T_1	T_a		T_3
T_a	T_3	T_2		T_2
$\cdot$	$\cdot$	$\cdot$		$\cdot$
$\cdot$	$\cdot$	$\cdot$	$\cdots\cdots$	$\cdot$
$\cdot$	$\cdot$	$\cdot$		$\cdot$
T_1	T_a	T_1		T_a
T_3	T_2	T_3		T_1

It should be noticed that (1) the assignment of the treatments $(T_1, T_2, \ldots, T_a)$ to the experimental units inside each block must be done at random, and (2) each treatment must appear in each block only one time.

The analysis of variance in the RCBD is based on partitioning the total variation in the observations of the response variable into three components; each component measures some source of variation.

Suppose that we have a treatments and b blocks, and let y_{ij} be the observation of the ith treatment in the jth block, where $(i = 1, 2, \ldots, a)$ and $(j = 1, 2, \ldots, b)$. The total variation in the observations of the response variable (Y) can be measured by the quantity $\text{SSTOT} = \sum_{i=1}^{a} \sum_{j=1}^{b} (y_{ij} - \bar{y}_{..})^2$, where $\bar{y}_{..}$ is the grand average of all observations. The degrees of freedoms associated with this sum of squares is $df_{TOT} = ab - 1 = N - 1$.

The observations can be arranged in the following layout:

		Blocks				Treatment total	Treatment average
		1	2	...	b		
Treatments	1	y_{11}	y_{12}	...	y_{1b}	$y_{1\cdot}$	$\bar{y}_{1\cdot}$
	2	y_{21}	y_{22}	...	y_{2b}	$y_{2\cdot}$	$\bar{y}_{2\cdot}$
	$\vdots$	$\vdots$	$\vdots$	$\vdots$	$\vdots$	$\vdots$	$\vdots$
	A	y_{a1}	y_{a2}	...	y_{ab}	$y_{a\cdot}$	$\bar{y}_{a\cdot}$
Block total		$y_{\cdot1}$	$y_{\cdot2}$	...	$y_{\cdot b}$	Grand Total $= y_{\cdot\cdot}$	
Block average		$\bar{y}_{\cdot1}$	$\bar{y}_{\cdot2}$	...	$\bar{y}_{\cdot b}$	Grand Average $= \bar{y}_{\cdot\cdot}$	

We define the total and the average of the observations of the ith treatment, respectively, by

$$y_{i\cdot} = \sum_{j=1}^{b} y_{ij}$$

$$\bar{y}_{i\cdot} = \frac{y_{i\cdot}}{b} = \frac{\sum_{j=1}^{b} y_{ij}}{b}$$

We define the total and the average of the observations of the jth block, respectively, by

$$y_{\cdot j} = \sum_{i=1}^{a} y_{ij}$$

$$\bar{y}_{\cdot j} = \frac{y_{\cdot j}}{a} = \frac{\sum_{i=1}^{a} y_{ij}}{a}.$$

We define the grand total and the grand average of all observations, respectively, by

$$y_{\cdot\cdot} = \sum_{i=1}^{a}\sum_{j=1}^{b} y_{ij} = \sum_{i=1}^{a} y_{i\cdot} = \sum_{j=1}^{b} y_{\cdot j}$$

$$\bar{y}_{\cdot\cdot} = \frac{y_{\cdot\cdot}}{ab} = \frac{\sum_{i=1}^{a}\sum_{j=1}^{b} y_{ij}}{N} = \frac{\sum_{i=1}^{a} y_{i\cdot}}{N} = \frac{\sum_{j=1}^{b} y_{\cdot j}}{N}.$$

We define the total number of observations by

$$N = ab.$$

The goal of ANOVA in the RCBD is to test the equality of the treatments' means $(H_0: \mu_1 = \mu_2 = \cdots = \mu_a)$ after eliminating the effect of the nuisance factor. In the RCBD, there are three sources of the total variation which are as follows:

(1) The first kind of variation is due to the differences between the treatments.
(2) The second kind of variation is due to the differences between the blocks.
(3) The third kind of variation is due to the random error.

According to these three sources of variation, we can partition the total sum of squares, $\text{SSTOT} = \sum_{i=1}^{a} \sum_{j=1}^{b} (y_{ij} - \bar{y}_{..})^2$, into three components which are as follows:

(1) The treatment sum of squares (SSTRT):

$$\text{SSTRT} = b \sum_{i=1}^{a} (\bar{y}_{i.} - \bar{y}_{..})^2$$

The degrees of freedom associated with this sum of squares are

$$\text{df}_{\text{TRT}} = a - 1.$$

(2) The block sum of squares (SSBLK):

$$\text{SSBLK} = a \sum_{j=1}^{b} (\bar{y}_{.j} - \bar{y}_{..})^2.$$

The degrees of freedom associated with this sum of squares are

$$\text{df}_{\text{BLK}} = b - 1.$$

(3) The error sum of squares (SSE):

$$\text{SSE} = \sum_{i=1}^{a} \sum_{j=1}^{b} (y_{ij} - \bar{y}_{i.} - \bar{y}_{.j} + \bar{y}_{..})^2.$$

The degrees of freedom associated with this sum of squares are

$$\text{df}_{\text{E}} = (a - 1)(b - 1).$$

Algebraically, it can be shown that the total sum of squares, $\text{SSTOT} = \sum_{i=1}^{a} \sum_{j=1}^{b} (y_{ij} - \bar{y}_{..})^2$ can be portioned into the sum of three components as follows:

$$SSTOT = SSTRT + SSBLK + SSE$$

and equivalently, we may write

$$\sum_{i=1}^{a}\sum_{j=1}^{b}(y_{ij}-\bar{y}_{..})^2 = b\sum_{i=1}^{a}(\bar{y}_{i.}-\bar{y}_{..})^2 + a\sum_{j=1}^{b}(\bar{y}_{.j}-\bar{y}_{..})^2$$

$$+ \sum_{i=1}^{a}\sum_{j=1}^{b}(y_{ij}-\bar{y}_{i.}-\bar{y}_{.j}+\bar{y}_{..})^2.$$

Similarly, we can partition the degrees of freedom associated with the total sum of squares ($df_{TOT} = ab - 1 = N - 1$) into three components as follows:

$$df_{TOT} = df_{TRT} + df_{BLK} + df_E$$

and equivalently, we may write

$$ab - 1 = (a - 1) + (b - 1) + (a - 1)(b - 1).$$

For the RCBD, the relevant mean of squares is as follows:

(1) The treatment mean square (MSTRT) is

$$MSTRT = \frac{SSTRT}{df_{TRT}} = \frac{SSTRT}{a - 1}.$$

(2) The block mean square (MSBLK) is

$$MSBLK = \frac{SSBLK}{df_{BLK}} = \frac{SSBLK}{b - 1}.$$

(3) The error mean square (MSE) is

$$MSE = \frac{SSE}{df_E} = \frac{SSE}{(a - 1)(b - 1)}.$$

10.3.2   Testing the Equality of Treatment Means

The test statistic used to test the equality of treatments' means $H_0: \mu_1 = \mu_2 = \cdots = \mu_a$ is

$$F_0 = \frac{\text{MSTRT}}{\text{MSE}}.$$

Under H_0 (i.e., when H_0 is correct), the test statistic $F_0 = \frac{\text{MSTRT}}{\text{MSE}}$ has an F-distribution with the following degrees of freedoms:

$$\text{df}_1 = \text{df}_{\text{TRT}} = a - 1$$
$$\text{df}_2 = \text{df}_{\text{E}} = (a - 1)(b - 1).$$

That is $F_0 \sim F(a - 1, (a - 1)(b - 1))$. We reject $H_0: \mu_1 = \mu_2 = \cdots = \mu_a$ at the significant level α if:

$$F_0 > F_\alpha(a - 1, (a - 1)(b - 1)).$$

ANOVA Table

The information needed to perform the ANOVA procedure for the RCBD is usually summarized in the following ANOVA table:

Source of variation	Sum of squares	Degrees of freedom	Mean squares	F-ratio (F_0)
Treatments	SSTRT	$a - 1$	$\text{MSTRT} = \frac{\text{SSTRT}}{a-1}$	$F_0 = \frac{\text{MSTRT}}{\text{MSE}}$
Blocks	SSBLK	$b - 1$	$\text{MSBLK} = \frac{\text{SSBLK}}{b-1}$	
Errors	SSE (by subtraction)	$(a - 1)(b - 1)$	$\text{MSE} = \frac{\text{SSE}}{(a-1)(b-1)}$	
Total	SSTOT	$ab - 1$		

Computational Formulas

In order to simplify calculating the sum of squares used in ANOVA table, we may use the following equivalent formulas:

$$\text{SSTOT} = \sum_{i=1}^{a} \sum_{j=1}^{b} y_{ij}^2 - \frac{y_{..}^2}{N}$$

$$\text{SSTRT} = \frac{1}{b} \sum_{i=1}^{a} y_{i\cdot}^2 - \frac{y_{..}^2}{N}$$

$$\text{SSBLK} = \frac{1}{a} \sum_{j=1}^{b} y_{\cdot j}^2 - \frac{y_{..}^2}{N}$$

$$\text{SSE} = \text{SSTOT} - \text{SSTRT} - \text{SSBLK}$$

Example 10.3 An experiment was conducted to compare the effects of four different medical training programs (T_1, T_2, T_3, T_4) on the students attainment. In order to compare the efficiency of these training programs, the researcher selected twenty medical students; four of them were in the first year of study (B_1), four of them were in the second year of study (B_2), four of them were in the third year of study (B_3), four of them were in the fourth year of study (B_4), and four of them were in the fifth year of study (B_5). Considering the level of study as the blocking factor (nuisance factor), an RCBD was used by randomly applying each training program $(T_i;\ i = 1, 2, 3, 4)$ once in each block $(B_j;\ j = 1, 2, 3, 4, 5)$.

In the end of the training program, the researcher obtained the marks of the students (out of 15), which are summarized in the following table:

		Blocks (level of study)				
		B_1	B_2	B_3	B_4	B_5
Treatments (training program)	T_1	12.1	13.9	12.2	14.5	15.0
	T_2	12.3	15.0	12.3	14.8	15.0
	T_3	6.7	9.9	11.1	10.3	10.7
	T_4	9.9	11.9	11.9	11.4	14.4

Are there significant differences between the treatment means? In other words, does the program type affect the students' attainment? Use $\alpha = 0.05$.

Solution

We want to test:

$H_0: \mu_1 = \mu_2 = \mu_3 = \mu_4$ (no differences between the treatment means)

$$H_1: \mu_i \neq \mu_j \text{ for some } i \text{ and } j$$

$\alpha = 0.05$.

There are four treatments (programs): $a = 4$.

There are five blocks (levels of study): $b = 5$.

The total number of observation is $N = an = 20$.

The following table summarizes the totals and the averages:

		Blocks (level of study)					Treatment total	Treatment average
		B_1	B_2	B_3	B_4	B_5		
Treatments (training program)	T_1	12.1	13.9	12.2	14.5	15.0	$y_{1.} = 67.7$	$\bar{y}_{1.} = 13.54$
	T_2	12.3	15.0	12.3	14.8	15.0	$y_{2.} = 69.4$	$\bar{y}_{2.} = 13.88$
	T_3	6.7	9.9	11.1	10.3	10.7	$y_{3.} = 48.7$	$\bar{y}_{3.} = 9.74$
	T_4	9.9	11.9	11.9	11.4	14.4	$y_{4.} = 59.5$	$\bar{y}_{4.} = 11.9$
Block total		$y_{.1} = 41.0$	$y_{.2} = 50.7$	$y_{.3} = 47.5$	$y_{.4} = 51.0$	$y_{.5} = 55.1$	Grand Total $= y_{..}$ $= 245.3$	
Block average		$\bar{y}_{.1} = 10.25$	$\bar{y}_{.2} = 12.675$	$\bar{y}_{.3} = 11.875$	$\bar{y}_{.4} = 12.75$	$\bar{y}_{.5} = 13.775$	Grand Average $= \bar{y}_{..}$ $= 12.265$	

In order to calculate the sums of squares, we first calculate the following quantities:

$$\frac{y_{..}^2}{N} = \frac{(245.3)^2}{20} = 3008.6045$$

$$\sum_{i=1}^{a}\sum_{j=1}^{b} y_{ij}^2 = (12.1)^2 + \cdots + (14.4)^2 = 3100.57$$

$$\sum_{i=1}^{a} y_{i.}^2 = (67.7)^2 + (69.4)^2 + (48.7)^2 + (59.5)^2 = 15311.59$$

$$\sum_{j=1}^{b} y_{.j}^2 = (41.0)^2 + (50.7)^2 + (47.5)^2 + (51.0)^2 + (55.1)^2 = 12144.75.$$

Calculate the sums of squares (SS) using the calculating formulas:

$$\text{SSTOT} = \sum_{i=1}^{a}\sum_{j=1}^{b} y_{ij}^2 - \frac{y_{..}^2}{N} = 3100.57 - 3008.6045 = 91.9655$$

$$\text{SSTRT} = \frac{1}{b}\sum_{i=1}^{a} y_{i.}^2 - \frac{y_{..}^2}{N} = \frac{1}{5}(15311.59) - 3008.6045 = 53.7135$$

$$\text{SSBLK} = \frac{1}{a}\sum_{j=1}^{b} y_{.j}^2 - \frac{y_{..}^2}{N} = \frac{1}{4}(12144.75) - 3008.6045 = 27.583$$

$$\text{SSE} = \text{SSTOT} - \text{SSTRT} - \text{SSBLK} = 91.9655 - 53.7135 - 27.583 = 10.669.$$

Calculate the degrees of freedom (df):

$$\text{df}_{\text{TRT}} = a - 1 = 4 - 1 = 3$$
$$\text{df}_{\text{BLK}} = b - 1 = 5 - 1 = 4$$
$$\text{df}_{\text{E}} = (a-1)(b-1) = 3 \times 4 = 12$$
$$\text{df}_{\text{TOT}} = N - 1 = 20 - 1 = 19.$$

Calculate the means of squares (MS):

$$\text{MSTRT} = \frac{\text{SSTRT}}{a-1} = \frac{53.7135}{4-1} = 17.9045$$

$$\text{MSBLK} = \frac{\text{SSBLK}}{a-1} = \frac{27.583}{5-1} = 6.8958$$

$$\text{MSE} = \frac{\text{SSE}}{(a-1)(b-1)} = \frac{10.669}{12} = 0.8891.$$

We notice that the value of the treatment mean squares (MSTRT) is much higher than the value of the error mean squares (MSE), and this indicates that the treatment means are likely to be different.

Calculate the value of the test statistics (F_0):

$$F_0 = \frac{\text{MSTRT}}{\text{MSE}} = \frac{17.9045}{0.8891} = 20.1378.$$

Finding the critical value $(F_\alpha(a-1, (a-1)(b-1)))$:

$$F_{0.05}(3, 12) = 3.49.$$

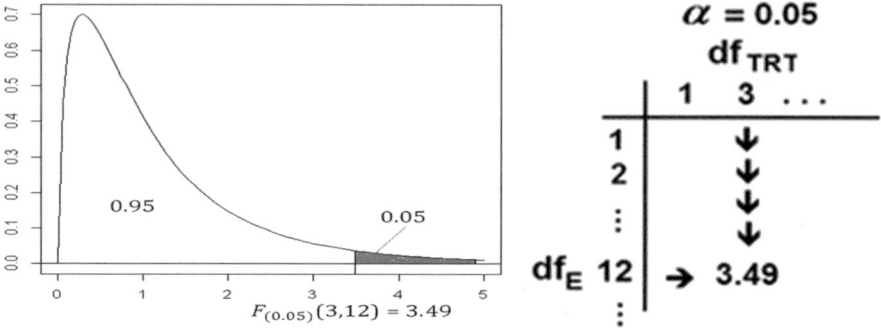

ANOVA Table
We summarize the above calculations in the following ANOVA table

Source of variation	Sum of squares	Degrees of freedom	Mean squares	F-ratio (F_0)
Treatments	53.7135	3	17.9045	20.1378
Blocks	27.583	4	6.8958	
Error	10.669	12	0.8891	
Total	91.9655	19		

Decision
Since $F_0 > F_{0.05}(3, 12)$, we reject $H_0: \mu_1 = \mu_2 = \mu_3 = \mu_4$ at the significance level $\alpha = 0.05$, and we conclude that the treatments' means are significantly different, which mean that the type of the training program has an effect on the student attainment.

10.4   Summary

The basic concepts and models of analysis of variance are introduced in this chapter. This chapter includes self-explanatory discussion on both one-way and two-way classifications. For both one-way and two-way analysis of variance, the models and assumptions, the analysis of variance techniques, decomposition of total sum of squares, pooled estimate of variance, mean squares, and test for the equality of treatment means are discussed elaborately. The analysis of variance tables is shown. The computational techniques are illustrated with examples. The estimation of the differences between the treatment means, separation of means, and pairwise comparisons are also illustrated in this chapter. The Fisher's least significant difference method is shown with example.

Exercises

10.1 The following hypothetical data represent the outcome of an experiment (temperature in degree Fahrenheit) with two different dose types of medicines (types A and B), and third type is a placebo (C) administered randomly to patients with high fever.Type of dose

A	B	C
100.2	101.5	102.3
101.3	100.3	103.1
100.4	99.8	102.6
102.5	102.3	102.4
	101.5	101.5
		102.7

(a) Write a suitable model that describes the variation in temperature attributable to three different dose types of medicine. What are the assumptions?

(b) Perform the analysis of data and display the analysis of variance table.

(c) Perform an appropriate test to determine whether there is variation in body temperature due to three dose types of medicines.

(d) Construct 95% one-sided and two-sided confidence intervals for the difference between all pairs of mean temperatures.

10.2 In a study let us consider that four different procedures (A, B, C, and D) are applied to randomly selected Type 2 diabetic subjects to find whether there is difference in the mean performance in controlling their preprandial blood glucose level (mmol/l).

A	B	C	D
7.4	8.2	7.5	8.1
5.8	7.2	6.8	7.6
6.2	7.0	7.1	8.4
7.5	8.9	9.3	9.6
7.8	6.4	8.1	9.3

(a) Write a suitable analysis of variance model that describes the variation in blood glucose level due to different procedures. What are the assumptions?

(b) Analyze the data and summarize the results in an analysis of variance table.

(c) Is there evidence in support of variation in preprandial blood glucose level? Perform an appropriate test and comment.

(d) Construct 95% two-sided confidence intervals for the difference between all pairs of mean blood glucose levels using a suitable least significant difference method.

10.3 Consider that a study is performed on borderline high total cholesterol level patients (200–239 mg/dL) and three different treatment options are applied to patients living in three different communities.

City	Treatment options		
	$T1$	$T2$	$T3$
City 1	204	223	227
	203	212	228
	190	212	207
City 2	215	214	215
	178	203	206
	200	204	204
City 3	213	213	217
	178	193	207
	190	194	206

(a) Write the appropriate analysis of variance model and indicate the underlying assumptions.

(b) Find the treatment sum of squares, block sum of squares, and error sum of squares. What are the corresponding mean squares?

(c) How can you test the equality of treatment means? What is your decision?

(d) How can you test the equality of block means? What is your comment?

(e) Interpret your overall findings.

10.4 The following data show outcomes of a study on seven different treatments applied to three different groups (blocks) of people. In each group, treatments were assigned randomly. The outcomes, on a scale from 0 to 100, are displayed below:

Group	Treatments						
	T_1	T_2	T_3	T_4	T_5	T_6	T_7
G_1	75	77	68	69	93	74	43
	82	80	70	73	81	78	53
	77	81	72	75	88	76	62
G_2	83	73	78	57	79	65	71
	76	72	78	67	87	68	64
	80	75	72	69	78	76	62
G_3	87	77	78	63	86	75	64
	78	73	75	67	79	71	65
	81	77	69	79	82	70	55

(a) Write the appropriate analysis of variance model and indicate the underlying assumptions.

(b) Find the treatment sum of squares, block sum of squares, and error sum of squares.

(c) How can you test the equality of treatment means? What is the test statistic? Comment on the findings of the treatments from the study.

(d) How can you test the equality of block means? What is the test statistic? What is your comment?

(e) Interpret your overall findings.

Chapter 11
Survival Analysis

11.1 Introduction

In this chapter, some important survival analysis techniques are introduced. Survival analysis deals with the time until occurrence of event of interest. We consider situations in which the analysis of times to the occurrence of events such as death attributable to a certain cause, recovery from a disease, duration in disease-free state before recurrence of a disease, etc. are of interest. The time to the occurrence of an event varies depending on the underlying risk or prognostic factors of the subjects included in the study. Mathematically, one can think of time to event as merely meaning a nonnegative valued variable. Although the term time to event is used for general reference, other terms such as survival time and failure time will also be frequently used. The time to event refers to beginning to end (or the length or duration) prior to occurrence of an event. This requires a very well defined event along with the understanding through which that event may occur. To define the recurrence of a disease, for instance, we need to confirm the time of initiation of the disease, duration of suffering from the disease before recovery at the first instance, duration of disease-free spell since recovery from the first spell before recurrence of the disease. In this case, the time to recurrence of disease is of interest. The starting time is the time at recovery from the disease after first spell of the disease and the end point refers to the time at relapse of the disease indicating end of disease-free spell.

For collecting survival data, we may use the following basic study designs:

(a) Cohort Study,
(b) Case-Control Study, and
(c) Cross-sectional Study.

The first two types, cohort or follow-up and case-control or retrospective, are known as longitudinal study designs. In a cohort/follow-up/prospective study, the individuals are followed over time to observe incidence of disease as well as to observe the changes in the status of disease. Here, the sampling is conducted on the

© Springer Nature Singapore Pte Ltd. 2018
M. A. Islam and A. Al-Shiha, *Foundations of Biostatistics*,
https://doi.org/10.1007/978-981-10-8627-4_11

basis of exposure status, and the incidence of the disease is observed at a subsequent time for both the groups with or without exposure. This study design makes it easier to study the natural history of a disease. On the other hand, if the association between a factor and disease is based on information in the past, then the study design is called a case-control study design. In this design, the sampling is performed on the basis of disease status, instead of exposure status, and data on exposure status are collected from the past information provided by the respondents for both the groups with disease or without disease. The cross-sectional study designs are easier to conduct practically both in terms of cost and time because the data on both exposure and disease status are collected at a particular point in time. However, it becomes difficult to assess whether there exists a time-dependent incidence of the disease as an effect of the hypothesized exposure from the data collected by using a cross-sectional study design.

The survival analysis deals with human as the host and the forces within host and environment that cause the events related to change in health conditions. One of our major objectives is to explore the relationships between the host and environmental factors with state of health in a cause–effect framework. However, in most of the cases, even if there is cause–effect relationship for certain events, the presence of multiple causes and their interactive processes make it difficult to establish the relationships using the data collected from various studies. The host factors include various personal traits termed as intrinsic factors. On the other hand, the environmental factors, classified by biological, social, and physical characteristics, are termed as extrinsic factors (Mausner and Kramer 1985). It is also noteworthy that the interrelations between host, agent, and environment, which may be in a broader sense considered as the interaction between host and environment due to the presence of multiplicity of causes, need to be conceptualized in the studies of survival analysis.

In a survival analysis study, the events are usually observed over time implying that some of the individuals may experience the event during the study period but others may experience it later beyond the scope of the study resulting in incomplete observations. These incomplete observations are called censoring. If we fix a predetermined time to end the study, then an individual's lifetime will be known exactly only if it is less than some predetermined value. In such situations, the data are said to be Type I (or time) censored. A Type II censored sample is one for which only the r smallest observations in a random sample of n items or subjects are observed $(1 \leq r \leq n)$. Experiments involving Type II censoring are often used, for example, in life testing; a total of n items is placed on test, but instead of continuing until all n items have failed, the test is terminated at the time of the rth item failure. Such tests can save time and money, since it could take a very long time for all items to fail in some instances. If both event time and censoring time occur randomly, then it is called random censoring.

11.2   Some Measures of Association

One of the major concerns in a survival analysis study is to measure the extent and nature of association between the risk factor or exposure (E) and the disease (D). The measure of association usually involves a direct association between outcome and exposure or study factor as well as a comparison between outcome and exposure with respect to a reference group which may not be considered as an exposure. That is why it becomes a challenge in many instances to measure the association with adequate epidemiologic reasoning. Let us consider that D denotes the occurrence of disease and $\bar{D}$ denotes nonoccurrence of the event. Similarly, let us denote E for presence of exposure and $\bar{E}$ for absence of exposure. Then, we can display the bivariate frequency distribution for presence or absence of exposure and occurrence or nonoccurrence of disease under three basic study designs: (i) prospective or cohort, (ii) retrospective or case-control, and (iii) cross-sectional study design.

(i) Prospective Study: Under the prospective or cohort study designs, the incidence of a disease can be measured for selected level of exposure or presence and absence of the exposure over the study period. In this design, the role of exposure level or presence and absence of exposure can be studied very carefully, and the measure of association provided on the basis of a prospective study may be considered as ideal for estimating measure of association. In a prospective study design, the fundamental condition of cause–effect is taken into consideration, may not be in a very strict sense due to likely presence of multiple causes for an effect, but still provides a more specific measure of association under given conditions in a relative sense. Mausner and Kramer (1985) observed that it is necessary to follow prospectively a defined group of people and determine the rate at which new cases of disease occur to determine incidence.

In Table 11.1, we follow up two groups with or without exposure and subsequently note the disease status among the subjects belonging to exposed and nonexposed groups.

(ii) Case-Control Study: The prospective or cohort studies are always preferred for studying the role of a specific exposure. However, it may not be a very practical study design if time and cost factors are involved. For a prospective study more time and costs are necessary and it is even more difficult if the event of concern or the disease under study is rare. In that

Table 11.1 Table for displaying exposure and disease status from a prospective study disease status

Disease status			
Exposure	D	$\bar{D}$	Total
E	a	b	$a + b$
$\bar{E}$	c	d	$c + d$
Total	$a + c$	$b + d$	n

case, the study needs to consider a very large number of subjects for a meaningful decision-making. Another important point is that for a prospective study, the setting up of specific hypothesis is of prime concern because the study is based on exposure status to determine its role in disease status. In addition, multiplicity of cause in explaining a disease status makes the prospective study constrained. In case of the case-control studies, the cases and controls are selected on the basis of disease status and the status regarding factors that might be considered as exposures are looked for past exposures to factors. Then, Table 11.2 displays the exposure and disease status frequencies.

In Table 11.2 for case-control studies, the cases and controls are selected first and the exposures are looked for retrospectively. In prospective study, the disease status is observed longitudinally as outcomes of follow-up of exposed and nonexposed groups of subjects. On the other hand, the approach is opposite in direction in respect of time for a case-control study where cases and controls are selected as disease status and their status in respect of exposures to factors are noted retrospectively. It may be noted here that there may be ambiguity in the data from retrospective studies about past events which may either be unavailable or may be misreported.

For a matched case-control study, the frequencies are presented in the format where matched pairs are considered (Table 11.3).

(iii) Cross-sectional Study: In a cross-sectional study, both risk factor or exposure and disease status are observed at the same time. These data are collected generally by surveys. Although the cross-sectional studies are easy to conduct and also less costly, the temporal sequence of events, necessary to establish a causal relationship, cannot be established due to lack of adequate information on occurrence of the disease and exposure to factors over time. The data from a cross-sectional study may only represent a snapshot view that represents the current status of both

Table 11.2 Table for displaying exposure and disease status from a case-control study disease status

Disease status

Exposure	Case	Control	Total
E	a	b	$a + b$
$\bar{E}$	c	d	$c + d$
Total	$a + c$	$b + d$	n

Table 11.3 Table for displaying exposure and disease status from a matched case-control study cases

Cases

Controls	E	$\bar{E}$	Total
E	a	b	$a + b$
$\bar{E}$	c	d	$c + d$
Total	$a + c$	$b + d$	n

Table 11.4 Table for displaying exposure and disease status from a cross-sectional study

Disease status			
Exposure	D	$\bar{D}$	Total
E	a	b	$a+b$
$\bar{E}$	c	d	$c+d$
Total	$a+c$	$b+d$	n

disease and exposure without providing any clue regarding the causal inference. However, these studies can be used to explore potential risk factors.

Table 11.4 looks similar as the one for the prospective study but it has to be remembered that in case of a prospective study, the disease status is observed by a follow-up study for exposed and nonexposed groups. In a cross section study, we know about disease and exposure to factors at the same time.

We can estimate the association between exposure and disease status using the following measures referring the tables displayed above.

1. **Relative Risk (RR) for Prospective Study**: Relative risk shows the ratio of risk of incidence in the exposed group as compared to the risk of incidence in the nonexposed group. Here, the risks of incidence in the exposed and nonexposed groups can be defined as follows:

Estimated risk of incidence for the exposed group $= \hat{P}(D|E) = \frac{a}{a+b}$.

Estimated risk of incidence for the nonexposed group $= \hat{P}(D|\bar{E}) = \frac{c}{c+d}$.

The estimated relative risk is

$$\hat{RR} = \frac{\text{risk for exposed group}}{\text{risk for non-exposed group}} = \frac{\hat{P}(D|E)}{\hat{P}(D|\bar{E})}$$
$$= \frac{a/(a+b)}{c/(c+d)}.$$

This measure is based on prospective study data. We cannot express the risks for incidence of disease from case-control or retrospective data.

Interpretation: If the relative risk,

(i) RR = 1, or ln RR = 0, then there is no association between exposure and disease;

(ii) RR > 1, or ln RR > 0, then there is positive association between exposure and disease indicating higher risk of incidence for the exposed group as compared to that of the nonexposed group;

(iii) RR < 1, or ln RR < 0, then there is protective association indicating lower risk of incidence in the exposed group as compared to that of the nonexposed group.

Confidence Interval and Test for RR
We know that RR = 1 indicates no association between the exposure and disease which is equivalent to testing for ln RR = 0. Let us show the test for the null hypothesis $H_0: \ln \text{RR} = 0$.

$\hat{\text{RR}} = \frac{a/(a+b)}{c/(c+d)}$ and $\ln \hat{\text{RR}} = \ln\left(\frac{a}{a+b}\right) - \ln\left(\frac{c}{c+d}\right)$.

It can be shown that the $\text{Var}(\ln \hat{\text{RR}}) = \frac{b/(a+b)}{a} + \frac{d/(c+d)}{c}$.

Similarly, the $\hat{se}(\ln \hat{\text{RR}}) = \sqrt{\frac{b/(a+b)}{a} + \frac{d/(c+d)}{c}}$.

Assuming asymptotic normality, we can use the following test statistic

$$Z = \frac{\ln \hat{\text{RR}}}{\hat{se}(\ln \hat{\text{RR}})} = \frac{\ln \hat{\text{RR}}}{\sqrt{\frac{b/(a+b)}{a} + \frac{d/(c+d)}{c}}} \sim N(0, 1).$$

Acceptance of the null hypothesis indicates that the evidence from the sample data is not sufficient to reject the null hypothesis of no association between exposure and disease, and rejection indicates a possible association.

For moderate or large sample, assuming normality, we can show that the 95% confidence limits for lnRR are

$$\ln \hat{\text{RR}} \pm 1.96 \text{ se } (\ln \hat{\text{RR}}),$$

which are $\ln \hat{\text{RR}} \pm 1.96 \sqrt{\frac{b/(a+b)}{a} + \frac{d/(c+d)}{c}}$.

The 95% confidence limits for RR can be shown as

Lower Limit: $\hat{\text{RR}} e^{-1.96 \hat{se}(\ln \hat{\text{RR}})} = \hat{\text{RR}} e^{-1.96 \sqrt{\frac{b/(a+b)}{a} + \frac{d/(c+d)}{c}}}$.

Upper Limit: $\hat{\text{RR}} e^{1.96 \hat{se}(\ln \hat{\text{RR}})} = \hat{\text{RR}} e^{1.96 \sqrt{\frac{b/(a+b)}{a} + \frac{d/(c+d)}{c}}}$.

2. **Risk Odds Ratio (ROR)**: A more convenient and popular measure for measuring the association between occurrence of disease in the exposed and non-exposed groups is the odds ratio. The odds ratio summarizes the ratio of odds of incidence of disease to non-disease in the exposed group with that of the nonexposed group. The risk odds ratio is defined as

$$\text{ROR} = \frac{P(D|E)/[1 - P(D|E)]}{P(D|\bar{E})/[1 - P(D|\bar{E})]},$$

where the odds of disease in the exposed group are in the numerator and the odds of disease in the nonexposed group are in the denominator. This is popularly known as the odds ratio or OR. For two independent groups by exposure status, the conditional probabilities represent the probabilities of number of incidence cases in the exposed and nonexposed groups. The probability distributions of number of cases in the exposed and nonexposed groups are binomial distributions with parameters $(a+b, P(D|E))$ and $(c+d, P(D|\bar{E}))$, respectively.

The estimates of $P(D|E)$ and $P(D|\bar{E})$ are

$$\hat{P}(D|E) = \frac{a}{a+b} \text{ and } \hat{P}(D|\bar{E}) = \frac{c}{c+d}.$$

We can also show that

$$1 - \hat{P}(D|E) = 1 - \frac{a}{a+b} = \frac{b}{a+b} \text{ and } 1 - \hat{P}(D|\bar{E}) = 1 - \frac{c}{c+d} = \frac{d}{c+d}.$$

Hence, the estimator of the OR can be shown as

$$\hat{OR} = \frac{\hat{P}(D|E)/[1 - \hat{P}(D|E)]}{\hat{P}(D|\bar{E})/[1 - \hat{P}(D|\bar{E})]}.$$

The variances of $\hat{P}(D|E)$ and $\hat{P}(D|\bar{E})$ are

$$\text{Var}\,[\hat{P}(D|E)] = \frac{[P(D|E)][1 - P(D|E)]}{(a+c)}, \text{ and}$$

$$\text{Var}\,[P(D|\bar{E})] = \frac{[P(D|\bar{E})][1 - P(D|\bar{E})]}{(b+d)}.$$

Then taking logarithm of $\hat{OR}$, we find

$$\ln \hat{OR} = \ln[\hat{P}(D|E)/[1 - \hat{P}(D|E)]] - \ln[\hat{P}(D|\bar{E})/[1 - \hat{P}(D|\bar{E})]],$$

where the first term is a function of the proportion of disease cases in the exposed group which is the familiar odds for the exposed group, and the second term is a function of the proportion of disease cases in the nonexposed group which is the odds for the nonexposed group. We can obtain the variance of the odds for both the exposed and nonexposed groups using the delta method as shown below:

$$\text{Var}\left[\ln O\hat{R}\right] = \text{Var}\left[\ln\{\hat{P}(D|E)/[1-\hat{P}(D|E)]\}\right] + \text{Var}\left[\ln\{\hat{P}(D|\bar{E})/[1-\hat{P}(D|\bar{E})]\}\right]$$

$$= \left[\frac{1}{P(D|E)} + \frac{1}{[1-P(D|E)]}\right]^2 \text{Var}\left[\hat{P}(D|E)\right]$$

$$+ \left[\frac{1}{P(D|\bar{E})} + \frac{1}{[1-P(D|\bar{E})]}\right]^2 \text{Var}\left[\hat{P}(D|\bar{E})\right]$$

$$= \left[\frac{1}{P(D|E)} + \frac{1}{[1-P(D|E)]}\right]^2 \frac{P(D|E)[1-P(D|E)]}{(a+b)}$$

$$+ \left[\frac{1}{P(D|\bar{E})} + \frac{1}{[1-P(D|\bar{E})]}\right]^2 \frac{P(D|\bar{E})[1-P(D|\bar{E})]}{(c+d)}$$

$$= \frac{1}{(a+b)\{P(D|E)/[1-P(D|E)]\}} + \frac{1}{(c+d)\{P(D|\bar{E})/[1-P(D|\bar{E})]\}}.$$

The estimate of the variance of $\ln O\hat{R}$ is

$$\text{Va}\hat{\text{r}}\left[\ln O\hat{R}\right] = \frac{1}{(a+b)\{\hat{P}(D|E)/[1-\hat{P}(D|E)]\}} + \frac{1}{(c+d)\{\hat{P}(D|\bar{E})/[1-\hat{P}(D|\bar{E})]\}}.$$

This can be rewritten as

$$\text{Va}\hat{\text{r}}\left[\ln O\hat{R}\right] = \frac{1}{(a+b)\left\{\frac{a}{(a+b)} \times \frac{b}{(a+b)}\right\}} + \frac{1}{(c+d)\left\{\frac{c}{(c+d)} \times \frac{b}{(c+d)}\right\}}$$

$$= \frac{1}{a} + \frac{1}{b} + \frac{1}{c} + \frac{1}{d}.$$

We can now obtain the estimate of the variance of $O\hat{R}$

$$\text{Va}\hat{\text{r}}\left[O\hat{R}\right] = O\hat{R}^2\left(\frac{1}{a} + \frac{1}{b} + \frac{1}{c} + \frac{1}{d}\right).$$

The estimate of the standard error of $O\hat{R}$ is

$$\text{s}\hat{\text{e}}\left[O\hat{R}\right] = O\hat{R}\sqrt{\left(\frac{1}{a} + \frac{1}{b} + \frac{1}{c} + \frac{1}{d}\right)}.$$

Interpretation: The interpretation of an odds ratio is similar to that of the relative risk as stated below:

(i)   OR = 1 or ln OR = 0 shows that there is no association between exposure and disease;

(ii) OR > 1, or ln OR > 0 shows that there is positive association between exposure and disease indicating higher risk of incidence for the exposed group as compared to that of the nonexposed group;

(iii) OR < 1, or ln OR < 0 shows that there is protective association indicating lower risk of incidence in the exposed group as compared to that of the nonexposed group.

Confidence Interval and Test for OR

We know that OR = 1 indicates no association between the exposure and disease which is equivalent to testing for ln OR = 0. Let us show the test for the null hypothesis $H_0: \ln \text{OR} = 0$.

$\hat{\text{OR}} = \frac{ad}{bc}$ and $\ln \hat{\text{OR}} = \ln(a) - \ln(b) - \ln(c) + \ln(d)$.

It can be shown that the $\hat{\text{Var}}(\ln \hat{\text{OR}}) = \frac{1}{a} + \frac{1}{b} + \frac{1}{c} + \frac{1}{d}$.

Similarly, the $\hat{\text{se}}(\ln \hat{\text{OR}}) = \sqrt{\frac{1}{a} + \frac{1}{b} + \frac{1}{c} + \frac{1}{d}}$.

Assuming asymptotic normality for large sample size, we can use the following test statistic:

$$Z = \frac{\ln \hat{\text{OR}}}{\hat{\text{se}}(\ln \hat{\text{OR}})} = \frac{\ln \hat{\text{OR}}}{\sqrt{\frac{1}{a} + \frac{1}{b} + \frac{1}{c} + \frac{1}{d}}} \sim N(0, 1).$$

Non-rejection of null hypothesis indicates that there is not sufficient evidence from the sample data in favor of rejecting the null hypothesis of no association between exposure and disease and rejection indicates possible association.

For moderate or large sample, assuming normality, we can show that the 95% confidence limits for lnOR are

$$\ln \hat{\text{OR}} \pm 1.96 \; \hat{\text{se}}(\ln \hat{\text{OR}}),$$

which are $\ln \hat{\text{OR}} \pm 1.96 \sqrt{\frac{1}{a} + \frac{1}{b} + \frac{1}{c} + \frac{1}{d}}$.

The 95% confidence limits for OR can be shown as

Lower Limit: $\hat{\text{OR}} \, e^{-1.96 \text{se}(\ln \hat{\text{OR}})} = \hat{\text{OR}} \, e^{-1.96 \sqrt{\frac{1}{a} + \frac{1}{b} + \frac{1}{c} + \frac{1}{d}}}$.

Upper Limit: $\hat{\text{OR}} \, e^{1.96 \text{se}(\ln \hat{\text{OR}})} = \hat{\text{OR}} \, e^{1.96 \sqrt{\frac{1}{a} + \frac{1}{b} + \frac{1}{c} + \frac{1}{d}}}$.

3. Risk Ratio for Case-Control Study

The case-control study is retrospective over time and the study is conducted among cases and controls to find the exposure to factor in the past which might have caused the disease. Two essential risks or probabilities for obtaining risk ratio,

$P(D|E)$ and $P(D|\bar{E})$, cannot be defined from the case-control study design. However, an approximation can be obtained for case-control study as shown below.

Let the risk ratio RR $= \frac{P(D|E)}{P(D|\bar{E})}$, where the risks can be expressed alternatively as

$$P(D|E) = \frac{P(D) \times P(E|D)}{P(D) \times P(E|D) + P(\bar{D}) \times P(E|\bar{D})}, \text{ and}$$

$$P(D|\bar{E}) = \frac{P(D) \times P(\bar{E}|D)}{P(D) \times P(\bar{E}|D) + P(\bar{D}) \times P(\bar{E}|\bar{D})}.$$

Replacing these expressions in the risk ratio, we obtain

$$RR = \frac{P(D|E)}{P(D|\bar{E})} = \frac{P(E|D)}{P(\bar{E}|D)} \times \frac{P(D) \times P(\bar{E}|D) + P(\bar{D}) \times P(\bar{E}|\bar{D})}{P(D) \times P(E|D) + P(\bar{D}) \times P(E|\bar{D})}.$$

For rare diseases, $P(D) \simeq 0$ and $P(\bar{D}) \simeq 1$ and the risk ratio is approximately

$$RR \simeq \frac{P(E|D)}{P(\bar{E}|D)} \times \frac{P(\bar{E}|\bar{D})}{P(E|\bar{D})}.$$

The following form resembles the risk ratio for exposure:

$$RR \simeq \frac{P(E|D)/P(\bar{E}|D)}{P(E|\bar{D})/P(\bar{E}|\bar{D})}.$$

This can be estimated as

$$\hat{RR} \simeq \frac{[a/(a+c)]/[c/(a+c)]}{[b/(b+d)]/[d/(b+d)]} = \frac{ad}{bc} = \hat{OR}.$$

This approximation is called the exposure odds ratio (EOR).

The Confidence Interval and Test for Exposure Odds Ratio
We know that OR $= 1$ indicates no association between the exposure and disease which is equivalent to testing for ln OR $= 0$. Let us show the test for the null hypothesis H_0: ln OR $= 0$.

$\hat{OR} = \frac{ad}{bc}$ and $\ln \hat{OR} = \ln(a) - \ln(b) - \ln(c) + \ln(d)$.

It can be shown that the variance is $\hat{Var}(\ln \hat{OR}) = \frac{1}{a} + \frac{1}{b} + \frac{1}{c} + \frac{1}{d}$.

Similarly, the estimate of the standard error is $\hat{se}(\ln \hat{OR}) = \sqrt{\frac{1}{a} + \frac{1}{b} + \frac{1}{c} + \frac{1}{d}}$.

Assuming asymptotic normality for large sample size, we can use the following test statistic

$$Z = \frac{\ln \hat{OR}}{s\hat{e}(\ln \hat{OR})} = \frac{\ln \hat{OR}}{\sqrt{\frac{1}{a} + \frac{1}{b} + \frac{1}{c} + \frac{1}{d}}} \sim N(0, 1).$$

Non-rejection of null hypothesis indicates that there is not sufficient evidence from the sample data in favor of rejecting the null hypothesis of no association between exposure and disease and rejection indicates possible association between exposure and disease status.

For moderate or large sample, assuming normality, we can show that the 95% confidence limits for ln OR are

$$\ln \hat{OR} \pm 1.96 \text{ se } (\ln \hat{OR}),$$

which are $\ln \hat{OR} \pm 1.96 \sqrt{\frac{1}{a} + \frac{1}{b} + \frac{1}{c} + \frac{1}{d}}$.

The 95% confidence limits for OR can be shown as

Lower Limit: $\hat{OR} \, e^{-1.96se(\ln \hat{OR})} = \hat{OR} \, e^{-1.96 \sqrt{\frac{1}{a}+\frac{1}{b}+\frac{1}{c}+\frac{1}{d}}}$.
Upper Limit: $\hat{OR} \, e^{1.96se(\ln \hat{OR})} = \hat{OR} \, e^{1.96 \sqrt{\frac{1}{a}+\frac{1}{b}+\frac{1}{c}+\frac{1}{d}}}$.

4. Odds Ratio from Cross-Sectional Data

Despite serious limitations of the odds ratio from a cross-sectional study design, we still use it as a measure of prevalence odds ratio. These limitations are well documented in the literature but still, the need for cross-sectional study designs is sometimes necessary to provide quick understanding about the potential relationships between exposure and disease. A careful attention is to be given to the limitations of such findings though.

The estimated probabilities can be obtained from cross-sectional cell frequencies for exposure status and disease status. The estimated probabilities, using the cell frequencies shown in Table 11.4, are presented.

The estimated probabilities are (Table 11.5)

$$p_{11} = \frac{a}{n}, p_{10} = \frac{b}{n}, p_{01} = \frac{c}{n}, p_{10} = \frac{d}{n}.$$

Table 11.5 Probabilities of exposure and disease status from a cross-sectional study

Exposure status	Disease status		
	D	$\bar{D}$	Total
E	p_{11}	p_{10}	$p_{1.}$
$\bar{E}$	p_{01}	p_{00}	$p_{0.}$
Total	$p_{.1}$	$p_{.0}$	1

Similarly, the marginal probabilities for exposure status are $p_{1.} = \frac{a+b}{n}$ and $p_{0.} = \frac{c+d}{n}$.

The odds for presence or absence of exposure may be defined as

$$\hat{O}_E = \frac{\hat{P}(D|E)}{\hat{P}(\bar{D}|E)} = \frac{p_{11}/p_{1.}}{p_{10}/p_{1.}} = \frac{a}{b},$$

and

$$\hat{O}_{\bar{E}} = \frac{\hat{P}(D|\bar{E})}{\hat{P}(\bar{D}|\bar{E})} = \frac{p_{01}/p_{0.}}{p_{00}/p_{0.}} = \frac{c}{d}.$$

The odds ratio is

$$\hat{OR} = \frac{\hat{O}_E}{\hat{O}_{\bar{E}}} = \frac{a/b}{c/d} = \frac{ad}{bc}.$$

The variance of the estimator of odds ratio can be shown by using the multinomial distribution and using the delta method it can be shown that

$$\hat{Var}\left[\ln \hat{OR}\right] = \frac{1}{a} + \frac{1}{b} + \frac{1}{c} + \frac{1}{d}.$$

Confidence Interval and Test for OR
The null hypothesis is $H_0: \ln OR = 0$.

Assuming asymptotic normality for large sample size, we can use the following test statistic:

$$Z = \frac{\ln \hat{OR}}{\hat{se}(\ln \hat{OR})} = \frac{\ln \hat{OR}}{\sqrt{\frac{1}{a} + \frac{1}{b} + \frac{1}{c} + \frac{1}{d}}} \sim N(0,1).$$

The 95% confidence limits for lnOR are

$$\ln \hat{OR} \pm 1.96 \, \hat{se}(\ln \hat{OR}),$$

which are $\ln \hat{OR} \pm 1.96 \sqrt{\frac{1}{a} + \frac{1}{b} + \frac{1}{c} + \frac{1}{d}}$.

It can also be shown that 95% confidence limits for OR can be shown as

Lower Limit: $\hat{OR} \, e^{-1.96 se(\ln \hat{OR})} = \hat{OR} \, e^{-1.96 \sqrt{\frac{1}{a} + \frac{1}{b} + \frac{1}{c} + \frac{1}{d}}}$.

Upper Limit: $\hat{OR} \, e^{1.96 se(\ln \hat{OR})} = \hat{OR} \, e^{1.96 \sqrt{\frac{1}{a} + \frac{1}{b} + \frac{1}{c} + \frac{1}{d}}}$.

Example 11.1 Let us consider a hypothetical example on incidence of a disease among the infants with low and normal birth weight from a prospective study

Table 11.6 Table for displaying hypothetical data on birth weight and disease status from a prospective study

Disease status			
Birth weight	D	$\bar{D}$	Total
Low	60	540	600
Normal	50	1950	2000
Total	110	2490	2600

continued for one year on the newly born babies in a community. The data are presented in Table 11.6.

In this example, low birth weight is an exposure and normal birth weight is considered as nonexposed for the incidence of disease being studied. The estimate of relative risk is obtained from the ratio of the risks for the exposed and nonexposed groups as follows:

$$\text{Estimate of risk for the low birthweight group} = \frac{a}{a+b} = \frac{60}{600} = 0.1000, \text{ and}$$

$$\text{Estimate of risk for the normal group} = \frac{c}{c+d} = \frac{50}{1950} = 0.0256.$$

The estimate of the relative risk is

$$\hat{RR} = \frac{R_E}{R_{\bar{E}}} = \frac{0.1}{0.0256} = 3.9062.$$

The estimate of the relative risk shows that the risk of disease for low birth weight babies is about 3.91 times higher than the risk for normal birth weight babies.

To test for the statistical significance of no association between birth weight and the disease, the null hypothesis is $H_0 : \ln RR = 0$.

The estimate of log relative risk is

$$\ln \hat{RR} = \ln\left(\frac{a}{a+b}\right) - \ln\left(\frac{c}{c+d}\right) = -2.3026 - (-3.6652) = 1.3626.$$

The estimate of the standard error of the log relative risk is

$$\hat{se}(\ln \hat{RR}) = \sqrt{\frac{540/600}{60} + \frac{1950/2000}{50}} = \sqrt{0.015 + 0.0195} = 0.1857.$$

The test statistic for large sample size is

$$Z = \frac{\ln \hat{RR}}{\hat{se}(\ln \hat{RR})} = \frac{\ln \hat{RR}}{\sqrt{\frac{b/(a+b)}{a} + \frac{d/(c+d)}{c}}} \sim N(0, 1)$$

and for the sample data, the test statistic value can be computed

$$z = \frac{\ln R\hat{R}}{s\hat{e}(\ln R\hat{R})} = \frac{1.3626}{0.1857} = 7.3376.$$

The null hypothesis of no association is rejected (*p*-value < 0.01). The 95% confidence limits for $\ln RR$ are

$$\ln R\hat{R} \pm 1.96 \text{ se } (\ln R\hat{R}).$$

Using the sample data, we obtain

$$1.3626 \pm 1.96 \times 0.1857$$

and the lower and upper limits are (0.9986,1.7265).

The 95% confidence limits for RR can be shown as

Lower Limit: $R\hat{R}\, e^{-1.96se(\ln R\hat{R})} = 3.9062 \times e^{-1.96 \times 1.3626} = 2.7145.$

Upper Limit: $R\hat{R}\, e^{1.96se(\ln R\hat{R})} = 3.9062 \times e^{1.96 \times 1.3626} = 5.6212.$

The null hypothesis for no association using the prospective data is $H_0: \ln OR = 0.$

The estimate of the odds ratio is

$$O\hat{R} = \frac{ad}{bc} = \frac{60 \times 1950}{540 \times 50} = 4.33 \text{ and } \ln O\hat{R} = 1.4656.$$

It can be shown that the

$$Va\hat{r}\,(\ln O\hat{R}) = \frac{1}{a} + \frac{1}{b} + \frac{1}{c} + \frac{1}{d} = \frac{1}{60} + \frac{1}{540} + \frac{1}{50} + \frac{1}{1950} = 0.0390$$

and taking positive square root, we obtain the estimate of the standard error $s\hat{e}(\ln O\hat{R}) = \sqrt{\frac{1}{a} + \frac{1}{b} + \frac{1}{c} + \frac{1}{d}} = 0.1975.$

The test statistic is

$$Z = \frac{\ln O\hat{R}}{s\hat{e}(\ln O\hat{R})} = \frac{\ln O\hat{R}}{\sqrt{\frac{1}{a} + \frac{1}{b} + \frac{1}{c} + \frac{1}{d}}}$$

and using the sample data, we obtain

$$z = \frac{\ln O\hat{R}}{s\hat{e}(\ln O\hat{R})} = \frac{1.4656}{0.1975} = 7.4207.$$

Like the test for the relative risk, in this case also, we reject the null hypothesis of no association between birth weight and the disease under study. In other words, there is evidence in support of rejection of the null hypothesis of no association between birth weight of babies and disease status.

The 95% confidence limits for ln OR are

$$\ln \hat{OR} \pm 1.96 \ se \ (\ln \hat{OR})$$

and using the sample data, we obtain the lower and upper limits from

$$1.4656 \pm 1.96 \times 0.1975$$

which are (1.0785, 1.8527).

We can construct the 95% confidence limits for OR can be shown as

Lower Limit: $\hat{OR} \ e^{-1.96se(\ln \hat{OR})} = 4.33 \times e^{-1.96 \times 0.1975} = 2.9402.$
Upper Limit: $\hat{OR} \ e^{1.96se(\ln \hat{OR})} = 4.33 \times e^{1.96 \times 0.1975} = 6.3768.$

11.3 Nonparametric Estimation

There are two different types of nonparametric methods extensively used for nonparametric estimation of survival function, $S(t)$. These are (i) the actuarial method and (ii) the product-limit or Kaplan–Meier method. First one is used mostly in actuarial science and the second method in both epidemiology and survival analysis in addition to extensive use in other fields as well. In this section, the actuarial method of constructing a life table and the product-limit method are discussed.

The Actuarial Method
Let time be partitioned into a fixed sequence of intervals I_1, I_2, $...{_k}I_k$. These intervals may or may not be of equal lengths, although mostly they are of equal lengths. We can show the intervals as follows:

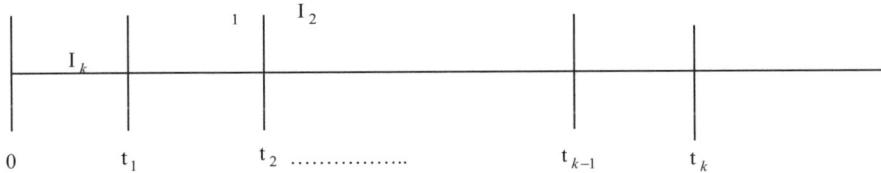

For a life table let us define the following:

n_i = number alive at the beginning of I_i,
d_i = number of deaths during I_i,
l_i = number lost to follow-up during I_i,

w_i = number withdrew during I_i, and
p_i = P (surviving through $I_i|$ alive at beginning of I_i), and
$q_i = 1 - p_i$.

To estimate a survival function, we can use the actuarial method.

By definition, the survival probability, $S(t_k)$, is the probability that an individual will survive greater than time t_k

$$S(t_k) = P(t > t_k)$$

which can be expressed as product of probabilities of surviving through intervals until t_k as shown below:

$$S(t_k) = P(T > t_1) \cdot P(T > t_2|T > t_1)...P(T > t_k|T > t_{k-1})$$
$$= p_1 \cdot p_2 \cdots p_k$$
$$= \prod_{i=1}^{k} p_i,$$

where $p_i = P(T > t_i|T > t_{i-1}), i = 1,...,k$.

For estimating p_i, we assume that the individuals who are lost or withdrawn during I_i are at risk for half the interval. Hence, we need to define the effective sample size

$$n_i' = n_i - 1/2(l_i + w_i).$$

The estimates for p_i and q_i are

$$\widehat{q}_i = \frac{d_i}{n_i'},$$

and $\widehat{p}_i = 1 - \widehat{q}_i$.

The actuarial estimate of survivor function is

$$\widehat{S}(t_k) = \prod_{i=1}^{k} \widehat{p}_i.$$

Variance of $\widehat{S}(t_k)$
We know that

$$\widehat{S}(t_k) = \prod_{i=1}^{k} \widehat{p}_i.$$

The variance of the survivor function can be shown as

$$\widehat{\text{Var}}\left(\hat{S}(t_k)\right) = \left(\hat{S}(t_k)\right)^2 \cdot \sum_{i=1}^{k} \frac{\hat{q}_i}{n_i' \hat{p}_i}$$

which can be further simplified as shown below:

$$\widehat{\text{Var}}\left(\hat{S}(t_k)\right) = \left(\hat{S}(t_k)\right)^2 \cdot \sum_{i=1}^{k} \frac{d_i}{n_i'(n_i' - d_i)}.$$

This is called the Greenwood's formula.

The Product-Limit Method

The most extensively used technique in survival analysis for estimating survival function for censored data is the product-limit (P-L) method developed by Kaplan and Meier in 1958. This is known as Kaplan–Meier (K-M) method too. The product-limit method is similar to the actuarial estimator except that the length of the interval I_i is a variable. In addition, the actuarial method is obtained for grouped data but the product-limit method is employed for ungrouped data, with exceptions for ties.

Let us consider t_i be the right endpoint of I_i which is the ith ordered censored or uncensored observation.

Let us consider that $T_{(1)} < T_{(2)} < \cdots < T_{(n)}$ be the order statistics of $T_1, \ldots, T_n$ where T_i is the variable for the ith time, censored or uncensored. The corresponding censored or uncensored values are $t_{(1)} < t_{(2)} < \cdots < t_{(n)}$. Let r be the total number of uncensored cases then $(n - r)$ is the number of censored cases in the lifetime data being considered in the experiment. Let us also consider that

$\delta_{(i)} = 1$ if $T_{(i)}$ is uncensored, and

$\quad\ = 0$ if $T_{(i)}$ is censored.

Then, we observe the pairs $(T_1, \delta_1), (T_2, \delta_2), \ldots, (T_n, \delta_n)$. For simplicity, let us consider the case of no ties first.

Let us assume that all the T_i's are distinct, and there is no tie. Hence, the ordered survival times $T_{(1)} < T_{(2)} < \cdots < T_{(n)}$ are associated with corresponding values of censoring indicators. Let $R(t)$ denote the risk set at time t, which is the set of subjects still surviving at time $t-$, and let

$n_i = $ risk set $R(t_{(i)}) = $ number of subjects still surviving at time $t_{(i)}-$,

$d_i = $ number of items failed at time $t_{(i)}$,

$p_i = P(\text{surviving through } I_i | \text{ alive at beginning of } I_i)$,

$\quad\ = P(T > t_{(i)} | T > t_{(i-1)}))$, and

$q_i = 1 - p_i$.

The estimates under the assumption of no ties are

$$\widehat{q}_i = \frac{1}{n_i},$$

$$\widehat{p}_i = 1 - \widehat{q}_i = 1 - \frac{1}{n_i} \text{ if } \delta_{(i)} = 1 \text{ (uncensored)}$$

$$= 1 \text{ if } \delta_{(i)} = 0 \text{ (censored.)}$$

Then, the estimate for the survival function, $S(t)$, under the assumption of no ties is

$$\hat{S}(t) = \prod_{t_{(i)} \le t} \widehat{p}_i = \prod_{t_{(i)} \le t} \left(1 - \frac{1}{n_i}\right)^{\delta_{(i)}}$$

$$= \prod_{t_{(i)} \le t} \left(1 - \frac{1}{n-i+1}\right)^{\delta_{(i)}} = \prod_{t_{(i)} \le t} \left(\frac{n-i}{n-i+1}\right)^{\delta_{(i)}}.$$

If censored and uncensored observations are tied, let us consider that uncensored observations occurred just before the censored observations.

Now let us consider that there are r distinct survival times that can be arranged as order statistics as follows:

$$t'_{(1)} < t'_{(2)} < \cdots < t'_{(r)}.$$

Then, let us define the following:

$$\delta_{(i)} = 1 \text{ if the observations at time } t'_{(i)} \text{ are uncensored,}$$

$$= 0, \text{ if censored,}$$

$$n_i = \text{ number of subjects at risk in } R(t'_{(i)}),$$

$$d_i = \text{ number of failures at } t'_{(i)}.$$

Then, the PL estimate for survival function can be obtained as follows for ties:

$$\widehat{S}(t) = \prod_{t'_i \le t} \left(1 - \frac{d_i}{n_i}\right)^{\delta_{(i)}}.$$

Variance of $\widehat{S}(t)$
We know that

$$\widehat{S}(t) = \prod_{t'_{(i)} \le t} \left(1 - \frac{d_i}{n_i}\right)^{\delta_{(i)}}.$$

Taking $\log_e$, we obtain

$$\ln\widehat{S}(t) = \sum_{t_{(i)} \leq t} \delta_{(i)} \ln \left(1 - \frac{d_i}{n_i}\right).$$

The estimate of the variance of survivor function can be shown as

$$\text{Var}(\widehat{S}(t)) = \left[\widehat{S}(t)\right]^2 \cdot \sum_{t_{(i)} \leq t} \frac{\delta_{(i)}\widehat{q}_i}{n_i\widehat{p}_i}$$

which can be further simplified as shown below:

$$\text{Var}(\widehat{S}(t)) = \left[\widehat{S}(t)\right]^2 \cdot \sum_{t_{(i)} \leq t} \frac{\delta_{(i)}d_i}{n_i(n_i - d_i)}.$$

This is the same Greenwood's formula for estimating variance of survival function displayed for the actuarial method.

Example 11.2 Suppose that a test has been carried out on a sample of 16 items, and the observed lifetimes are (given in months)

$$5, 7, 9+, 14, 17, 19+, 20, 26, 30+, 40, 45, 46, 49+, 55, 61+, 69$$

where + indicates a censoring.

The computation of P-L estimates is shown below for time of survival. The censoring indicator 1 denotes uncensored and 0 denotes censored times (Table 11.7; Fig. 11.1).

Log-Rank Test
We know that

$$\widehat{S}(t) = \prod_{t'_{(i)} \leq t} \left(1 - \frac{d_i}{n_i}\right)^{\delta_{(i)}}.$$

If we want to compare survivor functions of two groups, such as treatment is group 1 and placebo is group 2, then we can use the log-rank test which is essentially a large sample chi-square test.

Let us consider that the combined set is ordered and the distinct times are denoted by t_i. Then

n_{1i} = number of subjects in group 1 at risk at time t_i,
n_{2i} = number of subjects in group 2 at risk at time t_i,
d_{1i} = number of failures in group 1 at time t_i,
d_{2i} = number of failures in group 2 at time t_i,

Table 11.7 Computation of the P-L estimates of survival function

	Time (months)	Censoring indicator	Estimate of survival function and standard error		Number of cumulative events	Number of remaining cases
			Estimate	Std. error		
1	5	1	0.938	0.061	1	15
2	7	1	0.875	0.083	2	14
3	9	0			2	13
4	14	1	0.808	0.100	3	12
5	17	1	0.740	0.112	4	11
6	19	0			4	10
7	20	1	0.666	0.123	5	9
8	26	1	0.592	0.130	6	8
9	30	0			6	7
10	40	1	0.508	0.136	7	6
11	45	1	0.423	0.137	8	5
12	46	1	0.338	0.133	9	4
13	49	0			9	3
14	55	1	0.226	0.128	10	2
15	61	0			10	1
16	69	1	0.000	0.000	11	0

δ_{1i} = 1, if t_i is uncensored for failures in group 1; 0, otherwise, and
δ_{2i} = 1, if t_i is uncensored for failures in group 2; 0, otherwise.

Let the survivor functions for groups 1 and 2 at time t_j, where $j = 1, 2,..., n'$ then

$$\widehat{S}_1(t_j) = \prod_{t'_{(i)} \leq t_j} \left(1 - \frac{d_{1i}}{n_{1i}}\right)^{\delta_{(1i)}}, \text{ for group 1}$$

$$\widehat{S}_2(t_j) = \prod_{t'_{(i)} \leq t_j} \left(1 - \frac{d_{2i}}{n_{2i}}\right)^{\delta_{(2i)}}, \text{ for group 2.}$$

The expected number of failures in two groups is

$$e_{1i} = \left(\frac{n_{1i}}{n_{1i} + n_{2i}}\right) \times (d_{1i} + d_{2i})$$

$$e_{2i} = \left(\frac{n_{2i}}{n_{1i} + n_{2i}}\right) \times (d_{1i} + d_{2i}).$$

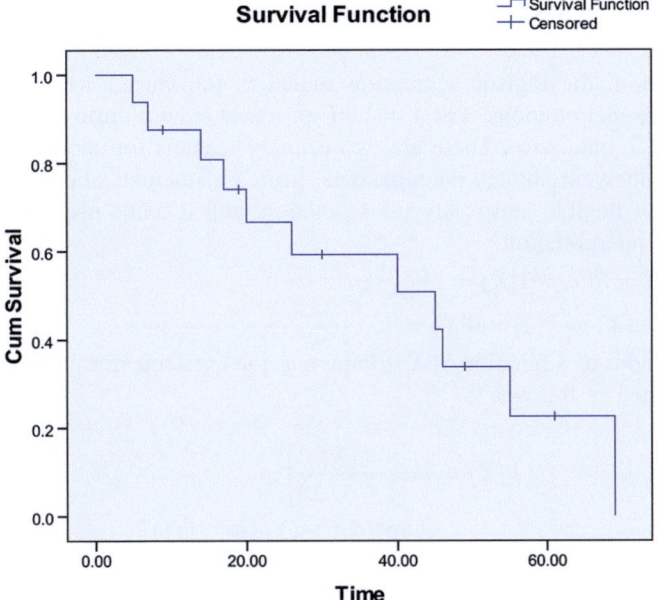

Fig. 11.1 Survival curve for the observed lifetimes of a sample of 16 subjects in a test

Then, the (observed − expected) deaths in group 1 is

$$O_1 - E_1 = \sum_{i=1}^{n} (d_{1i} - e_{1i})$$

and for group 2 is

$$O_2 - E_2 = \sum_{i=1}^{n} (d_{2i} - e_{2i}).$$

Then, the log-rank statistic is defined as

$$\chi^2 = \frac{(O_2 - E_2)^2}{\text{Var}\,(O_2 - E_2)}$$

$$= \frac{(O_2 - E_2)^2}{\sum_{i=1}^{n} \frac{n_{1i}n_{2i}(d_{1i} + d_{2i})(n_{1i} + n_{2i} - d_{1i} - d_{2i})}{(n_{1i} + n_{2i})^2 (n_{1i} + n_{2i} - 1)}}$$

which is chi-square with 1 df under H_0.

11.4 Logistic Regression Model

In this section, the logistic regression model is introduced where the outcome variables are dichotomous. Let $Y = 1$, if an event occurs during a defined study period, $Y = 0$, otherwise. There are two primary reasons for choosing the logistic function in analyzing binary outcome data, from a mathematical point of view, it is an extremely flexible and easily used function, and it lends itself to biologically meaningful interpretation.

Let $\pi(X) = P(Y = 1|X) = \frac{e^{\beta_0 + \beta_1 X}}{1 + e^{\beta_0 + \beta_1 X}}$

and $1 - \pi(X) = P(Y = 0|X) = 1 - \frac{e^{\beta_0 + \beta_1 X}}{1 + e^{\beta_0 + \beta_1 X}} = \frac{1}{1 + e^{\beta_0 + \beta_1 X}}.$

The log odds as a function of X is known as the logit transformation of $\pi(X)$ that can be defined as follows:

$$g(X) = \ln\left[\frac{\pi(X)}{1 - \pi(X)}\right]$$
$$= \ln\left[\frac{e^{\beta_0 + \beta_1 X}/(1 + e^{\beta_0 + \beta_1 X})}{1/(1 + e^{\beta_0 + \beta_1 X})}\right]$$
$$= \ln\left[e^{\beta_0 + \beta_1 X}\right] = \beta_0 + \beta_1 X.$$

This is a linear function and the logit function provides a linear logistic regression model.

Suppose we have a random sample of n pairs of observations (X_i, Y_i), $i = 1, 2,\ldots, n$. The outcome variable, Y, is a binary variable and X is the explanatory variable. The binary outcome variable represents presence or absence of the characteristic. The outcome variable can be represented by a Bernoulli distribution with parameter $\pi(X)$ and the likelihood function is

$$L(\beta) = \prod_{i=1}^{n} L_i(X_i) = \prod_{i=1}^{n} [\pi(X_i)]^{Y_i}[1 - \pi(X_i)]^{1-Y_i}$$
$$= \prod_{i=1}^{n} \left[\frac{e^{\beta_0 + \beta_1 X_i}}{1 + e^{\beta_0 + \beta_1 X_i}}\right]^{Y_i} \left[\frac{1}{1 + e^{\beta_0 + \beta_1 X_i}}\right]^{1-Y_i}.$$

Taking log and differentiating with respect to the regression parameters, we obtain the estimating equations

$$\sum_{i=1}^{n} [Y_i - \pi(X_i)] = 0, \text{and}$$

$$\sum_{i=1}^{n} X_i[Y_i - \pi(X_i)] = 0.$$

Solving the above equations, we obtain the estimates for β_0 and β_1.

To test the hypothesis that $H_0 : \beta_1 = 0$, a likelihood ratio test can be used. The statistic $\chi^2 = -2[\ln L(\hat{\beta}_0) - \ln L(\hat{\beta}_0, \hat{\beta}_1)]$ is distributed as chi-square with one degree of freedom under the hypothesis that β_1 is equal to zero.

An alternative test for the significance of the coefficients is the Wald test which uses the following test statistic:

$$W = \frac{\hat{\beta}_1}{se\left(\hat{\beta}_1\right)}$$

which follows the standard normal distribution asymptotically under the null hypothesis $H_0 : \beta_1 = 0$. Though the Wald test is used by many, it is less powerful than the likelihood ratio test. The Wald test often misleads the user to conclude that the coefficient (consequently the corresponding risk factor) is not significant when it indeed is.

We can extend the above model for p covariates. Let X be a vector of p independent variables

$$X = \begin{bmatrix} 1 \\ X_1 \\ \cdot \\ \cdot \\ \cdot \\ X_p \end{bmatrix}, \quad \text{and} \quad \beta = \begin{bmatrix} \beta_0 \\ \beta_1 \\ \cdot \\ \cdot \\ \cdot \\ \beta_p \end{bmatrix}$$

then

$$\pi(X) = \frac{e^{g(X)}}{1 + e^{g(X)}},$$

where $g(X) = X'\beta = \beta_0 + \beta_1 X_1 + \cdots + \beta_p X_p$.

Assume that we have a sample of n independent observations of the pair (X_i, Y_i) where

$$X_i = \begin{bmatrix} X_{i1} \\ X_{i2} \\ \cdot \\ \cdot \\ \cdot \\ X_{ip} \end{bmatrix} = \text{observations on the } p \text{ independent variables for the } i\text{th individual.}$$

Hence, the fitting of the model requires estimation of the vector of parameters

$$\beta = \begin{bmatrix} \beta_0 \\ \beta_1 \\ \cdot \\ \cdot \\ \cdot \\ \beta_p \end{bmatrix}.$$

The likelihood function is identical to that given for a single independent variable, with the only change being that $\pi(X)$ is defined in terms of a multivariate logit. There are $(p + 1)$ likelihood equations which are obtained by differentiating the log-likelihood function with respect to the $(p + 1)$ parameters $\beta_0, \beta_1, \ldots, \beta_p$. The estimating equations are

$$\sum_{i=1}^{n} [Y_i - \pi(X_i)] = 0$$

$$\sum_{i=1}^{n} X_{ij}[Y_i - \pi(X_i)] = 0, \quad j = 1, 2, \ldots, p.$$

From the second derivatives, we obtain

$$I_{ju}^* = -\sum_{i=1}^{n} X_{ij} X_{iu} \pi_i (1 - \pi_i), \quad j, u = 0, 1, \ldots, p$$

where $\pi_i = \pi(X_i)$. The information matrix is defined by the $(p + 1) \times (p + 1)$ matrix with (j, u)th element $I_{ju} = (-1) \cdot I_{ju}^*$. Then, the variance–covariance matrix can be defined as the inverse of the information matrix

$$\Sigma(\beta) = I^{-1}(\beta),$$

where jth diagonal element is the variance of the estimator of $\beta_j, j = 0, 1, \ldots, p$.

An approximate $100(1 - \alpha)$ percent confidence interval for β_j can be obtained as

$$\hat{\beta}_j \pm z_{1-\alpha/2} \sqrt{I_{jj}^{-1}},$$

where $z_{1-\alpha/2}$ is the $100(1 - \alpha/2)$ percentile of the standard normal distribution.

To test the hypothesis that some of the β_j's are zero, a likelihood ratio test can be used. For testing the null hypothesis

$$H_0 : \beta_1 = \beta_2 = \cdots = \beta_p = 0$$

we can use the test statistic

$$\chi^2 = -2\left[\ln L\left(\hat{\beta}_0\right) - \ln L\left(\hat{\beta}_0, \hat{\beta}_1, \ldots, \hat{\beta}_p\right)\right]$$

which is asymptotically chi square with p degrees of freedom.

Example 11.3 Let us consider the following hypothetical data where the dependent variable, Y, represents occurrence of a certain disease for $Y = 1$ and absence of disease for $Y = 0$. Similarly, X is an exposure with $X = 1$ for presence of exposure and $X = 0$ for absence of exposure.

Disease status			
Exposure	$Y = 1$	$Y = 0$	Total
$X = 1$	17	30	47
$X = 0$	2	20	22
Total	19	50	69

Here, the logistic regression model is

$$\pi(X) = P(Y = 1|X) = \frac{e^{\beta_0 + \beta_1 X}}{1 + e^{\beta_0 + \beta_1 X}}.$$

The estimates of the parameters and corresponding standard errors are

$$\hat{\beta}_0 = -2.4026 \quad \text{and} \quad \hat{\beta}_1 = 1.7346, \text{and}$$
$$\text{sê}\left(\hat{\beta}_0\right) = 0.7416 \quad \text{and} \quad \text{sê}\left(\hat{\beta}_1\right) = 0.8013.$$

The point estimate of $\ln OR$ is $\hat{\beta}_1 = 1.7346$ and the estimate for OR

$$e^{\hat{\beta}_1} = e^{1.7346} = 5.667.$$

The 95% confidence limits for OR are as follows: lower limit = 1.178 and upper limit = 27.254.

The fitted regression model is

$$\hat{\pi}(X) = \hat{P}(Y = 1|X) = \frac{e^{-2.3026 + 1.7346X}}{1 + e^{-2.3026 + 1.7346X}}.$$

Using the likelihood ratio test for $H_0: \beta_1 = 0$ against the alternative $H_1: \beta_1 \neq 0$, we obtain $\chi^2 = -2[\ln L(\hat{\beta}_0) - \ln L(\hat{\beta}_0, \hat{\beta}_1)] = 81.216 - 74.917 = 6.2989$ (p-value = 0.0121). Asymptotically, the distribution is chi-square with 1 degree of freedom in this case. Here, the null hypothesis that there is no association between the exposure and the disease may be rejected.

Alternatively, the Wald test which uses the following test statistic:

$$W = \frac{\hat{\beta}_1}{se\left(\hat{\beta}_1\right)} = \frac{1.7346}{0.8013} = 2.1647 \ (p\text{-value} = 0.0340)$$

confirms the result based on the likelihood ratio test.

Example 11.4 This example uses a five percent random sample data from the wave five of the Health and Retirement Study (HRS). Three hundred one subjects included in this sample after removing the missing values for outcomes and risk factors. The outcome is the depression status ($Y = 0$, 1), dichotomized (0 no depression, 1 depression) based on a score using the scale proposed by the Center for Epidemiologic Studies of Depression (CESD). The explanatory variables considered are age (in years) denoted by X_1, gender (male = 1, female = 0) denoted by X_2, marital status (MStatus) (married/partnered = 1, single/separated = 0) denoted by X_3, BMI is denoted by X_4, white race (1 yes, 0 no) denoted by X_5 (other race is the reference category), black race (1 yes, 0 no) denoted by X_6 (other race is the reference category), drink (yes = 1, no = 0) denoted by X_7, and number of conditions ever had (NCond) denoted by X_8.

The overall fit of the model appears to be significant that means we may reject the null hypothesis

$$H_0{:}\beta_1 = \beta_2 = \cdots = \beta_8 = 0.$$

The rejection of this null hypothesis implies that there is at least one logistic regression variable significantly associated with depression status. The likelihood ratio chi-square value is 61.5393 (p-value < 0.0001). The model fit statistics are shown in Table 11.8.

Among the selected variables, it appears that age, gender, and BMI do not show any statistically significant association with depression. However, the negative association of depression status with marital status (p-value $= 0.05$), white race (p-value < 0.01) compared to other races, black race (p-value $= 0.06$) compared to other races, and drinking habit (p-value < 0.01) are observed. The number of conditions shows a positive association with depression status (p-value < 0.001).

11.5 Models Based on Longitudinal Data

Survival analysis deals with events concerning survival status of subjects over time longitudinally. The event status of the under consideration is observed repeatedly over time. In contrast to longitudinal studies, cross-sectional studies provide single outcome for each individual at a point in time. The major advantages of a longitudinal study are that cohort and age effects can be studied in survival analysis using longitudinal data. In addition, the period effect can also be taken into account. The longitudinal data can be collected either prospectively, following subjects forward

Table 11.8 Model fit statistics, estimates, and tests on the logistic regression model for depression status among elderly people

A. Model fit statistics

Criterion	Intercept only	Intercept and covariates
AIC	440.671	395.132
SC	444.443	429.075
−2 Log L	438.671	377.132

B. Testing global null hypothesis beta = 0

Test	Chi-square	DF	Pr > ChiSq
Likelihood ratio	61.5393	8	<0.0001
Score	53.4166	8	<0.0001
Wald	44.8382	8	<0.0001

C. Estimates and tests of parameters of the logistic regression model

Covariate	Estimate	Standard error	Wald χ^2	p-value	Odds ratio estimates point estimate	95% Wald confidence limits	
Intercept	2.4501	2.8389	0.7449	0.3881			
Age	0.00318	0.0401	0.0063	0.9369	1.003	0.927	1.085
Gender	−0.0663	0.2631	0.0636	0.8010	0.936	0.559	1.567
MStatus	−0.5893	0.3009	3.8348	0.0502	0.555	0.308	1.001
BMI	0.0158	0.0248	0.4058	0.5241	1.016	0.968	1.067
White	−2.8780	1.0854	7.0304	0.0080	0.056	0.007	0.472
Black	−2.1319	1.1340	3.5341	0.0601	0.119	0.013	1.095
Drink	−0.7812	0.2561	9.3008	0.0023	0.458	0.277	0.756
NCond	0.4364	0.1109	15.475	<0.0001	1.547	1.245	1.923

in time, or retrospectively, by extracting multiple measurements on each person from historical records. The longitudinal data require special statistical methods because the set of observations on one subject tends to be intercorrelated. This correlation needs to be taken into account to draw valid scientific inferences. Furthermore, the longitudinal data analysis involves the problem of censoring or loss to follow-up. This problem requires special attention as well for any valid scientific conclusion.

Some important terms usually found in survival analysis are defined below.

Lifetime
We consider situations in which the time to the occurrence of some event is of interest for some population of individuals. The time to the occurrences of event is termed as lifetime. Mathematically, one can think of lifetime as merely meaning nonnegative valued variable. Although the term lifetime is used for general reference, other terms such as survival time and failure time are also frequently used.

Survival Function
Survival function is defined as the probability that an individual is surviving till time t and is defined by

$$S(t) = P[T \geq t], t \geq 0.$$

It is assumed that $S(t) = 1$ for $t = 0$.

A survival function is the complementary to cumulative distribution function since $S(t) = 1 - F(t)$ for continuous random variables, where $F(t) = P[T < t]$ is the cumulative distribution function. All survival functions must satisfy three conditions: $S(0) = 1$, $\lim_{t \to \infty} S(t) = 0$, and $S(t)$ is nonincreasing.

The conditional survival function, $S_{T|T \geq a}(t)$, is the survival function of a randomly chosen subject given that the subject is surviving at time a. The conditional survival function can be shown as

$$S_{T|T \geq a}(t) = \frac{P(T \geq t \text{ and } T \geq a)}{P(T \geq a)} = \frac{P(T \geq t)}{P(T \geq a)} = \frac{S(t)}{S(a)}, t \geq a.$$

Probability Density Function
The probability density function of lifetime is defined by

$$f(t) = \frac{dF(t)}{dt} = -\frac{dS(t)}{dt}$$

because $S(t) = 1 - F(t)$. The probability of failure between times a and b is calculated by an integral

$$P(a \leq T \leq b) = \int_a^b f(t) dt.$$

Hazard Function
The hazard function is used most extensively for its ability to provide a measure of the amount of risk associated with a subject at time t and for making comparison of the risks and possible change in the risks over time. The hazard function is known as the hazard rate, failure rate, force of mortality, force of decrement, intensity function, and age-specific death rate, and its reciprocal is known as Mill's ratio in economics.

The hazard function can be derived by using the conditional probability. Let us consider the probability of failure between t and $t + \Delta t$

$$P(t \leq T \leq t + \Delta t) = \int_{t}^{t + \Delta t} f(\tau) d\tau = S(t) - S(t + \Delta t).$$

Conditioning on the event that the subject is surviving at time t and then fails during t and $t + \Delta t$

$$P(t \leq T \leq t + \Delta t | T \geq t) = \frac{P(t \leq T \leq t + \Delta t)}{P(T \geq t)} = \frac{S(t) - S(t + \Delta t)}{S(t)}.$$

The average rate of failure is obtained if we divide by Δt

$$\frac{S(t) - S(t + \Delta t)}{S(t) \Delta t}.$$

As $\Delta t \to 0$, this becomes the instantaneous failure rate, which is the hazard function

$$h(t) = \lim_{\Delta t \to 0} \frac{S(t) - S(t + \Delta t)}{S(t) \Delta t}$$
$$= \frac{-S'(t)}{S(t)} = \frac{f(t)}{S(t)}, t \geq 0.$$

This shows that the hazard function is defined as the ratio of probability density function and survival function at time t. All the hazard functions must satisfy the following conditions:

$$\int_{0}^{\infty} h(t) dt = \infty \text{ and } h(t) \geq 0 \text{ for all } t \geq 0.$$

The hazard function is important because it has a direct physical interpretation, and information about the nature of the function is useful in selecting an appropriate model for lifetime.

Cumulative Hazard Function
The cumulative hazard function, $H(t)$, is defined as

$$H(t) = \int_{0}^{t} h(\tau) d\tau, \quad t \geq 0.$$

The cumulative hazard function satisfies three conditions: $H(0) = 0$, $\lim_{t \to \infty} H(t) = \infty$, and $H(t)$ is nondecreasing.

Mean Time to Failure (MTTF)
In survival analysis, the mean time to failure (MTTF) is often of interest. This is defined by

$$E(T) = \mu,$$

where

$$\mu = \int_0^\infty t f(t) \, dt,$$

which can be obtained equivalently from the following equation:

$$\mu = \int_0^\infty S(t) \, dt.$$

Median Life
The pth quantile (also known as the $100\,p$th percentile) of the distribution of T is the value t_p so that $F(t_p) \leq p$ and $S(t_p) \geq 1 - p$. If T is a continuous random variable then the pth quantile is found by solving the equation

$$S(t_p) = 1 - p.$$

The median lifetime is the 50th percentile $t_{0.5}$ so that $S(t_{0.5}) = 0.5$.

Relationship between Survival Function and Hazard Function
It can be shown that the survival function and hazard function are associated in the following form:

$$S(t) = e^{-\int_0^t h(\tau)d\tau},$$

and in terms of the cumulative hazard function, the survival function is

$$S(t) = e^{-H(t)}.$$

Using the definition of the hazard function, it is also evident that the probability density function of failure time is

$$f(t) = h(t) \cdot S(t)$$

and using the relationships between $S(t)$ and cumulative hazard or hazard functions, it can also be shown that

$$f(t) = h(t) \cdot e^{-H(t)} = h(t) \cdot e^{-\int_0^t h(\tau)d\tau}.$$

11.6 Proportional Hazards Model

The logistic regression is introduced in Sect. 11.4. Although the logistic regression model is considered as a very important model for analyzing survival status, it does not address some of the important aspects necessary for understanding the survival status adequately. In survival analysis, the lifetime or failure time is of core interest. In addition, the problems of censoring and truncation need to be considered in survival analysis. It is noteworthy that time to failure data needs special attention, and modeling of survival data needs to consider censoring time along with failure time of each subject in the sample. There is rarely any longitudinal data, particularly in case of studies conducted for a longer duration for chronic diseases, where the problem of censoring is not encountered. The dependence of failure times on risk or prognostic factors are of prime concern in analyzing survival data. We have to identify the factors associated with the failure time not only by analyzing the survival status ignoring the time of event but by considering the time of event as the response variable. To address such problems, the proportional hazards model provides a regression model for analyzing failure time data that takes into account partial censoring. The proportional hazards model is expressed as a function of two components: one component depends on time only, and the other component depends on risk or prognostic factors independent of time.

Let us represent the set of covariates by

$$Z = (Z_1, Z_2, \ldots, Z_p)$$

and the corresponding regression parameters are

$$\beta' = (\beta_1, \beta_2, \ldots, \beta_p).$$

The failure time is T. The survivor function is defined as

$$S(t; z) = P(T \geq t | Z = z).$$

The probability density function of survival or failure time is

$$f(t; z)$$

and it can be obtained by differentiating the distribution function as follows:

$$\frac{\partial F(t;z)}{\partial t} = f(t;z)$$

where $F(t;z) = 1 - S(t;z)$ which is the distribution function of the failure time, T.

In the proportional hazards model, proposed by Cox (1972), the combined effect of the Z variables is to scale the hazard function up or down. The hazard function satisfies

$$h(t,z) = h_0(t) \cdot g(z),$$

where $h_0(t)$ is the baseline hazard function. The regression model based on hazard function as proposed by Cox is

$$h(t,z) = h_0(t)e^{z\beta}$$
$$= h_0(t)e^{\beta_1 z_1 + \cdots + \beta_p z_p},$$

where $g(z) = e^{z\beta}$.

The ratio of hazard functions at time t for two subjects with covariate values z_1 and z_2 is

$$\frac{h(t,z_1)}{h(t,z_2)} = \frac{h_0(t)g(z_1)}{h_0(t)g(z_2)} = \frac{g(z_1)}{g(z_2)}$$

which is independent of time, t. The hazards at different z values are in constant proportion over time. That is why the model is known as the proportional hazards model. The function $g(z)$ may take a variety of forms involving covariates z.

After taking natural log of the survival function, we obtain

$$\ln S(t,z) = g(z) \cdot \ln S_0(t).$$

It is known that

$$S(t;z) = e^{-\int_0^t h(\tau,z)d\tau},$$

where $h(t,z) = h_0(t) \cdot g(z)$. Hence,

$$S(t,z) = [S_0(t)]^{g(z)}$$

that can be rewritten as

$$S(t,z) = [S_0(t)]^{e^{z\beta}}.$$

The baseline survival function is defined as

$$S_0(t) = e^{-\int_0^t h(\tau)d\tau}$$

which is a function of time only, independent of covariates.

Simple graphical analysis of data follows by plotting $\ln(-\ln S(t,z))$ for different z values against some function of t, typically t or $\log t$. If the proportional hazards assumption holds, the plots should be similar curves shifted in the y-axis direction resulting in parallel lines.

The parameters are estimated by applying marginal or partial likelihood approaches. We cannot use the likelihood method directly for estimating the parameters of a proportional hazards model and the unknown arbitrary hazard functions cannot be estimated directly as well. As the estimates of the regression parameters do not depend on the arbitrary or baseline hazard functions, the method of estimation for proportional hazards regression produces estimates of regression parameters without complicating the estimation procedure with estimation of baseline hazards at each time point.

If all the times are uncensored then the marginal likelihood is

$$L(\beta) = \prod_{i=1}^{n} \frac{e^{z_{(i)}\beta}}{\sum_{l \in R(t_{(i)})} e^{(z_l\beta)}}$$

where $R(t_{(i)})$ is the risk set exposed to failure at ordered time $t_{(i)}$, that is,

$$R(t_{(i)}) = \{(i), (i+1), \ldots, (n)\}.$$

If there are censoring cases, then let us suppose that k distinct failure times are denoted by the following order based on the rank of failure times as

$$(1), (2), \ldots, (k)$$

where ordered failure times are

$$t_{(1)} < t_{(2)} < \cdots < t_{(k)}$$

with corresponding covariates

$$z_{(1)}, z_{(2)}, \ldots, z_{(k)}$$

then the partial likelihood is

$$L(\beta) = \prod_{i=1}^{k} \frac{e^{z_{(i)}\beta}}{\sum_{l \in R(t_{(i)})} e^{z_l\beta}},$$

where $R(t_{(i)}) = \{[(j), j_1, \ldots, j_{c_j}], \quad j = i, \ldots \ldots, k\}$ is the risk set for a failure at time $t_{(i)}$ and c_i being number of censored cases during the interval $[t_{(i)}, t_{(i+1)})$. Similarly, the likelihood for ties can also be shown.

The value that maximizes the likelihood function can be obtained by a Newton–Raphson method. In the absence of ties, we can show that

$$\hat{\beta} \approx N(\beta, I^{-1}(\hat{\beta})).$$

There may be asymptotic bias in the estimation of both regression parameters and the variance–covariance of the estimators.

To test $H_0 : \beta = \beta_0$, the score statistic $U(\beta_0)$ can be used where under H_0

$$U(\beta_0) \approx N(0, I(\beta_0))$$
$$\chi^2 \approx U'(\beta_0)I^{-1}(\beta_0)U(\beta_0)$$

can be shown approximately as χ^2 with p degrees of freedom.

Model Checking: Test for Proportionality
A simple test for proportionality assumption is introduced here. There are several methods including graphical methods but in this section, a simple procedure is introduced so that anyone may use the method without any further complexity in the application of the proportional hazards model. Let us consider the proportional hazards model

$$h(t, z) = h_0(t)e^{\beta_1 z_1 + \cdots + \beta_p z_p}$$

where T is the survival time and $Z_1, \ldots, Z_p$ are the covariates. Now for testing whether the proportionality assumption is violated by Z_p, let us introduce a new variable.

Now for testing whether the proportionality assumption is violated by Z_p, let us introduce a new variable

$$Z_{p+1} = Z_p \times u(t)$$

where $u(t)$ is a function of time such as (Kleinbaum and Klein 2012, p. 184)

$$u(t) = t,$$
$$u(t) = \log t, \text{ and}$$
$$u(t) = 1 \text{ if } t \geq t_0$$
$$= 0 \text{ if } t < t_0.$$

Then, the extended proportional hazards model including the additional term as

$$h(t, z) = h_0(t)e^{\beta_1 z_1 + \cdots + \beta_p z_p + \beta_{p+1} z_{p+1}}$$

and after fitting the model let us test for the null hypothesis $H_0:\beta_{p+1} = 0$ versus $H_1:\beta_{p+1} \neq 0$.

The test statistic is

$$W = \frac{\hat{\beta}_{p+1}}{\mathrm{se}\left(\hat{\beta}_{p+1}\right)},$$

where W is called a Wald test statistic and this can be shown as asymptotically $N(0, 1)$.

If the null hypothesis is rejected, then there is sufficient evidence that the proportionality assumption might be violated due to covariate Z_p. In that case, either we have to drop the covariate from the model and redo the estimation and test once again to arrive at a model that performs better. Another alternative is to perform a stratified analysis in modeling the sample data. This procedure can be repeated by considering each variable as Z_p and then continue the procedure until all the covariates finally considered in the model are not causing violation of the proportionality assumption.

Now an extended method of assessing r ($r < p$) predictors at a time, $Z_{p+1}, \ldots, Z_{p+r}$, where these variables are defined by multiplying r selected covariates by $u(t)$. The extended hazards model is

$$h(t, z) = h_0(t)e^{\beta_1 z_1 + \cdots + \beta_p z_p + \beta_{p+1} z_{p+1} + \cdots + \beta_{p+r} z_{p+r}}.$$

We can employ the Wald test for all the interaction terms between covariates and time (or function of time) as shown for a single variable previously.

If the null hypothesis is rejected, then it may be concluded that there is sufficient evidence in favor of violation of proportionality assumption by one or more of the selected covariates.

Example 11.5 Let us consider the data from a prospective study on maternal morbidity in Bangladesh conducted by the Bangladesh Institute of Research for Promotion of Essential Reproductive Health and Technologies (BIRPERHT), during November 1992 to December 1993 (Akhter et al. 1996). The study was conducted to identify the risk factors of complications at antenatal, delivery and postnatal stages. In this example, excessive hemorrhage is considered as the outcome event. The outcome variable is defined as the time to excessive hemorrhage during pregnancy. The women who did not experience any excessive hemorrhage complication during pregnancy are considered as censored and the censoring time is the duration of pregnancy. The total number of pregnant women followed up was 1020 out of which complete information was obtained on 993 pregnant women. The potential risk factors are age at marriage (<15 years = 0, as reference category, 15–19 years = 1, 20 + years = 2), desired pregnancy (No = 0, Yes = 1), education (no education as reference category, primary, secondary +), economic status (low = 0, high = 1).

The mean and median survival times, the corresponding standard errors, and 95% confidence intervals are displayed. The mean survival time that is mean time from the beginning of the pregnancy to the time of first occurrence of excessive hemorrhage is 7.2 months with 95% confidence limits of 7.0 months to 7.4 months. This is estimated by using the Kaplan–Meier or Product-Limit method of survival function. Out of 993 subjects, 12.5% had excessive hemorrhage complication. It is found from the results displayed in Table 11.9 that age at marriage is negatively and economic status is positively associated with excessive hemorrhage during pregnancy (p-value < 0.05). We can say with caution that there might be a lower risk of excessive hemorrhage among pregnant women with higher level of education (p-value = 0.07). The test for proportionality shows that both age at marriage and economic status variables may be sources of violation of proportionality assumption. Hence, a further examination of potential risk factors and outcome variable is necessary. A careful investigation of the underlying relationships between the outcome variable and the potential risk factors as well as among potential risk factors may provide important insights in modeling the time to excessive hemorrhage event during pregnancy (Table 11.10).

Table 11.9 Estimates of mean and median survival times and estimation and tests on the proportional hazards model on time to pregnancy complication of excessive hemorrhage

A. Data summary			
Total N	No. of events	Censored	
		N	Percent
993	124	869	87.5

B. Means and medians for survival time							
Mean[a]				Median			
Estimate	Std. error	95% C.I.		Estimate	Std. error	95% C.I.	
		Lower	Upper			Lower	Upper
7.212	0.092	7.031	7.393	7.566	0.246	7.083	8.048

C. Estimation of parameters of proportional hazards model and tests						
	B	SE	Wald	df	Sig.	Exp(B)
Age at marriage	−0.430	0.185	5.387	1	0.020	0.651
Desired pregnancy	−0.062	0.191	0.103	1	0.748	0.940
Education	−0.346	0.192	3.273	1	0.070	0.707
Economic status	0.541	0.211	6.547	1	0.011	1.718

Table 11.10 Test for proportionality assumption

	B	SE	Wald	df	Sig.	Exp(B)
Age at marriage	−0.353	0.739	0.228	1	0.633	0.703
Desired pregnancy	1.710	0.660	6.715	1	0.010	5.528
Education	0.563	0.807	0.487	1	0.485	1.756
Economic status	1.917	0.787	5.931	1	0.015	6.803
Age at marriage * time	−0.256	0.093	7.512	1	0.006	0.775
Desired pregnancy * time	−0.128	0.116	1.217	1	0.270	0.880
Education * time	0.006	0.105	0.003	1	0.956	1.006
Economic status * time	−0.222	0.120	3.410	1	0.065	0.801

Model chi-square = 55.825, df = 8 (p-value < 0.001)

11.7 Summary

In this chapter, the basic concepts and techniques of analyzing survival data are introduced. Different study designs for collecting survival data are discussed, and the corresponding procedures for estimating association between exposure and disease such as relative risk or odds ratio are discussed. Also, the procedures for constructing confidence intervals as well as for testing the hypothesis concerning any association between exposure and disease are highlighted for data from prospective, case-control, and cross-sectional study designs. The nonparametric methods of estimating survivor function are shown including the product-limit method. The variance of the estimator of survivor function is also obtained and the log-rank test for comparing two survivor functions are also introduced in this chapter. One of the most widely used models in biostatistical data analysis is the logistic regression model which is introduced in this chapter with examples. The estimation and test procedures are discussed too. The basic concepts of longitudinal data analysis are discussed and the proportional hazards model is introduced in this chapter with example. A simple method of model checking is also shown.

Exercises

11.1 Suppose the following data on Type 2 diabetes show the post prandial blood glucose levels (<8.5 mmol/L = $\bar{E}$ and ≥ 8.5 mmol/L = E) and status of certain complication (developed complication = D and did not develop complication = $\bar{D}$) among the randomly selected subjects for groups E and $\bar{E}$ in a follow-up study.

Blood glucose level	Developed complication or not	
	D	$\bar{D}$
E	20	80
$\bar{E}$	7	93

(a)   (i) Estimate the odds of developing complications in exposed and nonexposed groups.
       (ii) Estimate the odds ratio of developing complications and interpret.
      (iii) Estimate the variance of the log odds ratio.
       (iv) Estimate the variance of the odds ratio.
        (v) Construct the 95% confidence intervals for the odds ratio.
       (vi) Test for the null hypothesis of H_0: ln OR $= 0$ against the alternative H_1: ln OR $\neq 0$.
      (vii) What is your conclusion?

(b)   (i) Estimate the risks of developing complications.
       (ii) Estimate the relative risk and interpret.
      (iii) Estimate the variance of the relative risk.
       (iv) Construct the 95% confidence interval for the relative risk.
        (v) Test for the null hypothesis of H_0: ln RR $= 0$ against the alternative H_1: ln RR $\neq 0$.
       (vi) Comment on the association between exposure and developing complication for Type 2 diabetes mellitus.

11.2 Consider the following table from a retrospective study to find the association between exposure ($\bar{E}$ = not exposed and E = exposed) and occurrence of disease ($\bar{D}$ = case and D = control).

Disease status		
Exposure status	Case	Control
E	25	30
$\bar{E}$	475	1900

     (i) Estimate the odds of developing complications in exposed and nonexposed groups.
    (ii) Estimate the odds ratio of developing complications and interpret.
   (iii) Estimate the variance of the log odds ratio.
    (iv) Estimate the variance of the odds ratio.
     (v) Construct the 95% confidence intervals for the odds ratio.
    (vi) Test for the null hypothesis of H_0: ln OR $= 0$ against the alternative H_1: ln OR $\neq 0$.
   (vii) What is your conclusion?

11.3 In a cross-sectional study, the relationship between presence or absence of a disease and presence or absence of an exposure is obtained as displayed in the following table:

Disease status		
Exposure status	Present (D)	Absent ($\bar{D}$)
Present (E)	30	50
Absent ($\bar{E}$)	970	2450

(i) Estimate the odds ratio of presence of disease in the randomly selected population and interpret the value of the odds ratio.
(ii) Estimate the variance of the log odds ratio.
(iii) Estimate the variance of the odds ratio.
(iv) Construct the 95% confidence interval for the odds ratio.
(v) Test for the null hypothesis of $H_0: \ln OR = 0$ against the alternative $H_1: \ln OR \neq 0$.
(vi) What is your conclusion?

11.4 Consider the following data on time to event in months.

$$7, 10, 12, 15, 15+, 17+, 20, 22, 23+, 26, 35+, 39, 45, 54$$

(i) Estimate the survivor function using the product-limit method.
(ii) Find the variance of the estimated survivor functions.
(iii) Plot the product-limit estimates of the survivor function and interpret the estimates of the survival function over time.

11.5 Consider the following hypothetical data show the remission times (in days) from high fever of patients selected in groups 1 and 2. The censored times are denoted by a + sign.

$$\text{Group } 1: 1, 2, 2, 3, 3+, 5, 5, 5+, 7, 10, 11, 12, 14, 15, 16+, 17, 19$$

$$\text{Group } 2: 3, 4, 7, 7+, 9, 10, 11, 11+, 15, 15, 16, 17, 18, 20, 21+, 22, 24$$

(i) Estimate the survivor function for both groups 1 and 2, using the product-limit method.
(ii) Graphically plot the survivor functions, compare the survivor functions, and comment on the survival probabilities.
(iii) Estimate the variance of the estimated survivor functions for both groups 1 and 2.

(iv) Is there any statistically significant difference between remission times of patients in groups 1 and 2? Use the log-rank test to compare two survivor functions and comment on your findings.

11.6 Following data set is a random sample of 120 subjects from the panel data from the Health and Retirement Study (HRS), sponsored by the National Institute of Aging (grant number NIA U01AG09740) and conducted by the University of Michigan (2002). This set of panel data is from the first round or wave for 1992. The high blood pressure (HBP) denotes the HRS diagnosed by doctors (yes = 1, no = 0). The potential risk factors considered in this study are age of the respondent in years, gender (male = 1, female = 0), marital status (Mstat: married/partnered = 1, single/widowed/divorced = 0), white (yes = 1, no = 0), black (yes = 1, no = 0), other races which are considered as reference category, BMI (kg/m^2), smoking (yes = 1, no = 0), felt sad (yes = 1, no = 0), and vigorous physical activity or exercise 3+ per week (yes = 1, no = 0).

HBP	Age	Gender	Mstat	White	Black	BMI	Smoking	Felt sad	Activity
0	57	0	0	1	0	18.5	1	0	0
0	59	0	0	1	0	32.3	0	0	1
1	53	0	0	0	1	31.3	0	1	0
0	51	1	1	1	0	28.1	0	0	1
1	61	1	1	1	0	30.3	0	0	0
0	56	0	1	0	1	25.1	1	0	0
1	60	1	1	0	1	30.7	0	0	0
0	54	1	1	1	0	26.1	0	0	0
0	54	0	0	1	0	20.8	0	1	0
0	59	1	1	1	0	25.1	1	1	0
1	61	0	1	1	0	32.1	0	0	0
0	51	0	1	1	0	21.9	1	0	0
0	55	0	1	1	0	24.8	1	0	1
0	55	0	1	1	0	22.4	0	1	0
0	54	0	0	0	1	31.8	0	0	1
1	51	0	1	1	0	27.8	0	1	0
0	59	0	1	1	0	25.5	0	1	0
1	61	0	0	1	0	28.5	1	0	0
0	55	0	1	1	0	23.3	0	0	0
0	60	0	1	1	0	29.6	0	0	0
0	50	0	1	1	0	31.9	0	1	0
0	53	1	1	1	0	22.2	1	0	0
0	61	0	0	1	0	21.8	0	0	1
0	55	1	1	0	0	26.2	0	0	1
0	59	0	1	1	0	22.3	0	0	0

(continued)

(continued)

HBP	Age	Gender	Mstat	White	Black	BMI	Smoking	Felt sad	Activity
0	55	0	1	1	0	23.4	0	0	0
0	59	1	1	1	0	29.4	0	0	0
1	61	1	1	1	0	24.7	0	0	1
0	57	0	0	1	0	20.2	0	1	0
0	58	0	1	1	0	25.7	0	0	1
0	51	1	1	1	0	25.8	0	1	0
0	61	1	1	1	0	27.3	0	0	0
1	52	1	1	1	0	28.4	0	0	1
0	51	1	1	1	0	27.6	1	1	0
0	57	0	1	1	0	28.2	0	0	0
0	51	1	0	1	0	23.7	0	0	1
1	60	1	1	1	0	38	0	0	0
1	53	0	1	0	1	32.3	0	0	0
0	56	0	1	1	0	27.1	1	1	0
0	56	0	1	1	0	27.9	0	1	1
0	58	0	1	1	0	25.8	0	1	0
0	52	1	1	1	0	21.6	1	0	0
0	56	0	0	1	0	24.1	0	1	0
0	55	1	1	1	0	30.4	1	0	0
0	60	0	1	1	0	32	0	1	0
1	59	0	1	1	0	25.5	0	1	0
1	56	1	1	1	0	35.3	0	0	0
1	51	0	0	1	0	23	1	1	1
1	51	0	0	1	0	29.3	0	1	0
1	60	0	1	0	1	24.8	1	1	1
0	52	1	1	1	0	23.6	0	1	0
0	56	0	1	1	0	21.3	0	1	0
0	55	0	1	1	0	23.8	0	0	1
0	55	1	1	1	0	31.7	0	0	1
0	56	0	1	1	0	23.5	0	0	0
0	52	1	1	1	0	29	0	0	0
0	61	1	1	1	0	23.7	0	0	1
1	60	0	1	1	0	34.3	0	1	1
1	54	0	1	1	0	31.3	0	0	0
1	54	1	1	0	0	27	0	1	0
0	61	0	1	1	0	20.3	0	0	0
0	52	1	0	1	0	24.4	0	1	1
0	59	1	1	1	0	26.9	0	0	0
0	53	1	1	1	0	24	1	0	0
1	52	0	1	1	0	35.4	0	0	0

(continued)

(continued)

HBP	Age	Gender	Mstat	White	Black	BMI	Smoking	Felt sad	Activity
0	58	0	1	1	0	32.9	0	1	1
1	55	0	1	1	0	25.6	1	0	1
0	60	1	1	1	0	25.7	0	1	1
0	58	1	1	1	0	32.8	0	0	0
1	59	1	1	1	0	29.6	0	0	0
0	55	1	1	1	0	29.4	0	0	0
0	55	0	1	1	0	25.2	0	1	0
1	54	0	1	1	0	23.4	0	1	0
1	56	1	1	1	0	28.5	0	0	0
1	51	0	0	1	0	24.5	1	0	0
1	52	0	1	1	0	31.9	1	1	0
0	55	1	1	1	0	22.7	0	0	0
0	57	0	0	1	0	24.6	0	0	1
0	58	1	1	0	1	20.8	1	1	0
1	54	0	0	0	0	35.4	0	0	0
1	57	0	0	0	1	26.2	0	0	0
1	61	0	1	0	1	27.3	0	0	1
1	56	1	1	0	1	28.1	1	1	0
1	54	0	1	0	1	32.1	0	0	1
1	53	0	0	1	0	31.3	0	1	0
0	56	1	1	1	0	27.3	0	1	0
0	52	0	1	1	0	27.8	0	1	0
1	55	0	0	1	0	20.5	0	0	0
0	53	1	1	1	0	32.1	0	0	0
0	61	0	0	1	0	20.6	0	1	0
1	60	1	0	1	0	28.8	0	0	0
0	57	1	1	1	0	23.1	0	0	0
0	57	1	0	0	1	27.3	1	0	0
0	54	1	1	0	1	27.3	0	0	0
0	51	1	1	1	0	24	0	0	0
0	56	0	1	1	0	24.2	0	0	0
0	56	0	1	1	0	23.5	0	1	0
0	53	0	1	1	0	19.9	0	1	0
0	58	1	1	1	0	27.3	0	1	0
0	54	1	1	1	0	25	1	0	0
0	51	0	1	1	0	22	0	1	0
0	53	1	1	1	0	45.3	0	1	0
1	52	0	1	1	0	33.7	0	1	1
0	59	1	1	1	0	27.7	0	0	0
1	57	0	1	1	0	26.6	0	0	0

(continued)

(continued)

HBP	Age	Gender	Mstat	White	Black	BMI	Smoking	Felt sad	Activity
1	59	1	1	1	0	25.7	0	1	0
1	55	0	1	1	0	35.4	0	1	0
1	55	1	1	1	0	25.1	0	0	0
0	58	1	0	0	1	27.9	1	0	0
1	56	0	1	0	1	36.6	0	1	0
0	56	1	1	1	0	21.6	1	0	0
0	55	0	1	1	0	22.5	0	0	0
0	55	0	1	1	0	18.3	0	0	1
1	58	1	1	1	0	38.4	0	0	0
1	55	1	1	0	1	31	1	0	1
0	61	1	1	1	0	21.6	1	0	1
0	56	1	1	1	0	28	1	0	1
0	57	0	1	1	0	19.9	1	1	0
0	59	1	1	1	0	27.3	0	1	0
0	55	1	1	1	0	28.5	0	0	0

HRS (2017). *Health and Retirement Study*, University of Michigan, Ann Arbor, 1992–2014. The authors gratefully acknowledge the support of HRS (Health and Retirement Study) which is sponsored by the National Institute of Aging (grant number NIA U01AG09740) and conducted by the University of Michigan for the data

(i)   Conduct an exploratory analysis to find the association between high blood pressure (HBP) and selected potential risk factors.

(ii) Fit a logistic regression model for high blood pressure to identify the nature of relationship between potential risk factors and HBP.

(iii) Comment on the goodness of fit of the model.

(iv) Test for the significance of the parameters and comment on the association between high blood pressure and potential risk factors.

(v)   Estimate the odds ratios from the model and interpret.

(vi) Find the 95% confidence interval for the population odds ratios.

11.7 Following data set is a random sample of 155 subjects from the panel data from the Health and Retirement Study (HRS), sponsored by the National Institute of Aging (grant number NIA U01AG09740) and conducted by the University of Michigan (2002). We have used the panel data from the second to eleventh round or wave. The variable "Time" is time to event since the entry to the study. The event of interest is the first time occurrence of heart problem since the last interview. The event heart (yes = 1, no = 0) denotes whether heart disease was diagnosed or not, yes indicating event and no for censored cases. Covariates are age (in years), gender (male = 1, female = 0), Hispanic (yes = 1, no = 0), drink (yes = 1, no = 0), smoking (yes = 1, no = 0), body mass index (BMI), doctor diagnosed high blood pressure (Hibps) (yes = 1, no = 0), and the number of previous conditions.

Time	Heart	Age	Gender	Hispanic	Drink	BMI	Number of prev. condition	Hibps	Smoke
17.9	0	61	0	1	1	25.2	0	0	0
23.0	0	70	1	0	1	31.3	4	0	0
16.9	0	72	1	0	1	29.1	4	0	0
24.7	1	53	0	0	0	26.6	5	0	1
21.9	1	67	0	0	0	21.0	3	0	0
23.0	1	74	1	0	1	27.1	2	0	0
25.0	0	77	0	0	0	32.4	3	1	0
23.0	1	60	0	0	0	28.1	2	0	1
18.0	0	72	1	0	0	29.1	3	0	0
29.0	0	71	0	0	0	31.9	3	0	0
19.0	0	81	0	0	1	27.4	4	0	0
22.0	0	65	0	0	0	25.6	2	1	0
25.9	1	67	0	0	0	30.9	6	0	0
20.7	1	56	1	0	0	24.5	2	0	1
17.9	0	74	0	0	0	28.2	3	0	0
21.9	0	65	0	0	0	23.6	5	0	0
20.0	0	79	0	0	0	31.4	3	0	0
24.5	0	55	0	0	1	24.5	1	0	0
13.0	0	72	1	1	1	23.6	2	0	1
21.7	1	62	1	0	0	25.1	3	0	0
26.0	0	72	1	0	0	28.9	3	0	0
24.2	0	55	1	0	0	27.1	2	0	0
25.9	0	69	1	0	1	27.5	2	0	0
25.0	0	75	1	0	0	27.1	2	0	0
22.0	0	79	0	0	1	22.3	1	0	0
19.0	0	75	1	0	0	29.3	1	0	0
23.0	0	76	0	0	1	25.2	3	0	0
24.9	0	55	0	0	0	32.7	2	0	0
23.1	0	57	0	0	0	20.4	3	0	0
21.0	1	65	1	0	0	29.8	2	0	0
21.0	0	69	1	0	0	29.7	3	1	1
22.0	1	64	0	0	0	36.8	4	0	0
21.0	0	73	0	0	1	25.1	4	0	0
25.9	1	63	0	0	1	30.2	6		0
21.0	0	68	0	0	1	22.1	4	0	1
26.0	0	74	0	1	1	23.7	3	0	0
26.0	0	75	0	0	0	35.7	2	0	0
24.9	0	73	0	0	0	27.5	4	0	0
19.0	0	71	0	0	1	19.4	1	0	0
20.5	0	52	0	0	1	29.5	0	0	0
28.0	0	77	1	0	0	31.0	4	0	0

(continued)

(continued)

Time	Heart	Age	Gender	Hispanic	Drink	BMI	Number of prev. condition	Hibps	Smoke
24.0	0	62	1	0	1	23.7	1	0	0
26.0	0	63	1	0	1	31.4	2	0	0
25.0	0	76	1	0	0	32.1	2	0	0
26.0	0	60	0	0	1	22.5	0	0	0
17.9	0	75	0	0	1	30.0	3	0	0
22.2	1	60	0	0	0	32.9	4	0	0
22.9	0	66	1	0	1	44.8	1	0	0
19.0	1	77	1	0	1	21.8	4	0	0
25.0	1	69	1	0	1	35.5	3	0	0
21.9	1	70	1	0	1	29.3	3	0	0
22.0	1	67	0	0	0	23.4	5	0	0
29.9	0	67	1	0	0	26.3	0	0	1
28.0	0	69	0	0	1	27.4	4	0	0
19.0	0	79	0	0	1	33.9	6	0	0
19.0	0	80	1	0	1	30.8	4	0	0
17.0	0	72	0	0	0	24.4	1	0	0
23.0	0	78	1	0	0	28.4	5	0	0
25.0	0	78	0	0	1	27.6	3	0	0
23.0	0	66	0	0	1	23.6	4	0	1
21.0	0	62	1	0	0	19.2	3	0	1
20.6	0	58	1	0	1	24.5	2	0	0
32.0	1	74	1	0	1	22.0	3	0	0
19.9	0	60	0	1	0	30.3	0	0	0
21.9	0	67	1	0	0	27.0	7	0	0
23.0	0	64	0	1	0	15.6	4	0	1
25.4	0	63	0	0	1	25.1	3	0	0
19.0	0	80	0	0	0	29.3	3	1	0
32.0	0	59	0	0	0	17.9	1	0	0
29.0	0	68	1	0	1	32.1	2	0	0
26.0	1	63	1	0	1	28.0	2	0	1
24.0	0	61	0	0	1	27.3	2	0	0
23.9	0	66	0	0	1	28.3	2	0	0
15.9	0	75	1	0	1	25.1	3	0	0
17.0	0	79	1	0	0	22.2	1	0	0
18.0	0	75	0	0	0	29.1	2	0	0
26.0	1	77	0	0	0	25.2	4	0	0
20.0	0	68	0	0	0	22.7	0	0	0
22.0	0	75	0	0	0	22.6	2	0	0
20.0	0	78	0	0	0	22.5	3	0	1
25.9	0	69	1	0	1	25.6	0	0	0

(continued)

(continued)

Time	Heart	Age	Gender	Hispanic	Drink	BMI	Number of prev. condition	Hibps	Smoke
27.0	0	73	0	0	0	20.2	2	0	1
20.9	0	73	1	0	0	31.4	4	0	0
26.6	0	61	1	0	0	23.8	3	0	1
23.9	0	56	1	0	1	28.7	0	0	0
19.0	0	73	0	0	0	21.6	3	0	0
23.9	0	71	1	0	0	21.7	3	0	0
25.0	1	59	0	0	0	22.4	3	0	0
25.8	1	63	0	0	0	39.2	4	0	0
24.0	0	73	1	0	1	27.0	2	0	0
28.0	1	70	1	0	1	22.2	2	0	0
21.0	0	73	1	0	0	25.8	3	0	0
19.0	0	79	1	0	1	24.3	1	0	0
19.0	0	81	0	0	0	32.9	1	0	0
23.0	0	71	0	0	1	40.9	2	0	0
19.9	0	74	0	0	1	28.9	1	0	0
17.0	0	77	0	0	0	20.4	1	0	1
21.0	0	75	1	0	1	30.7	2	0	0
24.5	1	54	1	1	0	25.8	2	1	0
24.9	0	73	1	0	0	25.8	0	0	0
17.9	0	76	0	0	0	32.0	1	0	0
23.0	1	57	0	0	0	26.5	2	0	0
31.0	0	59	1	0	0	19.7	2	0	1
25.9	1	78	1	0	0	29.0	5	0	0
19.9	0	57	1	1	1	25.4	0	0	0
16.9	0	71	0	0	0	21.8	1	0	0
19.5	0	56	1	0	1	28.1	0	0	1
24.0	0	76	1	0	0	26.9	3	0	0
29.0	0	61	0	0	0	26.6	0	0	0
19.9	0	79	0	0	0	26.8	4	0	0
20.9	1	57	1	0	0	33.7	3	0	0
23.0	1	65	0	0	0	23.1	4	0	1
21.9	1	66	0	0	0	34.8	5	0	0
29.9	0	72	0	0	0	31.6	3	0	0
23.9	0	68	0	0	1	20.5	1	0	1
31.9	0	69	1	0	1	31.9	1	0	0
31.0	1	74	1	0	0	22.9	6	0	0
22.0	0	74	1	1	0	28.7	3	0	1
21.0	0	78	0	1	0	24.8	3	0	0
25.5	0	65	1	0	0	25.8	1	0	1

(continued)

(continued)

Time	Heart	Age	Gender	Hispanic	Drink	BMI	Number of prev. condition	Hibps	Smoke
26.0	0	65	0	0	1	26.1	3	0	1
23.1	0	59	1	0	1	25.1	1	0	1
26.0	0	71	1	0	0	28.7	4	0	0
23.0	1	75	0	0	0	28.3	1	0	0
23.4	0	62	0	0	1	24.2	3	0	
17.9	0	71	0	0	0	24.9	3	0	0
23.0	0	58	0	0	0	27.5	1	0	1
27.0	0	73	0	0	0	37.4	4	0	0
18.0	0	72	1	0	1	28.1	3	0	0
22.0	0	72	0	0	1	25.4	3	0	1
23.3	0	65	1	0	0	23.5	3	0	0
19.9	0	73	0	0	1	19.0	5	0	1
27.0	0	80	1	0	1	25.8	4	0	0
17.0	0	76	1	0	0	30.4	3	0	0
19.0	1	65	0	1	0	33.8	4	1	0
21.0	1	57	1	0	0	25.5	2	0	1
21.2	0	62	0	0	0	23.0	3	0	0
14.9	0	71	0	0	1	24.2	1	0	0
17.0	0	71	1	0	1	23.0	1	0	0
25.0	0	81	1	0	1	21.6	2	0	1
20.0	0	78	0	0	0	25.1	3	0	0
30.0	0	59	0	0	0	21.3	1	0	0
21.0	0	77	1	0	0	25.8	2	0	0
27.0	0	71	1	0	0	27.4	1	0	0
21.0	0	65	0	0	1	26.5	1	0	0
22.9	0	60	1	0	0	29.0	2	0	0
29.9	0	68	0	0	0	23.5	1	0	0
25.0	0	68	1	0	0	30.0	3	0	0
27.0	1	58	1	0	1	33.1	3	1	1
21.0	0	66	0	0	0	32.6	3	0	0
17.0	0	70	1	0	0	23.3	1	0	0
26.0	1	69	0	0	1	33.2	5	0	0
17.9	0	70	1	0	0	33.9	2	0	0
23.1	0	55	0	0	0	23.0	0	0	1
17.5	0	72	0	0	1	39.8	2	0	0

HRS ((Health And Retirement Study) 2017). *Health and Retirement Study*, University of Michigan, Ann Arbor, 1992–2014. The authors gratefully acknowledge the support of HRS (Health and Retirement Study) which is sponsored by the National Institute of Aging (grant number NIA U01AG09740) and conducted by the University of Michigan for the data

(i) Estimate the relative risk and odds ratio of the occurrence of heart disease for each of the potential risk factors considered in this example. Comment on your results.

(ii) Test for the association between exposure and occurrence of heart disease from the data.

(iii) Propose a proportional hazards model for analyzing the time to occurrence of heart disease.

(iv) Fit a proportional hazards model and comment on the overall fit as well as significance of each variable included in the model.

(v) Check for the proportionality assumption for each covariate selected in the model and summarize your comments.

(vi) Summarize your findings from (i) to (v) and comment on the suitability of your model for analyzing the heart disease data.

References

Akhter, H. H., Chowdhury, M. E. E. K., & Sen, A. (1996). *A cross-sectional study on maternal morbidity in Bangladesh*. Dhaka, Bangladesh: BIRPERHT.

Cox, D. R. (1972). Regression models and life tables (with discussion). *Journal of the Royal Statistical Society B, 34*, 187–220.

HRS (Health And Retirement Study) (2017). *Public use dataset*. Produced and distributed by the University of Michigan with funding from the National Institute on Aging (grant number NIAU01AG09740). Ann Arbor, MI.

Kaplan, E. L., & Meier, P. (1958). Nonparametric estimation from incomplete observations. *Journal of the American Statistical Association, 53*, 457–481.

Kleinbaum, D. G., & Klein, M. (2012). *Survival analysis a self-learning text* (3rd ed.). New York: Springer Publishers.

Mausner, J. S., & Kramer, S. (1985). *Mausner & Bahn Epidemiology- An Introductory Text* (2nd ed.). Philadelphia: W.B. Saunders Company.

Appendix

Table A.1:   Binomial Cumulative Distribution Function

The tabulated value is $P(X \leq -x)$, where X has the binomial distribution with index n and parameter p, for a selection of values of n and p.

p =	0.05	0.10	0.15	0.20	0.25	0.30	0.35	0.40	0.45	0.50
n = 5, x = 0	0.7738	0.5905	0.4437	0.3277	0.2373	0.1681	0.1160	0.0778	0.0503	0.0312
1	0.9774	0.9185	0.8352	0.7373	0.6328	0.5282	0.4284	0.3370	0.2562	0.1875
2	0.9988	0.9914	0.9734	0.9421	0.8965	0.8369	0.7648	0.6826	0.5931	0.5000
3	1.0000	0.9995	0.9978	0.9933	0.9844	0.9692	0.9460	0.9130	0.8688	0.8125
4	1.0000	1.0000	0.9999	0.9997	0.9990	0.9976	0.9947	0.9898	0.9815	0.9688
n = 10, x = 0	0.5987	0.3487	0.1969	0.1074	0.0563	0.0282	0.0135	0.0060	0.0025	0.0010
1	0.9139	0.7361	0.5443	0.3758	0.2440	0.1493	0.0860	0.0464	0.0233	0.0107
2	0.9885	0.9298	0.8202	0.6778	0.5256	0.3828	0.2616	0.1673	0.0996	0.0547
3	0.9990	0.9872	0.9500	0.8791	0.7759	0.6496	0.5138	0.3823	0.2660	0.1719
4	0.9999	0.9984	0.9901	0.9672	0.9219	0.8497	0.7515	0.6331	0.5044	0.3770
5	1.0000	0.9999	0.9986	0.9936	0.9803	0.9527	0.9051	0.8338	0.7384	0.6230
6	1.0000	1.0000	0.9999	0.9991	0.9965	0.9894	0.9740	0.9452	0.8980	0.8281
7	1.0000	1.0000	1.0000	0.9999	0.9996	0.9984	0.9952	0.9877	0.9726	0.9453
8	1.0000	1.0000	1.0000	1.0000	1.0000	0.9999	0.9995	0.9983	0.9955	0.9893
9	1.0000	1.0000	1.0000	1.0000	1.0000	1.0000	1.0000	0.9999	0.9997	0.9990
n = 15, x = 0	0.4633	0.2059	0.0874	0.0352	0.0134	0.0047	0.0016	0.0005	0.0001	0.0000
1	0.8290	0.5490	0.3186	0.1671	0.0802	0.0353	0.0142	0.0052	0.0017	0.0005
2	0.9638	0.8159	0.6042	0.3980	0.2361	0.1268	0.0617	0.0271	0.0107	0.0037
3	0.9945	0.9444	0.8227	0.6482	0.4613	0.2969	0.1727	0.0905	0.0424	0.0176
4	0.9994	0.9873	0.9383	0.8358	0.6865	0.5155	0.3519	0.2173	0.1204	0.0592
5	0.9999	0.9978	0.9832	0.9389	0.8516	0.7216	0.5643	0.4032	0.2608	0.1509
6	1.0000	0.9997	0.9964	0.9819	0.9434	0.8689	0.7548	0.6098	0.4522	0.3036
7	1.0000	1.0000	0.9994	0.9958	0.9827	0.9500	0.8868	0.7869	0.6535	0.5000
8	1.0000	1.0000	0.9999	0.9992	0.9958	0.9848	0.9578	0.9050	0.8182	0.6964
9	1.0000	1.0000	1.0000	0.9999	0.9992	0.9963	0.9876	0.9662	0.9231	0.8491
10	1.0000	1.0000	1.0000	1.0000	0.9999	0.9993	0.9972	0.9907	0.9745	0.9408

(continued)

(continued)

$p =$	0.05	0.10	0.15	0.20	0.25	0.30	0.35	0.40	0.45	0.50
11	1.0000	1.0000	1.0000	1.0000	1.0000	0.9999	0.9995	0.9981	0.9937	0.9824
12	1.0000	1.0000	1.0000	1.0000	1.0000	1.0000	0.9999	0.9997	0.9989	0.9963
13	1.0000	1.0000	1.0000	1.0000	1.0000	1.0000	1.0000	1.0000	0.9999	0.9995
14	1.0000	1.0000	1.0000	1.0000	1.0000	1.0000	1.0000	1.0000	1.0000	1.0000
$n = 20, x = 0$										
1	0.3585	0.1216	0.0388	0.0115	0.0032	0.0008	0.0002	0.0000	0.0000	0.0000
2	0.7358	0.3917	0.1756	0.0692	0.0243	0.0076	0.0021	0.0005	0.0001	0.0000
3	0.9245	0.6769	0.4049	0.2061	0.0913	0.0355	0.0121	0.0036	0.0009	0.0002
4	0.9841	0.8670	0.6477	0.4114	0.2252	0.1071	0.0444	0.0160	0.0049	0.0013
5	0.9974	0.9568	0.8298	0.6296	0.4148	0.2375	0.1182	0.0510	0.0189	0.0059
6	0.9997	0.9887	0.9327	0.8042	0.6172	0.4164	0.2454	0.1256	0.0553	0.0207
7	1.0000	0.9976	0.9781	0.9133	0.7858	0.6080	0.4166	0.2500	0.1299	0.0577
8	1.0000	0.9996	0.9941	0.9679	0.8982	0.7723	0.6010	0.4159	0.2520	0.1316
9	1.0000	0.9999	0.9987	0.9900	0.9591	0.8867	0.7624	0.5956	0.4143	0.2517
10	1.0000	1.0000	0.9998	0.9974	0.9861	0.9520	0.8782	0.7553	0.5914	0.4119
11	1.0000	1.0000	1.0000	0.9994	0.9961	0.9829	0.9468	0.8725	0.7507	0.5881
12	1.0000	1.0000	1.0000	0.9999	0.9991	0.9949	0.9804	0.9435	0.8692	0.7483
13	1.0000	1.0000	1.0000	1.0000	0.9998	0.9987	0.9940	0.9790	0.9420	0.8684
14	1.0000	1.0000	1.0000	1.0000	1.0000	0.9997	0.9985	0.9935	0.9786	0.9423
15	1.0000	1.0000	1.0000	1.0000	1.0000	1.0000	0.9997	0.9984	0.9936	0.9793
16	1.0000	1.0000	1.0000	1.0000	1.0000	1.0000	1.0000	0.9997	0.9985	0.9941
17	1.0000	1.0000	1.0000	1.0000	1.0000	1.0000	1.0000	1.0000	0.9997	0.9987
18	1.0000	1.0000	1.0000	1.0000	1.0000	1.0000	1.0000	1.0000	1.0000	0.9998

Acknowledged that the copyright belongs to the Royal Statistical Society and reproduced from the Royal Statistical Society Tables, Royal Statistical Society, 2004 with permission from the Royal Statistical Society.

Table A.2:   Poisson Cumulative Distribution Function

The tabulated value is $P(X \leq -x)$, where X has the Poisson distribution with parameter μ for a selected values of μ

x	0.5	1.0	1.5	2.0	2.5	3.0	3.5	4.0	4.5	5.0
0	0.6065	0.3679	0.2231	0.1353	0.0821	0.0498	0.0302	0.0183	0.0111	0.0067
1	0.9098	0.7358	0.5578	0.4060	0.2873	0.1991	0.1359	0.0916	0.0611	0.0404
2	0.9856	0.9197	0.8088	0.6767	0.5438	0.4232	0.3208	0.2381	0.1736	0.1247
3	0.9982	0.9810	0.9344	0.8571	0.7576	0.6472	0.5366	0.4335	0.3423	0.2650
4	0.9998	0.9963	0.9814	0.9473	0.8912	0.8153	0.7254	0.6288	0.5321	0.4405
5	1.0000	0.9994	0.9955	0.9834	0.9580	0.9161	0.8576	0.7851	0.7029	0.6160
6	1.0000	0.9999	0.9991	0.9955	0.9858	0.9665	0.9347	0.8893	0.8311	0.7622
7	1.0000	1.0000	0.9998	0.9989	0.9958	0.9881	0.9733	0.9489	0.9134	0.8666
8	1.0000	1.0000	1.0000	0.9998	0.9989	0.9962	0.9901	0.9786	0.9597	0.9319
9	1.0000	1.0000	1.0000	1.0000	0.9997	0.9989	0.9967	0.9919	0.9829	0.9682
10	1.0000	1.0000	1.0000	1.0000	0.9999	0.9997	0.9990	0.9972	0.9933	0.9863
11	1.0000	1.0000	1.0000	1.0000	1.0000	0.9999	0.9997	0.9991	0.9976	0.9945
12	1.0000	1.0000	1.0000	1.0000	1.0000	1.0000	0.9999	0.9997	0.9992	0.9980
13	1.0000	1.0000	1.0000	1.0000	1.0000	1.0000	1.0000	0.9999	0.9997	0.9993
14	1.0000	1.0000	1.0000	1.0000	1.0000	1.0000	1.0000	1.0000	0.9999	0.9998
15	1.0000	1.0000	1.0000	1.0000	1.0000	1.0000	1.0000	1.0000	1.0000	0.9999
16	1.0000	1.0000	1.0000	1.0000	1.0000	1.0000	1.0000	1.0000	1.0000	1.0000

x	5.5	6.0	6.5	7.0	7.5	8.0	8.5	9.0	9.5	10.0
0	0.0041	0.0025	0.0015	0.0009	0.0006	0.0003	0.0002	0.0001	0.0001	0.0000
1	0.0266	0.0174	0.0113	0.0073	0.0047	0.0030	0.0019	0.0012	0.0008	0.0005
2	0.0884	0.0620	0.0430	0.0296	0.0203	0.0138	0.0093	0.0062	0.0042	0.0028
3	0.2017	0.1512	0.1118	0.0818	0.0591	0.0424	0.0301	0.0212	0.0149	0.0103
4	0.3575	0.2851	0.2237	0.1730	0.1321	0.0996	0.0744	0.0550	0.0403	0.0293
5	0.5289	0.4457	0.3690	0.3007	0.2414	0.1912	0.1496	0.1157	0.0885	0.0671
6	0.6860	0.6063	0.5265	0.4497	0.3782	0.3134	0.2562	0.2068	0.1649	0.1301

(continued)

(continued)

	0.5	1.0	1.5	2.0	2.5	3.0	3.5	4.0	4.5	5.0
7	0.8095	0.7440	0.6728	0.5987	0.5246	0.4530	0.3856	0.3239	0.2687	0.2202
8	0.8944	0.8472	0.7916	0.7291	0.6620	0.5925	0.5231	0.4557	0.3918	0.3328
9	0.9462	0.9161	0.8774	0.8305	0.7764	0.7166	0.6530	0.5874	0.5218	0.4579
10	0.9747	0.9574	0.9332	0.9015	0.8622	0.8159	0.7634	0.7060	0.6453	0.5830
11	0.9890	0.9799	0.9661	0.9467	0.9208	0.8881	0.8487	0.8030	0.7520	0.6968
12	0.9955	0.9912	0.9840	0.9730	0.9573	0.9362	0.9091	0.8758	0.8364	0.7916
13	0.9983	0.9964	0.9929	0.9872	0.9784	0.9658	0.9486	0.9261	0.8981	0.8645
14	0.9994	0.9986	0.9970	0.9943	0.9897	0.9827	0.9726	0.9585	0.9400	0.9165
15	0.9998	0.9995	0.9988	0.9976	0.9954	0.9918	0.9862	0.9780	0.9665	0.9513
16	0.9999	0.9998	0.9996	0.9990	0.9980	0.9963	0.9934	0.9889	0.9823	0.9730
17	1.0000	0.9999	0.9998	0.9996	0.9992	0.9984	0.9970	0.9947	0.9911	0.9857
18	1.0000	1.0000	0.9999	0.9999	0.9997	0.9993	0.9987	0.9976	0.9957	0.9928
19	1.0000	1.0000	1.0000	1.0000	0.9999	0.9997	0.9995	0.9989	0.9980	0.9965
20	1.0000	1.0000	1.0000	1.0000	1.0000	0.9999	0.9998	0.9996	0.9991	0.9984
21	1.0000	1.0000	1.0000	1.0000	1.0000	1.0000	0.9999	0.9998	0.9996	0.9993
22	1.0000	1.0000	1.0000	1.0000	1.0000	1.0000	1.0000	0.9999	0.9999	0.9997
23	1.0000	1.0000	1.0000	1.0000	1.0000	1.0000	1.0000	1.0000	0.9999	0.9999
24	1.0000	1.0000	1.0000	1.0000	1.0000	1.0000	1.0000	1.0000	1.0000	1.0000

Acknowledged that the copyright belongs to the Royal Statistical Society and reproduced from the Royal Statistical Society Tables, Royal Statistical Society, 2004 with permission from the Royal Statistical Society.

Table A.3: Normal Cumulative Distribution Function

For $Z \sim N(0, 1)$, the function tabulated is $\phi(z) = P(Z \le z) = \frac{1}{\sqrt{2\pi}} \int_{-\infty}^{z} e^{-\frac{1}{2}t^2} dt$.

Z	$\Phi(z)$	z	$\Phi(z)$	z	$\Phi(z)$	z	$\Phi(z)$	z	$\Phi(z)$
0.00	0.5000	0.50	0.6915	1.00	0.8413	1.50	0.9332	2.00	0.9772
0.01	0.5040	0.51	0.6950	1.01	0.8438	1.51	0.9345	2.02	0.9783
0.02	0.5080	0.52	0.6985	1.02	0.8461	1.52	0.9357	2.04	0.9793
0.03	0.5120	0.53	0.7019	1.03	0.8485	1.53	0.9370	2.06	0.9803
0.04	0.5160	0.54	0.7054	1.04	0.8508	1.54	0.9382	2.08	0.9812
0.05	0.5199	0.55	0.7088	1.05	0.8531	1.55	0.9394	2.10	0.9821
0.06	0.5239	0.56	0.7123	1.06	0.8554	1.56	0.9406	2.12	0.9830
0.07	0.5279	0.57	0.7157	1.07	0.8577	1.57	0.9418	2.14	0.9838
0.08	0.5319	0.58	0.7190	1.08	0.8599	1.58	0.9429	2.16	0.9846
0.09	0.5359	0.59	0.7224	1.09	0.8621	1.59	0.9441	2.18	0.9854
0.10	0.5398	0.60	0.7257	1.10	0.8643	1.60	0.9452	2.20	0.9861
0.11	0.5438	0.61	0.7291	1.11	0.8665	1.61	0.9463	2.22	0.9868
0.12	0.5478	0.62	0.7324	1.12	0.8686	1.62	0.9474	2.24	0.9875
0.13	0.5517	0.63	0.7357	1.13	0.8708	1.63	0.9484	2.26	0.9881
0.14	0.5557	0.64	0.7389	1.14	0.8729	1.64	0.9495	2.28	0.9887
0.15	0.5596	0.65	0.7422	1.15	0.8749	1.65	0.9505	2.30	0.9893
0.16	0.5636	0.66	0.7454	1.16	0.8770	1.66	0.9515	2.32	0.9898
0.17	0.5675	0.67	0.7486	1.17	0.8790	1.67	0.9525	2.34	0.9904
0.18	0.5714	0.68	0.7517	1.18	0.8810	1.68	0.9535	2.36	0.9909
0.19	0.5753	0.69	0.7549	1.19	0.8830	1.69	0.9545	2.38	0.9913
0.20	0.5793	0.70	0.7580	1.20	0.8849	1.70	0.9554	2.40	0.9918
0.21	0.5832	0.71	0.7611	1.21	0.8869	1.71	0.9564	2.42	0.9922
0.22	0.5871	0.72	0.7642	1.22	0.8888	1.72	0.9573	2.44	0.9927
0.23	0.5910	0.73	0.7673	1.23	0.8907	1.73	0.9582	2.46	0.9931
0.24	0.5948	0.74	0.7704	1.24	0.8925	1.74	0.9591	2.48	0.9934
0.25	0.5987	0.75	0.7734	1.25	0.8944	1.75	0.9599	2.50	0.9938
0.26	0.6026	0.76	0.7764	1.26	0.8962	1.76	0.9608	2.55	0.9946
0.27	0.6064	0.77	0.7794	1.27	0.8980	1.77	0.9616	2.60	0.9953

(continued)

(continued)

Z	$\Phi(z)$	z	$\Phi(z)$	z	$\Phi(z)$	z	$\Phi(z)$	z	$\Phi(z)$
0.28	0.6103	0.78	0.7823	1.28	0.8997	1.78	0.9625	2.65	0.9960
0.29	0.6141	0.79	0.7852	1.29	0.9015	1.79	0.9633	2.70	0.9965
0.30	0.6179	0.80	0.7881	1.30	0.9032	1.80	0.9641	2.75	0.9970
0.31	0.6217	0.81	0.7910	1.31	0.9049	1.81	0.9649	2.80	0.9974
0.32	0.6255	0.82	0.7939	1.32	0.9066	1.82	0.9656	2.85	0.9978
0.33	0.6293	0.83	0.7967	1.33	0.9082	1.83	0.9664	2.90	0.9981
0.34	0.6331	0.84	0.7995	1.34	0.9099	1.84	0.9671	2.95	0.9984
0.35	0.6368	0.85	0.8023	1.35	0.9115	1.85	0.9678	3.00	0.9987
0.36	0.6406	0.86	0.8051	1.36	0.9131	1.86	0.9686	3.05	0.9989
0.37	0.6443	0.87	0.8078	1.37	0.9147	1.87	0.9693	3.10	0.9990
0.38	0.6480	0.88	0.8106	1.38	0.9162	1.88	0.9699	3.15	0.9992
0.39	0.6517	0.89	0.8133	1.39	0.9177	1.89	0.9706	3.20	0.9993
0.40	0.6554	0.90	0.8159	1.40	0.9192	1.90	0.9713	3.25	0.9994
0.41	0.6591	0.91	0.8186	1.41	0.9207	1.91	0.9719	3.30	0.9995
0.42	0.6628	0.92	0.8212	1.42	0.9222	1.92	0.9726	3.35	0.9996
0.43	0.6664	0.93	0.8238	1.43	0.9236	1.93	0.9732	3.40	0.9997
0.44	0.6700	0.94	0.8264	1.44	0.9251	1.94	0.9738	3.50	0.9998
0.45	0.6736	0.95	0.8289	1.45	0.9265	1.95	0.9744	3.60	0.9998
0.46	0.6772	0.96	0.8315	1.46	0.9279	1.96	0.9750	3.70	0.9999
0.47	0.6808	0.97	0.8340	1.47	0.9292	1.97	0.9756	3.80	0.9999
0.48	0.6844	0.98	0.8365	1.48	0.9306	1.98	0.9761	3.90	1.0000
0.49	0.6879	0.99	0.8389	1.49	0.9319	1.99	0.9767	4.00	1.0000
0.50	0.6915	1.00	0.8413	1.50	0.9332	2.00	0.9772		

Table A.4:   Percentage Points of the Normal Distribution

The values z in the table are those which the random variable $Z \sim N(0, 1)$ exceeds with probability p; that is, $P(Z > z) = 1 - \Phi(z) = p$.

p	z	p	z
0.5000	0.0000	0.0500	1.6449
0.4000	0.2533	0.0250	1.9600
0.3000	0.5244	0.0100	2.3263
0.2000	0.8416	0.0050	2.5758
0.1500	1.0364	0.0010	3.0902
0.1000	1.2816	0.0005	3.2905

Acknowledged that the copyright belongs to the Royal Statistical Society and reproduced from the Royal Statistical Society Tables, Royal Statistical Society, 2004 with permission from the Royal Statistical Society.

Table A.5:   Percentage Points of E χ^2 Distribution

The values in the table are those which a random variable with the χ^2 distribution on v degrees of freedom exceeds with the probability shown.

	0.995	0.990	0.975	0.950	0.900	0.100	0.050	0.025	0.010	0.005
1	0.000	0.000	0.001	0.004	0.016	2.706	3.841	5.024	6.635	7.879
2	0.010	0.020	0.051	0.103	0.211	4.605	5.991	7.378	9.210	10.597
3	0.072	0.115	0.216	0.352	0.584	6.251	7.815	9.348	11.345	12.838
4	0.207	0.297	0.484	0.711	1.064	7.779	9.488	11.143	13.277	14.860
5	0.412	0.554	0.831	1.145	1.610	9.236	11.070	12.833	15.086	16.750
6	0.676	0.872	1.237	1.635	2.204	10.645	12.592	14.449	16.812	18.548
7	0.989	1.239	1.690	2.167	2.833	12.017	14.067	16.013	18.475	20.278
8	1.344	1.646	2.180	2.733	3.490	13.362	15.507	17.535	20.090	21.955
9	1.735	2.088	2.700	3.325	4.168	14.684	16.919	19.023	21.666	23.589
10	2.156	2.558	3.247	3.940	4.865	15.987	18.307	20.483	23.209	25.188
11	2.603	3.053	3.816	4.575	5.578	17.275	19.675	21.920	24.725	26.757
12	3.074	3.571	4.404	5.226	6.304	18.549	21.026	23.337	26.217	28.300
13	3.565	4.107	5.009	5.892	7.042	19.812	22.362	24.736	27.688	29.819
14	4.075	4.660	5.629	6.571	7.790	21.064	23.685	26.119	29.141	31.319
15	4.601	5.229	6.262	7.261	8.547	22.307	24.996	27.488	30.578	32.801
16	5.142	5.812	6.908	7.962	9.312	23.542	26.296	28.845	32.000	34.267
17	5.697	6.408	7.564	8.672	10.085	24.769	27.587	30.191	33.409	35.718
18	6.265	7.015	8.231	9.390	10.865	25.989	28.869	31.526	34.805	37.156
19	6.844	7.633	8.907	10.117	11.651	27.204	30.144	32.852	36.191	38.582
20	7.434	8.260	9.591	10.851	12.443	28.412	31.410	34.170	37.566	39.997
22	8.643	9.542	10.982	12.338	14.041	30.813	33.924	36.781	40.289	42.796
24	9.886	10.856	12.401	13.848	15.659	33.196	36.415	39.364	42.980	45.559
26	11.160	12.198	13.844	15.379	17.292	35.563	38.885	41.923	45.642	48.290
28	12.461	13.565	15.308	16.928	18.939	37.916	41.337	44.461	48.278	50.993
30	13.787	14.953	16.791	18.493	20.599	40.256	43.773	46.979	50.892	53.672

(continued)

(continued)

	0.995	0.990	0.975	0.950	0.900	0.100	0.050	0.025	0.010	0.005
40	20.707	22.164	24.433	26.509	29.051	51.805	55.758	59.342	63.691	66.766
50	27.991	29.707	32.357	34.764	37.689	63.167	67.505	71.420	76.154	79.490
60	35.534	37.485	40.482	43.188	46.459	74.397	79.082	83.298	88.379	91.952
70	43.275	45.442	48.758	51.739	55.329	85.527	90.531	95.023	100.425	104.215
80	51.172	53.540	57.153	60.391	64.278	96.578	101.879	106.629	112.329	116.321
90	59.196	61.754	65.647	69.126	73.291	107.565	113.145	118.136	124.116	128.299
100	67.328	70.065	74.222	77.929	82.358	118.498	124.342	129.561	135.807	140.169
110	75.550	78.458	82.867	86.792	91.471	129.385	135.480	140.917	147.414	151.948
120	83.852	86.923	91.573	95.705	100.624	140.233	146.567	152.211	158.950	163.648

Acknowledged that the copyright belongs to the Royal Statistical Society and reproduced from the Royal Statistical Society Tables, Royal Statistical Society, 2004 with permission from the Royal Statistical Society.

Table A.6:   Percentage Points of Student's *t*-Distribution

The values in the table are those which a random variable with Student's *t*-distribution on v degrees of freedom exceeds with the probability shown.

	0.100	0.050	0.025	0.010	0.005	0.001	0.0005
1	3.078	6.314	12.706	31.821	63.657	318.309	636.619
2	1.886	2.920	4.303	6.965	9.925	22.327	31.599
3	1.638	2.353	3.182	4.541	5.841	10.215	12.924
4	1.533	2.132	2.776	3.747	4.604	7.173	8.610
5	1.476	2.015	2.571	3.365	4.032	5.893	6.869
6	1.440	1.943	2.447	3.143	3.707	5.208	5.959
7	1.415	1.895	2.365	2.998	3.499	4.785	5.408
8	1.397	1.860	2.306	2.896	3.355	4.501	5.041
9	1.383	1.833	2.262	2.821	3.250	4.297	4.781
10	1.372	1.812	2.228	2.764	3.169	4.144	4.587
11	1.363	1.796	2.201	2.718	3.106	4.025	4.437
12	1.356	1.782	2.179	2.681	3.055	3.930	4.318
13	1.350	1.771	2.160	2.650	3.012	3.852	4.221
14	1.345	1.761	2.145	2.624	2.977	3.787	4.140
15	1.341	1.753	2.131	2.602	2.947	3.733	4.073
16	1.337	1.746	2.120	2.583	2.921	3.686	4.015
17	1.333	1.740	2.110	2.567	2.898	3.646	3.965
18	1.330	1.734	2.101	2.552	2.878	3.610	3.922
19	1.328	1.729	2.093	2.539	2.861	3.579	3.883
20	1.325	1.725	2.086	2.528	2.845	3.552	3.850
21	1.323	1.721	2.080	2.518	2.831	3.527	3.819
22	1.321	1.717	2.074	2.508	2.819	3.505	3.792
23	1.319	1.714	2.069	2.500	2.807	3.485	3.768
24	1.318	1.711	2.064	2.492	2.797	3.467	3.745
25	1.316	1.708	2.060	2.485	2.787	3.450	3.725
26	1.315	1.706	2.056	2.479	2.779	3.435	3.707
27	1.314	1.703	2.052	2.473	2.771	3.421	3.690
28	1.313	1.701	2.048	2.467	2.763	3.408	3.674

(continued)

(continued)

	0.100	0.050	0.025	0.010	0.005	0.001	0.0005
29	1.311	1.699	2.045	2.462	2.756	3.396	3.659
30	1.310	1.697	2.042	2.457	2.750	3.385	3.646
32	1.309	1.694	2.037	2.449	2.738	3.365	3.622
34	1.307	1.691	2.032	2.441	2.728	3.348	3.601
36	1.306	1.688	2.028	2.434	2.719	3.333	3.582
38	1.304	1.686	2.024	2.429	2.712	3.319	3.566
40	1.303	1.684	2.021	2.423	2.704	3.307	3.551
45	1.301	1.679	2.014	2.412	2.690	3.281	3.520
50	1.299	1.676	2.009	2.403	2.678	3.261	3.496
55	1.297	1.673	2.004	2.396	2.668	3.245	3.476
60	1.296	1.671	2.000	2.390	2.660	3.232	3.460
70	1.294	1.667	1.994	2.381	2.648	3.211	3.435
80	1.292	1.664	1.990	2.374	2.639	3.195	3.416
90	1.291	1.662	1.987	2.368	2.632	3.183	3.402
100	1.290	1.660	1.984	2.364	2.626	3.174	3.390
110	1.289	1.659	1.982	2.361	2.621	3.166	3.381
120	1.289	1.658	1.980	2.358	2.617	3.160	3.373
∞	1.282	1.645	1.960	2.326	2.576	3.090	3.291

Acknowledged that the copyright belongs to the Royal Statistical Society and reproduced from the Royal Statistical Society Tables, Royal Statistical Society, 2004 with permission from the Royal Statistical Society.

Table A.7: Percentage Points of the F-Distribution (Upper 10% Points)

The values in the table are those which a random variable with the F-distribution on v_1 and v_2 degrees of freedom exceeds with probability 0.10.

If an *upper* percentage point of the F-distribution on v_1 and v_2 degrees of freedom is f, then the corresponding *lower* percentage point of the F-distribution on v_2 and v_1 degrees of freedom is $1/f$

v_2 \ v_1	1	2	3	4	5	6	7	8	9	10	12	18	24	∞
1	39.86	49.50	53.59	55.83	57.24	58.20	58.91	59.44	59.86	60.19	60.71	61.57	62.00	63.33
2	8.53	9.00	9.16	9.24	9.29	9.33	9.35	9.37	9.38	9.39	9.41	9.44	9.45	9.49
3	5.54	5.46	5.39	5.34	5.31	5.28	5.27	5.25	5.24	5.23	5.22	5.19	5.18	5.13
4	4.54	4.32	4.19	4.11	4.05	4.01	3.98	3.95	3.94	3.92	3.90	3.85	3.83	3.76
5	4.06	3.78	3.62	3.52	3.45	3.40	3.37	3.34	3.32	3.30	3.27	3.22	3.19	3.10
6	3.78	3.46	3.29	3.18	3.11	3.05	3.01	2.98	2.96	2.94	2.90	2.85	2.82	2.72
7	3.59	3.26	3.07	2.96	2.88	2.83	2.78	2.75	2.72	2.70	2.67	2.61	2.58	2.47
8	3.46	3.11	2.92	2.81	2.73	2.67	2.62	2.59	2.56	2.54	2.50	2.44	2.40	2.29
9	3.36	3.01	2.81	2.69	2.61	2.55	2.51	2.47	2.44	2.42	2.38	2.31	2.28	2.16
10	3.29	2.92	2.73	2.61	2.52	2.46	2.41	2.38	2.35	2.32	2.28	2.22	2.18	2.06
11	3.23	2.86	2.66	2.54	2.45	2.39	2.34	2.30	2.27	2.25	2.21	2.14	2.10	1.97
12	3.18	2.81	2.61	2.48	2.39	2.33	2.28	2.24	2.21	2.19	2.15	2.08	2.04	1.90
13	3.14	2.76	2.56	2.43	2.35	2.28	2.23	2.20	2.16	2.14	2.10	2.02	1.98	1.85
14	3.10	2.73	2.52	2.39	2.31	2.24	2.19	2.15	2.12	2.10	2.05	1.98	1.94	1.80
15	3.07	2.70	2.49	2.36	2.27	2.21	2.16	2.12	2.09	2.06	2.02	1.94	1.90	1.76
16	3.05	2.67	2.46	2.33	2.24	2.18	2.13	2.09	2.06	2.03	1.99	1.91	1.87	1.72
17	3.03	2.64	2.44	2.31	2.22	2.15	2.10	2.06	2.03	2.00	1.96	1.88	1.84	1.69
18	3.01	2.62	2.42	2.29	2.20	2.13	2.08	2.04	2.00	1.98	1.93	1.85	1.81	1.66
19	2.99	2.61	2.40	2.27	2.18	2.11	2.06	2.02	1.98	1.96	1.91	1.83	1.79	1.63
20	2.97	2.59	2.38	2.25	2.16	2.09	2.04	2.00	1.96	1.94	1.89	1.81	1.77	1.61
22	2.95	2.56	2.35	2.22	2.13	2.06	2.01	1.97	1.93	1.90	1.86	1.78	1.73	1.57
24	2.93	2.54	2.33	2.19	2.10	2.04	1.98	1.94	1.91	1.88	1.83	1.75	1.70	1.53
26	2.91	2.52	2.31	2.17	2.08	2.01	1.96	1.92	1.88	1.86	1.81	1.72	1.68	1.50
28	2.89	2.50	2.29	2.16	2.06	2.00	1.94	1.90	1.87	1.84	1.79	1.70	1.66	1.48

(continued)

(continued)

v_2 \ v_1	1	2	3	4	5	6	7	8	9	10	12	18	24	∞
30	2.88	2.49	2.28	2.14	2.05	1.98	1.93	1.88	1.85	1.82	1.77	1.69	1.64	1.46
40	2.84	2.44	2.23	2.09	2.00	1.93	1.87	1.83	1.79	1.76	1.71	1.62	1.57	1.38
50	2.81	2.41	2.20	2.06	1.97	1.90	1.84	1.80	1.76	1.73	1.68	1.59	1.54	1.33
60	2.79	2.39	2.18	2.04	1.95	1.87	1.82	1.77	1.74	1.71	1.66	1.56	1.51	1.29
70	2.78	2.38	2.16	2.03	1.93	1.86	1.80	1.76	1.72	1.69	1.64	1.55	1.49	1.27
80	2.77	2.37	2.15	2.02	1.92	1.85	1.79	1.75	1.71	1.68	1.63	1.53	1.48	1.24
90	2.76	2.36	2.15	2.01	1.91	1.84	1.78	1.74	1.70	1.67	1.62	1.52	1.47	1.23
100	2.76	2.36	2.14	2.00	1.91	1.83	1.78	1.73	1.69	1.66	1.61	1.52	1.46	1.21
110	2.75	2.35	2.13	2.00	1.90	1.83	1.77	1.73	1.69	1.66	1.61	1.51	1.45	1.20
120	2.75	2.35	2.13	1.99	1.90	1.82	1.77	1.72	1.68	1.65	1.60	1.50	1.45	1.19
∞	2.71	2.30	2.08	1.94	1.85	1.77	1.72	1.67	1.63	1.60	1.55	1.44	1.38	1.00

Acknowledged that the copyright belongs to the Royal Statistical Society and reproduced from the Royal Statistical Society Tables, Royal Statistical Society, 2004 with permission from the Royal Statistical Society.

Table A.7:   Percentage Points of the F-Distribution
(Upper 5% Points)

The values in the table are those which a random variable with the F-distribution on v_1 and v_2 degrees of freedom exceeds with probability 0.05.

   If an *upper* percentage point of the F-distribution on v_1 and v_2 degrees of freedom is f, then the corresponding *lower* percentage point of the F-distribution on v_2 and v_1 degrees of freedom is $1/f$

v_2 \ v_1	1	2	3	4	5	6	7	8	9	10	12	18	24	∞
1	161.4	199.5	215.7	224.6	230.2	234.0	236.8	238.9	240.5	241.9	243.9	247.3	249.1	254.3
2	18.51	19.00	19.16	19.25	19.30	19.33	19.35	19.37	19.38	19.40	19.41	19.44	19.45	19.50
3	10.13	9.55	9.28	9.12	9.01	8.94	8.89	8.85	8.81	8.79	8.74	8.67	8.64	8.53
4	7.71	6.94	6.59	6.39	6.26	6.16	6.09	6.04	6.00	5.96	5.91	5.82	5.77	5.63
5	6.61	5.79	5.41	5.19	5.05	4.95	4.88	4.82	4.77	4.74	4.68	4.58	4.53	4.36
6	5.99	5.14	4.76	4.53	4.39	4.28	4.21	4.15	4.10	4.06	4.00	3.90	3.84	3.67
7	5.59	4.74	4.35	4.12	3.97	3.87	3.79	3.73	3.68	3.64	3.57	3.47	3.41	3.23
8	5.32	4.46	4.07	3.84	3.69	3.58	3.50	3.44	3.39	3.35	3.28	3.17	3.12	2.93
9	5.12	4.26	3.86	3.63	3.48	3.37	3.29	3.23	3.18	3.14	3.07	2.96	2.90	2.71
10	4.96	4.10	3.71	3.48	3.33	3.22	3.14	3.07	3.02	2.98	2.91	2.80	2.74	2.54
11	4.84	3.98	3.59	3.36	3.20	3.09	3.01	2.95	2.90	2.85	2.79	2.67	2.61	2.40
12	4.75	3.89	3.49	3.26	3.11	3.00	2.91	2.85	2.80	2.75	2.69	2.57	2.51	2.30
13	4.67	3.81	3.41	3.18	3.03	2.92	2.83	2.77	2.71	2.67	2.60	2.48	2.42	2.21
14	4.60	3.74	3.34	3.11	2.96	2.85	2.76	2.70	2.65	2.60	2.53	2.41	2.35	2.13
15	4.54	3.68	3.29	3.06	2.90	2.79	2.71	2.64	2.59	2.54	2.48	2.35	2.29	2.07
16	4.49	3.63	3.24	3.01	2.85	2.74	2.66	2.59	2.54	2.49	2.42	2.30	2.24	2.01
17	4.45	3.59	3.20	2.96	2.81	2.70	2.61	2.55	2.49	2.45	2.38	2.26	2.19	1.96
18	4.41	3.55	3.16	2.93	2.77	2.66	2.58	2.51	2.46	2.41	2.34	2.22	2.15	1.92
19	4.38	3.52	3.13	2.90	2.74	2.63	2.54	2.48	2.42	2.38	2.31	2.18	2.11	1.88
20	4.35	3.49	3.10	2.87	2.71	2.60	2.51	2.45	2.39	2.35	2.28	2.15	2.08	1.84
22	4.30	3.44	3.05	2.82	2.66	2.55	2.46	2.40	2.34	2.30	2.23	2.10	2.03	1.78
24	4.26	3.40	3.01	2.78	2.62	2.51	2.42	2.36	2.30	2.25	2.18	2.05	1.98	1.73
26	4.23	3.37	2.98	2.74	2.59	2.47	2.39	2.32	2.27	2.22	2.15	2.02	1.95	1.69
28	4.20	3.34	2.95	2.71	2.56	2.45	2.36	2.29	2.24	2.19	2.12	1.99	1.91	1.65

(continued)

(continued)

v_2 \ v_1	1	2	3	4	5	6	7	8	9	10	12	18	24	∞
30	4.17	3.32	2.92	2.69	2.53	2.42	2.33	2.27	2.21	2.16	2.09	1.96	1.89	1.62
40	4.08	3.23	2.84	2.61	2.45	2.34	2.25	2.18	2.12	2.08	2.00	1.87	1.79	1.51
50	4.03	3.18	2.79	2.56	2.40	2.29	2.20	2.13	2.07	2.03	1.95	1.81	1.74	1.44
60	4.00	3.15	2.76	2.53	2.37	2.25	2.17	2.10	2.04	1.99	1.92	1.78	1.70	1.39
70	3.98	3.13	2.74	2.50	2.35	2.23	2.14	2.07	2.02	1.97	1.89	1.75	1.67	1.35
80	3.96	3.11	2.72	2.49	2.33	2.21	2.13	2.06	2.00	1.95	1.88	1.73	1.65	1.32
90	3.95	3.10	2.71	2.47	2.32	2.20	2.11	2.04	1.99	1.94	1.86	1.72	1.64	1.30
100	3.94	3.09	2.70	2.46	2.31	2.19	2.10	2.03	1.97	1.93	1.85	1.71	1.63	1.28
110	3.93	3.08	2.69	2.45	2.30	2.18	2.09	2.02	1.97	1.92	1.84	1.70	1.62	1.27
120	3.92	3.07	2.68	2.45	2.29	2.18	2.09	2.02	1.96	1.91	1.83	1.69	1.61	1.25
∞	3.84	3.00	2.60	2.37	2.21	2.10	2.01	1.94	1.88	1.83	1.75	1.60	1.52	1.00

Acknowledged that the copyright belongs to the Royal Statistical Society and reproduced from the Royal Statistical Society Tables, Royal Statistical Society, 2004 with permission from the Royal Statistical Society.

Table A.7: Percentage Points of the F-Distribution (Upper 2.5% Points)

The values in the table are those which a random variable with the F-distribution on v_1 and v_2 degrees of freedom exceeds with probability 0.025.

If an *upper* percentage point of the F-distribution on v_1 and v_2 degrees of freedom is f, then the corresponding *lower* percentage point of the F-distribution on v_2 and v_1 degrees of freedom is $1/f$

v_2 \ v_1	1	2	3	4	5	6	7	8	9	10	12	18	24	∞
1	647.8	799.5	864.2	899.6	921.8	937.1	948.2	956.7	963.3	968.6	976.7	990.3	997.2	1018.3
2	38.51	39.00	39.17	39.25	39.30	39.33	39.36	39.37	39.39	39.40	39.41	39.44	39.46	39.50
3	17.44	16.04	15.44	15.10	14.88	14.73	14.62	14.54	14.47	14.42	14.34	14.20	14.12	13.90
4	12.22	10.65	9.98	9.60	9.36	9.20	9.07	8.98	8.90	8.84	8.75	8.59	8.51	8.26
5	10.01	8.43	7.76	7.39	7.15	6.98	6.85	6.76	6.68	6.62	6.52	6.36	6.28	6.02
6	8.81	7.26	6.60	6.23	5.99	5.82	5.70	5.60	5.52	5.46	5.37	5.20	5.12	4.85
7	8.07	6.54	5.89	5.52	5.29	5.12	4.99	4.90	4.82	4.76	4.67	4.50	4.41	4.14
8	7.57	6.06	5.42	5.05	4.82	4.65	4.53	4.43	4.36	4.30	4.20	4.03	3.95	3.67
9	7.21	5.71	5.08	4.72	4.48	4.32	4.20	4.10	4.03	3.96	3.87	3.70	3.61	3.33
10	6.94	5.46	4.83	4.47	4.24	4.07	3.95	3.85	3.78	3.72	3.62	3.45	3.37	3.08
11	6.72	5.26	4.63	4.28	4.04	3.88	3.76	3.66	3.59	3.53	3.43	3.26	3.17	2.88
12	6.55	5.10	4.47	4.12	3.89	3.73	3.61	3.51	3.44	3.37	3.28	3.11	3.02	2.72
13	6.41	4.97	4.35	4.00	3.77	3.60	3.48	3.39	3.31	3.25	3.15	2.98	2.89	2.60
14	6.30	4.86	4.24	3.89	3.66	3.50	3.38	3.29	3.21	3.15	3.05	2.88	2.79	2.49
15	6.20	4.77	4.15	3.80	3.58	3.41	3.29	3.20	3.12	3.06	2.96	2.79	2.70	2.40
16	6.12	4.69	4.08	3.73	3.50	3.34	3.22	3.12	3.05	2.99	2.89	2.72	2.63	2.32
17	6.04	4.62	4.01	3.66	3.44	3.28	3.16	3.06	2.98	2.92	2.82	2.65	2.56	2.25
18	5.98	4.56	3.95	3.61	3.38	3.22	3.10	3.01	2.93	2.87	2.77	2.60	2.50	2.19
19	5.92	4.51	3.90	3.56	3.33	3.17	3.05	2.96	2.88	2.82	2.72	2.55	2.45	2.13
20	5.87	4.46	3.86	3.51	3.29	3.13	3.01	2.91	2.84	2.77	2.68	2.50	2.41	2.09
22	5.79	4.38	3.78	3.44	3.22	3.05	2.93	2.84	2.76	2.70	2.60	2.43	2.33	2.00
24	5.72	4.32	3.72	3.38	3.15	2.99	2.87	2.78	2.70	2.64	2.54	2.36	2.27	1.94
26	5.66	4.27	3.67	3.33	3.10	2.94	2.82	2.73	2.65	2.59	2.49	2.31	2.22	1.88
28	5.61	4.22	3.63	3.29	3.06	2.90	2.78	2.69	2.61	2.55	2.45	2.27	2.17	1.83

(continued)

(continued)

v_2 \ v_1	1	2	3	4	5	6	7	8	9	10	12	18	24	∞
30	5.57	4.18	3.59	3.25	3.03	2.87	2.75	2.65	2.57	2.51	2.41	2.23	2.14	1.79
40	5.42	4.05	3.46	3.13	2.90	2.74	2.62	2.53	2.45	2.39	2.29	2.11	2.01	1.64
50	5.34	3.97	3.39	3.05	2.83	2.67	2.55	2.46	2.38	2.32	2.22	2.03	1.93	1.55
60	5.29	3.93	3.34	3.01	2.79	2.63	2.51	2.41	2.33	2.27	2.17	1.98	1.88	1.48
70	5.25	3.89	3.31	2.97	2.75	2.59	2.47	2.38	2.30	2.24	2.14	1.95	1.85	1.44
80	5.22	3.86	3.28	2.95	2.73	2.57	2.45	2.35	2.28	2.21	2.11	1.92	1.82	1.40
90	5.20	3.84	3.26	2.93	2.71	2.55	2.43	2.34	2.26	2.19	2.09	1.91	1.80	1.37
100	5.18	3.83	3.25	2.92	2.70	2.54	2.42	2.32	2.24	2.18	2.08	1.89	1.78	1.35
110	5.16	3.82	3.24	2.90	2.68	2.53	2.40	2.31	2.23	2.17	2.07	1.88	1.77	1.33
120	5.15	3.80	3.23	2.89	2.67	2.52	2.39	2.30	2.22	2.16	2.05	1.87	1.76	1.31
∞	5.02	3.69	3.12	2.79	2.57	2.41	2.29	2.19	2.11	2.05	1.94	1.75	1.64	1.00

Acknowledged that the copyright belongs to the Royal Statistical Society and reproduced from the Royal Statistical Society Tables, Royal Statistical Society, 2004 with permission from the Royal Statistical Society.

Table A.7:   Percentage Points of the F-Distribution (Upper 1% Points)

The values in the table are those which a random variable with the F-distribution on v_1 and v_2 degrees of freedom exceeds with probability 0.01.

If an *upper* percentage point of the F-distribution on v_1 and v_2 degrees of freedom is f, then the corresponding *lower* percentage point of the F-distribution on v_2 and v_1 degrees of freedom is $1/f$

v_2 \ v_1	1	2	3	4	5	6	7	8	9	10	12	18	24	∞
1	4052	5000	5403	5625	5764	5859	5928	5981	6022	6056	6106	6192	6235	6366
2	98.50	99.00	99.17	99.25	99.30	99.33	99.36	99.37	99.39	99.40	99.42	99.44	99.46	99.50
3	34.12	30.82	29.46	28.71	28.24	27.91	27.67	27.49	27.34	27.23	27.05	26.75	26.60	26.13
4	21.20	18.00	16.69	15.98	15.52	15.21	14.98	14.80	14.66	14.55	14.37	14.08	13.93	13.46
5	16.26	13.27	12.06	11.39	10.97	10.67	10.46	10.29	10.16	10.05	9.89	9.61	9.47	9.02
6	13.74	10.93	9.78	9.15	8.75	8.47	8.26	8.10	7.98	7.87	7.72	7.45	7.31	6.88
7	12.25	9.55	8.45	7.85	7.46	7.19	6.99	6.84	6.72	6.62	6.47	6.21	6.07	5.65
8	11.26	8.65	7.59	7.01	6.63	6.37	6.18	6.03	5.91	5.81	5.67	5.41	5.28	4.86
9	10.56	8.02	6.99	6.42	6.06	5.80	5.61	5.47	5.35	5.26	5.11	4.86	4.73	4.31
10	10.04	7.56	6.55	5.99	5.64	5.39	5.20	5.06	4.94	4.85	4.71	4.46	4.33	3.91
11	9.65	7.21	6.22	5.67	5.32	5.07	4.89	4.74	4.63	4.54	4.40	4.15	4.02	3.60
12	9.33	6.93	5.95	5.41	5.06	4.82	4.64	4.50	4.39	4.30	4.16	3.91	3.78	3.36
13	9.07	6.70	5.74	5.21	4.86	4.62	4.44	4.30	4.19	4.10	3.96	3.72	3.59	3.17
14	8.86	6.51	5.56	5.04	4.70	4.46	4.28	4.14	4.03	3.94	3.80	3.56	3.43	3.00
15	8.68	6.36	5.42	4.89	4.56	4.32	4.14	4.00	3.90	3.81	3.67	3.42	3.29	2.87
16	8.53	6.23	5.29	4.77	4.44	4.20	4.03	3.89	3.78	3.69	3.55	3.31	3.18	2.75
17	8.40	6.11	5.18	4.67	4.34	4.10	3.93	3.79	3.68	3.59	3.46	3.21	3.08	2.65
18	8.29	6.01	5.09	4.58	4.25	4.01	3.84	3.71	3.60	3.51	3.46	3.13	3.00	2.57
19	8.19	5.93	5.01	4.50	4.17	3.94	3.77	3.63	3.52	3.43	3.30	3.05	2.92	2.49
20	8.10	5.85	4.94	4.43	4.10	3.87	3.70	3.56	3.46	3.37	3.23	2.99	2.86	2.42
22	7.95	5.72	4.82	4.31	3.99	3.76	3.59	3.45	3.35	3.26	3.12	2.88	2.75	2.31
24	7.82	5.61	4.72	4.22	3.90	3.67	3.50	3.36	3.26	3.17	3.03	2.79	2.66	2.21
26	7.72	5.53	4.64	4.14	3.82	3.59	3.42	3.29	3.18	3.09	2.96	2.71	2.59	2.13
28	7.64	5.45	4.57	4.07	3.75	3.53	3.36	3.23	3.12	3.03	2.90	2.65	2.52	2.06

(continued)

(continued)

v_2 \ v_1	1	2	3	4	5	6	7	8	9	10	12	18	24	∞
30	7.56	5.39	4.51	4.02	3.70	3.47	3.30	3.17	3.07	2.98	2.84	2.60	2.47	2.01
40	7.31	5.18	4.31	3.83	3.51	3.29	3.12	2.99	2.89	2.80	2.67	2.42	2.29	1.80
50	7.17	5.06	4.20	3.72	3.41	3.19	3.02	2.89	2.79	2.70	2.56	2.32	2.18	1.68
60	7.08	4.98	4.13	3.65	3.34	3.12	2.95	2.82	2.72	2.63	2.50	2.25	2.12	1.60
70	7.01	4.92	4.07	3.60	3.29	3.07	2.91	2.78	2.67	2.59	2.45	2.20	2.07	1.54
80	6.96	4.88	4.04	3.56	3.25	3.04	2.87	2.74	2.64	2.55	2.42	2.17	2.03	1.49
90	6.92	4.85	4.01	3.54	3.23	3.01	2.85	2.71	2.61	2.52	2.39	2.14	2.00	1.46
100	6.89	4.82	3.98	3.51	3.21	2.99	2.82	2.69	2.59	2.50	2.37	2.12	1.98	1.43
110	6.87	4.80	3.96	3.50	3.19	2.97	2.81	2.68	2.57	2.49	2.35	2.10	1.97	1.40
120	6.85	4.79	3.95	3.48	3.17	2.96	2.79	2.66	2.56	2.47	2.34	2.09	1.95	1.38
∞	6.63	4.61	3.78	3.32	3.02	2.80	2.64	2.51	2.41	2.32	2.19	1.93	1.79	1.00

Acknowledged that the copyright belongs to the Royal Statistical Society and reproduced from the Royal Statistical Society Tables, Royal Statistical Society, 2004 with permission from the Royal Statistical Society.

Table A.7: Percentage Points of the F-Distribution (Upper 0.5% Points)

The values in the table are those which a random variable with the F-distribution on v_1 and v_2 degrees of freedom exceeds with probability 0.005.

If an *upper* percentage point of the F-distribution on v_1 and v_2 degrees of freedom is f, then the corresponding *lower* percentage point of the F-distribution on v_2 and v_1 degrees of freedom is $1/f$

v_2 \ v_1	1	2	3	4	5	6	7	8	9	10	12	18	24	∞
1	16211	20000	21615	22500	23056	23437	23715	23925	24091	24224	24426	24767	24940	25464
2	198.5	199.0	199.2	199.3	199.3	199.3	199.4	199.4	199.4	199.4	199.4	199.4	199.5	199.5
3	55.55	49.80	47.47	46.19	45.39	44.84	44.43	44.13	43.88	43.69	43.39	42.88	42.62	41.83
4	31.33	26.28	24.26	23.15	22.46	21.97	21.62	21.35	21.14	20.97	20.70	20.26	20.03	19.32
5	22.78	18.31	16.53	15.56	14.94	14.51	14.20	13.96	13.77	13.62	13.38	12.98	12.78	12.14
6	18.63	14.54	12.92	12.03	11.46	11.07	10.79	10.57	10.39	10.25	10.03	9.66	9.47	8.88
7	16.24	12.40	10.88	10.05	9.52	9.16	8.89	8.68	8.51	8.38	8.18	7.83	7.64	7.08
8	14.69	11.04	9.60	8.81	8.30	7.95	7.69	7.50	7.34	7.21	7.01	6.68	6.50	5.95
9	13.61	10.11	8.72	7.96	7.47	7.13	6.88	6.69	6.54	6.42	6.23	5.90	5.73	5.19
10	12.83	9.43	8.08	7.34	6.87	6.54	6.30	6.12	5.97	5.85	5.66	5.34	5.17	4.64
11	12.23	8.91	7.60	6.88	6.42	6.10	5.86	5.68	5.54	5.42	5.24	4.92	4.76	4.23
12	11.75	8.51	7.23	6.52	6.07	5.76	5.52	5.35	5.20	5.09	4.91	4.59	4.43	3.90
13	11.37	8.19	6.93	6.23	5.79	5.48	5.25	5.08	4.94	4.82	4.64	4.33	4.17	3.65
14	11.06	7.92	6.68	6.00	5.56	5.26	5.03	4.86	4.72	4.60	4.43	4.12	3.96	3.44
15	10.80	7.70	6.48	5.80	5.37	5.07	4.85	4.67	4.54	4.42	4.25	3.95	3.79	3.26
16	10.58	7.51	6.30	5.64	5.21	4.91	4.69	4.52	4.38	4.27	4.10	3.80	3.64	3.11
17	10.38	7.35	6.16	5.50	5.07	4.78	4.56	4.39	4.25	4.14	3.97	3.67	3.51	2.98
18	10.22	7.21	6.03	5.37	4.96	4.66	4.44	4.28	4.14	4.03	3.86	3.56	3.40	2.87
19	10.07	7.09	5.92	5.27	4.85	4.56	4.34	4.18	4.04	3.93	3.76	3.46	3.31	2.78
20	9.94	6.99	5.82	5.17	4.76	4.47	4.26	4.09	3.96	3.85	3.68	3.38	3.22	2.69
22	9.73	6.81	5.65	5.02	4.61	4.32	4.11	3.94	3.81	3.70	3.54	3.24	3.08	2.55
24	9.55	6.66	5.52	4.89	4.49	4.20	3.99	3.83	3.69	3.59	3.42	3.12	2.97	2.43
26	9.41	6.54	5.41	4.79	4.38	4.10	3.89	3.73	3.60	3.49	3.33	3.03	2.87	2.33
28	9.28	6.44	5.32	4.70	4.30	4.02	3.81	3.65	3.52	3.41	3.25	2.95	2.79	2.25

(continued)

(continued)

v_2 \ v_1	1	2	3	4	5	6	7	8	9	10	12	18	24	∞
30	9.18	6.35	5.24	4.62	4.23	3.95	3.74	3.58	3.45	3.34	3.18	2.89	2.73	2.18
40	8.83	6.07	4.98	4.37	3.99	3.71	3.51	3.35	3.22	3.12	2.95	2.66	2.50	1.93
50	8.63	5.90	4.83	4.23	3.85	3.58	3.38	3.22	3.09	2.99	2.82	2.53	2.37	1.79
60	8.49	5.79	4.73	4.14	3.76	3.49	3.29	3.13	3.01	2.90	2.74	2.45	2.29	1.69
70	8.40	5.72	4.66	4.08	3.70	3.43	3.23	3.08	2.95	2.85	2.68	2.39	2.23	1.62
80	8.33	5.67	4.61	4.03	3.65	3.39	3.19	3.03	2.91	2.80	2.64	2.35	2.19	1.56
90	8.28	5.62	4.57	3.99	3.62	3.35	3.15	3.00	2.87	2.77	2.61	2.32	2.15	1.52
100	8.24	5.59	4.54	3.96	3.59	3.33	3.13	2.97	2.85	2.74	2.58	2.29	2.13	1.49
110	8.21	5.56	4.52	3.94	3.57	3.30	3.11	2.95	2.83	2.72	2.56	2.27	2.11	1.46
120	8.18	5.54	4.50	3.92	3.55	3.28	3.09	2.93	2.81	2.71	2.54	2.25	2.09	1.43
∞	7.88	5.30	4.28	3.72	3.35	3.09	2.90	2.74	2.62	2.52	2.36	2.06	1.90	1.00

Acknowledged that the copyright belongs to the Royal Statistical Society and reproduced from the Royal Statistical Society Tables, Royal Statistical Society, 2004 with permission from the Royal Statistical Society.

Table A.7: Percentage Points of the F-Distribution
(Upper 0.1% Points)

The values in the table are those which a random variable with the F-distribution on v_1 and v_2 degrees of freedom exceeds with probability 0.001.

Note: All percentage points in the row for $v_2 = 1$ must be multiplied by 100; for example, the percentage point for $F_{8,1}$ is 598100 (to 4 significant figures)

If an *upper* percentage point of the F-distribution on v_1 and v_2 degrees of freedom is f, then the corresponding *lower* percentage point of the F-distribution on v_2 and v_1 degrees of freedom is $1/f$

v_2	v_1													
	1	2	3	4	5	6	7	8	9	10	12	18	24	∞
1	4053*	5000*	5404*	5625*	5764*	5859*	5929*	5981*	6023*	6056*	6107*	6192*	6235*	6366*
2	998.5	999.0	999.2	999.3	999.3	999.3	999.4	999.4	999.4	999.4	999.4	999.4	999.5	999.5
3	167.0	148.5	141.1	137.1	134.6	132.8	131.6	130.6	129.9	129.2	128.3	126.7	125.9	123.5
4	74.14	61.25	56.18	53.44	51.71	50.53	49.66	49.00	48.47	48.05	47.41	46.32	45.77	44.05
5	47.18	37.12	33.20	31.09	29.75	28.83	28.16	27.65	27.24	26.92	26.42	25.57	25.13	23.79
6	35.51	27.00	23.70	21.92	20.80	20.03	19.46	19.03	18.69	18.41	17.99	17.27	16.90	15.75
7	29.25	21.69	18.77	17.20	16.21	15.52	15.02	14.63	14.33	14.08	13.71	13.06	12.73	11.70
8	25.41	18.49	15.83	14.39	13.48	12.86	12.40	12.05	11.77	11.54	11.19	10.60	10.30	9.33
9	22.86	16.39	13.90	12.56	11.71	11.13	10.70	10.37	10.11	9.89	9.57	9.01	8.72	7.81
10	21.04	14.91	12.55	11.28	10.48	9.93	9.52	9.20	8.96	8.75	8.45	7.91	7.64	6.76
11	19.69	13.81	11.56	10.35	9.58	9.05	8.66	8.35	8.12	7.92	7.63	7.11	6.85	6.00
12	18.64	12.97	10.80	9.63	8.89	8.38	8.00	7.71	7.48	7.29	7.00	6.51	6.25	5.42
13	17.82	12.31	10.21	9.07	8.35	7.86	7.49	7.21	6.98	6.80	6.52	6.03	5.78	4.97
14	17.14	11.78	9.73	8.62	7.92	7.44	7.08	6.80	6.58	6.40	6.13	5.66	5.41	4.60
15	16.59	11.34	9.34	8.25	7.57	7.09	6.74	6.47	6.26	6.08	5.81	5.35	5.10	4.31
16	16.12	10.97	9.01	7.94	7.27	6.80	6.46	6.19	5.98	5.81	5.55	5.09	4.85	4.06
17	15.72	10.66	8.73	7.68	7.02	6.56	6.22	5.96	5.75	5.58	5.32	4.87	4.63	3.85
18	15.38	10.39	8.49	7.46	6.81	6.35	6.02	5.76	5.56	5.39	5.13	4.68	4.45	3.67
19	15.08	10.16	8.28	7.27	6.62	6.18	5.85	5.59	5.39	5.22	4.97	4.52	4.29	3.51
20	14.82	9.95	8.10	7.10	6.46	6.02	5.69	5.44	5.24	5.08	4.82	4.38	4.15	3.38
22	14.38	9.61	7.80	6.81	6.19	5.76	5.44	5.19	4.99	4.83	4.58	4.15	3.92	3.15
24	14.03	9.34	7.55	6.59	5.98	5.55	5.23	4.99	4.80	4.64	4.39	3.96	3.74	2.97
26	13.74	9.12	7.36	6.41	5.80	5.38	5.07	4.83	4.64	4.48	4.24	3.81	3.59	2.82
28	13.50	8.93	7.19	6.25	5.66	5.24	4.93	4.69	4.50	4.35	4.11	3.69	3.46	2.69

(continued)

(continued)

v_2	v_1													
	1	2	3	4	5	6	7	8	9	10	12	18	24	∞
30	13.29	8.77	7.05	6.12	5.53	5.12	4.82	4.58	4.39	4.24	4.00	3.58	3.36	2.59
40	12.61	8.25	6.59	5.70	5.13	4.73	4.44	4.21	4.02	3.87	3.64	3.23	3.01	2.23
50	12.22	7.96	6.34	5.46	4.90	4.51	4.22	4.00	3.82	3.67	3.44	3.04	2.82	2.03
60	11.97	7.77	6.17	5.31	4.76	4.37	4.09	3.86	3.69	3.54	3.32	2.91	2.69	1.89
70	11.80	7.64	6.06	5.20	4.66	4.28	3.99	3.77	3.60	3.45	3.23	2.83	2.61	1.79
80	11.67	7.54	5.97	5.12	4.58	4.20	3.92	3.70	3.53	3.39	3.16	2.76	2.54	1.72
90	11.57	7.47	5.91	5.06	4.53	4.15	3.87	3.65	3.48	3.34	3.11	2.71	2.50	1.66
100	11.50	7.41	5.86	5.02	4.48	4.11	3.83	3.61	3.44	3.30	3.07	2.68	2.46	1.62
110	11.43	7.36	5.82	4.98	4.45	4.07	3.79	3.58	3.41	3.26	3.04	2.65	2.43	1.58
120	11.38	7.32	5.78	4.95	4.42	4.04	3.77	3.55	3.38	3.24	3.02	2.62	2.40	1.54
∞	10.83	6.91	5.42	4.62	4.10	3.74	3.47	3.27	3.10	2.96	2.74	2.35	2.13	1.00

Acknowledged that the copyright belongs to the Royal Statistical Society and reproduced from the Royal Statistical Society Tables, Royal Statistical Society, 2004 with permission from the Royal Statistical Society.

Table A.8: Critical Values for Correlation Coefficients

These tables concern tests of the hypothesis that a population correlation coefficient ρ is 0. The values in the tables are the minimum values which need to be reached by a sample correlation coefficient in order to be significant at the level shown, on a one-tailed test.

Product moment coefficient					Sample size	Spearman's coefficient		
Level						Level		
0.10	0.05	0.025	0.01	0.005		0.05	0.025	0.01
0.8000	0.9000	0.9500	0.9800	0.9900	4	1.0000	–	–
0.6870	0.8054	0.8783	0.9343	0.9587	5	0.9000	1.0000	1.0000
0.6084	0.7293	0.8114	0.8822	0.9172	6	0.8286	0.8857	0.9429
0.5509	0.6694	0.7545	0.8329	0.8745	7	0.7143	0.7857	0.8929
0.5067	0.6215	0.7067	0.7887	0.8343	8	0.6429	0.7381	0.8333
0.4716	0.5822	0.6664	0.7498	0.7977	9	0.6000	0.7000	0.7833
0.4428	0.5494	0.6319	0.7155	0.7646	10	0.5636	0.6485	0.7455
0.4187	0.5214	0.6021	0.6851	0.7348	11	0.5364	0.6182	0.7091
0.3981	0.4973	0.5760	0.6581	0.7079	12	0.5035	0.5874	0.6783
0.3802	0.4762	0.5529	0.6339	0.6835	13	0.4835	0.5604	0.6484
0.3646	0.4575	0.5324	0.6120	0.6614	14	0.4637	0.5385	0.6264
0.3507	0.4409	0.5140	0.5923	0.6411	15	0.4464	0.5214	0.6036
0.3383	0.4259	0.4973	0.5742	0.6226	16	0.4294	0.5029	0.5824
0.3271	0.4124	0.4821	0.5577	0.6055	17	0.4142	0.4877	0.5662
0.3170	0.4000	0.4683	0.5425	0.5897	18	0.4014	0.4716	0.5501
0.3077	0.3887	0.4555	0.5285	0.5751	19	0.3912	0.4596	0.5351
0.2992	0.3783	0.4438	0.5155	0.5614	20	0.3805	0.4466	0.5218
0.2914	0.3687	0.4329	0.5034	0.5487	21	0.3701	0.4364	0.5091
0.2841	0.3598	0.4227	0.4921	0.5368	22	0.3608	0.4252	0.4975
0.2774	0.3515	0.4133	0.4815	0.5256	23	0.3528	0.4160	0.4862
0.2711	0.3438	0.4044	0.4716	0.5151	24	0.3443	0.4070	0.4757
0.2653	0.3365	0.3961	0.4622	0.5052	25	0.3369	0.3977	0.4662
0.2598	0.3297	0.3882	0.4534	0.4958	26	0.3306	0.3901	0.4571
0.2546	0.3233	0.3809	0.4451	0.4869	27	0.3242	0.3828	0.4487
0.2497	0.3172	0.3739	0.4372	0.4785	28	0.3180	0.3755	0.4401
0.2451	0.3115	0.3673	0.4297	0.4705	29	0.3118	0.3685	0.4325

(continued)

(continued)

Product moment coefficient					Sample size	Spearman's coefficient		
Level						Level		
0.10	0.05	0.025	0.01	0.005		0.05	0.025	0.01
0.2407	0.3061	0.3610	0.4226	0.4629	30	0.3063	0.3624	0.4251
0.2070	0.2638	0.3120	0.3665	0.4026	40	0.2640	0.3128	0.3681
0.1843	0.2353	0.2787	0.3281	0.3610	50	0.2353	0.2791	0.3293
0.1678	0.2144	0.2542	0.2997	0.3301	60	0.2144	0.2545	0.3005
0.1550	0.1982	0.2352	0.2776	0.3060	70	0.1982	0.2354	0.2782
0.1448	0.1852	0.2199	0.2597	0.2864	80	0.1852	0.2201	0.2602
0.1364	0.1745	0.2072	0.2449	0.2702	90	0.1745	0.2074	0.2453
0.1292	0.1654	0.1966	0.2324	0.2565	100	0.1654	0.1967	0.2327

Acknowledged that the copyright belongs to the Royal Statistical Society and reproduced from the Royal Statistical Society Tables, Royal Statistical Society, 2004 with permission from the Royal Statistical Society.

Table A.9:   Random Digits

86 13	84 10	07 30	39 05	97 96	88 07	37 26	04 89	13 48	19 20
60 78	48 12	99 47	09 46	91 33	17 21	03 94	79 00	08 50	40 16
78 48	06 37	82 26	01 06	64 65	94 41	17 26	74 66	61 93	24 97
80 56	90 79	66 94	18 40	97 79	93 20	41 51	25 04	20 71	76 04
99 09	39 25	66 31	70 56	30 15	52 17	87 55	31 11	10 68	98 23
56 32	32 72	91 65	97 36	56 61	12 79	95 17	57 16	53 58	96 36
66 02	49 93	97 44	99 15	56 86	80 57	11 78	40 23	58 40	86 14
31 77	53 94	05 93	56 14	71 23	60 46	05 33	23 72	93 10	81 23
98 79	72 43	14 76	54 77	66 29	84 09	88 56	75 86	41 67	04 42
50 97	92 15	10 01	57 01	87 33	73 17	70 18	40 21	24 20	66 62
90 51	94 50	12 48	88 95	09 34	09 30	22 27	25 56	40 76	01 59
31 99	52 24	13 43	27 88	11 39	41 65	00 84	13 06	31 79	74 97
22 96	23 34	46 12	67 11	48 06	99 24	14 83	78 37	65 73	39 47
06 84	55 41	27 06	74 59	14 29	20 14	45 75	31 16	05 41	22 96
08 64	89 30	25 25	71 35	33 31	04 56	12 67	03 74	07 16	49 32
86 87	62 43	15 11	76 49	79 13	78 80	93 89	09 57	07 14	40 74
94 44	97 13	77 04	35 02	12 76	60 91	93 40	81 06	85 85	72 84
63 25	55 14	66 47	99 90	02 90	83 43	16 01	19 69	11 78	87 16
11 22	83 98	15 21	18 57	53 42	91 91	26 52	89 13	86 00	47 61
01 70	10 83	94 71	13 67	11 12	36 54	53 32	90 43	79 01	95 15

Acknowledged that the copyright belongs to the Royal Statistical Society and reproduced from the Royal Statistical Society Tables, Royal Statistical Society, 2004 with permission from the Royal Statistical Society.

Table A.10:   Cumulative Standardized Normal Distribution

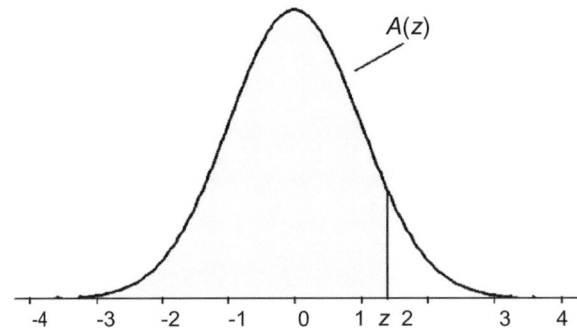

$A(z)$ is the integral of the standardized normal distribution from $-\infty$ to z (in other words, the area under the curve to the left of z). It gives the probability of a normal random variable not being more than z standard deviations above its mean. Values of z of particular importance:

z	$A(z)$	
1.645	0.9500	Lower limit of right 5% tail
1.960	0.9750	Lower limit of right 2.5% tail
2.326	0.9900	Lower limit of right 1% tail
2.576	0.9950	Lower limit of right 0.5% tail
3.090	0.9990	Lower limit of right 0.1% tail
3.291	0.9995	Lower limit of right 0.05% tail

z	0.00	0.01	0.02	0.03	0.04	0.05	0.06	0.07	0.08	0.09
0.0	0.5000	0.5040	0.5080	0.5120	0.5160	0.5199	0.5239	0.5279	0.5319	0.5359
0.1	0.5398	0.5438	0.5478	0.5517	0.5557	0.5596	0.5636	0.5675	0.5714	0.5753
0.2	0.5793	0.5832	0.5871	0.5910	0.5948	0.5987	0.6026	0.6064	0.6103	0.6141
0.3	0.6179	0.6217	0.6255	0.6293	0.6331	0.6368	0.6406	0.6443	0.6480	0.6517
0.4	0.6554	0.6591	0.6628	0.6664	0.6700	0.6736	0.6772	0.6808	0.6844	0.6879
0.5	0.6915	0.6950	0.6985	0.7019	0.7054	0.7088	0.7123	0.7157	0.7190	0.7224
0.6	0.7257	0.7291	0.7324	0.7357	0.7389	0.7422	0.7454	0.7486	0.7517	0.7549
0.7	0.7580	0.7611	0.7642	0.7673	0.7704	0.7734	0.7764	0.7794	0.7823	0.7852
0.8	0.7881	0.7910	0.7939	0.7967	0.7995	0.8023	0.8051	0.8078	0.8106	0.8133
0.9	0.8159	0.8186	0.8212	0.8238	0.8264	0.8289	0.8315	0.8340	0.8365	0.8389
1.0	0.8413	0.8438	0.8461	0.8485	0.8508	0.8531	0.8554	0.8577	0.8599	0.8621
1.1	0.8643	0.8665	0.8686	0.8708	0.8729	0.8749	0.8770	0.8790	0.8810	0.8830
1.2	0.8849	0.8869	0.8888	0.8907	0.8925	0.8944	0.8962	0.8980	0.8997	0.9015
1.3	0.9032	0.9049	0.9066	0.9082	0.9099	0.9115	0.9131	0.9147	0.9162	0.9177
1.4	0.9192	0.9207	0.9222	0.9236	0.9251	0.9265	0.9279	0.9292	0.9306	0.9319
1.5	0.9332	0.9345	0.9357	0.9370	0.9382	0.9394	0.9406	0.9418	0.9429	0.9441
1.6	0.9452	0.9463	0.9474	0.9484	0.9495	0.9505	0.9515	0.9525	0.9535	0.9545
1.7	0.9554	0.9564	0.9573	0.9582	0.9591	0.9599	0.9608	0.9616	0.9625	0.9633
1.8	0.9641	0.9649	0.9656	0.9664	0.9671	0.9678	0.9686	0.9693	0.9699	0.9706
1.9	0.9713	0.9719	0.9726	0.9732	0.9738	0.9744	0.9750	0.9756	0.9761	0.9767
2.0	0.9772	0.9778	0.9783	0.9788	0.9793	0.9798	0.9803	0.9808	0.9812	0.9817
2.1	0.9821	0.9826	0.9830	0.9834	0.9838	0.9842	0.9846	0.9850	0.9854	0.9857
2.2	0.9861	0.9864	0.9868	0.9871	0.9875	0.9878	0.9881	0.9884	0.9887	0.9890
2.3	0.9893	0.9896	0.9898	0.9901	0.9904	0.9906	0.9909	0.9911	0.9913	0.9916
2.4	0.9918	0.9920	0.9922	0.9925	0.9927	0.9929	0.9931	0.9932	0.9934	0.9936

(continued)

(continued)

z	0.00	0.01	0.02	0.03	0.04	0.05	0.06	0.07	0.08	0.09
2.5	0.9938	0.9940	0.9941	0.9943	0.9945	0.9946	0.9948	0.9949	0.9951	0.9952
2.6	0.9953	0.9955	0.9956	0.9957	0.9959	0.9960	0.9961	0.9962	0.9963	0.9964
2.7	0.9965	0.9966	0.9967	0.9968	0.9969	0.9970	0.9971	0.9972	0.9973	0.9974
2.8	0.9974	0.9975	0.9976	0.9977	0.9977	0.9978	0.9979	0.9979	0.9980	0.9981
2.9	0.9981	0.9982	0.9982	0.9983	0.9984	0.9984	0.9985	0.9985	0.9986	0.9986
3.0	0.9987	0.9987	0.9987	0.9988	0.9988	0.9989	0.9989	0.9989	0.9990	0.9990
3.1	0.9990	0.9991	0.9991	0.9991	0.9992	0.9992	0.9992	0.9992	0.9993	0.9993
3.2	0.9993	0.9993	0.9994	0.9994	0.9994	0.9994	0.9994	0.9995	0.9995	0.9995
3.3	0.9995	0.9995	0.9995	0.9996	0.9996	0.9996	0.9996	0.9996	0.9996	0.9997
3.4	0.9997	0.9997	0.9997	0.9997	0.9997	0.9997	0.9997	0.9997	0.9997	0.9998
3.5	0.9998	0.9998	0.9998	0.9998	0.9998	0.9998	0.9998	0.9998	0.9998	0.9998
3.6	0.9998	0.9998	0.9999							

References

Armitage, P., & Berry, G. (1987). *Statistical methods in medical research* (2nd ed.). London: Blackwell Scientific Publications.

Benjamini, Y. (1988). Opening the box of a boxplot. *The American Statistician, 42*(4), 257–262.

Berkson, J., & Gage, R. P. (1952). Survival curve for cancer patients following treatment. *Journal of the. American Statistical Association, 47,* 501–515.

Breslow, N. E., & Day, N. E. (1980). *Statistical methods in cancer research: Volume I—The analysis of case-control studies.* Lyon: International Agency for Research on Cancer.

Cornfield, J., & Haenszel, W. (1960). Some aspects of retrospective studies. *Journal of Chronic Diseases, 11,* 523–534.

Cox, D. R., & Hinkley, D. V. (1974). *Theoretical statistics.* London: Chapman and Hall.

Cox, D. R., & Oakes, D. (1984). *Analysis of survival data.* London: Chapman & Hall.

Daniel, W. W. (2010). *Biostatistics basic concepts and methodology for the health sciences* (9th ed.). New York: Wiley.

Draper, N., & Smith, H. (1981). *Applied regression analysis* (2nd ed.). New York: Wiley.

Fieller, E. C., Hartley, H. O., & Pearson, E. S. (1957). Tests for rank correlation coefficients. I. *Biometrika, 44*(3/4), 470–481.

Fleiss, J. L. (1981). *Statistical methods for rates and proportions* (2nd ed.). New York: Wiley.

Frigge, M., Hoaglin, D. C., & Iglewicz, B. (1989). Some implementations of boxplot. *The American Statistician, 43*(1), 50–54.

Gardner, M. J., & Altman, D. G. (1986). Confidence intervals rather than P values: Estimation rather than hypothesis testing. *Statistics in Medicine, 292,* 746–750.

Hogg, R. V., Craig, A., & McKean, J. W. (2005). *Introduction to mathematical statistics* (6th ed.). New Delhi: Pearson Prentice Hall.

Hosmer, D. W., & Lemeshow, S. (2008). *Applied survival analysis* (2nd ed.). New York: Wiley.

Kahn, H. A., & Sempos, C. T. (1989). *Statistical methods in epidemiology.* New York: Oxford University Press.

Kalbfleisch, J. D., & Prentice, R. L. (2002). *The statistical analysis of failure time data* (2nd ed.). New York: Wiley.

Kirkwood, B. R., & Sterne, J. A. (2003). *Essential medical statistics* (2nd ed.). Malden, Massachusetts: Blackwell Science Limited.

Kleinbaum, D. G. (1996). *Survival analysis.* New York: Springer.

Kleinbaum, D. G., Kupper, L. L., & Morgenstern, H. (1982). *Epidemiologic research: Principles and quantitative methods.* New York: Wiley.

Lawless, J. F. (1982). *Statistical models and methods for lifetime data.* New York: Wiley.

Lee, E. T., & Wang, J. W. (2003). *Statistical methods for survival data analysis* (3rd ed.). New York: Wiley.

Lichman, M. (2013). *UCI machine learning repository.* Irvine, CA: School of Information and Computer Science, University of California [http://archive.ics.uci.edu/ml].

MacDonald, A. D. (1982). A stem-leaf plot: An approach to statistics. *The Mathematics Teacher,* *75*(1), 27–28.

MacMahon, B., & Pugh, T. F. (1970). *Epidemiology: Principles and methods.* Brown, Boston: Little.

McGill, R., Tukey, J. W., & Larsen, W. A. (1978). Variations of box plots. *The American Statistician, 32*(1), 12–16.

Mood, A. M., Graybill, F. A., & Boes, D. C. (1963). *Introduction to the theory of statistics* (3rd ed.). New Delhi: Tata McGraw-Hill Publishing Company Limited.

National Institute of Population Research and Training (NIPORT). (2012). *Bangladesh maternal mortality and health care survey 2010.* MEASURE, Evaluation, and icddrb.

National Institute of Population Research and Training (NIPORT). (2016). *Bangladesh demographic and health survey 2014.* Dhaka, Bangladesh and Rockville, Maryland, USA, NIPORT, Mitra and Associates, and ICF International.

Neutra, R. R., & Drolette, M. E. (1978). Estimating exposure-specific disease rates from case-control studies using Bayes' theorem. *American Journal of Epidemiology, 108,* 214–222.

Ott, L. (1994). *An Introduction to statistical methods and data analysis* (4th ed.). Boston: Duxbury Press.

Reiczigel, J. (2003). Confidence intervals for the binomial parameter: Some new considerations. *Statistics in Medicine, 22,* 611–621.

Ross, S. (1980). *Introduction to applied probability models* (2nd ed.). New York: Academic Press Inc.

Rothman, K. J. (2002). *Epidemiology: An introduction.* New York: Oxford University Press.

Snedecor, G., & Cochran, W. G. (1989). *Statistical methods* (8th ed.). Ames, Iowa: The Iowa University Press.

Thompson, M. L., Myers, J. E., & Kriebel, D. Prevalence odds ratio or prevalence ratio in the analysis of cross sectional data: What is to be done? *Occupational and Environmental Medicine, 55,* 272–277.

Tukey, J. W. (1977). *Exploratory data analysis.* Reading, Mass: Addison-Wesley Publishing Co.

Walpole, R. E., Myers, R. H., Myers, S. L., & Ye, K. (2002). *Probability & statistics for engineers and scientists* (7th ed.). New Jersey: Pearson Education International Prentice Hall.

Zelen, M. (2006). Biostatisticians, biostatistical science and the future. *Statistics in Medicine, 25,* 3409–3414.

Index

© Springer Nature Singapore Pte Ltd. 2018
M. A. Islam and A. Al-Shiha, *Foundations of Biostatistics*,
https://doi.org/10.1007/978-981-10-8627-4

MIX
Papier aus verantwortungsvollen Quellen
Paper from responsible sources
FSC® C105338

If you have any concerns about our products,
you can contact us on
ProductSafety@springernature.com

In case Publisher is established outside the EU,
the EU authorized representative is:
Springer Nature Customer Service Center GmbH
Europaplatz 3, 69115 Heidelberg, Germany

Printed by Libri Plureos GmbH
in Hamburg, Germany